Lecture Notes in Computer Science 13550

Formal Methods

Subline of Lectures Notes in Computer Science

More information about this series at https://link.springer.com/bookseries/558

Bernd-Holger Schlingloff ·
Ming Chai (Eds.)

Software Engineering and Formal Methods

20th International Conference, SEFM 2022
Berlin, Germany, September 26–30, 2022
Proceedings

Springer

Editors
Bernd-Holger Schlingloff 🆔
Humboldt-Universität zu Berlin
Berlin, Germany

Ming Chai 🆔
Beijing Jiaotong University
Beijing, China

ISSN 0302-9743   ISSN 1611-3349   (electronic)
Lecture Notes in Computer Science
ISBN 978-3-031-17107-9   ISBN 978-3-031-17108-6   (eBook)
https://doi.org/10.1007/978-3-031-17108-6

Preface

This volume contains the papers accepted for SEFM 2022, the 20th International Conference on Software Engineering and Formal Methods, held in Berlin, Germany, during September 28–30, 2022.

The SEFM conference series aims to bring together researchers and practitioners from academia, industry, and government to advance the state of the art in formal methods, to facilitate their uptake in the software industry, and to encourage their integration within practical software engineering methods and tools. This year marks the 20th anniversary of the series. Within these 20 years, the field has matured and extended focus: whereas in the 1st edition, which was held in 2003 in Brisbane, topics like verification, testing, object-oriented modeling, and integration of formal and informal methods prevailed, today additional topics like verification of machine learning, program synthesis from formal specifications, and correctness of cyber-physical and multi-agent systems have been added to the range. To reflect this extension, special emphasis was placed on the topic of "Software Engineering and Formal Methods for Intelligent and Learning Systems" at SEFM 2022.

SEFM 2022 was jointly organized by the Institute of Computer Science of the Humboldt University of Berlin (Germany) and the School of Electronic and Information Engineering of Beijing Jiaotong University (China). We also kindly acknowledge the support of Fraunhofer FOKUS, the Fraunhofer Institute for Open Communication Systems, Berlin. Following the online editions of SEFM in 2020 and 2021, it was the general opinion that we should have a physical face-to-face meeting again. Nevertheless, talks were streamed to an open website to allow online participation of a worldwide audience.

There were three invited talks at SEFM 2022: Uwe Nestmann (Technische Universität Berlin, Germany) reported on "Distributed process calculi with local states"; Mariëlle Stoelinga (Radboud University Nijmegen and University of Twente, The Netherlands) spoke on "Maintenance meets model checking: predictive maintenance via fault trees and formal methods"; and Alessio Lomuscio (Imperial College London, UK) gave a talk titled "Towards verifying neural-symbolic multi-agent systems". The abstracts of these talks are contained in this volume; we thank all three invited speakers for their insights.

Following the call for papers, there were 68 announced submissions, of which six were retracted or not submitted in time. The remaining 62 submissions were each reviewed independently by three reviewers, and this was followed by an online discussion amongst the reviewers. Based on the reviewing results, the Program Committee selected 19 full papers and three tool papers for presentation at the conference and publication in this volume. The editors thank the members of the Program Committee and the additional reviewers for their reviews and discussions. We also thank all authors for their submissions, whether accepted or not, and hope that they will keep contributing to future editions of this conference series. All SEFM submissions have to be original, unpublished, and not submitted concurrently for publication elsewhere.

Associated with the main SEFM 2022 conference was a SEFM summer school and six workshops: AI4EA 2022, FMAS 2022, F-IDE 2022, ASYDE 2022, CIFMA 2022, and CoSim-CPS 2022. We thank all organizers of the associated events for contributing to the success of SEFM. The proceedings of these events will appear in a separate LNCS volume.

Furthermore, we thank Antonio Cerone for his guidance in the organization, and the team at Springer for their support of SEFM 2022 and these proceedings. We also gratefully acknowledge Andrei Voronkov and the University of Manchester for the EasyChair system, which was used to handle the submission and review processes, and we wish the new EasyChair registration services and the whole EasyChair team success. Finally, we thank GFaI (Gesellschaft zur Förderung angewandter Informatik e.V.) for providing rooms and materials, the support team from Beijing Jiaotong University (Haoyuan Liu, Haoxiang Su, Dong Xie, and Qi Wang) for their help in editing the proceeding, and the support team from the Humboldt University of Berlin (Marc Carwehl, Eric Faust, Luisa Gerlach, Galina Greil, Philipp Jass, Sami Kharma, and Merlin von Wartburg) for their help in organizing SEFM 2022.

August 2022   Bernd-Holger Schlingloff
                                                                                        Ming Chai

Organization

Program Committee Chairs

Bernd-Holger Schlingloff   Fraunhofer FOKUS and Humboldt University of
Berlin, Germany
Ming Chai   Beijing Jiaotong University, China

Program Committee

Jiri Barnat	Masaryk University, Czech Republic
Dirk Beyer	LMU München, Germany
Radu Calinescu	University of York, UK
María-Emilia Cambronero	University of Castilla-La Mancha, Spain
Ana Cavalcanti	University of York, UK
Alessandro Cimatti	Fondazione Bruno Kessler, Italy
Gabriel Ciobanu	Romanian Academy, Iasi, Romania
Corina Cirstea	University of Southampton, UK
Antonio Filieri	Imperial College London, UK
Mario Gleirscher	University of Bremen, Germany
Marie-Christine Jakobs	TU Darmstadt, Germany
Raluca Lefticaru	University of Bradford, UK
Antónia Lopes	Universidade de Lisboa, Portugal
Tiziana Margaria	University of Limerick – Lero, Ireland
Paolo Masci	National Institute of Aerospace, USA
Claudio Menghi	McMaster University, Canada
Rocco De Nicola	IMT School for Advanced Studies Lucca, Italy
Hans de Nivelle	Nazarbayev University, Kazakhstan
Peter Ölveczky	University of Oslo, Norway
Gordon Pace	University of Malta, Malta
Corina Pasareanu	Carnegie Mellon University, NASA, and KBR, USA
Violet Ka I Pun	Western Norway University of Applied Sciences, Norway
Markus Roggenbach	Swansea University, UK
Gwen Salaün	University of Grenoble Alpes, France
Augusto Sampaio	Federal University of Pernambuco, Brazil
Ina Schaefer	Karlsruhe Institute of Technology, Germany
Gerardo Schneider	Chalmers University of Technology and University of Gothenburg, Sweden
Marjan Sirjani	Malardalen University, Sweden
Elena Troubitsyna	KTH Royal Institute of Technology, Sweden
Graeme Smith	University of Queensland, Australia
Silvia Lizeth Tapia Tarifa	University of Oslo, Norway

Marina Waldén   Abo Akademi University, Finland
Heike Wehrheim   University of Oldenburg, Germany
Gianluigi Zavattaro   University of Bologna, Italy

List of Additional Reviewers

Filipe Arruda	Christoph König
Anna Becchi	Frédéric Lang
Lukas Birkemeyer	Michael Lienhardt
Tabea Bordis	Enrico Lipparini
Marco Bozzano	Mariano Moscato
Gabriele Costa	Cláudia Nalon
Dana Dghaym	Felix Pauck
Neil Evans	Ehsan Poorhadi
Xinwei Fang	Cedric Richter
Marco Feliu Gabaldon	Lionel Rieg
Letterio Galletta	Cleyton Rodrigues
Sinem Getir Yaman	Rudolf Schlatte
Alberto Griggio	Arnab Sharma
George Hagen	Fedor Shmarov
Jan Haltermann	Colin Snook
William Hughes	Marielle Stoelinga
Calum Imrie	Matteo Tadiello
Omar Inverso	Francesco Tiezzi
Eduard Kamburjan	Catia Trubiani
Alexander Kittelmann	Gricel Vazquez

Organizing Committee

Bernd-Holger Schlingloff   Fraunhofer FOKUS and Humboldt University of
                                     Berlin, Germany
Ming Chai   Beijing Jiaotong University, China

Steering Committee

Radu Calinescu   University of York, UK
Antonio Cerone   Nazarbayev University, Kazakhstan
Rocco De Nicola   IMT School for Advanced Studies Lucca, Italy
Gwen Salaün   University of Grenoble Alpes, France
Marjan Sirjani   Mälardalen University, Sweden

Webmaster

Ming Chai   Beijing Jiaotong University, China

Invited Talks

Distributed Process Calculi with Local States

Uwe Nestmann

Process calculi are popular for several reasons: (1) they precisely capture concurrent computation models via the syntax and semantics of minimalistic languages; (2) they are equipped with rich algebraic theories that build upon behavioural equivalences, often with precise logical counterparts; and (3) they support powerful action-based proof techniques. While these advantages of process calculi are good for many concurrent applications, the reasoning about distributed algorithms often requires analyses in a state-based style, e.g., using (global) invariants. Thus, we study extensions of process calculi with explicit support for distribution, where processes dispose of a private memory component representing their own explicit local state. In the talk, I addressed the motivation behind distributed process calculi with local states as well as the engineering principles when developing the design and theory of such calculi.

Maintenance Meets Model Checking—Predictive Maintenance via Fault Trees and Formal Methods

Mariëlle Stoelinga

Proper maintenance is crucial to keep our trains, power plants and robots up and running. Since maintenance is also expensive, effective maintenance is a typical optimization problem, where one balances costs against system performance (in terms of availability, reliability, and remaining useful lifetime).

Predictive maintenance is a promising technique that aims at predicting failures more accurately, so that just-in-time maintenance can be performed, doing maintenance exactly when and where needed. Thus, predictive maintenance promises higher availability and fewer failures at lower costs. In this talk, I advocated a combination of model-driven (esp. fault trees) and data analytical techniques to get more insight in the costs versus performance of maintenance strategies. I showed the results of several case studies from railroad engineering, namely rail track (with Arcadis), and HVAC (heating, ventilation, and air conditioning; with Dutch railroads).

Towards Verifying Neural-Symbolic Multi-Agent Systems

Alessio Lomuscio

A challenge in the deployment of multi-agent systems (MAS) remains the inherent difficulty of predicting with confidence their run-time behaviour. Over the past twenty years, increasingly scalable verification methods, including model checking and parameterised verification, have enabled the validation of several classes of MAS against AI-based specifications, and several MAS applications in services, robotics, security, and beyond.

Yet, a new class of agents is emerging in applications. Differently from traditional MAS, which are typically directly programmed (and less often purely neural), they combine both connectionist and symbolic aspects. We will refer to these as neural-symbolic MAS. These agents include a neural layer, often implementing a perception function, and symbolic or control-based layers, typically realising decision making and planning. Implementations of neural-symbolic agents permeate many present and forthcoming AI applications, including autonomous vehicles and robotics. Due to the neural layer, as well as their heterogeneity, verifying the behaviours of neural-symbolic MAS is particularly challenging. Yet, I argued that, given the safety-critical applications they are used in, methods and tools to address their formal verification should be developed.

In this talk I shared some of the contributions on this topic developed at the Verification of Autonomous Systems Lab at Imperial College London. I began by describing traditional approaches for the verification of symbolic MAS, and parameterised verification to address arbitrary collections of agents such as swarms. I then summarised our present efforts on verification of neural perception systems, including MILP-based approaches, linear relaxations, and symbolic interval propagation, introduce our resulting toolkits, Venus and Verinet, and exemplified their use.

This lead to existing methods for closed-loop, neural-symbolic MAS. In this context, I shared existing results that enable us to perform reachability analysis, and verify systems against bounded temporal specifications and Alternating Temporal Logic (ATL).

I concluded by highlighting some of the many challenges that lie ahead.

Contents

Formal Methods for Intelligent and Learning Systems

Specification and Contracts

Program Synthesis

Temporal Logic

Runtime Methods

Software Verification

A Unifying Approach for
Control-Flow-Based Loop Abstraction

Dirk Beyer, Marian Lingsch Rosenfeld, and Martin Spiessl

LMU Munich, Munich, Germany

Abstract. Loop abstraction is a central technique for program analysis, because loops can cause large state-space representations if they are unfolded. In many cases, simple tricks can accelerate the program analysis significantly. There are several successful techniques for loop abstraction, but they are hard-wired into different tools and therefore difficult to compare and experiment with. We present a framework that allows us to implement different loop abstractions in one common environment, where each technique can be freely switched on and off on-the-fly during the analysis. We treat loops as part of the abstract model of the program, and use counterexample-guided abstraction refinement to increase the precision of the analysis by dynamically activating particular techniques for loop abstraction. The framework is independent from the underlying abstract domain of the program analysis, and can therefore be used for several different program analyses. Furthermore, our framework offers a sound transformation of the input program to a modified, more abstract output program, which is unsafe if the input program is unsafe. This allows loop abstraction to be used by other verifiers and our improvements are not 'locked in' to our verifier. We implemented several existing approaches and evaluate their effects on the program analysis.

Keywords: Software verification · Program analysis · Loop abstraction · Precision adjustment · Counterexample-guided abstraction refinement · CPAchecker

1 Introduction

Software programs are among the most complex systems that mankind produces. Programs tend to have a complex state space and hence verifying the correctness of software programs is a difficult task. Abstraction is a key ingredient to every successful approach to prove the correctness of large programs. Let us look at a few examples: Constant propagation [21] abstracts from concrete values for a variable if the value of the variable is not constant. Counterexample-guided abstraction refinement (CEGAR) [14] is an algorithm to incrementally refine the level of abstraction until the abstract model is detailed enough to prove the correctness, while the abstract model is still coarse enough to make the analysis feasible. Predicate abstraction [18,20] uses an abstract domain where the abstract state is described as a combination of predicates from a certain

© The Author(s) 2022
B.-H. Schlingloff and M. Chai (Eds.): SEFM 2022, LNCS 13550, pp. 3–19, 2022.
https://doi.org/10.1007/978-3-031-17108-6_1

given precision [8] (a set of predicates). The precision is refined with CEGAR by adding new predicates to the precision. Shape analysis [25] abstracts from concrete data structures on the heap and stores only their shape for the analysis.

Finally, *loop abstraction* is a technique to abstract the behavior of a program with a loop in such a way that the correctness of the abstract program implies the correctness of the original program. There are several approaches for loop abstraction proposed in the literature [15,16,19,22]. While we will concentrate on reachability here, this technique can also be applied to other properties.

We contribute a formalism that treats loop abstraction as an abstraction in the sense of CEGAR: The precision is a choice of a certain approach to loop abstraction (level of abstraction of the loop). If the abstract model of the program defined by this precision (= loop abstraction) is too coarse to prove correctness, then we refine the abstract model by setting the precision to a different (more precise) loop abstraction.

Example. Let us consider the small program in Fig. 1a. The program uses one variable x, which is initialized with some large, even value and decreased by 2 in a loop. The specification requires that the value of x is even after the loop terminates. It is easy for a human to see that an even number, decreased by an even number, always yields an even number, no matter how often this is done. In other words, we discover the invariant that x is even and check if it is preserved. However, in this example there exists an even simpler invariant: The data type of x is unsigned int, which means values greater or equal to zero. The control flow cannot leave the loop as long as x is greater than 0. Once the control flow leaves the loop, we know that the value is 0, and thus, even. The loop-exit condition, together with the above argument, implies the specification. A program analysis that cannot discover this (e.g., bounded model checking, explicit-value analysis, interval analysis) has to unroll the loop many times.

But we can construct the loop abstraction in Fig. 1b, which executes the new body only if the loop condition x > 0 is fulfilled, and the new body models all behaviors that occur when the original program enters the loop. The new body havocs (sets to an arbitrary value) the variable x. Then it constrains the values of x by blocking the further control flow if the loop condition still holds, i.e., the original program would stay in the loop. Surprisingly, since the loop-exit condition now implies the specification, this overapproximation of the original program still satisfies the specification.

Contributions. This paper makes the following contributions:

- We propose a framework that can express several existing approaches for loop abstraction and makes it possible to compare those different approaches.
- The framework allows to switch dynamically, on-the-fly, between different loop-abstraction techniques, selecting different abstraction levels.
- The framework is independent from the underlying abstract domain of the program analysis. The loop abstractions work using transformations of the control flow. Once implemented, a strategy for loop abstraction is applicable to several abstract domains.

```
1  unsigned int x = 0x0ffffff0;
2  while (x > 0) {
3    x -= 2;
4  }
5  assert(!(x % 2)));
```
(a) Original program

```
1  unsigned int x = 0x0ffffff0;
2  if (x > 0) {
3    x = nondet_uint();
4    if (x > 0) {
5      return 0;
6    }
7  }
8  assert(!(x % 2)));
```
(b) Havoc abstraction

```
1  unsigned int x = 0x0ffffff0;
2  if (x > 0) {
3    long long iterations = x/2;
4    x -= 2*iterations;
5    if (x > 0) {
6      x -= 2;
7    }
8  }
9  assert(!(x % 2)));
```
(c) Constant extrapolation

```
1   unsigned int x = 0x0ffffff0;
2   if (x > 0) {
3     x = nondet_uint();
4     if (x <= 0) {
5       return 0;
6     }
7     x -=2;
8     if (x > 0) {
9       return 0;
10    }
11  }
12  assert(!(x % 2)));
```
(d) Naive abstraction

Fig. 1. Application of various loop abstraction strategies on the benchmark program `simple_4-2.c` from the SV-Benchmarks set; only the body of the main function is shown here

- We export the modified C program, such that the loop-abstraction techniques can be used by other verifiers.
- The framework is publicly available as an extension of the open-source verification framework CPACHECKER.
- We evaluate the effectiveness and efficiency of the framework on a benchmark set from the publicly available collection of verification tasks SV-Benchmarks, and compare it with state-of-the-art tools.

Related Work. In the following we discuss the most related existing approaches.

Loop Acceleration. As this is an obvious way to speed up verification, many different approaches have been proposed to calculate the effects of a loop execution [17, 19, 26]. We present only a very basic form where we accelerate variables that are incremented by a fixed value in loops with a known number of iterations, since our interest is rather into gaining insights into how different existing approaches can be combined to further improve their usefulness. As such we are interested in implementing other approaches for loop acceleration as strategies into our framework, rather than coming up with new ways of accelerating single loops.

Loop Abstraction. While loop acceleration is useful also in other areas, e.g., for compiler optimizations, verifiers have the possibility of using loop abstractions (i.e., overapproximatons) instead, for aiding the generation of correctness proofs. Since loop abstraction is closely related to invariant generation, and this is the main challenge in software verification, there is a large body of literature. We will therefore look at only those publications that also make use of the idea to encode the abstractions into the source code. The abstraction techniques we describe in this paper are taken taken from existing publications [15, 16]. As with loop accelerations, our goal is not to invent new strategies, but rather investigate how existing strategies can be combined. Also VERIABS [1] uses a variety of loop-abstraction techniques, but only statically generates a program that is then checked by a third-party verifier. As fallback, the original program is verified.

Encoding Loop Abstractions into the Program. We found one publication that also encodes loop accelerations into a modified program [23]. Here, the accelerated loop variant is added in such a way that the alternative code will be entered based on non-deterministic choice. The main motivation is to investigate how this can create synergies with invariant generation, i.e., whether existing invariant generators can be improved by also providing the results of the acceleration in the program. Compared to that, our approach is more general, as we also consider overapproximating loop abstractions. Instead of non-deterministic choice, we present an approach to determine which strategies to use automatically using CEGAR.

2   Preliminaries

We quickly introduce some notation and common concepts that will later be used in Sect. 3.1.

Program Semantics. For simplicity we will consider a programming language where the set Ops of possible program operations consists of simple assignments and assumptions. We represent the programs as control-flow automata (CFA). A CFA $C = \{L, l_0, G\}$ consists of a set L of program locations (modeling the progam counter), an initial program location l_0, and a relation $G \subseteq L \times Ops \times L$ that describes the control-flow edges (each modeling the flow from one program location via a program operation to a successor program location). The concrete semantics of such a CFA is given by the (labeled) transition relation $\rightarrow \subseteq C \times G \times C$ over the set C of concrete program states. We will write $c_1 \xrightarrow{g} c_2$ if the concrete state c_2 can be reached from c_1 via the control-flow edge $g \in G$.

Program Analysis. Our approach will work for many different kinds of program analysis. Typically, a program analysis is characterized by some abstract domain D that defines a set E of abstract states as well as an abstract transfer relation $\leadsto \subseteq E \times G \times E$, which determines which abstract states can be reached from the initial state $e_0 \in E$. One common way to design a program analysis is to determine the set of reachable abstract states by keeping track of a set $\texttt{reached} \subseteq E$ of already reached abstract states and a set (or list) `waitlist` $\subseteq E$ of abstract states that still need to be explored.[1]

CEGAR. Whenever a program analysis finds a counterexample, there are two possibilities. Either this turns out to correspond to an actual execution trace of the original program, and we have shown that the program violates the specification, or the counterexample is infeasible, meaning that it is only found because the abstraction level of the analysis is too coarse. This has led to the development of *counterexample-guided abstraction refinement*, or CEGAR for short [14]. The idea here is that one can extract information from the counterexample with which the abstract domain can be refined. For example with predicate abstraction[2], one can use the counterexample to compute predicates that —if tracked— rule out the infeasible counterexample. In order to formalize CEGAR, we will introduce the refinement operator:

$$\texttt{refine} : (\texttt{reached}, \texttt{waitlist}) \mapsto (\texttt{reached'}, \texttt{waitlist'})$$

Once an infeasible counterexample is found, the refinement operator is called with the current set of reached abstract states and the waitlist. This operator then extracts information from its inputs and returns a new set of reached states and a new waitlist which will then be used for further state-space exploration. In case the counterexample is feasible, the refinement operator will not remove the violation state(s) from the set of reached abstract states, which signals that the analysis found a bug and can terminate.

3   Loop Abstractions

We propose the approach of multi-strategy program analysis, which enables one tool to use several different loop-abstraction strategies simultaneously in one state-space exploration. In the following, we will first look at the theory behind loop abstractions and some practical examples for such strategies. After that, we will introduce our CEGAR refinement approach for loop abstractions in Sect. 3.2.

3.1   Theory

For verification, we usually use overapproximations if the goal is to find a proof of correctness. For loop control flow, such an overapproximation is called a *loop abstraction*, while precise methods are called *loop acceleration*. Whenever it is not important whether the technique is precise or overapproximating, we will just refer to the techniques as loop abstraction.

It is common to apply loop abstractions by replacing the loop statement S with some alternative program statement S' [1,23]. Intuitively, it is often clear whether this will overapproximate the program behavior, but we can also formalize this

---

[1] In the literature, this is also know as a worklist algorithm [24]; here we will adhere to the terminology used in the Handbook of Model Checking [6].

using strongest postconditions. We write $sp(S, P)$ for the strongest postcondition of a program statement S and a predicate P. Assume we have a program statement S that contains a loop, i.e., $S = \texttt{while (C) do B}$, where the body B inside S may itself contain loops. For a loop abstraction, the goal is to find an alternative program statement S' such that $\{P\}S\{sp(S', P)\}$ is a valid Hoare triple. If this requirement is fulfilled, then we can soundly replace S by S' in the program for the purpose of verification. In other words, S' is an abstraction of S if $sp(S, P) \Rightarrow sp(S', P)$. It is possible to find such rewriting schemes for a loop without knowing the exact form of the loop. This is best shown by two examples.

Havoc Abstraction. Let us look at the rather simple loop abstraction that served as example in Sect. 1, which we call *havoc abstraction*. Here we replace the loop $\texttt{while C do B}$ by a havoc statement $\texttt{havoc(mod(B))}$ that is guarded in such a way to ensure it is only executed if the loop condition holds, and after it is executed, the loop condition does not hold anymore. The havoc statement discards any information about the values of a set of variables. Here we use the set $\texttt{mod(B)}$ of variables that are modified in the loop body B. We denote the strongest postcondition of this havoc statement by $H_{B,P} = sp(\texttt{havoc(mod(B))}, P)$. We can easily prove soundness of the havoc abstraction by establishing that $H_{B,P}$ is actually a loop invariant and therefore the Hoare triple $\{P\}$ $\texttt{while C do B}$ $\{H_{B,P} \wedge \neg C\}$ holds.[2]

It is obvious that we can find an alternative statement S' for the while-loop that has the same post condition:

$$sp(\texttt{havoc(mod(B))};\texttt{assume(!C)}, P) = H_{B,P} \wedge \neg C$$

We therefore have found a statement whose strongest post is an overapproximation of the strongest post of the while loop.

Naive Abstraction. Another way to abstract a loop is the so-called naive loop abstraction [16]. An application to the example program from Fig. 1a is shown in Fig. 1d. Here one assigns non-deterministic values to all the variables that are modified in the loop (provided the loop condition holds when reaching the loop). Then the loop body is executed once, after which the negated loop condition is added as assumption. This essentially encodes the information that if the loop was entered, there is a "last" iteration of the loop after which the loop condition does not hold anymore and the loop therefore terminates. This is overapproximating the behavior of the original loop, since a loop, in general, is not guaranteed to terminate. From the Hoare proof of the naive abstraction, we get that $sp(B, C \wedge H_{B,P}) \vee P$ is an invariant of the while loop.[3]

The postcondition $(sp(B, C \wedge H_{B,P}) \vee P) \wedge \neg C$ that is shown in the proof is also the post condition of the alternative code for the loop described above:

$$sp(\texttt{if C then } \{\texttt{havoc(mod(B))};\texttt{assume(C)};\texttt{B};\texttt{assume(!C)}\}, P) =$$
$$(sp(B, C \wedge H_{B,P}) \vee P) \wedge \neg C$$

---

[2] Proof can be found at: https://www.sosy-lab.org/research/loop-abstraction/
[3] Proof can be found at: https://www.sosy-lab.org/research/loop-abstraction/

Observations. We can make three interesting observations by looking at these proofs. Firstly, we eliminated the outermost loop from the statement S, at the cost of overapproximation. If this can be achieved iteratively until no loops are left, the resulting overapproximation can be quickly checked by a (possibly bounded) model checker, as no loops need to be unrolled anymore.

Secondly, in the proof we actually used an invariant for applying the while-rule. Every loop-abstraction strategy can therefore be seen as a way to generate invariants for a loop based on some structural properties of the loop. In the example of the havoc abstraction, we used the fact that for a precondition P, $H_{B,P}$ is always preserved by a loop (provided there is no aliasing). The invariant depends on the precondition P, so for every precondition with which the loop can be reached, the loop abstraction yields a different state invariant. Without knowing P it can only be expressed as a transition invariant that may refer to the "old" values of variables before entering the loop. One can compute a state invariant by assuming the most general precondition $P = true$, but this will often eliminate most of the useful information from the invariant. As transition invariants can often be expressed precisely by program statements, this explains why for loop abstraction, we choose to replace the loop statement with alternative program statements that capture the corresponding transition invariant. This invariant view on loop abstraction works in both ways, meaning that if an invariant is provided for a loop, we can use this invariant for abstracting the loop. It is even possible to construct an inductive proof this way, i.e., transforming the loop in such a way that model checking of the resulting program will essentially carry out a combined-case (k-)inductive proof [15].

The third observation is that the invariant of one loop abstraction might sometimes imply the invariant of another loop abstraction. This is the case in the two examples: the invariant for havoc loop abstraction is implied by the invariant we use in the naive loop abstraction. This means we can build a hierarchy, where naive loop abstraction overapproximates the original loop, and havoc abstraction overapproximates naive abstraction. We will exploit the idea of this abstraction hierarchy later in Sect. 3.2 for an abstraction-refinement scheme.

Constant Extrapolation. For loops where we can calculate the exact number of iterations as well as the final values of the variables assigned in the loop (e.g., because the loop is linear or otherwise easily summarizable) we can simply accelerate the loop by replacing it with assignment statements for the final variable values. The application of constant extrapolation to the program from Fig. 1a is shown in Fig. 1c. For the program in Fig. 2, this would replace the loop with a statement that increments the variable i by N. For programs like the one shown in Fig. 3 that contains a potential property violation inside the loop, one has to be careful to preserve those violations that can occur in any of the loop iterations.

3.2   Combining Strategies for Loop Abstraction

In Sect. 3.1 we already introduced various ways to abstract loops, which we will in the following refer to as strategies. Intuitively, a strategy is a way to compute an abstraction of a loop that is helpful to verify a program.

Since there are often many different strategies that could be applied to a loop in the program, we need to make some choice about which strategies to use. The simplest approach that is used in the state-of-the-art verification tool VERIABS is to choose the most promising that can be applied for each loop, generate a program where the loops are rewritten according to these strategies, and hand this program over to a (possibly bounded) verifier for verification.

This has the downside that in cases where the program contains multiple loops, the chosen approximations might be either not abstract enough for the verifier to calculate the proof efficiently or too abstract, such that the proof of the property does not succeed. Choosing a good abstraction level is one of the key challenges in software verification. One successful way how this can be solved is counterexample-guided abstraction refinement (CEGAR) [14].

Our idea is therefore to use CEGAR in order to refine the abstraction of the program dynamically during the program analysis, which allows us to try multiple strategies for the same loop in the program, and even different strategies for the same loop at different locations in the state-space exploration. Because a program analysis operates on the CFA, and loop abstractions correspond to transition invariants that can often be expressed naturally as a sequence of progam instructions, we choose to encode the loop abstractions directly into the CFA. This allows us to realize the CEGAR approach for loop abstractions independently of the details of the exact program analysis that is used.

Encoding of Strategies. We encode strategies that are to be considered directly into the CFA of the program. The CFA for a program statement S such as a loop has a unique entry node α and a unique exit node ω. The application of a strategy to this statement results in the statement S' and a CFA with an entry node α' and an exit node ω'. We attach the CFA for the statement S' of a strategy with two dummy transitions $\alpha \to \alpha'$ and $\omega' \to \omega$, as depicted in Fig. 4. Here, we explicitly denoted the entry edge for the strategy application with the keyword `enter` followed by an identifier that makes clear which strategy was applied (here, h stands for havoc). The resemblance to function call and return edges is not a coincidence. By keeping track of the currently entered strategy applications, e.g. in form of a stack, it will always be clear which parts of the execution trace correspond to executions in the original program, and which parts are part of some —potentially overapproximating— strategy application. For nested loops, we can apply the strategies starting from the inner-most loop and construct alternatives in the CFA for all possible strategy combinations.

A CFA that is augmented with strategies in this way contains all program traces of the original program, and can non-deterministically branch into any of the strategy applications. In order to make use of this modified CFA, the analysis needs to be able to distinguish between the original control flow and nodes in the CFA at which we start to apply a particular strategy. The important nodes for this are the entry nodes for each of the strategy applications, so we augment the modified CFA $C = (L, l_{init}, G)$ with a strategy map $\sigma : L \to N$ that maps each CFA node $l \in L$ to a strategy identifier $\sigma(l) \in N$ and call the resulting tuple $\Gamma = (C, \sigma)$ a *strategy-augmented CFA*. The set N of strategy identifiers

```
1  void main() {
2    int i = 0;
3    while (i<N) {
4      i=i+1;
5    }
6    assert (i==N);
7  }
```

Fig. 2. Example program 1: potential property violation outside the loop

```
1  void main() {
2    int i = 0;
3    while (i<N) {
4      i=i+2;
5      assert(i%2==0);
6    }
7  }
```

Fig. 3. Example program 2: potential property violation inside the loop

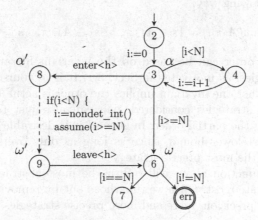

Fig. 4. CFA C of example program from Fig. 2, with an additional application of the havoc strategy

contains a special strategy b, which we call the base strategy. The strategy map σ maps the entry node for each strategy application to the corresponding strategy's identifier, while all other nodes are mapped to the base strategy b.

In a program analysis, we can now use the strategy map for selecting exactly the transitions we want to follow. For example, we can always follow the original program by excluding all transitions to CFA nodes with an associated strategy identifier that is different from the base strategy. By using a more general selection function, we have fine-grained control over which strategies we are applying, which we will describe in the following. As this modifies only the transition relation of the state-space exploration, it can be seamlessly applied to a wide variety of such algorithms.

Selection of Strategies. At any node l in an augmented CFA, we can calculate the set $A \subseteq N$ of available strategies as:

$$A = \{\sigma(l') \mid \exists g \in G : l \xrightarrow{g} l'\}$$

In order to define which strategies should be applied (e.g., because others overapproximate too much and lead to false alarms), we define a precision set $\pi_S \subseteq N$

which we call the *strategy precision*. This precision can be tracked along each abstract state of the program analysis. In practice this precision is tracked for each program location separately, but for simplicity of presentation, we will only consider a global precision here. Semantically the precision expresses which strategies are allowed to be taken from the current abstract state. We can now express different selection approaches by defining a function $\texttt{select} : \mathcal{P}(N) \times \mathcal{P}(N) \rightarrow \mathcal{P}(N)$, which needs to fulfill the property $\texttt{select}(A, \pi_S) \subseteq A \cap \pi_S$.

The exact choice of the function $\texttt{select}$ depends on the use case and the set of available strategies. One possibility which we will use is to define a partial order $\sqsubseteq$ over the set of available strategy identifiers, and derive the selection function in the following way:

$$\texttt{select}(A, \pi_S) = \{s \in A \cap \pi_s \mid \nexists s' \in A \cap \pi_s : s \sqsubseteq s'\} \tag{1}$$

Such a partial order can be based on the invariant hierarchy of the loop-abstraction strategies, as motivated in Sect. 3.1. It is of course not guaranteed that deciding whether one invariant implies the other is actually decidable. But depending on the strategies considered, one can also just take some design decisions regarding the partial order. In general it is desirable to have the base strategy as greatest lower bound, since as long as only overapproximation is considered, this is the most precise strategy.

The selection function above will return the most abstract strategies, i.e., that overapproximate most. Once we rule those out by removing their strategy identifier from the precision, more and more precise strategies will be returned.

CEGAR Refinement Chaining. We can now define the refinement operator $\texttt{refine}$ for precision-based loop acceleration on top of any refiner of an existing analysis, which we will call the wrapped refiner $\texttt{refine}_W$. This can be done by composing the refinement operator $\texttt{refine}_W$ with the strategy-refinement operator $\texttt{refine}_S$, which updates the strategy precision with information from the error path:

$$\texttt{refine} = \texttt{refine}_S \circ \texttt{refine}_W \tag{2}$$

Since the wrapped refinement operator is executed first, it gets the possibility to remove all error states from the reached set, in which case $\texttt{refine}_S$ has nothing to do and will just return its inputs. If there are still error states left in the reached set after $\texttt{refine}_W$ was executed, this means that the inner refinement has discovered a feasible error path for the augmented CFA. Now it depends on whether any overapproximating strategies were used on the error paths that are present in the reached set. If there are none, then the error path is indeed also present in the real program and $\texttt{refine}_S$ returns the reached set with the error state(s), indicating that a bug has been found. An example for this would be the case where only constant extrapolation has been used along the path. If there are overapproximating strategies such as the havoc abstraction on an error path, we can adapt the strategy precision in order to rule out that we will find the same error path again after the refinement. For that, we locate the first abstract state on the path whose successor enters an overapproximating strategy (the so-called pivot state) and adapt the strategy precision such that this strategy can not be selected in the future. We then remove all (transitive) successor abstract states of that pivot state from the set of reached abstract states.

Example. The chaining of the refinement operators is best visualized by looking at an example. Using the running example from Fig. 2, we can look at the key steps in the CEGAR refinement. Let us assume we are only using the havoc strategy, i.e., the augmented CFA will look like shown in Fig. 4. Based on this CFA, an example for how a generic state-space exploration could look like is depicted in Fig. 5. In Fig. 5a we start at an abstract state with three components. The first one encodes the program location and is set to 2, since program location 2 is the initial progam location in the CFA. Component e_0 encodes the analysis-specific domain part of the abstract state, e.g., for predicate abstraction this could be a set of predicates. The last component is the strategy precision. It contains the base strategy (b) as well as the havoc strategy (h). From this state, the state-space exploration continues to program location 3, where the selection of strategies in the transition relation only allows us to proceed into the application of the havoc abstraction. From there, we eventually reach the error location.

This is where the CEGAR refinement operator is first called. Since the path formula to the error location is actually feasible, the wrapped refinement operator return the inputs unchanged, and our strategy refinement operator takes over. Here we discover that an overapproximating strategy was used on the path. We update the strategy precision of the second state (the one at program location 3) such that the havoc strategy cannot be chosen anymore. We then remove all successors of the pivot state from the set of reached abstract states (and the waitlist), add the modified state to the waitlist, and return both sets.

The resulting reachability graph will look like in Fig. 5b. From there, the state-space exploration can continue as shown in Fig. 5c. We again discover an error path, this time however the wrapped refinement operator can determine that this error path is infeasible. In case of a predicate abstraction, a predicate like $i < N$ would be discovered and added to the predicate precision of e'_1 at program location 3. All successors after location 3 are removed again and the wrapped refinement operator returns. Since there is no error state present anymore in the set of reached states, the strategy refinement operator returns its inputs unchanged. The state-space exploration then continues by adding a new abstract state for program location 4 and so on, as depicted in Fig. 5d.

Transformation into Source Code. We also provide functionality to convert the loop abstractions we found back into source code, such that our findings can be used and validated by others. For that, we provide two different mechanisms. The first is that whenever we are able to generate a proof using some loop-abstraction strategy, we generate a modified version of the input program where just the loops are changed to reflect the effect of the loop abstraction. The second mechanism is that we provide a way to analyze a C program such that for each loop in the program and each loop-abstraction strategy, we create a patch file for the program (in case the strategy is applicable) that —when applied— will apply the loop abstraction on the source-code level.

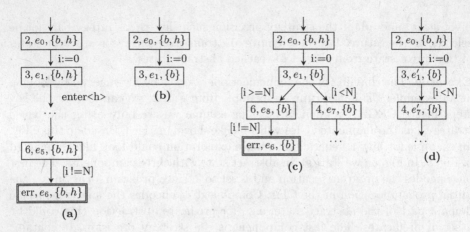

Fig. 5. Example for constructing a reachability graph of a program analysis on Fig. 4 using chained CEGAR refinements: **(a)** initial ARG until first refinement, **(b)** strategy precision updated after refinement (strategy h removed from precision), **(c)** state-space exploration on the original program continues, **(d)** exploration continues after a regular CEGAR refinement (e_1 replaced by e_1')

4 Evaluation

As a first step, we implemented the three loop-abstraction strategies that we described in Sect. 3.1 into the state-of-the-art verification framework CPACHECKER: havoc abstraction (h), naive abstraction (n), and constant extrapolation (c). In addition, we also implemented so-called output abstraction (o) [15]. For the evaluation, we define the following (partial) order on which the function `select` will be based:

$$b \sqsubseteq o \sqsubseteq c \sqsubseteq n \sqsubseteq h \tag{3}$$

We are interested in answering the following research questions:

- **RQ1:** Can our CEGAR-style loop-abstraction scheme soundly improve a verifier like CPACHECKER independently of the underlying analysis?
- **RQ2:** Are these abstractions also useful for other verifiers?

We conduct an experiment for each RQ in Sect. 4.2 to abtain answers.

4.1 Benchmark Environment

For conducting our evaluation, we use BENCHEXEC to ensure reliable benchmarking [12]. All benchmarks are performed on machines with an Intel Xeon E5-1230 CPU (4 physical cores with 2 processing units each), 33GB of RAM, and running Ubuntu 20.04 as operating system. All benchmarks are executed with resources limited to 900 s of CPU time, 15 GB of memory, and 1 physical core (2 processing units).

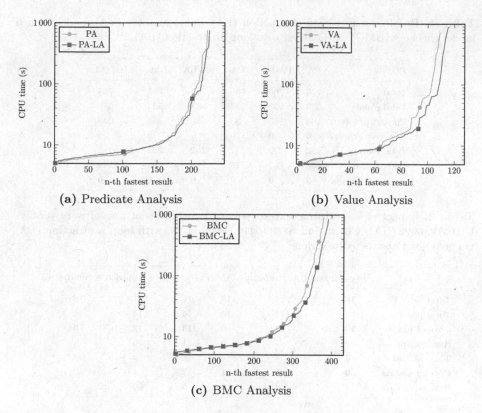

(a) Predicate Analysis   **(b)** Value Analysis

(c) BMC Analysis

Fig. 6. Quantile plots comparing performance of plain analyses with their versions that use loop-abstraction strategies; only correct results are considered

4.2   Experiments

For our experiments we use verification tasks taken from the SV-Benchmarks set of SV-COMP 2022 [3,4]. Here we selected only the 765 reachability tasks from the subcategory ReachSafety-Loops, as these cover a wide range of interesting loop constructs while at the same time only using a limited set of features of the programming language C, which allows us to focus on the algorithms instead of having to deal with lots of special cases.

RQ1. In a first experiment, we evaluate whether our approach can improve the overall results, and whether our new framework introduces significant overhead, for three analyses of CPACHECKER: (1) predicate analysis (PA) [5] configured to use predicate abstraction [7,9,18], (2) value analysis (VA) [6,11], which is an extension of constant propagation [21], and (3) predicate analysis configured to work as bounded model checking (BMC) [13]. For improvements we will look at effectiveness as well as efficiency. By effectiveness we mean an increase in the number of solved verification tasks while at the same time preserving soundness of the results, i.e., no increase of the number of wrong proofs or wrong alarms. For efficiency we will take a look at how our approach affects the verification time of successfully verified tasks.

Table 1. Results for predicate abstraction (PA), value analysis (VA), and bounded model checking (BMC), without vs. with loop abstraction (LA)

	PA	PA-LA	VA	VA-LA	BMC	BMC-LA
Total	765	765	765	765	765	765
Total proofs	533	533	533	533	533	533
Correct proofs	164	163	33	35	235	248
Incorrect proofs	0	0	0	0	0	0
Total alarms	232	232	232	232	232	232
Correct alarms	58	62	76	81	144	144
Incorrect alarms	0	0	0	0	0	0

Table 2. Impact of loop abstractions on solving capabilities of the software verifiers UAUTOMIZER (UA), CBMC, and SYMBIOTIC, without vs. with loop abstraction (LA) via generated abstracted programs

	UAUTOMIZER	UAUTOMIZER-LA	CBMC	CBMC-LA	SYMBIOTIC	SYMBIOTIC-LA
Total	18	18	18	18	18	18
Total proofs	14	14	14	14	14	14
Correct proofs	12	13	0	13	12	13
Incorrect proofs	0	1	0	1	0	1
Total alarms	4	4	4	4	4	4
Correct alarms	0	3	1	3	1	3
Incorrect alarms	0	0	0	0	0	0

The quantile plots in Fig. 6 show that we are able to slightly improve the results for all analyses. Both effectiveness and efficiency is improved, and thus, there is no noticeable overhead. We use PA-LA, VA-LA, and BMC-LA to refer to the variants of the analyses that use our CEGAR-style loop-abstraction scheme. As expected, the overhead of applying loop abstraction in cases where this does not help with solving the verification task does not add a significant overhead to the verification time. Table 1 shows that our approach is also sound, i.e., it does not increase the number of incorrect results.

Another observation is that there are more proofs as well as property violations found this way. The latter is possible because constant extrapolation is a precise abstraction, meaning that a counterexample found using this strategy corresponds to a feasible error path in the program.

The experimental data so far suggests that if loop abstraction helps with verification, the verification will usually succeed very quickly. For all tasks where the verdict improves, the application of loop abstraction reduces the verification time from a timeout, i.e., more than 900 seconds, to less than 10 seconds. On closer inspection, we find a total of 18 verification tasks where the loop abstraction is essential in proving the program correct with the used analyses. When comparing the different analyses, the effect is most noticeable with bounded model checking, which is not surprising given the fact that BMC alone can not prove programs with unbounded loops. There are 6 tasks where predicate analysis improved, 5 tasks for value analysis, and 17 tasks for BMC.[4] Since our framework supports exporting the accelerated loops into the source code, we can use the 18 abstracted programs that improved CPACHECKER's results in the next experiment, where we check whether these are also useful for other software verifiers.

RQ2. In the second experiment we take a look at whether our approach has the potential to improve the results of other state-of-the-art verification tools as well. In order to be able to do so without having to modify the existing tools, we take those programs where loop-abstraction strategies were able to improve the results for CPACHECKER and automatically generate the abstracted programs that can then be fed to other verifiers. In our case, we use the three well-known verifiers CBMC, SYMBIOTIC, and UAUTOMIZER.

The results of all three verifiers improve if loop abstraction is applied, as shown in Table 2. The table shows the results for the verifiers on the original verification tasks (columns without suffix LA) and on the abstracted programs (column with suffix LA). Note that this will not be the case in general, but for the selected verification tasks, we know that one of our implemented loop abstraction strategies is actually sufficient to prove the program correct. In general, if a loop abstraction over-approximates too much, the verifier will quickly find an error path, in which case we would execute the verifier on the original program. There is also one program for which our loop abstraction leads to a wrong proof, which is due to a bug in our translation back into source code.

The main observation here regarding our research question is that the results of all three verifiers can be improved by applying loop abstraction. We get the largest improvement for the bounded model checker CBMC. This is not surprising and in line with the results from the bounded model checking with CPACHECKER.

5 Conclusion

Loop abstraction is a technique for program verification that is currently not used by many of the state-of-the-art verification tools. In our experiments we have shown that mature verifiers can still benefit even from very simple loop abstractions. By adding more sophisticated loop-abstraction strategies in the future, we hope to achieve even better results that further improve the state-of-the-art. We make the loop abstractions that we implemented available to other tools by generating modified versions of the input programs, such that also other tools can benefit from loop abstractions in the future.

In this paper, we have also addressed the problem of how to select the right combination of loop abstractions for programs with multiple loops. Instead of deciding upfront which combination to choose, we use a novel approach based on CEGAR to automatically refine the loop abstractions as the analysis progresses. By using the control flow as interface for program analyses, we are able to apply our approach to a wide range of existing analyses and abstract domains, without additional implementation overhead.

---

[4] Detailed results at: https://www.sosy-lab.org/research/loop-abstraction/

Data-Availability Statement. The software and programs that we used for our experiments, including the generated programs with abstracted loops, are open source and available on our supplementary web page at https://www. sosy-lab.org/research/loop-abstraction/ and in the reproduction package at Zenodo [10].

Funding Statement. This project was funded in part by the Deutsche Forschungsgemeinschaft (DFG) – 378803395 (ConVeY).

References

1. Afzal, M., Asia, A., Chauhan, A., Chimdyalwar, B., Darke, P., Datar, A., Kumar, S., Venkatesh, R.: VeriAbs: Verification by abstraction and test generation. In: Proc. ASE. pp. 1138–1141 (2019). https://doi.org/10.1109/ASE.2019.00121
2. Ball, T., Majumdar, R., Millstein, T.D., Rajamani, S.K.: Automatic predicate abstraction of C programs. In: Proc. PLDI. pp. 203–213. ACM (2001). https://doi.org/10.1145/378795.378846
3. Beyer, D.: Progress on software verification: SV-COMP 2022. In: Proc. TACAS (2). pp. 375–402. LNCS 13244, Springer (2022). https://doi.org/10.1007/978-3-030-99527-0_20
4. Beyer, D.: SV-Benchmarks: Benchmark set for software verification and testing (SV-COMP 2022 and Test-Comp 2022). Zenodo (2022). https://doi.org/10.5281/zenodo.5831003
5. Beyer, D., Dangl, M., Wendler, P.: A unifying view on SMT-based software verification. J. Autom. Reasoning **60**(3), 299–335 (2017). https://doi.org/10.1007/s10817-017-9432-6
6. Beyer, D., Gulwani, S., Schmidt, D.: Combining model checking and data-flow analysis. In: Handbook of Model Checking, pp. 493–540. Springer (2018). https://doi.org/10.1007/978-3-319-10575-8_16
7. Beyer, D., Henzinger, T.A., Jhala, R., Majumdar, R.: The software model checker BLAST. Int. J. Softw. Tools Technol. Transfer **9**(5–6), 505–525 (2007). https://doi.org/10.1007/s10009-007-0044-z
8. Beyer, D., Henzinger, T.A., Théoduloz, G.: Program analysis with dynamic precision adjustment. In: Proc. ASE. pp. 29–38. IEEE (2008). https://doi.org/10.1109/ASE.2008.13
9. Beyer, D., Keremoglu, M.E., Wendler, P.: Predicate abstraction with adjustable-block encoding. In: Proc. FMCAD. pp. 189–197. FMCAD (2010)
10. Beyer, D., Lingsch Rosenfeld, M., Spiessl, M.: Reproduction package for SEFM 2022 article 'A unifying approach for control-flow-based loop abstraction'. Zenodo (2022). https://doi.org/10.5281/zenodo.6793834
11. Beyer, D., Löwe, S.: Explicit-state software model checking based on CEGAR and interpolation. In: Proc. FASE. pp. 146–162. LNCS 7793, Springer (2013). https://doi.org/10.1007/978-3-642-37057-1_11
12. Beyer, D., Löwe, S., Wendler, P.: Reliable benchmarking: Requirements and solutions. Int. J. Softw. Tools Technol. Transfer **21**(1), 1–29 (2017). https://doi.org/10.1007/s10009-017-0469-y
13. Biere, A., Cimatti, A., Clarke, E.M., Zhu, Y.: Symbolic model checking without BDDs. In: Proc. TACAS. pp. 193–207. LNCS 1579, Springer (1999). https://doi.org/10.1007/3-540-49059-0_14

14. Clarke, E.M., Grumberg, O., Jha, S., Lu, Y., Veith, H.: Counterexample-guided abstraction refinement for symbolic model checking. J. ACM **50**(5), 752–794 (2003). https://doi.org/10.1145/876638.876643
15. Darke, P., Chimdyalwar, B., Venkatesh, R., Shrotri, U., Metta, R.: Over-approximating loops to prove properties using bounded model checking. In: Proc. DATE. pp. 1407–1412. IEEE (2015). https://doi.org/10.7873/DATE.2015.0245
16. Darke, P., Khanzode, M., Nair, A., Shrotri, U., Venkatesh, R.: Precise analysis of large industry code. In: Proc. APSEC. pp. 306–309. IEEE (2012). https://doi.org/10.1109/APSEC.2012.97
17. Frohn, F.: A calculus for modular loop acceleration. In: Proc. TACAS (1). pp. 58–76. LNCS 12078, Springer (2020). https://doi.org/10.1007/978-3-030-45190-5_4
18. Graf, S., Saïdi, H.: Construction of abstract state graphs with Pvs. In: Proc. CAV. pp. 72–83. LNCS 1254, Springer (1997). https://doi.org/10.1007/3-540-63166-6_10
19. Jeannet, B., Schrammel, P., Sankaranarayanan, S.: Abstract acceleration of general linear loops. In: Proc. POPL. pp. 529–540. ACM (2014). https://doi.org/10.1145/2535838.2535843
20. Jhala, R., Podelski, A., Rybalchenko, A.: Predicate abstraction for program verification. In: Handbook of Model Checking, pp. 447–491. Springer (2018). https://doi.org/10.1007/978-3-319-10575-8_15
21. Kildall, G.A.: A unified approach to global program optimization. In: Proc. POPL. pp. 194–206. ACM (1973). https://doi.org/10.1145/512927.512945
22. Kumar, S., Sanyal, A., Venkatesh, R., Shah, P.: Property checking array programs using loop shrinking. In: Proc. TACAS (1). pp. 213–231. LNCS 10805, Springer (2018). https://doi.org/10.1007/978-3-319-89960-2_12
23. Madhukar, K., Wachter, B., Kröning, D., Lewis, M., Srivas, M.K.: Accelerating invariant generation. In: Proc. FMCAD. pp. 105–111. IEEE (2015)
24. Nielson, F., Nielson, H.R., Hankin, C.: Principles of Program Analysis. Springer (1999). https://doi.org/10.1007/978-3-662-03811-6
25. Sagiv, M., Reps, T.W., Wilhelm, R.: Parametric shape analysis via 3-valued logic. ACM Trans. Program. Lang. Syst. **24**(3), 217–298 (2002)
26. Silverman, J., Kincaid, Z.: Loop summarization with rational vector addition systems. In: Proc. CAV, Part 2. pp. 97–115. LNCS 11562, Springer (2019). https://doi.org/10.1007/978-3-030-25543-5_7

Auto-Active Verification of Floating-Point Programs via Nonlinear Real Provers

Junaid Rasheed$^{(\boxtimes)}$ and Michal Konečný

Aston University, Birmingham B4 7ET, UK
rasheeja@aston.ac.uk

Abstract. We give a process for verifying numerical programs against their functional specifications. Our implementation is capable of automatically verifying SPARK programs against tight error bounds featuring common elementary functions. We demonstrate and evaluate our implementation on several examples, yielding the first fully verified SPARK implementations of the sine and square root functions.

The process integrates existing tools using a series of transformations and derivations, building on the proving process in SPARK where Why3 produces Verification Conditions (VCs) and tools such as SMT solvers attempt to verify them. We add steps aimed specifically at VCs that contain inequalities with both floating-point operations and exact real functions. PropaFP is our open-source implementation of these steps.

Keywords: Floating-point computation · Software verification · Automated proving · Interval methods · Software assurance

1 Introduction

Context. Safety-critical software often includes numerical calculations. Since most processors now contain a floating-point (FP) unit, these calculations often use FP arithmetic to utilise the speed of FP units.

Those developing safety-critical programs need to provide guarantees that the program behaves in a precisely specified way. This can be achieved via formal verification, i.e., proving that the program adheres to some specification.

For example, consider the Ada function in Listing 1.1 that computes a Taylor approximation of the sine function. We specify that this function gives a result very close to the exact sine function under some conditions:

$$X \in [-0.5, 0.5] \implies |\texttt{Taylor\_Sin'Result} - \sin(X)| \leq 0.00025889 \qquad (1)$$

We would like a tool to automatically verify this specification or obtain a counterexample if it is not valid. This is an example of auto-active verification [18], i.e., automated proving of inline specifications such as post-conditions and loop invariants.

M. Konečný—This project has received funding from AdaCore Ltd and from the European Union's Horizon 2020 research and innovation programme under the Marie Skłodowska-Curie grant agreement No 731143.

B.-H. Schlingloff and M. Chai (Eds.): SEFM 2022, LNCS 13550, pp. 20–36, 2022.
https://doi.org/10.1007/978-3-031-17108-6_2

Listing 1.1. Sine function in Ada

```
function Taylor_Sin (X : Float) return Float is
   (X - ((X * X * X) / 6.0));
```

To this end, we deploy SPARK technology [14], which represents the state-of-the-art in industry-standard formal software verification. Specifically, we use SPARK Pro 22.1 which includes the GNAT Studio IDE and GNATprove. GNATprove manages Why3 and a selection of bundled SMT solvers (Alt-Ergo [6], Colibri [19], CVC4 [3], and Z3 [20]) as shown in Fig. 1.

As a language, SPARK is based on Ada with a focus on program verification. GNATprove translates SPARK programs to WhyML programs and Why3 [4] then derives proof obligations in the form of verification conditions (VCs), which are formulas comprising traditional mathematical features such as numbers, numerical functions, and sets, and do not mention programming constructs such as loops and mutable variables. The VCs imply that the program satisfies the given specification. Finally, these VCs are sent to various solvers which attempt to decide them. Why3 plays a key role in SPARK as well as other toolchains, effectively harnessing available solvers and provers for software verification.

Problem. With a SPARK version of the specification (1), the toolchain automatically verifies absence of overflow in the `Taylor_Sin` function. This is not difficult since the input x is restricted to the small domain $[-0.5, 0.5]$. However, the current SPARK toolchain and other frameworks we know of are unable to automatically verify that the result of `Taylor_Sin(X)` is close to the exact sin(x).

Part of the problem is that the VCs feature a mixture of exact real and FP operations. For example, in the VCs derived from (1), `Taylor_Sin'Result` is replaced with

$$X \ominus ((X \otimes X \otimes X) \oslash 6.0)$$

where $\ominus$, $\otimes$, and $\oslash$ are FP subtraction, multiplication, and division, respectively. Although SPARK has some support for FP verification [10,12], automatically verifying (1) requires further work.

Solution. To automatically verify functional specifications analogous to (1), we have designed and implemented an extension of the SPARK proving process, called PropaFP. The following steps are applied to quantifier-free VCs that contain real inequalities:

1. Derive bounds for variables and simplify the VC.
2. Safely replace FP operations with the corresponding exact real operations.
3. Again simplify the VC.
4. Attempt to decide the resulting VCs with provers for nonlinear real theorems.

Listing 1.2. SPARK formal specification of `Taylor_Sin`

```
function Taylor_Sin (X : Float) return Float with
  Pre => X >= -0.5 and X <= 0.5,
  Post =>
    abs(Real_Sin(Rf(X)) - Rf(Taylor_Sin'Result))
                      <= Ri(25889) / Ri(100000000);  -- 0.00025889
```

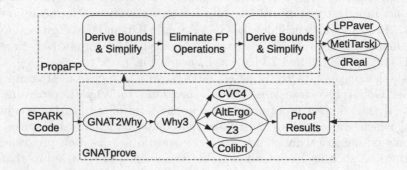

Fig. 1. Overview of Automated Verification via GNATprove with PropaFP

PolyPaver [11] is a nonlinear real theorem prover that integrates with an earlier version of SPARK in a similar way, but lacks the simplification steps and has a much less powerful method of safely replacing FP operations.

Paper Outline. Section 2 describes PropaFP steps in detail, and Sect. 3 analyses the components of the least error bound that is provable in this way. Sections 4 and 5 illustrate the process on further examples, featuring a loop, domain reduction using integers, and calling non-trivial subprograms. Section 6 analyses the performance of the new proving process and Sect. 7 concludes the paper.

2   Our Proving Process Steps

We will illustrate the steps using the program `Taylor_Sin` from Listing 1.1. First consider its SPARK formal specification shown in Listing 1.2.

To write more intuitive specifications, we use the Ada `Big_Real` and `Big_Integer` libraries to get exact rational arithmetic in specifications. Although in Ada the type `Big_Real` contains only rationals, Why3 treats `Big_Real` as the type of reals. We added non-rational functions such as `Real_Sin` as ghost functions; functions with no implementation, only a specification. Their specifications give a collection of basic axioms for solvers that do not understand the function natively. For example, the specification of `Real_Sin` declares the range and special values of sine.

The listings in this paper use shortened versions of some functions to aid readability. Functions `FC.To_Big_Real`, `FLC.To_Big_Real`, and `To_Real` respectively embed `Floats`, `Long_Floats` (doubles), and `Integers` to `Big_Reals`. We have shortened these functions to `Rf`, `Rlf`, and `Ri`, respectively.

Listing 1.3. NVC corresponding to the post-condition from Listing 1.2

```
— assertions regarding axioms for sin and pi omitted
assert to_float(RNA , 1) = 1.0
assert isFiniteFloat(x)
assert (-0.5) ≤ x ∧ x ≤ 0.5
assert isFiniteFloat(x⊙x)
assert isFiniteFloat((x⊙x)⊙x)
assert isFiniteFloat(x ⊖ (((x⊙x)⊙x)⊘6.0))
assert
¬((
    sin(x) + (-1·(x ⊖ (((x⊙x)⊙x)⊘6.0))) ≥ 0.0
    ⟹
    sin(x) + (-1·(x ⊖ (((x⊙x)⊙x)⊘6.0))) ≤ 25889/100000000
 )∧(
    ¬(sin(x) + (-1·(x ⊖ (((x⊙x)⊙x)⊘6.0))) ≥ 0.0)
    ⟹
    -1⊙(sin(x) + (-1·(x ⊖ (((x⊙x)⊙x)⊘6.0)))) ≤ 25889/100000000
 ))
```

2.1 Generating and Processing Verification Conditions

If a VC is not decided by the included SMT solvers, we use the Manual Proof feature in GNAT Studio to invoke PropaFP via a custom Why3 driver based on the driver for CVC4. This driver applies selected Why3 transformations and saves the VC in SMT format. Since in this format the VC is a negation of the specification from which it was produced, we shall refer to it as 'the negated VC' (NVC). The VC contextAsConjunction ⟹ goal becomes the NVC contextAsConjunction ∧ ¬goal. During further processing, we may weaken the conjunction of assertions by, for example, dropping assertions. A model that satisfies the weakened NVC will not necessarily be a counter-example to the original VC or the original specification. However, if the weakened NVC has no model, then both the original VC and the original specification are correct.

When parsing the SMT files, we ignore the definitions of basic arithmetic operations and transcendental functions. Instead of using these definitions, we use each prover's built-in interpretations of such operations and functions. In more detail, the parsing stage comprises the following steps:

– Parse the SMT file as a list of Lisp S-expressions. Drop everything except assertions and variable and function type declarations.
– Scan the assertions and drop any that contain unsupported functions.
– Determine the precision of FP operations by a bottom-up type derivation. The precision of literals is clear since they are given as bit vectors and the precision of variables is given in their declarations.

Dealing with π. Similar to Real_Sin, we have added a ghost parameterless function, Real_Pi, whose specification contains selected axioms for the exact π. Why3 tùrns this into the function `real_pi` with no input. To help provers understand that this is the exact π, all calls to `real_pi` are substituted with π.

For `Taylor_Sin`, the only VC that the SMT solvers included with GNAT Studio cannot solve is the post-condition VC. The NVC for this post-condition is in Listing 1.3. It has been reformatted for better readability by, e.g., removing redundant brackets, using circled symbols for FP operations, and omitting some irrelevant statements. The predicate `isFiniteFloat(X)` is short for the inequalities `MinFloat <= X, X <= MaxFloat`.

2.2   Simplifications and Bounds Derivation

As some of the tools used by PropaFP require bounds on all variables, we attempt to derive bounds from the assertions in the NVC. First, we make the following symbolic simplifications to help derive better bounds:

- Reduce vacuous propositions and obvious tautologies, such as:
  $\varphi = \varphi \longrightarrow$ true   (NOT φ OR true) AND (φ OR false) $\longrightarrow \varphi$
- Eliminate variables by substitution as follows:
  - Find variable-defining equations in the NVC, except circular definitions.
  - Pick a variable definition and make substitutions accordingly.
    * E.g., pick `i=i1+1`, and replace all occurrences of `i` with `i1+1`.
  - If the variable has multiple definitions, pick the shortest one.
    * E.g., if there are both `x=1` and `x=0+1`, pick the first one.
- Perform simple arithmetic simplifications, such as:
  φ / 1 $\longrightarrow \varphi$;   0 + 1 $\longrightarrow$ 1;   MIN (e, e) $\longrightarrow$ e.
- Repeat the above steps until no further simplification can be made.

  Deriving bounds for variables proceeds as follows:

- Identify inequalities which contain only a single variable on either side.
- Iteratively improve bounds by interval-evaluating the expressions given by these inequalities.
  - Initially the bounds for each variable are $-\infty$ and ∞.
  - For floating-point rounding $rnd(x)$, we overestimate the rounding error by the interval expression $x \cdot (1 \pm \epsilon) \pm \zeta$ where ϵ is the machine epsilon, and ζ is the machine epsilon for denormalized numbers for the precision of the rounded operation.
- Variables are assumed to be real unless they are declared integer.
- For integer variables, trim their bounds to nearest integers inside the interval.

  Next, use the derived bounds to potentially further simplify the NVC:

- Evaluate all formulas in the NVC using interval arithmetic.
- If an inequality is decided by this evaluation, replace it with `True` or `False`.

  Finally, repeat the symbolic simplification steps, e.g., to remove any tautologies that have arisen from the interval evaluation. Repeat deriving bounds, evaluations, and simplifications until we have no further improvement.

Listing 1.4. `Taylor_Sin` NVC after simplification and bounds derivation

```
Bounds on variables:
x (real) ∈ [-0.5, 0.5]

NVC:
assert to_float(RNA, 1) = 1.0
— The last assertion is unchanged from Listing 1.3 except turning ≥s into equivalent ≤s.
```

Similarities with Abstract Interpretation. This iterative process can be thought of as a simple form of Abstract Interpretation (AI) over the interval domain [7], but instead of scanning program steps along paths in loops, we scan a set of mutually recursive variable definitions.

The NVC arising from `Taylor_Sin`, shown in Listing 1.3, is already almost in its simplest form. The symbolic steps described in this section applied on this NVC only remove the assertions bounding x. The resulting bounded NVC is outlined in Listing 1.4.

2.3   Eliminating Floating-Point Operations

VCs arising from FP programs are likely to contain FP operations. As most provers for real inequalities do not natively support FP operations, we need to eliminate the FP operations before passing the NVCs to these provers. We propose computing a bound on the size of the overall rounding errors in expressions using a tool specialised in this task, replacing FP operations with the corresponding real operations, and compensating for the loss of rounding by adding/subtracting the computed error bound. Note that this action weakens the NVCs. Recall that weakening is safe for proving correctness but may lead to incorrect counter-examples.

Currently, in our implementation, we use FPTaylor [25] which supports most of the operations we need. In principle, we can use any tool that gives reliable absolute bounds on the rounding error of our FP expressions, such as Gappa [9], Rosa [8], or PRECiSA [26], perhaps enhanced by FPRoCK [24].

There are expressions containing FP operations in the `Taylor_Sin` NVC. The top-level expressions with FP operators are automatically passed to FPTaylor. Listing 1.5 shows an example of how the expressions are specified to FPTaylor. The error bounds computed by FPTaylor for the `Taylor_Sin` NVC expressions with FP operators are summarised in Table 1.

We can now use these error bounds to safely replace FP operations with exact real operations. Listing 1.6 shows the resulting NVC for `Taylor_Sin`.

There may be statements which can be further simplified thanks to the elimination of FP operations. For example, in Listing 1.6, we have the trivial tautology $1 \pm 0.0 = 1.0$. To capitalise on such occurrences, we could once again interval-evaluate each statement in the NVC. Instead, we invoke the steps from Sect. 2.2

Table 1. Error bounds computed by FPTaylor

rnd32(1.0)	0
sin(x) + (-1 * rnd32((x - rnd32((rnd32((rnd32((x * x)) * x)) / 6)))))	1.769513e-8
-1 * (sin(x) + (-1 * rnd32((x - rnd32((rnd32((rnd32((x * x)) * x)) / 6))))))	1.769513e-8

Listing 1.5. FPTaylor file to compute an error bound of the Taylor_Sin VC

```
Variables
  real x in [-0.5, 0.5];


Expressions
  sin(x) + (-1 * rnd32((x - rnd32((rnd32((rnd32((x*x))*x)) / 6)))));
// Computed absolute error bound: 1.769513e-8
```

again, which not only include interval evaluation, but also make any consequent simplifications. In Table 3 this NVC is referred to as Taylor_Sin.

We now have derived bounds for variables and a weakened and simplified NVC with no FP operations, ready for provers. We will call this the 'simplified exact NVC'.

Alternative Methods to Verify FP Problems. Why3 includes a formalization of the FP IEEE-754 standard [1]. For SMT solvers that natively support FP operations, this formalization is mapped to the SMT-LIB FP theory, and for SMT solvers that do not support FP operations, an axiomatization of the formalization is given [12]. This approach is currently unable to verify our examples, as SMT solvers and their FP theories are not yet sufficiently powerful to decide problems with nonlinear real expressions and FP operations. This includes Colibri, as currently integrated with GNATprove. Recent advances in FP support for SMT solvers [17,21,27] may help if combined with more powerful non-linear real solving. Recently, a FP SPARK program computing a weighted average has been verified using these techniques with additional lemmas supplied to the solvers via 'ghost' code [10]. Nevertheless, this approach still does not help SMT solvers prove inequalities featuring elementary functions.

3   Deriving Provable Error Bounds

The specification in Listing 1.2 bounds the difference between Taylor_Sin(X) and the exact sine function. Such a bound can be broken down as follows:

- The **subprogram specification error**, i.e. the error inherited from the specification of any subprograms that the implementation relies on.
    - If an implementation relies on some subprogram, the specification, not the implementation, of that subprogram would be used in the Why3 VC.
    - For Taylor_Sin this component is 0 as it does not call any subprograms.

Listing 1.6. Taylor_Sin NVC after removal of FP operations

```
Bounds on variables:
x (real) ∈ [-0.5, 0.5]

NVC:
assert 1 ± 0.0 = 1.0
assert
 ¬((
  0.0 ≤ (sin(x) + (-1·(x − ((x·x)·x/6.0))) + 1.769513e⁻⁸)
  ⟹
  (sin(x) + (-1·(x − ((x·x)·x/6.0))) + 1.769513e⁻⁸) ≤ (25889/100000000)
 )∧(
  ¬ (0.0 ≤ (sin(x) + (-1·(x − ((x·x)·x/6.0))) − 1.769513e⁻⁸))
  ⟹
  (-1·(sin(x) + (-1·(x − ((x·x)·x/6.0))) + 1.769513e⁻⁸))≤(25889/100000000)
 ))
```

- The **maximum model error** [5], i.e. the maximum difference between the *model* used in the computation and the exact *intended* result.
  - For Taylor_Sin this is the difference between the degree 3 Taylor polynomial for the sine function and the sine function.
- The **maximum rounding error** [5], i.e. the maximum difference between the *exact model* and the *rounded model* computed with FP arithmetic.
- A **rounding analysis cushion** arising when eliminating FP operations. This is the difference between the *actual maximum* rounding error and the *bound* on the rounding error calculated by a tool such as FPTaylor as well as over-approximations made when deriving bounds for variables.
  - The derived bounds are imperfect due to the accuracy loss of interval arithmetic as well as the over-approximation of FP operations.
  - Imperfections in the bounds for variables inflate the computed rounding error bound as more values have to be considered.
- A **proving cushion** is added so that the specification can be decided by the approximation methods in the provers. Without this *cushion*, the provers could not decide the given specification within certain bounds on resources, such as a timeout.

To justify our specification in Listing 1.2, we estimated the values of all five components. Our estimates can be seen in Table 2. The **maximum model error** and the **maximum rounding error** were calculated using the Monte-Carlo method. We ran a simulation comparing the Taylor series approximation of degree 3 of the sine function and an exact sine function. This simulation was ran for one million pseudo-random inputs, giving us an approximate model error. To estimate the maximum rounding error, we compared a single precision and a quadruple precision FP implementation of the model for one hundred million pseudo-random inputs. (FP operations are much faster than exact real operations.) We estimated the **rounding analysis cushion** as the difference between the **maximum rounding error** and the bound given by FPTaylor

Table 2. Error bound components for `Taylor_Sin`

	Single precision	Double precision
Subprogram specification error	0	0
Maximum model error	$\sim 2.59E-4$	$\sim 2.59E-4$
Maximum rounding error	$\sim 1.61E-8$	$\sim 2.89E-17$
Rounding analysis cushion	$\sim 1.57E-9$	$\sim 4.04E-18$
Proving cushion	$\sim 2.11E-9$	$\sim 1.80E-9$

($\sim 1.77E-8$). Note that the actual **rounding analysis cushion** may be larger due to over approximations made when deriving bounds for variables.

The sum of the **maximum model error**, the **maximum rounding error**, and the **rounding analysis cushion** is around 0.0002588878950. Raising the specification bound to 0.00025889 enables provers LPPaver and dReal to verify the specification, using a **proving cushion** of around $2.11E-9$.

In this case, most of the error in the program comes from the **maximum model error**. If we increased the number of Taylor terms, the **maximum model error** would become smaller and the **maximum rounding error** would become larger. Increasing the input domain would make both the **maximum model error** and the **maximum rounding error** larger.

Increasing the precision of the FP numbers used is a simple way to reduce both the maximum **rounding error** and the **rounding analysis cushion**. Table 2 on the right shows estimates for the components in a double-precision version of `Taylor_Sin`. The simplified exact NVC resulting from this example is referred to as Taylor_Sin_Double in Table 3.

To see how the **subprogram specification error** affects provable error bounds, consider function `SinSin` given in Listings 1.7 and 1.8.

Procedure `Taylor_Sin_P` is like function `Taylor_Sin` but the result is returned via the parameter `R`[1]. The specification for `Taylor_Sin_P` has two additional inequalities, bounding the output value `R` to allow us to derive tight bounds for `R` when proving VCs involving calls of this procedure. Verifying this procedure in GNATprove gives one NVC for our proving process, corresponding to the final postcondition. This NVC is referred to as Taylor_Sin_P in Table 3. The exact NVC is in folder examples/taylor_sine/txt in the PropaFP code repository[2].

Function `SinSin` calls `Taylor_Sin_P` with the parameter `X`, storing the result in variable `OneSin`. `Taylor_Sin_P` is then called again with the parameter `OneSin`, storing the result in `TwoSin`, which is then returned. The post-condition for the `SinSin` function specifies the difference between its result and the exact $\sin(\sin(X))$. The VC resulting from this post-condition is referred to as SinSin in Table 3.

---

[1] Our implementation currently does not support function calls, but it does support procedure calls. This limitation is not conceptually significant.

[2] https://github.com/rasheedja/PropaFP/tree/SEFM2022.

Listing 1.7. SinSin function definition in SPARK

```
procedure Taylor_Sin_P (X : Float; R : out Float) is
begin
    R := X - ((X * X * X) / 6.0);
end Taylor_Sin_P;

function SinSin (X : Float) return Float is
    OneSin, TwoSin : Float;
begin
    Taylor_Sin_P(X, OneSin);
    Taylor_Sin_P(OneSin, TwoSin);
    return TwoSin;
end SinSin;
```

Listing 1.8. SinSin function specification in SPARK

```
procedure Taylor_Sin_P (X : Float; R : out Float) with
  Pre => X >= -0.5 and X <= 0.5,
  Post =>
    Rf(R) >= Ri(-48) / Ri(100) and  — Helps verification of calling functions
    Rf(R) <= Ri(48) / Ri(100) and
    abs(Real_Sin(Rf(X)) - Rf(R)) <= Ri(25889) / Ri(100000000);

function SinSin ( X : Float) return Float with
  Pre => X >= -0.5 and X <= 0.5,
  Post =>
    abs(Real_Sin(Real_Sin(Rf(X))) - Rf(SinSin'Result))
      <= Ri(51778) / Ri(100000000);
```

Since the steps of SinSin involve only subprogram calls, there is no **model error** or **rounding error**, and thus no **rounding analysis cushion**. As the value of SinSin comes from Taylor_Sin_P applied twice, and the derivative of sin has the maximum value 1, the **subprogram specification error** is a little below $0.00025889 + 0.00025889 = 0.00051778$. Experimenting with different bounds, we estimate the LPPaver **proving cushion** is around 10^{-13}.

There is a delicate trade-off between the five components that a programmer would need to manage by a careful choice of the model used, FP arithmetic tricks, and proof tools used to obtain a specification for a program that is both accurate and does not require large cushions or specification errors. It is not our goal to make this type of optimisation for the example programs, rather we have calculated these values to help improve the understanding of how difficult it is to estimate them in practice. In simple cases, it would be sufficient to tighten and loosen the 'bound' in the specification until the proving process fails and succeeds, respectively.

Listing 1.9. Heron's Method Specification

```
function Certified_Heron (X : Float; N : Integer) Return Float with
  Pre => X >= 0.5 and X <= 2.0 and N >= 1 and N <= 5,
  Post =>
    abs(Real_Square_Root(Rf(X)) - Rf(Certified_Heron'Result))
      <= (Ri(1) / (Ri(2 ** (2 ** N)))) --- 1/2^{2^N} model error
          + Ri(3*N)*(Ri(1)/Ri(8388608)); --- 3·N·ε, rounding error bound
```

Listing 1.10. Heron's Method Implementation

```
function Certified_Heron (X : Float; N : Integer) return Float is
  Y : Float := 1.0;
begin
  for i in 1 .. N loop
    Y := (Y + X/Y) / 2.0;

    pragma Loop_Invariant (Y >= 0.7);
    pragma Loop_Invariant (Y <= 1.8);
    pragma Loop_Invariant
      (abs (Real_Square_Root (Rf(X)) - Rf(Y))
        <= (Ri(1) / (Ri(2 ** (2 ** i)))) --- 1/2^{2^i}
            + Ri(3*i)*(Ri(1)/Ri(8388608))); --- 3·i·ε
  end loop;
  return Y;
end Certified_Heron;
```

4   Verification of Heron's Method for Approximating the Square Root Function

We used PropaFP to verify an implementation of Heron's method. This is an interesting case study because it requires the use of loops and loop invariants.

In Listing 1.9, the term $3 \cdot N \cdot \varepsilon$ is a heuristic bound for the compound rounding error, guessed by counting the number of operations. Note that five iterations are more than enough to get an accurate approximation of the square root function for x in the range $[0.5, 2]$.

The implementation in Listing 1.10 contains loop invariants. The bounds on Y here help generate easier VCs for the loop iterations and post-loop behaviour. The main loop invariant is very similar to the post-condition in the specification, except substituting i for n, essentially specifying the difference between the exact square root and Heron's method for each iteration of the loop.

Why3 produces 74 NVCs from our implementation of Heron's method. 72 of these NVCs are either trivial or verified by SMT solvers. PropaFP is required for 2 NVCs that come from the main loop invariant. One NVC specifies that the loop invariant holds in the initial iteration of the loop, where i is equal to 1. Another VC specifies that the loop invariant is preserved from one iteration to the next, where i ranges from 1 to n. We refer to these NVCs as as Heron_Init and Heron_Pres in Table 3. Note that the third NVC derived from the invariant, i.e., that the invariant on the last iteration implies the postcondition, is trivial here. The corresponding simplified exact NVCs can be found in folder examples/heron/txt in the PropaFP repository.

5 Verifying AdaCore's Sine Implementation

With the help of PropaFP, we developed a verified version of an Ada sine implementation written by AdaCore for their high-integrity math library[3]. First, we removed SPARK-violating code such as generic FP types, fixing the type to the single-precision `Float`. We then translated functions into procedures since PropaFP currently does not support function calls.

The code consists of six procedures:

- `Multiply_Add` is a helper routine computing `X*Y + Z`.
- `Approx_Sin` and `Approx_Cos` approximate $\sin(x)$ and $\cos(x)$, respectively, for x near 0, evaluating a Taylor polynomial in Horner form, using `Multiply_Add`.
- `My_Machine_Rounding` rounds an FP number x to the nearest integer, replacing the SPARK-violating function `Float'Machine_Rounding`.
- `Reduce_Half_Pi` translates an angle $x \in [0, 802]$ to a quadrant near 0 by subtracting an integer multiple of $\pi/2$, using `My_Machine_Rounding`.
- `Sin` approximates $\sin(x)$ for $x \in [-802, 802]$ using the above procedures.

The original code has a loop that extends the domain beyond $[-802, 802]$. We have removed the loop for now. The complete code and specification can be found in folder examples/spark and NVCs can be found in folder examples/hie_sine/txt in the PropaFP repository. A more complete explanation of the code and specification is in the extended preprint [23].

`My_Machine_Rounding`$(x, \text{out } y)$ specifies $-0.500000001 \leq x - y \leq 0.500000001$. The "padding" added to 0.5 avoids "touching" VCs (such as $x > 0 \implies x > 0$), which solvers using interval methods usually cannot prove.

`Reduce_Half_Pi`$(\text{in out } x, \text{out } Q, \text{out } R)$ needs the integer result parameter R only so that the postcondition can state that $x_{\text{new}} \sim x_{\text{old}} - R \cdot \pi/2$.

`Apprix_Sin`, `Apprix_Cos`, and `Sin` specify bounds on their deviation from the exact sine or cosine at $5.8E{-}8$, $1.4E{-}7$ and $1.9E{-}4$, respectively.

Why3 derived 158 NVCs from the six procedures. SMT solvers have proved 146 of these NVCs and the remaining 12 have been proved using our process.

6 Benchmarking the Proving Process

Table 3 shows the performance of our implementation of the proving process on the verification examples described earlier. "VC processing" is the time it takes

---

[3] We obtained the original code from file `src/ada/hie/s-libsin.adb` in archive `gnat-2021-20210519-19A70-src.tar.gz` downloaded from "More packages, platforms, versions and sources" at https://www.adacore.com/download.

Table 3. Proving process on described examples

VC	VC Processing	dReal	MetiTarski	LPPaver
My_Machine_Rounding$_\geq$	0.53 s	n/s	n/s	0.47 s
My_Machine_Rounding$_<$	0.56 s	n/s	n/s	0.42 s
Reduce_Half_Pi_X$_\geq$	1.76 s	n/s	0.07 s	0.35 s
Reduce_Half_Pi_X$_<$	1.77 s	n/s	0.04 s	0.33 s
Reduce_Half_Pi$_\geq$	65.02 s	n/s	g/u	0.02 s
Reduce_Half_Pi$_<$	61.32 s	n/s	g/u	0.01 s
Approx_Sin$_\geq$	1.85 s	1 m 08.95 s	0.17 s	5.63 s
Approx_Sin$_<$	1.86 s	1 m 06.16 s	0.15s	5.61s
Approx_Cos$_\geq$	0.95 s	3.28 s	0.05 s	1.83 s
Approx_Cos$_<$	1.00 s	1.53 s	0.04 s	1.50 s
Sin$_\geq$	1.29 s	n/s	n/s	6 m 34.62 s
Sin$_<$	1.30 s	n/s	n/s	6 m 29.8 s
Taylor_Sin	2.04 s	0.01 s	0.14 s	0.06 s
Taylor_Sin_Double	2.07 s	n/s	0.11 s	0.05 s
Taylor_Sin_P	2.05 s	0.01 s	0.14 s	0.06 s
SinSin	0.53 s	3 m 19.81 s	g/u	8.20 s
Heron_Init	2.01 s	0.00 s	0.07 s	0.01 s
Heron_Pres	3.05 s	5 m 06.14 s	g/u	1 m 19.99 s

PropaFP to process the NVCs generated by GNATprove/Why3, including calls to FPTaylor. The remaining columns show the performance of the following provers applied to the resulting simplified exact NVCs:

- dReal v4.21.06.2 [13] – solver using numerical branch-and-prune methods.
- MetiTarski v2.4 [2] – symbolic theorem prover deciding real inequalities via cylindrical algebraic decomposition (CAD).
- LPPaver v0.0.1 [22] – our prover that uses methods similar to dReal.

In Table 3, g/u means that the prover gave up while n/s means the NVC cannot be applied to this prover for the following reasons:

- The My_Machine_Rounding NVC contains integer rounding with ties going away from zero, which is not supported by dReal and MetiTarski.
- After our proving process, the bound on the **maximum rounding error** computed by FPTaylor in the Reduce_Half_Pi and the Taylor_Sin_Double NVCs are very small. This number is represented as a fraction, and the denominator is outside the range of integers supported by dReal.
- The Sin NVCs contain integer rounding with ties going to the nearest even integer and uses the modulus operator.
    - dReal does not support integer rounding.
    - MetiTarski does not support the modulus operator.

Table 4. Effect of specification bound on proving time

VC	Bound	VC processing	dReal	MetiTarski	LPPaver
Approx_Sin$_\leq$	0.000000058	1.86 s	1 m 06.16 s	0.15 s	5.61 s
Approx_Sin$_\leq$	0.000000075	1.85 s	28.73 s	0.16 s	3.72 s
Approx_Sin$_\leq$	0.0000001	1.86 s	15.42 s	0.15 s	2.69 s
Approx_Sin$_\leq$	0.00001	1.85 s	0.09 s	0.15 s	0.25 s

Table 5. Proving process on described counter-examples

VC	VC processing	dReal	CE	LPPaver	CE
Taylor_Sin_Plus	2.05 s	0.00 s	$x = -0.166\ldots$	0.02 s	$x = -0.5$
Taylor_Sin_Swap	2.05 s	0.00 s	$x = 0.166\ldots$	0.03 s	$x = 0.499\ldots$
Taylor_Sin_Tight	2.1 s	0.00 s	$x = 0.499\ldots$	0.03 s	$x = 0.499\ldots$

All of the NVCs were solved by at least one of the provers in a reasonable time frame. VC processing takes, at most, a few seconds for most of the NVCs. For Reduce_Half_Pi$\{\geq,\leq\}$, the VC processing step takes around one minute. This is because FPTaylor takes a while to run its branch-and-bound algorithm on non-trivial formulas featuring π.

For provers using numerical approximation, the tightness of the specification bound is often correlated with the time it takes for a prover to decide a VC arising from said specification. We illustrate this in Table 4. The proving time for symbolic provers does not improve with looser bounds. However, MetiTarski failed to decide Reduce_Half_Pi$\{\geq,\leq\}$, but it could decide these NVCs when the specification bounds were loosened from $1.8E{-}4$ to $2.0E{-}4$.

6.1 Counter-examples

To demonstrate how the proving process produces potential counter-examples, we modify our Taylor_Sin example, introducing three different mistakes which a programmer may feasibly make:

1. Replace the - with + in the Taylor_Sin implementation in Listing 1.1.
2. Invert the inequality in the Taylor_Sin post-condition in Listing 1.2.
3. Make our specification bound slightly tighter than the **maximum model error + maximum rounding error + rounding analysis cushion** in the post-condition from Listing 1.2, changing the value of the right hand side of the inequality in the post-condition from 0.00025889 to 0.00025887.

These three 'mistakes' are referred to as Taylor_Sin_Plus, Taylor_Sin_Swap, and Taylor_Sin_Tight, respectively, in Table 5.

If a specification is incorrect, the resulting NVC must be true or 'sat'. dReal would report a 'delta-sat' result, which means the given file was 'sat' with a configurable tolerance, which we set to 1^{-100}. This makes models produced by dReal a *potential* model for the NVC. Models produced by LPPaver are actual models for the given NVC, but for files produced by the proving process, these should still be thought of as *potential* counter-examples due to the weakening of the NVC. The computed potential counter-examples shown in Table 5 are all actual counter-examples except those for Taylor_Sin_Tight.

7   Conclusion

Summary. In this paper, we have presented an automated proving process for deciding VCs that arise in the verification of floating-point programs with a strong functional specification. Our implementation of the process builds on SPARK, GNATprove, and Why3, and utilises FPTaylor and the nonlinear real provers dReal, MetiTarski, and LPPaver. This process could be adapted for other tools and languages, as long as one can generate NVCs similar to those generated by GNATprove.

We demonstrated our proving process on three examples of increasing complexity, featuring loops, real-integer interactions, and subprogram calls. The examples demonstrate an improvement on the state-of-the-art in the power of automated FP software verification. Table 3 indicates that our proving process can automatically and fairly quickly decide certain VCs that are currently considered difficult. Table 4 demonstrates how the process speeds up when using looser bounds in specifications. Table 5 shows that our proving process can quickly find potential, often even actual, counter-examples for a range of common incorrect specifications.

We conclude with thoughts on how our process could be further improved.

Executable Exact Real Specifications. We plan to make specifications containing functions such as $\sqrt{\cdot}$ executable via high-accuracy interval arithmetic, allowing the developer or IDE to check whether the suggested counter-examples are valid.

Adapting the Provers. To make dReal and MetiTarski more effective in our process, support for integer rounding could be added to both provers, and the modulo operator to MetiTarski.

More Provers. Connect PropaFP to other provers, notably Colibri.

Why3 Integration. Our VC processing steps could be integrated into Why3. This would include simplifications, bound derivation, and floating-point elimination. As Why3 transformations, the VC processing steps would be more accessible for users who are familiar with Why3. Also, the proving process would become easily available to the many tools that support Why3.

Support Function Calls. Having to manually translate functions into procedures is undesirable. Support for function calls could be added, e.g., by a Why3 transformation that translates functions into procedures.

Use Abstract Interpretation. We currently derive bounds for variables using our own iterative process similar to Abstract Interpretation. We could try integrating an established Abstract Interpretation implementation instead.

Verified Implementation. We would like to formally verify some elements of our process to ensure that the transformation steps are performed correctly. As PropaFP and LPPaver utilise Haskell and AERN2 [15], rewriting these tools in Coq with coq-aern [16] may be a feasible verification route.

References

1. IEEE Standard for Floating-Point Arithmetic. IEEE Std 754–2019 (Revision of IEEE 754–2008), pp. 1–84 (2019). https://doi.org/10.1109/IEEESTD.2019. 8766229
2. Akbarpour, B., Paulson, L.C.: MetiTarski: an automatic theorem prover for real-valued special functions. J. Autom. Reason. **44**(3), 175–205 (2010). https://doi. org/10.1007/s10817-009-9149-2
3. Barrett, C., et al.: CVC4. In: Gopalakrishnan, G., Qadeer, S. (eds.) CAV 2011. LNCS, vol. 6806, pp. 171–177. Springer, Heidelberg (2011). https://doi.org/10. 1007/978-3-642-22110-1_14
4. Bobot, F., Filliâtre, J.C., Marché, C., Paskevich, A.: Why3: shepherd your herd of provers. In: Boogie 2011: First International Workshop on Intermediate Verification Languages, pp. 53–64 (2011). https://hal.inria.fr/hal-00790310
5. Boldo, S., Clément, F., Filliâtre, J.C., Mayero, M., Melquiond, G., Weis, P.: Wave equation numerical resolution: a comprehensive mechanized proof of a C program. J. Autom. Reason. **50**(4), 423–456 (2013). https://doi.org/10.1007/s10817-012-9255-4
6. Conchon, S., Coquereau, A., Iguernlala, M., Mebsout, A.: Alt-Ergo 2.2. In: SMT Workshop: International Workshop on Satisfiability Modulo Theories (2018). https://hal.inria.fr/hal-01960203
7. Cousot, P., Cousot, R.: Abstract interpretation: a unified lattice model for static analysis of programs by construction or approximation of fixpoints. In: Proceedings of the 4th ACM SIGACT-SIGPLAN Symposium on Principles of Programming Languages, pp. 238–252. POPL 1977, Association for Computing Machinery, New York, NY, USA (1977). https://doi.org/10.1145/512950.512973
8. Darulova, E., Kuncak, V.: Towards a compiler for reals. ACM Trans. Program. Lang. Syst. (TOPLAS) **39**(2), 1–28 (2017). https://doi.org/10.1145/3014426
9. Daumas, M., Melquiond, G.: Certification of bounds on expressions involving rounded operators. ACM Trans. Math. Softw. **37**(1), 1–20 (2010). https://doi. org/10.1145/1644001.1644003
10. Dross, C., Kanig, J.: Making proofs of floating-point programs accessible to regular developers. In: Bloem, R., Dimitrova, R., Fan, C., Sharygina, N. (eds.) Software Verification, pp. 7–24. LNCS, Springer International Publishing, Cham (2022). https://doi.org/10.1007/978-3-030-95561-8_2
11. Duracz, J., Konečný, M.: Polynomial function intervals for floating-point software verification. Ann. Math. Artif. Intell. **70**(4), 351–398 (2014). https://doi.org/10. 1007/s10472-014-9409-7

12. Fumex, C., Marché, C., Moy, Y.: Automated verification of floating-point computations in Ada programs. report, Inria Saclay Ile de France (2017). https://hal.inria.fr/hal-01511183/document
13. Gao, S., Kong, S., Clarke, E.M.: dReal: an SMT solver for nonlinear theories over the reals. In: Bonacina, M.P. (ed.) CADE 2013. LNCS (LNAI), vol. 7898, pp. 208–214. Springer, Heidelberg (2013). https://doi.org/10.1007/978-3-642-38574-2_14
14. Hoang, D., Moy, Y., Wallenburg, A., Chapman, R.: SPARK 2014 and GNATprove. Int. J. Softw. Tools Technol. Transfer **17**(6), 695–707 (2015). https://doi.org/10.1007/s10009-014-0322-5
15. Konečný, M., et al.: AERN2 (2022). https://github.com/michalkonecny/aern2
16. Konečný, M., Park, S., Thies, H.: Axiomatic reals and certified efficient exact real computation. In: Silva, A., Wassermann, R., de Queiroz, R. (eds.) WoLLIC 2021. LNCS, vol. 13038, pp. 252–268. Springer, Cham (2021). https://doi.org/10.1007/978-3-030-88853-4_16
17. Leeser, M., Mukherjee, S., Ramachandran, J., Wahl, T.: Make it real: effective floating-point reasoning via exact arithmetic. In: 2014 Design, Automation & Test in Europe Conference & Exhibition (DATE), pp. 1–4 (2014). https://doi.org/10.7873/DATE.2014.130
18. Leino, K.R.M., Moskal, M.: Usable auto-active verification. In: Usable Verification Workshop (2010). http://fm.csl.sri.com/UV10.Citeseer
19. Marre, B., Bobot, F., Chihani, Z.: Real behavior of floating point numbers. In: SMT Workshop, p. 12 (2017)
20. de Moura, L., Bjørner, N.: Z3: an efficient SMT solver. In: Ramakrishnan, C.R., Rehof, J. (eds.) TACAS 2008. LNCS, vol. 4963, pp. 337–340. Springer, Heidelberg (2008). https://doi.org/10.1007/978-3-540-78800-3_24
21. Ramachandran, J., Wahl, T.: Integrating proxy theories and numeric model lifting for floating-point arithmetic. In: 2016 Formal Methods in Computer-Aided Design (FMCAD), pp. 153–160 (2016). https://doi.org/10.1109/FMCAD.2016.7886674
22. Rasheed, J.: LPPaver code repository (2022). https://github.com/rasheedja/LPPaver
23. Rasheed, J., Konečný, M.: Auto-active verification of floating-point programs via nonlinear real provers (extended preprint) (2022). arXiv:2207.00921
24. Salvia, R., Titolo, L., Feliú, M.A., Moscato, M.M., Muñoz, C.A., Rakamarić, Z.: A mixed real and floating-point solver. In: Badger, J.M., Rozier, K.Y. (eds.) NFM 2019. LNCS, vol. 11460, pp. 363–370. Springer, Cham (2019). https://doi.org/10.1007/978-3-030-20652-9_25
25. Solovyev, A., Baranowski, M.S., Briggs, I., Jacobsen, C., Rakamarić, Z., Gopalakrishnan, G.: Rigorous estimation of floating-point round-off errors with symbolic Taylor expansions. ACM Trans. Program. Lang. Syst. **41**(1), 1–39 (2019)
26. Titolo, L., Feliú, M.A., Moscato, M., Muñoz, C.A.: An abstract interpretation framework for the round-off error analysis of floating-point programs. In: VMCAI 2018. LNCS, vol. 10747, pp. 516–537. Springer, Cham (2018). https://doi.org/10.1007/978-3-319-73721-8_24
27. Zeljić, A., Backeman, P., Wintersteiger, C.M., Rümmer, P.: Exploring approximations for floating-point arithmetic using UppSAT. In: Galmiche, D., Schulz, S., Sebastiani, R. (eds.) IJCAR 2018. LNCS (LNAI), vol. 10900, pp. 246–262. Springer, Cham (2018). https://doi.org/10.1007/978-3-319-94205-6_17

Information Exchange Between Over- and Underapproximating Software Analyses

Jan Haltermann[(✉)] [iD] and Heike Wehrheim [iD]

University of Oldenburg, Oldenburg, Germany
{jan.haltermann,heike.wehrheim}@uol.de

Abstract. Cooperative software validation aims at having verification and/or testing tools *cooperate* on the task of correctness checking. Cooperation involves the exchange of information about currently achieved results in the form of (verification) artifacts. These artifacts are typically specialized to the type of analysis performed by the tool, e.g. bounded model checking, abstract interpretation or symbolic execution, and hence requires the definition of a new artifact for every new cooperation to be built.

In this paper, we introduce a unified artifact (called Generalized Information Exchange Automaton, short GIA) supporting the cooperation of *overapproximating* with *underapproximating* analyses. It provides all the information gathered by an analysis to its partner in a cooperation, independent of the type of analysis and usage context. We provide a formal definition of this artifact as an automaton together with two operators on GIAs, the first *reducing* a program with respect to results in a GIA and the second *combining* partial results in two GIAs into one. We show that computed analysis results are never lost when connecting tools via reducers and combiners. To experimentally demonstrate the feasibility, we have implemented one such cooperation and report on the achieved results, in particular how the new artifact is able to overcome some of the drawbacks of existing artifacts.

Keywords: Cooperative software verification · Verification artifact · Test case generation · Component-based CEGAR

1 Introduction

Over the past years, automatic software validation (i.e., verification and testing) has become a mature field, with numerous tools pro6iding various sorts of analysis (see e.g. the annual competitions on software verification and testing [3,4]). Still, the one-fits-all approach to software validation has not yet been found. All tools have their specific strengths and weaknesses, and tools efficiently solving one sort of analysis tasks might be slow at or even unable to solve other tasks.

J. Haltermann—This author was partially supported by the German Research Foundation (DFG) - WE2290/13-1 (Coop).

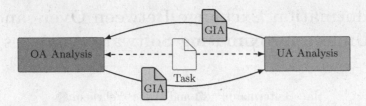

Fig. 1. Cooperation of over- and underapproximating analyses

To remedy this situation, cooperative software verification (term coined by Beyer and Wehrheim [15]) aims at having different tools cooperate on the task of software verification. This principle can not only be applied to verification but also to testing, and a number of different approaches combining various sorts of analyses exist today (e.g. [1,2,8,9,13,16,18–21,23–25,28]). To achieve cooperation, tools need to *exchange information* gathered about a program during its analysis. To leverage the strengths of tools, we need to make sure that no results computed about a program are lost during this information exchange. To this end, existing cooperative approaches use various sorts of so-called *verification artifacts* [15] for information exchange, e.g. correctness witnesses [5], predicate maps [13] or violation witnesses [6]. The artifacts are, however, often specialized to the type of analysis performed, with the consequence of having to define a new form of artifact with every new cooperation.

In this work, we introduce a novel *uniform* verification artifact (called GIA) for the exchange of information, specifically focusing on the cooperation of *over- and underapproximating software analyses* (see Fig. 1). Overapproximating (OA) analyses build an overapproximation of the state space of a program while underapproximating (UA) analyses inspect specific program paths. An underapproximating analysis typically aims at finding errors; an overapproximating analysis aims at proving program correctness. Before defining the new type of artifact, we first of all studied existing (cooperative and non-cooperative) analyses and the information they assemble and possibly exchange during an analysis. We also investigated what input formats existing tools accept. The majority of tools just take a program as input, however, there are also some tools already allowing for verification artifacts as additional inputs. With these insights at hand, we defined a new artifact in the form of a *generalized information exchange automaton* (GIA) which can express all the information generated by over- and underapproximating analyses. More specifically, our artifact needs to be able to cover (1) program paths which definitely or potentially lead to an error, i.e. (potential) counter examples, (2) program paths which are already known to be safe, (3) program paths which are already known to be infeasible plus (4) additional constraints on program paths like state invariants. The unification of all such information in one artifact should in particular make the artifact *independent* of its usage, i.e. the semantics of the GIA should be the same in all usage contexts. Current artifacts, in particular the protocol automata of Beyer and Wehrheim [15], have differing meanings depending on their usage: sometimes the paths described by an automaton are the safe paths and sometimes the paths leading to a property violation.

Along with this new artifact we also introduce two operations on it: *reducers* [10,22] and *combiners*. A reducer allows to (syntactically) reduce a program to the part which a (prior) analysis has not yet completed (e.g., not yet proven safe). Reducers are required for cooperation of analysis tools which only take programs as inputs. A combiner allows to combine computed analysis results given in two GIAs into one. We formally show that connecting tools via reducers and combiners guarantees computed analysis results to never be lost.

To demonstrate the feasibility of our approach, we have implemented one such cooperation employing GIAs as exchange format. We have experimentally evaluated this cooperation on benchmarks of SV-COMP [4] and report on the outcomes, in particular how existing drawbacks in cooperation approaches caused by information loss can be overcome with this new artifact.

2   Background

We generally aim at the validation of programs written in C. To be able to discuss and define formats for the information exchange, especially their semantics, we first provide some basic definitions on the syntax and semantics of programs, and then survey existing artifacts.

2.1   Program Syntax and Semantics

We represent a program as a *control-flow automaton (CFA)*. Intuitively, a CFA is a control-flow graph, where each edge is labeled with a program statement. More formally, a CFA C is a graph $C = (Loc, \ell_0, G)$ with a set of program locations Loc, the initial location $\ell_0 \in Loc$ and a transition relation $G \subseteq Loc \times Ops \times Loc$, where Ops contains all possible operations on integer variables[1], namely assignments, conditions (for both loops and branches), function calls and return statements. We let $\mathcal{C}$ denote the set of all CFAs. Note that any program can be transferred into a CFA and any deterministic CFA into a program.

We assume the existence of two specific functions `error` and `random` which programs can call; the former can be used to represent violations of a specification (reachability of an error), the latter returns a non-deterministic value and is typically used to model inputs. We assume our programs to be deterministic except for the function `random`.

For defining the semantics of CFAs, we let Var denote the set of all integer variables present in the program, $AExpr$ the set of arithmetic and $BExpr$ the set of boolean expressions over the variables in Var. A *state* c is a mapping of the program variables to integers, i.e., $c : Var \to \mathbb{Z}$. We lift this mapping to also contain evaluations of the arithmetic and boolean expressions, such that c maps $AExpr$ to $\mathbb{Z}$ and $BExpr$ to $\mathbb{B} = \{0, 1\}$. A finite *syntactic program path* is a sequence $\tau = \ell_0 \xrightarrow{g_1} \ldots \xrightarrow{g_n} \ell_n$ s.t. $(\ell_i, g_{i+1}, \ell_{i+1}) \in G$ for each transition. We

---

[1] We restrict the operations to integer variables for presentation only; the implementation covers C programs.

```
1  int main(){
2    int x = random();
3    if (x < 5) {
4      return 0;
5    } else {
6      x++;
7      if (x == 5) {
8        return 1;
9      } else {
10       return 2;
11     }
12   }
13 }
```

(a) An example program for test case generation

(b) CFA for program in Fig. 2a, where nodes after branching points are marked gray.

Fig. 2. Example program for test case generation and corresponding CFA.

extend a syntactic path to a *semantic program path* $\pi = \langle c_0, \ell_0 \rangle \xrightarrow{g_1} \dots \xrightarrow{g_n} \langle c_n, \ell_n \rangle$, by adding states to each location, where c_0 assigns the value 0 to all variables, and state changes for $\langle c_i, \ell_i \rangle \xrightarrow{g_{i+1}} \langle c_{i+1}, \ell_{i+1} \rangle$ are defined as follows: If g_{i+1} is an assignment of the form $x = a$, $x \in Var, a \in AExpr$, $c_{i+1} = c_i[x \mapsto c_i(a)]$, for assignments $x = \mathtt{random}()$ $c_{i+1} = c_i[x \mapsto z]$, $z \in \mathbb{Z}$, otherwise $c_{i+1} = c_i$. Note that we do not require that a semantic path meets all its boolean conditions, as we want to distinguish between feasible and infeasible semantic paths: A semantic path is called *feasible*, if for each condition $g_{i+1} = b$ in the path $c_i(b) = true$ holds, otherwise it is called *infeasible*. We say that a path π *reaches* location $\ell \in Loc$ if $\ell = \ell_n$. If no feasible semantic path reaches a location $\ell \in Loc$, it is called *unreachable*. The set of all semantic paths (or in short, paths) of a CFA C is denoted by $\mathcal{P}(C)$.

Figure 2 contains a C-program and its corresponding CFA. Let's assume our validation task on this program is *test case generation*, more specifically generating test inputs (values returned by $\mathtt{random}$) which cover all branches of the program. A tool would then need to generate inputs leading to paths such that each node of the CFA marked in gray is reached by at least one path. A feasible path that reaches the location ℓ_3 is: $\langle \{x \mapsto 0\}, \ell_1 \rangle \xrightarrow{x=\mathtt{random}();} \langle \{x \mapsto 3\}, \ell_2 \rangle \xrightarrow{x<5} \langle \{x \mapsto 3\}, \ell_3 \rangle \xrightarrow{\text{return } 0;} \langle \{x \mapsto 3\}, \ell_4 \rangle$. The location ℓ_7 is unreachable, as x is always greater than 5 at ℓ_6, and thus it cannot be covered.

2.2 Existing Artifacts

We next briefly explain some existing artifacts already used either for cooperative validation, for witness validation or storage of correctness proofs [5,6,10,15, 23,25,27] and discuss their suitability for representing information exchanged between underapproximating (UA) and overapproximating (OA) analysis. Most of the presented formats are automaton-based, where nodes are labeled with program locations and edges labeled with program operations from *Ops*. As the formats encode information about (non-)violation of properties, we call CFA nodes violating the property *target nodes*.

Violation Witness. A violation witness [6] is a automaton-based exchange format to encode a set of paths that lead to a property violation. These paths may contain path constraints on the variable values. By design, the violation witness does not allow using state invariants. Thus, its semantics does neither allow to encode that a path does not reach a target node (i.e., is safe) or is infeasible nor some justification of this in the form of state invariants.

Correctness Witnesses. A correctness witness [5] is a automaton-based exchange format used to encode that a program is safe (no target node reachable) together with a justification in form of invariants. Correctness witnesses do not allow to specify target nodes nor to encode partial results. Therefore, encoding path to target nodes as well as marking that only certain paths of the program (and not the whole program) is safe is impossible.

Condition Automaton. A condition automaton [10] is a automaton-based format, stating which paths of the program are already successfully verified and under which condition. Based on the precisely defined semantics, paths accepted by the condition automaton do not reach target nodes. Thus, paths (potentially) leading to a target node cannot be encoded. In addition, condition automata do not allow adding state invariants.

Abstract Reachability Graph (ARG). An ARG [7] represents the abstract state space computed by an analysis as a graph and is used within different tools, e.g. CPACHECKER [12]. ARG states contain a combination of analysis dependent information from different domains, e.g. predicates, live variables or variable values and can contain meta-information, e.g. whether the ARG state is a target or that certain successors are unreachable. Edges are labeled with program operations from *Ops*. The ARG can be used to represent all desired information that should be exchanged. Due to the analysis dependent information, ARG states generated for different analyses may however have different shapes, which makes an exchange of ARGs between different analyses in a general setting impossible.

Protocol Automaton. Protocol automata [6,15] are a flexible, automaton based exchange format, potentially allowing to express all desired information exchanged between OA and UA analyses. The major drawback (and the price of that flexibility) of protocol automaton is the *context-dependent* semantics. Thus, each tool working with protocol automata has to be aware of the type of protocol automaton given to it and its semantics. Depending on the encoded artifact, accepting paths encode either a path to a target node, an infeasible path or a path not reaching a target node. Consequently, it is impossible to mark within one protocol automaton both, a path to a target node as unreachable and state that a different path reaches another target node.

In summary, none of the existing artifacts is able to encode all desired information and is usable independent of the tools used while maintaining one semantics. Next, we introduce a new format that overcomes these limitations.

3   Validation Artifact GIA

In this work, we focus on two different validation tasks on programs, verification and test case generation, performed by over- and underapproximating analyses. For *verification*, the goal is to show the non-reachability of certain error locations. To this end, we fix a *safety property* $S = (\ell, \omega)$ as a pair of location $\ell \in Loc$ and condition $\omega \in BExpr$ which has to hold at ℓ. In practice, this is encoded in the CFA using two edges $(\ell \xrightarrow{\neg\omega} \ell_e \xrightarrow{error();} \ell_{e'})$. Note that there can be multiple safety properties for a program. For *test case generation*, the goal is to find paths from ℓ_0 reaching all locations from a set L_{cover}, containing e.g. each branch or statement in the program (branch-, statement-coverage) or certain function calls, especially `error`. To specify these paths, a sequence of return values (called *test suite*) for the calls to `random` suffices (as `random` models inputs to programs).

For cooperation, we prefer a uniform way of describing these tasks which we get by introducing the notion of *target nodes*, denoted by L, $L \subseteq Loc$. A target node is a node that either has a single outgoing edge labeled `error` (for verification) or is in L_{cover} (for test case generation). We can now reformulate the two tasks: the goal of verification is to show that no target node is reachable, the goal of test case generation is to find a test suite such that all target nodes are reached. In Fig. 2b, the target nodes for test case generation are $L = \{\ell_3, \ell_5, \ell_7, \ell_9\}$.

Our overall objective is next to define an artifact with one semantics which is valid for every type of exchanged information. In general, UA and OA tools either aim at showing that target nodes are reachable (for example a call to `error` or a branch that needs to be covered) or that (a part of) the program does not reach any target node (i.e., program is safe). The overall goal is achieved when for each target node either a path reaching it is found or it is proven unreachable.

The information exchanged between UA and OA tools thus need to be about (1) feasible paths definitely leading to a target node, (2) paths definitely not leading to a target node (either as they do not reach one or are infeasible) and (3) *candidate* paths potentially leading to target nodes and hence interesting to consider for the analysis, but where the definite result about it is unknown so far. The latter information is used in two cases: When an UA tool has not yet covered a path, either due to resource/time limitations or because it is infeasible, and when an OA tool has discovered a path to a target node, which might be feasible. In addition, we need the artifact to be able to pass helpful information about invariants of program locations or constraints about program transitions.

So far, none of the existing artifacts discussed in Sect. 2 is able to encode all this information while maintaining one semantics for the automaton. Inspired by the idea of three-valued logics (e.g. for three-valued model checking [17]), we extend the condition automata of [10] by introducing *three* different, disjoint sets of accepting states, one for each type of exchanged information.

Definition 1. *A generalized information exchange automaton for over- and under-approximative analysis (GIA) $A = (\mathcal{Q}, \Sigma, \delta, q_0, F_{ut}, F_{rt}, F_{cand})$ consists of*

- *a finite set $\mathcal{Q} \subseteq \Omega \times BExpr$ of states (each being a pair of a name of some set Ω and a boolean condition) and an initial state $(q_0, true) \in \mathcal{Q}$,*

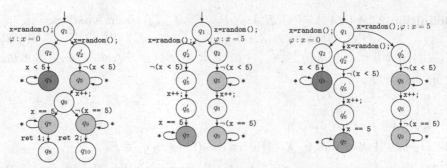

(a) GIA A_1 after appli- (b) GIA A_2 after applica- (c) Combined GIA of A_1 and A_2
cation of an UA tool   tion of an OA tool

Fig. 3. GIAs generated during cooperative test case generation for example program of Fig. 2 with states of F_{ut} marked green, of F_{rt} blue and of F_{cand} yellow. We elide state invariants (all *true*) and depict for transitions only the operation and non-true conditions. (Color figure online)

- *an alphabet* $\Sigma \subseteq 2^G \times BExpr$,
- *a transition relation* $\delta \subseteq \mathcal{Q} \times \Sigma \times \mathcal{Q}$, *and*
- *three pairwise disjoint sets of* accepting states: F_{ut} *(for unreachable targets)*, F_{rt} *(for reachable targets) and* F_{cand} *(for candidates)*.

Automaton states have (arbitrary) names and potentially *invariants* associated with them which come in the form of boolean expressions over program variables. Transitions are labelled over the alphabet Σ with elements being sets of transitions of the CFA plus additional *assumptions* (again out of *BExpr*) about program variables describing conditions when executing these transitions (see Definition 2 below). When drawing automata, we use $*$ to denote an edge that matches any operation from *Ops*. We additionally require for each GIA, that (1) the each state in the sets of accepting states F_{ut} and F_{rt} has no transitions to states not in F_{ut} (resp. F_{rt}) and (2) each accepting state from F_{cand} has at least a transition to itself[2]. More formally, we require that:

1. $\forall q_{ut} \in F_{ut} : \neg \exists q \in \mathcal{Q} : (q_{ut}, op, q) \in \delta \wedge q \notin F_{ut}$,
2. $\forall q_{rt} \in F_{rt} : \neg \exists q \in \mathcal{Q} : (q_{rt}, op, q) \in \delta \wedge q \notin F_{rt}$,
3. $\forall q_{cand} \in F_{cand} : (q_{cand}, *, q_{cand}) \in \delta$.

An example of a GIA for the program of Fig. 2 with target nodes $L = \{\ell_3, \ell_5, \ell_7, \ell_9\}$ is depicted in Fig. 3c, where $F_{rt} = \{q_3\}, F_{ut} = \{q_7\}$ and $F_{cand} = \{q_5, q_9\}$.

We let $\mathcal{A}$ denote the set of all GIAs. For the semantics, the three sets of accepting states are employed to describe three different languages of a GIA: the set of paths leading to (1) F_{ut}, (2) F_{rt} and (3) F_{cand}. We first of all define what it means that an automaton covers a path.

---

[2] This property is useful to have a single path π covering several nodes from F_{cand} (e.g. for branch coverage).

Definition 2. *A GIA* $A = (\mathcal{Q}, \Sigma, \delta, q_0, F_{ut}, F_{rt}, F_{cand})$ *covers a path* $\pi = \langle c_0, \ell_0 \rangle$ $\xrightarrow{g_1} \dots \xrightarrow{g_n} \langle c_n, \ell_n \rangle$ *if there is a sequence* $\rho = (q_0, \psi_0) \xrightarrow{(G_1, \varphi_1)} \dots \xrightarrow{(G_k, \varphi_k)}$ $(q_k, \psi_k), 0 \le k \le n$, *with* $(q_{i-1}, \psi_{i-1}) \xrightarrow{(G_i, \varphi_i)} (q_i, \psi_i) \in \Sigma$ *(called run), such that*

1. $q_k \in F_{ut} \cup F_{rt} \cup F_{cand}$,
2. $\forall i, 1 \le i \le k : g_i \in G_i$,
3. $\forall i, 1 \le i \le k : c_i \models \varphi_i$,
4. $\forall i, 0 \le i \le k : c_i \models \psi_i$.

We say that A *X-covers* π, $X \in \{ut, rt, cand\}$, *when* $q_k \in F_X$.

Depending on the parameter value for X-cover, we define three sets of paths (languages) of a GIA A: $\mathcal{P}_{ut}(A), \mathcal{P}_{rt}(A)$ and $\mathcal{P}_{cand}(A)$. These sets are used to establish the connection between a GIA A and a CFA C: If e.g. a path $\pi \in \mathcal{P}(C)$ reaches a target node ℓ and $\pi \in \mathcal{P}_{rt}(A)$, ℓ is denoted reachable by A. The GIA depicted in Fig. 3c thus contains the information that ℓ_3 is reachable when the condition $x = 0$ holds, ℓ_7 is unreachable and that ℓ_5 and ℓ_9 are candidates for being reached when the condition $x = 5$ holds.

With these definitions at hand, we can formally define the *correctness* of the analysis information in a GIA.

Definition 3. *Let* A *be a GIA,* C *a CFA and* $L \subseteq Loc$ *a set of target nodes.* A *is said to be* correct *wrt.* C *and* L *if* $\mathcal{P}_{ut}(A) \subseteq \{\pi \in \mathcal{P}(C) \mid \pi$ *is infeasible or* π *is feasible and reaches no* $\ell \in L\}$ *and* $\mathcal{P}_{rt}(A) \subseteq \{\pi \in \mathcal{P}(C) \mid \pi$ *is feasible and reaches some* $\ell \in L\}$.

Correctness thus means the automaton correctly (according to the program) marks paths as infeasible, as reaching no target or reaching some target nodes. Similarly, we can define the *soundness* of an OA or UA analysis, assuming that the target nodes L are encoded within the program C.

Definition 4. *Let* tool *be an OA or UA analysis producing a GIA as output, i.e. we assume the tool to encode a mapping* tool $: \mathcal{C} \times \mathcal{A} \to \mathcal{A}$.

If tool *is an OA analysis, it is* sound *whenever for all* $A, A' \in \mathcal{A}$, $C \in \mathcal{C}$ *with* tool$(A, C) = A'$ *we have*

- $\mathcal{P}_{ut}(A') \supseteq \mathcal{P}_{ut}(A)$ *and* $\mathcal{P}_{rt}(A') = \mathcal{P}_{rt}(A)$, *and*
- $\forall \pi \in \mathcal{P}_{ut}(A') \backslash \mathcal{P}_{ut}(A)$: π *is an infeasible path of* C *or is feasible but reaches no* $\ell \in L$.

If tool *is an UA analysis, it is* sound *whenever for all* $A, A' \in \mathcal{A}$, $C \in \mathcal{C}$ *with* tool$(A, C) = A'$ *we have*

- $\mathcal{P}_{rt}(A') \supseteq \mathcal{P}_{rt}(A)$ *and* $\mathcal{P}_{ut}(A') = \mathcal{P}_{ut}(A)$, *and*
- $\forall \pi \in \mathcal{P}_{rt}(A') \backslash \mathcal{P}_{rt}(A)$: π *is a feasible path of* C *reaching some* $\ell \in L$.

Consequently, a sound tool always generates correct GIAs when started with a correct GIA.

Finally, we can define when verification or test case generation is *completed*, namely, when a correct GIA A is generated for a CFA $C = (Loc, l_0, G)$ such that for all target nodes t there exists some $\pi \in \mathcal{P}_{rt}(A) \cup \mathcal{P}_{ut}(A)$ such that π reaches t (all target nodes covered or unreachable).

4   Using GIAs in Cooperative Validation

The basic idea of cooperation is to store analysis results computed by one tool in an artifact and let another tool start its work *using this additional information*. We next briefly discuss some such cooperations and how they could make use of GIAs.

Cooperative test case generation. The goal of test case generation is the computation of a test suite leading to paths covering all target nodes. This can be implemented as a cooperation of an UA analysis Under (e.g. concolic execution) with an OA analysis Over (e.g. explicit value analysis). Under is responsible for generating the test suite and Over for identifying target nodes which are unreachable. Hence, Under reports in a GIA within $\mathcal{P}_{rt}$ the set of already found paths to targets and in $\mathcal{P}_{cand}$ the set of not yet covered target paths; Over tries to show infeasibility of paths in $\mathcal{P}_{cand}$ and if it succeeds, moves these into $\mathcal{P}_{ut}$. Next, Under continues on the remaining targets, and this cycle continues until all target nodes are covered by the test suite. In addition, Over might add *assumptions* on program transitions to guide Under to uncovered targets. This form of analysis has been proposed by Daca et al. [23].

Cooperative verification using CEGAR. The goal of software verification is to show that none of the target nodes are reachable. This can be implemented as a cooperation of an OA analysis Over (e.g. predicate analysis) with an UA analysis Under (e.g. bounded model checking). Over is responsible for building an abstraction of the state space of the program while Under rules out potential counter examples. Hence, Over reports in a GIA within $\mathcal{P}_{cand}$ the candidates for counter examples which Under inspects and moves to $\mathcal{P}_{rt}$ when it can show them to be real. In that case, the verification stops with outcome "not safe", else Over next uses the spurious counter examples to refine its abstraction of the state space (CEGAR = counter example guided abstraction refinement), and the cycle starts anew. Here, we can actually view Over as consisting of *two* overapproximating analyses: one for the entire program and another one just operating on path programs describing spurious counter examples and computing new predicates via interpolation. Such a form of analysis appears in [2,29] in a non-cooperative form and in [13] in a cooperative form, but using different artifacts (see also Sect. 5 for a comparison).

Cooperative verification via Conditional Model Checking. Conditional model checking [8,10] can be viewed as a cooperation of several overapproximating analyses Over_1 to Over_n in which an analysis Over_i transfers the obtained partial results within $\mathcal{P}_{ut}$ to Over_{i+1} so that it can work on the remaining target nodes.

The sketched scenarios assume that all tools potentially employed as Over or Under understand GIAs. This is however (or rather, of course) not the case. To still enable cooperation of tools, in particular while still using the existing tools in a black box manner, we need two more operators on GIAs: (1) a way

---

Algorithm 1. X-REDUCER

Input: CFA $C = (Loc, \ell_0, G)$ ▷ *original program*
        GIA $A = (\mathcal{Q}, \Sigma, \delta, (q_0, \psi_0), F_{ut}, F_{rt}, F_{cand})$ ▷ *GIA*
Output: CFA $C_r = (Loc_r, \ell_0^r, G_r)$ ▷ *reduced program*
1: $(Loc_r, \ell_0^r, G_r) :=$ REDUCER$(C, (\mathcal{Q}, \Sigma, \delta, (q_0, \psi_0), F_X))$ ▷ *Call the existing reducer*
2: **if** $F_{cand} \neq \emptyset$ **then:**
3:     $toKeep := \emptyset$ ▷ *Locations on a path containing a node in F_{cand}*
4:     **for each** $\ell = (l_i, (q_i, \psi_i)) \in Loc_r$ s.t. $(q_i, \psi_i) \in F_{cand}$ **do**
5:        add all predecessors and successors of ℓ in Loc_r to $toKeep$
6:     **for each** $\ell \in Loc_r$ **do**
7:        **if** $\ell \notin toKeep$ **then**
8:           Remove ℓ from Loc_r; Remove all $(\ell, \cdot, \cdot), (\cdot, \cdot, \ell)$ from G_r
9: **return** (Loc_r, ℓ_0^r, G_r)

---

of encoding the information in the artifact into the only form of input accepted by the majority of tools, i.e. programs, and (2) a way of combining several partial results about programs as given by GIAs into one GIA as not to lose any information.

Reducer. For (1), we use the concept of *reducers* as introduced in [10, 22]. A reducer reduces a program to a certain part, removing some paths.

Definition 5. *An X-reducer for $X \in \{ut, rt\}$ is a mapping $red_X : \mathcal{C} \times \mathcal{A} \to \mathcal{C}$ satisfying*
$$\forall C \in \mathcal{C}, A \in \mathcal{A} : P \subseteq \mathcal{P}(red_X(C, A)) \subseteq \mathcal{P}(C),$$
where $P = \begin{cases} \mathcal{P}(C) \backslash \mathcal{P}_X(A) & \text{if } F_{cand} = \emptyset \text{ in } A \\ \mathcal{P}_{cand}(A) \backslash \mathcal{P}_X(A) & \text{otherwise.} \end{cases}$

A reducer for $X = ut$ in the case that $F_{cand} = \emptyset$ is already existing [10]. In Algorithm 1 we provide a parameterized reducer for both values of X, building on the existing one[3]. It first calls the existing reducer and obtains a program reduced wrt. X. As $\mathcal{P}_{cand}$ contains the set of interesting paths whereon the succeeding tool should focus, X-REDUCER minimizes the computed reduced CFA wrt. these paths (in line 2 to 8).

We get the following result:

Theorem 1. *Algorithm 1 is an X-reducer according to Definition 5.*

Proof. The proof follows from the correctness of the existing reducer in [10] (that works correctly in case $F_{cand} = \emptyset$) and the fact that the construction in line 2–8 only removes path not in $\mathcal{P}_{cand}(A)$.

---

[3] Algorithm 1 assumes for representation purposes that the GIA does not contain state invariants. A full construction, covering this aspect is given in the extended version of this paper, that can be found as part of the artifact at Zenodo [26].

Algorithm 2. COMBINER

Input: GIA $A_1 = (\mathcal{Q}_1, \Sigma, \delta_1, q_0, F_{ut}^1, F_{rt}^1, F_{cand}^1)$ ▷ *First GIA*

          GIA $A_2 = (\mathcal{Q}_2, \Sigma, \delta_2, s_0, F_{ut}^2, F_{rt}^2, F_{cand}^2)$ ▷ *Second GIA*

Output: GIA $A = (\mathcal{Q}, \Sigma, \delta, p_0, F_{ut}, F_{rt}, F_{cand})$ ▷ *Combined GIA*

1:   $\mathcal{Q} := \{((q_0, s_0), true)\}, p_0 := ((q_0, s_0), true), \delta := \emptyset, \text{waitlist} := \{((q_0, s_0), true)\}$

2:   **while** waitlist $\neq \emptyset$ **do**

3:      select $((q_i, s_i), \psi_i)$ from waitlist and remove it

4:      **for each** $t_1 = ((q_i, \psi_i) \xrightarrow{g_i, \varphi_i} (q_{i+1}, \psi_{i+1})) \in \delta_1$ **do**

5:         **if** $s_i \in \{\circ, \bullet\} \vee \nexists((s_i, \psi_i) \xrightarrow{g_j, \varphi_j} (s_{i+1}, \psi'_{i+1})) \in \delta_2 : g_i = g_j$ **then**

6:           **if** $s_i \in \{\circ, \bullet\}$ **then** $s_{i+1} = s_i$ **else** $s_{i+1} = \circ$

7:           $\mathcal{Q} := \mathcal{Q} \cup \{(q_{i+1}, s_{i+1}), \psi_{i+1}\}$,

8:           $\delta := \delta \cup \{((q_i, s_i), \psi_i) \xrightarrow{g_i, \varphi_i} ((q_{i+1}, s_{i+1}), \psi_{i+1})\}$

9:           **if** $q_{i+1} \notin F_{rt}^1 \cup F_{ut}^1$ **then** waitlist := wailist $\cup\{((q_{i+1}, s_{i+1}), \psi_{i+1})\}$

10:        **else**

11:           **for each** $t_2 = ((s_i, \psi_i) \xrightarrow{g_j, \varphi_j} (s_{i+1}, \psi'_{i+1})) \in \delta_2 : g_i = g_j$ **do**

12:             waitlist, $\mathcal{Q}, \delta := $ MERGE(waitlist, $\mathcal{Q}, \delta, t_1, t_2$)

13:      **for each** $((s_i, \psi_i) \xrightarrow{g_j, \varphi_j} (s_{i+1}, \psi_{i+1}) \in \delta_2$ **do** analogously to line 4–12

14:   F_{rt} $= \{(q_i, s_i) \in \mathcal{Q} \mid q_i \in F_{rt}^1 \vee s_i \in F_{rt}^2\}$

15:   F_{ut} $= \{(q_i, s_i) \in \mathcal{Q} \mid q_i \in F_{ut}^1 \vee s_i \in F_{ut}^2\}$

16:   $F_{cand} = \{(q_i, s_i) \in \mathcal{Q} \mid q_i \in F_{cand}^1 \cup \{\bullet\} \wedge s_i \in F_{cand}^2 \cup \{\bullet\}\}$

17:   **if** $F_{rt} \cap F_{ut} \neq \emptyset$ **then return** ERROR

18:   **return** $A = (\mathcal{Q}, \Sigma, \delta, p_0, F_{ut}, F_{rt}, F_{cand})$

     where $\circ, \bullet$ are replacements for a state used during splitting and are not processed.

Combiner. When several tools compute analysis information, we have to make sure that all this information is preserved. To this end, we introduce a *combiner* for the combination of GIAs. The combiner's goal is to keep all information on $\mathcal{P}_{ut}$ and $\mathcal{P}_{rt}$ from both GIAs.

Definition 6. *A combiner is a partial mapping* $comb : \mathcal{A} \times \mathcal{A} \to \mathcal{A}$ *which is defined on* consistent *GIAs A_1 and A_2 with* $\mathcal{P}_{ut}(A_1) \cap \mathcal{P}_{rt}(A_2) = \emptyset = \mathcal{P}_{rt}(A_1) \cap \mathcal{P}_{ut}(A_2)$ *such that*

$$\forall A_1, A_2 \in \mathcal{A} : \mathcal{P}_{ut}(comb(A_1, A_2)) = \mathcal{P}_{ut}(A_1) \cup \mathcal{P}_{ut}(A_2) \wedge$$
$$\mathcal{P}_{rt}(comb(A_1, A_2)) = \mathcal{P}_{rt}(A_1) \cup \mathcal{P}_{rt}(A_2) \ .$$

An algorithm for a combiner is given in Algorithm 2, for presentation purposes assuming that each edge in δ_1, δ_2 contains only a single transition. The intuitive idea of the COMBINER is to build the union of the two GIAs and consider newly computed information: For example, if there is a path $\pi \in \mathcal{P}_{cand}(A_1)$ and $\pi \in \mathcal{P}_{ut}(A_2)$, COMBINER ensures that $\pi \in \mathcal{P}_{ut}(A)$ for the combined GIA A. Therefore, COMBINER builds the new GIA A by searching for common sub-paths in the input-GIAs A_1 and A_2. A state in A is a tuple (a_1, a_2) of two states, $a_1 \in Q_1$ and $a_2 \in Q_2$, both reachable on the same path. If the paths diverge, the state is split, where the placeholders '$\circ$' and '$\bullet$' are used to replace either a_1 or a_2. We use e.g. '$\circ$' if the transitions from a_1 and from a_2 contain different CFA

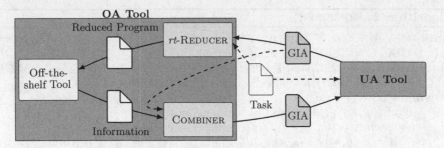

Fig. 4. Cooperative test case generation using rt-REDUCER and COMBINER

edges and e.g. '•' if the successor states have different state invariants. More details on how splitting works can be found in the method MERGE, that is given in the extended version of this paper, that can be found as part of the artifact at Zenodo [26].

Additionally, COMBINER maintains more precise information on paths from $\mathcal{P}_{cand}$: If a path π is present in $\mathcal{P}_{cand}(A_1)$ and $\mathcal{P}_{cand}(A_2)$, once with and once without condition, the condition is also present on the path in the combined GIA. For this, we need to use two different placeholders '○' and '•'. The resulting GIA is not guaranteed to be minimal, meaning that it may contain some paths multiple times and contains paths that do not lead to an accepting state.

Theorem 2. *Algorithm 2 is a combiner according to Definition 6.*

Proof. The proof can be found in the extended version [26].

Finally, we can state that connecting tools via reducers and combiners does not lose any of the already computed analysis results.

Theorem 3. *Let $A \in \mathcal{A}$ be a GIA, $C \in \mathcal{C}$ a CFA, tool a sound UA or OA analysis and $X \in \{ut, rt\}$. Then for a GIA $A' = comb(\text{tool}(red_X(A,C)), A)$ we get*

– $\mathcal{P}_{rt}(A') = \mathcal{P}_{rt}(A) \wedge \mathcal{P}_{ut}(A') \supseteq \mathcal{P}_{ut}(A)$ *if tool is an OA, and*
– $\mathcal{P}_{ut}(A') = \mathcal{P}_{ut}(A) \wedge \mathcal{P}_{rt}(A') \supseteq \mathcal{P}_{rt}(A)$ *if tool is an UA.*

Proof. Follows directly from Theorem 2 and Definition 4.

Figure 4 exemplifies this construction in the setting of cooperative test case generation. It uses an UA tool called UA tool working on GIA as well as rt-REDUCER and COMBINER for an off-the-shelf OA tool called OA tool, that does not understand GIAs. When started on the program from Fig. 2, UA tool finds a test suite covering ℓ_3 and generates the GIA A_1 depicted in Fig. 3a. Next, the rt-REDUCER computes the reduced program containing only the else-branch starting in line 5. It is given to OA tool which (1) computes that ℓ_7 is unreachable and (2) computes a path potentially leading to ℓ_5 and ℓ_9 under the condition $x = 5$. This is then encoded as GIA A_2 visualized in Fig. 3b. To not lose the information on

ℓ_3, A_1 and A_2 are combined to A_3. A_3 is given to UA tool, which confirms that ℓ_5 and ℓ_9 are covered. when all target nodes are either covered or identified as unreachable, the computation terminates.

5 Implementation and Evaluation

To demonstrate the feasibility of GIAs as exchange format and to show that the developed theoretical concepts work in practice, we exemplarily realized component-based CEGAR (C-CEGAR [13]) using only GIAs as exchange format, as explained in Sect. 4. The original implementation of C-CEGAR (here called CC-WIT) contains three components, a model explorer, a feasibility checker and a precision refiner, which are executed in a loop and exchange correctness and violation witnesses. The tool called Over in Sect. 4 comprises the two components model explorer (working on the full program) and precision refiner (computing new predicates). The tool Under is called feasibility checker in C-CEGAR.

Implementation. We implemented GIAs based on condition automata and realized our instance of C-CEGAR (called CC-GIA) in CoVeriTeam [11], alike the original implementation. CoVeriTeam is a framework that provides an easy way to build different forms of cooperative software verification. It provides a language to describe the communication between different components and their inputs and outputs. For CC-GIA, we integrated the GIA as an exchange format in CoVeriTeam. Additionally, we built modules within CPAchecker [12] that allow processing a GIA as input as well as generating a GIA as output, applicable for the existing realizations of model explorer, feasibility checker and precision refiner in CPAchecker. As the precision refiner in C-CEGAR focuses on refining the latest infeasible counter example generated by the model explorer, we additionally use a combiner to ensure that the precision increments computed in previous iterations are maintained. To this end, we built the combiner described in Algorithm 2 within CPAchecker, forming a standalone-executable component, also fully integrated in CoVeriTeam. Note that exchange formats like violation and correctness witnesses can be translated into GIAs, allowing to use any off-the-shelf tool that produces these artifacts as outputs.

Evaluation. The goal of the evaluation is two-fold: First, we exemplarily show that GIAs are feasible as exchange format and can be used in an existing cooperative verification setting. Second, we exemplify the advantages of the clearly defined semantics of GIA, allowing to precisely encode information for the exchange between analyses. Therefore, we compare effectiveness and efficiency of the existing implementation of C-CEGAR (CC-WIT), using violation and correctness witnesses as exchange formats between the three components, with our re-implementation (CC-GIA) which only makes use of GIAs for the information exchange.

Evaluation Setup. All experiments were run on machines with an Intel Xeon E3-1230 v5, 3.40 GHz (8 cores), 33 GB of memory, and Ubuntu 18.04 LTS with Linux kernel 5.4.0-96-generic. Each tool is limited to use 15 GB of memory,

Table 1. Comparison of the existing CC-WIT and the cooperation
using only GIA for information
exchange (CC-GIA)

Result	CC-GIA	CC-WIT
Correct overall	2 641	2 819
Correct proof	2 068	2 100
Correct alarm	573	719
Add. solved	114	–
Incorrect	5	7

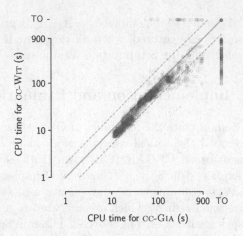

Fig. 5. Comparison of CPU time for CC-WIT and CC-GIA

4 CPU cores and 15 min of CPU time per verification run. All experiments were executed using BENCHEXEC [14], ensuring the resource limitations.

We evaluated both approaches on the SV-BENCHMARKS, the largest publicly available benchmark for C-programs, in the version used for the SV-COMP'22[4] containing in total 8 347 tasks. We used CPACHECKER in the version 2.1.2, CoVERITEAM in version 0.9 and BENCHEXEC in version 3.11.

Evaluation Results (Effectiveness). Table 1 contains the experimental results of CC-GIA and CC-WIT. It contains the number of overall correct answers, the correct proofs (where an approach correctly detects that no target node is reachable) and correct alarms (where a feasible path to a target node is computed). In addition, the incorrect answers are reported, as well as the number of tasks where CC-GIA computes the correct result but CC-WIT does not (row add. solved).

For the total number of correctly solved tasks, we observe that CC-GIA can solve 94% of all tasks solved by CC-WIT. Within the 94%, the number of iterations and the computed refinements are almost always equal. The decrease originates mostly in the fact that CC-GIA is not able to compute a solution in the given time limit for 259 tasks, for which CC-WIT computes a solution within 900 s.

When looking at the additionally solved tasks, we can see the advantages of using GIAs: In 114 cases, CC-GIA computes the correct result, whereas CC-WIT either runs in a timeout or aborts the computation as it eventually makes no progress and gets stuck. Both situations are caused by the fact that not all information computed by the precision refiner is added in the correctness witness, a situation not happening when using GIA. In [13], the authors argue that this situation is caused by the fact that correctness witnesses are not primarily designed for the exchange of a precision increment. The semantics of the GIA allows the

---

[4] https://gitlab.com/sosy-lab/benchmarking/sv-benchmarks/-/tree/svcomp22

precision refiner to encode the information, i.e., encode that a newly discovered predicate holds at a certain point of the infeasible counter example path. Therefore, the refiner builds a GIA that only contains the infeasible counter example, of which the last An example is given in the extended version [26].

Evaluation Results (Efficiency). Figure 5 compares the efficiency of CC-GIA and CC-WIT per task in a logarithmic scale. A point (x, y) contains the CPU time taken by CC-GIA (as x) and by CC-WIT (as y) for all tasks where both compute the correct solution or one runs into a timeout (TO). We observe that CC-GIA needs in general more time for finding a solution, as most points are below the diagonal. The increase is in the vast majority of all cases smaller than the factor two (lower dashed line). The CPU time increases on average by 1.4 (standard deviation is 0.4), the median increase is 1.3. In CC-WIT, information from correctness witnesses are joined using a *syntactic* approach, which is fast and, as it is only applied within this setting, expresses the precision increment in a way optimized for C-CEGAR. In contrast, CC-GIA employs the COMBINER, which takes the *semantics* of the two GIAs that are combined into account as to guarantee that no information is lost. The resulting GIA is significantly larger (contains more states and edges) and not optimized for C-CEGAR, which is the reason most likely causing the increasing runtime and the number of timeouts.

The evaluation shows that GIAs are a flexible, precise and practically suitable exchange format, applicable for C-CEGAR. In particular, we see that the drawbacks of CC-WIT, namely losing information on precision increments computed, can be overcome. As a downside, the overall efficiency slightly decreases when using GIA, due to their size and the fact that they are non optimized for specific applications.

6   Conclusion

In this paper, we have proposed general information exchange automata as an exchange format for the cooperation of over- and underapproximative analyses. It has a fixed well-defined semantics allowing its application in different scenarios. We have furthermore defined and implemented two operations on GIAs, reducing a program to the (remaining) task and combining results with previously computed information. These operations allow a re-use of off-the-shelf tools. We have formally shown that applying reducer and combiner maintains all relevant computed information. The feasibility of GIAs as exchange format has been demonstrated by applying it in an existing cooperative verification setting (C-CEGAR).

For future work, we plan to implement other existing forms of combinations of OA and UA off-the-shelf tools in a cooperative setting using GIAs for the information exchange, such as for conditional model checking, test case generation or k-induction. GIAs are also well suited for being applied in a parallelized cooperative setting, where multiple tools work side-by-side on the same task to increase the overall performance, as the combiner of arbitrary GIAs guarantees that no information is lost.

Data Availability Statement. Our implementation is open-source and available as part of CPACHECKER and COVERITEAM. We archived the implementation and all experimental data for reproduction at Zenodo [26].

References

1. Albarghouthi, A., Gurfinkel, A., Chechik, M.: From under-approximations to over-approximations and back. In: Flanagan, C., König, B. (eds.) TACAS 2012. LNCS, vol. 7214, pp. 157–172. Springer, Heidelberg (2012). https://doi.org/10.1007/978-3-642-28756-5_12
2. Beckman, N.E., Nori, A.V., Rajamani, S.K., Simmons, R.J.: Proofs from tests. In: Ryder, B.G., Zeller, A. (eds.) Proceedings ISSTA, pp. 3–14. ACM (2008). https://doi.org/10.1145/1390630.1390634
3. Beyer, D.: Advances in automatic software testing: Test-Comp 2022. In: FASE 2022. LNCS, vol. 13241, pp. 321–335. Springer, Cham (2022). https://doi.org/10.1007/978-3-030-99429-7_18
4. Beyer, D.: Progress on software verification: SV-COMP 2022. In: TACAS 2022. LNCS, vol. 13244, pp. 375–402. Springer, Cham (2022). https://doi.org/10.1007/978-3-030-99527-0_20
5. Beyer, D., Dangl, M., Dietsch, D., Heizmann, M.: Correctness witnesses: Exchanging verification results between verifiers. In: Zimmermann, T., Cleland-Huang, J., Su, Z. (eds.) Proceedings of FSE, pp. 326–337. ACM (2016). https://doi.org/10.1145/2950290.2950351
6. Beyer, D., Dangl, M., Dietsch, D., Heizmann, M., Stahlbauer, A.: Witness validation and stepwise testification across software verifiers. In: Nitto, E.D., Harman, M., Heymans, P. (eds.) Proceedings of ESEC/FSE, pp. 721–733. ACM (2015). https://doi.org/10.1145/2786805.2786867
7. Beyer, D., Henzinger, T.A., Jhala, R., Majumdar, R.: The software model checker Blast. Int. J. Softw. Tools Technol. Transf. **9**(5–6), 505–525 (2007). https://doi.org/10.1007/s10009-007-0044-z
8. Beyer, D., Henzinger, T.A., Keremoglu, M.E., Wendler, P.: Conditional model checking: a technique to pass information between verifiers. In: Tracz, W., Robillard, M.P., Bultan, T. (eds.) Proceedings of FSE, p. 57. ACM (2012). https://doi.org/10.1145/2393596.2393664
9. Beyer, D., Jakobs, M.-C.: CoVeriTest: cooperative verifier-based testing. In: Hähnle, R., van der Aalst, W. (eds.) FASE 2019. LNCS, vol. 11424, pp. 389–408. Springer, Cham (2019). https://doi.org/10.1007/978-3-030-16722-6_23
10. Beyer, D., Jakobs, M., Lemberger, T., Wehrheim, H.: Reducer-based construction of conditional verifiers. In: Chaudron, M., Crnkovic, I., Chechik, M., Harman, M. (eds.) Proceedings of ICSE, pp. 1182–1193. ACM (2018). https://doi.org/10.1145/3180155.3180259
11. Beyer, D., Kanav, S.: CoVeriTeam: on-demand composition of cooperative verification systems. In: TACAS 2022. LNCS, vol. 13243, pp. 561–579. Springer, Cham (2022). https://doi.org/10.1007/978-3-030-99524-9_31
12. Beyer, D., Keremoglu, M.E.: CPACHECKER: a tool for configurable software verification. In: Gopalakrishnan, G., Qadeer, S. (eds.) CAV 2011. LNCS, vol. 6806, pp. 184–190. Springer, Heidelberg (2011). https://doi.org/10.1007/978-3-642-22110-1_16

13. Beyer, D., Lemberger, T., Haltermann, J., Wehrheim, H.: Decomposing software verification into off-the-shelf components: an application to CEGAR. In: ICSE, pp. 536–548. ACM (2022). https://doi.org/10.1145/3510003.3510064
14. Beyer, D., Löwe, S., Wendler, P.: Reliable benchmarking: requirements and solutions. Int. J. Softw. Tools Technol. Transfer **21**(1), 1–29 (2017). https://doi.org/10.1007/s10009-017-0469-y
15. Beyer, D., Wehrheim, H.: Verification artifacts in cooperative verification: survey and unifying component framework. In: Margaria, T., Steffen, B. (eds.) ISoLA 2020. LNCS, vol. 12476, pp. 143–167. Springer, Cham (2020). https://doi.org/10.1007/978-3-030-61362-4_8
16. Blicha, M., Hyvärinen, A.E.J., Marescotti, M., Sharygina, N.: A cooperative parallelization approach for property-directed k-induction. In: Beyer, D., Zufferey, D. (eds.) VMCAI 2020. LNCS, vol. 11990, pp. 270–292. Springer, Cham (2020). https://doi.org/10.1007/978-3-030-39322-9_13
17. Bruns, G., Godefroid, P.: Model checking partial state spaces with 3-valued temporal logics. In: Halbwachs, N., Peled, D. (eds.) CAV 1999. LNCS, vol. 1633, pp. 274–287. Springer, Heidelberg (1999). https://doi.org/10.1007/3-540-48683-6_25
18. Christakis, M., Müller, P., Wüstholz, V.: Collaborative verification and testing with explicit assumptions. In: Giannakopoulou, D., Méry, D. (eds.) FM 2012. LNCS, vol. 7436, pp. 132–146. Springer, Heidelberg (2012). https://doi.org/10.1007/978-3-642-32759-9_13
19. Christakis, M., Müller, P., Wüstholz, V.: Guiding dynamic symbolic execution toward unverified program executions. In: Dillon, L.K., Visser, W., Williams, L. (eds.) Proceedings of ICSE, pp. 144–155. ACM (2016). https://doi.org/10.1145/2884781.2884843
20. Csallner, C., Smaragdakis, Y.: Check 'n' crash: combining static checking and testing. In: Roman, G., Griswold, W.G., Nuseibeh, B. (eds.) Proceedings of ICSE, pp. 422–431. ACM (2005). https://doi.org/10.1145/1062455.1062533
21. Csallner, C., Smaragdakis, Y., Xie, T.: DSD-crasher: a hybrid analysis tool for bug finding. TOSEM **17**(2), 8:1–8:37 (2008). https://doi.org/10.1145/1348250.1348254
22. Czech, M., Jakobs, M.-C., Wehrheim, H.: Just test what you cannot verify! In: Egyed, A., Schaefer, I. (eds.) FASE 2015. LNCS, vol. 9033, pp. 100–114. Springer, Heidelberg (2015). https://doi.org/10.1007/978-3-662-46675-9_7
23. Daca, P., Gupta, A., Henzinger, T.A.: Abstraction-driven concolic testing. In: Jobstmann, B., Leino, K.R.M. (eds.) VMCAI 2016. LNCS, vol. 9583, pp. 328–347. Springer, Heidelberg (2016). https://doi.org/10.1007/978-3-662-49122-5_16
24. Ge, X., Taneja, K., Xie, T., Tillmann, N.: DyTa: dynamic symbolic execution guided with static verification results. In: Taylor, R.N., Gall, H.C., Medvidovic, N. (eds.) Proceedings of ICSE, pp. 992–994. ACM (2011). https://doi.org/10.1145/1985793.1985971
25. Haltermann, J., Wehrheim, H.: CoVEGI: cooperative verification via externally generated invariants. In: FASE 2021. LNCS, vol. 12649, pp. 108–129. Springer, Cham (2021). https://doi.org/10.1007/978-3-030-71500-7_6
26. Haltermann, J., Wehrheim, H.: Extended version of 'information exchange between over- and underapproximating software analyses (2022). https://doi.org/10.5281/zenodo.6749669
27. Jakobs, M.-C., Wehrheim, H.: Compact proof witnesses. In: Barrett, C., Davies, M., Kahsai, T. (eds.) NFM 2017. LNCS, vol. 10227, pp. 389–403. Springer, Cham (2017). https://doi.org/10.1007/978-3-319-57288-8_28

28. Mukherjee, R., Schrammel, P., Haller, L., Kroening, D., Melham, T.: Lifting CDCL to template-based abstract domains for program verification. In: D'Souza, D., Narayan Kumar, K. (eds.) ATVA 2017. LNCS, vol. 10482, pp. 307–326. Springer, Cham (2017). https://doi.org/10.1007/978-3-319-68167-2_21
29. Nori, A.V., Rajamani, S.K., Tetali, S.D., Thakur, A.V.: The YOGI project: software property checking via static analysis and testing. In: Kowalewski, S., Philippou, A. (eds.) TACAS 2009. LNCS, vol. 5505, pp. 178–181. Springer, Heidelberg (2009). https://doi.org/10.1007/978-3-642-00768-2_17

Program Analysis

A Query Language for Language Analysis

Matteo Cimini[✉] ⓘD

University of Massachusetts Lowell, Lowell, MA 01854, USA
matteo_cimini@uml.edu

Abstract. Language analysis aims at establishing properties of languages, which provides strong guarantees on the behavior of every program written in such languages. Tools that automate language analysis often need to browse a language definition given as input and retrieve information from grammars, typing rules, reduction rules, and other components of the language.

In this paper, we propose a *languages-as-databases* approach where language definitions are stored as database tables. Our main contribution is LANG-SQL, a SQL-inspired query language that can express queries over languages. The key characteristic of LANG-SQL is that it contains linguistic features that are specific to query operational semantics aspects.

To demonstrate that LANG-SQL can be used in practical applications, we have used LANG-SQL queries to rewrite the majority of LANG-N-CHECK, a tool that analyzes languages and establishes their type soundness. Our queries are declarative, and concisely express complicated operations.

Keywords: Language analysis · Type soundness · SQL

1 Introduction

After designing a programming language (PL), there are many properties that are interesting to validate such as type soundness and strong normalization, for example. Language analysis aims at automatically establishing properties of languages from their description [1,2,4,13–16,18,22]. The benefit of doing that is that once a property of a language is established then *every program* that is written in such a language affords the property. The body of work in language analysis is not as rich as that of program analysis, and has primarily focused on type soundness and bisimilarity laws of process algebras.

A number of approaches have been proposed in the context of type soundness. In the approach with intrinsic typing [2,4,22], a language is implemented within a type theory with a strong meta-theory, and it is written in such a way that if its interpreter type checks then the language is type sound. Veritas [14–16], instead, relies on automated theorem proving and compiles languages into formulae that are checked with a theorem prover. Roberson et al. [21] propose an

© The Author(s), under exclusive license to Springer Nature Switzerland AG 2022
B.-H. Schlingloff and M. Chai (Eds.): SEFM 2022, LNCS 13550, pp. 57–73, 2022.
https://doi.org/10.1007/978-3-031-17108-6_4

approach based on model checking in which programs/states are generated, steps are computed from them, and then they are type checked. LANG-N-CHECK [13] proposes an approach in which a language definition must conform to a language organization that is known to guarantee type soundness. Meta SOS [1] and the tool of Mousavi and Reniers [18] analyze process algebras, instead, and their approach is based on syntactic templates for inference rules called rule formats [19]. These tools check whether bisimilarity is a congruence, and whether operators obey laws such as commutativtiy and associativity (modulo bisimilarity).

A common characteristic of this type of tools is that they need to retrieve information from grammars, typing rules, reduction rules, and other components of the language given as input. (We give full details of LANG-N-CHECK in this paper, and we offer some examples w.r.t. other tools in Sect. 6.) Interrogating language definitions is akin to asking queries to databases. In the field of databases queries can be written declaratively in a query language such as SQL. Queries are concise, mostly readable, and can be used in multiple projects. Language analysis tools, on the other hand, typically store languages as a data type of a specific PL, and implement their queries with several lines of code of this specific PL. As a consequence, the retrieval methods used in these tools are hard to locate, understand, maintain, and share among different tools.

Our question: *Can we develop a declarative query language that can express interesting questions about languages and be used to build practical applications?*

We have developed LANG-SQL [12], a SQL-inspired query language that can express queries over languages. LANG-SQL works with languages defined with operational semantics. The first characteristic of LANG-SQL is that it adopts a *languages-as-databases* approach where languages are stored as database tables. Consider a language with booleans with grammars $Type\ T ::= bool\ |\ \cdots$ and $Expression\ e ::= true\ |\ false\ |\ \cdots$, where the dots represent the rest. LANG-SQL accommodates this information in the following table called `grammar`.

category	term
Type	*bool*
Expression	*true*
Expression	*false*
...	...

This table has two attributes: `category`, which stores the name of the category, and `term`, which stores the grammar production. LANG-SQL also includes tables to link the metavariables T and e to their syntactic categories, and to store inference rules. (A complete description of our tables is in Sect. 2.)

The second characteristic of LANG-SQL is that it contains linguistic features that are specific to query operational semantics aspects. For example, LANG-SQL includes operations to check whether a term is a binder, to check whether a term is derived by a grammar, and to extract the top-level constructor of a term. (We cover all the features of LANG-SQL in Sect. 3.)

Evaluation. We have implemented LANG-SQL in OCaml [12]. The tool takes a language definition and a LANG-SQL query as input, and generates an output table in the style of SQL. LANG-SQL reads language definitions that are defined in a textual representation of operational semantics. Our tool compiles them into the tables that we have mentioned above, and applies the query on these tables.

To demonstrate that LANG-SQL can be used to develop practical applications, we target LANG-N-CHECK [13], which implements an analysis that has been proved to establish type soundness for a certain class of pure functional languages [13]. This tool performs several checks. For example, it checks that an elimination form has a reduction rule for each of the canonical forms that it is supposed to handle, and that the appropriate evaluation contexts exist.

We have rewritten the majority of LANG-N-CHECK as queries of LANG-SQL. Why do we not capture all LANG-N-CHECK? The reason is that we chose to be faithful to SQL, and avoid general forms of recursion (and always terminate). Therefore, there are two checks of LANG-N-CHECK that we cannot express. (We discuss this in Sect. 5.) Nonetheless, we have used LANG-SQL to rewrite most of the tool. Our queries amount to 23 lines of LANG-SQL code. This is remarkable: The part of LANG-N-CHECK's implementation that we have rewritten is over a thousand lines of OCaml code. We also have applied our queries to the same repo of languages of LANG-N-CHECK, and we obtain the same results.

Our work shows that LANG-SQL can be used to build practical language analysis tools. Overall, our queries are declarative, mostly readable, and concise.

The paper is organized as follows. Section 2 presents our approach based on languages-as-databases. Section 3 presents LANG-SQL. Section 4 provides our LANG-SQL implementation of LANG-N-CHECK. Section 5 discusses our evaluation and the limitations of our work. Section 6 discusses related work, and Sect. 7 concludes the paper.

2   Languages as Databases

LANG-SQL works with languages defined with operational semantics. To recall, Fig. 1 shows an example of language, which we call $\lambda_{b,[]}$, and is our running example. A language definition has a grammar, and an inference rule system. This section proposes a database schema for language definitions.

A grammar is a sequence of *grammar rules.* Each grammar rule defines a category, its metavariable, and provides a series of terms. In our example language, the category Expression is formed with the λ-calculus, booleans (**true** and **false**) and the **if**-statement, lists (**nil** and **cons**) and the **head** operation, a **let**-declaration, and the error **error**. The category Type defines types, which are the types for booleans, functions and lists. Values are the outcome of successful evaluations, and they are defined with the grammar Value. Values can be booleans, functions, and lists. The grammar Error contains **error**, which is the outcome of failed computations when **head** is applied to the empty list **nil**. $\lambda_{b,[]}$ is defined in small-step semantics with evaluation contexts. Therefore, EvalCtx declares within which contexts we allow reduction to take place.

$$\begin{array}{lll}
\text{Type} & T & ::= \text{Bool} \mid T \rightarrow T \mid \text{List } T \\
\text{Expression} & e & ::= \text{true} \mid \text{false} \mid \text{if } e \text{ then } e \text{ else } e \\
& & \mid x \mid \lambda x : T.e \mid e \, e \\
& & \mid \text{nil} \mid \text{cons } e \, e \mid \text{head } e \\
& & \mid \text{let } x = e \text{ in } e \\
& & \mid \text{error} \\
\text{Value} & v & ::= \text{true} \mid \text{false} \mid \lambda x : T.e \mid \text{nil} \mid \text{cons } v \, v \\
\text{Error} & er & ::= \text{error} \\
\text{EvalCtx} & E & ::= \square \mid \text{if } E \text{ then } e \text{ else } e \\
& & \mid E \, e \mid v \, E \\
& & \mid \text{cons } E \, e \mid \text{cons } v \, E \mid \text{head } E \\
& & \mid \text{let } x = E \text{ in } e \\
\text{TypeEnv} & \Gamma & ::= \emptyset \mid \Gamma, x : T
\end{array}$$

Type System $\boxed{\Gamma \vdash e : T}$

$$\Gamma, x : T \vdash x : T \qquad \Gamma \vdash \text{true} : \text{Bool} \qquad \Gamma \vdash \text{false} : \text{Bool}$$

$$\frac{\Gamma \vdash e_1 : \text{Bool} \quad \Gamma \vdash e_2 : T \quad \Gamma \vdash e_3 : T}{\Gamma \vdash \text{if } e_1 \text{ then } e_2 \text{ else } e_3 : T}$$

$$\frac{\Gamma, x : T_1 \vdash e : T_2}{\Gamma \vdash \lambda x : T_1.e : T_1 \rightarrow T_2} \qquad \frac{\Gamma \vdash e_1 : T_1 \rightarrow T_2 \quad \Gamma \vdash e_2 : T_1}{\Gamma \vdash e_1 \, e_2 : T_2}$$

$$\Gamma \vdash \text{nil} : \text{List } T \qquad \frac{\Gamma \vdash e_1 : T \quad \Gamma \vdash e_2 : \text{List } T}{\Gamma \vdash \text{cons } e_1 \, e_2 : \text{List } T}$$

$$\frac{\Gamma \vdash e : \text{List } T}{\Gamma \vdash \text{head } e : T} \qquad \frac{\Gamma \vdash e_1 : T_1 \quad \Gamma, x : T_1 \vdash e_2 : T_2}{\Gamma \vdash \text{let } x = e_1 \text{ in } e_2 : T_2}$$

$$\Gamma \vdash \text{error} : T$$

Reduction Semantics $\boxed{e \longrightarrow e}$

$$\text{if true then } e_1 \text{ else } e_2 \longrightarrow e_1$$

$$\text{if false then } e_1 \text{ else } e_2 \longrightarrow e_2$$

$$(\lambda x : T.e) \, v \longrightarrow e[v/x] \qquad (\beta \text{ rule})$$

$$\text{head nil} \longrightarrow \text{error}$$

$$\text{head } (\text{cons } v_1 \, v_2) \longrightarrow v_1$$

$$\text{let } x = v \text{ in } e \longrightarrow e[v/x]$$

$$\frac{e \longrightarrow e'}{E[e] \longrightarrow E[e']} \; (\text{CTX}) \qquad E[er] \longrightarrow er \; (\text{ERR-CTX})$$

Fig. 1. Language definition of $\lambda_{b.[]}$

The general shape of a grammar rule is $cname \; X ::= t_1 \mid \cdots \mid t_n$ where $cname \in \text{CATEGORY}$, and $X \in \text{METAVAR}$. CATEGORY is a set of grammar category names such as *Expression* and *Type*. METAVAR is a set of metavariables such as T and e. Terms t have the form Term $t ::= X \mid (opname \; t \cdots t) \mid (X)t \mid$

$t[t/X]$, where *opname* $\in$ OPERATOR. OPERATOR is a set of constructors such as *if*, *list*, and *app*. Terms have a top-level constructor applied to a finite sequence of terms. Terms can use unary binding $(X)t$ [6], where X is bound in the term t. Terms can also use $t[t/X]$ for the capture-avoiding substitution.

We model grammars with two entity sets: grammar-info and grammar. Entity set grammar-info declares a category, its metavariable and its object variable (like x in $\lambda x : T.e$). It has three attributes: category$_{info}$ contains a *cname*, meta-var contains an X, and obj-var contains an X. (We use an unused variable _ when there is no object level variable.) Entity set grammar has a category and its grammar productions (terms), i.e., two attributes: category contains a *cname*, and term contains a term t. Below is our ER diagram in Crow's foot notation. (PK is a primary key. When no key is indicated, all attributes are keys.)

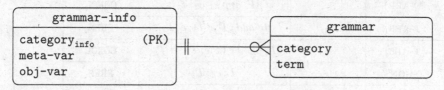

An entity of grammar-info is uniquely identified by its name category$_{info}$. Such a category may have many terms (grammar productions), so there is a one-to-many relationship between the two entity sets through category$_{info}$. The instantiation of an entity set is a table of the same name with zero or more rows and a column for each attribute. For example, the first rows of grammar-info and of grammar for $\lambda_{b,[]}$ are the following.

grammar-info

category$_{info}$	meta-var	obj-var
Type	T	-
Expression	e	x
Value	v	-
...	...	...

grammar

category	term
Type	*bool*
Type	*arrow T T*
Type	*list T*
Expression	*true*
Expression	*false*
Expression	*abs T (x)e*
...	...

An inference rule system defines the relations of the language. $\lambda_{b,[]}$ defines a typing relation $\Gamma \vdash e : T$, where Γ is a type environment that maps variables to types. It also has a reduction relation $e \longrightarrow e$ that models a small-step evaluation. An inference rule system defines these relations with *rules*. Figure 1 shows the declaration$_{\text{rel}}$

relation	rel-args
$\vdash$	$[TypeEnv;\ Expression;\ Type]$
$\longrightarrow$	$[Expression;\ Expression]$

rule

rulename	predname	args	role
(T-APP)	$\vdash$	$[\Gamma; e_1; T_1 \rightarrow T_2]$	PREM
(T-APP)	$\vdash$	$[\Gamma; e_2; T_1]$	PREM
(T-APP)	$\vdash$	$[\Gamma;\ app\ e_1\ e_2; T_2]$	CONCL
(T-ABS)	$\vdash$	$[te\dot{\ }add\ \ \Gamma\ x\ T_1; e; T_2]$	PREM
(T-ABS)	$\vdash$	$[\Gamma;\ abs\ T_1\ (x)e; T_1 \rightarrow T_2]$	CONCL
(T-CONS)	$\vdash$	$[\Gamma; e_1; T]$	PREM
(T-CONS)	$\vdash$	$[\Gamma; e_2;\ list\ T]$	PREM
(T-CONS)	$\vdash$	$[\Gamma;\ cons\ e_1\ e_2;\ list\ T]$	CONCL
(R-IF-TRUE)	$\longrightarrow$	$[if\ true\ e_1\ e_2; e_1]$	CONCL
(R-IF-FALSE)	$\longrightarrow$	$[if\ false\ e_1\ e_2; e_2]$	CONCL
(BETA)	$\longrightarrow$	$[app\ (abs\ T\ (x)e)\ v; e[v/x]]$	CONCL
...	...	...	...

declaration$_{\text{op}}$

	declaration$_{\text{op}}$
constructor	(PK)
constr-args	

declaration$_{\text{op}}$

constructor	constr-args
$true$	[]
$false$	[]
nil	[]
$cons$	$[Expression;\ Expression]$
$head$	$[Expression]$
...	...

Fig. 2. Table declaration$_{\text{rel}}$ (top), first rows of rule (center), our ER diagram of declaration$_{\text{op}}$ (bottom-left), and the first rows of its table (bottom-right)

rules for the typing and reduction relation of our running example. These rules are standard, including (CTX) for evaluating within evaluation contexts, and (ERR-CTX) for detecting an error and failing the overall evaluation.

Each rule has a series of *premises* and a *conclusion*. These are formulae that are built with a predicate name *pname* ∈ PREDICATE that is applied to a finite sequence of terms, where PREDICATE is a set of predicates such as ⊢ and ⟶. We also assume a set of names of rules RULENAME ranged over by *rname*.

We model inference rules with two entity sets: `declaration`$_{rel}$, and `rule`. Entity set `declaration`$_{rel}$ has two attributes: `relation` contains the name of the predicate (*pname*), and `rel-args` contains a list of category names (*cname*) that determines the sort of the arguments. Entity set `rule` records the name of a rule, a formula, and whether the formula is a premise or the conclusion. A formula, in turn, is represented with its predicate name, and its list of terms. Therefore, `rule` has four attributes: `rulename` contains a *rname* ∈ RULENAME, `predname` contains a *pname*, `args` contains a list of terms, and `role` contains either the constant `PREM` or the constant `CONCL`. Below is our ER diagram.

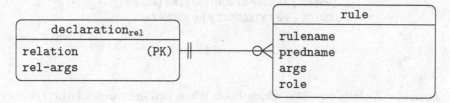

An entity of `declaration`$_{rel}$ is uniquely identified by `relation`. As many premises and conclusions may be formulae about this relation, there is a one-to-many relationship between the two entity sets through `declaration`$_{rel}$ (linked with `predname`). Figure 2 shows the first rows of `declaration`$_{rel}$ and `rule` for our running example. It also shows the entity set `declaration`$_{op}$, which declares constructors with `constructor` (an *opname*) and `constr-args` (a list of terms).

3   The Lang-SQL Query Language

Figure 3 presents the syntax of LANG-SQL. The notation ⁻ denotes finite sequences.

LANG-SQL includes the tables of Sect. 2. Expressions ultimately evaluate to elements that can be stored in tables. Expressions can be numbers (n), terms (t), attributes (*attr*), constructor names (*opname*), categories (*cname*), predicate names (*pname*), rule names (*rname*), CONCL, and PREM. LANG-SQL also includes lists, and some operations on lists. NTH(l, n) retrieves the n-th element of the list l. The first argument has index 0. LAST(l, n) retrieves the element that is n elements away from the end of l. In particular, LAST($l, 0$) is the last element of l.

GET-OPNAME(e) applies to an expression e that evaluates to a term of the form (*opname* $t_1 \cdots t_n$), and returns *opname*. GET-ARGS(e), instead, returns the list $[t_1; \cdots ; t_n]$ from (*opname* $t_1 \cdots t_n$). GET-BOUND-TERM(e) applies to an expression that evaluates to a term of the form $(X).t$ and returns t. GET-BOUND-VAR(e), instead, returns X from $(X).t$. The operator COUNT(), as standard in SQL, returns the number of rows returned by a query.

ATTRIBUTE includes the attributes from Section 2 (category, term, rulename, etc.).
$attr \in$ ATTRIBUTE

Table	tbl	::=	grammar $\mid$ grammar-info $\mid$ rule $\mid$ declaration$_{rel}$ $\mid$ declaration$_{op}$
			$\mid$ $cname$
Expression	e	::=	$n \mid t \mid attr \mid opname \mid cname \mid pname \mid rname \mid$ CONCL $\mid$ PREM
			$\mid [e; e \cdots ; e] \mid$ NTH$(e, e) \mid$ LAST(e, e)
			$\mid$ GET-OPNAME$(e) \mid$ GET-ARGS(e)
			$\mid$ GET-BOUND-TERM$(e) \mid$ GET-BOUND-VAR$(e) \mid$ COUNT$()$
Formula	f	::=	$e = e \mid e$ IS e VAR $\mid e$ IS CONSTRUCTED $\mid e$ IS DERIVED BY e
			$\mid f$ AND $f \mid f$ OR $f \mid$ NOT f
Select Item	e^*	::=	$\star \mid e$ AS (ROWS) $attr$
Query	q	::=	tbl
			$\mid$ SELECT e^* (DISTINCT) FROM $\overline{q}$
			(WHERE f (GROUP BY $\overline{attr}$ (HAVING (ALL) f)))
			$\mid q$ UNION $q \mid q$ INTERSECT $q \mid q$ EXCEPT q

Fig. 3. Syntax of LANG-SQL

Formulae include equality, which holds when two arguments (whether they are terms, numbers, category names, etc.) are syntactically the same. The formula e_1 IS e_2 VAR evaluates e_1 to a term, and evaluates e_2 to a category $cname$, and is true when the term is an instance of the metavariable of $cname$. To make an example, while $v_3 = v$ does not hold, v_3 IS $Value$ VAR holds. The formula e IS CONSTRUCTED is true when e evaluates to some $(opname\ t_1 \cdots t_n)$, and is false otherwise. The formula e_1 IS DERIVED BY e_2 evaluates e_1 to a term, and evaluates e_2 to a category $cname$, and is true when the term can be derived by the grammar of $cname$. Formulae can also be combined with OR, AND and NOT.

Queries produce collections of records. As in SQL, tables are queries themselves. Queries can also be computed with a SELECT statement of the form:

SELECT e^* (DISTINCT) FROM $\overline{q}$ (WHERE f_1 (GROUP BY $\overline{attr}$ (HAVING (ALL) f_2))).

Notation such as (DISTINCT) denotes that the part within parenthesis is optional. Our SELECT statement is typical and behaves as expected. First, it evaluates the queries $\overline{q}$. Then, the formula f_1 acts on the product of the tables just computed from $\overline{q}$, and selects zero or more rows. The GROUP BY part of the statement is optional. When it is present, groups of rows are formed depending on the rows that have the same values for $\overline{attr}$. The HAVING clause is optional, and when it is present it acts on these groups, not the whole collection of rows, and filters rows of these groups based on the formula f_2. The keyword ALL after HAVING is optional. When it is present the formula f_2 must be true for all the rows of a group for the group not to be discarded. Finally, when e^* is $\star$ then all columns are returned. When e^* is a sequence of n expressions, then they form a table with n attributes, which e^* can assign a name to using the keyword AS. Each expression is evaluated for each of the rows that remained after HAVING.

These expressions may invoke the operators that we have described above. Also, the select statement may use the optional keyword DISTINCT. When DISTINCT is present then duplicate rows are removed, and do not appear in the result.

Queries can also be combined with UNION, INTERSECT, and EXCEPT (all rows of the first query except the rows that are also in the second query).

For linguistic convenience, names of grammar categories can be used to denote the part of table grammar that is about such category. For example, SELECT ⋆ FROM *Value* produces the table (a) here on the left.

(a)

term
true
false
abs T (x)e
...

(b)

--	arg	arg-number
abs	T	0
abs	$(x)e$	1
cons	v	0
cons	v	1

LANG-SQL also introduces the keywords AS ROWS to conveniently handle lists. Consider the query SELECT GET-ARGS(term) AS *arg* FROM *Value*. This query returns a row for each item of the grammar *Value* with one column that contains a list. That is, an element in the table is an entire list. However, it is sometimes convenient to expand lists as a series of rows. LANG-SQL does so by adding "AS ROWS *attr*". The resulting table contains the column *attr* with an element of the list, and an *additional* column called *attr-number* that contains a number, which is the position of such element in the list. For example,

SELECT GET-OPNAME(term), GET-ARGS(term) AS ROWS *arg* FROM *Value*

produces the table (b) above on the right. Notice that *true*, *false*, and *nil* have no arguments and so they do not generate any row.

Next, we provide some examples of queries. As language designers can choose any shape for their relations, we fix some conventions. Whichever the typing relation, we assume that the second last argument of ⊢ is the expression being typed. This would be LAST(args, 1) in a row of the table rule. We assume that the last argument is the type being assigned. This would be LAST(args, 0) in rule. Whichever the reduction relation, the expression being evaluated, i.e., the source of the step, is the first argument of ⟶ (that is NTH(args, 0) in rule).

Example 1 (How Many Typing Rules Does a Constructor Have?). Unless carefully structured, for example with a subtyping relation or polymorphism, some language designers may be reluctant to give multiple types to an expression. A common design choice is to restrict each constructor to have only one typing rule. The following query computes the number of typing rules per constructor.

```
1      SELECT opname, COUNT() AS count
2      FROM (SELECT GET-OPNAME(LAST(args,1)) AS opname
3              FROM rule WHERE predname = ⊢ AND role = CONCL)
4      GROUP BY opname
```

Lines 2 and 3 select all the conclusions of the typing rules, focus on the expression to which they apply (this expression is at LAST(args, 1)), and save its operator name with GET-OPNAME. The SELECT statement at Line 1 acts on the table produced by lines 2 and 3. GROUP BY belongs to SELECT of Line 1, and makes groups based on the same *opname*. SELECT calls COUNT() to compute the number of rows in each group, that is, the number of typing rules for a constructor.

When we apply this query to $\lambda_{b,[]}$ we obtain a table with a record for each expression constructor, and each record has the column *count* set to 1.

Example 2 (What Are the Canonical Forms of the Language?). The canonical forms of a language tell, for each type, the shape that values of that type can have. Determining the canonical forms is essential to prove type soundness. The following query computes the canonical forms.

canonicalForms ≜
```
        SELECT GET-OPNAME(term) AS val,
                GET-OPNAME(LAST(args, 0)) AS type
        FROM Value, rule
        WHERE predname = ⊢ AND role = CONCL
                AND GET-OPNAME(term) = GET-OPNAME(LAST(args, 1))
```

canonicalForms selects terms in the grammar *Value*, and selects the conclusions of the typing rules that assign a type to such terms (last line). This query returns records with the constructor name of a value and the constructor name of the type that the typing rule assigns to it (LAST(args, 0)). For $\lambda_{b,[]}$, we obtain the following table. (Rows continue on the left).

val	type		abs	arrow
true	bool		nil	list
false	bool		cons	list

Example 3 (What Are the Elimination Forms of the Language?). Elimination forms of a type are operations that handle values of that type. In $\lambda_{b,[]}$, *if* is an elimination form of *bool*, *app* is an elimination form of *arrow*, and *head* is an elimination form of *list*. The reduction rules of elimination forms have one of the arguments of the operator, sometimes called *principal argument* [17], that pattern-matches against a value. The following queries compute the elimination forms of the language. We assume that the principal argument is the first.

$sourceOpWithArgs \triangleq$

```
    SELECT GET-OPNAME(NTH(args,0)) AS opname,
           GET-ARGS(NTH(args,0)) AS ROWS arg
    FROM rule WHERE predname = ⟶ AND role = CONCL
```

$eliminationForms \triangleq$

```
    SELECT DISTINCT opname FROM sourceOpWithArgs
    WHERE arg-number = 0 GROUP BY opname
    HAVING ALL (arg IS CONSTRUCTED AND arg IS DERIVED BY Value)
```

$sourceOpWithArgs$ selects each reduction rule and then records the top-level operator of the source of the step (NTH($\mathbf{args}, 0$)). The arguments that are applied to this operator are also recorded (one for each row). For example, the β rule makes the rows $app, (abs\,(x)e), 0$ and $app, v, 1$. $eliminationForms$ selects the rows of the principal arguments ($arg\text{-}number = 0$) from $sourceOpWithArgs$. It makes groups of rows with the same $opname$. After this, for example, we have two rows for $head$, one with nil and one with $(cons\ v_1\ v_2)$. HAVING ALL keeps the groups where all the rows have the argument, which is a principal argument, such that it makes use of a value constructor and is derived with the grammar $Value$. For our example, we obtain a table with if, app, and $head$ as rows of column $opname$.

4 Rewriting Lang-n-Check as Lang-SQL Queries

In this section, we use LANG-SQL to rewrite a majority of LANG-N-CHECK [13]. This tool takes a language definition as input and checks whether type soundness holds. Loosely speaking, it targets functional languages with no state nor dependent/refinement types, but its restrictions on input languages are several, and due to lack of space we refer to [13] for a detailed account of them.

Do Evaluation Contexts Cover for the Principal Arguments of Eliminators? LANG-N-CHECK checks that principal arguments of elimination forms are subjects of an evaluation context. This means that since app is an elimination form then $(app\ E\ e)$ must exist, otherwise the first argument cannot become a value and expressions can get stuck in the middle of a computation, hence jeopardizing type soundness. For the same reason, $(if\ E\ e\ e)$ and $(head\ E)$ must exist in $\lambda_{b,[]}$. The following queries check this aspect.

```
1   principalArgPosition ≜
2       SELECT opname, 0 AS arg-number FROM eliminationForms
3   evalPositions ≜
4       SELECT opname, arg-number
5       FROM (SELECT GET-OPNAME(term) AS opname,
6                    GET-ARGS(term) AS ROWS arg FROM EvalCtx)
7       WHERE arg IS EvalCtx VAR
8
9   principalArgPosition EXCEPT evalPositions
```

We first discuss *evalPositions*. The nested SELECT at Line 5 retrieves constructor names, arguments, and their position from *EvalCtx*. SELECT of Line 4 selects only the rows of those arguments that are subject to an evaluation context (Line 7), and only keeps *opname* and the argument position. For example, $(app\ E\ e)$ and $(app\ v\ E)$ make two rows for *app*, one with 0 and one with 1.

principalArgPosition creates a table with the constructors of elimination forms paired with the number 0 (that is, the position of the principal argument). Line 9 removes *evalPositions* from *principalArgPosition*. This query should be empty, and it is for $\lambda_{b,[]}$. Otherwise, the query provides the name of the elimination forms whose principal argument is missing an evaluation context.

Do Evaluation Contexts Cover for the Evaluated Arguments of Values? Another part of the analysis of Lang-n-Check checks that value declarations that require some arguments to be values are covered by an evaluation context. This means that since $(cons\ v\ v)$ is in *Value* then evaluation contexts such as $(cons\ E\ e)$ and $(cons\ v\ E)$ must exist. The following queries check this aspect.

```
1   valuePositions ≜
2        SELECT opname, arg-number
3        FROM (SELECT GET-OPNAME(term) AS opname,
4                     GET-ARGS(term) AS ROWS arg FROM Value)
5        WHERE arg IS Value VAR
6
7   valuePositions EXCEPT evalPositions
```

valuePositions is similar to *evalPositions* except that it selects constructors from *Value*, and Line 5 selects arguments that are value variables. For example, $(cons\ v\ v)$ makes two rows for *cons*, one with 0 and one with 1. The query at Line 7 should be empty, and it is for our running example. Otherwise, the query provides the name of the value constructors and the position of those arguments that are required to be values though are missing an evaluation context.

Do Evaluation Contexts Cover for the Evaluated Arguments of Reduction Rules? Lang-n-Check checks that arguments that are required to be values by reduction rules have an evaluation context. This means that since the second argument of *app* in $(app\ (abs\ (x)e)\ v)$ in the source of β is a v, then $(app\ v\ E)$ must exist in *EvalCtx*. If it did not exist, the argument of the function would not be evaluated, hence jeopardizing type soundness. The following queries check this aspect.

```
1   valuePosInRules ≜ SELECT opname, arg-number
2                     FROM sourceOpWithArgs WHERE arg IS Value VAR
3   valuePosInRules EXCEPT evalPositions
```

valuePosInRules selects rows from *sourceOpWithArgs*, which contains the arguments of the operator of the source of reduction rules. It selects only those rows where the argument is a value variable. The query at Line 3 should be empty, and it is for our running example. Otherwise, the query provides the constructor name and the position of those among its arguments that are required to be values by some rule for that to fire, but are missing an evaluation context.

Do Reduction Rules of Elimination Forms Handle All the Values of Their Type? LANG-N-CHECK checks that elimination forms handle each of the values that they are supposed to handle. This means that since *head* is an elimination form of *list* then we must have a reduction rule for *nil*, and one for *cons*. Missing one of them jeopardizes type soundness. The following queries check this aspect.

```
elimWithPArg ≜
        SELECT opname, GET-OPNAME(arg) AS parg
        FROM sourceOpWithArgs WHERE arg-number = 0
        GROUP BY opname
        HAVING ALL (arg IS CONSTRUCTED AND arg IS DERIVED BY Value)
```

elimWithPArg is similar to *eliminationForms*, though each row has a constructor name of an elimination form together with the constructor name of the principal argument handled by one of its reduction rules.

```
elimWithType ≜ SELECT DISTINCT opname, type AS elimType
                FROM elimWithPArg, canonicalForms WHERE parg = val
```

elimWithType produces a table that pairs each elimination form with the type they are elimination form of. It does so by selecting constructors from *elimWithPArg*, and retrieving the type of their principal arguments from *canonicalForms*.

```
elimWithValues ≜ SELECT opname, val AS parg
                FROM elimWithType, canonicalForms
                WHERE elimType = type
elimWithValues EXCEPT elimWithPArg
```

elimWithValues pairs each elimination form with the values of the type it eliminates. In other words, *elimWithValues* contains all the values that an elimination form must handle. *elimWithPArg*, instead, contains the values that an elimination form actually handles, as retrieved from its reduction rules. Then, EXCEPT at the last line should return an empty table, and it is the case for $\lambda_{b,[]}$. If the query returns some records, they display an elimination form and a value constructor that is not handled by any of the reduction rules of that elimination form. We do not show one query, as it mirrors the above. It checks that operators such as try/with handle errors at the principal argument rather than values.

5   Evaluation

Implementation. We have implemented LANG-SQL in OCaml [12]. Our tool takes 1) a language definition and 2) a LANG-SQL query as input. We use the syntax of LANG-N-CHECK for language definitions. (See [11] for an example.) Our tool compiles language definitions into tables grammar, rule, and so on, and applies the query on these tables. The output is a table in the style of SQL. As many lightweight implementations of SQL, we use lists of records to store tables.

Evaluation. We have applied the queries of Sect. 4 to the repo of languages of LANG-N-CHECK, described in [13]: The simply-typed λ-calculus (STLC), STLC with integers, the unit type, booleans, pairs, sums, option types, tuples, fix, let, letrec, universal and recursive types, lists and operations such as append, map, mapi, filter, filteri, range, list length, and reverse, and the natural recursor.

Additionally, the repo contains variations of these languages: call-by-value, call-by-name, and parallel reduction, and pairs, lists, and tuples are also considered in their lazy version. Languages are also defined with or without exceptions. The repo consists of 145 language definitions. This high number of languages is due to the many variations on the same languages, however.

The languages of this repo are all type sound. We confirm that the queries of Sect. 4 succeed our checks on all these languages. We also have created versions of the languages that are not type sound, by removing evaluation contexts or rules, for example. We confirm that our queries fail our checks on these modified languages. The website of the tool reports also on these experiments [12].

LANG-N-CHECK performs two checks that we cannot capture because we have decided to be faithful to SQL and avoid general forms of recursion (and always terminate). The first is the type preservation check for reduction rules. This is based on type checking source and target, and it is a recursive process, thus out of our scope. The second check is the acyclicity of the dependencies of evaluation contexts. Contexts with circular dependencies such as cons $E\ v$ | cons $v\ E$ lead to stuck expressions. LANG-N-CHECK detects cycles by computing a topological sort, but LANG-SQL cannot express this recursive computation.

Despite the lack of these checks, we could rewrite most of LANG-N-CHECK. For a fair comparison, we have excluded parsing, pretty-printing, the two checks that we omit, and the other unrelated parts of the LANG-N-CHECK implementation [7]. Even so, we have counted over 1200 lines of OCaml code. In contrast, our LANG-SQL queries amount to 23 lines. Furthermore, our queries are declarative and, we believe, easier to read and maintain.

We have tested Example 1–3 of Sect. 3, and also tested additional queries, for example to output the state of languages with state, and whether the language allows reduction under binders. Our website documents these tests [12].

Limitations. Standard SQL forbids general forms of recursion, and we have aligned with that choice. As a consequence, LANG-SQL cannot ask queries such as "What is the type of this program?", i.e., type checking, and cannot ask "Does this program evaluate to a value?", i.e., program execution. Some variants of SQL make use of recursive common table expressions but it is unclear whether they can express type checking and evaluation queries on languages like those of the LANG-N-CHECK repo, and whether they can solve the type preservation and topological sort problems necessary to capture the entirety of LANG-N-CHECK.

We handle only unary binding [6]. In the future, we would like to integrate more sophisticated approaches to binding. Also, LANG-SQL does not rule out type errors at compile-time. For example, GET-OPNAME(e) throws an error at run-time when e evaluates to, say, a number. We would like to design a type system that rules out these and similar type errors.

6   Related Work

SQL is the query language that is closest to our work. LANG-SQL differs in that it is tailored to interrogate language definitions. In particular, there are two main reasons why we did not use SQL and existing database implementations. 1) They do not primitively store terms and terms with binders. 2) It is not clear whether SQL can perform LANG-SQL operations such as deriving a term from a user-defined BNF grammar. On the other hand, SQL provides a wider range of operations, and offers a greater flexibility by adding a NULL value.

Statix [3] and scope graphs [20] use queries to solve name resolution problems but they cannot express the queries that we have seen in this paper. On the other hand, LANG-SQL cannot solve name resolution problems.

Can we use LANG-SQL to help implement other tools? We have mentioned some tools in the introduction. They are comparable to LANG-N-CHECK or larger, and it is impossible to address them here. We can offer only some examples. Veritas [14–16] generates inversion lemmas. LANG-SQL can be used to retrieve premises and conclusions of typing rules to build these lemmas. Veritas generates also a lemma for each operator to say, for example, that ($app\ e_1\ e_2$) "progresses", and so on for all constructors. LANG-SQL can be used to retrieve all constructors, their arguments and their categories, to build these lemmas. As for intrinsic typing, it is unclear how that translates to queries. Roberson et al. [21] computes steps from programs as it model checks. LANG-SQL cannot compute steps but can retrieve the reduction rules that apply. Meta SOS [1] and the tool of Mousavi and Reniers [18] implement several rule formats, each of which may have a dozen of restrictions. We provide an example. GSOS format [5] imposes that t and t' be variables in premises $t \longrightarrow t'$, which can be checked with IS VAR. It also needs t' not to occur in the source of the conclusion nor other premises. LANG-SQL can perform this check by grouping by arguments of the source of the conclusion and targets of premises, and checking that COUNT() = 1.

As future work, we would like to explore how far LANG-SQL can be used to implement (parts of) the above-mentioned tools.

7   Conclusion

We have designed and implemented LANG-SQL, a SQL-like language for querying languages. LANG-SQL adopts a languages-as-databases approach, and contains features that are specific to query operational semantics aspects. To demonstrate that LANG-SQL can be used in practical applications, we have rewritten the majority of LANG-N-CHECK with LANG-SQL. Our queries amount to 23 lines of LANG-SQL code while the corresponding part in LANG-N-CHECK is over a thousand lines of code. Our queries are declarative, mostly readable, and concise.

In the future, we would like to address the limitations that we have described in Sect. 6, and also formulate more queries. For example, it would be interesting to write queries that compute the variance of types. We would like to use LANG-SQL to implement other language analysis tools. We also plan to integrate LANG-SQL into a calculus with first-class languages [8–10].

References

1. Aceto, L., Goriac, E., Ingólfsdóttir, A.: Meta SOS - a maude based SOS meta-theory framework. In: Borgström, J., Luttik, B. (eds.) Proceedings Combined 20th International Workshop on Expressiveness in Concurrency and 10th Workshop on Structural Operational Semantics, EXPRESS/SOS 2013, Buenos Aires, Argentina, 26th August 2013. EPTCS, vol. 120, pp. 93–107 (2013). https://doi.org/10.4204/EPTCS.120.8
2. Altenkirch, T., Reus, B.: Monadic presentations of lambda terms using generalized inductive types. In: Flum, J., Rodriguez-Artalejo, M. (eds.) CSL 1999. LNCS, vol. 1683, pp. 453–468. Springer, Heidelberg (1999). https://doi.org/10.1007/3-540-48168-0_32
3. van Antwerpen, H., Bach Poulsen, C., Rouvoet, A., Visser, E.: Scopes as types. Proc. ACM Program. Lang. (PACMPL) 2(OOPSLA), 1–30 (2018). https://doi.org/10.1145/3276484
4. Bach Poulsen, C., Rouvoet, A., Tolmach, A., Krebbers, R., Visser, E.: Intrinsically-typed definitional interpreters for imperative languages. Proc. ACM Program. Lang. (PACMPL) 2(POPL), 1–34 (2017). https://doi.org/10.1145/3158104
5. Bloom, B., Istrail, S., Meyer, A.R.: Bisimulation can't be traced. J. ACM 42(1), 232–268 (1995). https://doi.org/10.1145/200836.200876
6. Cheney, J.: Toward a general theory of names: binding and scope. In: Pollack, R. (ed.) Proceedings of the 3rd ACM SIGPLAN Workshop on Mechanized Reasoning about Languages with Variable Binding, MERLIN 2005, pp. 33–40. Association for Computing Machinery, New York (2005). https://doi.org/10.1145/1088454.1088459
7. Cimini, M.: Lang-n-check. https://github.com/mcimini/TypeSoundnessCertifier (2015)
8. Cimini, M.: Languages as first-class citizens (vision paper). In: Pearce, D.J., Mayerhofer, T., Steimann, F. (eds.) Proceedings of the 11th ACM SIGPLAN International Conference on Software Language Engineering, SLE 2018, pp. 65–69. Association for Computing Machinery, New York (2018). https://doi.org/10.1145/3276604.3276983
9. Cimini, M.: On the effectiveness of higher-order logic programming in language-oriented programming. In: Nakano, K., Sagonas, K. (eds.) FLOPS 2020. LNCS, vol. 12073, pp. 106–123. Springer, Cham (2020). https://doi.org/10.1007/978-3-030-59025-3_7
10. Cimini, M.: A calculus for multi-language operational semantics. In: Bloem, R., Dimitrova, R., Fan, C., Sharygina, N. (eds.) Software Verification. NSV VSTTE 2021 2021. Lecture Notes in Computer Science, vol. 13124, pp. 25–42. Springer (2021). https://doi.org/10.1007/978-3-030-95561-8_3
11. Cimini, M.: Example of language in lang-SQL. https://github.com/mcimini/lang-sql/blob/main/Lang-n-Check/languages/stlc_cbv.lan (2022)
12. Cimini, M.: Lang-SQL. https://github.com/mcimini/lang-sql (2022)

13. Cimini, M., Miller, D., Siek, J.G.: Extrinsically typed operational semantics for functional languages. In: Lämmel, R., Tratt, L., de Lara, J. (eds.) Proceedings of the 13th ACM SIGPLAN International Conference on Software Language Engineering, SLE 2020, Virtual Event, USA, November 16–17 2020, pp. 108–125. ACM (2020). https://doi.org/10.1145/3426425.3426936

14. Grewe, S., Erdweg, S., Mezini, M.: Using vampire in soundness proofs of type systems. In: Kovács, L., Voronkov, A. (eds.) Proceedings of the 1st and 2nd Vampire Workshops. EPiC Series in Computing, vol. 38, pp. 33–51. EasyChair (2016). https://doi.org/10.29007/22x6

15. Grewe, S., Erdweg, S., Mezini, M.: Automating proof steps of progress proofs: comparing vampire and Dafny. In: Kovács, L., Voronkov, A. (eds.) Vampire 2016. Proceedings of the 3rd Vampire Workshop. EPiC Series in Computing, vol. 44, pp. 33–45. EasyChair (2017). https://doi.org/10.29007/5zjp

16. Grewe, S., Erdweg, S., Wittmann, P., Mezini, M.: Type systems for the masses: deriving soundness proofs and efficient checkers. In: Murphy, G.C., Steele Jr., G.L. (eds.) 2015 ACM International Symposium on New Ideas, New Paradigms, and Reflections on Programming and Software (Onward!), pp. 137–150. Onward! 2015, ACM, New York (2015). https://doi.org/10.1145/2814228.2814239

17. Harper, R.: Practical Foundations for Programming Languages, 2nd edn. Cambridge University Press, Cambridge (2016). https://doi.org/10.1017/CBO9781316576892

18. Mousavi, M.R., Reniers, M.A.: Prototyping SOS meta-theory in Maude. Electron. Notes . Theor. Comput. Sci. **156**(1), 135–150 (2006). https://doi.org/10.1016/j.entcs.2005.09.030

19. Mousavi, M.R., Reniers, M.A., Groote, J.F.: SOS formats and meta-theory: 20 years after. Theor. Comput. Sci. **373**(3), 238–272 (2007). https://doi.org/10.1016/j.tcs.2006.12.019

20. Neron, P., Tolmach, A., Visser, E., Wachsmuth, G.: A theory of name resolution. In: Vitek, J. (ed.) ESOP 2015. LNCS, vol. 9032, pp. 205–231. Springer, Heidelberg (2015). https://doi.org/10.1007/978-3-662-46669-8_9

21. Roberson, M., Harries, M., Darga, P.T., Boyapati, C.: Efficient software model checking of soundness of type systems. In: Harris, G.E. (ed.) Proceedings of the 23rd ACM SIGPLAN Conference on Object-Oriented Programming Systems Languages and Applications, pp. 493–504. OOPSLA 2008, Association for Computing Machinery, New York (2008). https://doi.org/10.1145/1449764.1449803

22. Rouvoet, A., Bach Poulsen, C., Krebbers, R., Visser, E.: Intrinsically-typed definitional interpreters for linear, session-typed languages. In: Blanchette, J., Hritcu, C. (eds.) Proceedings of the 9th ACM SIGPLAN International Conference on Certified Programs and Proofs, CPP 2020, New Orleans, LA, USA, January 20–21 2020, pp. 284–298. ACM (2020). https://doi.org/10.1145/3372885.3373818

Field-Sensitive Program Slicing

Carlos Galindo[1], Jens Krinke[2], Sergio Pérez[1](✉), and Josep Silva[1]

[1] VRAIN, Universitat Politècnica de València, Valencia, Spain
{cargaji,serperu,jsilva}@vrain.upv.es
[2] CREST Centre, University College London, London, UK
j.krinke@ucl.ac.uk

Abstract. The granularity level of the program dependence graph
(PDG) for composite data structures (tuples, lists, records, objects,
etc.) is inaccurate when slicing their inner elements. We present the
constrained-edges PDG (CE-PDG) that addresses this accuracy problem. The CE-PDG enhances the representation of composite data structures by decomposing statements into a subgraph that represents the
inner elements of the structure, and the inclusion and propagation of
data constraints along the CE-PDG edges allows for accurate slicing of
complex data structures. Both extensions are conservative with respect
to the PDG, in the sense that all slicing criteria (and more) that can be
specified in the PDG can be also specified in the CE-PDG, and the slices
produced with the CE-PDG are always smaller or equal to the slices
produced by the PDG. An evaluation of our approach shows a reduction
of the slices of 11.67%/5.49% for programs without/with loops.

Keywords: Program analysis · Program slicing · Composite data
structures

1 Introduction

The *Program Dependence Graph* (PDG) [18] represents the statements of a program as a collection of nodes; and their control and data dependencies are represented as edges. The PDG is used in *program slicing* [23], a technique for program
analysis and transformation whose main objective is to extract from a program
the set of statements, the so-called *program slice* [30], that affect the values of a
set of variables v at a program point p ($\langle p, v \rangle$), called *slicing criterion* [18].

Unfortunately, the original PDG is not able to properly handle the slicing of
composite data structures. Finite composite data structures can be atomized [19]

This work has been partially supported by grant PID2019-104735RB-C41 funded
by MCIN/AEI/ 10.13039/501100011033, by the *Generalitat Valenciana* under grant
Prometeo/2019/098 (DeepTrust), and by TAILOR, a project funded by EU Horizon
2020 research and innovation programme under GA No 952215. Sergio Pérez was partially supported by *Universitat Politècnica de València* under FPI grant PAID-01-18.
Carlos Galindo was partially supported by the Spanish Ministerio de Universidades
under grant FPU20/03861.

B.-H. Schlingloff and M. Chai (Eds.): SEFM 2022, LNCS 13550, pp. 74–90, 2022.
https://doi.org/10.1007/978-3-031-17108-6_5

and then sliced as usual, however, infinite data structures cannot be atomized and slicing them is therefore imprecise.

In this paper, we propose a general method that solves the problem of accurately representing and slicing any composite data structure, even if it is recursive (infinite data structures can be also sliced) or if it is collapsed and expanded again (we solve the *slicing pattern matching* problem [24], explained in Sect. 2).

The rest of the paper is structured as follows: The next section demonstrates the problems in slicing composite data structures. Section 3 presents the CE-PDG and how it is used for slicing. In Sect. 4 we present an implementation and an empirical evaluation of the proposed technique. It is followed by a discussion of related work and the conclusions.

2 Slicing Composite Data Structures

In this section, we show the inaccuracy problems caused by the PDG when it is used to slice programs with complex data structures. It is important to remark that the problem of data structure slicing can be studied and solved at the level of the PDG (i.e., for intra-procedural programs). Because we can present the fundamental ideas and solutions of field-sensitive slicing at this level, we avoid the representation in the *System Dependence Graph* (SDG) [9] (i.e., for inter-procedural programs). In this way, we keep the presentation easier to understand, avoiding the complexity introduced by the SDG (procedure calls, input/output edges, summary edges...). Of course, an extension of our work for the SDG is possible and will increase the precision of our technique by propagating dependencies throughout procedures[1]. We also want to highlight that, for the sake of clarity, we ignore aliasing, pointers, and other programming features that are orthogonal to the problem we want to solve: slicing (recursive) data structures. The pointer analysis needs to be field-sensitive in the same way our approach is.

Example 1. Consider the fragment of Erlang code in Fig. 1a, where we are interested in the values computed at variable C (the slicing criterion is $\langle 4,C \rangle$). The only

```
1 foo(X,Y) ->        1 foo(X,Y) ->        1 foo(X,Y) ->
2   {A,B} = {X,Y},   2   {A,B} = {X,Y},   2   {A,B} = {X,Y},
3   Z = {[8],A},      3   Z = {[8],A},      3   Z = {[8],A},
4   {[C],D} = Z.      4   {[C],D} = Z.      4   {[C],D} = Z.
```

  (a) Original Program   (b) PDG Slice   (c) Minimal Slice

Fig. 1. Slicing Erlang tuples (slicing criterion underlined and blue, slice in green) (Color figure online)

---

[1] Our implementation is already inter-procedural. However, due to lack of space, and because it is an important problem by itself, we have limited the paper to the intra-procedural version.

part of the code that can affect the values at C (i.e., the minimal slice) is coloured in green in Fig. 1c. Nevertheless, the slice computed with the PDG (shown in Fig. 1b) contains the whole program. This is a potential source of more imprecisions outside this function because it wrongly includes in the slice the parameters of function foo and, thus, all calls to foo are also included together with their arguments and the code on which they depend.

The fundamental problem in this particular example is pattern matching: a whole data structure (the tuple {[8],A}) has been collapsed to a variable (Z) and then expanded again ({[C],D}). Therefore, the list [C] depends on the list [8]. Nevertheless, the traditional PDG represents that [C] flow depends on Z, and in turn, Z flow depends on A. Because flow dependence is usually considered to be transitive, slicing the PDG wrongly infers that C depends on A (A is in the slice for C). This problem becomes worse in presence of recursive data types. For instance, trees or objects (consider a class A with a field of type A, which produces an infinite data type) can prevent the slicer to know statically what part of the collapsed structure is needed. An interesting discussion and example about this problem can be found in [26, pp. 2–3]. In the next section we propose an extension of the PDG that solves the above problem.

3   Constrained-Edges Program Dependence Graph

This section introduces the CE-PDG, for which the key idea is to expand all those PDG nodes where a composite data structure is defined or used. This expansion augments the PDG with a tree representation for composite data structures. We describe how this structure is generated and we introduce a new kind of dependence edge used to build this tree structure. For this, we formally define the concepts of constraint and constrained edge; describe the different types, and how they affect the graph traversal in the slicing process.

3.1   Extending the PDG

Figure 1b shows that PDGs are not accurate enough to differentiate the elements of composite structures. For instance, the whole statement in line 4 is represented by a single node, so it is not possible to distinguish the data structure {A,B} nor its internal subexpressions. This can be solved by transforming the PDG into a CE-PDG. The transformation is made following three steps.

Step 1. The first step is to decompose all nodes that contain composite data structures so that each component is represented by an independent node. As in most ASTs, we represent data structures with a tree-like representation (similar to the one used in object-oriented programs to represent objects in calls [13,29]). The decomposition of PDG nodes into CE-PDG nodes is straightforward from the AST. It is a recursive process that unfolds the composite structure by levels, i.e., if a subelement is another composite structure, it is recursively unfolded until the whole syntax structure is represented in the tree. The CE-PDG only unfolds data types as much as they are in the source code, thus unfolding is always finite (unlike atomization). In contrast to the PDG nodes (which represent complete statements), the nodes of this tree structure represent expressions. Therefore, we need a new kind of edge to connect these intra-statement nodes. We call these edges *structural edges* because they represent the syntactical structure.

Definition 1 (Structural Edge). *Let $G = (N, E)$ be a CE-PDG where N is the set of nodes and E is the set of edges. Given two CE-PDG nodes $n, n' \in N$, there exists a structural edge $n \dashrightarrow n'$ if and only if:*

- *n contains a data structure for which n' is a subcomponent, and*
- *$\forall n'' \in N : n \dashrightarrow n' \wedge n' \dashrightarrow n'' \rightarrow n \not\dashrightarrow n''$.*

Structural edges point to the components of a composite data structure, composing the inner skeleton of its abstract syntax tree. More precisely, each field in a data type is represented with a separate node that is a child of the PDG node that contains the composite data structure. For instance, the structural edges of the CE-PDG in Fig. 2 represent the tuples of the code in Fig. 1. The second condition of the definition enforces the tree structure as otherwise "transitive" edges could be established. For example, without the second condition a structural edge between {[C],D} = Z and C could exist.

Step 2. The second step is to identify the flow dependencies that arise from the decomposition of the data structure. Clearly, the new nodes can be variables that flow depend on other nodes, so we need to identify the flow dependencies that exist among the new (intra-statement) nodes. They can be classified according to two different scenarios: (i) composite data structures being defined, and (ii) composite data structures being used. In Fig. 1 we have a definition (line 4), a use (line 3) and a definition and use in the same node (line 2). The explicit definition of a whole composite data structure (e.g., a tuple in the left-hand side of an assignment, see line 4) always defines every element inside it, so the values of all subelements depend on the structure that immediately contains them. Hence, the subexpressions depend on the structure being defined (i.e., flow edges follow

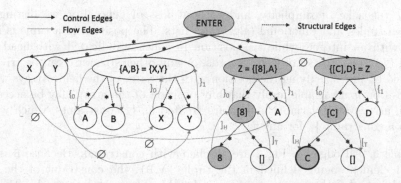

Fig. 2. CE-PDG of the code in Fig. 1.

the same direction as structural edges. See {[C],D}=Z in Fig. 2). Conversely, the structure being used depends on its subexpressions (i.e., flow edges follow the opposite direction than structural edges. See Z={[8],A} in Fig. 2). Additionally, because the decomposition of nodes augments the precision of the graph, all flow edges that pointed to original PDG nodes that have been decomposed, now point to the corresponding node in the new tree structure. An example of a flow edge that has been moved due to the decomposition is the flow edge between the new A nodes. In the original PDG, this flow edge linked the nodes {A,B}={X,Y} and Z={[8],A}.

Step 3. The last step to obtain the CE-PDG is labelling the edges with constraints that are used during the slicing phase. The idea is that the slicing algorithm traverses the edges and collects the labels in a stack that is used to decide what edges should be traversed and what edges should be ignored. We call the new labelled edges *constrained edges*.

Definition 2 (Constraint). *A constraint C is a label defined as follows:*

$$C ::= \varnothing \mid * \mid Tuple \mid List \qquad Pos ::= H \mid T$$
$$Tuple ::= \{_{int} \mid \}_{int} \qquad List ::= [_{Pos} \mid]_{Pos}$$

The meaning of each kind of constraint is the following:

- **Empty Constraint** ($n \xrightarrow{\varnothing} n'$). It specifies that an edge can always be traversed by the slicing algorithm.
- **Asterisk Constraint** ($n \xrightarrow{*} n'$). It also indicates that an edge can always be traversed; but it ignores all the collected restrictions so far, meaning that the whole data structure is needed. This kind of constraint is the one used in control and structural edges, which are traversed ignoring the previous constraints collected.
- **Access Constraint** ($n \xrightarrow{op_{position}} n'$). It indicates that an element is the *position*-th component of another data structure that is a tuple if $op=Tuple$ or a list if $op=List$. op also indicates whether the element is being defined ("{", "[") or used ("}", "]").

For the sake of simplicity, and without loss of generality, we distinguish between tuples and functional (algebraic) lists. The position in a tuple is indicated with an integer, while the position in a list is indicated with head (H) or tail (T). The case of objects, records, or any other structure can be trivially included by just specifying the position with the name of the field. Arrays where the position is a variable imply that any position of the array may be accessed. Hence, arrays with variable indices are treated as {$_*$ constraints, which would match a constraint }$_x$ for any x.

Example 2. All edges in Fig. 2 are labelled with constraints. Because B is the second element being defined in the tuple {A,B}, the constraint of the flow dependence edge that connects them is {$_1$. Also, because 8 is the head in the list [8], the constraint of the flow dependence edge that connects them is]$_H$.

At this point, the reader can see that the constraints can accurately slice the program in Fig. 1a. In the CE-PDG (Fig. 2), the slicing criterion (C) is the head of a list (indicated by the constraint $[_H$), and this list is the first element of a tuple. When traversing backward the flow dependencies, we do not want the whole Z, but the head of its first element (i.e., the cumulated constraints $[_H \{_0$). Then, when we reach the definition of Z, we find two flow dependencies ([8] and A). But looking at their constraints, we exactly know that we want to traverse first $\}_0$ and then $]_H$ to reach the 8. The slice computed in this way is composed of the grey nodes, and it is exactly the minimal slice in Fig. 1c. Note that no structural edge is traversed during the slice in the above example. How structural edges are handled during slicing is discussed in the next section.

The CE-PDG is a generalization of the PDG because the PDG is a CE-PDG where all edges are labelled with empty constraints ($\varnothing$). In contrast, all edges in the CE-PDG are labelled with different constraints:

- Structural and control edges are always labelled with asterisk constraints.
- Flow edges for definitions inside a data structure are labelled with opening ($\{,[$) access constraints.
- Flow edges for uses inside a data structure are labelled with closing ($\},]$) access constraints.
- The remaining data edges are labelled with empty constraints.

The behaviour of access constraints and asterisk constraints in the graph traversal is further detailed in the next section.

3.2   Slicing the CE-PDG: Constrained Traversal

In this section, we show how constraints can improve the accuracy of the slices computed with the CE-PDG. The paths of the CE-PDG that can be traversed are formed by any combination of closing constraints followed by opening constraints. Any number of empty constraints ($\varnothing$) can be placed along the path. On the other hand, asterisk constraints ($*$) always ignore any constraints already collected. Therefore, after traversing an asterisk constraint, the paths that can be traversed are the same as if no constraint was previously collected.

The slicing algorithm uses a stack to store the words while it traverses the CE-PDG. When a node is selected as the slicing criterion, the algorithm starts from this node with an empty stack ($\perp$) and accumulates constraints with each edge traversed. Only opening constraints impose a restriction on the symbols that can be pushed onto the stack: when an opening constraint is on the top of the stack, the only closing constraint accepted to build a realizable word is its complementary closing constraint.

Table 1 shows how the stack is updated in all possible situations. The constraints are collected or resolved depending on the last constraint added to the word (the one at the top of the *Input stack*) and the new one to be treated (column *Edge Constraint*). All cases shown in Table 1 can be summarized in four different situations:

Table 1. Processing edges' stacks. x and y are positions (int or H/T). $\varnothing$ and $*$ are empty and asterisk constraints, respectively. S is a stack, $\perp$ the empty stack.

	Input stack	Edge constraint	Output stack
(1)	S	$\varnothing$	S
(2)	S	$\{_x$ or $[_x$	$S\{_x$ or $S[_x$
(3)	$\perp$	$\}_x$ or $]_x$	$\perp$
(4)	$S\{_x$ or $S[_x$	$\}_x$ or $]_x$	S
(5)	$S\{_x$ or $S[_x$	$\}_y$ or $]_y$	$error$
(6)	S	$*$	$\perp$

- **Traverse constraint (cases 1 and 3):** The edge is traversed without modifying the stack.
- **Collect constraint (case 2):** The edge can be traversed by pushing the edge's constraint onto the stack.
- **Resolve constraint (cases 4 and 5):** There is an opening constraint at the top of the stack and an edge with a closing constraint that matches it (case 4), so the edge is traversed by popping the top of the stack; or they do not match (case 5), so the edge is not traversed.
- **Ignore constraints (case 6):** Traversing the edge empties the stack.

3.3   The Slicing Algorithm

Algorithm 1 illustrates the process to slice the CE-PDG. It works similar to the standard algorithm [21], traversing backwards all edges from the slicing criterion and collecting nodes to form the final slice. The algorithm uses a work list with the states that must be processed. A state represents the (backward) traversal of an edge. It includes the node reached, the current stack, and the sequence of already traversed edges (line 6). In every iteration the algorithm processes one state. First, it collects all edges that target the current node (function GETINCOMINGEDGES in line 7). If the previous traversed edge is structural, we avoid traversing flow edges (lines 9–10) and only traverse structural or control dependence edges. The reason for this is that structural edges are only traversed to collect the structure of a data type so that the final slice is syntactically correct (for instance, to collect the tuple to which an element belongs). Flow edges are not further traversed to avoid collecting irrelevant dependencies of the structural parent. Function PROCESSCONSTRAINT checks the existence of a loop (reaching an already traversed edge) during the slicing traversal and implements Table 1 to produce the new stack generated by traversing the edge to the next node (line 11). If the edge cannot be traversed according to Table 1 ($newStack == error$), then the reachable node is ignored (line 12). Otherwise, the node is added to the work list together with the new stack (line 13). Finally, the state is added to a list of processed states, used to avoid the multiple evaluation of the same state, and the current node is included in the slice (lines 14–16).

Algorithm 1. Intraprocedural slicing algorithm for CE-PDGs

Input: The slicing criterion node n_{sc}.
Output: The set of nodes that compose the slice.

```
1:  function SLICINGALGORITHMINTRA(n_sc)
2:    slice ← ∅; processed ← ∅
3:    workList ← {⟨n_sc, ⊥, []⟩}
4:    while workList ≠ ∅ do
5:      select some state ∈ workList;
6:      ⟨node, stack, traversedEdges⟩ = state
7:      for all edge ∈ GETINCOMINGEDGES(node) do
8:        ⟨sourceNode, type, _⟩ ← edge
9:        if GETLASTEDGETYPE(traversedEdges) = structural     then
                        ∧ type = flow
10:         continue for all
11:       newStack ← PROCESSCONSTRAINT(stack, edge)
12:       if newStack ≠ error then
13:         workList ← workList ∪
                {⟨sourceNode, newStack, traversedEdges ++ edge⟩}
14:       processed ← processed ∪ {state}
15:       workList ← {(n, s, t) ∈ workList | (n, s, _) ∉ processed}
16:       slice ← slice ∪ {node}
17:   return slice

18: function PROCESSCONSTRAINT(stack, edge)
19:   ⟨_, _, constraint⟩ ← edge
20:   if constraint = AsteriskConstraint then return ⊥
21:   else
22:     if edge ∈ traversedEdges then
23:       if ISINCREASINGLOOP(FINDLOOP(traversedEdges),edge) then return ⊥
24:     if constraint = EmptyConstraint then return stack
25:     else return PROCESSACCESS(stack, constraint)

26: function PROCESSACCESS(stack, constraint = ⟨op, position⟩)
27:   if stack = ⊥ then
28:     if op = { ∨ op = [ then return PUSH(constraint, stack)
29:     else return ⊥
30:   lastConstraint ← top(stack)
31:   if (op = } ∧ lastConstraint = ⟨{, position⟩)    then
          ∨ (op = ] ∧ lastConstraint = ⟨[, position⟩)
32:     return POP(stack)
33:   else
34:     if op = } ∨ op = ] then return error
35:     else return PUSH(constraint, stack)
36:   return stack
```

Function PROCESSCONSTRAINT computes a new stack for all possible types of constraint: First, it returns an empty stack for asterisk constraints (line 20), Then, the condition in line 22 checks the existence of a loop (reaching an already traversed edge) during the slicing traversal. Function FINDLOOP (line 23) returns the shortest suffix of the sequence of traversed edges that form the last loop, while function ISINCREASINGLOOP (line 23), whose rationale is extensively explained in Sect. 3.4, consequently empties the stack when needed. If no dangerous loop is detected, the function returns the same stack for empty constraints (line 24), or it processes access constraints following Table 1 with function PROCESSACCESS (line 25).

Example 3. Consider again function `foo` in the code of Fig. 1a, the selected slicing criterion ($\langle$ 4,C$\rangle$), and its CE-PDG, shown in Fig. 2. The slicing process starts from the node that represents the slicing criterion (the expanded representation of the CE-PDG allows us to select C, the bold node, inside the tuple structure, excluding the rest of the tuple elements). Algorithm 1 starts the traversal of the graph with an empty stack ($\perp$). The evolution of the stack after traversing each flow edge is the following: $\perp \xrightarrow{[_H} [_H \xrightarrow{\{o} [_H\{o \xrightarrow{\varnothing} [_H\{o \xrightarrow{\}o} [_H \xrightarrow{]_H} \perp$. Due to the traversal limitations imposed by the row 5 in Table 1, node A is never included in the slice because the following transition is not possible: $[_H\{o \xrightarrow{\}_1} error$. As already noted, the resulting slice provided by Algorithm 1 is exactly the minimal slice shown in Fig. 1c.

3.4 Dealing with Loops

In static slicing we rarely know the values of variables (they often depend on dynamic information), so we cannot know how many iterations will be performed in a program loop[2] (see the programs in Fig. 3, where the value of `max` is unknown). For the sake of completeness, we must consider any number of iterations, thus program loops are often seen as potentially infinite. Program loops produce cycles in the PDG. Fortunately, the traversal of cycles in the PDG is not a problem, since every node is only visited once. In contrast, the traversal of a cycle in the CE-PDG could produce a situation in which the stack grows infinitely (see Fig. 3a[3]), generating an infinite number of states. Fortunately, not all cycles produce this problem:[4] To keep the discussion precise, we need to formally define when a cycle in the CE-PDG is a *loop*.

Definition 3 (Loop). *A cyclic flow dependence path* $P = n_1 \xleftarrow{C_1} n_2 \ldots \xleftarrow{C_n} n_1$ *is a* loop *if P can be traversed $n > 1$ times with an initial empty stack ($\perp$) following the rules of Table 1.*

There exist three kinds of loops:

(1) Loops that decrease the size of the stack in each iteration can only produce a finite number of states because the stack will eventually become empty. Such loops can be traversed collecting the elements specified by the stack, without a loss of precision.

---

[2] Note the careful wording in this section, where we distinguish between "program loops" (`while`, `for`...), "cycles" (paths in the PDG that repeat a node), and "loops" (repeated sequence of nodes during the graph traversal).

[3] It is easier to see how the stack changes by reading the code backwards from the slicing criterion.

[4] The interested reader has a developed example for each kind of loop, which includes their CE-PDGs, in the technical report https://mist.dsic.upv.es/techreports/2022/06/field-sensitive-program-slicing.pdf.

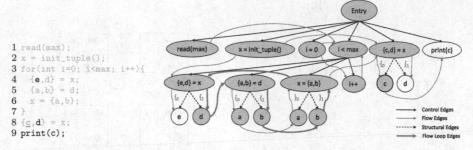

```
1 read(max);
2 x = init_tuple();
3 for(int i=0; i<max; i++){
4   {e,d} = x;
5   {a,b} = d;
6   x = {a,b};
7 }
8 {c,d} = x;
9 print(c);
```

(a) Increasing stack size

(b) CE-PDG of code in Figure 3a

Fig. 3. Slicing flow-dependence cycles in the CE-PDG (slicing criterion underlined and blue, slice in green). (Color figure online)

(2) Loops that keep the same stack in each iteration are also not a problem because traversing the loop multiple times does not generate new states. Again, they can be traversed as many times as required by the stack, without a loss of precision.

(3) Loops that increase the size of the stack in each iteration (Fig. 3a) could produce an infinite number of states because the stack grows infinitely. It is important to remark that not all cycles formed from more opening constraints than closing constraints are increasing loops. They may not even be loops (see Definition 3). Cycles that are not loops are not dangerous because the cycle's edges constraints prevent us to traverse them infinitely. One illustrative example is the code in Fig. 3a where we have the flow dependence cycle $(6, x) \overset{\}_0}{\leftarrow} (6, a) \overset{\varnothing}{\leftarrow} (5, a) \overset{\{_0}{\leftarrow} (5, d) \overset{\varnothing}{\leftarrow} (4, d) \overset{\{_1}{\leftarrow} (4, x) \overset{\varnothing}{\leftarrow} (6, x)$. But this is not a loop because no matter with what stack we enter the cycle, when $\{_1$ is pushed on the stack, the cycle cannot be entered again due to the constraint $\}_0$ that does not match the top of the stack. In contrast, in the same code there exist a loop (highlighted in bold red) that can infinitely increase the stack with $\{_1$ in each iteration: $(6, x) \overset{\}_1}{\leftarrow} (6, b) \overset{\varnothing}{\leftarrow} (5, b) \overset{\{_1}{\leftarrow} (5, d) \overset{\varnothing}{\leftarrow} (4, d) \overset{\{_1}{\leftarrow} (4, x) \overset{\varnothing}{\leftarrow} (6, x)$.

We formally define a special kind of loop which is the only potentially dangerous: *increasing loop*.

Definition 4 (Increasing Loop). *A loop L is an* increasing loop *if the number of opening constraints along L is greater than the number of closing constraints.*

To define and detect the increasing loops (those that can grow the stack infinitely) we have designed the pushdown automaton (PDA) of Fig. 4. The input of this automaton is the sequence of constraints that form a dependence cycle. The PDA contains two states and two different stacks (closing stack and opening stack). Initial state 0 represents the case where all opening constraints

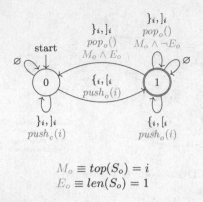

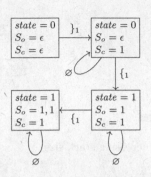

$$M_o \equiv top(S_o) = i$$
$$E_o \equiv len(S_o) = 1$$

Fig. 4. Pushdown automaton to recognize increasing loops.

Fig. 5. States produced by the PDA in Fig. 4 with the word $\}_1 \varnothing \{_1 \varnothing \{_1 \varnothing$

of the sequence are balanced by the corresponding closing constraint. When a closing constraint is reached, the PDA pushes the constraint into the closing stack ($push_c$). When an opening constraint is processed, the PDA pushes the opening constraint into the opening stack ($push_o$) and moves to state 1. Final state 1 represents the case where an opening constraint has been processed but not balanced yet. In state 1, when a closing constraint that matches a previous opening constraint (condition M_o) is processed, we pop the opening constraint from the stack (pop_o). If the popped element of the opening stack is the last element of the stack (condition E_o), the PDA returns to state 0. Finally, if a path is accepted by this automaton, the path forms an increasing loop if and only if the reversed stack S_c is a prefix of S_o and they are not equal. The rationale of this condition is that it ensures that, in each iteration, there are more opening constraints (those in S_o) than closing constraints (those in S_c), and all the closing constraints close some but not all opening constraints (because they are a prefix), thus the number of opening constraints grows infinitely. Note that * constraints do not appear in the PDA because they cannot appear in a loop (an * constraint empties the stack and thus the same state would be repeated).

Example 4. Consider the dependence cycle formed from lines 4, 5, and 6 of Fig. 3a: $(6, x) \xleftarrow{\}_1} (6, b) \xleftarrow{\varnothing} (5, b) \xleftarrow{\{_1} (5, d) \xleftarrow{\varnothing} (4, d) \xleftarrow{\{_1} (4, x) \xleftarrow{\varnothing} (6, x)$, which contains the word: $\}_1 \varnothing \{_1 \varnothing \{_1 \varnothing$.

Now, if we parse this word with the PDA we produce the sequence of states shown in Fig. 5. The final state is an accepting state, and the reverse of S_c (1) is a prefix of S_o (1, 1) (but they are not equal), so this path corresponds to an increasing loop. Moreover, the PDA also detects that this loop adds $\{_1$ (the remainder of S_o once the prefix is removed) to the stack in every iteration.

An increasing loop $n_1 \xleftarrow{C_1} n_2 \xleftarrow{C_2} \ldots \xleftarrow{C_n} n_1$ can be identified because $C_1 C_2 \ldots C_n$ belongs to the language induced by the PDA in Fig. 4 and the two final stacks computed with the PDA, S_c and S_o, satisfy that $reverse(S_c)$ is a prefix of S_o and $reverse(S_c) \neq S_o$.

Only increasing loops can produce non-termination. For this reason, Algorithm 1 detects loops (Line 22) and checks whether they are increasing with function PROCESSEDGECIRCUIT (Line 23). This function uses the PDA of Fig. 4 to determine whether the loop is increasing and in such a case the stack is emptied, i.e., the traversal continues unconstrained.

The reader could think that it would be a good idea to identify all increasing loops at CE-PDG construction time. Unfortunately, finding all cycles has an average complexity $\mathcal{O}(N^2 EL)$, where L is the number of cycles. The worst complexity is exponential $\mathcal{O}(2^N)$ [7]. Our approach avoids the problem of finding all loops. We just treat them on demand, when they are found by the slicing algorithm (i.e., we do not search for loops, we just find them during the CE-PDG traversal). So we only process those loops found in the slicing process; and processing a loop has a linear cost (in the worst case $\mathcal{O}(N)$, if the loop includes all program statements).

4   Implementation and Empirical Evaluation

Comparing our implementation against other slicers is not the best way to assess the proposed stack extension to the PDG, because we would find big differences in the PDG construction time, slicing time, and slicing precision due to differences in the libraries used, different treatment for syntax constructs such as list comprehensions, guards, etc. Therefore, we would not be able to assess the specific impact of the stack on the slicer's precision and performance. The only way to do a fair comparison is to implement a single slicer that is able to build and slice the PDG with and without constraints.

All the algorithms and ideas described in this paper have been implemented in a slicer for Erlang called e-Knife. e-Knife can produce slices based on either the PDG or the CE-PDG. Thus, it allows us to know exactly the additional cost required to build and traverse the constraints, and the extra precision obtained by doing so. e-Knife is a Java program with 12186 LOC (excluding comments and empty lines). It is an open-source project and is publicly available[5].

Additionally, anyone can slice a program via a web interface[6], without the need to build the project locally. Large or very complex programs may run into the memory and time limitations that are in place to avoid abuse.

To evaluate e-Knife, we used Bencher, a program slicing benchmark suite for Erlang. All the benchmarks were interprocedural programs, so we have created a new intraprocedural version of them (by inlining functions). This intraprocedural version has been made publicly available[7]. To evaluate the techniques proposed throughout this work, we have built both graphs (PDG and CE-PDG) for each of the intraprocedural benchmarks. Then, we sliced both graphs with respect

---

[5] https://mist.dsic.upv.es/git/program-slicing/e-knife-erlang.

[6] https://mist.dsic.upv.es/e-knife-constrained/.

[7] https://mist.dsic.upv.es/bencher/.

Table 2. Summary of experimental results, comparing the PDG (without constraints) to the CE-PDG (with constraints).

Program	Graph generation		Slice					
	PDG	CE-PDG	Function	#SCs	PDG	CE-PDG	Slowdown	Red. Size
bench1A.erl	5468.10 ms	5474.38 ms	getLast/2	26	82.55 μs	392.39 μs	4.40 ± 0.50	14.88 ± 3.23%
			getNext/3	174	308.66 μs	1645.44 μs	4.94 ± 0.16	13.06 ± 1.58%
			getStringDate/1	11	30.18 μs	93.71 μs	3.22 ± 0.18	8.67 ± 4.07%
			main/1	57	1121.93 μs	2869.79 μs	2.59 ± 0.30	38.76 ± 7.22%
bench3A.erl	49.58 ms	49.59 ms	tuples/2	22	38.39 μs	153.21 μs	3.69 ± 0.44	5.46 ± 2.08%
bench4A.erl	79.70 ms	79.76 ms	main/2	31	89.80 μs	376.33 μs	4.23 ± 0.42	20.79 ± 5.47%
bench5A.erl	48.69 ms	48.73 ms	lists/2	18	60.92 μs	265.87 μs	3.82 ± 0.43	6.51 ± 2.08%
bench6A.erl	403.52 ms	403.66 ms	ft/2	34	82.59 μs	333.51 μs	3.60 ± 0.36	12.25 ± 2.72%
			ht/2	16	21.39 μs	71.55 μs	2.94 ± 0.29	10.79 ± 3.81%
bench9A.erl	199.53 ms	199.71 ms	main/2	18	197.94 μs	458.68 μs	2.25 ± 0.14	1.38 ± 1.07%
bench11A.erl	15.49 ms	15.52 ms	lists/2	16	43.09 μs	141.87 μs	3.30 ± 0.16	6.47 ± 2.22%
bench12A.erl	1661.91 ms	1663.25 ms	add/4	26	104.88 μs	454.55 μs	4.27 ± 0.49	15.21 ± 4.29%
			from_ternary/2	9	22.92 μs	103.17 μs	4.28 ± 0.44	3.56 ± 2.76%
			main/3	39	103.42 μs	408.30 μs	4.03 ± 0.51	8.43 ± 6.27%
			mul/3	21	55.05 μs	261.14 μs	4.57 ± 0.35	2.74 ± 1.31%
			to_ternary/2	13	71.93 μs	199.70 μs	3.05 ± 0.28	1.02 ± 1.37%
bench14A.erl	3841.95 ms	3842.62 ms	main/2	81	85.94 μs	451.66 μs	4.01 ± 0.40	8.76 ± 2.56%
bench15A.erl	1948.76 ms	1949.37 ms	main/4	71	246.97 μs	609.24 μs	2.94 ± 0.19	2.31 ± 1.73%
bench16A.erl	276.60 ms	276.79 ms	word_count/5	36	83.79 μs	289.83 μs	3.96 ± 0.30	8.91 ± 2.93%
bench17A.erl	63.47 ms	63.60 ms	mug/3	19	55.44 μs	202.33 μs	3.78 ± 0.18	5.59 ± 3.10%
bench18A.erl	71.38 ms	71.50 ms	mbe/2	19	83.69 μs	278.30 μs	3.73 ± 0.31	7.38 ± 4.71%
			Totals and averages for set A	**757**	218.65 μs	814.51 μs	3.88 ± 0.10	**11.67±3.02%**
bench1B.erl	4689.59 ms	4695.39 ms	main/1	273	2375.91 μs	52978.07 μs	19.04 ± 1.48	5.78 ± 2.23%
bench2B.erl	122.07 ms	122.10 ms	main/2	17	100.30 μs	160.02 μs	2.54 ± 0.47	0.25 ± 0.34%
bench3B.erl	53.70 ms	53.71 ms	tuples/2	18	73.09 μs	283.20 μs	3.70 ± 0.42	4.33 ± 1.25%
bench4B.erl	38.34 ms	38.40 ms	main/2	39	136.43 μs	351.29 μs	2.98 ± 0.33	11.78 ± 3.70%
bench5B.erl	24.67 ms	24.72 ms	lists/2	11	83.64 μs	316.45 μs	3.83 ± 0.20	6.88 ± 0.89%
bench6B.erl	89.36 ms	89.49 ms	tuples/2	44	64.04 μs	241.37 μs	3.65 ± 0.39	6.54 ± 1.65%
bench8B.erl	144.54 ms	144.67 ms	main/2	42	317.21 μs	19641.19 μs	57.75 ± 7.30	0.73 ± 0.68%
bench9B.erl	53.57 ms	53.65 ms	main/2	17	305.20 μs	588.48 μs	2.02 ± 0.16	1.16 ± 0.88%
bench10B.erl	146.72 ms	146.98 ms	main/1	35	415.38 μs	7368.92 μs	26.06 ± 5.94	2.23 ± 1.17%
bench11B.erl	15.10 ms	15.15 ms	lists/2	13	69.71 μs	248.10 μs	3.58 ± 0.18	8.02 ± 2.17%
bench12B.erl	526.36 ms	527.29 ms	main/3	88	1445.05 μs	7244.07 μs	5.15 ± 1.32	2.61 ± 2.69%
bench13B.erl	41.00 ms	41.05 ms	main/0	22	212.20 μs	307.64 μs	1.88 ± 0.35	0.48 ± 0.40%
bench14B.erl	257.98 ms	258.50 ms	main/2	52	167.99 μs	522.23 μs	3.20 ± 0.40	12.84 ± 4.48%
bench15B.erl	376.22 ms	376.62 ms	main/4	73	394.71 μs	770.11 μs	2.39 ± 0.16	8.78 ± 2.86%
bench16B.erl	170.25 ms	170.42 ms	word_count/5	40	200.22 μs	3490.60 μs	30.73 ± 6.76	3.70 ± 1.53%
bench17B.erl	93.42 ms	93.55 ms	mug/3	19	248.47 μs	442.49 μs	1.88 ± 0.22	4.96 ± 2.45%
bench18B.erl	102.34 ms	102.48 ms	mbe/2	19	393.15 μs	607.97 μs	1.55 ± 0.15	0.05 ± 0.11%
			Totals and averages for set B	**822**	1060.16 μs	19742.28 μs	13.43 ± 1.18	**5.49 ± 2.16%**

to all possible slicing criteria[8], which guarantees that there is no bias in the selection of slicing criteria.

We strictly followed the methodology proposed by Georges et al. [6]. Each program's graph was built 1001 times, and the graphs were sliced 1001 times per criterion. To ensure real independence, the first iteration was always discarded (to avoid influence of dynamically loading libraries to physical memory, data

---

[8] Each variable use or definition in all functions that contain complex data structures.

persisting in the disk cache, etc.). From the 1000 remaining iterations we retained a window of 10 measurements when steady-state performance was reached, i.e., once the coefficient of variation (CoV, the standard deviation divided by the mean) of the 10 iterations falls below a preset threshold of 0.01 or the lowest CoV if no window reached it. It is with these 10 iterations that we computed the average time taken by each operation (building each graph or slicing each graph w.r.t. each criterion).

The results of the experiments performed are summarized in Table 2. The two columns (**PDG**, **CE-PDG**) display the average time required to build each graph. Building the CE-PDG, as in the PDG, is a quadratic operation; and the inclusion of labels in the edges is a linear operation. Thus, building the CE-PDG is only slightly slower than its counterpart. The other columns are as follows (average values are w.r.t. all slicing criteria):

Function: the name of the function where the slicing criterion is located.
#SCs: the number of slicing criteria in that function.
PDG, CE-PDG: the average time required to slice the corresponding graph.
Slowdown: the average additional time required (with 95% error margins), when comparing the CE-PDG with the PDG. For example, in the first row, the computation of each slice is on average 4.40 times slower in the CE-PDG.
Red. Size: the average reduction in the slices sizes (with 95% error margins). It is computed as $(A - B)/A$ where A is the size (number of AST nodes) of the slice computed with the standard (field-insensitive) algorithm and B is the size (number of AST nodes) of the slice computed with the field-sensitive algorithm (Algorithm 1). This way of measuring the size of the slices is much more precise and fair. LOC is not proper because it can ignore the removal of subexpressions. PDG/CE-PDG nodes is nor a good solution because the CE-PDG includes nodes and arcs not present in their PDG counterparts, therefore they are incomparable.

The averages shown at the bottom of the table are the averages of all slicing criteria, and not the averages of each function's average.

The first 13 benchmarks (set A) are benchmarks with complex data structures but without cycles, while the rest of benchmarks (set B) do contain cycles. In set A, each slice produced by the CE-PDG is around four times slower. However, this has little impact, as each slice consumes just hundreds of milliseconds. As can be seen in each row, generating the graph is at least 3 orders of magnitude slower than slicing it. This increase in time is offset by the average reduction of the slices, which is 8.45%. This increase goes up to 38.76% in function main/1 from bencher1A, as it contains complex data structures that can be efficiently sliced with the CE-PDG. The same happens in set B, but due to the analysis of loops, the slowdown is around thirteen times slower.

If we consider programs without cycles, and taking into account that this is an intra-procedural technique, the time required to compute a slice will be of at most a few hundred μs. Therefore, our technique reduces the size of the slices by $11.67 \pm 3.02\%$ at almost no cost (only a few μs). If we consider programs with cycles, the slowdown is 13.43, but since the technique has more opportunities for improvement (because, contrarily to the CE-PDG, the PDG includes the whole cycle in the slice in all cases), the reduction in the slices size is $5.49 \pm 2.16\%$. This is a very good result: for many applications, e.g., debugging, reducing the suspicious code over 11.67% with a cost of increasing the slicing time by only a few milliseconds is a good trade-off to make.

5   Related Work

Transitive data dependence analysis has been extensively studied [20,27]. Less attention has received, however, the problem of field-sensitive data dependence analysis [10,14,19,26]. The existing approaches can be classified into two groups: those that treat composite structures as a whole [14,15,17,18], and those that decompose them into small atomic data types [1-3,8,11,12,16,19]. The later approach is often called *atomization* or *scalar replacement*, and it basically consists of a program transformation that recursively disassembles composite structures to their primitive components. However, slicing over the decomposed structures usually uses traditional dependence graph based traversal [2,8,12] which limits the accuracy. Moreover, atomization cannot deal with recursive data structures. Other important approaches for field-sensitive data dependence analysis of this kind are [10,14,26]. Litvak et al. [14] proposed a field-sensitive program dependence analysis that identifies dependencies by computing the memory ranges written/read by definitions/uses. Späth et al. [26] proposed the use of pushdown systems to encode and solve field accesses and uses. Snelting et al. [25] present an approach to identify constraints over paths in dependence graphs. Our approach combines atomization with the addition of constraints checked by pushdown systems to improve the accuracy of slicing composite data structures.

Severals works have tried to adapt the PDG for functional languages dealing with tuple structures in the process [4,5,10,28]. Some of them with a high abstraction level [22], and other ones with a low granularity level. Silva et al. [24] propose a new graph representation for the sequential part of Erlang called the Erlang Dependence Graph. Their graph, despite being built with the minimum possible granularity (each node in the graph corresponds to an AST node) and being able to select subelements of a given composite data structure, does not have a mechanism to preserve the dependency of the tuple elements when a tuple is collapsed into a variable; i.e., they do not solve the *slicing pattern matching* problem (for instance, they cannot solve the program in Fig. 1). In contrast, although our graph is only fine-grained at composite data structures, we overcome their limitations by introducing an additional component to the graph, the constrained edges, which allow us to carry the dependence information between definition and use even if the composite structure is collapsed in the process.

6   Conclusion

To address the imprecision of PDG-based slicing of composite data structures, we present a generalization of the PDG called CE-PDG where (i) the inner components of the composite data structures are unfolded into a tree-like representation, providing an independent representation for their subexpressions and allowing us to accurately define intra-statement data dependencies, and (ii) the edges are augmented with constraints (constrained edges), which allows the propagation of the component dependence information through the traversal of the graph during the slicing process. As a result, the CE-PDG allows the user to select any subexpression of a data structure as the slicing criterion and it computes accurate slices for (recursive) composite data structures. An evaluation of our approach shows a slowdown of 3.88/13.43 and a reduction of the slices of 11.67%/5.49% for programs without/with cycles.

References

1. Agrawal, H., DeMillo, R.A., Spafford, E.H.: Dynamic slicing in the presence of unconstrained pointers. In: Proceedings of the Symposium on Testing, Analysis, and Verification, pp. 60–73 (1991)
2. Anderson, P., Reps, T., Teitelbaum, T.: Design and implementation of a fine-grained software inspection tool. IEEE Trans. Softw. Eng. **29**(8), 721–733 (2003)
3. Binkley, D., Gallagher, K.B.: Program slicing. Adv. Comput. **43**(2), 1–50 (1996)
4. Brown, C.M.: Tool support for refactoring Haskell programs. PhD thesis, School of Computing, University of Kent, Canterbury, Kent, UK (2008)
5. Cheda, D., Silva, J., Vidal, G.: Static slicing of rewrite systems. In: Proceedings of the 15th International Workshop on Functional and (Constraint) Logic Programming (WFLP 2006), pp. 123–136. Elsevier ENTCS 177 (2007)
6. Georges, A., Buytaert, D., Eeckhout, L.: Statistically rigorous Java performance evaluation. SIGPLAN Not. **42**(10), 57–76 (2007)
7. Gongye, X., Wang, Y., Wen, Y., Nie, P., Lin, P.: A simple detection and generation algorithm for simple circuits in directed graph based on depth-first traversal. Evol. Intell. (2020)
8. Graf, J.: Speeding up context-, object- and field-sensitive SDG generation. In: 2010 10th IEEE Working Conference on Source Code Analysis and Manipulation, pp. 105–114 (2010)
9. Horwitz, S., Reps, T., Binkley, D.: Interprocedural slicing using dependence graphs. ACM Trans. Program. Lang. Syst. **12**(1), 26–60 (1990)
10. Prasanna Kumar, K., Sanyal, A., Karkare, A., Padhi, S.: A static slicing method for functional programs and its incremental version. In: Proceedings of the 28th International Conference on Compiler Construction, CC 2019, pp. 53–64, New York, NY, USA, Association for Computing Machinery (2019)
11. Korel, B., Laski, J.: Dynamic slicing of computer programs. J. Syst. Softw. **13**(3), 187–195 (1990)
12. Krinke, J.: Advanced slicing of sequential and concurrent programs. PhD thesis, Universität Passau (2003)
13. Liang, D., Harrold, M.J.: Slicing objects using system dependence graphs. In: Proceedings of the International Conference on Software Maintenance, ICSM 1998, pp. 358–367, Washington, DC, USA, IEEE Computer Society (1998)
14. Litvak, S., Dor, N., Bodik, R., Rinetzky, N., Sagiv, M.: Field-sensitive program dependence analysis. In: Proceedings of the Eighteenth ACM SIGSOFT International Symposium on Foundations of Software Engineering, FSE 2010, pp. 287–296, New York, NY, USA, Association for Computing Machinery (2010)

15. Lyle, J.R.: Evaluating variations on program slicing for debugging (Data-Flow, Ada). PhD thesis, USA (1984)
16. Muchnick, S.S.: Advanced Compiler Design and Implementation, Chapter 12.2. Morgan Kaufmann, Burlington (1997)
17. Muchnick, S.S.: Advanced Compiler Design and Implementation Chapter 8.12. Morgan Kaufmann, Burlington (1997)
18. Ottenstein, K.J., Ottenstein, L.M.: The program dependence graph in a software development environment. SIGSOFT Softw. Eng. Notes 9(3), 177–184 (1984)
19. Ramalingam, G., Field, J., Tip, F.: Aggregate structure identification and its application to program analysis. In: Proceedings of the 26th ACM SIGPLAN-SIGACT Symposium on Principles of Programming Languages, POPL 1999, pp. 119–132, New York, NY, USA, Association for Computing Machinery (1999)
20. Reps, T., Horwitz, S., Sagiv, M.: Precise interprocedural dataflow analysis via graph reachability. In: Proceedings of the 22nd ACM SIGPLAN-SIGACT Symposium on Principles of Programming Languages, POPL 1995, pp. 49–61, New York, NY, USA, Association for Computing Machinery (1995)
21. Reps, T., Horwitz, S., Sagiv, M., Rosay, G.: Speeding up slicing. SIGSOFT Softw. Eng. Notes 19(5), 11–20 (1994)
22. Rodrigues, N.F., Barbosa, L.S.: Component identification through program slicing. In: Proceedings of Formal Aspects of Component Software (FACS 2005). Elsevier ENTCS, pp. 291–304. Elsevier (2005)
23. Silva, J.: A vocabulary of program slicing-based techniques. ACM Comput. Surv. 44(3), 1–41 (2012)
24. Silva, J., Tamarit, S., Tomás, C.: System dependence graphs in sequential erlang. In: de Lara, J., Zisman, A. (eds.) FASE 2012. LNCS, vol. 7212, pp. 486–500. Springer, Heidelberg (2012). https://doi.org/10.1007/978-3-642-28872-2_33
25. Snelting, G., Robschink, T., Krinke, J.: Efficient path conditions in dependence graphs for software safety analysis. ACM Trans. Softw. Eng. Methodol. 15(4), 410–457 (2006)
26. Späth, J., Ali, K., Bodden, E.: Context-, flow-, and field-sensitive data-flow analysis using synchronized pushdown systems. Proc. ACM Program. Lang. 3(POPL), 1–29 (2019)
27. Sridharan, M., Fink, S.J., Bodik, R.: Thin slicing. In: Proceedings of the 28th ACM SIGPLAN Conference on Programming Language Design and Implementation, PLDI 2007, pp. 112–122, New York, NY, USA, Association for Computing Machinery (2007)
28. Tóth, M., Bozó, I., Horváth, Z., Lövei, L., Tejfel, M., Kozsik, T.: Impact analysis of erlang programs using behaviour dependency graphs. In: Horváth, Z., Plasmeijer, R., Zsók, V. (eds.) CEFP 2009. LNCS, vol. 6299, pp. 372–390. Springer, Heidelberg (2010). https://doi.org/10.1007/978-3-642-17685-2_11
29. Walkinshaw, N., Roper, M., Wood, M.: The Java system dependence graph. In: Proceedings Third IEEE International Workshop on Source Code Analysis and Manipulation, pp. 55–64 (2003)
30. Weiser, M.: Program slicing. In: Proceedings of the 5th International Conference on Software Engineering (ICSE 1981), pp. 439–449, Piscataway, NJ, USA, IEEE Press 1981

SPouT: Symbolic Path Recording During Testing - A Concolic Executor for the JVM

Malte Mues[1]([⊠]) [iD], Falk Howar[1,2] [iD], and Simon Dierl[1] [iD]

[1] TU Dortmund University, Dortmund, Germany
{malte.mues,falk.howar,simon.dierl}@tu-dortmund.de
[2] Fraunhofer ISST, Dortmund, Germany

Abstract. In this paper, we present SPouT, a concolic executor for the Java virtual machine. To the user, SPouT is a java executable that takes some additional parameters for setting the values of concolic inputs and produces symbolic traces over variables under observation during the execution. Technically, SPouT extends the JVM implementation provided by the Espresso guest language for the GraalVM. Therefore, SPouT is the first concolic executor build on an industrial JVM. In this paper, we describe the architectural design of SPouT, detail how the partial symbolic analysis of Java's strings is implemented in SPouT, and show its performance and versatility by comparing it to other analysis tools for Java programs.

Keywords: Software verification · Java program analysis · Dynamic symbolic execution

1 Introduction

Symbolic analysis of Java applications at scale is a tough technical challenge. The Java platform has many semantically rich features (reflection, lambda expressions, annotations, etc.) and the Java Virtual Machine is a complex execution environment. Tools for the symbolic analysis of Java programs broadly fall into three categories: tools that translate Java code or some intermediate representations, e.g., bytecode, into a representation amenable to formal analysis (examples are KEY [1], JAYHORN [7], and JBMC [6]), tools that instrument bytecode and execute it on an unmodified Java Virtual Machine (COASTAL is one recent example), and tools that do not modify the programs, but instrument a Java Virtual Machine to analyze bytecode during execution. Java PathFinder [24] was the first successful model checker for Java and its analyzer JPF-VM, a Java-based JVM implementation running on top of a normal JVM, served as a basis for many tools in this third category (e.g., SPF [17], JAVA RANGER [21], and JDART [12]).

This work has been partially funded by an Amazon Research Award.

B.-H. Schlingloff and M. Chai (Eds.): SEFM 2022, LNCS 13550, pp. 91–107, 2022.
https://doi.org/10.1007/978-3-031-17108-6_6

For all three categories, the soundness of analyses hinges on correctly modeling (or not changing) the semantics of the Java language or the specified behavior of a JVM and all three approaches have distinct advantages and drawbacks: Working on Java code directly removes a big portion of complex technical machinery from the analysis but has to be adapted to new language features and manually transferred to other languages. Tools that instrument bytecode instructions are light-weight with respect to their execution environment (a standard JVM) but for a complete symbolic analysis, the symbolic semantics of stack and heap operations have to be woven into the analyzed code. Instrumenting a Java Virtual Machine enables analysis of all programs and language features that are compiled to JVM bytecode but requires a JVM implementation to instrument. Developing and maintaining a sufficiently feature-complete JVM that powers the analysis is cumbersome: e.g., as of today, the JPF-VM only supports the analysis of Java version 8 bytecode, while Java 11 has been the LTS version since 2018, and was succeeded by Java 17 (LTS) in September of 2021.

In this paper, we present SPouT, a concolic executor for the Java Virtual Machine. To the user, SPouT is a java executable that takes some additional parameters for setting the values of concolic inputs and produces symbolic traces over variables under observation during the execution. Technically, SPouT instruments the Espresso guest language for the GRAALVM [25]. Espresso is an existing full-fledged virtual machine written in Java and maintained by Oracle. We describe the architectural design of SPouT and detail how the partial symbolic analysis of Java's standard string library is implemented in SPouT.

We evaluate the performance of SPouT and its versatility by comparing it to other analysis tools for Java programs in a series of usage examples and by analyzing the results of SV-COMP 2022, where we used SPouT as a component in the GDart [15] tool ensemble for the dynamic symbolic execution of Java bytecode. Our results show that the architectural design of SPouT is a viable alternative to the design of existing research tools. Further, the described experiments demonstrate that SPouT analyzes programs that the JPF-VM cannot execute. This enables further research on dynamic symbolic execution for Java.

Related Work. There are two areas of research influencing the design of SPouT: The symbolic encoding of Java programs during the analysis and the encoding of string specific operations in general. In most cases, converting a program to its analysis representation is only one step, implemented as part of an analyzer. As we are only interested in the symbolic encoding approach in the context of SPouT, we shortly describe some selected techniques for preparing the analysis target in Java tools participating at SV-COMP without discussing the analysis approaches in detail. The encoding of string operations in the symbolic analysis is also a very active research area, and we cannot discuss all results here. Instead, we present selected examples with a strong influence on this paper.

All presented techniques generate a logical representation of the Java program. However, they vary in the concrete style of encoding and the involved abstraction level. JAYHORN [7] compiles the Java program into horn clauses and operates on the Java byte code. The analysis is completely executed on the symbolic encoding. JBMC converts Java code in to CBMC's [5] goto-language and continues the analysis on this intermediate format. SPF [17] was the first symbolic execution engine build on top of JPF and encodes the JVM byte-code under analysis into a symbolic representation using the JPF-VM. JAVA RANGER [21] reuses this infrastructure for encoding the program. COASTAL's[1] concolic executor uses the ASM[2] bytecode manipulation framework to weave the symbolic constraints recording code into the program under analysis. The tools conceptually closest to SPOUT are JDART [12] and SYMJEX [8]. JDART instruments the JPF-VM to record symbolic constraints during concrete execution, but behaves mostly identical to SPOUT except for the trace reporting. SYMJEX uses the GRAALVM compiler frontend to lift Java bytecode into an intermediate representation for performing symbolic execution. In contrast SPOUT executes bytecode using the Espresso VM running on the GRAALVM. As this paper focuses mainly on dynamic testing methods for Java, we skip most literature dealing with static testing methods for Java (e.g. Julia [22] or PMD[3]).

Previous work on encoding string operations for the analysis of Java generally uses bitvector encodings (e.g. [3,18]) or automata based encodings built from collected string graphs (e.g. [4,18,20]). Instead, SPOUT encodes the string operations using SMT-Lib's theory of strings [2] as an abstraction and leaves the decision making to the SMT solver working with SPOUT's output. This cleanly decouples the constraint generation (as part of concolic execution) and solving.

The Java String Analyzer (JSA) by Christensen et al. [4] is one of the first major static string analyzer for Java build using the automata theory stimulating many follow up work. Redelinghuys et al. [18] used it for deciding string graphs, their intermediate representation of string operations in Java programs. They compare the automata theory with a bitvector encoded version decided by Z3 [13]. Their main result is that there is no significant difference between using automatons or bitvectors for representing strings symbolically. Instead, the combination of constraints limiting the string content and its length influences performance. SMT-Lib allows to express these constraints in SPOUT's encoding and from our experience in previous work [14], today's string solvers support them well. Bjørner et al. [3] describe the integration of a bitvector based encoding for string operations in the dynamic symbolic execution of .NET programs with PEX [23]. They split the check into numeric checks first and the content constraint next, allowing the precise modelling of exceptions caused by wrong relations between indices and the string length, e.g., if the index is outside of the string size for the charAt method. SPOUT follows this encoding pattern, but instead of encoding the string content parts as bitvectors, we encode it in the SMT-Lib string theory. Shannon et al. [19] describe different techniques for instrumenting the analysis enabling to intercept the operations on string values on the Java standard library API level and evaluate replacing the String class with a SymbolicString class for interception the calls. SPOUT directly instruments the String class inside the JVM instead of replacing it in the implementation. As part of their experiments, Shannon et al. pointed out the

---

[1] https://github.com/DeepseaPlatform/coastal.

[2] https://asm.ow2.io.

[3] https://pmd.github.io.

$$trace ::= (decl \mid decision \mid err \mid abort \mid assume)^* \quad [\texttt{ENDOFTRACE}]$$

$$decl ::= [\texttt{DECLARE}] \quad def$$

$$decision ::= [\texttt{DECISION}] \quad expr \quad // \quad \texttt{branchCount} = i, \texttt{branchId} = j$$

$$err ::= [\texttt{ERROR}] \quad cause$$

$$abort ::= [\texttt{ABORT}] \quad cause$$

$$assume ::= [\texttt{ASSUMPTION}] \quad expr \quad // \quad \texttt{sat} = b$$

$def \in$ SMTLib Fun. Defs. $i, j \in \mathbb{N}_0$

$expr \in$ SMTLib Assertions $b \in \{true, \, false\}$ $cause \in$ Text

Fig. 1. The BNF grammar for a trace that summarizes a concolic execution run.

problem of domain crossing whenever strings are converted to numbers. Their encoding does not express the semantic implications precisely. We still have the same problems today with SPOUT.

Outline. Section 2 describes the internals of SPOUT. In Sect. 3, we provide usage examples and evaluate the performance of SPOUT by comparing it to several other analysis tools for the JVM.

2   SPOUT: Directing the Flow of Espresso

SPOUT[4] (*Symbolic Path Recording during Testing*) implements concolic execution in the Espresso[5] Java Virtual Machine for Oracle's GRAALVM[6]. As it extends Espresso, SPOUT – like Espresso – is licensed under the GPLv2. SPOUT's symbolic additions are bundled in a single `Concolic` class. This avoids scattering the functionality across the virtual machine. SPOUT extends *Espresso* with the functionality to (a) maintain symbolic annotations for values on the stack and on the heap, (b) compute the effect of bytecode instructions on these symbolic annotations, (c) record path constraints on branching points, and (d) inject concolic values into the analysis. Using substitution methods as a general extension method of the GRAALVM, we demonstrate how to intercept the invocation of standard library methods to encode them symbolically on higher levels than the executed bytecode instructions. SPOUT uses this technique for encoding operations of the `Java` string library.

2.1   SPOUT's Design

SPOUT is built as a `java` executable. Command-line arguments added to the invocation of SPOUT allow seeding the concolic variables. SPOUT will report back the collected symbolic constraints and the result using the trace language

---

[4] https://github.com/tudo-aqua/spout, available under GPLv2.

[5] https://github.com/oracle/graal/tree/master/espresso.

[6] https://github.com/oracle/graal/.

defined by the BNF grammar in Fig. 1. Trace logs can contain symbolic variable declarations, assumptions and decisions (i.e., SMT-Lib assertions over symbolic variables), as well as errors and abort statements. For decisions and assertions minimal information about the *shape* of a trace, i.e., branch counts and branch directions are communicated, furthering the easy integration of SPOUT as a component in other analyses. SPOUT uses a `Verifier` class with nondeterministic value factories for all supported concolic data types, e.g., `int`, `boolean`, `String`, etc., to allow programmatic definition of concolic variables in the driver method of an analysis.

We demonstrate the usage of SPOUT by analyzing the small Kotlin[7] program shown in Listing 2 (Kotlin is compiled to JVM bytecode). The program generates an integer value, using the `Verifier.nondetInt()` method that is instrumented by SPOUT during concolic execution, i.e., SPOUT will return the configured concrete value, create a symbolic variable for the return value and track its influence through path constraints. In the program, the returned concolic integer is used in the test (x > 0), guarding an assertion violation.

```
import tools.aqua.concolic.Verifier
fun main() {
    val x = Verifier.nondetInt()
    if (x > 0)
        assert(false)
}
```

Listing 2: A simple Kotlin program with a guarded assertion violation and a call to method `Verifier.nondetInt()` that returns concolic values.

The `kotlin` command basically wraps a `java` invocation and adds Kotlin resources to the classpath. We execute the compiled Kotlin program concolically by using the GraalVM with SPOUT as follows:

```
export JAVA_HOME=/path/to/spoutvm
/path/to/kotlin/bin/kotlin -J"-truffle" -J"-ea" \
  -Dconcolic.ints=0 \
  -cp [verifier-stub]:. MainKt
```

The argument `-J"-truffle"` is passed to the GRAALVM Java binary and selects the Truffle-based Java implementation, while `-J"-ea"` enables assertion checking. `-Dconcolic.ints=0` is parsed by SPOUT and instructs it to use 0 as the concrete value for the first concolic integer value. The argument takes a comma-separated list of values that seed the `Verifier` class and controls this way the execution along a specific path. Once the preseeded values are exhausted, default values are used. Similar arguments exist for all primitive data types and string values. For the sake of brevity, we omit parts of the executions output and only show the recorded trace with abbreviated decision branch information:

```
[DECLARE]   (declare-fun __int_0 () (_ BitVec 32))
[DECISION]  (assert (bvsle __int_0 #x00000000)) //b.Count = 2, b.Id = 1
[ENDOFTRACE]
```

In the trace, the concolic integer value is represented by the variable `__int_0`.

---

[7] https://kotlinlang.org/.

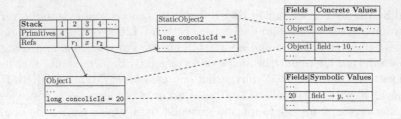

Fig. 2. Memory architecture of SPoUT. Black parts provided by Espresso. Red parts added by SPoUT.

2.2   Memory Architecture

The JVM state is represented in the memory using the stack and the heap. In the following, we describe how these memory structures are extended with symbolic annotations, the concolic bytecodes propagate the symbolic annotations and record symbolic constraints, and substitution methods enable the symbolic encoding of methods.

Symbolic Stack and Heap. As sketched in Fig. 2, Espresso uses two arrays of identical size to represent the stack; one for primitive values and one for object references. They are populated alternatingly (for each index, either a primitive or an object reference is stored). SPoUT leverages this layout and stores concolic information about primitive values at the (unused) corresponding index in the object reference array and vice versa. As a consequence, Espresso takes care of all stack operations (e.g., copying values and annotations between frames). On the heap, Espresso represents every instantiated object by a `StaticObject` that – among other things – maintains a field table and stores contents of field in an optimized (native) location. SPoUT extends these container objects with unique concolic ids and stores symbolic contents of fields in a map indexed by id. This mechanism operates lazily, creating map entries only for objects with concolically tainted fields, keeping the memory overhead of this analysis minimal. SPoUT extends the `getfield` and `setfield` instructions to propagate symbolic annotations between stack and heap.

Concolic Bytecodes. Concolic bytecode implementations are used for computing symbolic effects of instructions and for recording path constraints (e.g., on branching instructions). SPoUT extends the implementation of all bytecodes that compute values, e.g., `iadd`, or introduce branching conditions, e.g., `if_icmpne`. Listing 3 shows the concolic extension of the `iadd` instruction: After the concrete effect on the stack is computed by Espresso, SPoUT computes the symbolic effect only if needed, keeping the impact on performance as small as possible.

Substituting Methods. Espresso provides a mechanism for substituting individual methods with customized versions (i.e., executing custom code instead of the actual method). SPoUT leverages this mechanism for two purposes: (a) user-

```
void iadd(long[] primitives, Object[] refs, int top) {
    int i1 = popInt(primitives, top - 1);
    int i2 = popInt(primitives, top - 2);
    int iRes = i1 + i2;
    putInt(primitives, top - 2, iRes);
    // added concolic operation
    putConcolic(refs, top -2, sadd(i1, i2, iRes,
        popConcolic(refs, top-1), popConcolic(refs, top-2)));
}


Concolic sadd(int i1, int i2, int iRes, Concolic c1, Concolic c2) {
    if (c1 == null && c2 == null) return null;
    if (c1 == null) c1 = concFromConstant(i1);
    if (c2 == null) c2 = concFromConstant(i2);
    return new Conc(iRes, new Expression(IADD, c1.symb(), c2.symb()));
}
```

Listing 3: Implementation of Concolic `iadd` Bytecode.

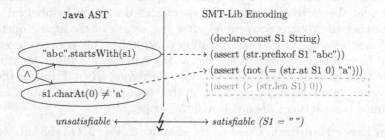

Fig. 3. The black boxes on the right demonstrate the naive mapping from the Java AST to an SMT-Lib encoding. The bottom part shows the semantic mismatch: the test is unsatisfiable in the Java language while the SMT-Lib semantics admit an empty string as a valid model for S1.

defined concolic values are injected via methods of the `Verifier` class[8], and (b) the concolic semantics of operations on strings are implemented in substituted implementations. A concolic semantic consists of two parts: the concrete computation that changes the heap state and the update of the symbolic values.

2.3 Symbolic Encoding of String Operations

The analysis of string operations is especially important for reasoning on Java programs [4,10,18] and encoding them on the string level has various benefits over instrumenting the primitive types that represent a string (c.f. [3,19]). In the following, we describe how SPOUT encodes string operations, present three concrete challenges in the encoding, and describe the limitations. The tree challenges are: faithful error handling, numeric and string semantic of characters, and regular expressions.

---

[8] https://github.com/tudo-aqua/verifier-stubs.

Table 1. Mapping from the `Java` standard string library to SMT-Lib.

Java operation	SMT-Lib operation	Java operation	SMT-Lib operation
CONCAT(s1, s2)	$(str.++ \; s1 \; s2)$	ISDIGIT(c1)	$(str.is\_digit \; c1)$
CONTAINS(s1, s2)	$(str.contains \; s1 \; s2)$	LENGTH(s1)	$(str.len \; s1)$
CONTENTEQUALS(s1, seq2)	$(= \; s1 \; seq2)$	REPLACE(s1, s2, s3)	$(str.replace\_all \; s1 \; s2 \; s3)$
ENDSWITH(s1, s2)	$(str.suffixof \; s1 \; s2)$	STARTSWITH(s1, s2)	$(str.prefixof \; s2 \; s1)$
EQUALS(s1, s2)	$(= \; s1 \; s2)$	SUBSTRING(s1, i1)	$(str.substr \; s1 \; i1 \; (str.len s1))$
INDEXOF(s1, s2)	$(str.indexof \; s1 \; s2 \; 0)$	SUBSTRING(s1, i1, i2)	$(str.substr \; s1 \; i1 \; (- \; i2 \; i1))$
INDEXOF(s1, s2, i1)	$(str.indexof \; s1 \; s2 \; i1)$		

Encoding. SPOUT encodes `Java`'s string operations symbolically using a mixture of integer and string theory constraints in the SMT-Lib language. While for some operations in `Java`, the SMT-Lib language contains matching counterparts (shown in Table 1), others exhibit different semantics in edge cases or are not expressible (shown in Table 2). String operations are the first datatype with symbolic encoding in SPOUT that introduce an abstraction of the bytecode semantics of the JVM in the symbolic operation. The substitution methods intercept the method invocation and encodes the effects symbolically. But for continuing the concrete execution after the return of the string operation, SPOUT must execute the string operation concretely. This concrete execution must not be visible in the constraint tree, as the symbolic encoding describes the semantic already using a higher abstraction. Therefore, SPOUT pauses the general bytecode level constraint recording in the scope of the substitution method and resumes it on return, when it leaves the scope.

Faithful Error Handling. Consider the example in Fig. 3. On the left, we have a path constraint that is similar to a previously discussed example by Redelinghuys et al. [18] for comparing automatons and bitvector encodings. Assume that s1 is a concolic string variable and recorded constraints require s1 to be a prefix of the string "abc" but the first character of s1 must not be 'a'. Under the `Java` semantics, this is unsatisfiable: the empty string throws an `IndexOutOfBoundsException` when accessing its 0-th character and non-empty strings cannot match both constraints. SMT-Lib defines the `str.prefixof` and `str.at` operations that are mostly comparable to the `Java` methods `startsWith` and `charAt`. The black part on the right of the figure shows the direct mapping from `Java` to these functions. But there are differences in the semantics of corner cases. In SMT-Lib, the problem is satisfiable by the empty string, since accessing an index beyond the string length yields an *error value* that is not equal to "a". Therefore, for the concolic analysis of the `charAt(i)` method on the symbolic string s1, a check on the index is required. The index i must be greater or equal to zero and less than the string length of s1 to be successful in the `Java` SE library. The green constraint on the right side is an added implicit assumption modeling that `charAt` did not throw an exception. This implies that encoding a single `Java` constraint may yield two path constraints in SMT-Lib, one modeling invalid access operations and one modeling valid ones. The exception path and the branching condition guarding it becomes visible in the tree.

```
void main(String[] args) {          //
  String arg =                      25: iload_2
    Verifier.nondetString();        26: invokestatic #6 //toUpperCase
  if (arg.length() < 1) return;     29: iload_2
  char c = arg.charAt(0);           30: invokestatic #7 //toLowerCase
  assert Character.toUpperCase(c)   33: if_icmpne    44
    != Character.toLowerCase(c);    36: new          #8
}                                   //
```

Fig. 4. The StaticCharMethods02 task from SV-COMP 2022.

Fig. 5. The bytecode for the assert statement from Fig. 4

Numeric and String Semantics of Characters. Java uses a character type for its string and numeric semantic, but the compiled bytecode only utilizes integer operations. In contrast, the SMT-Lib is only aware of the string semantic for a character. Therefore, for encoding a problem in SMT-Lib, the string theory semantic is sometimes easier. For example, consider the charAt method. In the SMT-Lib language, charAt returns a value of type string. In the Java language, it is a character. Inside the JVM, the character is represented as an integer. Figure 3 encodes the comparison of the charAt result against the character 'a' as a comparison in the string semantic using the SMT-Lib. Otherwise, this small example involves in the encoding of the numeric equality many cast operations from a string to an integer to a 32-bit bitvector. For this case, lifting from the Java representation to the string semantic is easier than using casting expressions in the symbolic encoding.

Consider the example in Fig. 4. The character at position zero is extracted from a nondeterministic string. Next, the assertion statement compares the result from the to upper case and lower case conversion. Figure 5 shows the compiled bytecode of the assertion check in Fig. 4. The invokestatic bytecode takes the integer from the stack and replace it with another integer. This is a lookup in a large map that cannot be encoded in SMT-Lib using an numeric value in the bitvector theory. On the other side, some solvers, e.g., CVC4, support the functions toUpper and toLower in the string theory. Using them, it is possible to encode the assertion semantic in the string theory. Assuming ARG represents the symbolic string, the logical encoding is: $(= (toUpper\,(str.at\,\text{ARG}\,0))\,(toLower\,(str.at\,\text{ARG}\,0)))$. To allow this flexible in encoding the semantic, the character values in the JVM require a string semantic and a bitvector semantic equivalent in the encoding. SMT-Lib supports str.to_code and nat2bv that allows to express the numeric code point of a String into a bitvector, but it is not a true semantic link representing the dual semantics of the character data type in the Java language in SMT-Lib. At the moment, SPouT uses mainly the string semantics, but we are still investigating the best way to deal with this representation problem in a more general solution that also support cases where the character is used numerically in the program.

Table 2. Functions that cannot be mapped directly and precisely from the Java standard string library to the SMT-Lib language, or do not maintain their semantic.

Java Operation	SMT-Lib Operation	Comment
CHARAT($s1$, $i1$)	$(str.at\ s1\ i1)$	The charAt function requires some error handling in Java not represented in the SMT-Lib function $str.at$.
COMPARETO($s1$, $s2$)	$(str. <\ s1\ s2)$ $(str. <=\ s1\ s2)$	SMT-Lib has lexicographic ordering operations but they need to be embedded in the evaluation of COMPARETO splitting the three value result logic to binary decisions
COMPARETO-INGORECASE($s1$, $s2$)	–	There is no mapping in SMT-Lib allowing the encoding of the ignore case semantic. Using solver specific operations as toUpper allow to work around this limitation
EQUALS-IGNORECASE($s1$, $s2$)	–	The same problem as for COMPARETOIGNORECASE applies
ISLETTER($c1$) ISUPPERCASE($c1$)	–	It is possible to use $str.to\_code$ to convert c1 into a code point. But afterwards the unicode table defining which code points are within the target domain have to be encoded as well. In practice, we have only archived to encode this for limited ranges on the code point
JOIN($s1$, $s2$[])	–	There is no way for expressing a join on a symbolic string array yet as we have not really a way to express the capacity of an array symbolically
LASTINDEXOF($s1$, $s2$)	(declare-const x Int) $(and\ (=\ (str.at\ s1\ x)\ s2)$ $(not\ (exists\ ((y\ Int))$ $(and\ (<\ x\ y)\ (<\ y\ (str.len\ s1))$ $(not\ (=\ (str.at\ s1\ y)\ s2))))))$	We can encode this using helper variables, but it is leaving the QF_SLIA theory as quantifiers are required. Therefore, the encoding is not within the official theory definition of the SMT-Lib anymore as $SLIA$ is not defined as official theory
MATCHES($s1$, $s2$)	$(str.in\_re\ s1\ ...)$	Depending on the complexity of the pattern involved in $s2$, this is possible. But the pattern contained in $s2$ needs to be transformed to SMT-Lib first
PARSEFP($s1$, FPSIZE) PARSEINT($s1$)	–	It is not possible to model this in SMT-Lib at the moment
SPLIT($s1$, $s2$)	–	It is not possible to transfer this except for a concrete example describing that the concatenation of the new subparts with the separator $s2$ are equal to $s1$
REVERSE($s1$)	–	Reversing a string is not supported in todays SMT solvers
STRIP($s1$)	$(and\ (not\ (=\ (str.at\ s1\ 0)\ "\ ")$ $(not\ (=\ (str.at\ s1\ (-$ $(str.len\ s1)\ 1))\ "\ ")))$	While this encoding implies that the first and last character are no whitespaces, it is no possible to express that a string might be shorter after strip in this encoding
STRIPINDENT($s1$) STRIPLEADING($s1$) STRIPTRAILING($s1$) TRIM($s1$)	–	See the problem with strip. The same applies for these methods
TOSTRING(FP1) TOSTRING($i1$) TOSTRING($c1$)	–	There is no symbolic encoding in SMT-Lib that allows to convert a numeric value in its string representation
TOUPPER($s1$) TOLOWER($s1$)	$(str.upper\ s1)$ $(str.lower\ s1)$	These functions are not supported in the official SMT-Lib standard. CVC4 supports it as a custom interface
INSERT($s1$, $s2$, $i1$) DELECTCHARAT($s1$, $i1$) DELETE($s1$, $i1$, $i2$)	–	These functions do not have a counterpart in SMT-Lib but can be encoded using $substring$ to split the existing string and gluing the remaining parts together using $concat$

Encoding Regular Expressions. In general, the Java string library separates two kinds of regular expressions: those that use backreferences and those that do not. Backreferences in regular expression work similar to the Perl regular expression language[9]. In the Java context they are also called capture groups. For example, a regular expression with a capture group is: *name: (*)?$*. It matches any character after the string "name:" until the end of the line. Java allows to extract the group, the part matched between the brackets, if the regular expression matches. E.g., if the string is "name: SPOUT", the group is SPOUT. SMT-Lib does not support backreferences in the regular expression language

---

[9] https://www.pcre.org.

and SPOUT does not support them in the encoding. However, Loring et al. [11] present ideas on encoding and solving constraints with regular expressions using groups for JavaScript by applying a CEGAR based algorithm in combination with SMT solvers.

Regular expressions without capture groups are supported and allow the encoding of string operations like `matches` or `replace`. The main technical challenge is transforming the regular expression into the automaton that is encoded in the SMT-Lib. For example, consider the following regular expression in the Java language: "Date: \d \d-\d\d-\d\d". It has to be decomposed into the different parts first and then combined into the SMT-Lib constraint. SPOUT only reports the regular expression in the Java syntax and the tool that uses this encoding has to parse the Java regular expression string into an SMT-Lib constraint. GDART uses the brics automaton library[10] for the conversion from the string representation into an automaton representation. The first step is resolving the Java specific range definition, in this case "\d" for a digit. An equivalent regular expression is "Date: [0-9][0-9]-[0-9][0-9]-[0-9][0-9]". This regular expression is then converted to SMT-Lib:

$$
\begin{aligned}
&(re.++(str.to\_re\,``Date:\,") \\
&\quad (re.range\,``0"\,``9")\,(re.range\,``0"\,``9")\,(str.to\_re\,``-") \\
&\quad (re.range\,``0"\,``9")\,(re.range\,``0"\,``9")\,(str.to\_re\,``-") \\
&\quad (re.range\,``0"\,``9")\,(re.range\,``0"\,``9"))
\end{aligned}
$$

In this final form, the regular expression can be used in the symbolic encoding of operations. The values produced in a SMT-Lib model for such an expression matches the Java semantic during concrete execution.

Limitations. The presented encoding method works well for modeling operations on strings and the concatenation helper methods that do not involve code point handling (e.g., `concat`, `startsWith`, `equals`, and `indexOf`). Table 2 shows methods that are part of the Java standard library, but currently have no direct semantic counter part in the SMT-Lib language. We partition them in roughly four groups: Those that can be expressed combining other SMT-Lib functions, those that cannot be expressed, those that require restrictions on character, and those that are used for value serialization and deserialization.

E.g., `compareTo` and `insert` can be modeled using a combination of multiple SMT-Lib functions. An insertion can be expressed by creating two substrings from a string and putting them together again by concatenating the first part, the new content between and the second part.

Some methods require unbounded path enumeration in the encoding. A prominent example is the `split` method that cannot be expressed in SMT-Lib yet. For the current path, it is possible to encode the structure of the concrete string and how a new string leading to an increased array looks like. A semantic-preserving encoding of the `split` result as a symbolic array is not yet possible.

---

[10] https://www.brics.dk/automaton/.

Many of the functions that are not expressible in SMT-Lib at the moment apply restriction on certain characters of the string or a single character, e.g., `isLetter`, `strip`, and `trim`. Without support in the string theory, e.g., encoding an equality comparison between a trimmed string value and its not trimmed counterpart is impossible. In `Java`, an example for this case that evaluates to true is: " Hello".trim().equals("Hello"). As SMT-Lib does not have a notion of a single character and custom range checks on them, encoding is impossible.

The last group of problems includes serialization and deserialization for different primitive data types, e.g. `parseFloat`, which converts a `String` into a `float`. This function cannot be expressed symbolically in the current version of SMT-Lib. Supporting the parsing function requires also linking the two theories as a single variable has a representation in both theories.

2.4 Supported Languages and Implemented Features

SPOUT aims to analyze JVM bytecode programs and can – in theory – process any program that is compiled to JVM bytecode using only primitive types (e.g., `Java`, SCALA, and KOTLIN programs with primitive types). As mentioned previously, for higher level data types, e.g., strings, a modeling of the standard library in the form of substitute methods is required. We developed substitutes for `Java` programs as a part of SPOUT. Using SPOUT with other languages as SCALA or KOTLIN requires additional standard library abstractions suitable to the language, although it is already possible to load programs in these languages, including their runtime libraries, using SPOUT.

SPOUT analyzes all JVM primitive types (i.e., `boolean`, `byte`, `char`, `short`, `int`, `long`, `float`, and `double`) concolically (including boxed objects) by generating symbolic constraints in SMT-Lib bitvector and floating point theory. It also tracks concolic array length for one-dimensional and multi-dimensional arrays and models `System.arraycopy`, enabling analysis of collections and arrays.

Since GraalVM is a polyglot virtual machine and Espresso implements a JVM as a guest language, SPOUT benefits from GraalVM's JIT optimization.

3 Demonstration and Evaluation

We evaluate the versatility SPOUT in a number of small usage examples by comparing it to other tools for the analysis of `Java` programs. We have demonstrated its performance in SV-COMP 2022 for the first time, where we used SPOUT as the concolic executor in the GDART tool ensemble. This paper, takes a closer look on the performance of the string encoding in comparison with other tools. In addition, we show two examples, why SPOUT will stimulate future research.

Performance of the String Encoding. Since modeling of string operations is a major challenge when analyzing the security of `Java` web applications, we added the securibench benchmark suite[11] [9,10] to the set of `Java` instances in

---

[11] https://github.com/tudo-aqua/securibench-micro.

Table 3. Comparison of the SV-COMP tools in the Java track on the securibench task subset consisting of 113 task in total. The results are taken from the official SV-COMP runs.

Result	Tool						
	GDART (using SPOUT)	JDART	SPF	JAVA RANGER	JAYHORN	COASTAL	JBMC
Correct	95	100	85	76	0	22	100
Incorrect	0	0	3	0	0	90	0
Unkown	10	12	22	37	113	1	8
Error	8	1	3	0	0	0	5

Table 4. Comparing GDART's capability enabled by SPouT with other Java tools from SV-COMP on the described examples. (+) means the tool solves the example with the expected verdict, (×) means the tool does not solve the example, (−) does not reach the expected verdict, and † means the tool crashes or times out (15 min). - means we could not run the tool on the example.

Tool	Example				
	java11	Scala	Kotlin	JIT	Maven
GDART (using SPOUT)	(+) 4.9 s	(+) 10.7 s	(+) 5.7 s	(+) 26.4 s	(+) 69.1 s
JDART	(−) 2.7 s	–	–	†	–
SPF	(×) 0.9 s	–	–	(×) 1.1 s	–
JAVA RANGER	(×) 0.9 s	–	–	(×) 2.3 s	–
JAYHORN	(−) 2.4 s	–	–	†	–
JBMC	(×) 1.1 s	–	–	(+) 1.5 s	–
COASTAL	(×) 1.1 s	–	–	(×) 1.2 s	–

SV-COMP 2022. The securibench benchmark set is inspired by web application security threats and contains many instances that use String operations. Table 3 compares the different tools reporting results for SV-COMP 2022 on this subset of tasks. JDART and JBMC both solve 100 tasks correctly, five more than GDART. Compared to JAVA RANGER, GDART correctly solves 19 more tasks. JAYHORN solves none of these tasks. The only tools reporting incorrect answers are SPF (3) and COASTAL (90). For the 10 tasks GDART reports as unknown, 5 are due to a triggered exception in the symbolic reasoning component, 3 cannot be solved as the StringTokenzier is not symbolically modeled in SPouT, and two are due to problem specific errors. For the 8 error tasks, GDART exhausts the resource limits. While the summary suggests that JDART and JBMC solve 5 more tasks than GDART, this is not the case. JDART solves 4 tasks for which GDART exhausts the resources and also solves 4 tasks for which GDART reports unknown results. The resource exhaustion happens in the symbolic execution of GDART and are not explicitly related to SPouT. However, GDART solves 3 tasks that JDART does not solve due to different instrumentations of the toLowerCase method. In direct comparison with JBMC, GDART solves 6 tasks that JBMC does not solve mostly, because GDART supports reflection within the JVM, and JBMC does not. On the other side, JBMC solves 5 tasks for which GDART exhausts the resource limit and 6 tasks that GDART does not solve. The distances for unknown tasks are less surprising considering that JDART and JBMC support operations on the `StringTokenizer`.

Performance in SV-COMP 2022. GDART solved 471 out of 586 tasks using SPOUT, which is the third highest amount of correctly solved task, following behind JBMC (506) and JDART (522). As GDART is by design stronger in finding errors (302) than proving the absence of an error (169), it ranks in the SV-COMP point schema fourth after JAVA RANGER (solving 466 tasks, 204 without error, 262 with error) (c.f. SV-COMP results[12]).

Demonstration of Versatility. We have implemented a number of demonstration examples[13] for GDART's capability enabled by SPOUT and report the performance of other `Java` tools in Table 4 in comparison. SPOUT allows GDART to run more examples than any other tool. The examples demonstrate the following:

Modern Java Byte Codes. Being built on top of a full-fledged JVM, SPOUT is capable of analyzing modern `Java` bytecode that uses `Java` 11 features as demonstrated by the `java11` example. This is a major advantage of SPOUT compared to JPF-VM based tools that load only `Java` 8 bytecode.

Analysis of arbitrary JVM languages. SPOUT allows execution of arbitrary JVM bytecode programs, even compiled KOTLIN and SCALA programs, if they are loaded along with their runtimes. The `Kotlin` and `Scala` examples demonstrate this. However, as mentioned previously, support for the KOTLIN and SCALA standard library is incomplete.

JIT Optimization. Since SPOUT runs on the GRAALVM, it benefits from the GRAALVM's just-in-time compiler. In the `jit` example, we can observe a 2.5-fold speed-up for hot code during concolic execution. On the other hand, it has to be noted that the execution with Espresso (version 21.2.0) is 10 to 20 times slower than the native GRAALVM in our examples.

Maven and SpringBoot. The `springboot` example shows how SPOUT can be used out-of-the-box as the JVM for concolically executing test cases in a Maven build process. We demonstrate this for a test case of a containerized Spring Boot web application with mocking and code injection that uses the complete Spring Boot application stack.

The `springboot` example, in particular, shows the strength of the tool architecture of SPOUT: We were not able to run the other tools on this example as the test is executed as a JUnit test case from within a build tool (maven). SPOUT is implemented as a feature of a `Java` executable and simply executes the build system. We enable the concolic execution feature only for the unit test.

---

[12] https://sv-comp.sosy-lab.org/2022/results/results-verified/.

[13] available on GitHub: https://github.com/tudo-aqua/gdart-examples.

We are confident, though we could not test it, that the other tools cannot analyze the unit test since it starts a Tomcat web container including database, injects mock code into the test case (generated and compiled at runtime), and relies on interception of method calls (also configured at runtime). As a consequence, the actual behavior of the application only emerges during execution in the Tomcat.

Enabler for Future Research Projects. The versatility of SPOUT and the industry grade GRAALVM running it allows scaling our security detection research further and investing into scalable dynamic symbolic execution engines. We will explain this in two examples. Both examples are currently not runnable with the JPF-VM and demonstrate the large potential for future research enabled in this area using the concolic runner SPOUT. The examples are:

Evaluating JAINT on Jenkins. The JAINT framework [16] combines dynamic symbolic execution and dynamic tainting. Today, it is build on top of the JPF-VM using JDART. After evaluating JAINT on benchmarks, the next scaling step is detecting existing injection vulnerabilities, e.g., the OS command injection in the Jenkins Git Client Plugin 2.8.4[14]. But the JPF-VM prevented that we have been able to analyze these kinds of tasks. Due to the incomplete support of the Java standard library in the JPF-VM, it was not possible to create temporary directories required to model a concrete driver for analyzing the plugin dynamically. Using the new SPOUT executor, we are today able to run the examples dynamically and record constraints. This enables future research project that focus on the application of dynamic symbolic execution for the analysis of Java and, therefore, also allows empirical experiments that measure JAINT's scalability.

Dynamic Symbolic Execution of Log4Shell. Using SPOUT, we have successfully analyzed the Log4Shell example project[15] with dynamic symbolic execution. As of today, we can demonstrate that the symbolic annotations for dynamic symbolic execution travel across the project and the method substitution pattern works on this spring boot application as well for injecting monitors on the Log4j classes.

4 Conclusion

In this paper, we presented SPOUT, a concolic executor build on top of the GRAALVM. We detailed the integration of the symbolic annotation recording into the concrete bytecode execution of the Espresso JVM and, for the first time, formalized SPOUT's symbolic trace format. Moreover, we present how GRAALVM features are used to encode symbolic operations on strings at the library level. We use SPOUT as the concolic executor of GDART, but are confident that the component might be useful for other research projects as well, e.g., for fuzzing Java programs.

---

[14] https://cve.mitre.org/cgi-bin/cvename.cgi?name=CVE-2019-10392.
[15] https://github.com/christophetd/log4shell-vulnerable-app.

References

1. Ahrendt, W., et al.: The KeY platform for verification and analysis of Java programs. In: Giannakopoulou, D., Kroening, D. (eds.) VSTTE 2014. LNCS, vol. 8471, pp. 55–71. Springer, Cham (2014). https://doi.org/10.1007/978-3-319-12154-3_4
2. Barrett, C., Fontaine, P., Tinelli, C.: The SMT-LIB standard: version 2.6. Technical report, Department of Computer Science, The University of Iowa (2021). https://smtlib.cs.uiowa.edu. Accessed 21 May 2021
3. Bjørner, N., Tillmann, N., Voronkov, A.: Path feasibility analysis for string-manipulating programs. In: Kowalewski, S., Philippou, A. (eds.) TACAS 2009. LNCS, vol. 5505, pp. 307–321. Springer, Heidelberg (2009). https://doi.org/10.1007/978-3-642-00768-2_27
4. Christensen, A.S., Møller, A., Schwartzbach, M.I.: Precise analysis of string expressions. In: Cousot, R. (ed.) SAS 2003. LNCS, vol. 2694, pp. 1–18. Springer, Heidelberg (2003). https://doi.org/10.1007/3-540-44898-5_1
5. Clarke, E., Kroening, D., Lerda, F.: A tool for checking ANSI-C programs. In: Jensen, K., Podelski, A. (eds.) TACAS 2004. LNCS, vol. 2988, pp. 168–176. Springer, Heidelberg (2004). https://doi.org/10.1007/978-3-540-24730-2_15
6. Cordeiro, L., Kesseli, P., Kroening, D., Schrammel, P., Trtik, M.: JBMC: a bounded model checking tool for verifying java bytecode. In: Chockler, H., Weissenbacher, G. (eds.) CAV 2018. LNCS, vol. 10981, pp. 183–190. Springer, Cham (2018). https://doi.org/10.1007/978-3-319-96145-3_10
7. Kahsai, T., Rümmer, P., Sanchez, H., Schäf, M.: JayHorn: a framework for verifying java programs. In: Chaudhuri, S., Farzan, A. (eds.) CAV 2016. LNCS, vol. 9779, pp. 352–358. Springer, Cham (2016). https://doi.org/10.1007/978-3-319-41528-4_19
8. Kloibhofer, S., Pointhuber, T., Heisinger, M., Mössenböck, H., Stadler, L., Leopoldseder, D.: SymJEx: symbolic execution on the GraalVM. In: Proceedings of the 17th International Conference on Managed Programming Languages and Runtimes, MPLR 2020, pp. 63–72. Association for Computing Machinery, New York (2020). https://doi.org/10.1145/3426182.3426187
9. Livshits, B.: Improving software security with precise static and runtime analysis. Ph.D. thesis, Stanford University (2006)
10. Livshits, V.B., Lam, M.S.: Finding security vulnerabilities in Java applications with static analysis. In: 14th USENIX Security Symposium, SEC 2005, pp. 271–286. USENIX Association, San Diego (2005). https://www.usenix.org/legacy/publications/library/proceedings/sec05/tech/livshits.html
11. Loring, B., Mitchell, D., Kinder, J.: Sound regular expression semantics for dynamic symbolic execution of JavaScript. In: Proceedings of the 40th ACM SIGPLAN Conference on Programming Language Design and Implementation, PLDI 2019, pp. 425–438. Association for Computing Machinery, New York (2019). https://doi.org/10.1145/3314221.3314645
12. Luckow, K., et al.: JDART: a dynamic symbolic analysis framework. In: Chechik, M., Raskin, J.-F. (eds.) TACAS 2016. LNCS, vol. 9636, pp. 442–459. Springer, Heidelberg (2016). https://doi.org/10.1007/978-3-662-49674-9_26
13. de Moura, L., Bjørner, N.: Z3: an efficient SMT solver. In: Ramakrishnan, C.R., Rehof, J. (eds.) TACAS 2008. LNCS, vol. 4963, pp. 337–340. Springer, Heidelberg (2008). https://doi.org/10.1007/978-3-540-78800-3_24
14. Mues, M., Howar, F.: Data-driven design and evaluation of SMT meta-solving strategies: balancing performance, accuracy, and cost. In: 2021 36th IEEE/ACM International Conference on Automated Software Engineering (ASE), ASE 2021,

pp. 179–190. IEEE, New York (2021). https://doi.org/10.1109/ASE51524.2021.9678881

15. Mues, M., Howar, F.: GDART: an ensemble of tools for dynamic symbolic execution on the java virtual machine (competition contribution). In: Fisman, D., Rosu, G. (eds.) TACAS 2022. LNCS, vol. 13244, pp. 435–439. Springer, Cham (2022). https://doi.org/10.1007/978-3-030-99527-0_27

16. Mues, M., Schallau, T., Howar, F.: Jaint: a framework for user-defined dynamic taint-analyses based on dynamic symbolic execution of java programs. In: Dongol, B., Troubitsyna, E. (eds.) IFM 2020. LNCS, vol. 12546, pp. 123–140. Springer, Cham (2020). https://doi.org/10.1007/978-3-030-63461-2_7

17. Păsăreanu, C.S., Visser, W., Bushnell, D., Geldenhuys, J., Mehlitz, P., Rungta, N.: Symbolic PathFinder: integrating symbolic execution with model checking for Java bytecode analysis. Autom. Softw. Eng. **20**(3), 391–425 (2013). https://doi.org/10.1007/s10515-013-0122-2

18. Redelinghuys, G., Visser, W., Geldenhuys, J.: Symbolic execution of programs with strings. In: Proceedings of the South African Institute for Computer Scientists and Information Technologists Conference, SAICSIT 2012, pp. 139–148. Association for Computing Machinery, New York (2012). https://doi.org/10.1145/2389836.2389853

19. Shannon, D., Ghosh, I., Rajan, S., Khurshid, S.: Efficient symbolic execution of strings for validating web applications. In: Proceedings of the 2nd International Workshop on Defects in Large Software Systems: Held in Conjunction with the ACM SIGSOFT International Symposium on Software Testing and Analysis (ISSTA 2009), DEFECTS 2009, pp. 22–26. Association for Computing Machinery, New York (2009). https://doi.org/10.1145/1555860.1555868

20. Shannon, D., Hajra, S., Lee, A., Zhan, D., Khurshid, S.: Abstracting symbolic execution with string analysis. In: Testing: Academic and Industrial Conference Practice and Research Techniques - MUTATION (TAICPART-MUTATION 2007), pp. 13–22. IEEE, New York (2007). https://doi.org/10.1109/TAIC.PART.2007.34

21. Sharma, V., Hussein, S., Whalen, M.W., McCamant, S., Visser, W.: Java ranger: statically summarizing regions for efficient symbolic execution of Java. In: Proceedings of the 28th ACM Joint Meeting on European Software Engineering Conference and Symposium on the Foundations of Software Engineering, ESEC/FSE 2020, pp. 123–134. Association for Computing Machinery, New York (2020). https://doi.org/10.1145/3368089.3409734

22. Spoto, F.: The Julia static analyzer for Java. In: Rival, X. (ed.) SAS 2016. LNCS, vol. 9837, pp. 39–57. Springer, Heidelberg (2016). https://doi.org/10.1007/978-3-662-53413-7_3

23. Tillmann, N., de Halleux, J.: Pex–white box test generation for .NET. In: Beckert, B., Hähnle, R. (eds.) TAP 2008. LNCS, vol. 4966, pp. 134–153. Springer, Heidelberg (2008). https://doi.org/10.1007/978-3-540-79124-9_10

24. Visser, W., Havelund, K., Brat, G., Park, S., Lerda, F.: Model checking programs. Autom. Softw. Eng. **10**(2), 203–232 (2003). https://doi.org/10.1023/A:1022920129859

25. Würthinger, T., et al.: One VM to rule them all. In: Proceedings of the 2013 ACM International Symposium on New Ideas, New Paradigms, and Reflections on Programming & Software, pp. 187–204. Association for Computing Machinery, New York (2013). https://doi.org/10.1145/2509578.2509581

Verifier Technology

Cooperation Between Automatic and Interactive Software Verifiers

Dirk Beyer⬦, Martin Spiessl⬦, and Sven Umbricht⬦

LMU Munich, Munich, Germany

Abstract. The verification community develops two kinds of verification tools: automatic verifiers and interactive verifiers. There are many such verifiers available, and there is steady progress in research. However, cooperation between the two kinds of verifiers was not yet addressed in a modular way. Yet, it is imperative for the community to leverage all possibilities, because our society heavily depends on software systems that work correctly. This paper contributes tools and a modular design to address the open problem of insufficient support for cooperation between verification tools. We identify invariants as information that needs to be exchanged in cooperation, and we support translation between two 'containers' for invariants: program annotations and correctness witnesses. Using our new building blocks, invariants computed by automatic verifiers can be given to interactive verifiers as annotations in the program, and annotations from the user or interactive verifier can be given to automatic verifiers, in order to help the approaches mutually to solve the verification problem. The modular framework, and the design choice to work with readily-available components in off-the-shelf manner, opens up many opportunities to combine new tools from existing components. Our experiments on a large set of programs show that our constructions work, that is, we constructed tool combinations that can solve verification tasks that the verifiers could not solve before.

Keywords: Software verification, Program analysis, Invariant generation, Automatic verification, Interactive verification, CPAchecker, Frama-C

1 Introduction

Software verification becomes more and more important, and large IT companies are investing into this technology [5,25,29]. There was a lot of progress in the past two decades and many software-verification tools exist [7,8,15,34,42]. But there are also obstacles that hinder the application of new technology in practice [3,35]. The verification tools can roughly be divided into two different flavors: automatic verifiers, which are more suited for automatic settings such as continuous-integration checks, and interactive verifiers, which can be fed with proof hints to solve verification tasks. These different tools have different strengths and often one verifier alone is not able to prove the correctness. Yet, the

© The Author(s) 2022
B.-H. Schlingloff and M. Chai (Eds.): SEFM 2022, LNCS 13550, pp. 111–128, 2022.
https://doi.org/10.1007/978-3-031-17108-6_7

potential from cooperation between different kinds of verifiers is a largely unused technology, although it is expected to significantly improve the state of the art.

In this paper, we contribute ideas to bridge the gap between automatic and interactive verifiers by introducing cooperation between tools of both kinds. As a starting point, we identify invariants as the objects that we need to exchange. Then we investigate which interfaces are supported by different verification tools. As a result, we choose verification witnesses [12] and annotations [6] as containers for the invariants. We implement various transformers for exchanging invariants between the different interfaces. This results in a modular composition framework that is based on off-the-shelf components (in binary format). We can use existing components because we base our work on existing interfaces (witnesses and annotations).

Automatic verifiers, such as CBMC [28], CPACHECKER [18], GOBLINT [49], KORN [32], PESCO [48], SYMBIOTIC [26], ULTIMATE AUTOMIZER [39], and VERIABS [1] (alphabetic order, just to name a few, for a larger list we refer to a competition report [8]), usually take as input a program and a specification (a.k.a. verification task) and compute invariants, in order to prove correctness. The above-mentioned verifiers can save the computed invariants into a standard witness file for later use (e.g., for result validation).

Interactive verifiers, such as DAFNY [46], FRAMA-C [30], KEY [2], KIV [33], and VERIFAST [43] (alphabetic order, just to name a few, for a larger list we refer to a competition report [34]), usually take as input a program with an inlined specification (contracts, asserts), and during the verification process, the verification engineer can interact with the verifier by providing invariants and other information as annotations in the program.

The automatic verifiers use a standardized exchange format for verification witnesses [12], and thus, we can easily plug-in all of them. The interactive verifiers come each with their own annotation language. We decided to consider only ACSL [6], which is supported by FRAMA-C [30], as a starting point for our study, because it is well documented. In practice, many of these annotation languages are similar, so our results apply to other annotation languages as well.

Contributions. This paper contributes the following in order to enable new verification technology:

- We develop a novel compositional design to construct new tools for software verification from existing 'off-the-shelf' components:
    1. We construct interactive verifiers from automatic verifiers and validators.
    2. We construct result validators from interactive verifiers.
    3. We improve interactive verifiers by feeding them with invariants computed by automatic verifiers.
- We identified an appropriate benchmark set of verification tasks with verification witnesses that contain provably useful invariants. We also created second benchmark set with manually added ACSL annotations containing (inductive) loop invariants and assertions. In order to make our evaluation reproducible and to offer the invariants to other researchers for further experiments, we make both benchmark sets available.

- We make all components and transformations available as open source, such that other researchers and practitioners can reuse and experiment with them, and verify our results (see Sect. 5 for the data-availability statement).
- We perform a sound experimental evaluation on a large benchmark set to investigate the effectivity of the new compositions. The results are promising and suggest that such compositions are worth to be considered in practice.

Combinations like the proposed cooperation approach can significantly impact the way in which verification tools are used in practice. Currently, engineers need to use both kinds of verifiers, automatic and interactive, in isolation, but our study has shown that there is much potential in leveraging cooperation.

Related Work. In the following we discuss the most related existing approaches.

Transform Programs. This is not the first work to convert the semantics of witness validation into a program. Some existing approaches [14] focus on violation witnesses, while we solely focus on correctness witnesses. Most similar in this regard is METAVAL [21]. The main difference is that we preserve the program structure while METAVAL does an automaton product between the *control-flow automaton (CFA)* of the program and witness automaton, and turns the result back into a C program, which will result in a different syntactic structure.

Interact via Conditions. The approach *conditional model checking* [16] also achieves cooperation between verifiers, but is limited to automatic verifiers that support the condition format and the verifier that comes second uses the condition to restrict the part of the state space that is explored. Our framework supports more tools via the usage of standardized exchange formats, also considers interactive verifiers, and the second verifier still performs a full proof. Another approach that builds on conditions is *alternating conditional analysis* [36,37]. Here, the witness format is also used as standardized exchange format and multiple verifiers are supported. However, the focus is on violation witnesses whereas we are focussing on correctness witnesses. Instead of removing parts of the state space, we actually extend the property that needs to be checked, such that it is (potentially) easier to be proven. The same holds if we compare our component WITNESS2ASSERT to *reducer-based conditional model checking* [17]. While both approaches encode the important information into the original program, we actually would need to assume the invariants instead of asserting them in order to act as a reducer. Conditions are also used to improve testing [19,27,31].

Store and Exchange Proofs. Another parallel can be drawn to *proof-carrying code* [44,45,47], where the proof of correctness is stored alongside the program. We do the same here in cases where the added annotations actually suffice for a full proof by FRAMA-C, but we also have the possibility to generate partial proofs. Correctness witnesses are used to store intermediate results and to validate results [11]. Proofs are also stored in the area of theorem provers [38] (https://www.isa-afp.org/) and SAT solvers [40,41].

```
1
2   int main() {
3     unsigned int x = 0;
4     unsigned int y = 0;
5
6     while (nondet_int()) {
7       x++;
8
9       y++;
10    }
11    assert(x==y);
12    return 0;
13  }
```

```
1   //@ensures \return==0;
2   int main() {
3     unsigned int x = 0;
4     unsigned int y = 0;
5     //@loop invariant x==y;
6     while (nondet_int()) {
7       x++;
8       //@assert x==y+1;
9       y++;
10    }
11    assert(x==y);
12    return 0;
13  }
```

Fig. 1. Example program with loop invariant x==y

Fig. 2. Example program with ACSL annotations

2 Preliminaries

For our framework that enables cooperation between automatic and interactive verifiers we need to take into account the interfaces that each of them provide, i.e., how the information important for the verification process is communicated. For automatic verifiers there exists a common exchange format [12] in which verifiers export the program invariants they found. For interactive verifiers, we look at ACSL [6], the specification language that is e.g. used by FRAMA-C. In the following, we will quickly introduce these formats and the general verification problem we are looking at using a small example program that is depicted in Fig. 1.

For the rest of the paper, we will focus on reachability properties, though our approach can also be extended to work for other properties as well.[1] The crucial part of verifying reachability properties is to find the right loop invariants. In the example program this would be the fact that x==y always holds before each loop iteration. Please note that while this invariant is also present in the assertion in line 11, for more complicated programs it is generally not the case that we can find the invariants written in the code. Also, since there might be more than one loop in a program, a verifier might only partially succeed and therefore only be able to provide invariants for some of these loops, or only invariants that are not yet strong enough to prove the program correct. This is why cooperation by exchange of these discovered invariants can potentially lead to better results.

2.1 Verification Witnesses

In case an automatic verifier can prove our example program correct, information like a discovered invariant is normally made available as shown in Fig. 3a in the standard witness exchange format (described in [12], maintained at https://github.com/sosy-lab/sv-witnesses) as correctness witness. There are also

---

[1] Also, we will concentrate only on intraprocedural analysis, though our approach works for interprocedural analysis as well.

```
1   ...
2   <node id="q1">
3   <data key="invariant">( y == x )</data>
4   <data key="invariant.scope">main</data>
5   </node>
6   <edge source="q0" target="q1">
7   <data key="enterLoopHead">true</data>
8   <data key="startline">6</data>
9   <data key="endline">6</data>
10  <data key="startoffset">157</data>
11  <data key="endoffset">165</data>
12  </edge>
13  ...
```

(a) Encoding of an invariant in a GraphML-based correctness witness

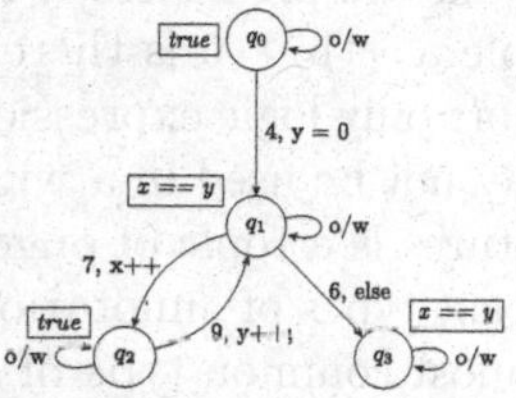

(b) Example witness automaton for the program from Fig. 1

Fig. 3. Example of the witness format and automaton; o/w stands for otherwise, i.e., all other possible program transitions

violation witnesses in case a violation has been found, but since we are mainly interested in the invariants, we will focus on correctness witnesses and omit the prefix "correctness" for the rest of the paper.

Such a witness contains a graph representation of an observer automaton. Invariants can be given for nodes if they always hold when the witness automaton is in the corresponding state. The semantics of the witness is given by constructing the product of the witness automaton and the CFA of the program. This might lead to edge cases where the exact semantics depends on how the tool interpreting the witness constructs a CFA from the program, but in practice a witness can be written such that it is mostly robust against those differences. For further details on the semantics of the witness automata we refer the reader the existing literature [12].

There are currently some restrictions on the contents of an invariant: An invariant has to be a valid C expression that can be evaluated to an int at the current scope in the program. It may contain conjunctions and disjunctions but no function calls.

2.2 ACSL

Interactive verifiers rely on the user to provide the (non-trivial) invariants for the proof. An example can bee seen in Fig. 2, where the loop invariant has been added as ACSL annotation in line 5. Only when this information is externally provided (usually by the user), an interactive verifier like FRAMA-C is able to prove that the assertion in line 11 can never be violated.

Loop annotations are only one of many kinds of annotation in ACSL. For example we can see a function contract in line 1 and an assertion in line 8. These annotations usually represent specifications which the implementation should adhere to, but they can also be seen as invariants, since they should hold for every possible program execution.

The basic building blocks of ACSL annotations are *logic expressions* that represent the concrete properties of the specification, e.g., `a + b > 0` or `x && y == z`. Logic expressions can be subdivided into terms and predicates, which behave similarly as terms and formulas in first-order logic. Basically, logic expressions that evaluate to a boolean value are predicates, while all other logic expressions are terms. The above example `a + b > 0` is therefore a predicate, while `a + b` is a term. We currently support only logic expressions that can also be expressed as C expressions, as they may not be used in a witness otherwise. Finding ways to represent more ACSL features is a topic of ongoing research.

ACSL also features different types of annotations. In this paper we will only present translations for the most common type of annotations, namely function contracts, and the simplest type, namely assertions. Our implementation also supports statement contracts and loop annotations.

All types of ACSL annotations when placed in a C source file must be given in comments starting with an @ sign, i.e., must be in the form `//@ annotation` or `/*@ annotation */`. ACSL assertions can be placed anywhere in a program where a statement would be allowed, start with the keyword `assert` and contain a predicate that needs to hold at the location where the assertion is placed.

3 A Component Framework for Cooperative Verification

The framework we developed consists of three core components that allow us to improve interaction between the existing tools.

WITNESS2ACSL acts as transformer that converts a program and a correctness witness given as witness automaton where invariants are annotated to certain nodes, into a program with ACSL annotations.

ACSL2WITNESS takes a program that contains ACSL annotations, encodes them as invariants into a witness automaton and produces a correctness witness in the standardized GraphML format.

WITNESS2ASSERT is mostly identical to WITNESS2ACSL. The main difference is that instead of adding assertions as ACSL annotations to the program, it actually encodes the semantics of the annotations directly into the program such that automatic verifiers will understand them as additional properties to prove. On the one hand, this component enables us to check the validity of the ACSL annotations for which ACSL2WITNESS generated a witness, with tools that do not understand the annotation language ACSL. On the other hand, this component is also useful on its own, since it allows us to validate correctness witnesses and give

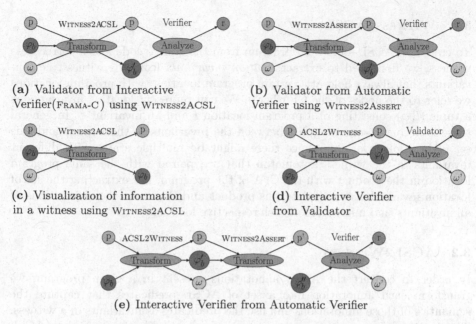

(a) Validator from Interactive Verifier(FRAMA-C) using WITNESS2ACSL

(b) Validator from Automatic Verifier using WITNESS2ASSERT

(c) Visualization of information in a witness using WITNESS2ACSL

(d) Interactive Verifier from Validator

(e) Interactive Verifier from Automatic Verifier

Fig. 4. Graphical visualization of the developed components to improve cooperation; we use the notation introduced in previous work [24]: p represents a program, ϕ_b a behavior specification, ω a witness, and r a verification result

witness producers a better feedback on how their invariants are interpreted and whether they are useful (validator developers can inspect the produced program).

These three components now enable us to achieve cooperation in many different ways. We can utilize a proposed component framework [24] to visualize this as shown in Fig. 4. The use case shown in Fig. 4a is to use FRAMA-C as a correctness witness validator. This is interesting because it can further reduce the technology bias (the currently available validators are based on automatic verifiers [4,11,13,21], test execution [14], and interpretation [50]). By using WITNESS2ASSERT instead of WITNESS2ACSL as shown in Fig. 4b we can also configure new correctness witness validators that are based on automatic verifiers, similar to what METAVAL [21] does, only with a different transformer. Figure 4c illustrates the use of WITNESS2ACSL (or similarly for WITNESS2ASSERT) to inspect the information from the witness as annotations in the program code.

The compositional framework makes it possible to leverage existing correctness witness validators and turn them into interactive verifiers that can understand ACSL, as shown in Fig. 4d. Since we also have the possibility now to construct a validator from an automatic verifier (Fig. 4b) we can turn automatic verifiers into interactive ones as depicted in Fig. 4e. While automatic verifiers can already make use of assertions that are manually added to the program, this now also allows us to use other types of high-level annotations like function contracts without having to change the original program.

3.1 Witness2ACSL

To create an ACSL annotated program from the source code and a correctness witness, we first need to extract *location invariants* from the witness, i.e., invariants that always hold at a certain program location (with program locations we refer to the nodes of the CFA here). We can represent location invariants as a tuple (l, ϕ) consisting of a program location l and an invariant ϕ. In general there is no one-to-one mapping between the invariants in the witness and this set of location invariants, since there might be multiple states with different invariants in the witness automaton that are paired with the same program location in the product with the CFA of the program. For extracting the set of location invariants, we calculate this product and then take the disjunctions of all invariants that might hold at each respective location.

3.2 ACSL2Witness

In order to convert the ACSL annotations present in a given program, we transform each annotation into a set of ACSL predicates that capture the semantics of those annotations and use the predicates as invariants in a witness. This mode of operation is based on two observations: Firstly, for a given ACSL annotation it is usually possible to find a number of ACSL assertions that are semantically equivalent to that annotation. For example, a loop invariant can be replaced by asserting that the invariant holds at the loop entry, i.e., before each loop iteration. Secondly, most ACSL assertions are logically equivalent to a valid invariant and can therefore be used in a witness. As mentioned in Sect. 2.2, we currently only support those predicates which can be converted into C expressions, which is a limitation of the witness format and might be lifted in future versions of the format.

3.3 Witness2Assert

This component is very similar to Witness2ACSL. The main difference is that instead of generating ACSL annotations we generate actual C code that encodes the invariants as assertions (i.e., additional reachability properties). This translation is sound since assertions added this way do not hide violations, i.e., every feasible trace that violates the original reachability property in the program before the modification will either still exist or have a corresponding trace that violates the additional reachability properties of the modified program. It is worth mentioning that this is an improvement compared to existing transformations like the one used in MetaVal [21], where the program is resynthesized from the reachability graph and the soundness can therefore easily be broken by a bug in MetaVal's transformation process.

4   Evaluation

We implemented the components mentioned in Sect. 3 in the software-verification framework CPACHECKER. In our evaluation, we attempt to answer the following research questions:

- **RQ 1:** Can we construct interactive verifiers from automatic verifiers, and can they be useful in terms of effectiveness?
- **RQ 2:** Can we improve the results of, or partially automate, interactive verifiers by annotating invariants that were computed by automatic verifiers?
- **RQ 3:** Can we construct result validators from interactive verifiers?
- **RQ 4:** Are verifiers ready for cooperation, that is, do they produce invariants that help other verifiers to increase their effectiveness?

4.1   Experimental Setup

Our benchmarks are executed on machines running Ubuntu 20.04. Each of these machines has an Intel E5-1230 processor with 4 cores, 8 processing units, and 33 GB of RAM. For reliable measurements we use BENCHEXEC [20]. For the automatic verifiers, we use the available tools that participated in the ReachSafety category of the 2022 competition on software verification (SV-COMP) in their submission version[2]. FRAMA-C will be executed via FRAMA-C-SV [22], a wrapper that enables FRAMA-C to understand reachability property and special functions used in SV-COMP. Unless otherwise noted we will use the EVA plugin of FRAMA-C. We limit each execution to 900 s of CPU time, 15 GB of RAM, and 8 processing units, which is identical to the resource limitations used in SV-COMP.

4.2   Benchmark Set with Useful Witnesses

In order to provide meaningful results, we need to assemble an appropriate benchmark set consisting of witnesses that indeed contain useful information, i.e., information that potentially improves the results of another tool.

As a starting point, we consider correctness witnesses from the final runs of SV-COMP 2022 [8,10]. This means that for one verification task we might get multiple correctness witnesses (from different participating verifiers), while for others we might even get none because no verifier was able to come up with a proof. We select the witnesses for tasks in the subcategory ReachSafety-Loops, because this subcategory is focussed on verifying programs with challenging loop invariants. This selection leaves us with 6242 correctness witnesses (without knowing which of those actually contain useful information).

For each of the selected witnesses we converted the contained invariants into both ACSL annotations (for verification with FRAMA-C) and assertions (for verification with automatic verifiers from SV-COMP 2022). Here we can immediately drop those witnesses that do not result in any annotations being generated, which results in 1931 witnesses belonging to 640 different verification tasks.

---

[2] https://gitlab.com/sosy-lab/sv-comp/archives-2022/-/tree/svcomp22/2022

Table 1. Impact of cooperation: in each row, a 'consuming' verifier is fed with information from witnesses of our benchmark set; 'Baseline' reports the number of programs that the verifier proved correct without any help; 'Improved via coop.' reports the number of programs that the verifier can prove *in addition*, if the information from the witness is provided

Consuming verifier	Benchmark tasks (434 total)		Projection on programs (230 total)	
	Baseline	Improved via coop.	Baseline	Improved via coop.
2Ls	157	179	83	111
UAutomizer	360	47	186	31
Cbmc	281	53	142	28
CPAchecker	300	69	149	53
Dartagnan	280	82	139	51
Esbmc	239	133	121	76
gazer-theta	266	118	135	64
Goblint	38	106	21	47
UKojak	191	134	97	76
Korn	183	46	98	27
PeSCo	180	162	87	99
Pinaka	258	105	127	59
Symbiotic	349	51	174	32
UTaipan	334	65	172	37
VeriAbs	343	31	186	28
Frama-C	211	31	105	20

We then run each verifier for each program where annotations have been generated, once with the original, unmodified program, and n times with the transformed program for each of the n witnesses. This allows us determine whether any improvement was achieved, by looking at the differences between verification of the unmodified program versus verification of a program that has been enhanced by information generated from some potentially different tool. Using this process, we further reduce our benchmark set of witnesses to those that are useful for at least one of the verifiers and thus enable cooperation. This leads to the final set of 434 witnesses that evidently contain information that enables cooperation between verifiers. These witnesses correspond to 230 different programs from the SV-Benchmarks repository (https://github.com/sosy-lab/sv-benchmarks). We made this benchmark set available to the community in a supplementary artifact of this paper [23].

4.3 Experimental Results

RQ 1. For the first research question, we need to show that we can construct interactive verifiers from automatic verifiers, and that they can be useful in terms of effectiveness. By "interactive verifier", we mean a verifier that can verify more programs correct if we feed it with invariants, for example, by annotating the input program with ACSL annotations. Using our building blocks from Sect. 3, an interactive verifier can be composed as illustrated in Fig. 4e (that is, configurations of the form ACSL2WITNESS|WITNESS2ASSERT|VERIFIER). For a meaningful evaluation we need a large number of annotated programs, which we would be able to get if we converted the witnesses from SV-COMP using WITNESS2ACSL in advance. But since the first component ACSL2WITNESS in Fig. 4e essentially does the inverse operation, we can generalize and directly consider witnesses as input, as illustrated in Fig. 4b (that is, configurations of the form WITNESS2ASSERT|VERIFIER).

Now we look at the results in Table 1: The first row reports that cooperation improves the verifier 2LS in 179 cases, that is, there are 179 witnesses that contain information that helps 2LS to prove a program that it could not prove without the information. In other words, for 179 witnesses, we ran WITNESS2ASSERT to transform the original program to one in which the invariants from the witness were written as assertions, and 2LS was then able to verify the program. Since there are often several witnesses for the same program, 2LS verified in total 111 unique unique programs that it was not able to verify without the annotated invariants as assertion.

In sum, the table reports that many programs that could not be proved by verifiers when ran on the unmodified program, could be proved when the verifier was given the program with invariants. Since we were able to show the effect using generated witnesses, it is clear that manually provided invariants will also help the automatic verifiers to prove the program. We will continue this argument in Sect. 4.4.

RQ 2. For the second research question, we need to show that our new design can improve the results of interactive verifiers by annotating invariants that were computed by automatic verifiers. Using our building blocks from Sect. 3, we assemble a construction as illustrated in Fig. 4a (i.e., configurations of the form WITNESS2ACSL|VERIFIER). We take a program and a witness and transform the program to a new program that contains the invariants from the witness as ACSL annotations.

Let us consider the last row in Table 1: FRAMA-C is able to prove 20 programs correct using invariants from 31 witnesses. Those 31 witnesses were computed by automatic verifiers, and thus, we can conclude that our new design enables using results of automatic verifiers to help the verification process of an interactive verifier.

RQ 3. For the third research question, we need to show that we can construct result validators from interactive verifiers and that they can effectively complement existing validators. A results validator is a tool that takes as input a verification task, a verdict, and a witness, and confirms or rejects the result. In essence, due to the modular components, the answer to this research question can be given by the same setup as for RQ 2: If the interactive verifier (FRAMA-C) was able to prove the program correct, then it also has proved that the invariants provided by the witnesses were correct, and thus, the witness should be confirmed. FRAMA-C has confirmed 31 correctness witnesses.

Table 2. Proof of cooperation: for each 'producing' verifier, we report the number of correctness witnesses that help another verifier to prove a program which it otherwise could not; we also list the number of cases where this cooperation was observed (some witnesses improve the results of multiple verifiers); we omit producers without improved results

Producing verifier	Useful witnesses	Cases of cooperation
2LS	1	1
CBMC	20	22
CPACHECKER	148	533
GOBLINT	2	3
GRAVES-CPA	151	823
KORN	10	15
PESCO	78	271
SYMBIOTIC	5	10
UAUTOMIZER	19	70
Sum	434	1748

New validators that are based on a different technology are a welcome complement because this reduces the technology bias and increases trust. Also, the proof goals for annotated programs might be interesting for verification engineers to look at, even or especially when the validation does not succeed completely.

RQ 4. For the fourth research question, we report on the status of cooperation-readiness of verifiers. In other words, the question is if the verifiers produce invariants that help other verifiers to increase their effectiveness.

In Table 2 we list how many useful witnesses each verifier contributed to our benchmark set of useful witnesses. The results show that there are several verifiers that produce significant amounts of witnesses that contain invariants that help to improve results of other verifiers.

4.4   Case Study on Interactive Verification with Manual Annotations

So far, we tested our approach using information from only the SV-COMP witnesses. For constructing interactive verifiers, we would also like to evaluate whether our approach is useful if the information is provided by an actual human in the form of ACSL annotations.

ACSL Benchmark Set. To achieve this, we need a benchmark set with tasks that contain sufficient ACSL annotations and also adhere to the conventions of SV-COMP. Since to our knowledge such a benchmark set does not exist yet, we decided to manually annotate assertions and loop invariants to the tasks from the SV-Benchmarks collection ourselves. While annotating all of the benchmark tasks is out of scope, we managed to add ACSL annotations to 125 tasks from the ReachSafety-Loops subcategory. This subcategory is particularly relevant, since it contains a selection of programs with interesting loop invariants. The loop invariants we added are sufficient to proof the tasks correct in a pen-and-paper,

Table 3. Case study with 125 correct verification tasks where sufficient, inductive loop invariants are manually annotated to the program; we either input these to FRAMA-C or automatically transform the annotations into witnesses and try to validate these witnesses using CPACHECKER's k-induction validator (with k fixed to 1); the listed numbers correspond to the number of successful proofs in each of the sub-folders; we also list the number of successful proofs if no invariants are provided to the tools

Subfolder	Tasks	FRAMA-C		k-induction	
		with invs.	without invs.	with invs.	without invs.
loop-acceleration	17	3	1	11	4
loop-crafted	2	0	0	2	2
loop-industry-pattern	1	0	0	1	1
loop-invariants	8	3	0	8	0
loop-invgen	5	0	0	2	0
loop-lit	11	6	0	10	2
loop-new	5	1	0	5	2
loop-simple	6	6	0	1	1
loop-zilu	20	9	0	19	7
loops	23	13	6	17	15
loops-crafted-1	27	0	0	12	1
total	125	41	7	88	35

Hoare-style proof. Our benchmark set with manually added ACSL annotations is available in the artifact for this paper [23].[3]

Construction of an Interactive Verifier. With our ACSL benchmark set, we can now convert a witness validator into an interactive verifier as depicted in Fig. 4d. For the validator we use CPACHECKER, which can validate witnesses by using the invariants for a proof by k-induction. By fixing the unrolling bound of the k-induction to $k = 1$, this will essentially attempt to prove the program correct via 1-induction over the provided loop invariants. If we do not fix the unrolling bound, the k-induction validation would also essentially perform bounded model checking, so we would not know whether a proof succeeded because of the provided loop invariants or simply because the verification task is bounded to a low number of loop iterations.

Since this 1-induction proof is very similar to what FRAMA-C's weakest-precondition analysis does, we can directly compare both approaches. As some tasks from the benchmark set do not require additional invariants (i.e., the

---

[3] Our benchmark set is continuously updated and can also be found at: https://gitlab.com/sosy-lab/research/data/acsl-benchmarks

property to be checked is already inductive) we also analyze how both tools perform on the benchmark set if we do not provide any loop invariants.

The experimental setup is the same described in Sect. 4.1, except that we use a newer version of FRAMA-C-SV in order to use the weakest-precondition analysis of FRAMA-C. The results are shown in Table 3, which lists the number of successful proofs by subfolder. We can observe that both FRAMA-C and our constructed interactive verifier based on CPACHECKER can make use of the information from the annotations and prove significantly more tasks compared to without the annotated loop invariants. This shows that the component described in Fig. 4d is indeed working and useful.

5   Conclusion

The verification community integrates new achievements into two kinds of tools: interactive verifiers and automatic verifiers. Unfortunately, the possibility of cooperation between the two kinds of tools was left largely unused, although there seems to be a large potential. Our work addresses this open problem, identifying witnesses as interface objects and constructing some new building blocks (transformations) that can be used to connect interactive and automatic verifiers. The new building blocks, together with a cooperation framework from previous work, make it possible to construct new verifiers, in particular, automatic verifiers that can be used interactively, and interactive verifiers that can be fed with information from automatic verifiers: Our new program transformations translate the original program into a new program that contains invariants in a way that is understandable by the targeted backend verifier (interactive *or* automatic). Our combinations do not require changes to the existing verifiers: they are used as 'off-the-shelf' components, provided in binary form.

We performed an experimental study on witnesses that were produced in the most recent competition on software verification and on programs with manually annotated loop invariants. The results show that our approach works in practice: We can construct various kinds of verification tools based on our new building blocks. Instrumenting information from annotations and correctness witnesses into the original program can improve the effectivity of verifiers, that is, with the provided information they can verify programs that they could not verify without the information. Our results have many practical implications: (a) automatic verification tools can now be used in an interactive way, that is, users or other verifiers can conveniently give invariants as input in order to prove programs correct, (b) new validators based on interactive verifiers can be constructed in order to complement the set of currently available validators, and (c) both kinds of verifiers can be connected in a cooperative framework, in order to obtain more powerful verification tools. This work opens up a whole array of new opportunities that need to be explored, and there are many directions of future work. We hope that other researchers and practitioners find our approach helpful to combine existing verification tools without changing their source code.

Data-Availability Statement. The witnesses that we used are available at Zenodo [10]. The programs are available at Zenodo [9] and on GitLab at https:// gitlab.com/sosy-lab/benchmarking/sv-benchmarks/-/tree/svcomp22. We implemented our transformations in the verification framework CPACHECKER, which is freely available via the project web site at https://cpachecker.sosy-lab.org. A reproduction package for our experimental results is available at Zenodo [23].

Funding Statement. This project was funded in part by the Deutsche Forschungsgemeinschaft (DFG) – 378803395 (ConVeY).

Acknowledgment. We thank Nikolai Kosmatov for an inspiring and motivating discussion at the conference ISoLA 2018 on the necessity to combine automatic and interactive verification.

References

1. Afzal, M., Asia, A., Chauhan, A., Chimdyalwar, B., Darke, P., Datar, A., Kumar, S., Venkatesh, R.: VERIABS: Verification by abstraction and test generation. In: Proc. ASE. pp. 1138–1141 (2019). https://doi.org/10.1109/ASE.2019.00121
2. Ahrendt, W., Baar, T., Beckert, B., Bubel, R., Giese, M., Hähnle, R., Menzel, W., Mostowski, W., Roth, A., Schlager, S., Schmitt, P.H.: The key tool. Software and Systems Modeling **4**(1), 32–54 (2005). https://doi.org/10.1007/s10270-004-0058-x
3. Alglave, J., Donaldson, A.F., Kröning, D., Tautschnig, M.: Making software verification tools really work. In: Proc. ATVA. pp. 28–42. LNCS 6996, Springer (2011). https://doi.org/10.1007/978-3-642-24372-1_3
4. Ayaziová, P., Chalupa, M., Strejček, J.: SYMBIOTIC-WITCH: A Klee-based violation witness checker (competition contribution). In: Proc. TACAS (2). pp. 468–473. LNCS 13244, Springer (2022). https://doi.org/10.1007/978-3-030-99527-0_33
5. Ball, T., Levin, V., Rajamani, S.K.: A decade of software model checking with SLAM. Commun. ACM **54**(7), 68–76 (2011). https://doi.org/10.1145/1965724.1965743
6. Baudin, P., Cuoq, P., Filliâtre, J.C., Marché, C., Monate, B., Moy, Y., Prevosto, V.: ACSL: ANSI/ISO C specification language version 1.17 (2021), available at https:// frama-c.com/download/acsl-1.17.pdf
7. Beckert, B., Hähnle, R.: Reasoning and verification: State of the art and current trends. IEEE Intelligent Systems **29**(1), 20–29 (2014). https://doi.org/10.1109/ MIS.2014.3
8. Beyer, D.: Progress on software verification: SV-COMP 2022. In: Proc. TACAS (2). pp. 375–402. LNCS 13244, Springer (2022). https://doi.org/10.1007/978-3-030-99527-0_20
9. Beyer, D.: SV-Benchmarks: Benchmark set for software verification and testing (SV-COMP 2022 and Test-Comp 2022). Zenodo (2022). https://doi.org/10.5281/ zenodo.5831003
10. Beyer, D.: Verification witnesses from verification tools (SV-COMP 2022). Zenodo (2022). https://doi.org/10.5281/zenodo.5838498
11. Beyer, D., Dangl, M., Dietsch, D., Heizmann, M.: Correctness witnesses: Exchanging verification results between verifiers. In: Proc. FSE. pp. 326–337. ACM (2016). https://doi.org/10.1145/2950290.2950351

12. Beyer, D., Dangl, M., Dietsch, D., Heizmann, M., Lemberger, T., Tautschnig, M.: Verification witnesses. ACM Trans. Softw. Eng. Methodol. (2022). https://doi.org/10.1145/3477579

13. Beyer, D., Dangl, M., Dietsch, D., Heizmann, M., Stahlbauer, A.: Witness validation and stepwise testification across software verifiers. In: Proc. FSE. pp. 721–733. ACM (2015). https://doi.org/10.1145/2786805.2786867

14. Beyer, D., Dangl, M., Lemberger, T., Tautschnig, M.: Tests from witnesses: Execution-based validation of verification results. In: Proc. TAP. pp. 3–23. LNCS 10889, Springer (2018). https://doi.org/10.1007/978-3-319-92994-1_1

15. Beyer, D., Gulwani, S., Schmidt, D.: Combining model checking and data-flow analysis. In: Handbook of Model Checking, pp. 493–540. Springer (2018). https://doi.org/10.1007/978-3-319-10575-8_16

16. Beyer, D., Henzinger, T.A., Keremoglu, M.E., Wendler, P.: Conditional model checking: A technique to pass information between verifiers. In: Proc. FSE. ACM (2012). https://doi.org/10.1145/2393596.2393664

17. Beyer, D., Jakobs, M.C., Lemberger, T., Wehrheim, H.: Reducer-based construction of conditional verifiers. In: Proc. ICSE. pp. 1182–1193. ACM (2018). https://doi.org/10.1145/3180155.3180259

18. Beyer, D., Keremoglu, M.E.: CPACHECKER: A tool for configurable software verification. In: Proc. CAV. pp. 184–190. LNCS 6806, Springer (2011). https://doi.org/10.1007/978-3-642-22110-1_16

19. Beyer, D., Lemberger, T.: Conditional testing: Off-the-shelf combination of test-case generators. In: Proc. ATVA. pp. 189–208. LNCS 11781, Springer (2019). https://doi.org/10.1007/978-3-030-31784-3_11

20. Beyer, D., Löwe, S., Wendler, P.: Reliable benchmarking: Requirements and solutions. Int. J. Softw. Tools Technol. Transfer 21(1), 1–29 (2017). https://doi.org/10.1007/s10009-017-0469-y

21. Beyer, D., Spiessl, M.: METAVAL: Witness validation via verification. In: Proc. CAV. pp. 165–177. LNCS 12225, Springer (2020). https://doi.org/10.1007/978-3-030-53291-8_10

22. Beyer, D., Spiessl, M.: The static analyzer FRAMA-C in SV-COMP (competition contribution). In: Proc. TACAS (2). pp. 429–434. LNCS 13244, Springer (2022). https://doi.org/10.1007/978-3-030-99527-0_26

23. Beyer, D., Spiessl, M., Umbricht, S.: Reproduction package for SEFM 2022 article 'Cooperation between automatic and interactive software verifiers'. Zenodo (2022). https://doi.org/10.5281/zenodo.6541544

24. Beyer, D., Wehrheim, H.: Verification artifacts in cooperative verification: Survey and unifying component framework. In: Proc. ISoLA (1). pp. 143–167. LNCS 12476, Springer (2020). https://doi.org/10.1007/978-3-030-61362-4_8

25. Calcagno, C., Distefano, D., Dubreil, J., Gabi, D., Hooimeijer, P., Luca, M., O'Hearn, P.W., Papakonstantinou, I., Purbrick, J., Rodriguez, D.: Moving fast with software verification. In: Proc. NFM. pp. 3–11. LNCS 9058, Springer (2015). https://doi.org/10.1007/978-3-319-17524-9_1

26. Chalupa, M., Strejček, J., Vitovská, M.: Joint forces for memory safety checking. In: Proc. SPIN. pp. 115–132. Springer (2018). https://doi.org/10.1007/978-3-319-94111-0_7

27. Christakis, M., Müller, P., Wüstholz, V.: Collaborative verification and testing with explicit assumptions. In: Proc. FM. pp. 132–146. LNCS 7436, Springer (2012). https://doi.org/10.1007/978-3-642-32759-9_13

28. Clarke, E.M., Kröning, D., Lerda, F.: A tool for checking ANSI-C programs. In: Proc. TACAS. pp. 168–176. LNCS 2988, Springer (2004). https://doi.org/10.1007/978-3-540-24730-2_15

29. Cook, B.: Formal reasoning about the security of Amazon web services. In: Proc. CAV (2). pp. 38–47. LNCS 10981, Springer (2018). https://doi.org/10.1007/978-3-319-96145-3_3

30. Cuoq, P., Kirchner, F., Kosmatov, N., Prevosto, V., Signoles, J., Yakobowski, B.: Frama-C. In: Proc. SEFM. pp. 233–247. Springer (2012). https://doi.org/10.1007/978-3-642-33826-7_16

31. Czech, M., Jakobs, M., Wehrheim, H.: Just test what you cannot verify! In: Proc. FASE. pp. 100–114. LNCS 9033, Springer (2015). https://doi.org/10.1007/978-3-662-46675-9_7

32. Ernst, G.: A complete approach to loop verification with invariants and summaries. Tech. Rep. arXiv:2010.05812v2, arXiv (January 2020). https://doi.org/10.48550/arXiv.2010.05812

33. Ernst, G., Pfähler, J., Schellhorn, G., Haneberg, D., Reif, W.: KIV: Overview and VerifyThis competition. Int. J. Softw. Tools Technol. Transf. **17**(6), 677–694 (2015). https://doi.org/10.1007/s10009-014-0308-3

34. Ernst, G., Huisman, M., Mostowski, W., Ulbrich, M.: VerifyThis: Verification competition with a human factor. In: Proc. TACAS. pp. 176–195. LNCS 11429, Springer (2019). https://doi.org/10.1007/978-3-030-17502-3_12

35. Garavel, H., ter Beek, M.H., van de Pol, J.: The 2020 expert survey on formal methods. In: Proc. FMICS. pp. 3–69. LNCS 12327, Springer (2020). https://doi.org/10.1007/978-3-030-58298-2_1

36. Gerrard, M.J., Dwyer, M.B.: Comprehensive failure characterization. In: Proc. ASE. pp. 365–376. IEEE (2017). https://doi.org/10.1109/ASE.2017.8115649

37. Gerrard, M.J., Dwyer, M.B.: ALPACA: A large portfolio-based alternating conditional analysis. In: Atlee, J.M., Bultan, T., Whittle, J. (eds.) Proceedings of the 41st International Conference on Software Engineering: Companion Proceedings, ICSE 2019, Montreal, QC, Canada, May 25–31, 2019. pp. 35–38. IEEE / ACM (2019). https://doi.org/10.1109/ICSE-Companion.2019.00032

38. Hales, T.C., Harrison, J., McLaughlin, S., Nipkow, T., Obua, S., Zumkeller, R.: A revision of the proof of the Kepler conjecture. Discret. Comput. Geom. **44**(1), 1–34 (2010). https://doi.org/10.1007/s00454-009-9148-4

39. Heizmann, M., Hoenicke, J., Podelski, A.: Software model checking for people who love automata. In: Proc. CAV. pp. 36–52. LNCS 8044, Springer (2013). https://doi.org/10.1007/978-3-642-39799-8_2

40. Heule, M.J.H.: The DRAT format and drat-trim checker. CoRR **1610**(06229) (October 2016)

41. Heule, M.J.H.: Schur number five. In: Proc. AAAI. pp. 6598–6606. AAAI Press (2018)

42. Howar, F., Isberner, M., Merten, M., Steffen, B., Beyer, D., Păsăreanu, C.S.: Rigorous examination of reactive systems. The RERS challenges 2012 and 2013. Int. J. Softw. Tools Technol. Transfer **16**(5), 457–464 (2014). https://doi.org/10.1007/s10009-014-0337-y

43. Jacobs, B., Smans, J., Philippaerts, P., Vogels, F., Penninckx, W., Piessens, F.: VeriFast: A powerful, sound, predictable, fast verifier for C and Java. In: Proc. NFM. pp. 41–55. LNCS 6617, Springer (2011). https://doi.org/10.1007/978-3-642-20398-5_4

44. Jakobs, M.C., Wehrheim, H.: Certification for configurable program analysis. In: Proc. SPIN. pp. 30–39. ACM (2014). https://doi.org/10.1145/2632362.2632372

45. Jakobs, M.C., Wehrheim, H.: Programs from proofs: A framework for the safe execution of untrusted software. ACM Trans. Program. Lang. Syst. **39**(2), 7:1–7:56 (2017). https://doi.org/10.1145/3014427
46. Leino, K.R.M.: Dafny: An automatic program verifier for functional correctness. In: Proc. LPAR. pp. 348–370. LNCS 6355, Springer (2010). https://doi.org/10.1007/978-3-642-17511-4_20
47. Necula, G.C.: Proof-carrying code. In: Proc. POPL. pp. 106–119. ACM (1997). https://doi.org/10.1145/263699.263712
48. Richter, C., Hüllermeier, E., Jakobs, M.-C., Wehrheim, H.: Algorithm selection for software validation based on graph kernels. Autom. Softw. Eng. **27**(1), 153–186 (2020). https://doi.org/10.1007/s10515-020-00270-x
49. Vojdani, V., Apinis, K., Rõtov, V., Seidl, H., Vene, V., Vogler, R.: Static race detection for device drivers: The Goblint approach. In: Proc. ASE. pp. 391–402. ACM (2016). https://doi.org/10.1145/2970276.2970337
50. Švejda, J., Berger, P., Katoen, J.P.: Interpretation-based violation witness validation for C: NITWIT. In: Proc. TACAS. pp. 40–57. LNCS 12078, Springer (2020). https://doi.org/10.1007/978-3-030-45190-5_3

Strategy Switching: Smart Fault-Tolerance for Weakly-Hard Resource-Constrained Real-Time Applications

Lukas Miedema[✉][iD] and Clemens Grelck[iD]

Faculty of Science, University of Amsterdam, Amsterdam, Netherlands
{l.miedema,c.grelck}@uva.nl

Abstract. The probability of data corruption as a result of *single event upsets* (SEUs) increases as transistor sizes decrease. Software-based fault-tolerance can help offer protection against SEUs on *Commercial off The Shelf* (COTS) hardware. However, such fault tolerance relies on replication, for which there may be insufficient resources in resource-constrained environments. Systems in the weakly-hard real-time domain can tolerate some faults as a product of their domain. Combining both the need for fault-tolerance and the intrinsic ability to tolerate faults, we propose a new approach for applying fault-tolerance named *strategy switching*. Strategy switching minimizes the effective unmitigated fault-rate by switching which tasks are to be run under a fault-tolerance scheme at runtime. Our method does not require bounding the number of faults for a given number of consecutive iterations.

We show how our method improves the steady-state fault rate by analytically computing the rate for our test set of generated DAGs and comparing this against a static application of fault-tolerance. Finally, we validate our method using UPPAAL.

Keywords: Cyber-physical systems · Resource constraint · Weakly-hard real-time · Fault-tolerance · Single event upset · Adaptivity

1 Introduction

As transistor density increases and gate voltages decreases, the frequency of *transient faults* or *single event upsets* (SEUs) increases. As such, fault-tolerance techniques are becoming a requirement in computer systems [12]. Fault-tolerance techniques can either be implemented in hardware or in software. Hardware-based techniques are (partially) implemented in silicon, and as such can offer transparent fault-tolerance with minimal overhead. However, an implementation in silicon may not be feasible, e.g. due to the cost of manufacturing special-purpose microprocessors. Software-based fault-tolerance offers an attractive alternative due to its ability to protect workloads on *Commercial Off The Shelf* (COTS) hardware. Code is protected by executing it multiple times

B.-H. Schlingloff and M. Chai (Eds.): SEFM 2022, LNCS 13550, pp. 129–145, 2022.
https://doi.org/10.1007/978-3-031-17108-6_8

(redundant execution). The process of managing replication, determining consensus between the replicas, as well as any mitigation mechanism is entirely done in software. Redundant execution often takes shape *N-Modular Redundancy* [11] (NMR). NMR uses two-out-of-N voting on the output of some unit of code to obtain a majority and mitigate the effects of a SEU. At least three replicas are needed to obtain a majority in case of fault, which is known as *Triple Modular Redundancy* (TMR). Higher levels of N offer robustness against multiple faults.

Modular redundancy can be implemented at different levels of granularity, e.g. by replicating individual instructions threefold like *SWIFT-R* [6], but also at the OS task level [1]. Regardless, significant overhead remains: instrumenting a binary with SWIFT-Rs technique increases its execution time by 99% [6]. As such, constrained real-time systems may have insufficient processing resources to complete protection with fault-tolerance. For applications consisting of multiple components or *tasks*, software-based fault-tolerance allows for protecting a subset of all tasks. This holds even when multiple tasks time-share the same processor, as the application of fault-tolerance is independent of the processor.

Control tasks may be able to tolerate non-consecutive deadline misses, which has led to the adoption of the *weakly hard model* [3]. Each task i has an (m_i, k_i) constraint, indicating that the task must complete at least m_i times successfully out of every k_i times. We use this (m_i, k_i) constraint with $m_i < k_i$ to deliver more effective fault-tolerance to resource-constrained systems.

Contribution. We propose *strategy switching*, a new approach for improving fault-tolerance for resource-constrained real-time applications. We minimize the effective unmitigated fault rate by selecting which tasks are to be run under the protection of a fault-tolerance mechanism. Our approach uses weakly-hard $(m_i, k_i) = (1, 2)$ constraints on tasks to improve the effective fault rate by varying which tasks are protected at runtime. Strategy switching does not require a fault model within which the number of faults are bound, but instead minimizes the effective fault rate regardless of whether complete fault prevention is feasible. Finally, we offer an analytical solution to computing the effective fault rate when using strategy switching, and validate this solution using UPPAAL [2].

Organization. In Sect. 2 we introduce our task and fault model. Strategies are organized in a *state machine*, which is discussed in Sect. 3. Our state machine construction algorithm is detailed in Sect. 4. To evaluate the effect of our solution on the steady-state fault rate, we propose an analytical technique for obtaining said rate in Sect. 5. We evaluate our strategy switching technique in Sect. 6. Validation of our analytical method is done using UPPAAL in Sect. 7. Related work is discussed in Sect. 8, after which the paper is concluded in Sect. 9. Finally in Sect. 10 we discuss various future directions and propose improvements for our strategy switching technique.

2   System Models

Task Model. We assume the application is structured as a set of periodic real-time tasks $\Gamma = \{\tau_1...\tau_n\}$ with a single, global period and deadline D such that

Table 1. Definitions of symbols and terms used in the task model

Item	Meaning
Task model	
Γ	Set of all tasks, $\Gamma = \{\tau_1...\tau_n\}$
$\tau_i \in \Gamma$	Task $i \in \Gamma$, e.g. τ_A is task A
E	Set of all precedence relations, $E = \{(\tau_i, \tau_j), ...\}$
C_i	*Worst Case Execution Time* (WCET) of task i
D	Global deadline (shared by all tasks)
Fault model	
λ	Fault rate (Poisson distribution)
(m_i, k_i)	Constraint indicating task i has to execute successfully for at least m_i iterations out of every k_i iterations
Unmitigated fault	Fault in a task not mitigated by a fault-tolerance technique
Catastrophic fault	Unmitigated fault that leads to the (m_i, k_i) constraint of the task being violated

the period is equal to or larger than the deadline (no pipelining). For each task τ_i, a worst-case execution time C_i is known. We also assume the effects of applying fault-tolerance to a task is known: fault-tolerance may create replicas that have to be scheduled, or the tasks' own C_i value may increase as a result of redundancy. Furthermore, we support non-cyclic precedence relations $E = \{(\tau_i, \tau_j)\}$ for any task τ_i and τ_j where τ_i must precede τ_j creating a *Directed Cyclic Graph* (DAG) of tasks. Our technique requires the presence of a (global, offline) scheduler that can schedule the task set efficiently across the processors. The scheduler must be able to deal with fault-tolerance applied to any subset of the task set and yield a schedule. As the use of fault-tolerance increases the utilization of the system, the scheduler must be able to identify whether a particular subset of tasks under fault-tolerance is *schedulable* – i.e. able to meet the real-time deadline. Finally, every time the subset of tasks under fault-tolerance changes constitutes a real-time *mode switch*, as the schedule effectively changes from that moment on. As such, we require a middleware capable of making such a switch at the end of every period (when no tasks are running).

Fault Model. We use the Poisson distribution as an approximation for the worst-case fault rate of SEUs, which was argued to be a good approximation by Broster et al. [4]. We do not assume universal fault detection: only when the task runs under a fault-tolerance scheme can a fault be detected and mitigated. When a task does not run with fault-tolerance, it is unknown whether or not it succeeded. Successor tasks rely on data produced by their predecessors, as such we consider faults to cascade across precedence relations. We use the term *catastrophic fault* to describe an unmitigated fault occurring in two consecutive iterations of a task that can tolerate a single unmitigated fault, i.e. the task i has an $(m_i, k_i) = (1, 2)$ constraint. We do not consider constraints beyond $k_i = 2$ in this paper.

Fault Mitigation. We assume the presence and implementation of a particular fault-tolerance scheme, and that any task can be run under that scheme. In this paper, we assume that SEUs always go undetected in tasks protected by a fault-tolerance mechanism. Fault-tolerance implemented using replication may fail (no consensus between the replicas). As such, we assume fault mitigation may fail, and that it is known when fault mitigation fails.

Other Definitions. Given the complexity and number of symbols used in this paper, a table of all symbols and terms is compiled in Table 1. Each symbol or term used will be defined prior to use, as well as being listed in the table.

3   A State Machine of Strategies

To swiftly select a new subset of the task set to protect with fault-tolerance, we precompute the best subset of tasks to protect next for each situation. The response to such a situation is identified by a *strategy*, dictating which tasks to run with fault-tolerance. Exactly one strategy is active at any moment in time, and switching between strategies is facilitated through a *strategy state machine*.

Table 2. Definitions of symbols and terms used in the strategy state machine

Item	Meaning
States in the state machine	
$\mathcal{S}$	Set of all strategies
$s \in \mathcal{S}$	A strategy
$\Gamma_s \subseteq \Gamma$	The tasks protected under strategy s
$s_{A,B}$	A strategy protecting task A and B, i.e. $\Gamma_{s_{A,B}} = \{\tau_A, \tau_B\}$
$\mathcal{R}$	Set of all results
$r \in \mathcal{R}$	A result
$r_{A,\overline{B}}$	A result where task A (τ_A) succeeded and task B (τ_B) failed
Transitions in the state machine	
Δ	The transition function for the strategy state machine
$\Delta(s)$	The set of successors of strategy s as per the transition function Δ. Due to the bipartite nature of the state machine, this is always a set of results
$\Delta(r)$	The successor of result r as per transition function Δ. Always a single element, and due to the bipartite nature of Δ it is always a strategy

The architecture of our strategy switching approach distinguishes between an online part at runtime, as well as an offline part executing ahead-of-time not beholden to any real-time constraints. The offline component prepares the state machine, which is then available for online playback. The strategy state machine is a bipartite state machine, consisting of *strategy* states and *result* states. Figure 1b shows such a state machine. All symbols used to define the strategy state machine is given in Table 2.

Online. We introduce a *strategy switching component*, which plays back the strategy state machine, taking transitions based on observed faults as the application runs. At runtime, this component selects a single strategy s ahead of every execution of the task set, which becomes active. The strategy s dictates which tasks to protect with a fault-tolerance scheme (Γ_s), and which ones not ($\Gamma \setminus \Gamma_s$). Fault-tolerance techniques are typically not a silver bullet solution, and unmitigated faults may still occur in tasks in Γ_s. Furthermore, these techniques can often report the fact that they failed to mitigate a fault (e.g. no consensus in N-modular redundancy). After executing all tasks, the online component uses this information from the execution of the task set to select the matching result r from the state machine. This result reflects the success or fail state, or probability thereof, of each of the tasks. Each possible result r directly maps to its best successor strategy, which is applied to the next iteration of the task set.

Offline. The full set of strategies $s \in \mathcal{S}$ is computed ahead of time, as well as the transition relation Δ from any given result $r \in \mathcal{R}$ to the best successor strategy $\Delta(r) = s$. Strategies which are not schedulable are pruned from $\mathcal{S}$. Furthermore, strategies which are dominated by other strategies (i.e. there is another strategy that protects a superset of tasks) are also not considered in $\mathcal{S}$.

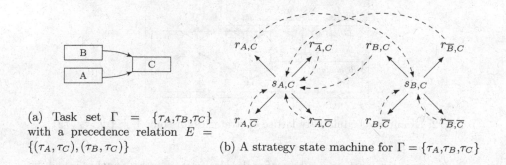

(a) Task set $\Gamma = \{\tau_A, \tau_B, \tau_C\}$ with a precedence relation $E = \{(\tau_A, \tau_C), (\tau_B, \tau_C)\}$

(b) A strategy state machine for $\Gamma = \{\tau_A, \tau_B, \tau_C\}$

Fig. 1. Example task set with a corresponding example state machine

4 Strategy State Machine Construction

Building the strategy state machine is a two-step process: (1) enumerating valid strategies and results, (2) determine the best successor strategy for each result. The state machine construction process is guaranteed to produce a state machine as long as the task set without any tasks under fault-tolerance is schedulable. However, in the case that no strategy applying fault-tolerance is schedulable, the strategy state machine becomes *degenerate*. Such a state machine consists exclusively of the empty strategy, i.e. $\mathcal{S} = \{s_\emptyset\}$ with $\Gamma_{s_\emptyset} = \emptyset$. Given that there is only one strategy protecting nothing, no meaningful switching can occur as there is no other strategy to switch to. Under a degenerate strategy state machine, the application behaves as if it runs without fault-tolerance or strategy switching.

4.1   Enumerating Strategies and Results

The set of all strategies $\mathcal{S}$ and set of all results $\mathcal{R}$ can be constructed by considering every subset $\Gamma_s \subseteq \Gamma$ and applying fault protection accordingly.

The scheduler is used to mark subsets as either schedulable or unschedulable, depending on its ability to produce a schedule that meets the deadline with that subset running with fault protection. Marking each subset in effect forms an annotated lattice over the subset relation. An example of such a lattice is shown in Fig. 2. The shown annotation could be the result of a high worst-case execution time C_X when compared to C_Y and C_Z. As such, the extra compute needed for running τ_A under fault-tolerance is much larger than doing the same for τ_Y or τ_Z. This in turn makes the strategy protecting both τ_Y and τ_Z ($s_{Y,Z}$) schedulable, while protecting any task together with τ_X makes the strategy unschedulable (i.e. $s_{X,Y}$ and $s_{X,Z}$).

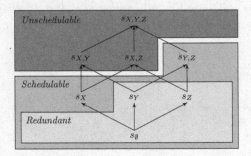

Fig. 2. Example schedulability lattice of strategies for some $\Gamma = \{\tau_X, \tau_Y, \tau_Z\}$

Some strategies protect a subset of tasks also protected by another schedulable strategy (e.g. s_Y protects a subset of $s_{X,Y}$). In Fig. 2, this is s_Y, s_Z and $s_\emptyset$. These strategies are annotated as *redundant* and as such are discarded together with the unschedulable strategies. Each strategy $s \in \mathcal{S}$ has one result $r \in \mathcal{R}$ for each possible outcome. As success or failure is only known for tasks in τ_s, a result r is constructed for every combination of outcomes for tasks in τ_s.

4.2   Strategy Linking

Each result r is linked to a successor strategy by a process called *linking*. When transitioning from a result r to a strategy s, there is knowledge about two consecutive iterations of the task set. This is used to compute the expected number of catastrophic faults as shown in Theorem 1 by means of $\delta(s, r)$. Then, our algorithm selects the best successor s by minimizing $\delta(s, r)$ per Definition 1.

Theorem 1. *Expected number of catastrophic faults given r was reached and s will be activated*

$$\delta(s, r) = \sum_{\tau_i \in \Gamma} P(\text{transitive fault in } \tau_i | r) \cdot P(\text{transitive fault in } \tau_i | s)$$

Definition 1. *Determining a successor strategy $\Delta(r) \in \mathcal{S}$*

$$\Delta(r) = \underset{s \in \mathcal{S}}{\arg \min}\, \delta(s, r)$$

The fault probability $P(\text{transitive fault in } \tau_i | r)$ and $P(\text{transitive fault in } \tau_i | s)$ can be derived from the tasks execution time, the fault rate λ, the fault-tolerance scheme (NMR), and the result r and strategy s. Given the Poisson distribution and the WCET C_i, the chance of a fault in τ_i is given as p_i in Definition 2, while the chance of a fault under NMR is given as q_i in Definition 3.

Definition 2. *Chance of a fault in any invocation of task τ_i when no fault tolerance ("NOFT") mechanism is applied*

$$P(\text{fault in } \tau_i | NOFT) = e^{-\lambda \cdot C_i} = p_i$$

Definition 3. *Chance of a fault in any invocation of task τ_i when NMR is used*

$$P(\text{fault in } \tau_i | NMR) = p_i^3 + \binom{3}{2} p_i^2 \cdot (1 - p_i) = q_i$$

The protection status of a task (either "NOFT" or "NMR") can be read from the strategy, as shown in Definition 4.

Definition 4. *Chance of a fault in any invocation of task τ_i under strategy s*

$$P(\text{fault in } \tau_i | s) = \begin{cases} \text{if } \tau_i \text{ protected by } s & = P(\text{fault in } \tau_i | NMR) \\ \text{otherwise} & = P(\text{fault in } \tau_i | NOFT) \end{cases}$$

We assume faults propagate along the DAG as invalid output is sent to successor tasks. Definition 5 defines the probability of a transitive fault, where the fault can either originate from itself or from a predecessor.

Definition 5. *Chance of a transitive fault in any invocation of task τ_i under strategy s*

$$P(\text{transitive fault in } \tau_i | s) = P(\text{fault in } \tau_i | s) + (1 - P(\text{fault in } \tau_i | s))$$
$$\cdot \left(1 - \prod_{\tau_j \in pred(\tau_i)} 1 - P(\text{fault in } \tau_j | s) \right)$$

The same idea of Definition 4 is used to define the chance of success given a result, which is given in Definition 6. The same mechanism for handling precedence relations as seen in Definition 5 can be applied using $P(\text{fault in } \tau_i|r)$ to derive $P(\text{transitive fault in } \tau_i|r)$, which we will omit for brevity.

Definition 6. *Chance of a fault in any invocation of task τ_i when result r of strategy s_r was reached*

$$P(\text{fault in } \tau_i|r) = \begin{cases} \text{if } \tau_i \text{ succeeded per } r & = 1 \\ \text{if } \tau_i \text{ failed per } r & = 0 \\ \text{otherwise} & = P(\text{fault in } \tau_i|s_r) \end{cases}$$

4.3 State Machine Construction Algorithm

We show the entire strategy state machine construction process in Algorithm 1.

① All strategies are enumerated and the scheduler is used to determine for each strategy its schedulability status. The lattice relation, as shown in Fig. 2, is used to significantly reduce the number of times the scheduler needs to be invoked. When a strategy is found to be unschedulable, all strategies protecting *more* tasks are immediately marked as unschedulable. Likewise, when an unschedulable strategy is encountered, all strategies protecting *fewer* tasks are marked as schedulable.

② The resulting S contains all strategies, and is pruned of unschedulable strategies and strategies that protect a subset of tasks than other schedulable strategies.

③ Set S is further pruned, removing all strategies that provide equal or worse protection when compared to some other strategy in S.

④ Results are constructed and their successor $\Delta(r) \in S$ is determined for each of the remaining strategies. Each result associated with strategy s is identified with a bitmask o over Γ_s such that index l in the bitmasks identifies whether task τ_l at index l in Γ_s is protected. The results are added to $\mathcal{R}$.

4.4 Algorithmic Complexity

The approach, as presented here, can easily become intractable for even small task sets due to the explosion of S and $\mathcal{R}$. In Sect. 10, we discuss ways to lower the algorithmic complexity. For completeness, we discuss the algorithmic complexity of the (naïve) state machine construction algorithm as presented.

The number of strategies is up to all combinations of tasks, i.e. $|S| \in \mathcal{O}(|\Gamma|!)$. Each strategy has $\leq 2^{|\Gamma_s|}$ results, $2^{|\Gamma_s|} \in \mathcal{O}(2^{|\Gamma|})$ and thus $|\mathcal{R}| \in \mathcal{O}(|\Gamma|! \cdot 2^{|\Gamma|})$. Let $n = |\Gamma|$, i.e. n is the number of tasks. Then, the final algorithmic time complexity is given in Theorem 2.

Algorithm 1. Complete state machine construction algorithm

① Collect all strategies and their schedulability status
1: $\mathcal{S} \leftarrow \emptyset$
2: **for all** $\Gamma_j \in$ subsets of Γ **do**
3:      **if** $\exists s \in \mathcal{S} : \Gamma_s = \Gamma_j$ **then**   ▷ Skip if a strategy for subset Γ_j already exists
4:          **continue**
5:      **end if**
6:      $\Gamma_s \leftarrow \{\, \text{NMR}(\tau_i)\ :\ \tau_i \in \Gamma_j\,\} \cup (\Gamma \setminus \Gamma_j)$ ▷ Set of all tasks with NMR applied
7:      **if** schedulable(Γ_s) **then**
8:          $s_j \leftarrow$ **new** Strategy$(\Gamma_s, \text{schedulable} = \textbf{true})$ ▷ Strategy is schedulable
9:          $\mathcal{S} \leftarrow \mathcal{S} \cup \{s_j\}$
10:          **for all** $\Gamma_k \in$ subsets of Γ where $\Gamma_j \subset \Gamma_k$ **do** ▷ Propagate down the lattice
11:              $s_k \leftarrow$ **new** Strategy$(\Gamma_k, \text{schedulable} = \textbf{true})$
12:              $\mathcal{S} \leftarrow \mathcal{S} \cup \{s_k\}$
13:          **end for**
14:      **else**
15:          $s_j \leftarrow$ **new** Strategy$(\Gamma_s, \text{schedulable} = \textbf{false})$ ▷ Strategy is unschedulable
16:          $\mathcal{S} \leftarrow \mathcal{S} \cup \{s_j\}$
17:          **for all** $\Gamma_k \in$ subsets of Γ where $\Gamma_k \subset \Gamma_j$ **do**   ▷ Propagate up the lattice
18:              $s_k \leftarrow$ **new** Strategy$(\Gamma_k, \text{schedulable} = \textbf{false})$
19:              $\mathcal{S} \leftarrow \mathcal{S} \cup \{s_k\}$
20:          **end for**
21:      **end if**
22: **end for**

② Prune strategies based on schedulability and redundancy
23: $\mathcal{S} \leftarrow \{s : s \in \mathcal{S}, s \text{ is schedulable}\}$ ▷ Using information in $s \in \mathcal{S}$
24: $\mathcal{S} \leftarrow \{s_i : s_i \in \mathcal{S}, \neg \exists s_j \in \mathcal{S} : \Gamma_{s_i} \subset \Gamma_{s_j}\}$ ▷ Remove redundant strategies

③ Prune strategies based on fault-tolerance quality
25: **for all** $s_i \in \mathcal{S}$ **do**
26:      **for all** $s_j \in \mathcal{S} \setminus s_i$ **do**
27:          **if** $\forall \tau_k \in \Gamma : P(\text{transitive fault in } \tau_k | s_i) \leq P(\text{transitive fault in } \tau_k | s_j)$ **then**
28:              $\mathcal{S} \leftarrow \mathcal{S} \setminus s_j$ ▷ s_j is equal or worse for all tasks than s_i
29:          **end if**
30:      **end for**
31: **end for**

④ Create and link results
32: $\mathcal{R} \leftarrow \emptyset$
33: $\Delta \leftarrow \emptyset$
34: **for all** $s_i \in \mathcal{S}$ **do**
35:      **for all** $o_j \in$ all combinations of success and failure for Γ_s **do** ▷ o_j is a bitmask
36:          $r_j \leftarrow$ **new** Result(o_j)
37:          $s_{\text{next}} \leftarrow s \in \mathcal{S} : \min_{s_k \in \mathcal{S}} \delta(s_k, r_j) = \delta(s, r_j)$ ▷ Linking per Definition 1
38:          $\Delta(r_j) \leftarrow s_{\text{next}}$
39:          $\Delta(s_i, o_j) \leftarrow r_j$
40:          $\mathcal{R} \leftarrow \mathcal{R} \cup \{r_j\}$
41:      **end for**
42: **end for**

Theorem 2. *Time-complexity for the construction of the strategy state machine for* $|\Gamma| = n$ *tasks*

$$\mathcal{O}(|\mathcal{R}| + |\mathcal{S}|) \approx \mathcal{O}(|\mathcal{R}|) \in \mathcal{O}(|\Gamma|! \cdot 2^{|\Gamma|}) = \mathcal{O}(n! \cdot 2^n)$$

Note that this is a high upper bound which is unlikely to be hit by an arbitrary task graph. Redundant strategies are identified and pruned before the results are enumerated as seen in Algorithm 1, reducing the number of results significantly. In further work, we intend to improve the tractability by improving the strategy enumeration process itself.

5   Evaluating State Machines

To evaluate and compare our algorithm against a static (non-switching) solution, a way of determining the effective fault rate is necessary. We define the effective fault rate as $\delta(\Delta)$. $\delta(\Delta)$ is the expected number of catastrophic faults for any arbitrary period of the task set managed according to state machine Δ. $\delta(\Delta)$ can be obtained analytically converting it to a Discrete-Time Markov Chain.

5.1   Discrete-Time Markov Chain Evaluation

The expected number of catastrophic faults in Δ is the weighted average of the $\delta(r, s) = \delta(r, \Delta(r))$ function from Theorem 1. The weight of result r can be derived from its strategy s, as shown in Theorem 3.

Theorem 3. *Probability of selecting result* r *given strategy* s

$$P(r|s) = \prod_{\tau_i \in \Gamma_s} \begin{cases} \textit{if } \tau_i \textit{ fails in } r & = P(\textit{transitive fault in } \tau_i | s) \\ \textit{otherwise} & = 1 - P(\textit{transitive fault in } \tau_i | s) \end{cases}$$

Theorem 4. *Expected number of catastrophic faults per period of the task set*

$$\delta(\Delta) = \sum_{r \in \mathcal{R}} P(s|\Delta) \cdot P(r|s) \cdot \delta(r, \Delta(r))$$

$P(s|\Delta)$ provides the steady-state probability of finding the strategy state machine in strategy s. $P(s|\Delta)$ can be computed by converting the state machine into a *Discrete-Time Markov Chain*. Conversion is applied as follows:

1. Result states are removed, and all incoming edges are transferred directly to the successor of each result state.
2. A transition matrix T_Δ is created from Δ.
3. The steady-state vector $\vec{SS}_\Delta$ of T_Δ is computed (e.g. using linear algebra).
4. $\vec{SS}_\Delta(s \in \mathcal{S}) = P(s|\Delta)$.

6 Evaluation

To evaluate our technique, we generate a set of task graphs and compute a strategy state machine for each graph across a variety of scenarios.

6.1 Dataset

We generate 500 task graphs with between 2 and 20 tasks using *Task Graphs For Free* (TGFF) [9]. Each task graph is statically scheduled once with Forward List Scheduling targeting a 4 core platform, without any fault-tolerance. These schedules are used to determine each task graphs' base makespan. We set the fault rate to $\lambda = 10^{-5}s^{-1}$ and determine fault probabilities using the Poisson distribution, i.e. $P(\text{fault in } \tau_i | \text{ NOFT}) = e^{\lambda \cdot C_i}$. As fault-tolerance technique we use TMR at the task level. The scheduler is tasked with scheduling the three replicas and voter according to their precedence relations.

To simulate resource-constrained scenarios, we obtain results for various deadlines. We define the deadline as a multiple of the base makespan. A multiple of 1 (i.e. deadline = 1×makespan) leaves only strategies that can place task replicas in existing gaps in the schedule, while a multiple of 3 leaves enough time available for every task to run three times.

6.2 Results

Figure 3 shows the results of the 500 task graphs with four different deadlines. For each plot, the x-axis represents utilization without fault-tolerance, while the y-axis presents the steady-state fault rate $\delta(\Delta)$ (lower is better).

The higher the utilization, the fewer unused resources there are to use for placing replicas. The effect of this is visible – the higher the utilization, the higher the fault rate in both the switching and non-switching case. Each plot compares our strategy-switching solution to a non-switching one where only a single strategy is selected, as well as one without fault-tolerance ("NOFT").

For the extremely constrained scenario of deadline = 1×makespan (Fig. 3a), our strategy-switching solution manages to hit a lower fault-rate than the non-switching solution in most cases. Our solution offers a 17.82% lower steady-state fault rate on average (±37.34% std. dev) when compared to the non-switching approach. At a more relaxed deadline = 1.2×makespan, these figures stay about the same (17.92% improvement with ±44.06% std. dev). But relaxing the deadline to 1.4×makespan yields a fault rate reduction of 24.79% (±50.29% std. dev). When the ratio matches the extra resource requirement of TMR (≤ 3), all solutions perform identical as seen in Fig. 3d.

We analyze this behavior at the hand of Fig. 4, where the relative improvement for the first 6 DAGs is shown across multiple makespan/deadline ratios. The strategy switching solution provides a reduction in fault-rate for intermediate makespan/deadline ratios.

With more relaxed deadlines, the number of possible strategies starts to overtake the tractability of our algorithm: at 1.2×, for 3 of the 500 task graphs

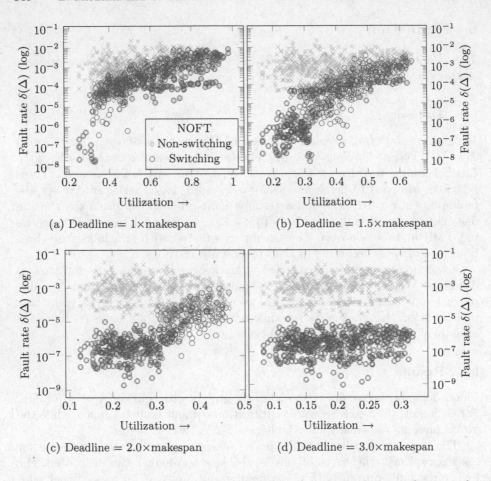

Fig. 3. Utilization vs. steady-state fault rate for a non-switching solution and our switching solution across various levels of resource constrainity. Lower fault rate is better.

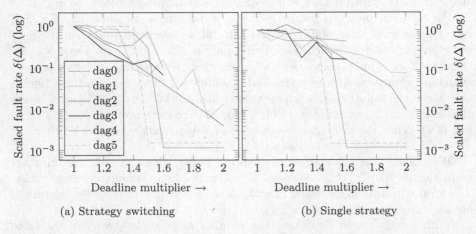

Fig. 4. Relative improvement in fault rate when the makespan multiplier increases for the first 6 DAGs

a state machine cannot be constructed within 30 minute on our hardware. This grows to 20 of the 500 graphs for a multiplier of 1.4×. However, this does not take away from the validity of the state machine for DAGs where it is feasible.

Our approach does not always yield an improvement. For 1× multiplier, strategy switching offered an improvement when compared to a static solution in 272 of the 500 cases. In 68 of the missing cases, our strategy-switching approach performs *worse* than the non-switching solution. Our greedy $\Delta(r)$ successor determination method as presented in Definition 1 is naive and susceptible to make locally-optimal decisions that are detrimental to the total fault-rate. Such cases can easily be avoided however: as we propose an analytical method for computing the fault rate in this paper, the algorithm can easily be extended to verify that the resulting state machine outperforms a static solution. When this is not the case, it can fall back to the static solution. In future work, we intent on creating a better linking algorithm that could also deliver in an improvement in these cases, and not have to fall back to a static non-switching solution.

7 Validation Using UPPAAL

To improve confidence in our analytical evaluation, we model the online part of the strategy switching using UPPAAL [2]. Online strategy switching is combined with UPPAAL processes for tasks, edges, processors, and a variety of monitoring models. These processes in effect build a complete runtime simulator with which we can study long-running behavior of a weakly-hard real-time application when experiencing a given incidence rate of faults. UPPAAL is used in *Stochastic Model Checking* (SMC) mode [5], which lets us estimate the expected number of catastrophic faults for a large number of periods of a particular task set. For validation to succeed, this estimation must match the analytical solution obtained per Sect. 5. As each model is specific to one task set and its strategy state machine, we develop a generator that produces a UPPAAL model automatically from a task set and strategy state machine.

7.1 UPPAAL Processes

Systems models constructed in UPPAAL [2] are composed of a set of concurrently-running UPPAAL *processes* derived from *process templates*. We define 12 templates for validation, in which three categories can be identified:

i) *Our contribution*: a strategy state machine process, plus a set of result matcher processes identifying when particular results is reached
ii) *Hardware & application*: task, edge, NMR voter and processor templates
iii) *Monitoring*: task and edge monitoring templates to propagate faults and register the actual catastrophic fault rate

For brevity we limit discussion to one template: the task process template. This template is shown in Fig. 5. A task process is created for each combination of a task τ_i and strategy s_j. It is parameterized with task index i, strategy id j, the release time r_i, its WCET C_i, the assigned core P_i.

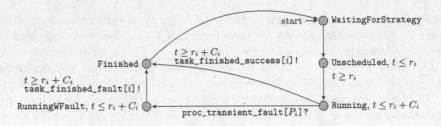

Fig. 5. Simplified UPPAAL process template for a task

When the strategy s_j is activated, the task process moves to the `Unscheduled` location. This location is left when clock t reaches $t = r_i$. In the `Running` state, it may encounter a fault signaled via the `proc_transient_fault[P_i]`. The fault is captured by moving to `RunningWFault`. The process finishes by either emitting a `task_finished_success[i]` or `task_finished_fault[i]` depending on its fault status, which is relayed to a voter process (omitted for brevity).

7.2 Validating Results

The UPPAAL model is periodic, and counts the number of catastrophic faults encountered by means of the monitoring processes. To determine the global steady-state fault rate $\delta(\Delta)$, we query the number of catastrophic faults for a large number of tasks set iterations. Then, validation succeeds when $\delta(\Delta) \approx \frac{\#\,\text{catastrophic faults}}{\#\,\text{iterations}}$. We set the confidence interval for this experiment to 95%.

We apply the UPPAAL model transformation to the first 10 task graphs with deadline $= 1\times$makespan, the validation results of which can be seen in Table 3. The raw data is shown in the "# **faults**" column, and is obtained using the query `E[<=`t`;128](max:catastrophic_faults)`. The formula estimates the number of catastrophic faults seen until time t. 128 such simulations are conducted to gain confidence in the stability of the value and get the bounds of the 95% confidence interval (shown with $\pm$). In the formula, parameter t is set to the period $\times$ 4096 to simulate 4096 consecutive iterations of the task set. As such, $\delta(\Delta)$ is approximated by dividing the output of the formula by 4096.

Two values (dag2 and dag8) are absent: the UPPAAL query did not return a result in 24 hour. The extremely low fault-rate of dag7 makes seeing a single fault in $4096 \cdot 128$ iterations is 0.029. The remaining values present in Table 3 are within their 95% confidence interval, giving good confidence in the accuracy of our analytical method and therefore our results.

8 Related Work

The (m_i, k_i) constraints have been used before to improve the efficacy of fault-tolerance in real-time scheduling. [8] proposed a scheduler and an efficient schedulability algorithm for a sporadic task set with tasks under (m_i, k_i) constraints. Their scheduler allows for scheduling task sets that would normally not

Table 3. Numerical evaluation using UPPAAL

DAG	# tasks	$|\mathcal{S}|$	# faults	$\delta(\Delta)$ (numerical)	$\delta(\Delta)$ (analytical)
dag0	19	1	18.9766 ± 1.543	$(4.633 \pm 0.377) \cdot 10^{-3}$	$4.34 \cdot 10^{-3}$
dag1	14	17	4.32812 ± 0.574086	$(1.057 \pm 0.141) \cdot 10^{-3}$	$1.01 \cdot 10^{-3}$
dag2	21	21	Did Not Finish		$3.14 \cdot 10^{-3}$
dag3	20	1	21.9219 ± 2.09571	$(5.352 \pm 0.512) \cdot 10^{-3}$	$5.25 \cdot 10^{-3}$
dag4	4	1	0.453125 ± 0.113753	$(1.106 \pm 0.278) \cdot 10^{-4}$	$1.09 \cdot 10^{-4}$
dag5	5	4	0.40625 ± 0.112856	$(9.918 \pm 2.755) \cdot 10^{-5}$	$9.36 \cdot 10^{-5}$
dag6	10	10	1.64844 ± 0.272017	$(4.025 \pm 0.664) \cdot 10^{-4}$	$3.78 \cdot 10^{-4}$
dag7	4	1	0 ± 0	$(0 \pm 0) \cdot 10^{0}$	$5.65 \cdot 10^{-8}$
dag8	12	26	Did Not Finish		$3.67 \cdot 10^{-4}$
dag9	4	2	0.148438 ± 0.0661748	$(3.624 \pm 1.616) \cdot 10^{-5}$	$4.46 \cdot 10^{-5}$

be schedulable, yet utilizing their (m_i, k_i) constraints allows them to be scheduled.

Chen et al. [7] proposed a solution that is similar to ours. Their method offers fault-tolerance with the goal of reducing the effective fault rate as well as lowering energy consumption. Chen et al. propose a static scheduling technique called *Static Pattern-Based Reliable Execution*, ensuring each (m_i, k_i) constraint is respected in the presence of transient faults. Furthermore, they propose delaying the execution of their static pattern if no fault is detected at runtime, opportunistically running more unprotected instances of the task with the goal of saving energy. However, if the static pattern is found to be unschedulable as per their schedulability test, their implementation is unable to provide a schedule that minimizes the fault rate for a given resource-constrained real-time system. While their approach offers more flexibility in the task model (specifically the support for (m_i, k_i) constraints with $k_i > 2$), it does not consider that fault mitigation may fail. Our approach optimally lowers the fault rate, regardless of the hardware constrains. Furthermore, our approach recognizes that fault mitigation may fail, and includes this in the calculation for lowering the fault rate.

[10] offers a technique for measuring the fault rate of an application with tasks under (m_i, k_i) constraints. Their technique provides an upper bound for the fault probability per iteration of a *Fault-tolerant Single-Input Single-Output* (FT-SISO) control loop, similar to our $\delta(\Delta)$ function. Their technique hopes to provide transparency to system designers, allowing analyzing the impact on the reliability when changing the hardware or software. However, while their approach is aware of (m_i, k_i) constraints, it does not provide schedules that utilize them. Instead, it merely includes them in the reliability calculation.

The domain of strategy switching shares some aspects with *Mixed-Criticality* (MC) systems. In an MC system, the system switches between different levels of criticality depending on the operating conditions of the system. Tasks are assigned a criticality level, and when the system criticality is higher than that of the task, the task is not scheduled to guarantee the successful and timely execution of tasks with a higher criticality level. Pathan [13] combines MC with fault-tolerance against transient faults. As is typical in MC research, as the level of criticality increases, the pessimism increases. Pathan increases the maximum fault rate when switching to a higher level of criticality. In our approach we do not vary the pessimism of any parameter. Instead, we assume the λ parameter provides a suitable upper bound to the fault rate in all conditions. Our approach offers some aspects typically not found in MC systems: while each strategy appears as is own a criticality level, it is a level applied to a subset of the tasks (specifically Γ_s). Finally, [13] requires bounding the number of faults that can occur in any window. As such, passing their sufficient schedulability test will (under their fault model) guarantee the system will never experience a fault.

9   Conclusion

In this paper, we introduced *strategy switching*, a technique to improve fault-tolerance for resource-constrained systems. By switching the subset of the set of tasks that receives fault-tolerance, we are able to reduce the effective fault-rate for resource-constrained weakly-hard real-time systems. We contribute a comprehensive algorithm for constructing the strategy state machine, as well as an evaluation of our technique across 500 DAGs. In our evaluation, we saw an improvement in the majority of cases when resource constraints are significant. Furthermore, we contribute an analytical technique for analyzing the strategy state machine, and use UPPAAL to validate our technique.

10   Future Work

We hope to address the issue of tractability in future work, as well as lower the steady-state fault rate of applications by means of an improved linking algorithm. Finally, we hope lift the limitation of (m_i, k_i) where $k_i \leq 2$ in a future paper.

Tractability may be improved by utilizing symmetry in the strategy set $\mathcal{S}$, as well as leveraging heuristic-driven strategy enumeration techniques. Furthermore, we intent to lower the steady-state fault rate of our strategy switching solution by developing a new divide-and-conquer linking algorithm. When not encountering any faults, the lowest steady-state fault rate is achieved by switching between two strategies or remaining in one strategy. This is a logical consequence of the $k_i = 2$ limitation, as it limits the effects of an unmitigated faults to two iterations (two strategies). By identifying these pairs and devising a merge operation, we hope to construct a high-quality composite strategy state machine.

Finally, we aim to support tasks with $k_i > 2$ constraints. The past $k - 1$ successes or fails of a task is needed in $\delta(s, r)$ to compute the expected number of catastrophic faults when evaluating successor strategy s. As such, a result should be allocated for each combination of previous fails/successes. Naively allocating these results is trivially intractable. Instead, we hope to create an efficient result enumeration and linking algorithm that can operate at runtime.

Acknowledgments. This project has received funding from the European Union's Horizon 2020 research and innovation program under grant agreement No. 871259 (ADMORPH project). We thank the reviewers for their suggestions on improving this paper.

References

1. Asghari, S.A., Binesh Marvasti, M., Rahmani, A.M.: Enhancing transient fault tolerance in embedded systems through an OS task level redundancy approach. Future Gener. Comput. Syst. **87** (2018). https://doi.org/10.1016/j.future.2018.04.049

2. Bengtsson, J., Larsen, K., Larsson, F., Pettersson, P., Yi, W.: UPPAAL—a tool suite for automatic verification of real-time systems. In: Alur, R., Henzinger, T.A., Sontag, E.D. (eds.) HS 1995. LNCS, vol. 1066, pp. 232–243. Springer, Heidelberg (1996). https://doi.org/10.1007/BFb0020949

3. Bernat, G., Burns, A., Liamosi, A.: Weakly hard real-time systems. IEEE Trans. Comput. **50**(4), 308–321 (2001)

4. Broster, I., Burns, A., Rodriguez-Navas, G.: Timing analysis of real-time communication under electromagnetic interference. Real-Time Syst. **30**(1–2), 55–81 (2005)

5. Bulychev, P., et al.: UPPAAL-SMC: statistical model checking for priced timed automata. arXiv e-prints (2012)

6. Chang, J., Reis, G.A., August, D.I.: Automatic instruction-level software-only recovery. IEEE (2006)

7. Chen, K.H., Bönninghoff, B., Chen, J.J., Marwedel, P.: Compensate or ignore? Meeting control robustness requirements through adaptive soft-error handling. In: LCTES 2016. Association for Computing Machinery, New York (2016). https://doi.org/10.1145/2907950.2907952

8. Choi, H., Kim, H., Zhu, Q.: Job-class-level fixed priority scheduling of weakly-hard real-time systems (2019). https://doi.org/10.1109/RTAS.2019.00028

9. Dick, R., Rhodes, D., Wolf, W.: TGFF: task graphs for free (1998). https://doi.org/10.1109/HSC.1998.666245

10. Gujarati, A., Nasri, M., Brandenburg, B.B.: Quantifying the resiliency of fail-operational real-time networked control systems. In: Leibniz International Proceedings in Informatics (LIPIcs), vol. 106. Schloss Dagstuhl–Leibniz-Zentrum fuer Informatik, Dagstuhl, Germany (2018). https://doi.org/10.4230/LIPIcs.ECRTS.2018.16

11. Lyons, R.E., Vanderkulk, W.: The use of triple-modular redundancy to improve computer reliability. IBM J. Res. Dev. **6**(2), 200–209 (1962)

12. Oz, I., Arslan, S.: A survey on multithreading alternatives for soft error fault tolerance. ACM Comput. Surv. **52**, 1–38 (2019)

13. Pathan, R.M.: Fault-tolerant and real-time scheduling for mixed-criticality systems. Real-Time Syst. **50**(4), 509–547 (2014). https://doi.org/10.1007/s11241-014-9202-z

A Program Slicer for Java (Tool Paper)

Carlos Galindo[✉][iD], Sergio Perez[iD], and Josep Silva[iD]

Departamento de Sistemas Informáticos y Computación, Universitat Politècnica de València, Camino de Vera s/n, 46022 Valencia, Spain
cargaji@vrain.upv.es, {serperu,jsilva}@dsic.upv.es

Abstract. Program slicing is a static analysis technique used in debugging, compiler optimization, program parallelization, and program specialization. However, current implementations for Java are proprietary software, pay-per-use, and closed source. Most public and open-source implementations for Java are not maintained anymore or they are obsolete because they do not cover novel Java features or they do not implement advanced techniques for the treatment of objects, exceptions, and unconditional jumps. This paper presents *JavaSlicer*, a public and open-source tool written in Java for slicing Java programs, which supports the aforementioned features. We present its usage, architecture, and performance.

Keywords: Program slicing · System Dependence Graph · Tool paper

1 Introduction

Program slicing is a static analysis technique used to automatically identify *what parts of a program may affect the value of a variable at a given position* (static backward slicing) or *what parts of a program may be affected by the value of a variable at a given position* (static forward slicing). The program point of interest (a set of variables in a line) is known as *slicing criterion*. The output, or *slice*, is the subset of the program that affects the slicing criterion.

Program slicing can be likened to automated scissors for code: given a pattern to target (a slicing criterion) it will remove all the code that is not relevant to that pattern. Consider Fig. 1, in which a very simple program has been sliced. The criterion ⟨10, *sum*⟩ indicates that we are interested in the elements that affect the value of the variable *sum* at line 10. The resulting slice has removed the lines used to compute *prod* because they have no influence on *sum*.

This work has been partially supported by the EU (FEDER) and the Spanish MCI/AEI under grant PID2019-104735RB-C41, by the *Generalitat Valenciana* under grant Prometeo/2019/098 (DeepTrust), and by TAILOR, a project funded by EU Horizon 2020 research and innovation programme under GA No 952215. Sergio Pérez was partially supported by Universitat Politècnica de València under FPI grant PAID-01-18. Carlos Galindo was partially supported by the Spanish Ministerio de Universidades under grant FPU20/03861.

B.-H. Schlingloff and M. Chai (Eds.): SEFM 2022, LNCS 13550, pp. 146–151, 2022.
https://doi.org/10.1007/978-3-031-17108-6_9

```
1   void f(int n, int m) {          7       prod *= n;
2     int sum = 0;                   8       i++;
3     int prod = 0;                  9   }
4     int i = 0;                     10    log(sum);
5     while (i < m) {                11    log(prod);
6       sum += n;                    12  }
```

Fig. 1. A simple Java program and its slice w.r.t. ⟨10, *sum*⟩ (in black).

Program slicing is particularly useful for debugging (where the slicing criterion is a variable containing an incorrect value and, thus, the slice must contain
the bug), but there are many other applications such as program specialization,
and program parallelisation. Unfortunately, currently, there does not exist a public and open-source program slicer for modern Java since the existing ones are
obsolete or proprietary. For instance, there does not exist a plug-in for IntelliJ
IDEA or Eclipse, two of the most popular Java IDEs in the market.

JavaSlicer is a library and terminal client that creates slices for Java programs, using the System Dependence Graph (SDG). Its current version is
JavaSlicer 1.3.1 (aka *scissorhands*). In this paper, we present its usage, structure,
underlying architecture, and performance.

2   Background

The most common data structure used to slice a program is the System Dependence Graph (SDG) [3], a directed graph that represents program statements as
nodes and the dependences between them as edges. Once built, a slice can be
computed in linear time as a graph reachability problem by selecting the node
that represents the slicing criterion and traversing the edges backwards/forwards
(for a backward/forward slice, respectively).

The SDG itself is built from a sequence of graphs: each method is used
to compute a Control-Flow Graph (CFG), then control and flow (aka data)
dependences are computed and they are stored in a Program Dependence Graph
(PDG). Finally, the calls in each PDG are connected to their corresponding
declarations to form the SDG, making it the union of all the PDGs.

To compute a slice, the slicing criterion is located, and then a two-phase
traversal process is used (so that the context of each call is preserved), which
produces a set of nodes that can then be converted back to code or processed in
other ways.

3   Producing Slices with *JavaSlicer*

JavaSlicer is a very sophisticated tool that implements the SDG and its corresponding slicing algorithms with advanced treatment for object-oriented (OO)
features [5], exception handling [1], and unconditional jumps [4] (in Java, break,

continue, `return` and `throw` are unconditional jumps). It includes novel techniques that improve the until now most advanced representation of OO programs, the *JSysDG* [2]. It is free/libre software and is publicly available at https://github.com/mistupv/JavaSlicer under the AGPL license. The sources can be built by using maven (following the instructions in the README), or a prebuilt jar can be downloaded from the releases page[1].

With the *sdg-cli.jar* file, an installation of Java 11 or later, and the Java sources that are to be sliced, producing a slice for is a simple task. E.g., for a file called *Example.java* and the slicing criterion $\langle 10, x \rangle$, the command would be:

```
$ java -jar sdg-cli.jar -c Example.java:10#x
```

The slice will be placed in a *slice* folder (which will be created if it does not already exist). The parameter `--output` or `-o` can set the output directory to any other location. The slicing criterion is given using the `--criterion` or `-c` parameter, with the following format: `FILE:LINE#VAR`. Alternatively, the criterion can be split into the `--file`, `--line`, and `--var` parameters.

3.1 Slicing More Than One File

Most non-trivial programs are spread across multiple files, so it is also possible to produce slices w.r.t. a whole project. An additional parameter (`--include` or `-i`) must be passed so that a SDG is generated with all the files that make up the program. Assuming that the project is inside *src* and that the slicing criterion is $\langle 10, x \rangle$ in *src/Main.java*, the command would be:

```
$ java -jar sdg-cli.jar -i src -c src/Main.java:10#x
```

Any file from the project from which statements are included in the slice will appear in the *slice* folder. If the project is spread across multiple modules, they can be concatenated with commas (i.e., `-i x/src,y/src`).

3.2 Slicing with External Libraries

A limitation of *JavaSlicer* is that the project must be compilable, so any external dependency must be included either in the SDG (as shown in the previous section) or added to Java's classpath. To do so, we can use the `-cp` parameter, concatenating multiple libraries with semicolons. For example, to slice a small program that depends on *JGraphT* with slicing criterion $\langle 25, res \rangle$, the command would be:

```
$ java -cp jgrapht-1.5.0.jar -jar sdg-cli.jar -c Graphing.java:25#res
```

---

[1] Available at https://github.com/mistupv/JavaSlicer/releases.

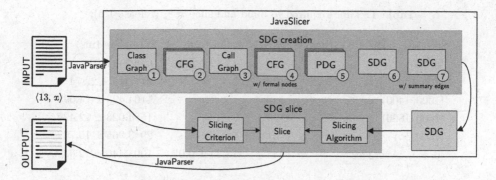

Fig. 2. Sequence of events that slice a program in *JavaSlicer*.

Of course, transitive dependencies must also be included (in our case, we would need to include *JGraphT*'s dependencies).

Each module, library, and dependency in a project must be included via `-i` or `-cp`. However, the SDG's behaviour changes in each. With the former, the files are included in the SDG (they are parsed, analysed, its dependences are computed, etc.), increasing precision but making the analysis take longer and more memory. The latter does not take into account the body of each function, speeding up the process at the cost of some precision. This gives the user the freedom of including/excluding specific libraries from the analysis.

4   Implementation

JavaSlicer is a Java project with 9.3K LOC[2] in two modules:

sdg-core: The main program slicing library, which contains multiple variants of the SDG with their corresponding slicing algorithms.
sdg-cli: A simple client that uses the core library to produce slices.

The main module contains all the data structures and algorithms required to run the slicer. Slicing a program with the library is as simple as creating a new SDG, building it with the parsed source code, and slicing it w.r.t. a slicing criterion. Internally, the construction of the SDG follows a 7-step process: (1) Compute the class graph (connecting classes, their parents and members) from the parsed sources. (2) Compute the control-flow arcs to create a CFG for each method in the program. (3) Compute the call graph, which represents methods as nodes and calls between them as edges. (4) Perform a data-flow analysis to locate the formal-in and formal-out variables, adding markers to the CFG such that formal nodes will be placed in the PDG. (5) Compute control and data dependence for each CFG, creating its corresponding PDG. (6) Transform the PDGs into the associated SDGs, connecting each call site to its corresponding

---

[2] Measured at release 1.3.1, excluding whitespace and comments, measured with `cloc`.

Table 1. Time required to build and slice *re2j* (release 1.6).

Slice size range (SDG nodes)	# SCs	Build time (s)	Slice time (ms)
[0, 100)	49	13.35 ± 0.07	0.927 ± 0.018
[100, 1000)	95		217.315 ± 2.874
[1000, 1400)	122		1164.423 ± 13.093
[1400, 1800)	146		1584.023 ± 12.429
[1800, ∞)	31		2943.965 ± 15.702
[0, ∞) - Averages	443	13.35 ± 0.07	1095.440 ± 12.039

declaration (using the call graph). (7) Compute the summary arcs between each pair of actual-in and actual-out nodes that belong to the same call.

Finally, the graph can be stored for repeated use or a slice can be generated. Each child class of SDG contains a reference to the correct slicing algorithm required to slice it. The user only has to provide enough information to locate the node(s) that represent the slicing criterion (via an instance of *SlicingCriterion*). The resulting slice is a set of nodes from the SDG, that can be studied as-is or converted back to source code via *JavaParser*.

Figure 2 summarises the process through which the source code and slicing criterion are employed to build and slice the SDG.

5   Empirical Evaluation

To evaluate the capabilities and performance of our tool, we chose *re2j*, a Java library written by Google to handle regular expressions. It contains 8.1K LOC across 19 Java files. We generated the SDG and then sliced it once per return statement (using the value being returned as the slicing criterion). In total we performed 443 slices. We repeated each action a hundred times to obtain the average execution time with error margins (99% confidence).

The results are summarised in Table 1. To show more relevant values, we grouped the slices by slice size, showing that the time required to slice scales linearly with the number of nodes traversed. Our tool produces slices between one and four orders of magnitude faster than it builds the SDG, which is expected and fits well into the typical usage of program slicers, in which the graph is built once and sliced multiple times. The amount of time dedicated to each phase in the creation of the graph can be seen in Fig. 3.

6   Related Work

The most similar tool in the state of the art is Codesonar, a proprietary tool for C, C++, and Java, that is being sold by *grammatech*©. On the public side, unfortunately, most Java slicers have been abandoned. For instance, Kaveri is an Eclipse plug-in that contains a program slicer, but it has not been updated since

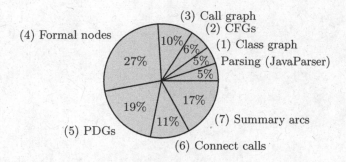

Fig. 3. Breakdown of the time dedicated to each step of the creation of the SDG.

2014 (8 years) and cannot work with maintained releases of Eclipse. The reason is, probably, the difficulty of dealing with the new features of Java (functional interfaces, lambda expressions, record types, sealed classes, etc.). There is still, however, a public program slicer maintained for Java: the slicer contained in the WALA (T. J. Watson Libraries for Analysis, for Java and JavaScript) libraries. Unfortunately, this slicer does not implement the advanced extensions of the SDG for object-oriented (OO) features, such as inclusion polymorphism, [5], exception handling [1], and unconditional jumps [4].

7   Conclusions

JavaSlicer is a novel free-software program slicing tool for Java. It efficiently implements the most advanced extensions of the SDG, including all the JSysDG extensions for object-oriented programs (inheritance, interfaces, polymorphism, etc.); specific exception handling treatment (`throw`, `try-catch`, etc.); and unconditional jumps (`return`, `break`, `continue`, etc.). It is both a library that can be used by other systems, and a standard program slicing tool.

References

1. Allen, M., Horwitz, S.: Slicing Java programs that throw and catch exceptions. SIGPLAN Not. **38**(10), 44–54 (2003)
2. Galindo, C., Pérez, S., Silva, J.: Data dependencies in object-oriented programs. In: 11th Workshop on Tools for Automatic Program Analysis (2020)
3. Horwitz, S., Reps, T., Binkley, D.: Interprocedural slicing using dependence graphs. In: Proceedings of the ACM SIGPLAN 1988 Conference on Programming Language Design and Implementation, PLDI 1988, pp. 35–46. ACM, New York (1988). https://doi.org/10.1145/53990.53994
4. Kumar, S., Horwitz, S.: Better slicing of programs with jumps and switches. In: Kutsche, R.-D., Weber, H. (eds.) FASE 2002. LNCS, vol. 2306, pp. 96–112. Springer, Heidelberg (2002). https://doi.org/10.1007/3-540-45923-5_7
5. Walkinshaw, N., Roper, M., Wood, M.: The Java system dependence graph. In: Proceedings Third IEEE International Workshop on Source Code Analysis and Manipulation, pp. 55–64 (2003)

Formal Methods for Intelligent and Learning Systems

Constrained Training of Recurrent Neural Networks for Automata Learning

Bernhard K. Aichernig[1] , Sandra König[2] , Cristinel Mateis[2] ,
Andrea Pferscher[1](✉) , Dominik Schmidt[2] , and Martin Tappler[1,3]

[1] Institute of Software Technology, Graz University of Technology, Graz, Austria
{aichernig,andrea.pferscher,martin.tappler}@ist.tugraz.at
[2] AIT Austrian Institute of Technology, Vienna, Austria
{sandra.koenig,cristinel.mateis}@ait.ac.at, t-dschmidt@microsoft.com
[3] Silicon Austria Labs, TU Graz - SAL DES Lab, Graz, Austria

Abstract. In this paper, we present a novel approach to learning finite automata with the help of recurrent neural networks. Our goal is not only to train a neural network that predicts the observable behavior of an automaton but also to learn its structure, including the set of states and transitions. In contrast to previous work, we constrain the training with a specific regularization term. We evaluate our approach with standard examples from the automata learning literature, but also include a case study of learning the finite-state models of real Bluetooth Low Energy protocol implementations. The results show that we can find an appropriate architecture to learn the correct automata in all considered cases.

Keywords: Automata learning · Machine learning · Recurrent neural networks · Bluetooth Low Energy · Model inference

1 Introduction

Models are at the heart of any engineering discipline. They capture the necessary abstractions to master the complexity in a systematic design and development process. In software engineering, models are used for a variety of tasks, including specification, design, code-generation, verification, and testing. In formal methods, these models are given formal mathematical semantics to reach the highest assurance levels. This is achieved through (automated) *deduction*, i.e. the reasoning about specific properties of a general model.

With the advent of machine learning, there has been a growing interest in the *induction* of models, i.e. the learning of formal models from data. We have seen techniques to learn deterministic and non-deterministic finite state machines, Mealy machines, Timed Automata, and Markov decision processes. In this research, called automata learning [10], model learning [1], or model inference [11], specific algorithms have been developed that either start from given data (passive learning) [25] or actively query a system during learning

B.-H. Schlingloff and M. Chai (Eds.): SEFM 2022, LNCS 13550, pp. 155–172, 2022.
https://doi.org/10.1007/978-3-031-17108-6_10

(active learning) [2]. Two prominent libraries that implement such algorithms are AALpy [21] and LearnLib [12].

An alternative to specific algorithms is to map the automata learning problem to another domain. For example, it was shown that the learning problem can be encoded as SAT [8] or SMT [29,30] problem, and then it is the task of the respective solver to find a model out of the given data.

In this work, we ask the question if machine learning can be exploited for automata learning. That is, we research if and how the problem of automata learning can be mapped to a machine learning architecture. Our results show that a specific recurrent neural network (RNN) architecture is able to learn a Mealy machine from given data. Specifically, we approach the classic NP-complete problem of inducing an automaton with at most k states that is consistent with a finite sample of a regular language [6].

The main contributions are: (i) a novel architecture for automata learning by enhancing classical RNNs, (ii) a specific constrained training approach exploiting regularization, (iii) a systematic evaluation with standard grammatical inference problems and a real-world case study, and (iv) evidence that we can find an appropriate architecture to learn the correct automata in all considered cases.

The rest of the paper is structured as follows. Section 2 introduces preliminary work. In Sect. 3, we present our automata learning technique based on RNNs. Section 4 discusses the results of the conducted case studies. We compare to related work in Sect. 5, followed by concluding remarks in Sect. 6.

2   Preliminaries

2.1   Recurrent Neural Networks

Recurrent Neural Networks (RNNs) are a popular choice for modeling sequential data, such as time-series data [5]. The classical version of an RNN with feedback from a hidden layer to itself is known as vanilla RNN [17].

A *vanilla recurrent neural network* with input x and output y is defined as

$$h^{<t>} = f(W_{hx}x^{<t>} + W_{hh}h^{<t-1>} + b_h)$$
$$\hat{y}^{<t>} = g(W_y h^{<t>} + b_y)$$

where f and g are activation functions for the recurrent and the output layer, respectively. Popular activation functions for the recurrent layer are rectified linear unit ($ReLU$) and hyperbolic tangent ($tanh$), whereas the *softmax* function may be used for g when categorial output values shall be predicted. The parameters, aka weights, $\Theta = (W_{hx}, W_{hh}, b_h, W_y, b_y)$ need to be learned. The input to the network at time step t is $x^{<t>}$, whereas $\hat{y}^{<t>}$ is the corresponding network's prediction. $h^{<t>}$ is referred to as the hidden state of the network and is used by the network to access information from past time steps or equivalently, pass relevant information from the current time step to future steps.

An RNN maps an input sequence $\mathbf{x}$ to an output sequence $\hat{y}$ of the same length. It is trained based on training data $\{(\mathbf{x}_1, \mathbf{y}_1), \ldots, (\mathbf{x}_m, \mathbf{y}_m)\}$ containing

m sequence pairs. While processing input sequences $\mathbf{x}_i = (x_i^{<1>}, \ldots, x_i^{<n>})$, values of the parameters Θ are learned that minimize the error between the true outputs $\mathbf{y}_i = (y_i^{<1>}, \ldots, y_i^{<n>})$ and the network's predictions $(\hat{y}_i^{<1>}, \ldots, \hat{y}_i^{<n>})$.

The error is measured through a predefined loss function. The most popular loss functions are the mean squared error for real-valued $y^{<t>}$, and the cross-entropy loss for categorical $y^{<t>}$. Gradient-based methods are used to minimize the error by iteratively changing each weight in proportion to the derivative of the actual error with respect to that weight until the error falls below a predefined threshold for a fixed number of iterations.

2.2   Finite State Machines

We consider finite-state machines (FSMs) in the form of Mealy machines:

Definition 1. *A **Mealy machine** is a 6-tuple $\langle Q, q_0, I, O, \delta, \lambda \rangle$ where*

- *Q is a finite set of states containing the initial state q_0,*
- *I and O are finite sets of input and output symbols,*
- *$\delta : Q \times I \to Q$ is the state transition function, and*
- *$\lambda : Q \times I \to O$ is the output function.*

Starting from a fixed initial state, a Mealy machine $\mathcal{M}$ responds to inputs $i \in I$, by changing its state according to δ and producing outputs $o \in O$ according to λ. Given an input sequence $\mathbf{i} \in I^*$, $\mathcal{M}$ produces an output sequence $\mathbf{o} = \lambda^*(q_0, \mathbf{i})$, where $\lambda^*(q, \epsilon) = \epsilon$ for the empty sequence ϵ and $\lambda^*(q, i \cdot \mathbf{i}) = \lambda(q, i) \cdot \lambda^*(\delta(q, i), \mathbf{i})$, i is an input, $\mathbf{i}$ is an input sequence, and $\cdot$ denotes concatenation. Given input and output sequences $\mathbf{i}$ and $\mathbf{o}$ of the same length, we use $t(\mathbf{i}, \mathbf{o})$ to create a sequence of input-output pairs in $(I \times O)^*$. We call such a sequence of pairs a *trace*.

A Mealy machine $\mathcal{M}$ defines a regular language over $I \times O$: $L(\mathcal{M}) = \{t(\mathbf{i}, \mathbf{o}) \mid \mathbf{i} \in I^*, \mathbf{o} = \lambda^*(q_0, \mathbf{i})\} \subseteq (I \times O)^*$. The language contains the deterministic response to any input sequence and excludes all other sequences. We can now formalize the problem that we tackle in this paper: *Given a finite set of traces $S \subset (I \times O)^*$, we learn a Mealy machine $\mathcal{M}$ with at most n states such that $S \subseteq L(\mathcal{M})$, by training an RNN.* This is a classic NP-complete problem in grammatical inference [6]. Usually, it is stated for deterministic finite automata (DFAs), but any DFA can be represented by a Mealy machine with *true* and *false* as outputs, denoting whether a word (input sequence) is accepted.

2.3   Automata Learning

Automata learning creates behavioral FSMs of black-box systems. Figure 1 illustrates the general framework for learning a reactive system model in the form of a Mealy machine. The goal of automata learning is to create a model $\mathcal{M}$ such that $L(\mathcal{M}) = L(\mathcal{M}_{\text{SUL}})$, where $\mathcal{M}_{\text{SUL}}$ is an unknown Mealy machine representing the System Under Learning (SUL).

We distinguish between active and passive learning algorithms. Passive learning creates a behavioral model from a given set of traces. To learn a Mealy

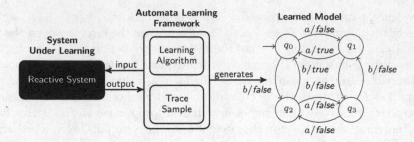

Fig. 1. The automata learning framework creates from a sample of traces a Mealy machine. The sample is generated from the executions of inputs on the reactive system.

machine $\mathcal{M}_P$, passive learning infers from a finite set of traces $S \subset (I \times O)^*$ a model $\mathcal{M}_P$ such that $S \subseteq L(\mathcal{M}_P)$, often restricting $\mathcal{M}_P$ to have at most k states. Given that $S \subseteq L(\mathcal{M}_{\mathrm{SUL}})$, most algorithms guarantee $L(\mathcal{M}_P) = L(\mathcal{M}_{\mathrm{SUL}})$ for large enough S and finite $\mathcal{M}_{\mathrm{SUL}}$ [9]. One challenge in the application of passive learning is to provide a finite set of traces such that $L(\mathcal{M}_P) = L(\mathcal{M}_{\mathrm{SUL}})$.

Active automata learning queries the SUL to create a behavioral model. Many active learning algorithms are based on the L^* algorithm [2] which is defined for different modeling formalisms like Mealy machines [28]. L^* queries the SUL to generate a finite set of traces $S \subset (I \times O)^*$ from which a hypothesis Mealy machine $\mathcal{M}_A$ is constructed that fulfills $S \subseteq L(\mathcal{M}_A)$. L^* guarantees that the $\mathcal{M}_A$ is minimal. The hypothesis $\mathcal{M}_A$ is then checked for equivalence to the language $L(\mathcal{M}_{\mathrm{SUL}})$. Since $\mathcal{M}_{\mathrm{SUL}}$ is unknown, checking the behavioral equivalence between $\mathcal{M}_{\mathrm{SUL}}$ and $\mathcal{M}_A$ is generally undecidable. Hence, conformance testing is used to substitute the equivalence oracle in active learning. Model-based testing techniques generate a finite set of traces $S_T \subset (I \times O)^*$ from executions on $\mathcal{M}_A$ and check if $S_T \subset L(\mathcal{M}_{\mathrm{SUL}})$. If $t(\mathbf{i}, \mathbf{o}) \notin L(\mathcal{M}_{\mathrm{SUL}})$, a counterexample to the behavioral equivalence between $\mathcal{M}_{\mathrm{SUL}}$ and $\mathcal{M}_A$ is found. Based on this trace, the set of traces $S \subset (I \times O)^*$ is extended by performing further queries. Again a hypothesis $\mathcal{M}_A$ is created and checked for equivalence. This procedure repeats until no counterexample to the equivalence between $L(\mathcal{M}_{\mathrm{SUL}})$ and $L(\mathcal{M}_A)$ can be found. The algorithm then returns the learned automaton $\mathcal{M}_A$. Note that L^* creates $\mathcal{M}_A$ such that $S \subset L(\mathcal{M}_A)$. With access to a perfect behavioral equivalence check between $\mathcal{M}_{\mathrm{SUL}}$ and $\mathcal{M}_A$, we could guarantee that the generated finite set of traces S enables learning a model $\mathcal{M}_A$ such that $L(\mathcal{M}_A) = L(\mathcal{M}_{\mathrm{SUL}})$.

3   Automata Learning with RNNs

In this section, we first present the problem that we tackle and propose an RNN architecture as a solution. After that, we cover (i) the constrained training of the proposed RNN architecture with our specific regularization term, and (ii) the usage of the trained RNN to extract an appropriate automaton.

3.1   Overview and Architecture

It is well known that recurrent neural networks (RNNs) can be used to efficiently model time-series data, such as data generated from interaction with a Mealy machine. Concretely, this can be done by using the machine inputs $x^{<t>}$ as inputs to the RNN and minimizing the difference between the machine's true outputs $y^{<t>}$ and the RNN's predictions $\hat{y}^{<t>}$. In other words, the RNN would predict the language $L(\mathcal{M})$ of a Mealy machine $\mathcal{M}$.

This optimization process can be performed via gradient descent. Even if such a trained RNN can model all interactions with perfect accuracy, one disadvantage compared to the original automaton is that it is much less interpretable. While each state in a Mealy machine can be identified by a discrete number, the hidden state of the RNN, which is the information passed from one time step to the next one, is a continuous real-valued vector. This vector may be needlessly large and contain mostly redundant information. Thus it would be useful if we could simplify such a trained RNN into a Mealy machine $\mathcal{M}_R$ that produces the language $\mathcal{M}$ that we want to learn, i.e., with $L(\mathcal{M}) = L(\mathcal{M}_R)$.

We approach the following problem. Given a sample $S \subset L(\mathcal{M})$ of traces $t(\mathbf{i}_j, \mathbf{o}_j)$ and the number of states k of $\mathcal{M}$, we train an RNN to correctly predict $\mathbf{o}_j$ from $\mathbf{i}_j$. To facilitate interpretation, we want to extract a Mealy machine $\mathcal{M}_R$ from the trained RNN with k states, modeling the same language. For $\mathcal{M}_R$, $S \subset L(\mathcal{M}_R)$ shall hold such that for large enough S we have $L(\mathcal{M}) = L(\mathcal{M}_R)$.

For this purpose, we propose an RNN architecture and learning procedure that ensure that the RNN hidden states can be cleanly translated into k discrete automata states. Compared to standard vanilla RNNs, the hidden states are transformed into an estimate of a categorical distribution over the k possible automaton states. This restricts the encoding of information in the hidden states since now all components need to be in the range $[0, 1]$ and sum up to 1. Figure 2 shows our complete RNN cell architecture, implementing the following equations.

$$h^{<t>} = af(W_{hx}x^{<t>} + W_{hs}s^{<t-1>} + b_h), \quad af \in \{ReLU, tanh\}$$
$$\hat{y}^{<t>} = softmax(W_y h^{<t>} + b_y)$$
$$\hat{s}^{<t>} = softmax(W_s h^{<t>} + b_s)$$
$$s^{<t>} = \begin{cases} softmax(W_s h^{<t>} + b_s), & \text{if mode} = \text{``train''} \\ hardmax(W_s h^{<t>} + b_s), & \text{else (i.e. mode} = \text{``infer''}) \end{cases}$$

In comparison to vanilla RNN cells, the complete hidden state $h^{<t>}$ is only an intermediate vector of values. Based on $h^{<t>}$, an output $\hat{y}^{<t>}$ is predicted using a softmax activation. A Mealy machine state $\hat{s}^{<t>}$ is predicted as well and passed to the next time step. It is computed via (i) softmax during RNN training, and (ii) via hardmax during inference. During training, we also compute the cross-entropy of $\hat{s}^{<t>}$ with $hardmax(\hat{s}^{<t>})$ as a label, which serves as a regularization term. Inference refers to extracting an automaton from the trained RNN, which takes as input the current system state and an input symbol and gives as output

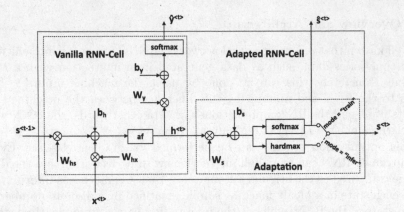

Fig. 2. RNN-cell architecture

the next system state and an output symbol. Hence, we use softmax to estimate a categorial distribution over possible states for training, whereas we use hardmax to concretely infer one state during inference.

Our algorithm for extracting a Mealy machine from a trained RNN is based on the idea that if the RNN achieves near-perfect accuracy when predicting the machine's true outputs, the hidden state $h^{<t>}$ encodes information corresponding to the state of a Mealy machine at time step t. Otherwise, the RNN would not be able to predict the expected outputs correctly, since those are a function of both the input and the current state. By adapting the RNN architecture, we enforce hidden states to correspond to discrete Mealy machine states.

3.2 Training and Automaton Extraction

In the following, we first discuss how to train an RNN with the structure shown in Fig. 2 such that it will encode an automaton. Secondly, we show how to extract the automaton from a trained RNN. We start by illustrating the basic operation of such an RNN, i.e., the prediction of an output sequence and a state sequence from an input sequence. This is called the *forward pass* and is used during training and automaton extraction.

Forward Pass. Algorithm 1 implements the forward pass taking an input sequence $\mathbf{x}$ and a mode variable as parameters. The mode variable distinguishes between training (*train*) and automaton extraction (*infer*). The algorithm returns a pair $(\hat{\mathbf{y}}, \hat{\mathbf{s}})$ comprising the predicted output sequence and the sequence of hidden states visited by the forward pass. We want to learn the language of a Mealy machine, i.e., map $\mathbf{i} \in I^*$ to $\mathbf{o} \in O^*$ for sets I, O of input and output symbols. Therefore, we encode every $i \in I$ using a one-hot-encoding to yield input sequences $\mathbf{x}$ from $\mathbf{i} \in I^*$. In this encoding, every i is associated with a unique $|I|$-dimensional vector, where exactly one element is equal to one and all others are zero. We use an analogous encoding for outputs and the hidden state shall approach a one-hot encoding in a k-dimensional vector space. For

---

Algorithm 1. Model forward pass $M(x, mode)$

Input: Input sequence $\mathbf{x}$, Forward pass mode $\in$ {"train", "infer"}
Output: Pair $(\hat{\mathbf{y}}, \hat{\mathbf{s}})$ of predicted outputs and automaton states, resp.
1 $\hat{\mathbf{y}}, \hat{\mathbf{s}} = [\,], [\,]$
2 $s = one\_hot\_encoding(q_0)$
3 **for** $t \leftarrow 1$ **to** $\#steps(\mathbf{x})$ **do**
4      $h = af(W_{hx}x^{<t>} + W_{hs}s + b_h)$ $//$ $af \in \{ReLU, \tanh\}$
5      $\hat{y}^{<t>} = softmax(W_y h + b_y)$
6      $\hat{s}^{<t>} = softmax(W_s h + b_s)$
7   **if** $mode ==$ "train" **then**
8          $s = \hat{s}^{<t>}$
9   **else**
10          $s = hardmax(W_s h + b_s)$ $//$ $mode =$ "infer"
11 **return** $(\hat{\mathbf{y}}, \hat{\mathbf{s}})$

Algorithm 2. RNN Training $train(M, D)$

Input: Initialized RNN model M, Training dataset $D = \{(\mathbf{x}_1, \mathbf{y}_1), \ldots, (\mathbf{x}_m, \mathbf{y}_m)\}$, $\#epochs$,
        Regularization factor C
Output: Trained RNN model M
1 $optimizer = Adam(M)$
2 **for** $i \leftarrow 1$ **to** $\#epochs$ **do**
3      $acc_{inf} = 0$
4   **foreach** $(\mathbf{x}, \mathbf{y}) \in D$ **do**
5          $\hat{\mathbf{y}}_{inf}, \hat{\mathbf{s}}_{inf} = M(\mathbf{x}, $ "infer"$)$
6          $acc_{inf} += accuracy(\mathbf{y}, \hat{\mathbf{y}}_{inf})/|D|$
7          $\hat{\mathbf{y}}_{tr}, \hat{\mathbf{s}}_{tr} = M(\mathbf{x}, $ "train"$)$
8          $loss = cross\_entropy(\mathbf{y}, \hat{\mathbf{y}}_{tr}) + C \times cross\_entropy(hardmax(\hat{\mathbf{s}}_{tr}), \hat{\mathbf{s}}_{tr})$
9          $loss.backward()$
10          $optimizer.step()$
11   **if** $acc_{inf} = 100\%$ **then**
12   **break**
13 **return** M

---

one-hot encoded outputs, we generally use the letter y and we use D to denote one-hot-encoded training datasets derived from a sample $S \subset L(\mathcal{M})$.

Algorithm 1 initializes the output and state sequences $\hat{\mathbf{y}}$ and $\hat{\mathbf{s}}$ to the empty sequences and the hidden state s of the RNN to the one-hot encoding of the fixed initial state q_0. For every input symbol $x^{<t>}$, Line 4 to Line 10 perform the equations defining the RNN, i.e., applying affine transformation using weights and an activation function. At each step t, we compute and store the predicted output $\hat{y}^{<t>}$ (Line 5) and the predicted state $\hat{s}^{<t>}$ (Line 6) in $\hat{\mathbf{y}}$ and $\hat{\mathbf{s}}$, respectively. In the "train" mode, we pass $\hat{s}^{<t>}$ as hidden state to the next time step (Line 8). In the "infer" mode used for automaton extraction, we apply a hardmax on the hidden state (Line 10) so that exactly one state is predicted.

Training. The architecture is trained by minimizing a prediction loss between $y^{<t>}$ and $\hat{y}^{<t>}$ along with a regularization loss: the cross-entropy of the state distribution $s^{<t>}$ w.r.t. to the state with the highest probability in $s^{<t>}$. Minimizing our regularization of choice forces the RNN to increase the certainty about the predicted state. This ensures that the hidden states tend to be approximately one-hot-encoded vectors where the index of the maximal component corresponds to the state of a Mealy machine accepting the same language. Note that directly using a discrete state representation is not beneficial when training with gradient descent. Algorithm 2 implements the training in PyTorch-like [26] style. Its parameters are the training dataset D, a sample of the language to be learned, the learning epochs, and a regularization factor, which controls the influence of state regularization. The training is performed using the gradient descent-based Adam optimizer [14]. The algorithm performs up to #epochs loops over the training data. An epoch processes each trace in the training data referred to as an episode (Line 4 to Line 10). Training stops when the prediction accuracy of the RNN operated as an automaton reaches 100% or #epochs episodes have been performed. To calculate accuracy, we perform a forward pass in "infer" mode in Line 5 and compute the average accuracy in Line 6. For the actual training, we perform a forward pass in "train" mode and compute the overall loss from the prediction and state regularization losses (Line 7 and Line 8). Line 9 and 10 update the RNN parameters, i.e., the weights. Upon finishing the training, Algorithm 2 returns the trained RNN.

The purpose of the trained RNN model is not to predict outputs of new inputs, unseen during training, but to help with inferring an automaton that produces the training data. This automaton shall be used to predict the outputs corresponding to (new) inputs. Thus, we use all available data for training the RNN and aim at achieving perfect accuracy on the training data. Perfect accuracy on the training set gives us the confidence that the internal state representation of the learned RNN model corresponds to the true (partial) automaton that produced that data. In cases where the training data does not cover all states and transitions of the full true automaton, we might learn a partial automaton missing some states and transitions. Using all available data for training reduces the possibility to learn just a partial automaton.

Automaton Extraction from a Trained RNN. Given a trained RNN model, we extract the corresponding automaton with Algorithm 3. We represent the automaton of a Mealy machine by its set of transitions in the following form:

$$T = \{(s, s', i/o) \mid s, s' \in Q \land i \in I \land o \in O \land \delta(s, i) = s' \land \lambda(s, i) = o\}.$$

Algorithm 3 starts by initializing T to the empty set. Then, it iterates through all episodes, i.e., all traces, from the training set D. At each iteration (Line 3 to Line 12), it first runs the RNN model M on the one-hot encoded input sequence $\mathbf{x}$ of the current episode (Line 3) to obtain the corresponding predicted output symbols and transition state sequences $\hat{\mathbf{y}}$ and $\hat{\mathbf{s}}$, respectively. Line 4 to Line 12 iterate through all steps of the current episode. All episodes start from the initial state q_0 which, by construction, is assigned the label 0. Thus, we initialize the first state to 0 (Line 4). If the predicted output symbol matches the label at the current step (Line 8), then T is extended by a triple encoding a transition, which is built from the starting/ending states and the input/output symbols of the current step. By applying $argmax$ on the one-hot encoded input $x^{<t>}$ and

---

Algorithm 3. Automaton extraction from RNN $extract(M, D)$

Input: Trained RNN model M, Training data $D = \{(\mathbf{x}_1, \mathbf{y}_1), \ldots, (\mathbf{x}_m, \mathbf{y}_m)\}$
Output: Automaton transitions T

1   $T \leftarrow \{\}$
2   **foreach** $episode = (\mathbf{x}, \mathbf{y}) \in D$ **do**
3     $(\hat{\mathbf{y}}, \hat{\mathbf{s}}) = M(\mathbf{x}, \text{"infer"})$
4     $s\_from, s\_to = 0$
5   **for** $t \leftarrow 1$ **to** $\#steps(episode)$ **do**
6       $s\_to = argmax(\hat{s}^{<t>})$
7       $in, out = argmax(x^{<t>}), argmax(y^{<t>})$
8   **if** $out = argmax(\hat{y}^{<t>})$ **then**
9        $T = T \cup \{(s\_from, s\_to, in/out)\}$
10   **else**
11   **break**
12      $s\_from = s\_to$
13   **return** T

Table 1. Description of Tomita Grammars.

Grammar	Description	# States
Tomita 1	strings of the form 1^*	2
Tomita 2	strings of the form $(1\ 0)^*$	4
Tomita 3	strings that do not include an odd number of consecutive 0 symbols Following an odd number of consecutive 1 symbols	5
Tomita 4	strings without more than 2 consecutive 0 symbols	4
Tomita 5	even strings with an even number of 0 and 1 symbols	4
Tomita 6	strings where the difference between the numbers of 0s and 1s is divisible by three	3
Tomita 7	strings of the form $0^*1^*0^*1^*$	5

output $y^{<t>}$ we get integer-valued discrete representations of them[1] (Line 7). If the predicted output does not match the expected value, the current and remaining steps of the current episode are ignored and the algorithm moves to the next episode (Line 2). Note that an episode consists of a sequence of adjacent steps (or transitions) in the automaton, that is, the next step starts from the state where the current step ended (Line 12). After processing all training data traces, Algorithm 3 returns the extracted automaton with transitions T.

4 Case Studies

4.1 Case Study Subjects

Tomita Grammars. We use Tomita Grammars [32] to evaluate our approach. These grammars are popular subjects in the evaluation of formal-language-

---

[1] The actual corresponding input, resp. output, symbol is obtained from the input, resp. output, symbol alphabet through an appropriate indexed mapping. For simplicity, we don't show this mapping here.

Table 2. Investigated BLE devices including the running application. The states indicate the state number of the models created by from active automata learning.

Manufacturer (board)	System-on-Chip	Application	# States
Texas instruments (LAUNCHXL-CC2650)	CC2650	Project zero	5
Cypress (CY8CPROTO-063-BLE)	CYBLE-416045-02	Find me target	3
Nordic (decaWave DWM1001-DEV)	nRF52832	Nordic GATTS	5

related work on RNNs [22,23,33], as they possess various features, while they are small enough to facilitate manual analysis. All of the grammars are defined over the input symbols 0 and 1. We transformed the ground-truth Deterministic Finite Automata (DFAs) into Mealy machines, thus the outputs are either *true* (string accepted) or *false* (string not accepted). Table 1 contains for each Tomita grammar a short description of the accepted strings and the number of states of the smallest Mealy machine accepting the corresponding language. For example, Tomita 5 accepts strings depending on parity of 0 and 1 symbols. The same language has been used to illustrate the L^* algorithm [2]. Automata accepting such languages are hard to encode using certain types of RNNs [7].

Bluetooth Low Energy (BLE). To evaluate the applicability to practical problems, we consider the BLE protocol. BLE was introduced in the Bluetooth standard 4.0 as a communication protocol for low-energy devices. The BLE protocol stack implementation is different from the Bluetooth classic protocol. Pferscher and Aichernig [27] learned with L^* behavioral models of BLE devices. They presented practical challenges in the creation of an interface to enable the interaction required by active automata learning. Especially, the requirement of adequately resetting the device after each performed query raises the need for a learning technique that requires less interaction with the SUL. We selected three devices from their case study. The selected devices have a similarly large state space and show more stable deterministic behavior than other devices in the case study by Pferscher and Aichernig [27] which would have required advanced data processing that filters out non-deterministic behavior. Table 2 states the investigated devices, the used System-on-Chip, and the running application. In the following, we refer to the devices by the Systems-on-Chip name. The running application initially sends BLE advertisements and accepts a connection with another BLE device. If a connection terminates, the device again sends advertisements. The generated behavioral model should formalize the implemented connection procedure. Compared to existing work [27], we extended the considered nine inputs by another input that implements the termination indication, which indicates the termination of the connection by one of the two devices. Since every input must be defined for every state, the complexity of learning increases with the size of the input alphabet. Hence, the BLE case study provides a first impression of the scalability of our presented learning technique.

Figure 3 depicts a behavioral model of the CYBLE-416045-02. Some input and output labels have been simplified by a '+'-symbol. The model shows that

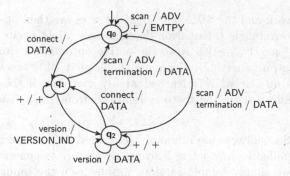

Fig. 3. Simplified model of the CYBLE-416045-02 ('+' abbreviates inputs/outputs).

a connection can be established with a connection request and terminated by a scan request or termination indication. A version indication is only answered once during an active connection. Pferscher and Aichernig [27] provide a link to complete models of all three considered examples.

4.2   Experimental Setup

We demonstrate the effectiveness of our approach on both (i) the canonical Tomita grammars used in the literature [4,22,33], and (ii) the physical BLE devices introduced in the previous section. We consider the automata learned with the active automata learning (AAL) algorithm L^* and the corresponding data produced by AAL as given. We call these the AAL automata and AAL data, respectively. In general, we do not require AAL to be executed in advance. AAL rather provides an outline for the evaluation of our proposed RNN architecture. The number of states k of the AAL automata is used to set the size of s in the RNN architecture. The AAL automaton itself is only used as ground truth. It does not affect the RNN training procedure in any way other than defining the size of s. We say that the RNN learned the correct automaton if the automaton extracted from the trained RNN according to Algorithm 3 is the same as the AAL automaton, modulo some states relabelling.

AAL Data. Firstly, we use the AAL data as RNN training data. This finite set of traces from AAL is complete in the sense that passive automata learning could learn a behavioral model that conforms to the model learned by AAL. For AAL data generation, we used the active automata learning library AALpy [21], which implements state-of-the-art algorithms including the L^*-algorithm variant for Mealy machines by Shahbaz and Groz [28]. The logged data includes all performed output queries and the traces generated for conformance testing during the equivalence check. The model-based testing technique used for conformance testing provides state coverage for the intermediate learned hypotheses.

For the BLE data generation, we use a similar learning framework as Pferscher and Aichernig [27]. To collect the performed output queries during automata learning, we logged the performed BLE communication between the learning framework and the SUL. The logged traces are then post-processed to exclude non-deterministic traces. Non-determinism might occur due to packet loss or delayed packets. In this case, the active automata learning framework repeated the output query. To clean up the logged BLE traces, we execute all input traces on the actively learned Mealy machine. If the observed output sequence differentiate, the trace is removed from the considered learning data set.

Random Data. Secondly, we use randomly generated data as training data. That is, we are not guided by any active learning procedure to generate the training data. Instead, we simply sample random inputs from the input alphabet and observe the outputs produced by the system, i.e. the Tomita grammars or the physical BLE devices. This corresponds to a more realistic real-world scenario where the data logged during regular system operation is the only available training data. To speed up the experiments, we use the AAL automaton instead of the real system to generate random data. More precisely, we achieve this through random walks on the AAL automaton. Each random walk represents a trace in the training data. It always starts from the initial state of the AAL automaton and collects the sequence of input-output pairs obtained by running the AAL automaton on the randomly generated inputs. We set a value max_length for the maximal length of the generated episodes.

- For Tomita grammars, we set the number of traces to be generated. At each iteration, we produce a trace through a random walk from the initial state with a length uniformly distributed within $[1, max\_length]$.
- For the BLE devices, we generate traces that simulate BLE sessions between real-world devices. For this, each trace ends with a terminate request indicating the end of the connection. Hence, we can extract such traces from a long random walk by extracting the subtraces between two subsequent terminate requests. Thus, we set the overall number of transitions n to be generated and start a random walk of length n from the initial state. At each step, we sample an input request or force a terminate request to (1) finish the walk or to (2) ensure a maximum individual trace length of max_length.

  Since each episode ends in the initial state due to the final terminate request, we exploit this knowledge during the RNN training by adding to the overall loss (s. Algorithm 2, line 8) the term $cross\_entropy(q_0, s^{<last>})$ corresponding to the deviation of the last RNN state $s^{<last>}$ from the initial state of the learned automaton, which is fixed to q_0 by construction.

For both Tomita grammars and BLE devices, we remove from the random data all duplicated traces, if any. We start with a smaller random dataset and progressively generate bigger random datasets until the RNN learns the correct automaton or a predefined time budget is consumed.

All experiments were performed with PyTorch 1.8 on a Dell Latitude 5501 laptop with Intel Hexa-Core I7-9850H, 32 GB RAM, 2.60 GHz, 512 GB SSD, NVIDIA GeForce MX150, and Windows-10 OS.

Table 3. RNN Automata Learning of Tomita Grammars. The correct automaton could be learned in all cases. Fixed parameters: #neurons per hidden layer = 256, learning rate = 0.001, C = 0.001.

Grammar	AAL Data			Random Data			
	Size	Episode Lengths {m; std}	RNN {af; #hl} {#e; t}	Size	AAL Data Coverage	Episode Lengths {m; std}	RNN {af; #hl} {#e; t}
Tomita 1	41	{8.4; 4.5}	{relu; 1} {5; 3 s}	10	3/41	{6.3; 3.3}	{relu; 1} {14; 2 s}
Tomita 2	73	{9.5; 5.3}	{tanh; 1} {9; 11 s}	38	13/73	{5.9; 3.0}	{tanh; 1} {76; 37 s}
Tomita 3	111	{10.4; 4.9}	{tanh; 2} {25; 59 s}	438	35/111	{7.7; 2.0}	{relu; 2} {26; 215 s}
Tomita 4	83	{10.4; 5.2}	{tanh; 1} {28; 45 s}	70	11/83	{6.5; 2.6}	{tanh; 1} {25; 25 s}
Tomita 5	91	{9.3; 4.7}	{relu; 1} {10; 16 s}	38	10/91	{5.9; 3.0}	{relu; 1} {25; 12 s}
Tomita 6	68	{8.6; 4.6}	{relu; 1} {7; 8 s}	14	5/68	{6.1; 3.2}	{relu; 2} {26; 6 s}
Tomita 7	115	{10.4; 5.1}	{relu; 1} {15; 33 s}	38	10/115	{5.5; 3.3}	{tanh; 1} {296; 151 s}

Table 4. RNN Automata Learning of BLE devices. The correct automaton could be learned in all cases. Fixed parameters: #neurons per hidden layer = 256, #hl = 1, af = relu, learning rate = 0.001.

Device	AAL Data			Random Data			
	Size	Episode Lengths {m; std}	RNN {C; #e; t}	Size	AAL Data Coverage	Episode Lengths {m; std}	RNN {C; #e; t}
CYBLE-416045-02	272	{4.0; 1.0}	{0.01; 8; 20 s}	75	13/272	{10.5; 7.6}	{0.01; 99; 216 s}
CC2650	473	{5.9; 2.1}	{0.001; 166; 17 m:40 s}	933	93/473	{10.1; 6.6}	{0.001; 50; 17 m:26 s}
nRF52832	447	{4.6; 1.1}	{0.001; 38; 4 m:15 s}	941	84/447	{10.0; 6.7}	{0.001; 36; 13 m:22 s}

4.3   Results and Discussion

Tables 3 and 4 illustrate the experimental results obtained by applying our approach to learn the automata of Tomita grammars and BLE devices, respectively, from both AAL data and random data. The number of traces contained in the training data is given in the column *Size* for both AAL data and random data. For the random data, it is interesting to know how many traces from the AAL data were contained also in the random data. This information is shown in the column *AAL Data Coverage* as the ratio between the number of AAL traces contained in the random data and the overall number of traces in the AAL data.

The column *Episode Lengths* contains the means and standard deviations of the lengths of the traces in the training data. The column *RNN* contains (i) the RNN architecture parameters which possibly changed across the experiments (i.e. the activation function af and the number of hidden layers #hl in Table 3 and the regularization factor C in Table 4), and (ii) the number of epochs #e and the time t required by the RNN training to learn the correct automaton.

The values of other RNN architecture parameters, which were the same in all experiments, are mentioned in the table captions. For instance, it turned out that the values 0.001 and 256 for the learning rate and the number of neurons per hidden layer, respectively, worked for all considered case studies.

For the Tomita grammars (Table 3), the value of the regularization factor C was also fixed and equal to 0.001, whereas different activation functions and numbers of hidden layers were used across the different grammars. For the BLE devices (Table 4), the number of the hidden layers and the activation function were also fixed and equal to 1 and *ReLU*, respectively, whereas different regularization factors were used across different devices.

The results show that we could find an appropriate architecture to learn the correct automata in all considered cases. This was expected when learning from AAL data, as the AAL data is fully representative for the underlying minimum automaton. More surprising is that we could learn the correct automaton also from relatively small random datasets with a low coverage of the AAL data. Even more surprising is that for all Tomita grammars, except Tomita 3, we could learn the correct automaton from random datasets which were much smaller than the AAL dataset - smaller in terms of both number of traces and average trace length. Moreover, only a small fraction of the AAL data happened to be included also in the random data. This suggests that the proposed RNN architecture and training may better generalize than AAL. The good performance on Tomita grammars might be attributed to the small number of automaton transitions and input/outputs alphabets that only consist of 0 and 1 symbols.

For the BLE device CYBLE-416045-02, which has much larger input and output alphabets, we could still learn the correct automaton from a random dataset containing fewer traces than the AAL data. The other two BLE devices required larger random datasets, approximately twice as large as the AAL dataset, due to the higher number of transitions to be covered.

For all case studies, except Tomita 3 and 6, the same RNN architecture worked for both AAL and random data. For Tomita 3, *tanh* worked for the AAL data, whereas *ReLU* worked for the random data. For Tomita 6, we needed two hidden layers for the random data, as opposed to a single hidden layer.

5   Related Work

Early work on the relationship between finite automata and neural networks dates back to Kleene, who showed that neural networks can simulate finite automata [15]. Minsky gave a general construction of neural networks that simulate finite automata [20]. In contrast, we do not simulate a known automaton, but we learn an automaton of bounded size from a sample of a regular language.

The relationship between RNNs and automata has also been exploited to explain RNN behavior, by extracting automata from RNNs. Omlin and Giles proposed an approach to construct finite automata from RNNs trained on regular languages [24]. The basis for their approach is that hidden states of RNNs form clusters, thus automata states can be identified by determining such clusters. This property was recently also used to learn deterministic finite automata (DFAs) [33] and Markov chains [4] from RNNs. Tiňo and Šajada [31] used self-organizing maps to identify clusters for modeling Mealy automata. Michalenko et al. [19] empirically analyzed this property and found that there is a correspondence between hidden-state clusters and automata states, but some clusters may overlap, i.e., some states may be indistinguishable. In contrast to relying on clustering, which may not be perfect, we enforce a clustering of the hidden states through regularization. Closest to our work in this regard is the work by Oliva and Lago-Fernández [23]. They enforce neurons with sigmoid activation to operate in a binary regime, thus leading to very dense clusters, by introducing Gaussian noise prior to applying the activation function during training.

Several approaches based on or related to the L^* algorithm [2] have been proposed recently. Weiss et al. proposed automata-learning-based approaches to extract DFAs [33], weighted automata [34], and subsets of context-free grammars from RNNs [35]. Mayr and Yovine [18] applied the L^* algorithm to extract automata from RNNs, where they provide probabilistic guarantees. Khmelnitsky et al. [13] propose a property-directed verification approach for RNNs. They use the L^* algorithm to learn automata models from RNNs and analyze these models through model checking. Dong et al. [4] also apply automata learning and verification to analyze RNNs. Muškardin et al. [22] examine the effect of different equivalence-query implementations in L^*-based learning of models from RNNs.

Koul et al. [16] introduce quantization through training of *quantized bottleneck networks* into RNNs that encode policies of autonomous agents. This allows them to extract FSMs in order to understand the memory usage of recurrent policies. Carr et al. [3] use quantized bottleneck networks to extract finite-state controllers from recurrent policies to enable formal verification.

6 Conclusion

In this work, we presented a new machine learning technique for learning finite-state models in the form of Mealy machines. Our new automata learning approach exploits a specialized RNN architecture together with a constrained training method in order to construct a minimal Mealy machine from given training data. We evaluated our method on example grammars from the literature as well as on a Bluetooth protocol implementation.

We see the encouraging results as a step towards learning more complex models comprising discrete and continuous behavior, as found in many control applications. Especially, the explainability of such hybrid systems is an open problem that could be addressed with automata learning.

In contrast to some classical passive automata learning methods, we have to know (or assume) the number of states k in advance. However, the current approach could be the starting point for learning also the minimum number of states. One possible way would be to start with a small number of states, e.g. $k = 2$, and progressively increase k until we can learn an automaton with k states which perfectly explains the training data. Another way would be to introduce a further regularization term aiming at reducing an initially overestimated value for k. We leave these investigations for future work. We will also apply our approach to case studies with larger numbers of states.

Finally, we dare to express the hope that this work might contribute to bridging the gap between the research communities in machine learning and automata learning ultimately leading to more trustworthy AI systems.

Acknowledgement. This work was collaboratively done in the TU Graz LEAD project Dependable Internet of Things in Adverse Environments project, the Learn-Twins project funded by FFG (Österreichische Forschungsförderungsgesellschaft) under grant 880852, and the "University SAL Labs" initiative of Silicon Austria Labs (SAL) and its Austrian partner universities for applied fundamental research for electronic based systems.

References

1. Aichernig, B.K., Mostowski, W., Mousavi, M.R., Tappler, M., Taromirad, M.: Model learning and model-based testing. In: Bennaceur, A., Hähnle, R., Meinke, K. (eds.) Machine Learning for Dynamic Software Analysis: Potentials and Limits. LNCS, vol. 11026, pp. 74–100. Springer, Cham (2018). https://doi.org/10.1007/978-3-319-96562-8_3
2. Angluin, D.: Learning regular sets from queries and counterexamples. Inf. Comput. **75**(2), 87–106 (1987). https://doi.org/10.1016/0890-5401(87)90052-6
3. Carr, S., Jansen, N., Topcu, U.: Verifiable RNN-based policies for POMDPs under temporal logic constraints. In: IJCAI, pp. 4121–4127. ijcai.org (2020). https://doi.org/10.24963/ijcai.2020/570
4. Dong, G., et al.: Towards interpreting recurrent neural networks through probabilistic abstraction. In: ASE, pp. 499–510. IEEE (2020). https://doi.org/10.1145/3324884.3416592
5. Elman, J.L.: Finding structure in time. Cogn. Sci. **14**(2), 179–211 (1990). https://doi.org/10.1207/s15516709cog1402_1
6. Gold, E.M.: Complexity of automaton identification from given data. Inf. Control **37**(3), 302–320 (1978). https://doi.org/10.1016/S0019-9958(78)90562-4
7. Goudreau, M.W., Giles, C.L., Chakradhar, S.T., Chen, D.: First-order versus second-order single-layer recurrent neural networks. IEEE Trans. Neural Netw. **5**(3), 511–513 (1994). https://doi.org/10.1109/72.286928
8. Heule, M., Verwer, S.: Software model synthesis using satisfiability solvers. Empir. Softw. Eng. **18**(4), 825–856 (2013)
9. de la Higuera, C.: Grammatical Inference: Learning Automata and Grammars. Cambridge University Press, New York (2010)
10. Howar, F., Steffen, B.: Active automata learning in practice. In: Bennaceur, A., Hähnle, R., Meinke, K. (eds.) Machine Learning for Dynamic Software Analysis: Potentials and Limits. LNCS, vol. 11026, pp. 123–148. Springer, Cham (2018). https://doi.org/10.1007/978-3-319-96562-8_5
11. Irfan, M.N., Oriat, C., Groz, R.: Model inference and testing. In: Advances in Computers, vol. 89, pp. 89–139. Elsevier (2013)

12. Isberner, M., Howar, F., Steffen, B.: The open-source LearnLib. In: Kroening, D., Păsăreanu, C.S. (eds.) CAV 2015, Part I. LNCS, vol. 9206, pp. 487–495. Springer, Cham (2015). https://doi.org/10.1007/978-3-319-21690-4_32
13. Khmelnitsky, I., et al.: Property-directed verification and robustness certification of recurrent neural networks. In: Hou, Z., Ganesh, V. (eds.) ATVA 2021. LNCS, vol. 12971, pp. 364–380. Springer, Cham (2021). https://doi.org/10.1007/978-3-030-88885-5_24
14. Kingma, D.P., Ba, J.: Adam: A method for stochastic optimization. In: ICLR (2015)
15. Kleene, S.C.: Representation of Events in Nerve Nets and Finite Automata. RAND Corporation, Santa Monica (1951)
16. Koul, A., Fern, A., Greydanus, S.: Learning finite state representations of recurrent policy networks. In: ICLR. OpenReview.net (2019)
17. Ma, Y., Principe, J.C.: A taxonomy for neural memory networks. IEEE Trans. Neural Netw. Learn. Syst. 31(6), 1780–1793 (2020). https://doi.org/10.1109/TNNLS.2019.2926466
18. Mayr, F., Yovine, S.: Regular inference on artificial neural networks. In: Holzinger, A., Kieseberg, P., Tjoa, A.M., Weippl, E. (eds.) CD-MAKE 2018. LNCS, vol. 11015, pp. 350–369. Springer, Cham (2018). https://doi.org/10.1007/978-3-319-99740-7_25
19. Michalenko, J.J., Shah, A., Verma, A., Baraniuk, R.G., Chaudhuri, S., Patel, A.B.: Representing formal languages: A comparison between finite automata and recurrent neural networks. In: ICLR. OpenReview.net (2019)
20. Minsky, M.L.: Computation: Finite and Infinite Machines. Prentice-Hall Inc., USA (1967)
21. Muškardin, E., Aichernig, B.K., Pill, I., Pferscher, A., Tappler, M.: AALpy: An active automata learning library. In: Hou, Z., Ganesh, V. (eds.) ATVA 2021. LNCS, vol. 12971, pp. 67–73. Springer, Cham (2021). https://doi.org/10.1007/978-3-030-88885-5_5
22. Muskardin, E., Aichernig, B.K., Pill, I., Tappler, M.: Learning finite state models from recurrent neural networks. In: ter Beek, M.H., Monahan, R. (eds.) IFM 2022. LNCS, vol. 13274, pp. 229–248. Springer, Cham (2022). https://doi.org/10.1007/978-3-031-07727-2_13
23. Oliva, C., Lago-Fernández, L.F.: Stability of internal states in recurrent neural networks trained on regular languages. Neurocomputing 452, 212–223 (2021). https://doi.org/10.1016/j.neucom.2021.04.058
24. Omlin, C.W., Giles, C.L.: Extraction of rules from discrete-time recurrent neural networks. Neural Netw. 9(1), 41–52 (1996). https://doi.org/10.1016/0893-6080(95)00086-0
25. Oncina, J., Garcia, P.: Identifying regular languages in polynomial time. In: Advances in Structural and Syntactic Pattern Recognition. Machine Perception and Artificial Intelligence, vol. 5, pp. 99–108. World Scientific (1992)
26. Paszke, A., et al.: PyTorch: An imperative style, high-performance deep learning library. In: NeurIPS, pp. 8024–8035. Curran Associates, Inc. (2019)
27. Pferscher, A., Aichernig, B.K.: Fingerprinting Bluetooth Low Energy devices via active automata learning. In: Huisman, M., Păsăreanu, C., Zhan, N. (eds.) FM 2021. LNCS, vol. 13047, pp. 524–542. Springer, Cham (2021). https://doi.org/10.1007/978-3-030-90870-6_28
28. Shahbaz, M., Groz, R.: Inferring Mealy machines. In: Cavalcanti, A., Dams, D.R. (eds.) FM 2009. LNCS, vol. 5850, pp. 207–222. Springer, Heidelberg (2009). https://doi.org/10.1007/978-3-642-05089-3_14

29. Smetsers, R., Fiterău-Broştean, P., Vaandrager, F.: Model learning as a satisfiability modulo theories problem. In: Klein, S.T., Martín-Vide, C., Shapira, D. (eds.) LATA 2018. LNCS, vol. 10792, pp. 182–194. Springer, Cham (2018). https://doi.org/10.1007/978-3-319-77313-1_14

30. Tappler, M., Aichernig, B.K., Lorber, F.: Timed automata learning via SMT solving. In: Deshmukh, J.V., Havelund, K., Perez, I. (eds.) NFM 2022. LNCS, vol. 13260, pp. 489–507. Springer, Cham (2022). https://doi.org/10.1007/978-3-031-06773-0_26

31. Tiňo, P., Šajda, J.: Learning and extracting initial Mealy automata with a modular neural network model. Neural Comput. **7**(4), 822–844 (1995). https://doi.org/10.1162/neco.1995.7.4.822

32. Tomita, M.: Dynamic construction of finite automata from examples using hill-climbing. In: Conference of the Cognitive Science Society, pp. 105–108 (1982)

33. Weiss, G., Goldberg, Y., Yahav, E.: Extracting automata from recurrent neural networks using queries and counterexamples. In: ICML. Proceedings of Machine Learning Research, vol. 80, pp. 5244–5253. PMLR (2018)

34. Weiss, G., Goldberg, Y., Yahav, E.: Learning deterministic weighted automata with queries and counterexamples. In: NeurIPS, pp. 8558–8569 (2019)

35. Yellin, D.M., Weiss, G.: Synthesizing context-free grammars from recurrent neural networks. In: Groote, J.F., Larsen, K.G. (eds.) TACAS 2021. LNCS, vol. 12651, pp. 351–369. Springer, Cham (2021). https://doi.org/10.1007/978-3-030-72016-2_19

Neural Network Verification Using Residual Reasoning

Yizhak Yisrael Elboher[✉] ⓘ, Elazar Cohen ⓘ, and Guy Katz ⓘ

The Hebrew University of Jerusalem, Jerusalem, Israel
{yizhak.elboher,elazar.cohen1,g.katz}@mail.huji.ac.il

Abstract. With the increasing integration of neural networks as components in mission-critical systems, there is an increasing need to ensure that they satisfy various safety and liveness requirements. In recent years, numerous sound and complete verification methods have been proposed towards that end, but these typically suffer from severe scalability limitations. Recent work has proposed enhancing such verification techniques with abstraction-refinement capabilities, which have been shown to boost scalability: instead of verifying a large and complex network, the verifier constructs and then verifies a much smaller network, whose correctness implies the correctness of the original network. A shortcoming of such a scheme is that if verifying the smaller network fails, the verifier needs to perform a refinement step that increases the size of the network being verified, and then start verifying the new network from scratch—effectively "wasting" its earlier work on verifying the smaller network. In this paper, we present an enhancement to abstraction-based verification of neural networks, by using *residual reasoning*: the process of utilizing information acquired when verifying an abstract network, in order to expedite the verification of a refined network. In essence, the method allows the verifier to store information about parts of the search space in which the refined network is guaranteed to behave correctly, and allows it to focus on areas where bugs might be discovered. We implemented our approach as an extension to the Marabou verifier, and obtained promising results.

Keywords: Neural networks · Verification · Abstraction refinement · Residual reasoning · Incremental reasoning

1 Introduction

In recent years, the use of deep neural networks (DNNs) [16] in critical components of diverse systems has been gaining momentum. A few notable examples include the fields of speech recognition [10], image recognition [17], autonomous driving [6], and many others. The reason for this unprecedented success is the ability of DNNs to generalize from a small set of training data, and then correctly handle previously unseen inputs.

Still, despite their success, neural networks suffer from various reliability issues. First, they are completely dependent on the training process, which may

© The Author(s), under exclusive license to Springer Nature Switzerland AG 2022
B.-H. Schlingloff and M. Chai (Eds.): SEFM 2022, LNCS 13550, pp. 173–189, 2022.
https://doi.org/10.1007/978-3-031-17108-6_11

include data that is anecdotal, partial, noisy, or biased [22,28]; further, the training process has inherent over-fitting limitations [34]; and finally, trained networks suffer from susceptibility to adversarial attacks, as well as from obscurity and lack of explainability [1]. Unless addressed, these concerns, and others, are likely to limit the applicability of DNNs in the coming years.

A promising approach for improving the reliability of DNN models is to apply *formal verification* techniques: automated and rigorous techniques that can ensure that a DNN model adheres to a given specification, in all possible corner cases [15,18,20,30]. While sound and complete formal verification methods can certify that DNNs are reliable, these methods can typically only tackle small or medium-sized DNNs; and despite significant strides in recent years, scalability remains a major issue [4].

In order to improve the scalability of DNN verification, recent studies have demonstrated the great potential of enhancing it with abstraction-refinement techniques [2,8,14,26]. The idea is to use a black-box DNN verifier, and feed it a series of *abstract networks*—i.e., DNNs that are significantly smaller than the original network being verified. Because the complexity of DNN verification is exponential in the size of the DNN in question [20], these queries can be solved relatively quickly; and the abstract networks are constructed so that their correctness implies the correctness of the original, larger network. The downside of abstraction is that sometimes, verifying the smaller network returns an inconclusive result—in which case, the abstract network is *refined* and made slightly larger, and the process is repeated. Is it well known that the heuristics used for performing the abstraction and refinement steps can have a significant impact on performance [8,14], and that poor heuristics can cause the abstraction-refinement sequence of queries to take longer to dispatch than the original query.

In this paper, we propose an extension that can improve the performance of an abstraction-refinement verification scheme. The idea is to use *residual reasoning* [3]: an approach for re-using information obtained in an early verification query, in order to expedite a subsequent query. Presently, a verifier might verify an abstract network N_1, obtain an inconclusive answer, and then verify a refined network, N_2; and it will verify N_2 from scratch, as if it had never verified N_1. Using residual reasoning, we seek to leverage the similarities between N_1 and N_2 in order to identify large portions of the verification search space that need not be explored, because we are guaranteed a-priori that they contain no violations of the property being checked.

More specifically, modern verifiers can be regarded as traversing a large search tree. Each branching in the tree is caused by an *activation function* within the neural network, which can take on multiple linear phases; and each branch corresponds to one of these phases. We show that when a verifier traverses a branch of the search tree and determines that no property violations occur therein, that information can be used to deduce that no violation can exist in some of the branches of the search tree traversed when verifying a refined network. The advantages of this approach are clear: by curtailing the search space, the verification process can be expedited significantly. The disadvantage is that, unlike in other abstraction-refinement based techniques, the verifier needs to be instrumented, and cannot be used as a black box.

Our contributions in this paper are as follows: (i) we formally define our residual reasoning scheme, in a general way that preserves the soundness and completeness of the underlying verifier; (ii) we specify how our approach can be used to extend the state-of-the-art Marabou DNN verification engine [21]; and (iii) we implement our approach, and evaluate it on the ACAS Xu set of benchmarks [19]. We regard this work as a step towards tapping into the great potential of abstraction-refinement methods in the context of DNN verification.

The rest of the paper is organized as follows. In Sect. 2 we recap the necessary background on DNNs and their verification. Next, in Sect. 3 we describe our general method for residual reasoning; followed by a discussion of how our technique can enhance a specific abstraction-refinement method, in Sect. 4. Sections 5 is then dedicated to explaining how our method can be applied using the Marabou DNN verifier as a backend, followed by our evaluation of the approach in Sect. 6. Related work is covered in Sect. 7, and we conclude in Sect. 8.

2   Background

Deep Neural Networks (DNNs). A neural network [16] $N : \mathbb{R}^n \to \mathbb{R}^m$ is a directed graph, organized into an input layer, multiple hidden layers, and an output layer. Each layer is a set of nodes (neurons), which can take on real values. When an input vector is passed into the input layer, it can be used to iteratively compute the values of neurons in the following layers, all through to neurons in the output layer—which constitute the network's output. We use L_i to denote the i'th layer of the DNN, and $v_{i,j}$ to denote the j'th node in L_i.

Typically, each neuron in the DNN is evaluated by first computing a weighted sum of the values assigned to neurons in the preceding layer, and then applying some activation function to the result. For simplicity, we restrict our attention to the popular ReLU activation function [16], which is a piecewise-linear function defined as $\text{ReLU}(x) = max(x, 0)$. When $x > 0$, we say that the ReLU is active; and otherwise, we say that it is inactive. A simple example appears in Fig. 1, and shows a DNN evaluated on input $\langle 0, 1 \rangle$. The value above each neuron is the weighted sum that it computes, prior to the application of the ReLU activation function. The network's output is 9.

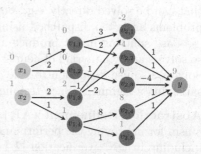

Fig. 1. A DNN with an input layer (green), two hidden layers (blue), and an output layer (red). (Color figure online)

Neural Network Verification. Neural network verification [23] deals with checking whether an input-output relation in a neural network holds. A verification query is a couple $\langle N, \varphi \rangle$, where N is a neural network and φ is a property of the form: $\vec{x} \in D_I \wedge \vec{y} \in D_O$, meaning that the input $\vec{x}$ is in some input domain D_I and the output $\vec{y}$ is in some output domain D_O. Typically, φ represents *undesirable* behavior; and so the verification problem is to find an input $\vec{x}$ and its matching output $\vec{y}$ that satisfy φ, and so constitute a counter-example (the SAT case), or to prove that no such $\vec{x}$ exists (the UNSAT case). Without loss of generality, we assume that verification queries only consists of a network N with a single output neuron y, and of a property φ of the form $\vec{x} \in D_I \wedge y > c$; other queries can be reduced to this setting in a straightforward way [14].

As a simple example, consider the DNN in Fig. 1 and the property $\varphi : x_1, x_2 \in [0,1] \wedge y > 14$. Checking whether input $x_1 = 0, x_2 = 1$ satisfies this property, we get that it does not, since $y = 9 \leq 14$. A sound verifier, therefore, would not return $\langle 0,1 \rangle$ as a satisfying assignment for this query.

Linear Programming and Case Splitting. A key technique for DNN verification, which is nowadays used by many leading verification tools, is called *case splitting* [21,29,31]. A DNN verification problem can be regarded as a satisfiability problem, where linear constraints and ReLU constraints must be satisfied simultaneously; and while linear constraints are easy to solve [9], the ReLUs render the problem NP-Complete [20]. In case splitting, the verifier sometimes transforms a ReLU constraint into an equivalent disjunction of linear constraints:

$$(y = \text{ReLU}(x)) \equiv ((x \leq 0 \wedge y = 0) \vee (x \geq 0 \wedge y = x))$$

and then each time *guesses* which of the two disjuncts holds, and attempts to satisfy the resulting constraints. This approach gives rise to a search tree, where internal nodes correspond to ReLU constraints, and their outgoing edges to the two linear constraints each ReLU can take. Each leaf of this tree is a problem that can be solved directly, e.g., because all ReLUs have been split upon. These problems are often dispatched using linear programming engines.

Case splitting might produce an exponential number of sub-problems, and so solvers apply a myriad of heuristics to avoid them or prioritize between them. Solvers also use deduction to rule out a-priori case splits that cannot lead to a satisfying assignment. Such techniques are beyond our scope.

Abstraction-Refinement (AR). Abstraction-refinement is a common mechanism for improving the performance of verification tools in various domains [8], including in DNN verification [2,14,26]. A sketch of the basic scheme of AR is illustrated in Fig. 8 in Appendix A of the full version of this paper [13]. The process begins with a DNN N and a property φ to verify, and then *abstracts* N into a different, smaller network N'. A key property is that N' *over-approximates* N: if $\langle N', \varphi \rangle$ is UNSAT, then $\langle N, \varphi \rangle$ is also UNSAT. Thus, it is usually preferable to verify the smaller N' instead of N.

If a verifier determines that $\langle N', \varphi \rangle$ is SAT, it returns a counter-example $\vec{x_0}$. That counter-example is then checked to determine whether it also constitutes a counterexample for $\langle N, \varphi \rangle$. If so, the original query is SAT, and we are done; but otherwise, $\vec{x_0}$ is a *spurious* counter-example, indicating that N' is inadequate for determining the satisfiability of the original query. We then apply *refinement*: we use N', and usually also $\vec{x_0}$, to create a new network N'', which is larger than N' but is still an over-approximation of N. The process is then repeated using N''. Usually, the process is guaranteed to converge: either we are able to determine the satisfiability of the original query using one of the abstract networks, or we end up refining N' all the way back to N, and solve the original query, which, by definition, cannot return a spurious result.

In this paper we focus on a particular abstraction-refinement mechanism for DNN verification [14]. There, abstraction and refinement are performed by merging or splitting (respectively) neurons in the network, and aggregating the weights of their incoming and outgoing edges. This merging and splitting is carried out in a specific way, which guarantees that if N is abstracted into N', then for all input $\vec{x}$ it holds that $N'(\vec{x}) \geq N(\vec{x})$; and thus, if $N'(\vec{x}) \geq c$ is UNSAT, then $N(\vec{x}) \geq c$ is also UNSAT, as is required of an over-approximation.

An illustrative example appears in Fig. 2. On the left, we have the network from Fig. 1, denoted N. The middle network, denoted N', is obtained by merging together neurons $v_{2,1}$ and $v_{2,2}$ into the single neuron $v_{2,1+2}$; and by merging neurons $v_{2,4}$ and $v_{2,5}$ into the single neuron $v_{2,4+5}$. The weights on the outgoing edges of these neurons are the sums of the outgoing edges of their original neurons; and the weights of the incoming edges are either the min or max or the original weights, depending on various criteria [14]. It can be proven [14] that N' over-approximates N; for example, $N(\langle 3, 1 \rangle) = -6 < N'(\langle 3, 1 \rangle) = 6$. Finally, the network on the right, denoted N'', is obtained from N by splitting a previously merged neuron. N'' is larger than N', but it is still an over-approximation of the original N: for example, $N''(\langle 3, 1 \rangle) = 1 > N(\langle 3, 1 \rangle) = -6$.

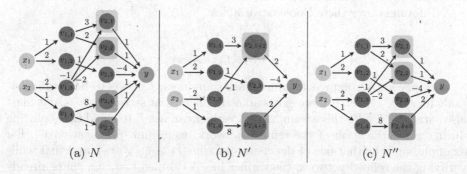

Fig. 2. Neural network abstraction and refinement through the merging and splitting of neurons [14].

3   Residual Reasoning (RR)

Consider again our running example, and observe that property φ is satisfiable for the most abstract network: for $\vec{x_0} = \langle 0, 1 \rangle$ we have $N'(\vec{x_0}) = 16$. However, this $\vec{x_0}$ is a spurious counterexample, as $N(\vec{x_0}) = 9$. Consequently, refinement is performed, and the verifier sets out to verify $\langle N'', \varphi \rangle$; and this query is solved from scratch. However, notice that the verification queries of φ in N', N'' are very similar: the networks are almost identical, and the property is the same. The idea is thus to re-use some of the information already discovered when $\langle N', \varphi \rangle$ was solved in order to expedite the solving of $\langle N'', \varphi \rangle$. Intuitively, an abstract network allows the verifier to explore the search space very coarsely, whereas a refined network allows the verifier to explore that space in greater detail. Thus, areas of that space that were determined safe for the abstract network need not be re-explored in the refined network.

In order to enable knowledge retention between subsequent calls to the verifier, we propose to introduce a *context* variable, Γ, that is passed to the verifier along with each verification query. Γ is used in two ways: (i) the verifier can store into Γ information that may be useful if a refined version of the current network is later verified; and (ii) the verifier may use information already in Γ to curtail the search space of the query currently being solved. A scheme of the proposed mechanism appears in Fig. 9 in Appendix A of the full version of this paper [13]. Of course, Γ must be designed carefully in order to maintain soundness.

Avoiding Case-Splits with Γ. In order to expedite subsequent verification queries, we propose to store in Γ information that will allow the verifier to *avoid case splits*. Because case splits are the most significant bottleneck in DNN verification [20, 29], using Γ to reduce their number seems like a natural strategy.

Let N' be an abstract network, and N'' its refinement; and observe the queries $\langle N', \varphi \rangle$ and $\langle N'', \varphi \rangle$. Let $R_1, \ldots, R_n$ denote the ReLU constraints in N'. For each ReLU R_i, we use a Boolean variable r_i to indicate whether the constraint is active (r_i is true), or inactive ($\neg r_i$ is true). We then define Γ to be a CNF formula over these Boolean variables:

$$\Gamma: \quad \bigwedge \Big(\bigvee_{l_j \in \bigcup_{i=1}^n \{r_i, \neg r_i\}} l_j \Big)$$

In order for our approach to maintain soundness, Γ needs to be a *valid formula* for $\langle N'', \varphi \rangle$; i.e., if there exists an assignment that satisfies $\langle N'', \varphi \rangle$, it must also satisfy Γ. Under this assumption, a verifier can use Γ to avoid case-splitting during the verification of the refined network, using unit-propagation [5]. For example, suppose that one of the clauses in Γ is $(r_1 \vee \neg r_2 \vee \neg r_3)$, and that while verifying the refined network, the verifier has performed two case splits already to the effect that r_1 is false (R_1 is inactive) and r_2 is true (R_2 is active). In this case, the verifier can immediately set r_3 to false, as it is guaranteed that no satisfying assignments exist where r_3 is true, as these would violate the clause above. This guarantees that no future splitting is performed on R_3.

More formally, we state the following Lemma:

Lemma 1 (Soundness of Residual Reasoning). *Let $\langle N', \varphi \rangle$ and $\langle N'', \varphi \rangle$ be verification queries on an abstract network N' and its refinement N'', being solved by a sound verifier; and let Γ be a valid formula as described above. If the verifier uses Γ to deduce the phases of ReLU constraints using unit propagation for the verification of $\langle N'', \varphi \rangle$, soundness is maintained.*

The proof is straightforward, and is omitted. We also note that when multiple consecutive refinement steps are performed, some renaming of variables within Γ is required; we discuss this in later sections.

4   Residual Reasoning and Neuron-Merging Abstraction

Our proposed approach for residual reasoning is quite general; and our definitions do not specify how Γ should be populated. In order to construct in Γ a lemma that will be valid for future refinements of the network, one must take into account the specifics of the abstraction-refinement scheme in use. In this section, we propose one possible integration with a recently proposed abstraction-refinement scheme that merges and splits neurons [14], which was discussed in Sect. 2.

We begin by revisiting our example from Fig. 2. Suppose that in order to solve query $\langle N, \varphi \rangle$, we generate the abstract network N' and attempt to verify $\langle N', \varphi \rangle$ instead. During verification, some case splits are performed; and it is discovered that when neuron $v_{2,1+2}$'s ReLU function is active, no satisfying assignment can be found. Later, the verifier discovers a satisfying assignment for which $v_{2,1+2}$ is inactive: $\vec{x} = \langle 0, 1 \rangle \Rightarrow N'(\vec{x}) = 16 > 14$. Unfortunately, this counterexample turns out to be spurious, because $N(\langle 0, 1 \rangle) = 9 \leq 14$, and so the network is refined: node $v_{2,1+2}$ is split into two new nodes, $(v_{2,1}, v_{2,2})$, giving rise to the refined network N''. The verifier then begins solving query $\langle N'', \varphi \rangle$.

We make the following claim: because no satisfying assignment exists for $\langle N', \varphi \rangle$ when $v_{2,1+2}$ is active, and because $v_{2,1+2}$ was refined into $(v_{2,1}, v_{2,2})$, then no satisfying assignment exists for $\langle N'', \varphi \rangle$ when $v_{2,1}$ and $v_{2,2}$ are both active. In other words, it is sound to verify $\langle N'', \varphi \rangle$ given $\Gamma = (\neg r_{2,1} \vee \neg r_{2,2})$, where $r_{2,1}$ and $r_{2,2}$ correspond to the activation phase of $v_{2,1}$ and $v_{2,2}$, respectively. Thus, e.g., if the verifier performs a case split and fixes $v_{2,1}$ to its active phase, it can immediately set $v_{2,2}$ to inactive, without bothering to explore the case where $v_{2,2}$ is also active.

In order to provide intuition as to why this claim holds, we now formally prove it; i.e., we show that if an input $\vec{x}$ satisfies $\langle N'', \varphi \rangle$ when $v_{2,1}$ and $v_{2,2}$ are both active, then it must also satisfy $\langle N'_1, \varphi \rangle$ when $v_{2,1+2}$ is active. First, we observe that because N'' is a refinement of N', it immediately follows that $N''(\vec{x}) \leq N'(\vec{x})$; and because the property φ is of the form $y > c$, if $\langle N'', \varphi \rangle$ is SAT then $\langle N', \varphi \rangle$ is also SAT. Next, we observe that N'' and N' are identical in all layers preceding $v_{2,1}, v_{2,2}$ and $v_{2,1+2}$, and so all neurons feedings into these three neurons are assigned the same values in both networks. Finally, we assume towards contradiction that $v_{2,1+2}$ is not active; i.e., that $3 \cdot \text{ReLU}(v_{1,1}) -$

$\text{ReLU}(v_{1,3}) < 0$; but because it also holds that $v_{2,1} = 3 \cdot \text{ReLU}(v_{1,1}) - \text{ReLU}(v_{1,3})$, this contradicts the assumption that $v_{2,1}$ and $v_{2,2}$ are both active. This concludes our proof, and shows that $\Gamma = (\neg r_{2,1} \vee \neg r_{2,2})$ is valid.

In the remainder of this section, we formalize the principle demonstrated in the example above. The formalization is complex, and relies on the details of the abstraction mechanism [14]; we give here the gist of the formalization, with additional details appearing in Appendix B of the full version of this paper [13].

Using the terminology of [14], two nodes can be merged as part of the abstraction process if they share a *type*: specifically, if they are both `inc` neurons, or if they are both `dec` neurons. An `inc` neuron has the property that *increasing* its value results in an increase to the network's single output; whereas a `dec` neuron has the property that *decreasing* its value increases the network's single output. In our running example, neuron $v_{2,1+2}$ is an `inc` neuron, whereas neuron $v_{2,3}$ is a `dec` neuron.

We use the term *abstract neuron* to refer to a neuron generated by the merging of two neurons from the same category, and the term *refined neuron* to refer to a neuron that was generated (restored) during a refinement step. An example for the merging of two `inc` neurons appears in Fig. 3.

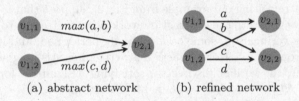

(a) abstract network   (b) refined network

Fig. 3. Abstraction/refinement of two *inc* neurons.

We now state our main theorem, which justifies our method of populating Γ. We then give an outline of the proof, and refer the reader to Theorem 2 in Appendix B of the full version of this paper [13] for additional details.

Theorem 1. *Let $\langle N, \varphi \rangle$ be a verification query, where $N : \vec{x} \to y$ has a single output node y, and φ is of the form $\varphi = (\vec{l} \leq \vec{x} \leq \vec{u}) \wedge (y > c)$. Let N' be an abstract network obtained from N using neuron merging, and let N'' be a network obtained from N' using a single refinement step in reverse order of abstraction. Specifically, let v be a neuron in N' that was split into two neurons v_1, v_2 in N''. Then, if a certain guard condition $\mathcal{G}$ holds, we have the following:*

1. *If v is `inc` neuron, and during the verification of $\langle N', \varphi \rangle$, the verifier determines that setting v to active leads to an UNSAT branch of the search tree, then $\Gamma = (\neg r_1 \vee \neg r_2)$ is a valid formula for $\langle N'', \varphi \rangle$ (where r_1 and r_2 correspond to v_1 and v_2, respectively).*
2. *Symmetrically, if setting a `dec` neuron v to inactive leads to an UNSAT branch, then $\Gamma = (r_1 \vee r_2)$ is a valid formula for $\langle N'', \varphi \rangle$.*

The guard condition $\mathcal{G}$ is intuitively defined as the conjunction of the following stipulations, whose goal is to enforce that the branches in both search trees (of $\langle N', \varphi \rangle$ and $\langle N'', \varphi \rangle$) are sufficiently similar:

1. The same case splits have been applied during the verification of N' and N'', for all neurons in the preceding layers of the abstract neuron and for any other neurons in the same layer as the abstract neuron.
2. The same case splits have been applied during the verification of N' and N'' for the abstract neuron and its refined neurons.
3. Every inc neuron in layers following the layer of v, v_1, v_2 has been split on and set to active, and every dec neuron in these layers has been split on and set to inactive.

We stress that the guard condition $\mathcal{G}$ does not change the way Γ is populated; but that the verifier must ensure that $\mathcal{G}$ holds before it applies unit-propagation based on Γ. The precise definitions and proof appear in Appendix B of the full version of this paper [13].

When the conditions of the theorem are met, a satisfying assignment within the specific branch of the search tree of the refined network would indicate that the corresponding branch in the abstract network is also SAT, which we already know is untrue; and consequently, that branch can be soundly skipped. To prove the theorem, we require the two following lemmas, each corresponding to one of the two cases of the theorem.

Lemma 2. *Given an input $\vec{x}$, if the value of an abstract inc node v is negative, then at least one of the values of the refined nodes v_1 and v_2 is negative for the same $\vec{x}$.*

Proof Outline. We explain how to prove the lemma using the general network from Fig. 3; and this proof can be generalized to any network in a straightforward way. Observe nodes $v_{2,1}$ and $v_{2,2}$ in Fig. 3(b), which are nodes refined from node $v_{2,1}$ in Fig 3(a). We need to prove that the following implication holds:

$$x_1 \cdot max(a, b) + x_2 \cdot max(c, d) < 0 \Rightarrow (x_1 \cdot a + x_2 \cdot c < 0 \lor x_1 \cdot b + x_2 \cdot d < 0)$$

The values of x_1, x_2 are the outputs of ReLUs, and so are non-negative. We can thus split into 4 cases:

1. If $x_1 = 0, x_2 = 0$, the implication holds trivially.
2. If $x_1 = 0, x_2 > 0$, then $x_2 \cdot max(c, d) < 0$, and so $c, d < 0$. We get that $x_1 \cdot a + x_2 \cdot c = x_2 \cdot c < 0$ and $x_1 \cdot b + x_2 \cdot d = x_2 \cdot d < 0$, and so the implication holds.
3. The case where $x_1 > 0, x_2 = 0$ is symmetrical to the previous case.
4. If $x_1 > 0, x_2 > 0$, the implication becomes

$$max(x_1 \cdot a, x_1 \cdot b) + max(x_2 \cdot c, x_2 \cdot d) < 0 \Rightarrow (x_1 \cdot a + x_2 \cdot c < 0 \lor x_1 \cdot b + x_2 \cdot d < 0)$$

Let us denote $a' = x_1 \cdot a$, $b' = x_1 \cdot b$ and $c' = x_2 \cdot c$, $d' = x_2 \cdot d$. The lemma then becomes:

$$max(a', b') + max(c', d') < 0 \Rightarrow a' + c' < 0 \lor b' + d' < 0$$

– If $a' \geq b'$, then $a' = max(a', b')$ and $a' + max(c', d') < 0$. We then get that

$$b' + d' \leq a' + d' \leq a' + max(c', d') < 0$$

as needed.
– If $a' < b'$, then $b' = max(a', b')$ and $b' + max(c', d') < 0$. We then get that

$$a' + c' \leq b' + max(c', d') < 0$$

again as needed.

Lemma 2 establishes the correctness of Theorem 1 for **inc** neurons. We also have the following, symmetrical lemma for **dec** neurons:

Lemma 3. *Given an input $\vec{x}$, if the value of an abstract **dec** node v is positive, then at least one of the values of the refined nodes v_1 and v_2 is positive for the same $\vec{x}$.*

The proof outline is similar to that of Lemma 2, and appears in Appendix B of the full version of this paper [13].

The result of applying Theorem 1 as part of the verification of our running example from Fig. 2 is illustrated in Fig. 4. There, each rectangle represents a single verification query, and blue lines indicate abstraction steps. Within each rectangle, we see the verifier's search tree, where triangles signify sub-trees— and red triangles are sub-trees where the verifier was able to deduce that no satisfying assignment exists. The figure shows that, when solving the query in the bottom rectangle, the verifier discovered an UNSAT sub-tree that meets the conditions of the Theorem. This allows the verifier to deduce that another sub-tree, in another rectangle/query, is also UNSAT, as indicated by a green arrow. Specifically, by discovering that setting $v_{2,1+2}$ to *active* results in UNSAT, the verifier can deduce that setting $v_{2,1}$ to *active* and then $v_{2,2}$ to *active* must also result in UNSAT.

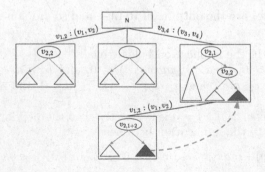

Fig. 4. Applying Theorem 1 while solving the query from Fig. 2.

Multiple Refinement Steps. So far, we have only discussed populating Γ for a single refinement step. However, Γ can be adjusted as multiple refinement steps are performed. In that case, each invocation of Theorem 1 adds another CNF clause to the formula already stored in Γ. Further, some book-keeping and renaming is required, as neuron identifiers change across the different networks: intuitively, whenever an abstract neuron v is split into neurons v_1 and v_2, the literal v must be replaced with $v_1 \vee v_2$. These notions are formalized in Sec. 5; and the soundness of this procedure can be proven using repeated invocations of Theorem 1.

5 Adding Residual Reasoning to Reluplex

Unlike in previous abstraction-refinement approaches for DNN verification [2, 14,26], residual reasoning requires instrumenting the DNN verifier in question, for the purpose of populating, and using, Γ. We next describe such an instrumentation for the Reluplex algorithm [20], which is the core algorithm used in the state-of-the-art verifier Marabou [21]. Reluplex, a sound and complete DNN verification algorithm, employs case-splitting as discussed in Sect. 2, along with various heuristics for curtailing the search space and reducing the number of splits [32,33]; and it has been integrated with abstraction-refinement techniques before [14], rendering it a prime candidate for residual reasoning. We term our enhanced version of Reluplex AR^4, which stands for Abstraction-Refinement with Residual Reasoning for Reluplex.

For our purposes, it is convenient to think of Reluplex as a set of derivation rules, applied according to an implementation-specific strategy. The most relevant parts of this calculus, borrowed from Katz et al. [20] and simplified, appear in Fig. 5; other rules, specifically those that deal with the technical aspects of solving linear problems, are omitted for brevity.

$$\text{Failure} \quad \frac{\exists x \in \mathcal{X}.\ l(x) > u(x)}{\text{UNSAT}} \qquad \text{ReluSplit} \quad \frac{\langle x_i, x_j \rangle \in R, \quad l(x_i) < 0, \quad u(x_i) > 0}{u(x_i) := 0 \qquad l(x_i) := 0}$$

$$\text{Success} \quad \frac{\forall x \in \mathcal{X}.\ l(x) \le \alpha(x) \le u(x), \quad \forall \langle x, y \rangle \in R.\ \alpha(y) = \max(0, \alpha(x))}{\text{SAT}}$$

Fig. 5. Derivation rules of Reluplex calculus (partial, simplified).

Internally, Reluplex represents the verification query as a set of linear equalities and lower/upper bounds over a set of variables, and a separate set of ReLU constraints. A *configuration* of Reluplex over a set of variables $\mathcal{X}$ is either a distinguished symbol from the set $\{\texttt{SAT}, \texttt{UNSAT}\}$, or a tuple $\langle T, l, u, \alpha, R \rangle$, where: T, the *tableau*, contains the set of linear equations; l, u are mappings that assign each variable $x \in \mathcal{X}$ a lower and an upper bound, respectively; α, the *assignment*, maps each variable $x \in \mathcal{X}$ to a real value; and R is the set of ReLU constraints, i.e. $\langle x, y \rangle \in R$ indicates that $y = \text{ReLU}(x)$. Reluplex will often derive *tighter bounds* as it solves a query; i.e., will discover greater lower bounds or smaller upper bounds for some of the variables.

Using these definitions, the rules in Fig. 5 can be interpreted follows: Failure is applicable when Reluplex discovers inconsistent bounds for a variable, indicating that the query is UNSAT. ReluSplit is applicable for any ReLU constraint whose linear phase is unknown; and it allows Reluplex to "guess" a linear phase for that ReLU, by either setting the upper bound of its input to 0 (the inactive case), or the lower bound of its input to 0 (the active case). Success is applicable when the current configuration satisfies every constraint, and returns SAT.

In order to support AR^4, we extend the Reluplex calculus with additional rules, depicted in Fig. 6. We use the context variable Γ, as before, to store a valid CNF formula to assist the verifier; and we also introduce two additional context variables, Γ_A and Γ_B, for book-keeping purposes. Specifically, Γ_A stores a mapping between abstract neurons and their refined neurons; i.e., it is comprised of triples $\langle v, v_1, v_2 \rangle$, indicating that abstract neuron v has been refined into neurons v_1 and v_2. Γ_B is used for storing past case splits performed by the verifier, to be used in populating Γ when the verifier finds an UNSAT branch. Given variable x of neuron v, we use $\mathcal{G}^{\text{inc}}(\Gamma_A, \Gamma_B, x)$ and $\mathcal{G}^{\text{dec}}(\Gamma_A, \Gamma_B, x)$ to denote a Boolean function that returns true if and only if the guard conditions required for applying Theorem 1 hold, for an inc or dec neuron v, respectively.

$$\text{ReluSplit} \quad \frac{\langle x_i, x_j \rangle \in R, \quad l(x_i) < 0, \quad u(x_i) > 0}{u(x_i) := 0 \qquad l(x_i) := 0} $$
$$\Gamma_B := \Gamma_B \vee r_i \qquad \Gamma_B := \Gamma_B \vee \neg r_i$$

$$\text{Failure} \quad \frac{\exists x_i \in \mathcal{X}. \; l(x_i) > u(x_i)}{\text{UNSAT}, \Gamma := \Gamma \wedge \Gamma_B} \qquad \text{AbstractionStep} \quad \frac{CanAbstract(x_1, x_2)}{\Gamma_A := \Gamma_A \cup \langle x_{1,2}, x_1, x_2 \rangle}$$

$$\text{RefinementStep} \quad \frac{\Gamma_A \neq \emptyset}{\Gamma_A := \Gamma_A[:-1]} \qquad \text{RealSuccess} \quad \frac{\text{SAT} \wedge isRealSAT(\Gamma_A)}{\text{RealSAT}}$$

$$\text{ApplyAbstraction} \quad \frac{true}{Abstract(\Gamma_A), UpdateContext(\Gamma, \Gamma_A, \Gamma_B)}$$

$$\text{Prune}_1 \quad \frac{\langle x, x_i, x_j \rangle \in \Gamma_A \wedge \neg r_i, \neg r_j \in \Gamma_B \wedge \mathcal{G}^{\text{inc}}(\Gamma_A, \Gamma_B, x) \wedge l(x_i) = 0}{u(x_j) = 0, \Gamma_B := \Gamma_B \vee r_j}$$

$$\text{Prune}_2 \quad \frac{\langle x, x_i, x_j \rangle \in \Gamma_A \wedge r_i, r_j \in \Gamma_B \wedge \mathcal{G}^{\text{dec}}(\Gamma_A, \Gamma_B, x) \wedge u(x_i) = 0}{l(x_j) = 0, \Gamma_B := \Gamma_B \vee \neg r_j}$$

Fig. 6. Derivation rules for the AR^4 calculus.

The rules in Fig. 6 are interpreted as follows. AbstractionStep is used for merging neurons and creating the initial, abstract network. RefinementStep is applicable when dealing with an abstract network (indicated by $\Gamma_A \neq \emptyset$), and performs a refinement step by canceling the last abstraction step. ApplyAbstraction is applicable anytime, and generates an abstract network according to the information in Γ_A, updating the relevant contexts correspondingly. The Success rule from the original Reluplex calculus in included, as is, in the AR^4 calculus; but we note that a SAT conclusion that it reaches is applicable only to the current, potentially abstract network, and could thus be spurious. To solve this issue, we add the RealSuccess rule, which checks whether a SAT result is true for the original network as well. Thus, in addition to SAT or UNSAT, the RealSAT state is also a terminal state for our calculus.

The Failure rule replaces the Reluplex rule with the same name, and is applicable when contradictory bounds are discovered; but apart from declaring UNSAT, it also populates Γ with the current case-split history in Γ_B, for future pruning of the search space. The ReluSplit rule, similarly to the Reluplex version, guesses a linear phase for one the ReLUs, but now also records that action in Γ_B. Finally, the $Prune_{1/2}$ rules are applicable when all the conditions of Theorem 1 (for the inc/dec cases, respectively) are met, and they trim the search tree and update Γ accordingly.

Side Procedures. We intuitively describe the four functions, *CanAbstract*, *Abstract*, *UpdateContext* and *isRealSat*, which appear in the calculus; additional details can be found in Appendix C of the full version of this paper [13].

- CanAbstract (Algorithm 1, Appendix C [13]) checks whether two neurons can be merged according to their types; and also checks whether the assignment to the variables did not change yet during the verification process.
- Abstract (Algorithm 3, Appendix C [13]) performs multiple abstraction steps. A single abstraction step (Algorithm 2, Appendix C [13]) is defined as the merging of two neurons of the same type, given that the assignments to their variables were not yet changed during verification.
- UpdateContext clears the case-splitting context by setting ($\Gamma_B = \emptyset$), and also updates clauses in Γ to use new variables: for variables representing inc nodes, $\neg r$ is replaced with $\neg r_1 \vee \neg r_2$; and for variables representing dec nodes, r is replaced with $r_1 \vee r_2$.
- *isRealSat* (Algorithm 5, Appendix C [13]) checks whether a counterexample holds in the original network.

Implementation Strategy. The derivation rules in Fig. 6 define the "legal moves" of AR^4—i.e., we are guaranteed that by applying them, the resulting verifier will be sound. We now discuss one possible *strategy* for applying them, which we used in our proof-of-concept implementation.

We begin by applying AbstractionStep to saturation, in order to reach a small abstract network; and then apply once the ApplyAbstraction rule, to properly initialize the context variables. Then, we enter into the loop of abstraction-based verification: we apply the Reluplex core rules using existing strategies [21], but every time the ReluSplit rule is applied we immediately apply $Prune_1$ and $Prune_2$, if they are applicable. The Failure and Success rules are applied as in Reluplex, and RealSuccess is applied immediately after Success if it is applicable; otherwise, we apply RefinementStep, and repeat the process. We also attempt to apply $Prune_1$ and $Prune_2$ after each application of Failure, since it updates Γ.

Table 1. Comparing AR^4 and AR.

	Adversarial		Safety		Total (weighted)	
	AR^4	AR	AR^4	AR	AR^4	AR
Timeouts	95/900	116/900	7/180	9/180	102/1080	125/1080
Instances solved more quickly	160	95	28	24	188	119
Uniquely solved	26	5	2	0	28	5
Visited tree states	6.078	7.65	3.569	4.98	5.634	7.178
Avg. instrumentation time	91.54	–	36.5	–	82.367	–

6   Experiments and Evaluation

For evaluation purposes, we created a proof-of-concept implementation of AR^4, and compared it to the only tool currently available that supports CEGAR-based DNN verification—namely, the extension of Marabou proposed in [14]. We used both tools to verify a collection of properties of the ACAS Xu family of 45 DNNs (each with 310 neurons, spread across 8 layers) for airborne collision avoidance [19]. Specifically, we verified a collection of 4 safety properties and 20 adversarial robustness properties for these networks, giving a total of 1080 benchmarks; and from these experiments we collected, for each tool, the runtime (including instrumentation time), the number of properties successfully verified within the allotted timeout of two hours, and the number of case splits performed. The experiments were conducted on x86-64 Gnu/Linux based machines using a single Intel(R) Xeon(R) Gold 6130 CPU @ 2.10 GHz core. Our code is publicly available online.[1]

The results of our experiments appear in Table 1 and Fig. 7, and demonstrate the advantages of AR^4 compared to AR. AR^4 timed out on 18.4% fewer benchmarks, and solved 188 benchmarks more quickly than AR, compared to 119 where AR was faster. We note that in these comparisons, we treated experiments in which both tools finished within 5 s of each other as ties. Next, we observe that residual reasoning successfully curtailed the search space: on average, AR^4 traversed 5.634 states of the search tree per experiment, compared to 7.178 states traversed by AR—a 21.5% decrease.

Despite the advantages it often affords, AR^4 is not always superior to AR—because the cost of instrumenting the verifier is not always negligible. In our experimenters, the verifier spent an average of 82 s executing our instrumentation code out of an average total runtime of 885 seconds—nearly 10%, which is quite significant. In order to mitigate this issue, moving forward we plan to strengthen the engineering of our tool, e.g., by improve its implementation of unit-propagation through the use of watch literals [5].

---

[1] https://drive.google.com/file/d/1onk3dW3yJeyXw8_rcL6wUsVFC1bMYvjL.

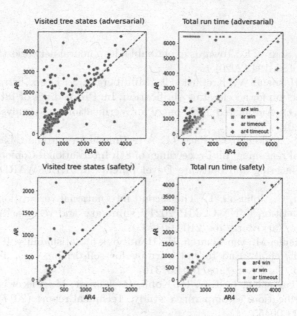

Fig. 7. Comparing AR^4 and AR.

7   Related Work

Modern DNN verification schemes leverage principles from SAT and SMT solving [12,18,20,21,25], mixed integer linear programming [7,11,12,29], abstract interpretation [15,24,27,31], and others. Many of these approaches apply case-splitting, and could benefit from residual reasoning.

Abstraction-refinement techniques are known to be highly beneficial in verifying hand-crafted systems [8], and recently there have been promising attempts to apply them to DNN verification as well [2,14,26]. As far as we know, ours is the first attempt to apply residual reasoning in this context.

8   Conclusion

As DNNs are becoming increasingly integrated into safety-critical systems, improving the scalability of DNN verification is crucial. Abstraction-refinement techniques could play a significant part in this effort, but they can sometimes create redundant work for the verifier. The residual reasoning technique that we propose can eliminate some of this redundancy, resulting in a speedier verification procedure. We regard our work here as another step towards tapping the potential of abstraction-refinement methods in DNN verification.

Moving forward, we plan to improve the engineering of our AR^4 tool; and to integrate it with other abstraction-refinement DNN verification techniques [2].

Acknowledgments. This work was supported by ISF grant 683/18. We thank Jiaxiang Liu and Yunhan Xing for their insightful comments about this work.

References

1. Angelov, P., Soares, E.: Towards explainable deep neural networks (xDNN). Neural Netw. **130**, 185–194 (2020)
2. Ashok, P., Hashemi, V., Kretinsky, J., Mühlberger, S.: DeepAbstract: neural network abstraction for accelerating verification. In: Proceedings of 18th International Symposium on Automated Technology for Verification and Analysis (ATVA), pp. 92–107 (2020)
3. Azzopardi, S., Colombo, C., Pace, G.: A technique for automata-based verification with residual reasoning. In: Proceedings of 8th International Conference on Model-Driven Engineering and Software Development (MODELSWARD), pp. 237–248 (2020)
4. Bak, S., Liu, C., Johnson, T.: The second international verification of neural networks competition (VNN-COMP 2021): summary and results. Technical report (2021). http://arxiv.org/abs/2109.00498
5. Biere, A., Heule, M., van Maaren, H.: Handbook of Satisfiability. IOS Press (2009)
6. Bojarski, M., et al.: End to end learning for self-driving cars. Technical report (2016). http://arxiv.org/abs/1604.07316
7. Bunel, R., Turkaslan, I., Torr, P., Kohli, P., Kumar, M.: Piecewise linear neural network verification: a comparative study. Technical report (2017). http://arxiv.org/abs/1711.00455
8. Clarke, E., Grumberg, O., Jha, S., Lu, Y., Veith, H.: Counterexample-guided abstraction refinement. In: Emerson, E.A., Sistla, A.P. (eds.) CAV 2000. LNCS, vol. 1855, pp. 154–169. Springer, Heidelberg (2000). https://doi.org/10.1007/10722167_15
9. Dantzig, G.: Linear Programming and Extensions. Princeton University Press, Princeton (1963)
10. Devlin, J., Chang, M.W., Lee, K., Toutanova, K.: BERT: pre-training of deep bidirectional transformers for language understanding. Technical report (2018). http://arxiv.org/abs/1810.04805
11. Dutta, S., Jha, S., Sanakaranarayanan, S., Tiwari, A.: Output range analysis for deep neural networks. In: Proceedings of 10th NASA Formal Methods Symposium (NFM), pp. 121–138 (2018)
12. Ehlers, R.: Formal verification of piece-wise linear feed-forward neural networks. In: D'Souza, D., Narayan Kumar, K. (eds.) ATVA 2017. LNCS, vol. 10482, pp. 269–286. Springer, Cham (2017). https://doi.org/10.1007/978-3-319-68167-2_19
13. Elboher, Y., Cohen, E., Katz, G.: Neural network verification using residual reasoning. Technical report (2022). http://arxiv.org/abs/2208.03083
14. Elboher, Y.Y., Gottschlich, J., Katz, G.: An abstraction-based framework for neural network verification. In: Lahiri, S.K., Wang, C. (eds.) CAV 2020. LNCS, vol. 12224, pp. 43–65. Springer, Cham (2020). https://doi.org/10.1007/978-3-030-53288-8_3
15. Gehr, T., Mirman, M., Drachsler-Cohen, D., Tsankov, E., Chaudhuri, S., Vechev, M.: AI2: safety and robustness certification of neural networks with abstract interpretation. In: Proceedings of 39th IEEE Symposium on Security and Privacy (S&P) (2018)
16. Goodfellow, I., Bengio, Y., Courville, A.: Deep Learning. MIT Press, Cambridge (2016)
17. He, K., Zhang, X., Ren, S., Sun, J.: Deep residual learning for image recognition. In: Proceedings of IEEE Conference on Computer Vision and Pattern Recognition (CVPR), pp. 770–778 (2016)

18. Huang, X., Kwiatkowska, M., Wang, S., Wu, M.: Safety verification of deep neural networks. In: Majumdar, R., Kunčak, V. (eds.) CAV 2017. LNCS, vol. 10426, pp. 3–29. Springer, Cham (2017). https://doi.org/10.1007/978-3-319-63387-9_1
19. Julian, K., Lopez, J., Brush, J., Owen, M., Kochenderfer, M.: Policy compression for aircraft collision avoidance systems. In: Proceedings of 35th Digital Avionics Systems Conference (DASC), pp. 1–10 (2016)
20. Katz, G., Barrett, C., Dill, D.L., Julian, K., Kochenderfer, M.J.: Reluplex: an efficient SMT solver for verifying deep neural networks. In: Majumdar, R., Kunčak, V. (eds.) CAV 2017. LNCS, vol. 10426, pp. 97–117. Springer, Cham (2017). https://doi.org/10.1007/978-3-319-63387-9_5
21. Katz, G., et al.: The marabou framework for verification and analysis of deep neural networks. In: Dillig, I., Tasiran, S. (eds.) CAV 2019. LNCS, vol. 11561, pp. 443–452. Springer, Cham (2019). https://doi.org/10.1007/978-3-030-25540-4_26
22. Kim, B., Kim, H., Kim, K., Kim, S., Kim, J.: Learning not to learn: training deep neural networks with biased data. In: Proceedings of IEEE Conference on Computer Vision and Pattern Recognition (CVPR), pp. 9004–9012 (2019)
23. Liu, C., Arnon, T., Lazarus, C., Barrett, C., Kochenderfer, M.: Algorithms for verifying deep neural networks. Technical report (2020). http://arxiv.org/abs/1903.06758
24. Müller, M., Makarchuk, G., Singh, G., Püschel, M., Vechev, M.: PRIMA: general and precise neural network certification via scalable convex hull approximations. In: Proceedings of 49th ACM SIGPLAN Symposium on Principles of Programming Languages (POPL) (2022)
25. Narodytska, N., Kasiviswanathan, S., Ryzhyk, L., Sagiv, M., Walsh, T.: Verifying properties of binarized deep neural networks. Technical report (2017). http://arxiv.org/abs/1709.06662
26. Prabhakar, P., Afzal, Z.: Abstraction based output range analysis for neural networks. Technical report (2020). http://arxiv.org/abs/2007.09527
27. Singh, G., Gehr, T., Puschel, M., Vechev, M.: An abstract domain for certifying neural networks. In: Proceedings of 46th ACM SIGPLAN Symposium on Principles of Programming Languages (POPL) (2019)
28. Song, H., Kim, M., Park, D., Shin, Y., Lee, J.G.: End to end learning for self-driving cars. Technical report (2020). http://arxiv.org/abs/2007.08199
29. Tjeng, V., Xiao, K., Tedrake, R.: Evaluating robustness of neural networks with mixed integer programming. Technical report (2017). http://arxiv.org/abs/1711.07356
30. Wang, S., Pei, K., Whitehouse, J., Yang, J., Jana, S.: Formal security analysis of neural networks using symbolic intervals. In: Proceedings of 27th USENIX Security Symposium (2018)
31. Wang, S., et al.: Beta-CROWN: efficient bound propagation with per-neuron split constraints for complete and incomplete neural network verification. In: Proceedings of 35th Conference on Neural Information Processing Systems (NeurIPS) (2021)
32. Wu, H., et al.: Parallelization techniques for verifying neural networks. In: Proceedings of 20th International Conference on Formal Methods in Computer-Aided Design (FMCAD), pp. 128–137 (2020)
33. Wu, H., Zeljić, A., Katz, G., Barrett, C.: Efficient neural network analysis with sum-of-infeasibilities. In: TACAS 2022. LNCS, vol. 13243, pp. 143–163. Springer, Cham (2022). https://doi.org/10.1007/978-3-030-99524-9_8
34. Ying, X.: An overview of overfitting and its solutions. J. Phys: Conf. Ser. **1168**, 022022 (2019)

Training Agents to Satisfy Timed and Untimed Signal Temporal Logic Specifications with Reinforcement Learning

Nathaniel Hamilton[✉] [iD], Preston K Robinette[iD], and Taylor T Johnson[iD]

Vanderbilt University, Nashville, TN 37212, USA
{nathaniel.p.hamilton,preston.k.robinette,taylor.johnson}@vanderbilt.edu

Abstract. Reinforcement Learning (RL) depends critically on how reward functions are designed to capture intended behavior. However, traditional approaches are unable to represent temporal behavior, such as "do task 1 before doing task 2." In the event they can represent temporal behavior, these reward functions are handcrafted by researchers and often require long hours of trial and error to shape the reward function just right to get the desired behavior. In these cases, the desired behavior is already known, the problem is generating a reward function to train the RL agent to satisfy that behavior. To address this issue, we present our approach for automatically converting timed and untimed specifications into a reward function, which has been implemented as the tool STLGym. In this work, we show how STLGym can be used to train RL agents to satisfy specifications better than traditional approaches and to refine learned behavior to better match the specification.

Keywords: Deep Reinforcement Learning · Safe Reinforcement Learning · Signal Temporal Logic · Curriculum Learning

1 Introduction

Reinforcement Learning (RL) and Deep Reinforcement Learning (DRL) are fast-growing fields with growing impact, spurred by success in training agents to beat human experts in games like Go [23], Starcraft [25], and Gran Turismo [28]. These results support the claims from [24] that "reward is enough to drive behavior that exhibits abilities studied in natural and artificial intelligence."

However, traditional reward functions are Markovian by nature; mapping states, or states and actions, to scalar reward values without considering previous states or actions [5]. This Markovian nature is in direct conflict with designing reward functions that describe complex, temporally-extended behavior. For example, the task of opening a freezer door, taking something out, and then closing the freezer door cannot be represented by Markovian reward functions, because the success of taking something out of the freezer is dependent on opening the freezer door first. This problem also extends to the context of

B.-H. Schlingloff and M. Chai (Eds.): SEFM 2022, LNCS 13550, pp. 190–206, 2022.
https://doi.org/10.1007/978-3-031-17108-6_12

safety-critical systems, where the desired behavior might include never entering some region or responding to a situation within a specified amount of time.

Therefore, if we want to use RL and DRL to solve complex, temporally-extended problems, we need a new way of writing and defining reward functions. This is a challenging problem with growing interest as RL research looks into new ways to formulate the reward function to solve these kinds of problems. The most promising approaches look at using temporal logic to write specifications describing the desired behavior, and then generating complex reward functions that help agents learn to satisfy the specifications. Temporal logics are formalism for specifying the desired behavior of systems that evolve over time [16]. Some approaches, like the one presented in this work, take advantage of quantitative semantics [1,2,14], while others construct reward machines that change how the reward function is defined depending on which states have been reached [5,11–13].

Despite the many successes of these approaches, only one is able to incorporate timing constraints [2] and many only work with a few RL algorithms that require researchers to write up the problem in a custom format to work with the implementation provided. By ignoring timing constraints, the approaches leave out reactive specifications where systems need to respond within a specified amount of time, like in power systems.

Our Contributions. In this work, we introduce our approach, and a tool implementation, STLGym, for training RL agents to satisfy complex, temporally-extended problems with and without timing constraints using RL. To the best of our knowledge, and compared to related works discussed in Sect. 6, our approach is the first that allows users to train agents to satisfy timed and untimed specifications, evaluate how well their agents satisfy those specifications, and retrain agents that do not already satisfy the specifications. We demonstrate the features of our tool and explore some best practices in five interesting example case studies. Our results show STLGym is an effective tool for training RL agents to satisfy a variety of timed and untimed temporal logic specifications.

2   Preliminaries

2.1   (Deep) Reinforcement Learning

Reinforcement Learning (RL) is a form of machine learning in which an agent acts in an environment, learning through experience to increase its performance based on rewarded behavior. *Deep Reinforcement Learning* (DRL) is a newer branch of RL in which a neural network is used to approximate the behavior function, i.e. policy π. The environment can be comprised of any dynamical system, from video game simulations [9,25,28] to complex robotics scenarios [4,8,17]. In this work, and to use our tool STLGym, the environment must be constructed using OpenAI's Gym API [4].

Reinforcement learning is based on the *reward hypothesis* that all goals can be described by the maximization of expected *return*, i.e. the cumulative reward. During training, the agent chooses an action, u, based on the input observation,

o. The action is then executed in the environment, updating the internal state, s, according to the plant dynamics. The agent then receives a scalar r, and the next observation vector, o'. The process of executing an action and receiving a reward and next observation is referred to as a *timestep*. Relevant values, like the input observation, action, and reward are collected as a data tuple, i.e. *sample*, by the RL algorithm to update the current policy, π, to an improved policy, π^*. How often these updates are done is dependent on the RL algorithm.

The return is the sum of all rewards collected over the course of an *episode*. An episode is a finite sequence of states, observations, actions, and rewards starting from an initial state and ending when some terminal, i.e. *done*, conditions are met. In this work, we refer to different elements of the episode by their corresponding timestep, t. Thus, r_t is the reward value at timestep $t \in [0, T]$, where T is the final timestep in the episode.

2.2   Signal Temporal Logic

Signal Temporal Logic (STL) was first introduced in [16] as an extension of previous temporal logics that allows for formalizing control-theoretic properties, properties of path-planning algorithms, and expressing timing constrains and causality relations.

STL specifications are defined recursively according to the *syntax*:

$$\phi := \psi | \neg\phi | \phi \wedge \varphi | \phi \vee \varphi | F_{[a,b]}\phi | G_{[a,b]}\phi | \phi U_{[a,b]}\psi, \tag{1}$$

where $a, b \in \mathbb{R}_{\geq 0}$ are finite non-negative time bounds; ϕ and φ are STL formulae; and ψ is a predicate in the form $f(w) < d$. In the predicate, $w : \mathbb{R}_{\geq 0} \to \mathbb{R}^n$ is a signal, $f : \mathbb{R}^n \to \mathbb{R}$ is a function, and $d \in \mathbb{R}$ is a constant. The Boolean operators $\neg$, $\wedge$, and $\vee$ are negation, conjunction, and disjunction respectively; and the temporal operators F, G, and U refer to *Finally* (i.e. eventually), *Globally* (i.e. always), and *Until* respectively. These temporal operators can be timed, having time boundaries where the specification must be met, or untimed without strict time boundaries.

w_t denotes the value of w at time t and (w, t) is the part of the signal that is a sequence of $w_{t'}$ for $t' \in [t, |w|)$, where $|w|$ is the end of the signal. The propositional semantics of STL are recursively defined as follows:

$$
\begin{aligned}
(w, t) &\models (f(w) < d) & \Leftrightarrow & \quad f(w_t) < d, \\
(w, t) &\models \neg\phi & \Leftrightarrow & \quad \neg((w, t) \models \phi), \\
(w, t) &\models \phi \wedge \varphi & \Leftrightarrow & \quad (w, t) \models \phi \text{ and } (w, t) \models \varphi, \\
(w, t) &\models \phi \vee \varphi & \Leftrightarrow & \quad (w, t) \models \phi \text{ or } (w, t) \models \varphi, \\
(w, t) &\models F_{[a,b]}\phi & \Leftrightarrow & \quad \exists t' \in [t+a, t+b] \text{ s.t. } (w, t') \models \phi, \\
(w, t) &\models G_{[a,b]}\phi & \Leftrightarrow & \quad (w, t') \models \phi \; \forall t' \in [t+a, t+b], \\
(w, t) &\models \phi U_{[a,b]}\varphi & \Leftrightarrow & \quad \exists t_u \in [t+a, t+b) \text{ s.t. } (w, t_u) \models \varphi \\
& & & \quad \wedge \; \forall t' \in [t+a, t_u)(w, t') \models \phi.
\end{aligned}
$$

For a signal $(w, 0)$, i.e. the whole signal starting at time 0, satisfying the timed predicate $F_{[a,b]}\phi$ means that "there exists a time within $[a, b]$ such that ϕ will eventually be true", and satisfying the timed predicate $G_{[a,b]}\phi$ means that "ϕ is true for all times between $[a, b]$". Satisfying the timed predicate $\phi U_{[a,b]}\varphi$ means "there exists a time within $[a, b]$ such that φ will be true, and *until* then, ϕ is true." Satisfying the untimed predicates have the same description as their timed counterpart, but with $a = 0$ and $b = |w|$.

Quantitative Semantics. STL has a metric known as *robustness degree* or "degree of satisfaction" that quantifies how well a given signal w satisfies a given formula ϕ. The robustness degree is calculated recursively according to the *quantitative semantics*:

$$\rho(w, (f(w) < d), t) = d - f(w_t),$$
$$\rho(w, \neg\phi, t) = -\rho(w, \phi, t),$$
$$\rho(w, (\phi \land \varphi), t) = \min\left(\rho(w, \phi, t), \rho(w, \varphi, t)\right),$$
$$\rho(w, (\phi \lor \varphi), t) = \max\left(\rho(w, \phi, t), \rho(w, \varphi, t)\right),$$
$$\rho(w, F_{[a,b]}\phi, t) = \max_{t' \in [t+a, t+b]} \rho(w, \phi, t'),$$
$$\rho(w, G_{[a,b]}\phi, t) = \min_{t' \in [t+a, t+b]} \rho(w, \phi, t'),$$
$$\rho(w, \phi U_{[a,b]}\varphi, t) = \max_{t_u \in [t+a, t+b]} \left(\min\{\rho(w, \varphi, t_u), \min_{t' \in [t, t_u]} \left(\rho(w, \phi, t')\right)\}\right).$$

3 Examples

In the remaining sections, we will be referring to these two example RL environments, *Pendulum* and *CartPole*, in order to explain how STLGym works and differs from other approaches. Figure 1 shows annotated screenshots of the simulated environments.

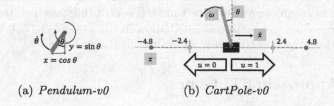

(a) *Pendulum-v0*   (b) *CartPole-v0*

Fig. 1. Annotated screenshots showing the simulated environments, *Pendulum* (left) and *CartPole* (right), from the OpenAI Gym benchmarks [4].

3.1 Pendulum

The Pendulum environment, shown in Fig. 1(a), consists of an inverted pendulum attached to a fixed point on one side. The agent's goal in this environment is to swing the free end of the pendulum to an upright position, $\theta = 0$, and maintain the position.

The interior plant model changes the state, $s = [\theta, \omega]$, according to the discrete dynamics given the control from the RL agent, u_t, in the range $[-2, 2]$ applied as a torque about the fixed end of the pendulum. Additionally, within the environment the pendulum's angular velocity, ω, is clipped within the range $[-8, 8]$, and the angle from upright, θ, is aliased within $[-\pi, \pi]$ radians. θ is measured from upright and increases as the pendulum moves clockwise. The values θ, ω, and u are used to determine the observation, $o = [\cos(\theta), \sin(\theta), \omega]^T$ and the reward,

$$r_t = -\theta_t^2 - 0.1(\omega_t)^2 - 0.001(u_t)^2. \tag{2}$$

For each episode, the pendulum is initialized according to a uniform distribution with $\theta \in [-\pi, \pi]$ and $\omega \in [-1, 1]$. The episode ends when 200 timesteps have occurred. That means T is always 200.

3.2 CartPole

In the CartPole environment[1], a pole is attached to a cart moving along a frictionless track. The agent's goal in this environment is to keep the pole upright, $-12° \leq \theta \leq 12°$, and the cart within the bounds $-2.4 \leq x \leq 2.4$ until the time limit, $t = 200$, is reached. The agent accomplishes this goal by applying a leftward or rightward force to move the cart along the track. The agent's actions are discretized for a "bang-bang" control architecture that moves the cart left when $u = 0$ and right when $u = 1$.

The interior plant model changes the state, $s = [x, \dot{x}, \theta, \dot{\theta}]$, until a terminal condition is met. These terminal conditions are: (1) the cart's position leaves the bounds $-2.4 \leq x \leq 2.4$, (2) the pole's angle is outside the bounds $-12° \leq \theta \leq 12°$, and/or (3) the goal time limit is reached, i.e. $t = 200$.

The original, baseline reward function with this environment gives the agent +1 for every timestep the first two terminal conditions are not violated. Thus, the return for an episode is the same as the episode's length. To ensure the agent has a chance to complete at least one timestep successfully, each state element is initialized according to a uniform distribution in the range $[-0.05, 0.05]$. In this implementation, the observation is equivalent to the state, $o = s$.

4 Our Approach: STLGym

Our approach focuses solely on augmenting the environment side of the RL process to add an STL monitor and replace the existing reward output with the

---

[1] The environment is based on the classic cart-pole system implemented for [3], where more information on the dynamics can be found.

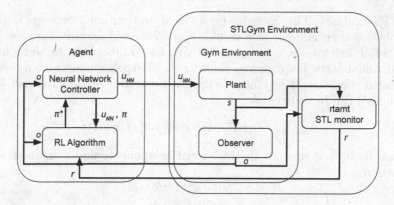

Fig. 2. A representation of how STLGym wraps around the user's environment to record signals and replace the reward function.

calculated *robustness degree* as it relates to the desired specification(s), as shown in Fig. 2. This process maintains the standards of the Gym API, so no changes to the RL algorithm are necessary to facilitate its use. As a result, our approach is *algorithm-agnostic*, since no modifications to the RL algorithm are required. Furthermore, since our approach makes use of existing environments, there is great potential for *retraining* learned policies to better optimize satisfying specifications. Our approach is implemented as the tool STLGym[2].

To use the tool, a user provides a YAML file that defines the variable(s) that need to be recorded for the multivariate signal, w, and the specification(s) that the signal needs to satisfy. Additionally, the user must provide the underlying Gym environment that will be augmented. Provided these two inputs, STLGym generates a new Gym environment where the specified variables are recorded so RTAMT can monitor the defined STL specification and return the robustness degree as the reward function.

4.1 Computing the Robustness Degree

To compute the robustness degree, we make use of RTAMT [19], a tool for monitoring STL specifications on recorded data. Given the recorded signal and specification, RTAMT computes the robustness degree according to the quantitative semantics described in Sect. 2.2. Whenever the robustness degree is calculated, it covers the full episode from time 0 to t.

4.2 Allowable Specifications

Our approach is amenable to a wide range of specifications and supports the full range of semantics described in Sect. 2.2 in addition to any described in

---

[2] STLGym implementation is available at https://github.com/nphamilton/stl-gym.

RTAMT's readme[3]. This includes both timed and untimed operators, adding more options than allowed in a similar tool *Truncated Linear Temporal Logic* TLTL [14]. Furthermore, our approach allows for specifications to be broken up into individual parts. For example, consider the Cartpole example from Sect. 3.2. The desired behavior ("Keep the pole upright between $\pm 12°$ and the cart within ± 2.4 units") can be written as

$$\Phi_{single} = G((|\theta| < 0.20944) \wedge (|x| < 2.4)) \tag{3}$$

or it can be broken up into the individual components and combined with a conjunction,

$$\phi_{angle} = G(|\theta| < 0.20944)$$
$$\phi_{position} = G(|x| < 2.4) \tag{4}$$
$$\Phi_{split} = \phi_{angle} \wedge \phi_{position}.$$

These specifications, Eq. 3 and Eq. 4, are equivalent and allowable in both TLTL and STLGym. However, STLGym allows users to treat ϕ_{angle} and $\phi_{position}$ as individual specifications and automatically applies the conjunction. Any number of individual specifications can be defined, and the resulting specification the RL agent will learn to satisfy is the conjunction of all of them. Thus, if n specifications are provided, the RL agent will learn to satisfy

$$\Phi = \bigwedge_{i=0}^{n} \phi_i. \tag{5}$$

4.3   Calculating Reward

STLGym replaces any existing reward function in the environment with the *robustness degree* calculated using the provided specification(s) and RTAMT. If the user defines n specifications, $\phi_0, \phi_1, ..., \phi_n$ with corresponding weight values[4], $c_0, c_1, ..., c_n$, the reward function is constructed as

$$r_t = \sum_{i=0}^{n} c_i \rho(s, \phi_i, 0). \tag{6}$$

We include optional weights to add more versatility. This allows for users to write specifications that build on each other, i.e. a specification is defined using another specification, but remove one from the reward function if desired by setting its weight to 0. Additionally, weights can help establish priorities in learning specifications. For example, we go back to the CartPole specification Eq. 4. The reward function generated, according to the quantitative semantics described in Sect. 2.2, for the specification is

$$r_t = c_{angle} \min_{t' \in [0,t]} (0.20944 - |\theta_{t'}|) + c_{position} \min_{t' \in [0,t]} (2.4 - |x_{t'}|). \tag{7}$$

---

[3] The RTAMT code is available at https://github.com/nickovic/rtamt.
[4] If a weight is not defined by the user, the default is 1.

If both $c_{angle} = c_{position} = 1$, then the maximum possible reward for satisfying both specifications is 2.60944. However, because the environment was designed to terminate if either specification is violated, if the agent only satisfies $\phi_{position}$ and lets the pole fall, the maximum possible reward is 2.4. Since the gain from keeping the pole upright is so small, it could be ignored. In contrast, if we make the weights $c_{angle} = 4.7746$ and $c_{position} = 0.41666$, then the maximum possible reward for satisfying both specifications is 2. If either of the specifications are ignored, the maximum possible reward drops to 1. Thus, we have enforced equal priority for satisfying the specifications.

Dense Vs Sparse. In addition to adding optional weights for each specification, STLGym allows users to specify if the reward function should be calculated densely or sparsely. This design decision was spurred on by the existing RL literature, where there are two main types of rewards utilized: dense and sparse. In the literature, dense rewards are returned at every timestep and are often a scalar representation of the agent's progresses toward the goal. For example, the baseline reward function in the Pendulum environment (Eq. 2) is a dense reward. In contrast, sparse rewards are not returned at each timestep, but instead are only returned if certain conditions are met. For example, an agent receiving +1 for passing a checkpoint would be considered a sparse reward. Each of these reward types have their advantages for different tasks and algorithms. However, we make use of these terms to make our own definitions of dense and sparse reward as they relate to frequency.

Definition 1 (Dense Reward). *When using the dense reward, the robustness degree is computed at every allowable timestep. Thus, at each timestep, the reward returned to the agent is the robustness degree of the episode from the beginning to the current time step.*

Definition 2 (Sparse Reward). *When using the sparse reward, the robustness degree is only computed once at the end of the episode. In all timesteps before that, the reward is 0. Thus, the return is the robustness degree for the entire episode.*

From our experiments, we found using dense rewards trained agents to satisfy the specification with fewer timesteps, while the sparse reward was better for evaluating their performance and understanding if they have successfully learned to satisfy the specification or not. An example is provided in Sect. 5.1.

5   Example Case Studies

In this section, we describe 5 case studies we conducted using the environments described in Sect. 3[5]. In all of our case studies, we use the Proximal Policy

---

[5] All training scripts are available at https://github.com/nphamilton/spinningup/tree/master/spinup/examples/sefm2022.

Optimization (PPO) [22] algorithm for training, unless otherwise specified. These case studies were designed to highlight features of STLGym and try to identify some potential "best practices" for future use in other environments.

5.1   Sparse vs Dense Reward

In this case study, we demonstrate why having the ability to swap between sparse and dense versions of our STL reward function is important. To this end, we train 30 agents in the pendulum environment from Sect. 3.1 to swing the pendulum upright and stay upright. Written as an STL specification, that is

$$\Phi = F(G((|\theta| < 0.5))). \tag{8}$$

Ten agents are trained using the baseline reward function (Eq. 2), ten agents are trained with the sparse version of our STL reward function, and ten agents are trained with the dense version of our STL reward function. Using the quantitative semantics from Sect. 2.2, our tool automatically generates the reward function,

$$r_t = \max_{t' \in [0,t]} \Big(\min_{t'' \in [t',t]} (0.5 - |\theta_{t''}|) \Big). \tag{9}$$

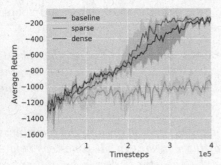

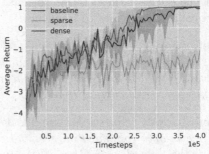

(a) Sample complexity of PPO agents trained in the Pendulum environment. The return is calculated using Equation 2.

(b) Sample complexity of PPO agents trained in the Pendulum environment. The return is calculated using Equation 9 defined sparsely.

Fig. 3. Plots comparing the sample complexity using PPO to train agents in the Pendulum environment using three reward functions: (baseline) the baseline reward function, Eq. 2; (sparse) the STLGym reward function, Eq. 9, defined sparsely; and (dense) the STLGym reward function defined densely. Each curve represents the average return from 10 agents trained the same way. The shaded region around each curve shows the 95% confidence interval.

We show the sample complexity plots of training these 30 agents with the 3 different reward functions in Fig. 3. Sample complexity is a measure of how quickly an RL agent learns optimal performance. Throughout training, the process is halted, and the agent is evaluated to see how well it performs with the policy learned so far. The policy is evaluated in ten episodes, and the performance, measured by the return, is recorded for the plot. A better sample complexity is shown by a higher return earlier in training. In Fig. 3, we show sample complexity measured by the (a) baseline reward function and (b) the sparse STL reward function to highlight how the agents trained with the dense STL reward have a better sample complexity than agents trained with the baseline reward function even according to the baseline metric.

While the agents trained using the sparse STL reward function failed to learn an optimal policy, using the sparse STL reward function for evaluating performance was very beneficial. Using the dense reward function for evaluating performance is very similar to the baseline reward function, in that neither provide any insight into whether or not the learned policy satisfies the desired behavior. In contrast, using the sparse STL reward function in Fig. 3(b), we see the exact point where the learned policies are successfully able to satisfy the specification when the return is greater than 0.

5.2   STLGym is Algorithm-Agnostic

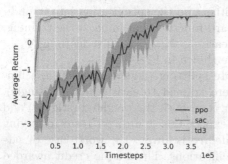
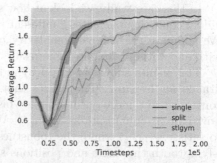

(a) Comparing multiple RL algorithms using STLGym to learn the Pendulum specification, Equation 8.

(b) Comparing the three options presented in Section 5.3 in the CartPole.

Fig. 4. These plots compare the sample complexity of agents trained using different methods. Each curve represents the average of 10 trained agents, and the shaded region shows the 95% confidence interval. In (b), the return is calculated using the sparse definition of Φ_{split} (reward function represented by Eq. 7) with $c_{angle} = 4.7746$ and $c_{position} = 0.41666$ so the maximum possible return is 2.0.

In this case study, we demonstrate that our approach is algorithm-agnostic by using multiple RL algorithms for the Pendulum example explained in Sect. 3.1. All algorithms are used to learn the optimal policy for satisfying the specification in Eq. 8. We demonstrate the following RL algorithms successfully learning to satisfy the specification using STLGym: Proximal Policy Optimization (PPO) [22], Soft Actor-Critic (SAC) [7], and Twin Delayed Deep Deterministic Policy Gradient (TD3) [6]. The sample complexity plot in Fig. 4(a) shows all RL algorithms successfully learn to satisfy the specification. While the results suggest SAC and TD3 work better with our STL reward function, these algorithms are known to learn the optimal policy for this environment very quickly. More examples, across different environments, are needed to make that claim.

5.3   On Separating Specifications and Scaling

The goal of the agent in the CartPole environment is to learn how to keep the pole upright so the angle, θ, is between $\pm 12°$ and the cart's position, x remains within the boundary of ± 2.4 for 200 timesteps. As explained in Sect. 4.2, this specification can be written as a singular specification, Eq. 3, or as the conjunction of individual components, Eq. 4.

Using STL's quantitative semantics, STLGym would generate the reward function for Φ_{single} as

$$r_t = \min_{t' \in [0,t]} \Big(\min \big((0.20944 - |\theta_{t'}|), (2.4 - |x_{t'}|) \big) \Big). \tag{10}$$

Similarly, STLGym would generate the reward function for Φ_{split} as Eq. 7

In this case study, we look at how splitting up the specification into its individual components creates a different reward function that impacts the training. We compare the sample complexity of learning Φ_{single} against learning Φ_{split} with and without weights. The results are shown in Fig. 4(b).

The results shown in Fig. 4(b) indicate splitting the specification is a hindrance for learning. The agents that were trained to satisfy Φ_{single} (single), converged to a more optimal policy faster than both the weighted (stlgym) and unweighted (split) options of Φ_{split}. We expect this is a direct result of trying to satisfy Φ_{single}, where the robustness degree is always the worst-case of satisfying both the angle and positions specifications. There is no credit awarded for satisfying one better than the other, like in the Φ_{split} definition. We believe that, while splitting the specification in this case study was more of a hindrance, in more complicated systems with more specifications, splitting could be more beneficial than shown here. In those cases, the option for weighting the individual specifications will be very helpful as the weighted and split option (stlgym), which is only supported in STLGym, learned faster than and outperformed the unweighted option.

5.4   Retraining with New Goal

There are many cases where the traditional reward functions successfully train agents to complete the desired behavior, but we want to refine/improve/augment that behavior to some other desired behavior. Instead of designing a new reward function and training a new agent from scratch, our tool can be leveraged to retrain the agent to satisfy the new desired behavior. This also makes our tool amenable to curriculum learning [26], an RL training strategy that trains agents in progressively harder environments or constraints. Similar to a learning curriculum used to teach students in a class, by starting with easier constraints and building upon what is learned from the easier tasks, the agent is better able to learn more complex behaviors.

In this case study, we look at an example with the CartPole environment described in Sect. 3.2. The baseline reward function trains agents to keep the pole upright very efficiently, but as [2] point out in their work, many of the learned policies are unstable. When they evaluated the policies for longer than 200 timesteps, they found many learned policies failed shortly after 200 timesteps. We saw similar results, which are shown in Fig. 5. To counteract this issue, we retrain the agents to maximize the measured robustness of the specifications

$$\phi_{position} = F(G(|x| < 0.5)), \text{ and}$$
$$\phi_{angle} = F(G(|\theta| < 0.0872665)). \tag{11}$$

In plain English, the specifications translate to "eventually the cart will always be within ± 0.5 units of the center of the track" and "eventually, the pole's angle will always be within $\pm 5°$."[6]

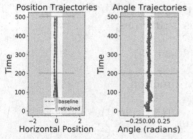 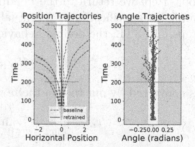

(a) 10 example episodes where the policy learned using the baseline reward function is stable.

(b) 10 example episodes where the policy learned using the baseline reward function is unstable.

Fig. 5. These plots show recorded episodes of trained policies evaluated in the CartPole environment. The red marks the region outside the specification and the horizontal green lines mark the goal during training at 200, and the goal at evaluation 500. In (a) we see the agent trained with the baseline reward function learned a stable policy and retraining with STLGym is able to further refine the learned policy to maximize the distance to the red region. In (b) we see the agent trained with the baseline reward learned an unstable policy, but after retraining with STLGym, the learned policy becomes stable. (Color figure online)

---

[6] These specifications came from [2].

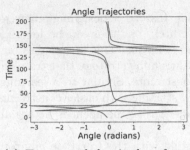
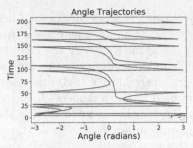

(a) Two recorded episodes of one trained policy.

(b) Two recorded episodes of a different trained policy.

Fig. 6. Episodes of policies trained to satisfy the timed specification in Eq. 12.

After some retraining, Fig. 5 shows the retrained policies converged to more stable and consistent behavior. In particular, Fig. 5(b) shows our approach corrects the unstable behavior.

5.5   Learning a Timed Specification

In this case study, we look at one of the features of our tool that sets it apart from almost all existing approaches in the literature—the ability to learn timed specifications. Here we return to the Pendulum environment described in Sect. 3.1. This time, the specification is "eventually the angle will be between $\pm 45°$ for 10 timesteps." In STL, the desired behavior is written as,

$$\Phi = F(G_{[0:10]}(|\theta| < 0.5)). \tag{12}$$

And is converted by our tool to the reward function,

$$r_t = \max_{t' \in [0,t]} \left(\min_{t'' \in [t',t'+10]} (0.5 - |\theta_{t''}|) \right). \tag{13}$$

The results of learning the specification in Eq. 12 are highlighted in Fig. 6 where we show a few example episodes. When we first wrote this specification, we believed the resulting behavior would closely match that of the agents in Sect. 5.1. Instead, the learned policies were more varied. Some stay close to the upright position for longer than others, but they always return. We believe this is a result of the circular state space, which puts the agent back in a starting position after it moves away from upright. This result shows STLGym can successfully train agents to satisfy timed specifications. However, it also highlights a limitation of our approach: we have no way of overwriting the terminal conditions. We would see more consistent results if we were able to stop the episode once the specification was satisfied, but that is a feature left for future work.

6   Related Work

Our work is not the first to use temporal logic specifications to create reward functions. The previous works can be grouped into two categories, (1) quantitative semantics and (2) reward machines. We describe the related works in greater detail below and provide a general comparison of our approach with others in Table 1. The RL algorithms listed in Table 1 are the following: Augmented Random Search (ARS) [17], Deep Deterministic Policy Gradient (DDPG) [15], Deep Q-Learning (DQN) [18], Neural Fitted Q-iteration (NFQ) [21], Relative Entropy Policy Search (REPS) [20], Q-Learning (Q) [27], and Twin Delayed Deep Deterministic Policy Gradient (TD3) [6].

Table 1. A comparison of our tool to similar tools in the literature, separated by category, filled in to the best of our knowledge. × indicates the feature is not supported, ✓ indicates the feature is supported, and ? indicates it should be supported, but we cannot say so with confidence.

Name	Env-API	Sparse/Dense	RL Algorithms	Retraining	Timed	Sequential
TLTL [14]	?	Dense	REPS	?	×	✓
BHNR [2]	Custom	Dense	DQN, PPO	?	✓	?
STLGym (ours)	Gym	Both	Any	✓	✓	✓
QRM [11]	Gym	Both	Q, DQN	×	×	✓
LCRL [10]	Custom	Both	Q, DDPG, NFQ	×	×	✓
SPECTRL [12]	Custom	Dense	ARS	×	×	✓
DIRL [13]	Gym	Dense	ARS, TD3	×	×	✓

6.1   Quantitative Semantics

The quantitative semantics category is where our work resides. These works, [1,2,14], generate reward functions based on the quantitative semantics of the temporal logics used to write the specifications the RL agents are tasked with learning to satisfy. In Truncated Linear Temporal Logic (TLTL), presented in [14], the authors create a new specification language, TLTL, that consciously removes the time bounds from STL to only have untimed operators. They made this decision, so specifications do not have to account for robotic limitations. In contrast, our STLGym is designed to handle both timed and untimed specifications, thus handling all TLTL problems and more.

Another work, [2], uses timed and untimed STL specifications similar to our STLGym. Their approach, Bounded Horizon Nominal Robustness (BHNR), computes a normalized robustness value over bounded horizons, i.e. small segments, of the episode, creating a reward vector. By only analyzing the robustness over smaller segments of the episode, their approach is able to speed up the robustness degree calculation for dense reward computation. However, because only a small portion of the episode is analyzed, their approach cannot be used to determine the robustness degree across an entire episode like our sparse reward function is able to do. Additionally, their implementation limits user's specifications to be defined only by variables in the environment's observation space. Thus, their tool cannot train our pendulum example without re-writing to specification in terms of x and y instead of θ.

6.2   Reward Machines

Reward machine approaches, [5,11–13], use finite state automata (FSA) to handle context switching in the reward function. Temporal logic specifications are used to generate FSA that monitor the episode for satisfaction. Additionally, depending on which state of the FSA is in, the reward function changes in order to guide the agent towards satisfying the next specification. This approach is optimal for solving sequential tasks because it allows the user to specify "go to the fridge; open the door; take something out; close the door; return to home" and the reward function changes depending on which part of the task is being done. To the best of our knowledge, however, none of these approaches can handle timed specifications yet.

7   Conclusions and Future Work

This paper presents our tool, STLGym, for training agents to satisfy timed and untimed STL specifications using RL. To demonstrate the features of our tool and explore some best practices for learning to satisfy STL specifications, we trained over 130 different RL agents in our 5 case studies. From these case studies we observed (1) RL agents learned STLGym's dense rewards better than sparse rewards, (2) STLGym is algorithm-agnostic and works with any RL algorithm designed to integrate with Gym environments, (3) leaving specifications combined is better for RL agents than splitting them into individual parts, (4) STLGym is effective for retraining RL agents to better satisfy specifications, and (5) STLGym is effective for training RL agents to satisfy timed STL specifications.

In future work, we hope to expand to other, more complicated environments and explore more scenarios with timed specifications. Additionally, we would like to explore how STLGym can be leveraged more effectively for curriculum learning.

Acknowledgments. The material presented in this paper is based upon work supported the Defense Advanced Research Projects Agency (DARPA) through contract number FA8750-18-C-0089, the Air Force Office of Scientific Research (AFOSR) award FA9550-22-1-0019, the National Science Foundation (NSF) through grant number 2028001, and the Department of Defense (DoD) through the National Defense Science & Engineering Graduate (NDSEG) Fellowship Program. Any opinions, findings, and conclusions or recommendations expressed in this publication are those of the authors and do not necessarily reflect the views of DARPA, AFOSR, NSF or DoD.

References

1. Aksaray, D., Jones, A., Kong, Z., Schwager, M., Belta, C.: Q-learning for robust satisfaction of signal temporal logic specifications. In: 2016 IEEE 55th Conference on Decision and Control (CDC), pp. 6565–6570. IEEE (2016)
2. Balakrishnan, A., Deshmukh, J.V.: Structured reward shaping using signal temporal logic specifications. In: 2019 IEEE/RSJ International Conference on Intelligent Robots and Systems (IROS), pp. 3481–3486. IEEE (2019)
3. Barto, A.G., Sutton, R.S., Anderson, C.W.: Neuronlike adaptive elements that can solve difficult learning control problems. IEEE Trans. Syst. Man Cybern. SMC-**13**(5), 834–846 (1983)
4. Brockman, G., et al.: Openai gym (2016)
5. Camacho, A., Icarte, R.T., Klassen, T.Q., Valenzano, R.A., McIlraith, S.A.: LTL and beyond: formal languages for reward function specification in reinforcement learning. In: IJCAI. vol. 19, pp. 6065–6073 (2019)
6. Fujimoto, S., Hoof, H., Meger, D.: Addressing function approximation error in actor-critic methods. In: International Conference on Machine Learning, pp. 1587–1596. PMLR (2018)
7. Haarnoja, T., Zhou, A., Abbeel, P., Levine, S.: Soft actor-critic: off-policy maximum entropy deep reinforcement learning with a stochastic actor. In: International Conference on Machine Learning, pp. 1861–1870. PMLR (2018)
8. Hamilton, N., Musau, P., Lopez, D.M., Johnson, T.T.: Zero-shot policy transfer in autonomous racing: reinforcement learning vs imitation learning. In: Proceedings of the 1st IEEE International Conference on Assured Autonomy (2022)
9. Hamilton, N., Schlemmer, L., Menart, C., Waddington, C., Jenkins, T., Johnson, T.T.: Sonic to knuckles: evaluations on transfer reinforcement learning. In: Unmanned Systems Technology XXII. vol. 11425, p. 114250J. International Society for Optics and Photonics (2020)
10. Hasanbeig, M., Abate, A., Kroening, D.: Logically-constrained reinforcement learning code repository. https://github.com/grockious/lcrl (2020)
11. Icarte, R.T., Klassen, T., Valenzano, R., McIlraith, S.: Using reward machines for high-level task specification and decomposition in reinforcement learning. In: International Conference on Machine Learning, pp. 2107–2116. PMLR (2018)
12. Jothimurugan, K., Alur, R., Bastani, O.: A composable specification language for reinforcement learning tasks. In: Advances in Neural Information Processing Systems 32: Annual Conference on Neural Information Processing Systems 2019, NeurIPS 2019 (2019)
13. Jothimurugan, K., Bastani, O., Alur, R.: Abstract value iteration for hierarchical reinforcement learning. In: International Conference on Artificial Intelligence and Statistics, pp. 1162–1170. PMLR (2021)
14. Li, X., Vasile, C.I., Belta, C.: Reinforcement learning with temporal logic rewards. In: 2017 IEEE/RSJ International Conference on Intelligent Robots and Systems (IROS), pp. 3834–3839. IEEE (2017)
15. Lillicrap, T.P., et al.: Continuous control with deep reinforcement learning. In: ICLR (2016)
16. Maler, O., Nickovic, D.: Monitoring temporal properties of continuous signals. In: Lakhnech, Y., Yovine, S. (eds.) FORMATS/FTRTFT -2004. LNCS, vol. 3253, pp. 152–166. Springer, Heidelberg (2004). https://doi.org/10.1007/978-3-540-30206-3_12

17. Mania, H., Guy, A., Recht, B.: Simple random search of static linear policies is competitive for reinforcement learning. In: Proceedings of the 32nd International Conference on Neural Information Processing Systems, pp. 1805–1814 (2018)
18. Mnih, V., et al.: Human-level control through deep reinforcement learning. Nature **518**(7540), 529–533 (2015)
19. Ničković, D., Yamaguchi, T.: RTAMT: online robustness monitors from STL. In: Hung, D.V., Sokolsky, O. (eds.) ATVA 2020. LNCS, vol. 12302, pp. 564–571. Springer, Cham (2020). https://doi.org/10.1007/978-3-030-59152-6_34
20. Peters, J., Mulling, K., Altun, Y.: Relative entropy policy search. In: Twenty-Fourth AAAI Conference on Artificial Intelligence (2010)
21. Riedmiller, M.: Neural fitted Q iteration – first experiences with a data efficient neural reinforcement learning method. In: Gama, J., Camacho, R., Brazdil, P.B., Jorge, A.M., Torgo, L. (eds.) ECML 2005. LNCS (LNAI), vol. 3720, pp. 317–328. Springer, Heidelberg (2005). https://doi.org/10.1007/11564096_32
22. Schulman, J., Wolski, F., Dhariwal, P., Radford, A., Klimov, O.: Proximal policy optimization algorithms. arXiv preprint arXiv:1707.06347 (2017)
23. Silver, D., et al.: Mastering the game of go with deep neural networks and tree search. Nature **529**, 484–489 (2016)
24. Silver, D., Singh, S., Precup, D., Sutton, R.S.: Reward is enough. Artif. Intell. **299**, 103535 (2021)
25. Vinyals, O., et al.: Grandmaster level in StarCraft ii using multi-agent reinforcement learning. Nature **575**(7782), 350–354 (2019)
26. Wang, X., Chen, Y., Zhu, W.: A survey on curriculum learning. IEEE Trans. Pattern Anal. Mach. Intell. **44**, 4555–4576 (2021)
27. Watkins, C.J., Dayan, P.: Q-learning. Mach. Learn. **8**(3), 279–292 (1992)
28. Wurman, P.R., et al.: Outracing champion Gran Turismo drivers with deep reinforcement learning. Nature **602**(7896), 223–228 (2022)

Specification and Contracts

Information Flow Control-by-Construction for an Object-Oriented Language

Tobias Runge[1,2](✉) (iD), Alexander Kittelmann[1,2] (iD), Marco Servetto[3],
Alex Potanin[4] (iD), and Ina Schaefer[1,2]

[1] TU Braunschweig, Braunschweig, Germany
[2] Karlsruhe Institute of Technology, Karlsruhe, Germany
{tobias.runge,alexander.kittelmann,ina.schaefer}@kit.edu
[3] Victoria University of Wellington, Wellington, New Zealand
marco@ecs.vuw.ac.nz
[4] Australian National University, Canberra, Australia
alex.potanin@anu.edu.au

Abstract. In security-critical software applications, confidential information must be prevented from leaking to unauthorized sinks. Static analysis techniques are widespread to enforce a secure information flow by checking a program after construction. A drawback of these systems is that incomplete programs during construction cannot be checked properly. The user is not guided to a secure program by most systems. We introduce IFbCOO, an approach that guides users incrementally to a secure implementation by using refinement rules. In each refinement step, confidentiality or integrity (or both) is guaranteed alongside the functional correctness of the program, such that insecure programs are declined by construction. In this work, we formalize IFbCOO and prove soundness of the refinement rules. We implement IFbCOO in the tool CorC and conduct a feasibility study by successfully implementing case studies.

Keywords: Correctness-by-construction · Information flow control · Security-by-design

1 Introduction

For security-critical software, it is important to ensure *confidentiality* and *integrity* of data, otherwise attackers could gain access to this secure data. For example, in a distributed system, one client A has a lower privilege (i.e., a lower security level) than another client B. When both clients send information to each other, security policies can be violated. If A reads secret data from B, confidentiality is violated. If B reads untrusted data from A, the integrity of B's data is no longer guaranteed. To ensure security in software, mostly static analysis techniques are used, which check the software after development [28]. A violation of

B.-H. Schlingloff and M. Chai (Eds.): SEFM 2022, LNCS 13550, pp. 209–226, 2022.
https://doi.org/10.1007/978-3-031-17108-6_13

security is only revealed after the program is fully developed. If violations occur, an extensive and repetitive repairing process of writing code and checking the security properties with the analysis technique is needed. An alternative is to check the security with language-based techniques such as type systems [28] during the development. In such a secure type system, every expression is assigned to a type, and a set of typing rules checks that the security policy is not violated [28]. If violations occur, an extensive process of debugging is required until the code is type-checked.

To counter these shortcomings, we propose a constructive approach to directly develop functionally correct programs that are secure by design without the need of a *post-hoc* analysis. Inspired by the correctness-by-construction (CbC) approach for functional correctness [18], we start with a security specification and refine a high-level abstraction of the program stepwise to a concrete implementation using a set of refinement rules. Guided by the security specification defining the allowed security policies on the used data, the programmer is directly informed if a refinement is not applicable because of a prohibited information flow. With IFbCOO (Information Flow control by Construction for an Object-Oriented language), programmers get a local warning as soon as a refinement is not secure, which can reduce debugging effort. With IFbCOO, functionally correct and secure programs can be developed because both, the CbC refinement rules for functional correctness and the proposed refinement rules for information flow security, can be applied simultaneously.

In this paper, we introduce IFbCOO which supports information flow control for an object-oriented language with type modifiers for mutability and alias control [13]. IFbCOO is based on IFbC [25] proposed by some of the authors in previous work, but lifts its programming paradigm from a simple imperative language to an object-oriented language. IFbC introduced a sound set of refinement rules to create imperative programs following an information flow policy, but the language itself is limited to a simple while-language. In contrast, IFbCOO is based on the secure object-oriented language SIFO [27]. SIFO's type system uses immutability and uniqueness properties to facilitate information flow reasoning. In this work, we translate SIFO's typing rules to refinement rules as required by our correctness-by-construction approach. This has the consequence that programs written in SIFO and programs constructed using IFbCOO are interchangeable. In summary, our contributions are the following. We formalize IFbCOO and establish 13 refinement rules. We prove soundness that programs constructed with IFbCOO are secure. Furthermore, we implement IFbCOO in the tool CorC and conduct a feasibility study.

2   Object-Oriented Language SIFO by Example

SIFO [27] is an object-oriented language that ensures secure information flow through a type system with precise uniqueness and (im)mutability reasoning. SIFO introduces four type modifiers for references, namely `read`, `mut`, `imm`, and `capsule`, which define allowed aliasing and mutability of objects in programs.

While, mut and imm point to mutable and immutable object respectively, a capsule reference points to a mutable object that cannot be accessed from other mut references. A read reference points to an object that cannot be aliased or mutated. In this section, SIFO is introduced with examples to give an overview of the expressiveness and the security mechanism of the language. We use in the examples two security levels, namely low and high. An information flow from low to high is allowed, whereas the opposite flow is prohibited. The security levels can be arranged in any user-defined lattice. In Sect. 4, we introduce SIFO formally. In Listing 1, we show the implementation of a class Card containing a low immutable int number and two high fields: a mutable Balance and an immutable Pin.

```
1  class Card{low imm int number; high mut Balance blc;
2    high imm Pin pin;}
3  class Balance{low imm int blc;}
4  class Pin{low imm int pin;}
```

Listing 1. Class declarations

In Listing 2, we show allowed and prohibited field assignments with immutable objects as information flow reasoning is the easiest with these references. In a secure assignment, the assigned expression and the reference need the same security level (Lines 6,7). This applies to mutable and immutable objects. The security level of expressions is calculated by the least upper bound of the accessed field security level and the receiver security level. A high int cannot be assigned to a low blc reference (Line 8) because this would leak confidential information to an attacker, when the attacker reads the low blc reference. The assignment is rejected. Updates of a high immutable field are allowed with a high int (Line 9) or with a low int (Line 10). The imm reference guarantees that the assigned integer is not changed, therefore, no new confidential information can be introduced and a promotion in Line 10 is secure. The promotion alters the security level of the assigned expression to be equal to the security level of the reference. As expected, the opposite update of a low field with a high int is prohibited in Line 11 because of the direct flow from higher to lower security levels.

```
5   low mut Card c = new low Card();//an existing Card reference
6   high mut Balance blc = c.blc;//correct access of high blc
7   high imm int blc = c.blc.blc;//correct access of high blc.blc
8   low imm int blc = c.blc.blc;//wrong high assigned to low
9   c.blc.blc = highInt;//correct field update with high int
10  c.blc.blc = c.number;//correct update with promoted imm int
11  high imm int highInt = 0;//should be some secret value
12  c.number = highInt;//wrong, high int assigned to low c.number
```

Listing 2. Examples with immutable objects

Next, in Listing 3, we exemplify which updates of mutable objects are legal and which updates are not. We have a strict separation of mutable objects with different security levels. We want to prohibit that an update through a higher reference is read by lower references, or that an update through lower references corrupt data of higher references. A new `Balance` object can be initialized as a `low` object because the `Balance` object itself is not confidential (Line 12). The association to a `Card` object makes it a confidential attribute of the `Card` class. However, the assignment of a `low mut` object to a `high` reference is prohibited. If Line 13 would be accepted, Line 14 could be used to insecurely update the confidential `Balance` object because the `low` reference is still in scope of the program. Only an assignment without aliasing is allowed (Line 16). With `capsule`, an encapsulated object is referenced to which no other `mut` reference points. The `low capsBlc` object can be promoted to a `high` security level and assigned. Afterwards, the `capsule` reference is no longer accessible. In the case of an immutable object, the aliasing is allowed (Line 18), since the object itself cannot be updated (Line 19). Both `imm` and `capsule` references are usable to communicate between different security levels.

```
12  low mut Balance newBlc = new low Balance(0);//ok
13  c.blc = newBlc;//wrong, mutable secret shared as low and high
14  newBlc.blc = 10;//ok? Insecure with previous line
15  low capsule Balance capsBlc = new low Balance(0);//ok
16  c.blc = capsBlc;//ok, no alias introduced
17  low imm Pin immPin = new low Pin(1234);//ok
18  c.pin = immPin;//ok, pin is imm and can be aliased
19  immPin.pin = 5678;//wrong, immutable object cannot be updated
```

Listing 3. Examples with mutable and encapsulated objects

3   IFbCOO by Example

With IFbCOO, programmers can incrementally develop programs, where the security levels are organized in a lattice structure to guarantee a variety of confidentiality and integrity policies. IFbCOO defines 13 refinement rules to create secure programs. As these rules are based on refinement rules for correctness-by-construction, programmers can simultaneously apply refinements rules for functional correctness [12,18,26] and security. We now explain IFbCOO in the following examples. For simplicity, we omit the functional specification. IFbCOO is introduced formally in Sect. 4.

In IFbCOO, the programmer starts with a class including fields of the class and declarations of method headers. IFbCOO is used to implement methods in this class successively. The programmer chooses one abstract method body and refines this body to a concrete implementation of the method. A starting IFb-COO tuple specifies the typing context Γ and the abstract method body eA. The expression eA is abstract in the beginning and refined incrementally to a concrete implementation. During the construction process, local variables can be added. The refinement process in IFbCOO results in a method implementation which can be exported to the existing class. First, we give a fine-grained example to show the application of refinement rules in detail. The second example illustrates that IFbCOO can be used to implement larger methods.

The first example in Listing 4 is a setter method. A field `number` is set with a parameter `x`. We start the construction with an abstract expression $eA : [\Gamma; \text{low imm void}]$ with a typing context $\Gamma = \text{low mut } C$ `this`, `low imm int x` extracted from the method signature (C is the class of the method receiver). The abstract expression eA contains all local information (the typing context and its type) to be further refined. A concrete expression that replaces the abstract expression must have the same type `low imm void`, and it can only use variables from the typing context Γ. The tuple $[\Gamma; \text{low imm void}]$ is now refined stepwise. First, we introduce a field assignment: $eA \rightarrow eA_1.\text{number} = eA_2$. The newly introduced abstract expressions are $eA_1 : [\Gamma; \text{low mut } C]$ and $eA_2 : [\Gamma; \text{low imm int}]$ according to the field assignment refinement rule. In the next step, eA_1 is refined to `this`, which is the following refinement: $eA_1.\text{number} = eA_2 \rightarrow \text{this.number} = eA_2$. As `this` has the same type as eA_1, the refinement is correct. The last refinement replaces eA_2 with `x`, resulting in $\text{this.number} = eA_2 \rightarrow \text{this.number} = \text{x}$. As `x` has the same type as eA_2, the refinement is correct. The method is fully refined since no abstract expression is left.

```
1  low mut method low imm void setNumber(low imm int x) {
2    this.number = x; }
```

Listing 4. Set method

To present a larger example, we construct a check of a signature in an email system (see Listing 5). The input of the method is an `email` object and a `client` object that is the receiver of the email. The method checks whether the key with which the `email` object was signed and the stored public key of the `client` object are a valid pair. If this is the case, the `email` object is marked as verified. The fields `isSignatureVerified` and `emailSignKey` of the class `email` have a high security level, as they contain confidential data. The remaining fields have `low` as security level.

```
1  static low imm void verifySignature(
2    low mut Client client, low mut Email email) {
3    low imm int pubkey = client.publicKey;
4    high imm int privkey = email.emailSignKey;
5    high imm boolean isVerified;
6    if (isKeyPairValid(privkey, pubkey)) {
7      isVerified = true;
8    } else {
9      isVerified = false;
10   }
11   email.IsSignatureVerified = isVerified;
12 }
```

Listing 5. Program of a secure signature verification

In Fig. 1, we show the starting IFbCOO tuple with the security level of the variables (type modifier and class name are omitted) at the top. In our example,

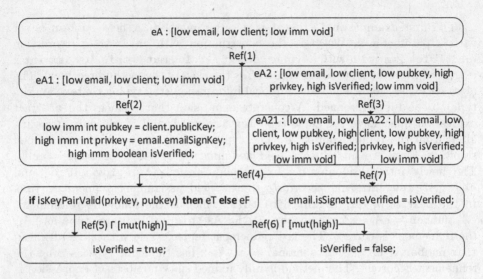

Fig. 1. Refinement steps for the signature example

we have two parameters `client` and `email`, with a `low` security level. To construct the algorithm of Listing 5, the method implementation is split into three parts. First, two local variables (private and public key for the signature verification) are initialized and a Boolean for the result of the verification is declared. Second, verification whether the keys used for the signature form a valid pair takes place. Finally, the result is saved in a field of the `email` object.

Using the refinement rule for composition, the program is initially split into the initialization phase and the remainder of the program's behavior (Ref(1)). This refinement introduces two abstract expressions $eA1$ and $eA2$. The typing contexts of the expressions are calculated by IFbCOO automatically during refinement. As we want to initialize two local variables by further refining $eA1$, the finished refinement in Fig. 1 already contains the local `high` variables `privkey` and `isVerified`, and the `low` variable `pubkey` in the typing context of expression $eA2$.

In Ref(2), we apply the assignment refinement[1] to initialize the integers `pubkey` and `privkey`. Both references point to immutable objects that are accessed via fields of the objects `client` and `email`. The security levels of the field accesses are determined with the field access rule checked by IFbCOO. The determined security level of the assigned expression must match the security level of the reference. In this case, the security levels are the same. Additionally, it is enforced that immutable objects cannot be altered after construction (i.e., it is not possible to corrupt the private and public key). In Ref(3), the next expression $eA2$ is split with a composition refinement into $eA21$ and $eA22$.

Ref(4) introduces an if-then-else-expression by refining $eA21$. Here, it is checked whether the public and private key pair is valid. As the `privkey`

---

[1] To be precise, it would be a combination of composition and assignment refinements, because an assignment refinement can only introduce one assignment expression.

$$
\begin{array}{ll}
T & ::= s \; mdf \; C \\
s & ::= \texttt{high} \mid \texttt{low} \mid \ldots (\text{user defined}) \\
mdf & ::= \texttt{mut} \mid \texttt{imm} \mid \texttt{capsule} \mid \texttt{read} \\
CD & ::= \texttt{class } C \texttt{ implements } \overline{C} \; \{ \overline{F \; MD} \; \} \mid \texttt{interface } C \texttt{ extends } \overline{C} \; \{\overline{MH}\} \\
F & ::= s \texttt{ mut } C \; f; \mid s \texttt{ imm } C \; f; \\
MD & ::= MH \; \{\texttt{return } e;\} \\
MH & ::= s \; mdf \; \texttt{method } T \; m(T_1 \; x_1, \; \ldots, \; T_n \; x_n) \\
e & ::= eA \mid x \mid e_0.f = e_1 \mid e.f \mid e_0.m(\overline{e}) \mid \texttt{new } s \; C(\overline{e}) \mid e_0; e_1 \\
& \quad \mid \texttt{if } e_0 \texttt{ then } e_1 \texttt{ else } e_2 \mid \texttt{while } e_0 \texttt{ do } e_1 \mid \texttt{declassify}(e) \\
\Gamma & ::= x_1 : T_1 \ldots x_n : T_n \\
\mathcal{E} & ::= [] \mid \mathcal{E}.f \mid \mathcal{E}.f = e \mid e.f = \mathcal{E} \mid \mathcal{E}.m(\overline{e}) \mid e.m(\overline{e} \; \mathcal{E} \; \overline{e}) \mid \texttt{new } s \; C(\overline{e} \; \mathcal{E} \; \overline{e})
\end{array}
$$

Fig. 2. Syntax of the extended core calculus of SIFO

object has a `high` security level, we have to restrict our typing context with $\Gamma[mut(\texttt{high})]$. This is necessary to prevent indirect information leaks. With the restrictions, we can only assign expressions to at least `high` references and mutate `high` objects ($mut(\texttt{high})$) in the then- and else-expression. If we assign a value in the then-expression to a `low` reference that is visible outside of the then-expression, an attacker could deduce that the guard was evaluated to true by reading that `low` reference.

Ref(5) introduces an assignment of an immutable object to a `high` reference, which is allowed in the restricted typing context. As explained, the assignment to `low` references is forbidden. The assigned immutable object `true` can be securely promoted to a `high` security level. In Ref(6), a similar assignment is done, but with the value `false`. Ref(7) sets a field of the `email` object by refining $eA22$. We update the `high` field of the `email` object by accepting the `high` expression `isVerified`. With this last refinement step, the method is fully concretized. The method is secure by construction and constitutes valid SIFO code (see Listing 5).

4 Formalizing Information Flow Control-by-Construction

In this section, we formalize IFbCOO for the construction of functionally correct and secure programs. Before, we introduce SIFO as the underlying programming language formally.

4.1 Core Calculus of SIFO

Figure 2 shows the syntax of the extended core calculus of SIFO [27]. SIFO is an expression-based language similar to Featherweight Java [17]. Every reference and expression is associated with a type T. The type T is composed of a security level s, a type modifier mdf and a class name C. Security levels are arranged in a lattice with one greatest level $\top$ and one least level $\bot$ forming the security policy. The security policy determines the allowed information flow. Confidentiality and integrity can be enforced by using two security lattices and two security annotations for each expression. Each property is enforced by a strict separation of security levels. In the interest of an expressive language, we allow the information flow from lower to higher levels (confidentiality or integrity security levels) using promotion rules while the opposite needs direct interaction with the programmer by using the `declassify` expression. For convenience, we will use only one lattice of confidentiality security levels in the explanations.

The type modifier mdf can be `mut`, `imm`, `capsule`, and `read` with the following subtyping relation. For all type modifier mdf : `capsule` $\leq mdf$, $mdf \leq$ `read`. In SIFO, objects are *mutable* or (deeply) *immutable*. The reachable object graph (ROG) from a mutable object is composed of mutable and immutable objects, while the ROG of an immutable object can only contain immutable objects. A `mut` reference must point to a mutable object; such an object can be aliased and mutated. An `imm` reference must point to an immutable object; such an object can be aliased, but not mutated. A `capsule` reference points to a mutable object. The object and the mutable objects in its ROG cannot be accessed from other references. As `capsule` is a subtype of `imm` and `mut` the object can be assigned to both. Finally, a `read` reference is the supertype that points to an object that cannot be aliased or mutated, but it has no immutability guarantee that the object is not modified by other references. These modifiers allow us to make precise decisions about the information flow by utilizing immutability or uniqueness properties of objects. For example, an immutable object cannot be altered, therefore it can be securely promoted to a higher security level. For a mutable object, a security promotion is insecure because an update through other references with lower security levels can corrupt the confidential information.

Additionally, the syntax of SIFO contains class definitions CD which can be classes or interfaces. An interface has a list of method headers. A class has additional fields. A field F has a type T and a name, but the type modifier can only be `mut` or `imm`. A method definition MD consists of a method header and a body. The header has a receiver, a return type, and a list of parameters. The parameters have a name and a type T. The receiver has a type modifier and a security level. An expression e can be a variable, field access, field assignment, method call, or object construction in SIFO. In the extended version presented in the paper, we also added abstract expressions, sequence of expressions, conditional expression, loop expression, and declassification. With the `declassify` operator a reverse information flow is allowed. The expression eA is abstract and typed by $[\Gamma; T]$. Beside the type T a local typing context Γ is used to have all needed information to further refine eA. We require a Boolean type for the guards in the conditional and loop expression. A typing context Γ assigns a type T_i to variable x_i. With the evaluation context $\mathcal{E}$, we define the order of evaluation for the reduction of the system. The typing rules of SIFO are shown in the report [24].

4.2   Refinement Rules for Program Construction

To formalize the IFbCOO refinement rules, in Fig. 3, we introduce basic notations, which are used in the refinement rules.

L is the lattice of security levels to define the information flow policy and *lub* is used to calculate the least upper bound of a set of security levels. The

L Bounded upper semi-lattice $(L, \leq)$ of security levels
$lub : \mathcal{P}(L) \to L$ Least upper bound of the security levels in L
$\{P; Q; \Gamma; T; eA\}$ Starting IFbCOO tuple
$eA : [P; Q; \Gamma; T]$ Typed abstract expression eA
$\Gamma[mut(s)]$ Restricted typing context
$sec(T) = s$ Returns the security level s in type T

Fig. 3. Basic notations for IFbCOO

functional and security specification of a program is defined by an IFbCOO tuple $\{P; Q; \Gamma; T; eA\}$. The IFbCOO tuple consists of a typing context Γ, a type T, an abstract expression eA, and a functional pre-/postcondition, which is declared in the first-order predicates P and Q. The abstract expression is typed by $[P; Q; \Gamma; T]$. In the following, we focus on security, so the functional specification is omitted.

The refinement process of IFbCOO starts with a method declaration, where the typing context Γ is extracted from the arguments and T is the method return type. Then, the user guides the construction process by refining the first abstract expression eA. With the notation $\Gamma[mut(s)]$, we introduce a restriction to the typing context. The function $mut(s)$ prevents mutation of mutable objects that have a security level lower than s. When the user chooses the lowest security level of the lattice, the function does not restrict Γ. The function $sec(T)$ extracts the security level of a type T.

Refinement Rules. The refinement rules are used to replace an IFbCOO tuple $\{\Gamma; T; eA\}$ with a concrete implementation by concretizing the abstract expression eA. This refinement is only correct if specific side conditions hold. On the right side of the rules, all newly introduced symbols are implicitly existentially quantified. The rules can introduce new abstract expressions eA_i which can be refined by further applying the refinement rules.

Refinement Rule 1 (Variable)
eA is refinable to x if $eA : [\Gamma; T]$ and $\Gamma(x) = T$.

The first IFbCOO rule introduces a variable x, which does not alter the program. It refines an abstract expression to an x if x has the correct type T.

Refinement Rule 2 (Field Assignment)
eA is refinable to $eA_0.f := eA_1$ if $eA : [\Gamma; T]$ and $eA_0 : [\Gamma; s_0 \text{ mut } C_0]$ and $eA_1 : [\Gamma; s_1 \text{ mdf } C]$ and $s \text{ mdf } C f \in fields(C_0)$ and $s_1 = lub(s_0, s)$.

We can refine an abstract expression to a field assignment if the following conditions hold. The expression eA_0 has to be mut to allow a manipulation of the object. The security level of the assigned expression eA_1 has to be equal to the least upper bound of the security levels of expression eA_0 and the field f. The field f must be a field of the class C_0 with the type $s \text{ mdf } C$. With the security promotion rule, the security level of the assigned expression can be altered.

Refinement Rule 3 (Field Access)
eA is refinable to $eA_0.f$ if $eA : [\Gamma; s \ mdf \ C]$ and $eA_0 : [\Gamma; s_0 \ mdf_0 \ C_0]$ and $s_1 \ mdf_1 \ C \ f \in fields(C_0)$ and $s = lub(s_0, s_1)$ and $mdf_0 \triangleright mdf_1 = mdf$.

We can refine an abstract expression to a field access if a field f exists in the class of receiver eA_0 with the type $s_1 \ mdf_1 \ C$. The accessed value must have the expected type $s \ mdf \ C$ of the abstract expression. This means, the class name of the field f and C must be the same. Additionally, the security level of the abstract expression eA is equal to the least upper bound of the security levels of expression eA_0 and field f. The type modifiers must also comply. The arrow between type modifiers is defined as follows. As we allow only mut and imm fields, not all possible cases are defined: $mdf \triangleright mdf' = mdf''$

- mut $\triangleright \ mdf =$ capsule $\triangleright \ mdf = mdf$
- imm $\triangleright \ mdf = mdf \triangleright$ imm $=$ imm
- read $\triangleright$ mut $=$ read.

Refinement Rule 4 (Method Call)
eA is refinable to $eA_0.m(eA_1, \ldots, eA_n)$ if $eA : [\Gamma; T]$ and $eA_0 : [\Gamma; T_0] \ldots eA_n : [\Gamma; T_n]$ and $T_0 \ldots T_n \to T \in methTypes(class(T_0), m)$ and $sec(T) \geq sec(T_0)$ and forall $i \in \{1, \ldots, n\}$ if $mdf(T_i) \in \{$mut, capsule$\}$ then $sec(T_i) \geq sec(T_0)$.

With the method call rule, an abstract expression is refined to a call to method m. The method has a receiver eA_0, a list of parameters $eA_1 \ldots eA_n$, and a return value. A method with matching definition must exist in the class of receiver eA_0. This method definition is returned by the *methTypes* function. The function *class* returns the class of a type T. The security level of the return type has to be greater than or equal to the security level of the receiver. This condition is needed because through dynamic dispatch information of the receiver may be leaked if its security level is higher than the security level of the return type. The same applies for mut and capsule parameters. The security level of these parameters must also be greater than or equal to the security level of the receiver. As the method call replaces an abstract expression eA, the return value must have the same type (security level, type modifier, and class name) as the refined expression. In the technical report [24], we introduce multiple methods types [27] to reduce writing effort and increase the flexibility of IFbCOO. A method can be declared with specific types for receiver, parameters and return value, and other signatures of this method are deduced by applying the transformations from the multiple method types definition, where security level and type modifiers are altered. All these deduced method declarations can be used in the method call refinement rule.

Refinement Rule 5 (Constructor)
eA is refinable to new $s \ C(eA_1 \ldots eA_n)$ if $eA : [\Gamma; s \ mdf \ C]$ and $fields(C) = T_1 \ f_1 \ldots T_n \ f_n$ and $eA_1 : [\Gamma; T_1[s]] \ldots eA_n : [\Gamma; T_n[s]]$.

The constructor rule is a special method call. We can refine an abstract expression to a constructor call, where a mutable object of class C is constructed with a security level s. The parameter list $eA_1 \ldots eA_n$ must match the list of declared fields $f_1 \ldots f_n$ in class C. Each parameter eA_i is assigned to field f_i. This assignment is allowed if the type of parameter eA_i is (a subtype of) $T_i[s]$. $T[s]$ is a helper function which returns a new type whose security level is the least upper bound of $sec(T)$ and s. It is defined as: $T[s] = lub(s, s')\ mdf\ C$, where $T = s'\ mdf\ C$, defined only if $s' \leq s$ or $s \leq s'$. By calling a constructor, the security level s can be freely chosen to use parameters with security levels that are higher than originally declared for the fields. In other words, a security level s is used to initialize lower security fields with parameters of higher security level s. This results in a newly created object with the security level s [27]. As the newly created object replaces an abstract expression eA, the object must have the same type as the abstract expression. If the modifier promotion rule is used (i.e., no mutable input value exist), the object can be assigned to a `capsule` or `imm` reference.

Refinement Rule 6 (Composition)
eA is refinable to $eA_0; eA_1$ if $eA : [\Gamma; T]$ and $eA_0 : [\Gamma; T_0]$ and $eA_1 : [\Gamma; T]$.

With the composition rule, an abstract expression eA is refined to two subsequent abstract expression eA_0 and eA_1. The second abstract expression must have the same type T as the refined expression.

Refinement Rule 7 (Selection)
eA is refinable to `if` eA_0 `then` eA_1 `else` eA_2 if $eA : [\Gamma; T]$ and $eA_0 : [\Gamma; s\ \mathrm{imm}$ `Boolean`$]$ and $eA_1 : [\Gamma[mut(s)]; T]$ and $eA_2 : [\Gamma[mut(s)]; T]$.

The selection rule refines an abstract expression to a conditional `if-then-else`-expression. Secure information can be leaked indirectly as the selected branch may reveal the value of the guard. In the branches, the typing context is restricted. The restricted typing context prevents updating mutable objects with a security level lower than s. The security level s is determined by the Boolean guard eA_0. When we add updatable local variables to our language, the selection rule must also prevent the update of local variables that have a security level lower than s.

Refinement Rule 8 (Repetition)
eA is refinable to `while` eA_0 `do` eA_1 if $eA : [\Gamma; T]$ and $eA_0 : [\Gamma; s\ \mathrm{imm}$ `Boolean`$]$ and $eA_1 : [\Gamma[mut(s)]; T]$.

The repetition rule refines an abstract expression to a `while`-loop. The repetition rule is similar to the selection rule. For the loop body, the typing context is restricted to prevent indirect leaks of the guard in the loop body. The security level s is determined by the Boolean guard eA_0.

Refinement Rule 9 (Context Rule)
$\mathcal{E}[eA]$ is refinable to $\mathcal{E}[e]$ if eA is refinable to e.

The context rule replaces in a context $\mathcal{E}$ an abstract expression with a concrete expression, if the abstract expression is refinable to the concrete expression.

Refinement Rule 10 (Subsumption Rule)
$eA : [\Gamma; T]$ *is refinable to* $eA_1 : [\Gamma; T']$ *if* $T' \leq T$.

The subsumption rule can alter the type of expressions. An abstract expression that requires a type T can be weakened to require a type T' if the type T' is a subtype of T.

Refinement Rule 11 (Security Promotion)
$eA : [\Gamma; s\ mdf\ C]$ *is refinable to* $eA_1 : [\Gamma; s'\ mdf\ C]$ *if* $mdf \in \{\texttt{capsule}, \texttt{imm}\}$ *and* $s' \leq s$.

The security promotion rule can alter the security level of expressions. An abstract expression that requires a security level s can be weakened to require a security level s' if the expression is $\texttt{capsule}$ or $\texttt{imm}$. Other expressions ($\texttt{mut}$ or $\texttt{read}$) cannot be altered because potentially existing aliases are a security hazard.

Refinement Rule 12 (Modifier Promotion)
$eA : [\Gamma; s\ \texttt{capsule}\ C]$ *is refinable to* $eA_1 : [\Gamma[\texttt{mut}\backslash\texttt{read}]; s\ \texttt{mut}\ C]$.

The modifier promotion rule can alter the type modifier of an expression eA. An abstract expression that requires a $\texttt{capsule}$ type modifier can be weakened to require a $\texttt{mut}$ type modifier if all $\texttt{mut}$ references are only seen as $\texttt{read}$ in the typing context. That means, that the mutable objects in the ROG of the expression cannot be accessed by other references. Thus, manipulation of the object is only possible through the reference on eA.

Refinement Rule 13 (Declassification)
$eA : [\Gamma; \perp\ mdf\ C]$ *is refinable to* $\texttt{declassify}(eA_1) : [\Gamma; s\ mdf\ C]$ *if* $mdf \in \{\texttt{capsule}, \texttt{imm}\}$.

In our information flow policy, we can never assign an expression with a higher security level to a variable with a lower security level. To allow this assignment in appropriate cases, the $\texttt{declassify}$ rule is used. An expression eA is altered to a $\texttt{declassify}$-expression with an abstract expression eA_1 that has a security level s if the type modifier is $\texttt{capsule}$ or $\texttt{imm}$. A $\texttt{mut}$ or $\texttt{read}$ expression cannot be declassified as existing aliases are a security hazard. Since we have the security promotion rule, the declassified $\texttt{capsule}$ or $\texttt{imm}$ expression can directly be promoted to any higher security level. Therefore, it is sufficient to use the bottom security level in this rule without restricting the expressiveness. For example, the rule can be used to assign a hashed password to a public variable. The programmer has the responsibility to ensure that the use of $\texttt{declassify}$ is secure.

4.3 Proof of Soundness

In the technical report, we prove that programs constructed with the IFbCOO refinement rules are secure according to the defined information flow policy. We prove this by showing that programs constructed with IFbCOO are well typed in SIFO (Theorem 1). SIFO itself is proven to be secure [27]. In the technical report [24], we prove this property for the core language of SIFO, which does not contain composition, selection, and repetition expressions. The SIFO core language is minimal, but using well-known encodings, it can support composition, selection, and repetition (encodings of the Smalltalk [14] style support control structures). We also exclude the declassify operation because this rule is an explicit mechanism to break security in a controlled way.

Theorem 1 (Soundness of IFbCOO)
An expression e constructed with IFbCOO is well typed in SIFO.

5   CorC Tool Support and Evaluation

IFbCOO is implemented in the tool CorC [12,26]. CorC itself is a hybrid textual and graphical editor to develop programs with correctness-by-construction. IFbC [25] is already implemented as extension of CorC, but to support object-orientation with IFbCOO a redesign was necessary. Source code and case studies are available at: https://github.com/TUBS-ISF/CorC/tree/CCorCOO.

5.1   CorC for IFbCOO

For space reasons, we cannot introduce CorC comprehensively. We just summarize the features of CorC to check IFbCOO information flow policies:

- Programs are written in a tree structure of refining IFbCOO tuples (see Fig. 1). Besides the functional specification, variables are labeled with a type T in the tuples.
- Each IFbCOO refinement rule is implemented in CorC. Consequently, functional correctness and security can be constructed simultaneously.
- The information flow checks according to the refinement rules are executed automatically after each refinement.
- Each CorC-program is uniquely mapped to a method in a SIFO class. A SIFO class contains methods and fields that are annotated with security labels and type modifiers.
- A properties view shows the type T of each used variable in an IFbCOO tuple. Violations of the information flow policy are explained in the view.

5.2   Case Studies and Discussion

The implementation of IFbCOO in the tool CorC enables us to evaluate the feasibility of the security mechanism by successfully implementing three case studies [16,32] from the literature and a novel one in CorC. The case studies are also implemented and type-checked in SIFO to confirm that the case studies are secure. The newly developed *Database* case study represents a secure system

Table 1. Metrics of the case studies

Name	#Security levels	# Classes	# Lines of code	# Methods in CorC
Database	4	6	156	2
Email [16]	2	9	807	15
Banking [32]	2	3	243	6
Paycard	2	3	244	5

that strictly separates databases of different security levels. *Email* [16] ensures that encrypted emails cannot be decrypted by recipients without the matching key. *Paycard* (http://spl2go.cs.ovgu.de/projects/57) and *Banking* [32] simulate secure money transfer without leaking customer data. The *Database* case study uses four security levels, while the others (*Email*, *Banking*, and *Paycard*) use two.

As shown in Table 1, the cases studies comprise three to nine classes with 156 to 807 lines of code each. 28 Methods that exceed the complexity of getter and setter are implemented in CorC. It should be noted that we do not have to implement every method in CorC. If only `low` input data is used to compute `low` output, the method is intrinsically secure. For example, three classes in the Database case study are implemented with only `low` security levels. Only the class `GUI` and the main method of the case study, which calls the `low` methods with higher security levels (using multiple method types) is then correctly implemented in CorC. The correct and secure promotion of security levels of methods called in the main method is confirmed by CorC.

Discussion and Applicability of IFbCOO. We emphasize that CbC and also IFbCOO should be used to implement correctness- and security-critical programs [18]. The scope of this work is to demonstrate the feasibility of the incremental construction of correctness- and security-critical programs. We argue that we achieve this goal by implementing four case studies in CorC.

The constructive nature of IFbCOO is an advantage in the secure creation of programs. Instead of writing complete methods to allow a static analyzer to accept/reject the method, with IFbCOO, we directly design and construct secure methods. We get feedback during each refinement step, and we can observe the status of all accessible variables at any time of the method. For example, we received direct feedback when we manipulated a `low` object in the body of a `high` then-branch. With this information, we could adjust the code to ensure security. As IFbCOO extends CorC, functional correctness is also guaranteed at the same time. This is beneficial as a program, which is security-critical, should also be functionally correct. As IFbCOO is based on SIFO, programs written with any of the two approaches can be used interchangeably. This allows developers to use their preferred environment to develop new systems, re-engineer their systems, or integrate secure software into existing systems. These benefits of IFbCOO are of course connected with functional and security specification effort, and the strict refinement-based construction of programs.

6   Related Work

In this section, we compare IFbCOO to IFbC [25,29] and other Hoare-style logics for information flow control. We also discuss information flow type systems and correctness-by-construction [18] for functional correctness.

IFbCOO extends IFbC [25] by introducing object-orientation and type modifiers. IFbC is based on a simple while language. As explained in Sect. 4, the language of IFbCOO includes objects and type modifiers. Therefore, the refinement rules of IFbC are revised to handle secure information flow with objects. The object-orientation complicates the reasoning of secure assignments because objects could be altered through references with different security levels. If private information is introduced, an already public reference could read this information. SIFO and therefore IFbCOO consider these cases and prevent information leaks by considering immutability and encapsulation and only allowing secure aliases.

Previous work using Hoare-style program logics with information flow control analyzes programs after construction, rather than guaranteeing security during construction. Andrews and Reitman [5] encode information flow directly in a logical form. They also support parallel programs. Amtoft and Banerjee [3] use Hoare-style program logics and abstract interpretations to detect information flow leaks. They can give error explanations based on strongest postcondition calculation. The work of Amtoft and Banerjee [3] is used in SPARK Ada [4] to specify and check the information flow.

Type system for information flow control are widely used, we refer to Sabelfeld and Myers [28] for a comprehensive overview. We only discuss closely related type systems for object-oriented languages [9–11,20,30,31]. Banerjee et al. [9] introduced a type system for a Java-like language with only two security levels. We extend this by operating on any lattice of security levels. We also introduce type modifiers to simplify reasoning in cases where objects cannot be mutated or are encapsulated. Jif [20] is a type system to check information flow in Java. One main difference is in the treatment of aliases: Jif does not have an alias analysis to reason about limited side effects. Therefore, Jif pessimistically discards programs that introduce aliases because Jif has no option to state immutable or encapsulated objects. IFbCOO allows the introduction of secure aliases.

In the area of correctness-by-construction, Morgan [19] and Back [8] propose refinement-based approaches which refine functional specifications to concrete implementations. Beside of pre-/postcondition specification, Back also uses invariants as starting point. Morgan's calculus is implemented in ArcAngel [22] with the verifier ProofPower [33], and SOCOS [6,7] implements Back's approach. In comparison to IFbCOO, those approaches do not reason about information flow security. Other refinement-based approaches are Event-B [1,2] for automata-based systems and Circus [21,23] for state-rich reactive systems. These approaches have a higher abstraction level, as they operate on abstract machines instead of source code. Hall and Chapman [15] introduced with CbyC another related approach that uses formal modeling techniques to analyze the development during all stages (architectural design, detailed design, code) to eliminate defects early. IFbCOO is tailored to source code and does not consider other development phases.

7 Conclusion

In this paper, we present IFbCOO, which establishes an incremental refinement-based approach for functionally correct and secure programs. With IFbCOO programs are constructed stepwise to comply at all time with the security policy. The local check of each refinement can reduce debugging effort, since the user is not warned only after the implementation of a whole method. We formalized IFbCOO by introducing 13 refinement rules and proved soundness by showing that constructed programs are well-typed in SIFO. We also implemented IFbCOO in CorC and evaluated our implementation with a feasibility study. One future direction is the conduction of comprehensive user studies for user-friendly improvements which is only now possible due to our sophisticated tool CorC.

Acknowledgments. This work was supported by KASTEL Security Research Labs.

References

1. Abrial, J.: Modeling in Event-B - System and Software Engineering. Cambridge University Press, Cambridge (2010)
2. Abrial, J.R., Butler, M., Hallerstede, S., Hoang, T.S., Mehta, F., Voisin, L.: Rodin: an open toolset for modelling and reasoning in Event-B. Int. J. Softw. Tools Technol. Transfer **12**(6), 447–466 (2010)
3. Amtoft, T., Banerjee, A.: Information flow analysis in logical form. In: Giacobazzi, R. (ed.) SAS 2004. LNCS, vol. 3148, pp. 100–115. Springer, Heidelberg (2004). https://doi.org/10.1007/978-3-540-27864-1_10
4. Amtoft, T., Hatcliff, J., Rodríguez, E.: Specification and checking of software contracts for conditional information flow. In: Cuellar, J., Maibaum, T., Sere, K. (eds.) FM 2008. LNCS, vol. 5014, pp. 229–245. Springer, Heidelberg (2008). https://doi.org/10.1007/978-3-540-68237-0_17
5. Andrews, G.R., Reitman, R.P.: An axiomatic approach to information flow in programs. ACM Trans. Program. Langu. Syst. (TOPLAS) **2**(1), 56–76 (1980)
6. Back, R.J.: Invariant based programming: basic approach and teaching experiences. Formal Aspects Comput. **21**(3), 227–244 (2009)
7. Back, R.-J., Eriksson, J., Myreen, M.: Testing and verifying invariant based programs in the SOCOS environment. In: Gurevich, Y., Meyer, B. (eds.) TAP 2007. LNCS, vol. 4454, pp. 61–78. Springer, Heidelberg (2007). https://doi.org/10.1007/978-3-540-73770-4_4
8. Back, R.J., Wright, J.: Refinement Calculus: A Systematic Introduction. Springer, Heidelberg (2012)
9. Banerjee, A., Naumann, D.A.: Secure information flow and pointer confinement in a Java-like language. In: Computer Security Foundations Workshop, vol. 2, p. 253 (2002)

10. Barthe, G., Pichardie, D., Rezk, T.: A certified lightweight non-interference Java bytecode verifier. In: De Nicola, R. (ed.) ESOP 2007. LNCS, vol. 4421, pp. 125–140. Springer, Heidelberg (2007). https://doi.org/10.1007/978-3-540-71316-6_10

11. Barthe, G., Serpette, B.P.: Partial evaluation and non-interference for object calculi. In: Middeldorp, A., Sato, T. (eds.) FLOPS 1999. LNCS, vol. 1722, pp. 53–67. Springer, Heidelberg (1999). https://doi.org/10.1007/10705424_4

12. Bordis, T., Cleophas, L., Kittelmann, A., Runge, T., Schaefer, I., Watson, B.W.: Re-CorC-ing KeY: correct-by-construction software development based on KeY. In: Ahrendt, W., Beckert, B., Bubel, R., Johnsen, E.B. (eds.) The Logic of Software. A Tasting Menu of Formal Methods. LNCS, vol. 13360, pp. 80–104. Springer, Cham (2022). https://doi.org/10.1007/978-3-031-08166-8_5

13. Giannini, P., Servetto, M., Zucca, E., Cone, J.: Flexible recovery of uniqueness and immutability. Theor. Comput. Sci. **764**, 145–172 (2019)

14. Goldberg, A., Robson, D.: Smalltalk-80: The Language and its Implementation. Addison-Wesley Longman Publishing Co., Inc. (1983)

15. Hall, A., Chapman, R.: Correctness by construction: developing a commercial secure system. IEEE Softw. **19**(1), 18–25 (2002)

16. Hall, R.J.: Fundamental nonmodularity in electronic mail. Autom. Softw. Eng. **12**(1), 41–79 (2005)

17. Igarashi, A., Pierce, B.C., Wadler, P.: Featherweight Java: a minimal core calculus for Java and GJ. ACM Trans. Program. Lang. Syst. (TOPLAS) **23**(3), 396–450 (2001)

18. Kourie, D.G., Watson, B.W.: The Correctness-by-Construction Approach to Programming. Springer, Heidelberg (2012)

19. Morgan, C.: Programming from Specifications, 2nd edn. Prentice Hall, Hoboken (1994)

20. Myers, A.C.: JFlow: practical mostly-static information flow control. In: Proceedings of the 26th ACM SIGPLAN-SIGACT Symposium on Principles of Programming Languages, pp. 228–241. ACM (1999)

21. Oliveira, M., Cavalcanti, A., Woodcock, J.: A UTP semantics for circus. Formal Aspects Comput. **21**(1), 3–32 (2009)

22. Oliveira, M.V.M., Cavalcanti, A., Woodcock, J.: ArcAngel: a tactic language for refinement. Formal Aspects Comput. **15**(1), 28–47 (2003)

23. Oliveira, M.V.M., Gurgel, A.C., Castro, C.G.: CRefine: support for the circus refinement calculus. In: 2008 Sixth IEEE International Conference on Software Engineering and Formal Methods, pp. 281–290. IEEE (2008)

24. Runge, T., Kittelmann, A., Servetto, M., Potanin, A., Schaefer, I.: Information flow control-by-construction for an object-oriented language using type modifiers (2022). https://arxiv.org/abs/2208.02672

25. Runge, T., Knüppel, A., Thüm, T., Schaefer, I.: Lattice-based information flow control-by-construction for security-by-design. In: Proceedings of the 8th International Conference on Formal Methods in Software Engineering (2020)

26. Runge, T., Schaefer, I., Cleophas, L., Thüm, T., Kourie, D., Watson, B.W.: Tool support for correctness-by-construction. In: Hähnle, R., van der Aalst, W. (eds.) FASE 2019. LNCS, vol. 11424, pp. 25–42. Springer, Cham (2019). https://doi.org/10.1007/978-3-030-16722-6_2

27. Runge, T., Servetto, M., Potanin, A., Schaefer, I.: Immutability and Encapsulation for Sound OO Information Flow Control (2022, under review)

28. Sabelfeld, A., Myers, A.C.: Language-based information-flow security. IEEE J. Sel. Areas Commun. **21**(1), 5–19 (2003)

29. Schaefer, I., Runge, T., Knüppel, A., Cleophas, L., Kourie, D., Watson, B.W.: Towards confidentiality-by-construction. In: Margaria, T., Steffen, B. (eds.) ISoLA 2018. LNCS, vol. 11244, pp. 502–515. Springer, Cham (2018). https://doi.org/10.1007/978-3-030-03418-4_30
30. Strecker, M.: Formal analysis of an information flow type system for MicroJava. Technische Universität München, Technical report (2003)
31. Sun, Q., Banerjee, A., Naumann, D.A.: Modular and constraint-based information flow inference for an object-oriented language. In: Giacobazzi, R. (ed.) SAS 2004. LNCS, vol. 3148, pp. 84–99. Springer, Heidelberg (2004). https://doi.org/10.1007/978-3-540-27864-1_9
32. Thüm, T., Schaefer, I., Apel, S., Hentschel, M.: Family-based deductive verification of software product lines. In: Proceedings of the 11th International Conference on Generative Programming and Component Engineering, pp. 11–20 (2012)
33. Zeyda, F., Oliveira, M., Cavalcanti, A.: Supporting ArcAngel in ProofPower. Electron. Notes Theor. Comput. Sci. 259, 225–243 (2009)

Specification is Law: Safe Creation and Upgrade of Ethereum Smart Contracts

Pedro Antonino[1]([✉]), Juliandson Ferreira[2], Augusto Sampaio[2],
and A. W. Roscoe[1,3,4]

[1] The Blockhouse Technology Limited, Oxford, UK
pedro@tbtl.com
[2] Centro de Informática, Universidade Federal de Pernambuco, Recife, Brazil
{jef,acas}@cin.ufpe.br
[3] Department of Computer Science, Oxford University, Oxford, UK
[4] University College Oxford Blockchain Research Centre, Oxford, UK

Abstract. Smart contracts are the building blocks of the "code is law" paradigm: the smart contract's code indisputably describes how its assets are to be managed - once it is created, its code is typically immutable. Faulty smart contracts present the most significant evidence against the practicality of this paradigm; they are well-documented and resulted in assets worth vast sums of money being compromised. To address this issue, the Ethereum community proposed (i) tools and processes to audit/analyse smart contracts, and (ii) design patterns implementing a mechanism to make contract code mutable. Individually, (i) and (ii) only partially address the challenges raised by the "code is law" paradigm. In this paper, we combine elements from (i) and (ii) to create a systematic framework that moves away from "code is law" and gives rise to a new "specification is law" paradigm. It allows contracts to be created and upgraded but only if they meet a corresponding formal specification. The framework is centered around *a trusted deployer*: an off-chain service that formally verifies and enforces this notion of conformance. We have prototyped this framework, and investigated its applicability to contracts implementing three widely used Ethereum standards: the ERC20 Token Standard, ERC3156 Flash Loans and ERC1155 Multi Token Standard, with promising results.

Keywords: Formal verification · Smart contracts · Ethereum · Solidity · Safe deployment · Safe upgrade

1 Introduction

A *smart contract* is a stateful reactive program that is stored in and processed by a trusted platform, typically a blockchain, which securely executes such a program and safely stores its persistent state. Smart contracts were created to

B.-H. Schlingloff and M. Chai (Eds.): SEFM 2022, LNCS 13550, pp. 227–243, 2022.
https://doi.org/10.1007/978-3-031-17108-6_14

provide an unambiguous, automated, and secure way to manage digital assets. They are the building blocks of the "code is law" paradigm, indisputably describing how their assets are to be managed. To implement this paradigm, many smart contract platforms - including Ethereum, the platform we focus on - disallow the code of a contract to be changed once deployed, effectively enforcing a notion of *code/implementation immutability*.

Implementation immutability, however, has two main drawbacks. Firstly, contracts cannot be patched if the implementation is found to be incorrect after being deployed. There are many examples of real-world contract instances with flaws that have been exploited with astonishing sums of cryptocurrencies being taken over [7,30]. The ever-increasing valuation of these assets presents a significant long-standing incentive to perpetrators of such attacks. Secondly, contracts cannot be optimised. The execution of a contract function has an explicit cost to be paid by the caller that is calculated based on the contract's implementation. Platform participants would, then, benefit from contracts being updated to a functionally-equivalent but more cost-effective implementation, which is disallowed by this sort of code immutability.

To overcome this limitation, the Ethereum community has adopted the *proxy pattern* [31] as a mechanism by which one can mimic contract upgrades. The simple application of this pattern, however, presents a number of potential issues. Firstly, the use of this mechanism allows for the patching of smart contracts but it does not address the fundamental underlying problem of correctness. Once an issue is detected, it can be patched but (i) it may be too late, and (ii) what if the patch is faulty too? Secondly, it typically gives an, arguably, unreasonable amount of power to the maintainers of this contract. Therefore, no guarantees are enforced by this updating process; the contract implementations can change rather arbitrarily as long as the right participants have approved the change. In such a context, the "code is law" paradigm is in fact nonexistent.

To address these issues, we propose a *systematic deployment framework* that requires contracts to be formally verified before they are created and upgraded; we target the Ethereum platform and smart contracts written in Solidity. We propose a *verification framework* based on the *design-by-contract methodology* [25]. The specification format that we propose is similar to what the community has used, albeit in an informal way, to specify the behaviour of common Ethereum contracts [35]. Our framework also relies on our own version of the proxy pattern to carry out updates but in a sophisticated and safe way. We rely on a *trusted deployer*, which is an off-chain service, to vet contract creations and updates. These operations are only allowed if the given implementation meets the expected specification - the contract specification is set at the time of contract creation and remains unchanged during its lifetime. As an off-chain service, our framework can be readily and efficiently integrated into existing blockchain platforms. Participants can also check whether a contract has been deployed via our framework so that they can be certain the contract they want to execute has the expected behaviour.

Our framework promotes a paradigm shift where the specification is immutable instead of the implementation/code. Thus, it moves away from "code is law" and proposes the *"specification is law" paradigm* - enforced by formal verification. This new paradigm addresses all the concerns that we have highlighted: arbitrary code updates are forbidden as only conforming implementations are allowed, and buggy contracts are prevented from being deployed as they are vetted by a formal verifier. Thus, contracts can be optimised and changed to meet evolving business needs and yet contract stakeholders can rely on the guarantee that the implementations always conform to their corresponding specifications. As specifications are more stable and a necessary element for assessing the correctness of a contract, we believe that a framework that focuses on this key artifact and makes it immutable improves on the current "code is law" paradigm.

We have created a prototype of our framework, and conducted a case study that investigates its applicability to real-world smart contracts implementing the widely used ERC20, ERC3156 and ERC1155 Ethereum token standards. We analysed specifically how the sort of formal verification that we use fares in handling practical contracts and obtained promising results.

In this paper, we assume the deployer is a trusted third party and focus on the functional aspect of our framework. We are currently working on an implementation of the trusted deployer that relies on a Trusted Execution Environment (TEE) [24], specifically the AMD SEV implementation [29]. Despite being an off-chain service, the use of a TEE to implement our deployer should give it a level of *execution integrity/trustworthiness*, enforced by the trusted hardware, comparable to that achieved by on-chain mechanisms relying on blockchains' *consensus*, with less computational overhead. However, on-chain mechanisms would enjoy better availability guarantees. We further discuss these trade-offs in Sect. 5.

Outline. Section 2 introduces the relevant background material. Section 3 introduces our framework, and Sect. 4 the evaluation that we conducted. Section 5 discusses related work, whereas Sect. 6 presents our concluding remarks.

2   Background

2.1   Solidity

A smart contract is a program running on a trusted platform, usually a blockchain, that manages the digital assets it owns. Solidity is arguably the most used language for writing smart contracts as it was designed for the development of contracts targeting the popular Ethereum blockchain platform [1]. A contract in Solidity is a concept very similar to that of a *class* in object-oriented languages, and a contract instance a sort of long-lived persistent object. We introduce the main elements of Solidity using the `ToyWallet` contract in Fig. 1. It implements a very basic "wallet" contract that participants and other contracts can rely upon to store their Ether (Ethereum's cryptocurrency). The *member variables* of a contract define the persistent state of the contract. This example contract has a single member variable `accs`, a mapping from addresses to 256-bit unsigned integers, which keeps track of the balance of Ether each "client" of the contract has in the ToyWallet; the integer accs[addr] gives the current balance for address addr, and an address is represented by a 160-bit number.

Public functions describe the operations that participants and other contracts can execute on the contract. The contract in Fig. 1 has *public functions* deposit and withdraw that can be used to transfer Ether into and out of the ToyWallet contract, respectively. In Solidity, functions have the implicit argument msg.sender designating the caller's address, and payable functions have the msg.value which depict how much *Wei* - the most basic (sub)unit of Ether - is being transferred, from caller to callee, with that function invocation; such a transfer is carried out implicitly by Ethereum. For instance, when deposit is called on an instance of ToyWallet, the caller can decide on some amount amt of Wei to be sent with the invocation. By the time the deposit body is about to execute, Ethereum will already have carried out the transfer from the balance associated to the caller's address to that of the ToyWallet instance - and amt can be accessed via msg.value. Note that, as mentioned, this balance is part of the blockchain's state rather than an explicit variable declared by the contract's code. One can programmatically access this implicit balance variable for address addr with the command addr.balance. Solidity's construct require (condition) aborts and reverts the execution of the function in question if condition does not hold - even in the case of implicit Ether transfers. The call addr.send(amount) sends amount Wei from the currently executing instance to address addr; it returns true if the transfer was successful, and false otherwise. For instance, the first require statement in the function withdraw requires the caller to have the funds they want to withdraw, whereas the second requires the msg.sender.send(value) statement to succeed, i.e. the value must have been correctly withdrawn from ToyWallet to msg.sender. The final statement in this function updates the account balance of the caller (i.e. msg.sender) in ToyWallet to reflect the withdrawal.

We use the transaction *create-contract* as a means to create an instance of a Solidity smart contract in Ethereum. In reality, Ethereum only accepts contracts in the *EVM bytecode* low-level language - Solidity contracts need to be compiled into that. The processing of a transaction *create-contract*$(c, args)$ creates an instance of contract c and executes its constructor with arguments $args$. Solidity contracts without a constructor (as our example in Fig. 1) are given an implicit one. A *create-contract* call returns the address at which the contract instance was created. We omit the $args$ when they are not relevant for a call. We use σ to denote the state of the blockchain where $\sigma[ad].balance$ gives the balance for address ad, and $\sigma[ad].storage.mem$ the value for member variable mem of the contract instance deployed at ad for this state. For instance, let c_{tw} be the code in Fig. 1, and $addr_{tw}$ the address returned by the processing of *create-contract*(c_{tw}). For the blockchain state σ' immediately after this processing, we have that: for any address $addr$, $\sigma'[addr_{tw}].storage.accs[addr] = 0$ and its balance is zero, i.e., $\sigma'[addr_{tw}].balance = 0$. We introduce and use this intuitive notation to present and discuss state changes as it can concisely and clearly capture them. There are many works that formalise such concepts [6,18,36].

```
contract ToyWallet {
  mapping (address => uint) accs;

  function deposit () payable public {
    accs[msg.sender] = accs[msg.sender] + msg.value;
  }

  function withdraw (uint value) public {
    require(accs[msg.sender] >= value);
    bool ok = msg.sender.send(value);
    require(ok);
    accs[msg.sender] = accs[msg.sender] - value;
  }
}
```

Fig. 1. ToyWallet contract example.

A transaction $call - contract$ can be used to invoke contract functions; processing $call\text{-}contract(addr, func\_sig, args)$ executes the function with signature $func\_sig$ at address $addr$ with input arguments $args$. When a contract is created, the code associated with its non-constructor public functions is made available to be called by such transactions. The constructor function is only run (and available) at creation time. For instance, let $addr_{tw}$ be a fresh ToyWallet instance and ToyWallet.deposit give the signature of the corresponding function in Fig. 1, processing the transaction $call\text{-}contract(addr_{tw}, \text{ToyWallet.deposit},$ $args)$ where $args = \{msg.sender = addr_{snd}, msg.value = 10\}$ would cause the state of this instance to be updated to σ'' where we have that $\sigma''[addr_{tw}].$ $storage.accs[addr_{snd}] = 10$ and $\sigma''[addr_{tw}].balance = 10$. So, the above transaction has been issued by address $addr_{snd}$ which has transferred 10 Wei to $addr_{tw}$.

2.2 Formal Verification with *solc-verify*

The modular verifier *solc-verify* [16,17] was created to help developers to formally check that their Solidity smart contracts behave as expected. Input contracts are manually annotated with contract *invariants* and their functions with *pre-* and *postconditions*. An annotated Solidity contract is then translated into a Boogie program which is verified by the Boogie verifier [9,20]. Its modular nature means that *solc-verify* verifies functions locally/independently, and function calls are abstracted by the corresponding function's specification, rather than their implementation being precisely analysed/executed. These specification constructs have their typical meaning. An invariant is valid if it is established by the constructor and maintained by the contract's public functions, and a function meets its specification if and only if from a state satisfying its preconditions, any state successfully terminating respects its postconditions. So the notion is that of partial correctness. Note that an aborted and reverted execution, such as one triggered by a failing require command, does not successfully terminate. We use Fig. 2 illustrates a *solc-verify* specification for an alternative version of the ToyWallet's withdraw function. The postconditions specify that the balance of the instance and the wallet balance associated with the caller must decrease by the withdrawn amount and no other wallet balance must be affected by the call.

```
/** @notice postcondition address(this).balance == __verifier_old_uint(
       address(this).balance) - value
 * @notice postcondition accs[msg.sender] == __verifier_old_uint(accs[msg.
       sender]) - value
 * @notice postcondition forall (address addr) addr == msg.sender ||
       __verifier_old_uint(accs[addr]) == accs[addr] */
function withdraw (uint value) public {
  require(accs[msg.sender] >= value);
  bool ok;
  (ok,) = msg.sender.call.value(value)("");
  require(ok);
  accs[msg.sender] = accs[msg.sender] - value;
}
```

Fig. 2. ToyWallet alternate buggy withdraw implementation with specification.

This alternative implementation uses `msg.sender.call.value(val)("")` instead of `msg.sender.send(val)`. While the latter only allows for the transfer of val Wei from the instance to address `msg.sender`, the former *delegates control* to `msg.sender` in addition to the transfer of value.[1] If `msg.sender` is a smart contract instance that calls withdraw again during this control delegation, it can withdraw all the funds in this alternative ToyWallet instance - even the funds that were not deposited by it. This *reentrancy* bug is detected by *solc-verify* when it analyses this alternative version of the contract. A similar bug was exploited in what is known as the DAO attack/hack to take over US$53 million worth of Ether [7,30].

3 Safe Ethereum Smart Contracts Deployment

We propose a framework for the *safe creation and upgrade of smart contracts* based around a *trusted deployer*. This entity is trusted to only create or update contracts that have been verified to meet their corresponding specifications. A smart contract development process built around it prevents developers from deploying contracts that have not been implemented as intended. Thus, stakeholders can be sure that contract instances deployed by this entity, even if their code is upgraded, comply with the intended specification.

Our trusted deployer targets the Ethereum platform, and we implement it as an off-chain service. Generally speaking, a trusted deployer could be implemented as a smart contract in a blockchain platform, as part of its consensus rules, or as an off-chain service. In Ethereum, implementing it as a smart contract is not practically feasible as a verification infrastructure on top of the EVM [1] would need to be created. Furthermore, blocks have an upper limit on the computing power they can use to process their transactions, and even relatively simple computing tasks can exceed this upper limit [37]. As verification is a notoriously complex computing task, it should exceed this upper limit even for reasonably small systems. Neither can we change the consensus rules for Ethereum.

---

[1] In fact, the function send also delegates control to `msg.sender` but it does in such a restricted way that it cannot perform any side-effect computation. So, for the purpose of this paper and to simplify our exposition, we ignore this delegation.

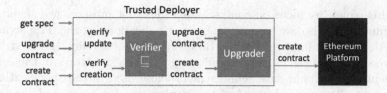

Fig. 3. Trusted deployer architecture.

We present the architecture of the *trusted deployer infrastructure* in Fig. 3. The trusted deployer relies on an internal *verifier* that implements the functions *verify-creation$_\sqsubseteq$* and *verify-upgrade$_\sqsubseteq$*, and an *upgrader* that implements functions *create-contract* and *upgrade-contract*; we detail what these functions do in the following. The deployer's *create-contract* (*upgrade-contract*) checks that an implementation meets its specification by calling *verify-creation$_\sqsubseteq$* (*verify-upgrade$_\sqsubseteq$*) before relaying this call to the upgrader's *create-contract* (*upgrade-contract*) which effectively creates (upgrades) the contract in the Ethereum platform. The *get-spec* function can be used to test whether a contract instance has been deployed by the trusted deployer and which specification it satisfies.

The *verifier* is used to establish whether an implementation meets a specification. A verification framework is given by a triple $(\mathcal{S}, \mathcal{C}, \sqsubseteq)$ where $\mathcal{S}$ is a language of smart contract specifications, $\mathcal{C}$ is a language of implementations, and $\sqsubseteq \in (\mathcal{S} \times \mathcal{C})$ is a satisfiability relation between smart contracts' specifications and implementations. In this paper, $\mathcal{C}$ is the set of Solidity contracts and $\mathcal{S}$ a particular form of Solidity contracts, possibly annotated with contract invariants, that include function signatures annotated with postconditions. The functions *verify-creation$_\sqsubseteq$* and *verify-upgrade$_\sqsubseteq$* both take a specification $s \in \mathcal{S}$ and a contract implementation $c \in \mathcal{C}$ and test whether c meets s - they work in slightly different ways as we explain later. When an implementation does not meet a specification, verifiers typically return an error report that points out which parts of the specification do not hold and maybe even witnesses/- counterexamples describing system behaviours illustrating such violations; they provide valuable information to help developers correct their implementations.

The *upgrader* is used to create and manage *upgradable smart contracts* - Ethereum does not have built-in support for contract upgrades. Function *create-contract* creates an upgradable instance of contract c - it returns the Ethereum address where the instance was created - whereas *upgrade-contract* allows for the contract's behaviour to be upgraded. The specification used for a successful contract creation will be stored and used as the intended specification for future upgrades. Only the creator of a *trusted contract* can update its implementation.

Note that once a contract is created via our trusted deployer, the instance's specification is fixed, and not only its initial implementation but all upgrades are guaranteed to satisfy this specification. Therefore, participants in the ecosystem interacting with this contract instance can be certain that its behaviour is as intended by its developer during the instance's entire lifetime, even if the implementation is upgraded as the contract evolves.

In this paper, we focus on contract upgrades that preserve the signature of public functions. Also, we assume contract specifications fix the data structures used in the contract implementation. However, we plan to relax these restrictions in future versions of the framework, allowing the data structures in the contract implementation to be a data refinement of those used in the specification; we also plan to allow the signature of the implementation to extend that of the specification, provided some notion of behaviour preservation is obeyed when the extended interface is projected into the original one.

3.1 Verifier

We propose *design-by-contract* [25] as a methodology to specify the behaviour of smart contracts. In this traditional specification paradigm, conceived for object-oriented languages, a developer can specify invariants for a class and pre-/postconditions for its methods. Invariants must be established by the constructor and guaranteed by the public methods, whereas postconditions are ensured by the code in the method's body provided that the preconditions are guaranteed by the caller code and the method terminates. Currently, we focus on partial correctness, which is aligned with our goal to ensure safety properties, and the fact that smart contracts typically have explicitly bound executions[2]. We propose a specification format that defines what the member variables and signatures of member functions should be. Additionally, the function signatures can be annotated with postconditions, and the specification with invariants; these annotations capture the expected behaviour of the contract. In ordinary programs, a function is called in specific *call sites* fixed in the program's code. Preconditions can, then, be enforced and checked in these call sites. In the context of public functions of smart contracts, however, any well-formed transaction can be issued to invoke such a function. Hence, we move away from preconditions in our specification, requiring, thus, postconditions to be met whenever public functions successfully terminate.

Figure 4 illustrates a specification for the `ToyWallet` contract. Invariants are declared in a comment block preceding the contract declaration, and function postconditions are declared in comment blocks preceding their signatures. Our specification language reuses constructs from Solidity and the *solc-verify* specification language, which in turn borrows elements from the Boogie language [9,20]. Member variables and function signature declarations are as prescribed by Solidity, whereas the conditions on invariants, and postconditions are side-effect-free Solidity expressions extended with quantifiers and the expression `__verifier_old_x(v)` that can only be used in a postcondition, and it denotes the value of v in the function's execution pre-state.

We choose to use Solidity as opposed to EVM bytecode as it gives a cleaner semantic basis for the analysis of smart contracts [6] and it also provides a high-level error message when the specification is not met. The satisfiability relation $\sqsubseteq$ that we propose is as follows.

---

[2] The Ethereum concept of *gas*, i.e. execution resources, is purposely abstracted away/disregarded in our exposition.

```
/** @notice invariant accs[address(this)] == 0 */
contract ToyWallet {
  mapping (address => uint) accs;

  /** @notice postcondition forall (address addr) accs[addr] == 0 */
  constructor() public;

  /** @notice postcondition address(this).balance == __verifier_old_uint(
        address(this).balance) + msg.value
   * @notice postcondition accs[msg.sender] == __verifier_old_uint(accs[msg.
        sender]) + msg.value
   * @notice postcondition forall (address addr) addr == msg.sender ||
        __verifier_old_uint(accs[addr]) == accs[addr] */
  function deposit () payable public;

  /** @notice postcondition address(this).balance == __verifier_old_uint(
        address(this).balance) - value
   * @notice postcondition accs[msg.sender] == __verifier_old_uint(accs[msg.
        sender]) - value
   * @notice postcondition forall (address addr) addr == msg.sender ||
        __verifier_old_uint(accs[addr]) == accs[addr] */
  function withdraw (uint value) public;
}
```

Fig. 4. ToyWallet specification.

Definition 1. *The relation $s \sqsubseteq c$ holds iff:*

- Syntactic obligation: *a member variable is declared in s if and only if it is declared in c with the same type, and they must be declared in the same order. A public function signature is declared in s if and only if it is declared and implemented in c.*
- Semantic obligation: *invariants declared in s must be respected by c, and the implementation of functions in c must respect their corresponding postconditions described in s.*

The purpose of this paper is not to provide a formal semantics to Solidity or to formalise the execution model implemented by the Ethereum platform. Other works propose formalisations for Solidity and Ethereum [5,17,36]. Our focus is on using the modular verifier *solc-verify* to discharge the semantic obligations imposed by our satisfaction definition.

The *verify-creation$_\sqsubseteq$* function works as follows. Firstly, the syntactic obligation imposed by Definition 1 is checked by a syntactic comparison between s and c. If it holds, we rely on *solc-verify* to check whether the semantic obligation is fulfilled. We use what we call a *merged contract* as the input to *solc-verify* - it is obtained by annotating c with the corresponding invariants and postconditions in s. If *solc-verify* is able to discharge all the proof obligations associated to this merged contract, the semantic obligations are considered fulfilled, and *verify-creation$_\sqsubseteq$* succeeds.

Function *verify-upgrade$_\sqsubseteq$* is implemented in a very similar way but it relies on a slightly different satisfiability relation and merged contract. While *verify-creation$_\sqsubseteq$* checks that the obligations of the constructor are met by its implementation, *verify-upgrade$_\sqsubseteq$* assumes they do, since the constructor is only executed - and, therefore, its implementation checked for satisfiability - at creation time. The upgrade process only checks conformance for the implementation of the (non-constructor) public functions.

3.2 Upgrader

Ethereum does not provide a built-in mechanism for upgrading smart contracts. However, one can simulate this functionality using the *proxy pattern* [31], which splits the contract across two instances: the *proxy instance* holds the persistent state and the upgrade logic, and rely on the code in an *implementation instance* for its business logic. The proxy instance is the *de-facto* instance that is the target of calls willing to execute the upgradable contract. It stores the address of the implementation instance it relies upon, and the behaviour of the proxy's public functions can be upgraded by changing this address. Our *upgrader* relies on our own version of this pattern to deploy *upgradable* contracts.

Given a contract c that meets its specification according to Definition 1, the upgrader creates the Solidity contract $proxy(c)$ as follows. It has the same member variable declarations, in the same order, as c - having the same order is an implementation detail that is necessary to implement the sort of delegation we use as it enforces proxy and implementation instances to share the same memory layout. In addition to those, it has a new *address* member variable called `implementation` - it stores the address of the implementation instance. The constructor of $proxy(c)$ extends the constructor of c with an initial setting up of the variable `implementation`.[3] This proxy contract also has a public function `upgrade` that can be used to change the address of the implementation instance. The trusted deployer is identified by a trusted Ethereum address $addr_{td}$. This address is used to ensure calls to `upgrade` can *only* be issued by the trusted deployer. In the process of creating and upgrading contracts the trusted deployer acts as an external participant of the Ethereum platform. We assume that the contract implementations and specifications do not have member variables named `implementation`, or functions named `upgrade` to avoid name clashes.

The proxy instance relies on the low-level `delegatecall` Solidity command to dynamically execute the function implementations defined in the contract instance at `implementation`. When the contract instance at address `proxy` executes `implementation.delegatecall(`sig`, args)`, it executes the code associated with the function with signature sig stored in the instance at address `implementation` but applied to the `proxy` instance - modifying its state - instead of `implementation`. For each (non-constructor) public function in c with signature sig, $proxy(c)$ has a corresponding function declaration whose implementation relies on `implementation.delegatecall(`sig`, args)`. This command was proposed as a means to implement and deploy contracts that act as a sort of dynamic library. Such a contract is deployed with the sole purpose of other contracts borrowing and using their code.

---

[3] Instead of using the proxy pattern `initialize` function to initialise the state of the proxy instance, we place the code that carries out the desired initialisation directly into the proxy's constructor. Our approach benefits from the inherent behaviour of constructors - which only execute once and at creation time - instead of having to implement this behaviour for the non-constructor function `initialize`. Our Trusted Deployer, available at https://github.com/formalblocks/safeevolution, automatically generates the code for such a proxy.

The upgrader function *create-contract*(c) behaves as follows. Firstly, it issues transaction *create-contract*($c, args$) to the Ethereum platform to create the initial implementation instance at address addr$_{impl}$. Secondly, it issues transaction *create-contract*($proxy(c), args$), such that implementation would be set to addr$_{impl}$, to create the proxy instance at address addr$_{px}$. Note that both of these transactions are issued by and using the trusted deployer's address addr$_{td}$. The upgrader function *upgrade-contract*(c) behaves similarly, but the second step issues transaction *call-contract*(addr$_{px}$, upgrade, $args$), triggering the execution of function upgrade in the proxy instance and changing its implementation address to the new implementation instance.

4   Case Studies: ERC20, ERC1155, and ERC3156

To validate our approach, we have carried out three systematic case studies of the ERC20 Token Standard, the ERC1155 Multi Token Standard, and the ERC3156 Flash Loans. For the ERC20, we examined 8 repositories and out of 32 commits analysed, our framework identified 8 *unsafe commits*, in the sense that they did not conform to the specification; for the ERC1155, we examined 4 repositories and out of 18 commits analysed, 5 were identified as unsafe; and for the ERC3156, we examined 5 repositories and out of 18 commits analysed, 7 were identified as unsafe. We have prototyped the entire framework in the form of our Trusted Deployer.[4] We have applied it to the commit history of the repository *0xMonorepo*, and our tool was able to identify and prevent unsafe evolutions while carrying out safe·ones. The design and promising findings of these case studies and commit history analyses are presented in full detail in the extended version of this paper [4]. In the remainder of this section, as our space is limited, we only present here a brief account of the ERC20 case study.

Our summary of the ERC20 case study presented here has focused specifically on the verification of the semantic obligation that we enforce. This task is the most important and computationally-demanding element of our methodology. So, in this case study, we try to establish whether: (a) can we use our notation to capture the ERC20 specification formally, (b) (if (a) holds) can *solc-verify* check that real-world ERC20 contracts conform to its formal specification, and (c) (if (b) holds) how long does *solc-verify* take to carry out such verifications.s

We were able to capture the ERC20 specification using our notation, an extract of which is presented in Fig. 5, so we have a positive answer to (a). To test (b) and (c), we relied on checking, using *solc-verify*, merged contracts involving our specification and real-world contracts. We selected contract samples from public github repositories that presented a reasonably complex and interesting commit history. The samples cover aspects of evolution that are related to improving the readability and maintenance of the code, but also optimisations where, for instance, redundant checks executed by a function were removed.

---

[4] The prototype is implemented as a standalone tool available at https://github.com/
formalblocks/safeevolution. We do not provide a service running inside a Trusted
Execution Environment yet but such a service will be provided in the future.

Table 1. ERC20 results

ERC20							
Repository	Commit	Time	Output	Repository	Commit	Time	Output
0xMonorepo	548fda	7.78 s	WOP	Uniswap	55ae25	6.89 s	WOP
DigixDao	5aee64	8.52 s	NTI	Uniswap	E382d7	7.08 s	IOU
DsToken	08412f	8.74 s	WOP	SkinCoin	25db99	1.95 s	NTI
Klenergy	60263d	2.40 s	VRE	SkinCoin	27c298	1.81 s	NTI

```
1   /** @notice invariant totalSupply == __verifier_sum_uint(balances) */
2   contract IERC20  {
3   uint256 totalSupply;
4   mapping (address => uint256) balances;
5   mapping (address => mapping (address => uint256)) allowance;
6
7   //... functions transfer, totalSupply, balanceOf, allowance, and approve
        omitted ...
8
9   /** @notice postcondition ((balances[from] == __verifier_old_uint(balances[
        from]) - value && from != to) || (balances[from] == __verifier_old_uint(
        balances[from]) && from == to) && ok) || !ok
10 *  @notice postcondition ((balances[to] == __verifier_old_uint(balances[to]) +
        value && from != to) || (balances[to] == __verifier_old_uint (balances[
        to]) && from == to) && ok) || !ok
11 *  @notice postcondition allowance[from][msg.sender] == __verifier_old_uint(
        allowance[from][msg.sender]) - value || from == msg.sender
12 *  @notice postcondition allowance[from][msg.sender] <= __verifier_old_uint(
        allowance[from][msg.sender]) || from == msg.sender
13 *  @notice postcondition forall (address addr) (addr == from || addr == to ||
        __verifier_old_uint(balances[addr]) == balances[addr]) && ok || (
        __verifier_old_uint(balances[addr]) == balances[addr]) && !ok*/
14 function transferFrom(address from, address to, uint256 value) public returns
        (bool ok);
15 }
```

Fig. 5. ERC20 reduced specification.

We checked these merged contracts using a Lenovo IdeapadGaming3i with Windows 10, Intel(R) Core(TM) i7-10750 CPU @ 2.60 GHz, 8 GB of RAM, with Docker Engine 20.15.5 and Solidity compiler version 0.5.17. Table 1 shows the results we obtained.[5] Our framework was able to identify errors in the following categories: Integer Overflow and Underflow (IOU); Nonstandard Token Interface (NTI), when the contract does not meet the syntactic restriction defined by the standard; wrong operator (WOP), for instance, when the < operator would be expected but ≤ is used instead; Verification Error (VRE) denotes that the verification process cannot be completed or the results were inconclusive. Our framework also found conformance for 24 commits analysed; we omitted those for brevity, each of them was verified in under 10 s.

The ERC20 standard defines member variables: `totalSupply` keeps track of the total number of tokens in circulation, `balanceOf` maps a wallet (i.e. address) to the balance it owns, and `allowance` stores the number of tokens that an address has made available to be spent by another one. It defines public functions: `totalSupply`, `balanceOf` and `allowance` are accessors for the

---

[5] All the instructions, the specifications, the sample contracts, and scripts used in this evaluation can be found at https://github.com/formalblocks/safeevolution.

```
function transferFrom(address from, address to, uint value) external
returns (bool success) {
    if (allowance_[from][msg.sender] != uint(-1)) {
        allowance_[from][msg.sender] =
        allowance_[from][msg.sender].sub(value);
    }
    _transfer(from, to, value);
    return true;
}
```

Fig. 6. Buggy ERC20 transferFrom function.

above variables; `transfer` and `transferFrom` can be used to transfer tokens between contracts; and `approve` allows a contract to set an "allowance" for a given address.

Figure 5 presents a reduced specification - focusing on function `transferFrom` for the purpose of this discussion - derived from the informal description in the standard [35]. In Line 1, we define a contract invariant requiring that the total number of tokens supplied by this contract is equal to the sum of all tokens owned by account holders. The `transferFrom` function has 4 postconditions; the operation is successful only when the tokens are debited from the source account and credited in the destination account, according to the specifications provided in the ERC20 standard. The first two postconditions (lines 9 to 10) require that the balances are updated as expected, whereas the purpose of the last two (lines 11 to 12) is to ensure that the tokens available for withdrawal have been properly updated.

We use the snippet in Fig. 6 - extracted from the Uniswap repository, commit 55ae25 - to illustrate the detection of wrong operator errors. When checked by our framework, the third postcondition for the `transferFrom` function presented in the specification in Fig. 5 is not satisfied. Note that the allowance amount is not debited if the amount to be transferred is equal to the maximum integer supported by Solidity (i.e. `uint(-1)`). A possible solution would consist of removing the `if` branching, allowing the branch code to always execute. We have also validated cases of safe evolution, namely, where our framework was able to show that consecutive updates conformed with the specification.

The results of our case study demonstrate that we can verify real-world contracts implementing a very popular Ethereum token standard efficiently - positively answering questions (b) and (c). The fact that errors were detected (and safe evolutions were checked) in real-world contracts attests to the necessity of our framework and its practical impact. More details about this case study and of the other two, with our commit history analyses, can be found in [4].

5   Related Work

Despite the glaring need for a safe mechanism to upgrade smart contracts in platforms, such as Ethereum, where contract implementations are immutable once deployed [15,19,32], surprisingly, we could only find three close related approaches [8,10,28] that try to tackle this specific problem. The work in [10] proposes a methodology based around special contracts that carry a proof that they meet the expected specification. They propose the addition of a special instruction to deploy these special proof-carrying contracts, and the adaptation of platform miners, which are responsible for checking and reaching a consensus on the validity of contract executions, to check these proofs. Our framework and the one presented in that work share the same goal, but our approach and theirs differ significantly in many aspects. Firstly, while theirs requires a fundamental change on the rules of the platform, ours can be implemented, as already prototyped, on top of Ethereum's current capabilities and rely on tools that are easier to use, i.e. require less user input, like program verifiers. The fact that their framework is on-chain makes the use of such verification methods more difficult as they would slow down consensus, likely to a prohibitive level.

Azzopardi *et al.* [8] propose the use of runtime verification to ensure that a contract conforms to its specification. Given a Solidity smart contract C and an automaton-based specification S, their approach produces an instrumented contract I that dynamically tracks the behaviour of C with respect to S. I's behaviour is functionally equivalent to C when S is respected. If a violation to S is detected, however, a reparation strategy (i.e. some user-provided code) is executed instead. This technique can be combined with a proxy to ensure that a monitor contract keeps track of implementation contracts as they are upgraded, ensuring their safe evolution. Unlike our approach, there is an inherent (on-chain) runtime overhead to dynamically keep track of specification conformance. An evaluation in that paper demonstrates that, for a popular type of contract call, it can add a 100% cost overhead. Our off-chain verification at deployment-time does not incur this sort of overhead. Another difference from our approach concerns the use of reparation strategies. One example given in the paper proposes the reverting of a transaction/behaviour that is found to be a violation. An improper implementation could, then, have most of its executions reverted. Our approach presents at (pre-)deployment-time the possible violated conditions, allowing developers to fix the contract before deployment. Their on-chain verification can be implemented on top of Ethereum's capabilities.

In [28], the authors propose a mechanism to upgrade contracts in Ethereum that works at the EVM-bytecode level. Their framework takes vulnerability reports issued by the community as an input, and tries to patch affected deployed contracts automatically using patch templates. It uses previous contract transactions and, optionally user-provided unit tests, to try to establish whether a patch preserves the behaviour of the contract. Ultimately, the patching process may require some manual input. If the deployed contract and the patch disagree on some test, the user must examine this discrepancy and rule on what should be done. Note that this manual intervention is always needed for attacked contracts, as the transaction carrying out the attack - part of the attacked contract's history - should be prevented from happening in the new patched contract. While they simply test patches that are reactively generated based on vulnerability reports, we proactively require the user to provide a specification of the expected behaviour of a contract and formally verify the evolved contract against such a formal specification. Their approach requires less human intervention, as a specification does not need to be provided - only optionally some unit tests - but it offers no formal guarantees about patches. It could be that a patch passes their validation (i.e. testing with the contract history), without addressing the underlying vulnerability.

Methodologies to carry out pre-deployment patching/repairing of smart contracts have been proposed [26,33,38]. However, they do not propose a way to update deployed contracts. A number of tools to verify smart contracts at both EVM and Solidity levels have been proposed [2,3,6,13,14,16,17,22,23,27,34,36]. Our paper proposes a verification-focused development process based around, supported, and enforced by such tools.

6   Conclusion

We propose a framework for the safe deployment of smart contracts. Not only does it check that contracts conform to their specification at creation time, but it also guarantees that subsequent code updates are conforming too. Upgrades can be performed even if the implementation has been proven to satisfy the specification initially. A developer might, for instance, want to optimise the resources used by the contract. Furthermore, our *trusted deployer* records information about the contracts that have been verified, and which specification they conform to, so that participants can be certain they are interacting with a contract with the expected behaviour; contracts can be safely executed. None of these capabilities are offered by the Ethereum platform by default nor are available in the literature to the extent provided by the framework proposed in this paper.

We have prototyped our trusted deployer and investigated its applicability - specially its formal verification component - to contracts implementing three widely used Ethereum standards: the ERC20 Token Standard, ERC3156 Flash Loans and ERC1155 Multi Token Standard, with promising results.

Our framework shifts immutability from the implementation of a contract to its specification, promoting the "code is law" to the "specification is law" paradigm. We believe that this paradigm shift brings a series of improvements. Firstly, developers are required to elaborate a (formal) specification, so they can, early in the development process, identify issues with their design. They can and should validate their specification; we consider this problem orthogonal to the framework that we are providing. Secondly, specifications are more abstract and, as a consequence, tend to be more stable than (the corresponding conforming) implementations. A contract can be optimised so that both the original and optimised versions must satisfy the same reference specification. Thirdly, even new implementations that involve change of data representation can still be formally verified against the same specification, by using data refinement techniques.

A limitation of our current approach is the restrictive notion of evolution for smart contracts: only the implementation of public functions can be upgraded - the persistent state data structures are fixed. However, we are looking into new types of evolution where the data structure of the contract's persistent state can be changed - as well as the interface of the specification, provided the projected behaviour with respect to the original interface is preserved, based on notions of class [21] and process [11] inheritance, and interface evolution such as in [12].

References

1. Ethereum White Paper. https://github.com/ethereum/wiki/wiki/White-Paper Accessed 5 Aug 2022
2. Ahrendt, W., Bubel, R.: Functional verification of smart contracts via strong data integrity. In: Margaria, T., Steffen, B. (eds.) ISoLA 2020. LNCS, vol. 12478, pp. 9–24. Springer, Cham (2020). https://doi.org/10.1007/978-3-030-61467-6_2
3. Alt, L., Reitwiessner, C.: SMT-based verification of solidity smart contracts. In: Margaria, T., Steffen, B. (eds.) ISoLA 2018. LNCS, vol. 11247, pp. 376–388. Springer, Cham (2018). https://doi.org/10.1007/978-3-030-03427-6_28
4. Antonino, P., Ferreira, J., Sampaion, A., Roscoe, A.W.:Specification is law: safe deployment of ethereum smart contracts - technical report. Technical report (2022). https://github.com/formalblocks/safeevolution
5. Antonino P., Roscoe, A. W.: Formalising and verifying smart contracts with solidifier: a bounded model checker for solidity. CoRR, abs/2002.02710 (2020)
6. Antonino P., Roscoe, A. W.: Solidifier: bounded model checking solidity using lazy contract deployment and precise memory modelling. In: Proceedings of the 36th Annual ACM Symposium on Applied Computing, pp. 1788–1797 (2021)
7. Atzei, N., Bartoletti, M., Cimoli, T.: A survey of attacks on ethereum smart contracts (SoK). In: Maffei, M., Ryan, M. (eds.) POST 2017. LNCS, vol. 10204, pp. 164–186. Springer, Heidelberg (2017). https://doi.org/10.1007/978-3-662-54455-6_8
8. Azzopardi, S., Ellul, J., Pace, G.J.: Monitoring smart contracts: contractlarva and open challenges beyond. In: Colombo, C., Leucker, M. (eds.) RV 2018. LNCS, vol. 11237, pp. 113–137. Springer, Cham (2018). https://doi.org/10.1007/978-3-030-03769-7_8
9. Barnett, M., Chang, B.-Y.E., DeLine, R., Jacobs, B., Leino, K.R.M.: Boogie: a modular reusable verifier for object-oriented programs. In: de Boer, F.S., Bonsangue, M.M., Graf, S., de Roever, W.-P. (eds.) FMCO 2005. LNCS, vol. 4111, pp. 364–387. Springer, Heidelberg (2006). https://doi.org/10.1007/11804192_17
10. Dickerson, T., Gazzillo, P., Herlihy, M., Saraph, V., Koskinen, E.: Proof-carrying smart contracts. In: Zohar, A., et al. (eds.) FC 2018. LNCS, vol. 10958, pp. 325–338. Springer, Heidelberg (2019). https://doi.org/10.1007/978-3-662-58820-8_22
11. Dihego, J., Antonino, P., Sampaio, A.: Algebraic laws for process subtyping. In: Groves, L., Sun, J. (eds.) ICFEM 2013. LNCS, vol. 8144, pp. 4–19. Springer, Heidelberg (2013). https://doi.org/10.1007/978-3-642-41202-8_2
12. Dihego, J., Sampaio, A., Oliveira, M.: A refinement checking based strategy for component-based systems evolution. J. Syst. Softw. **167**, 110598 (2020)
13. Frank, J., Aschermann, C., Holz, T.: ETHBMC: a bounded model checker for smart contracts. In: 29th USENIX Security Symposium (USENIX Security 2020), pp. 2757–2774. USENIX Association (2020)
14. Grishchenko, I., Maffei, M., Schneidewind, C.: Ethertrust: sound static analysis of ethereum bytecode. Technische Universität Wien, Technical report (2018)
15. Groce, A., Feist, J., Grieco, G., Colburn, M.: What are the actual flaws in important smart contracts (and how can we find them)? In: Bonneau, J., Heninger, N. (eds.) FC 2020. LNCS, vol. 12059, pp. 634–653. Springer, Cham (2020). https://doi.org/10.1007/978-3-030-51280-4_34
16. Hajdu, Á., Jovanović, D.: SMT-friendly formalization of the solidity memory model. In: FC 2020. LNCS, vol. 12059, pp. 224–250. Springer, Cham (2020). https://doi.org/10.1007/978-3-030-44914-8_9

17. Hajdu, Á., Jovanović, D.: SOLC-VERIFY: a modular verifier for solidity smart contracts. In: Chakraborty, S., Navas, J.A. (eds.) VSTTE 2019. LNCS, vol. 12031, pp. 161–179. Springer, Cham (2020). https://doi.org/10.1007/978-3-030-41600-3_11
18. Hildenbrandt, E., et al.: KEVM: a complete formal semantics of the ethereum virtual machine. In: CSF 2018, pp. 204–217. IEEE (2018)
19. Bin, H., et al.: A comprehensive survey on smart contract construction and execution: paradigms, tools, and systems. Patterns 2(2), 100179 (2021)
20. Leino K. R. M.: This is boogie 2. Manuscript KRML 178(131), 9 (2008)
21. Liskov, B.H., Wing, J.M.: A behavioral notion of subtyping. ACM Trans. Program. Lang. Syst. 16(6), 1811–1841 (1994)
22. Liu, C., Liu, H., Cao, Z., Chen, Z., Chen, B., Roscoe, B.: ReGuard: finding reentrancy bugs in smart contracts. In: ICSE 2018, pp. 65–68. ACM (2018)
23. Luu, L., Chu, D.-H., Olickel, H., Saxena, P., Hobor, A.: Making smart contracts smarter. In: CCS 2016, pp. 254–269. ACM (2016)
24. Maene, P., Götzfried, J., de Clercq, R., Müller, T., Freiling, F., Verbauwhede, I.: Hardware-based trusted computing architectures for isolation and attestation. IEEE Trans. Comput. 67(3), 361–374 (2018)
25. Meyer, B.: Applying 'design by contract'. Computer 25(10), 40–51 (1992)
26. Nguyen, T.D., Pham, L.H., Sun, J.: SGUARD: towards fixing vulnerable smart contracts automatically. In: 2021 IEEE Symposium on Security and Privacy (SP), pp. 1215–1229 (2021)
27. Permenev, A., Dimitrov, D., Tsankov, P., Drachsler-Cohen, D., Vechev, M.: VerX: safety verification of smart contracts. In: SP 2020, pp. 18–20 (2020)
28. Rodler, M., Li, W., Karame, G. O., Davi, L.: EVMPatch: timely and automated patching of ethereum smart contracts. In: (USENIX Security 2021), pp. 1289–1306. USENIX Association (2021)
29. AMD SEV-SNP. Strengthening VM isolation with integrity protection and more (2020)
30. Siegel, D.: Understanding the DAO attack. https://www.coindesk.com/understanding-dao-hack-journalists. Accessed 22 July 2021
31. OpenZeppelin team. Proxy Upgrade Pattern. https://docs.openzeppelin.com/upgrades-plugins/1.x/proxies. Accessed 5 Aug 2022
32. Tolmach, P., Li, Y., Lin, S.W., Liu, Y., Li, Z.: A survey of smart contract formal specification and verification. ACM Comput. Surv. 54(7), 1–38 (2021)
33. Torres, C. F., Jonker, H., State, R.: Elysium: Automagically healing vulnerable smart contracts using context-aware patching. CoRR, abs/2108.10071 (2021)
34. Tsankov, P., Dan, A., Drachsler-Cohen, D., Gervais, A., Buenzli, F., Vechev. M.: Securify: practical security analysis of smart contracts. In: CCS 2018, pp. 67–82. ACM (2018)
35. Vogelsteller, F., Buterin, V.: EIP-20: token standard. https://eips.ethereum.org/EIPS/eip-20. Accessed 5 Aug 2022
36. Wang, Y., et al.: Formal verification of workflow policies for smart contracts in azure blockchain. In: Chakraborty, S., Navas, J.A. (eds.) VSTTE 2019. LNCS, vol. 12031, pp. 87–106. Springer, Cham (2020). https://doi.org/10.1007/978-3-030-41600-3_7
37. Wüst, K., Matetic, S., Egli, S., Kostiainen, K., Capkun, S.: ACE: asynchronous and concurrent execution of complex smart contracts. In: CCS 2020, pp. 587–600 (2020)
38. Yu, X.L., Al-Bataineh, O., Lo, D., Roychoudhury, A.: Smart contract repair. ACM Trans. Softw. Eng. Methodol. 29(4), 1–32 (2020)

SKLEE: A Dynamic Symbolic Analysis Tool for Ethereum Smart Contracts (Tool Paper)

Namrata Jain[1] , Kosuke Kaneko[2] , and Subodh Sharma[1](✉)

[1] Indian Institute of Technology, Delhi, New Delhi, India
`svs@cse.iitd.ac.in`
[2] Kyushu University, Fukuoka, Japan
`kaneko.kosuke.437@m.kyushu-u.ac.jp`

Abstract. We present SKLEE, a dynamic symbolic framework to analyse Solidity smart contracts for various safety vulnerabilities. While there are many analysis tools for Solidity contracts, in this work we demonstrate that existing analysis infrastructures for other sequential programming languages, such as C, can be leveraged to construct a competitive analysis framework for Solidity contracts. Notably, SKLEE is bootstrapped on top of KLEE – a dynamic symbolic test-case generation tool for C programs – with modelling for Solidity primitives such as **send, call, transfer**, and others. Our experiments indicate that SKLEE is indeed competitive with other state-of-the-art tools in terms of (i) the number of bug classes it can identify, and (ii) the number of benchmarks it can analyse in a given time bound.

Keywords: Blockchain · Smart contract · Symbolic execution

1 Introduction

Broken smart contracts (or contracts) adversely impact the advertised desideratum of blockchain (such as trust, traceability and transparency). As a result, it becomes imperative to analyse smart contracts for safety and security vulnerabilities. Many recent works have designed and implemented analysis tools for smart contracts [1,7,8,10,12,13,15,16].

In this work, sharing the same objective with prior works of automated contract analysis, we present a *dynamic symbolic execution* (DSE) tool built on KLEE [5] to discover safety and security bugs in Ethereum Solidity contracts. In many prior works, the analysis infrastructure was specifically tailored for contract languages and specific blockchain platforms; in contrast, our work adopts the philosophy of *maximum software reuse*. This allows us to provide an appropriate context for presenting principles of contract modeling and design of adequately functional and efficient analysis infrastructure. While the presented contributions are specific to Ethereum, the modeling principles adopted are generic and can be adapted for other smart contract languages such as Go and Vyper.

© The Author(s), under exclusive license to Springer Nature Switzerland AG 2022
B.-H. Schlingloff and M. Chai (Eds.): SEFM 2022, LNCS 13550, pp. 244–250, 2022.
https://doi.org/10.1007/978-3-031-17108-6_15

Related Work. Several past contributions have analysed the bytecode of either *Ethereum Virtual Machine* (EVM) or its transformation to a custom intermediate representation (IR) [10,12,13,16]. In contrast, SKLEE translates to and analyses the LLVM bitcode. Similar to SKLEE several contributions work with source-code of contracts [3,6,8,9,11], thus leveraging the structured high-level information from the source-code. Some contributions offer *sound* guarantees [4,8,13], while others are heuristic-driven bug detectors [10,12,15]. SKLEE falls in the category of bug detection tools. The class of vulnerabilities that many prior contributions have addressed can be viewed as state *reachability* (or *safety*) properties (such as unchecked send or call to unknown functions). Recent work in [14] supports the verification of much richer temporal properties such as *liveness*. The focus of this work, however, is to analyse safety properties. Support for liveness properties is left for future work.

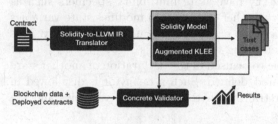

Fig. 1. SKLEE workflow

The contribution of this paper are as follows. As the first contribution within SKLEE[1] (C1) we design and implement a translator from Solidity to C++ code which is further compiled down to LLVM bitcode. The LLVM IR is robust with large user community and many robust analysis engines support it. The translation philosophy of SKLEE in many ways similar to the work in [3] where contract codes are converted to Java. However, it uses *KeY* prover to discharge verification conditions. As the second contribution, (C2) we implement the analyser for translated contracts by modifying the KLEE backend with the modeling of contract language primitives. SKLEE, in addition to detection of common reachability errors, also detects unsafe implementation practices in Solidity such as *mapping reads* and *address typecasts*. Finally, we validate the results of SKLEE by running the contracts with automatically generated test cases in a real setup – by forking a private copy of the Ethereum blockchain platform.

2   Overview of SKLEE

Figure 1 shows the framework of SKLEE. It takes as input a contract written in `Solidity` and produces as output tests that are generated by KLEE. SKLEE converts a contract to a corresponding `C++` program, which is subsequently converted to LLVM bitcode (required by KLEE) using the `clang` compiler, `llvm-gcc`. Since both, `C++` and `Solidity`, are object oriented languages, this allows for straightforward modeling of many features of `Solidity` in `C++`.

---

[1] SKLEE link: https://github.com/subodhvsharma/SKLEE.

2.1 Contract Translator

We convert `Solidity` code to LLVM bitcode by implementing a Lexer/Parser using the tool FLEX-BISON. `Solidity`'s constructs have been mapped to corresponding `C++` constructs. We briefly describe the conversion approach followed for some of the constructs.

Type and Function Library. `Solidity`'s pre-defined functions' definition and type system are implemented as a `Type library`. It contains `address, int, uint, byte` and `bytes` datatype as `C++` structures.

Modeling Contracts. Contracts with state variables, member functions and unique address are converted to a `C++` class. Since every contract is convertible to an `address` type, the equivalent class for a contract derives publicly from the `address` type. Functions in `Solidity` have state mutability specifiers such as `pure, view, payable` which specify whether the function modifies state variables of contract, performs only read operation or accepts payment, respectively. This information to be later used in identifying vulnerabilities.

`Solidity` allows a state variable to be used in the declaration of another state variable before it is actually declared/defined. Such a behavior is disallowed in `C++`. *Use-def* chain is used in our translation to detect such variables and are explicitly declared before their use.

`Solidity` implicitly declares default, parameterized constructors for struct members. During translation, SKLEE inserts default and parameterized constructors in struct definition when they are not explicitly defined.

In `Solidity` a *modifier* defines a condition that must be met before invoking a function. Modifiers are modeled as class functions returning `boolean` values; the modeled function returns true if the condition defined in the modifier is satisfied, otherwise false.

Inheritance. SKLEE models inheritance by using the public visibility level for each contract from which the immediate contract is derived. Multiple inheritance is supported in both `Solidity` and `C++`. While class names are used to resolve overridden functions in `C++`, `Solidity` uses 'C3 Linearization' [2] to force a specific order of base classes. SKLEE, instead, lists the base contracts in the reverse order in which they are specified. Then it uses this order to add scope (*i.e.*, contract name) before the overridden function.

2.2 Augmenting KLEE

Builtin functions in `Solidity` (such as `send, call`, and `transfer`) that are left uninterpreted during translation are modeled in KLEE. The decision to not translate them early on rests on the fast-changing nature of the language. Note that the symbolic simulation of KLEE remains untouched. KLEE treats the return values of `send, call, transfer` as *symbolic*. The modeling of `send` is shown in the following code.

```
1    bool address:send(unsigned amount) { bool success;
2      klee_make_symbolic(&success, sizeof(success), "ReturnValue"); if
3      (success) return true; return false; }
```

Since Solidity allows callbacks, in order to capture reentrancy issues arising from send or transfer we assign identifiers to contracts' fallback functions (if present). Then, in the modeling of the calls the fallback function is invoked as the last instruction.

2.3 Vulnerabilities and Their Detection

SKLEE targets many of the vulnerability classes that are discussed in prior works such as payable-without-fallback, unchecked sends, block- and transaction-state dependence *etc.* . We discuss briefly a couple of vulnerabilities below.

Unchecked send. A contract is vulnerable when it invokes send method, but does not explicitly check its return value and modifies the global state of the contract after the call. SKLEE throws an error in such a case.

Greedy Contract. A contract is greedy if it has a function which accepts payments, but does not contain any function which transfers ether to other contracts. It is originally defined as a trace property in [12]. SKLEE analyzes a contract to check whether it transacts through a transfer. If transfer is guarded by some condition which involves a state variable, then SKLEE checks if there is at least one function which writes to that variable, otherwise there is a possibility that the condition may never become true. SKLEE generates error if no such transacting function is found.

2.4 Validation

SKLEE uses a private fork of the original Ethereum blockchain with the last block as the input context to validate its results. It runs the contract with the concrete values of the transactions (obtained from the symbolic analysis) to check if the vulnerability holds in the concrete execution. If the concrete execution fails to exhibit a violation of the property, we mark the contract as a false positive. At the moment only unchecked send, overflow/underflow, greedy, prodigal and suicidal vulnerabilities are validated. The vulnerability validation approach is similar to MAIAN [12] – it analyzes the bytecode of smart contracts and has its custom symbolic execution framework.

2.5 Limitations

SKLEE supports a subset of Solidity. For instance, SKLEE does not currently support *assembly* blocks in the contract code and revert functions. Also, SKLEE does not model the gas consumption of any instruction or function as it is set by the transaction initiator and is not known during analysis. Vulnerabilities such as address typecasts cannot be analysed symbolically as checking it requires the

Table 1. SKLEE results

Bug	TP	FP	FN
Unchecked send	163	2	6
Overflow	106	7	3
Greedy	8	2	3
Prodigal	5	0	1
Suicidal	17	1	3
Re-entrancy	31	3	0
Typecast	21	2	0
TOD	179	0	0
Blockstate dep	8	0	2
Transaction state dep	9	0	2
Mapping read	78	2	3
Memory overlap	117	1	0
No fallback	18	4	0

Table 2. Comparison results. SC = SmartCheck. ∗: when multiplication after division can cause overflow/underflow.

Bug	SKLEE	SC	Mythril
Unchecked send	165	152	86
Overflow	113	54*	87
Greedy	10	20	-
Prodigal	5	-	4
Suicidal	18	0	1
Re-entrancy	34	0	-
Typecast	23	-	-
TOD	179	-	-
Blockstate dep	8	6	49
Transaction state dep	9	14	-
Mapping read	80	-	-
Memory overlap	118	122	-
No fallback	22	0	-

runtime state of the Blockchain. SKLEE only reports warning in typecast issues. Solidity, just like C/C++, does not enforce a sub-expression evaluation order. SKLEE can be unsound in the analysis of such nested expressions.

3   Experiments and Results

SKLEE is evaluated on a total of 575 unique smart contracts by scraping through etherscan.io (same as in [13]). SKLEE was able to successfully convert 515 contracts to C++ code. The unsuccessful conversions were due to unsupported features of Solidity (such as assembly and revert). Out of 515 contracts, 65 contracts had no vulnerability. Table 1 shows the number of smart contracts found corresponding to a vulnerability with false positive (FP), false negative (FN) and true positive (TP) numbers. Table 2 shows the comparison of SKLEE with other recent contract analysers – Mythril is used by industry and is partnered by Enterprise Ethereum Alliance; SmartCheck is a leading static analyser of Solidity contracts for the version that is also supported by SKLEE. Some of the scraped contracts required solc version <0.4.11 and could not be analyzed with Mythril (shown with a −).

Time Comparison. On a set of randomly selected 10 contracts, SKLEE took 2.05 min, while Mythril completed execution in 6.78 min. For the same set, SmartCheck took only 15 s. Note that SmartCheck does not generate test cases at all.

4   Conclusion

We presented a dynamic-symbolic execution SKLEE for Solidity smart contract analysis. The tool was built on top of existing and robust frameworks such as LLVM and KLEE. The paper demonstrated that the tool is competitive with existing smart contract analysis tools. As future work, we will support a larger subset of the Solidity language and try to obtain higher precision and recall.

References

1. Consensys: Mythril: a security analysis tool for ethereum smart contracts. https://github.com/ConsenSys/mythril-classic
2. Solidity c3 linearization. https://docs.soliditylang.org/en/v0.8.4/contracts.html
3. Ahrendt, W., et al.: Verification of smart contract business logic - exploiting a Java source code verifier. In: Hojjat, H., Massink, M. (eds.) Fundamentals of Software Engineering - 8th International Conference, FSEN, pp. 228–243 (2019)
4. Amani, S., Bégel, M., Bortin, M., Staples, M.: Towards verifying Ethereum smart contract bytecode in Isabelle/HOL. In: Proceedings of the 7th ACM SIGPLAN International Conference on Certified Programs and Proofs, pp. 66–77 (2018)
5. Cadar, C., Dunbar, D., Engler, D.: KLEE: unassisted and automatic generation of high-coverage tests for complex systems programs. In: Proceedings of the 8th USENIX Conference on Operating Systems Design and Implementation, OSDI 2008, pp. 209–224. USENIX Association (2008)
6. Feist, J., Grieco, G., Groce, A.: Slither: a static analysis framework for smart contracts. In: 2019 IEEE/ACM 2nd International Workshop on Emerging Trends in Software Engineering for Blockchain (WETSEB) (2019)
7. Hildenbrandt, E., et al.: KEVM: a complete formal semantics of the Ethereum virtual machine. In: 2018 IEEE 31st Computer Security Foundations Symposium (CSF), pp. 204–217 (2018)
8. Kalra, S., Goel, S., Dhawan, M., Sharma, S.: ZEUS: analyzing safety of smart contracts. In: 25th Annual Network and Distributed System Security Symposium, NDSS (2018)
9. Lu, N., Wang, B., Zhang, Y., Shi, W., Esposito, C.: NeuCheck: a more practical Ethereum smart contract security analysis tool. Softw. Practice Exp. **51**(10), 2065–2084 (2019). https://doi.org/10.1002/spe.2745
10. Luu, L., Chu, D.H., Olickel, H., Saxena, P., Hobor, A.: Making smart contracts smarter. In: Proceedings of the 2016 ACM SIGSAC Conference on Computer and Communications Security, CCS 2016, pp. 254–269. Association for Computing Machinery (2016)
11. Mossberg, M., et al.: Manticore: a user-friendly symbolic execution framework for binaries and smart contracts (2019)
12. Nikolić, I., Kolluri, A., Sergey, I., Saxena, P., Hobor, A.: Finding the greedy, prodigal, and suicidal contracts at scale. In: Proceedings of the 34th Annual Computer Security Applications Conference, ACSAC 2018, pp. 653–663. Association for Computing Machinery (2018)
13. Schneidewind, C., Grishchenko, I., Scherer, M., Maffei, M.: eThor: practical and provably sound static analysis of ethereum smart contracts. In: Proceedings of the 2020 ACM SIGSAC Conference on Computer and Communications Security, CCS 2020, pp. 621–640. Association for Computing Machinery (2020)

14. Stephens, J., Ferles, K., Mariano, B., Lahiri, S., Dillig, I.: Smartpulse: automated checking of temporal properties in smart contracts. In: 42nd IEEE Symposium on Security and Privacy. IEEE (2021)
15. Tikhomirov, S., Voskresenskaya, E., Ivanitskiy, I., Takhaviev, R., Marchenko, E., Alexandrov, Y.: Smartcheck: static analysis of Ethereum smart contracts. In: WETSEB 2018, pp. 9–16. Association for Computing Machinery (2018)
16. Tsankov, P., Dan, A., Drachsler-Cohen, D., Gervais, A., Bünzli, F., Vechev, M.: Securify: practical security analysis of smart contracts. In: CCS 2018, New York, NY, USA. Association for Computing Machinery (2018)

Program Synthesis

Weighted Games for User Journeys

Paul Kobialka[1]([✉])[iD], Silvia Lizeth Tapia Tarifa[1][iD],
Gunnar Rye Bergersen[1,2][iD], and Einar Broch Johnsen[1][iD]

[1] University of Oslo, Oslo, Norway
{paulkob,sltarifa,gunnab,einarj}@ifi.uio.no
[2] GrepS B.V., Utrecht, The Netherlands
gunnar@greps.com

Abstract. The servitisation of business is moving industry to business models driven by customer demand. Customer satisfaction is connected with financial rewards, forcing companies to investigate in their users' experience. User journeys describe how users manoeuvre through a service. Today, user journeys are typically modelled graphically, and lack formalisation and analysis support. This paper proposes to formalise user journeys as weighted games between the user and the service provider. We further propose a data-driven construction of such games, derived from system logs using process mining techniques. As user journeys may contain cycles, we bound the number of iterations in each cycle and develop an algorithm to unfold user journeys into acyclic weighted games. These can be model checked using UPPAAL STRATEGO to uncover potential challenges in how a company interacts with its users and to derive company strategies to guide users better in their journeys. Our analysis pipeline was evaluated on an industrial case study; it revealed design challenges within the studied service and could be used to derive suitable recommendations for improvement.

Keywords: User journeys · Data-driven model construction · Games · Model checking · UPPAAL

1 Introduction

The *servitisation of business* [37], a concept of creating added value to products by offering services, is a major practice embraced by most (if not all) successful companies. Such companies are interested in the analysis of their services, which until now has mostly focused on the *managerial* perspective, where the service is analysed with respect to the companies' view. Recent tendencies are shifting the focus from the company's view to the end-users view, where a positive experience and impression that a user has while engaging in the service, has shown to have a positive impact on the financial reward of a company [17]. Thus, companies aim to analyse and improve their services, based on their users' satisfaction.

This work is part of the *Smart Journey Mining* project, funded by the Research Council of Norway (grant no. 312198).

User journeys (also called customer journeys) analyse services from the user perspective [30]: A user journey is inherently a goal-oriented process, because humans engage in a service with a goal in mind. The user moves through the journey by engaging in so-called touchpoints, which are either actions performed by the user or a communication event between the user and a service provider. We here assume that users only engage in one touchpoint of a service at a time.

Tools are currently lacking the analysis of user journeys [21], which hinders their operational use. User journey diagrams are usually generated by hand, and the user perspective is derived from interviews with experts and users, e.g. [20,30]. This process has been highly successful, discovering points of failure in the studied services and, as a result, providing advice to companies on how to improve their services. However, this manual process is best suited for relatively small services and a restricted number of users. For services with thousands of users, journey diagrams need to be automatically generated and analysed.

This paper proposes a formalization of user journeys as *weighted games* [12] between users and a service provider, and a method to derive these games from process logs. Our aim is to use these games to analyse services and to suggest service improvements such that service providers always have a strategy to guide their users towards a desired goal. We capture the user perspective of services by means of so-called *gas*. The term is inspired by blockchain technology such as Ethereum, where gas refers to the cost necessary to perform a transaction on the network. In our work, the gas quantitatively reflects how moves in the user journey contribute to the users reaching their goal. Consequently, the moves in the derived games are weighted and accumulated into the gas of the journeys, which allows to compare and analyse journeys using model checkers such as UPPAAL STRATEGO [15] or PRISM-games [13], and to give strategic recommendations to service providers. In short, our contributions are: (1) a formalization of user journeys as weighted games; (2) a pipeline to automatically derive and model check weighted games; and (3) an industrial case study that evaluates the feasibility of our approach.

Related Work: We discuss related work with respect to the modelling of user journeys and the use of data-driven techniques to discover user journeys. We are not aware of prior work that uses automatic verification methods to check properties for user journeys.

User journeys aim to improve service design by describing how users interact with services [16,36]. Modelling notations for user journeys aim to support the so-called blueprinting [11], i.e., to create an anticipated model of a service. There are various notations to create diagrams for user journeys [5,14,19,24,29,30]; these diagrams are mostly handmade but some digital support exists; for example, a semantic lifting into ontologies has been used to visualize fixed aspects of a model [24]: the data sent, the communication channels and devices used, etc. Berendes *et al.* propose in [5] the *high street journey modelling language* (HSJML) tailored to journeys in shopping streets. Razo-Zapata *et al.* propose the *VIVA* modelling language with focus on interactions [29]. In contrast, our work aims to use data-driven techniques [2] to automatically discover user journey diagrams and formal methods to automatically check properties of user journeys and derive recommendations for improving the service under analysis.

The *Customer Journey Modelling Language* (CJML) [18,20] captures the end-users point of view. CJML distinguishes planned and actual user journeys, which represent the journey as planned as part of the service design and as perceived by the user, respectively. Our work is part of a project [21] on tool support for data-driven user journey modelling in CJML. Whereas previous work on CJML manually quantifies user experience collected through user feedback questionnaires, our work aims to capture the journeys as perceived by the user in a data-driven manner, based on system logs.

Data-driven techniques for process discovery allow us to discover user journeys. Harbich *et al.* [22] use mixtures of Markov models to derive user journey maps. Bernard *et al.* [8,10] study process mining [2] for user journeys, such as hierarchical clustering to explore large numbers of journeys [7] and process discovery techniques to generate user journey maps at different levels of granularity [9]. Terragni and Hassani [33] apply process mining to user journey web logs to build process models, and improve the results by clustering journeys. This work has been integrated with a recommender system to suggest service actions that maximize key performance indicators [34], e.g., how often the product page is visited. In our work we propose a data-driven method to discover models of user centric journeys with multiple actors, building on existing techniques.

Outline: Section 2 introduces foundational definitions needed for weighted games and the model checking suite UPPAAL that we use for analysis. The formal model for user journeys is introduced in Sects. 3–5 and model checked in Sect. 6. Section 7 discusses the implementation, Sect. 8 evaluates our approach in terms of an industrial case study and Sect. 9 concludes the paper.

2   Preliminaries

We briefly summarise the formal notations and tools that we build on for the proposed user journey pipeline to analyse a service.

A *transition system* [28] is a tuple $S = \langle \Gamma, A, E, s_0, T \rangle$ with a set Γ of states, a set A of actions (or labels), a transition relation $E \subseteq \Gamma \times A \times \Gamma$, an initial state $s_0 \in \Gamma$ and a set $T \subseteq \Gamma$ of final states. A *weighted transition system* [35] $\mathcal{S} = \langle S, w \rangle$ extends the transition system S with a weight function $w : E \to \mathbb{R}$ that assigns weights to transitions.

Weighted games [12] are obtained from weighted transition systems by partitioning the actions A into *controllable* actions A_c, and *uncontrollable* actions A_u, where only actions in A_c can be controlled by the analyser, while actions in A_u are nondeterministically decided by an adversarial environment. When analysing games, we look for a *strategy* that guarantees a desired outcome, i.e. winning the game by reaching a certain state. The strategy is given by a partial function $\Gamma \to A_c \cup \{\lambda\}$ that decides on the action of the controller in a given state (here, λ denotes the "wait" action, letting the adversary move).

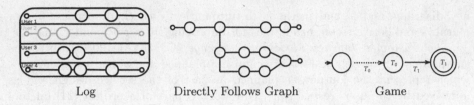

Log   Directly Follows Graph   Game

Fig. 1. Creation of the journey model.

UPPAAL TIGA [4] can be used to analyse reachability and safety properties for games expressed using (timed) transition systems, extending the model checker UPPAAL [25]. UPPAAL TIGA checks whether there is a strategy under which the behaviour satisfies a control objective, denoted `control: P` for a property P. Property P is expressed in computational tree logic [3], an extension of propositional logic that is used to express properties along paths in a transition system. Recall that computational tree logic *state properties* ϕ can be decided in a single state; while *reachability properties* `E <>`ϕ express that the formula ϕ is satisfiable in some reachable state in a transition system; *safety properties* `E []`ϕ express that the formula ϕ is always satisfied in all the states of *some path* in a transition system and `A []`ϕ expresses that ϕ is always satisfied in all the states of *all paths* of a transition system. Similarly, *liveness properties* `A <>`ϕ express that the formula ϕ will eventually be satisfied in all the paths in a transition system and the formula ϕ `-->`ψ expresses that satisfying formula ϕ leads to satisfying formula ψ.

UPPAAL STRATEGO [15] can be used to analyse and refine a strategy generated by UPPAAL TIGA with respect to a quantitative attribute like weights. UPPAAL STRATEGO is a statistical model checker [27]; it extends UPPAAL for stochastic priced timed games and combines simulations with hypothesis testing until statistical evidence can be deduced.

3   From User Logs to Games

To capture the *user perspective* in games that model user journeys, user actions (representing communication initiated by the user) can be seen as controllable and the service provider's actions as uncontrollable. However, from an analytical perspective, it is more interesting to treat user actions as uncontrollable and the service provider's actions as controllable. The service provider is expected to have suitable reactions for all possible user interactions. Ideally, the service provider should not rely on the user to make the journey pleasant. By treating user actions as uncontrollable, we can expose the worst behaviour of the service provider, and thereby strengthen the user-centric perspective promoted by journey diagrams. Games for user journeys are then defined as follows:

Definition 1 (User journey games). *A user journey game is a weighted game* $\langle \Gamma, A_c, A_u, E, s_0, T, T_s, w \rangle$, *where*

- Γ *are states that represent the touchpoints of the user journey,*
- A_c *and* A_u *are disjoint sets of actions respectively initiated by the service provider and the user,*
- $E \subseteq \Gamma \times A_c \cup A_u \times \Gamma$ *are the possible actions at the different touchpoints,*
- $s_0 \in \Gamma$ *is an initial state,*
- $T \subseteq \Gamma$ *are the final states of the game,*
- $T_s \subseteq T$ *are the final states in which the game is successful, and*
- $w : E \to \mathbb{R}$ *specifies the weight associated with the different transitions.*

The process of deriving such user journey games from user logs is illustrated in Fig. 1. In *Step 1*, we go from logs to a user journey model, expressed as a directly follows graph (DFG), and in *Step 2*, the DFG is extended to a game. The derivation of weights for the transitions is discussed in Sect. 4.

Step 1. We use a *directly follows graph* (DFG) as an underlying process model to capture the order of events in an event log; a DFG is well-suited as the process model provided that users only engage in one touchpoint at a time. DFGs are derived from event logs by means of *process discovery* [2]. An *event log L* is a multi-set of journeys. A journey $J = \langle a_0, \ldots, a_n \rangle$ is a finite and ordered sequence of events a_i from a universe $\mathscr{A}$. We construct the DFG of an event log L as a transition system $S = \langle \Gamma, A, E, s_0, T \rangle$ where the states Γ capture the event universe, $\Gamma \subseteq \mathscr{A} \cup \{s_0\} \cup T$. Every sequence of events is altered to start in the start state s_0 and to end in a dedicated final state $t \in T$. The set of actions A is the union of the event universe and the final states, $A = \mathscr{A} \cup T$. The transition relation E includes a triple (a_i, a_{i+1}, a_{i+1}) if a_i is directly followed by a_{i+1} in some $J \in L$; we can traverse from state a_i to state a_{i+1} by performing the action a_{i+1}. Here reaching a state in S is interpreted as the corresponding event in L has already been performed. By construction, the DFG S obtained from log L can replay every observed journey in L. However S may capture more journeys than those present in L, since for example S may contain transitions with loops.

Step 2. The DFG is now transformed into a game. Observe that the DFG captures the temporal ordering of events but it does not directly differentiate the messages sent by the user to the service provider from those sent by the service provider to the user. For simplicity, let us assume that this information is either part of the events in the logs or known in advance from domain knowledge concerning the event universe. The mined DFG can then be extended into a game by annotating the actions that are *(un)controllable.*

4   Capturing User Feedback in User Journey Games

We now extend the games derived from system logs into weighted games by defining a *gas* function reflecting user feedback. We develop a gas function that is automatically calculated and applied to the transitions of the game, depending on the traversal and entropy that is present in the corresponding event log. Informally, the gas function captures how much "steam" the consumer has left to continue the journey. Less steam means that the user is more likely to abort the journey and more steam means that the user is more likely to complete the journey successfully. Assuming that the service provider attempts to provide the best possible service, its goal is to maximize gas in a journey. The adversarial user aims for the weaknesses in the journey and therefore minimizes the gas. Formally, the weight function $w : E \rightarrow \mathbb{R}$ maps the transitions E of a game to weights, represented as reals. Given a log L and its corresponding game, we compute the weight for every transition $e \in E$.

Since user journeys are inherently goal-oriented, we distinguish successful and unsuccessful journeys; the journeys that reach the goal are called *successful* and the remaining journeys are considered to be *unsuccessful*. This is captured by a function majority $: E \times L \rightarrow \{-1, 1\}$ that maps every transition $e \in E$ to $\{-1, 1\}$, depending on whether the action in the transition appears in the majority of journeys in L that are unsuccessful or successful, respectively. Ties arbitrarily return -1 or 1.

Many actions might be part of both successful and unsuccessful journeys. For this reason, we use Shannon's notion of *entropy* [32]. Intuitively, if an action is always present in unsuccessful journeys and never in successful ones, there is certainty in this transition. The entropy is low, since we understand the context in which this transition occurs. In contrast, actions involved in both successful and unsuccessful journeys have high entropy. The entropy is calculated using

1. the number of occurrences of an event in the transitions of successful journeys within the event log L, denoted $\#_L^{pos} e$, and the number of transitions in unsuccessful ones, denoted $\#_L^{neg} e$; and
2. the total number of occurrences of the event in L, denoted $\#_L e$.

The entropy H of transition e given the event log L is now defined as

$$H(e, L) = -\frac{\#_L^{pos} e}{\#_L e} \cdot log_2(\frac{\#_L^{pos} e}{\#_L e}) - \frac{\#_L^{neg} e}{\#_L e} \cdot log_2(\frac{\#_L^{neg} e}{\#_L e}).$$

The weight function w that computes the weights of the transitions can now be defined in terms of the entropy function, inspired by decision tree learning [31]. Given an event log L, the weight of a transition e is given by

$$w(e) = ((1 - H(e, L)) \cdot \text{majority}(e, L) - C) \cdot M.$$

The constant C represents an aversion bias and is learned from the training set. It is used to model a basic aversion against continuous interactions. The sign of a transition depends on its majority. If the transition is mostly traversed on successful journeys, it is positive. Otherwise, it is negative. The inverse entropy factor quantifies the uncertainty of transitions. The constant M scales the energy weight to integer sizes (our implementation currently requires integer values, see Sect. 7).

The gas of a journey quantitatively reflects the history of that journey, allowing us to not only compare the weights of transitions but also to compare (partial)

Algorithm 1. k-bounded loop unrolling

Input: Weighted Game $S = \langle \Gamma, A_c, A_u, E, s_0, T, T_s, w \rangle$, constant $k \in \mathbb{N}^+$
Output: Acyclic Weighted Game $S' = \langle \Gamma', A_c, A_u, E', s_0, T', T_s, w' \rangle$
 1: Initialize $S' = \langle \emptyset, A'_c, A'_u, \emptyset, s_0, T', T_s, w \rangle$ and queue $Q = [s_0]$
 2: $C \leftarrow \{c \mid c$ is simple cycle in $S\}$
 3: **while** not EMPTY(Q) **do**
 4:     state $s \leftarrow$ FIRST(Q)
 5:     **for** $t \in \{t \mid (s, t) \in E\}$ **do**
 6:         hist $\leftarrow$ PUSH(HISTORY(s), t)
 7:         allSmaller $\leftarrow$ **True**
 8:         canTraverse $\leftarrow$ **False**
 9:         **if** REPETITIONS($c, hist$) $\geq k$ for all cycle $c \in C$ **then**
10:             allSmaller $\leftarrow$ **False**
11:         **if** !allSmaller **then**
12:             $P \leftarrow$ ALLSIMPLEPATHS(S, t, T)
13:             **for** path $p \in P$ **do**   ▷ check whether cycle might be partially traversed
14:                 $hist' \leftarrow$ MERGE($hist, p$)
15:                 **if** REPETITIONS($c, hist'$) $\leq k$ for all cycle $c \in C$ **then**
16:                     canTraverse $\leftarrow$ **True**   ▷ cycle can be partially traversed
17:         **if** allSmaller $\vee$ canTraverse **then**
18:             state t' copy of t with history $hist$
19:             PUSH(Q, t')
20:             ADDTRANSITION($(s, t'), S'$)   ▷ Copies weight to w' and actor to A'_c, A'_u
21: **return** S'

---

journeys. The gas $\mathcal{G}$ of a journey $J = \langle a_0, \ldots, a_n \rangle$ with transitions $e_0, \ldots e_{n-1}$ is defined as the sum of the weights along the traversed transitions:

$$\mathcal{G}(J) := \sum_{i=0}^{n-1} w(e_i).$$

5 Finite Unrolling of Games

The generated weighted games may contain loops, which capture unrealistic journeys (since no user endures indefinitely in a service) and hinder model checking. Therefore, the weighted games with loops are transformed into acyclic weighted games using a breadth-first search loop unrolling strategy bounded in the number of iterations per loop. The transformation is implemented in an algorithm that preserves the original decision structure and adds no additional final states.

The algorithm for k-*bounded loop unrolling* (shown in Algorithm 1) returns an acyclic weighted game, where each loop is traversed at most k times. The unrolling algorithm utilizes a breadth-first search from the initial state s_0 in combination with a loop counting to build an acyclic weighted game. In the algorithm, the state s denotes the current state that is being traversed. To traverse the paths in the weighted game, we use a queue Q to store the states that need to be traversed, a set C containing all the cycles in the graph (where each cycle is a sequence of states), and the function ALLSIMPLEPATHS(S, s, T) that returns all paths in the weighted game S from s to any final state $t \in T$. The extended graph is stored in the acyclic game S'. A state in a cycle can be traversed if it has been visited less than k times (see Lines 9–10). The function REPETITIONS checks the number of traversals. If the counter for one cycle is k, the algorithm checks whether the cycle can be partially traversed (see Lines 11–16).

Partial traversals guarantee that we reach a final state without closing another loop. The partial traversal does not increase the count of another cycle to $k+1$ (Lines 14–16). Every state stores its history (a sequence of visited states), which can be retrieved using the function HISTORY. Line 14 increases the current history by including a (partial) path through the loop. This check iterates through all paths from the current state to any final state. If state t can be traversed, it is added to the acyclic game (Lines 17–20). A copy t' of t is added to the queue Q, the transition (s, t'), its weight and actor are added to S' using the function ADDTRANSITION. The resulting weighted game can be reduced. All states outside a cycle can be merged into the same state. This can either be done after unrolling the whole game or on the fly while unrolling.

Example. Figure 2 illustrates the unrolling algorithm (for simplicity, we ignore transition weights and do not distinguish controllable and uncontrollable actions in the example). Starting from the cyclic weighted game in Fig. 2a, the algorithm with $k = 1$ generates the acyclic weighted game in Fig. 2b. The input contains two loops: $C = \{[2, 3], [2, 4, 3]\}$. Starting at state 1, we can traverse two neighbour states which both are part of the cycles. Thus, both transitions are inserted to S', and Q is updated to $[2, 3]$. Continuing with state 2, all reachable transitions are again inserted as the corresponding cycles have not been fully traversed. Names of copies of the states that are already present once in the graph are incremented (the first occurrence of state 3 is called 3, the second 3.1, the third, 3.2, etc.) The algorithm continues until the first loop 2, 3, 2 is closed. In this case, it is not possible to traverse again to state 3 without closing the loop $[2, 3]$. Only state 4 and its corresponding loop can be traversed (see Fig. 2b, left branch). As result of

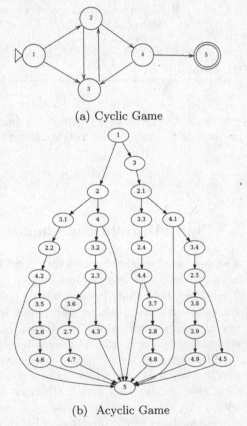

(a) Cyclic Game

(b) Acyclic Game

Fig. 2. Unrolling example.

the state reduction, all final states are merged into one (removing the copies originally introduced by the algorithm).

Properties. The unrolling algorithm preserves the decision structure of the initial weighted game. By construction, acyclic weighted games do not traverse cycles in the initial game $k+1$ times. Loops can be traversed partially to ensure that every final state in the acyclic weighted game is also a final state in the initial weighted game. Only unreachable states are excluded in the acyclic game. No further final states or "dead ends" are introduced. The algorithm also preserves the local decisions between controllable and uncontrollable actions, so the strategies found on the unrolled weighted game carry over to the initial weighted game.

6   Model Checking User Journeys

In this section we describe how to model check properties for user journeys and generate strategies to improve user journeys, using acyclic weighted games. The analysis of a weighted game gives formal insights into the performance of a service. We introduce generic properties that capture the user's point of view on a user journey. The analysis in this paper uses the STRATEGO extension for UPPAAL [15], which supports non-deterministic priced games and stochastic model checking. STRATEGO allows to model check reachability properties within a finite number of steps, when following a strategy (therefore the need for acyclic games). STRATEGO constructs a strategy that satisfies a property P, so that the controller can not be defeated by the non-deterministic environment. We detail some strategies and properties of interest for games derived from user journeys.

Guiding Users to a Target State. A company needs a suitable plan of (controllable) actions for all possible (uncontrollable) actions of their users when guiding them through a service. In UPPAAL STRATEGO we define the following strategy:

```
strategy goPos = control: A<> Journey.finPos.
```

Model checking this property returns true if and only if there exists a company-strategy `goPos` such that the positive target state `finPos`, indicating that the journey is successful, is eventually reached in all paths. The corresponding strategy (given as a pseudo-code) can be produced with the UPPAAL TIGA command-line tool VERIFYTGA. If the verification fails, the company should be advised to simplify their service and offer more support to avoid unsuccessful user journeys.

Analysing User Feedback. We can use the gas function and a liveness property to analyse the desired accumulated feedback at the end of successful user journeys:

```
Journey.finPos --> gas > 0 under goPos.
```

This property checks that in general users have balancing experiences within their journeys, when the company follows the `goPos` strategy.

We can also check the feedback levels along the journey. The following property checks that a user never falls below a defined constant feedback C:

```
control: A[] gas > C under goPos.
```

Fluctuations in the feedback level of users can be revealed using simulations. UPPAAL uses an implicit model for the passage of time to guarantee termination of statistical queries and simulations, using an upper time bound T, as specified in [15]. The following query simulates X runs through the system using the goPos strategy, where each run has T as a time bound:

```
simulate X [t<=T]{Journey.finPos, gas} under goPos.
```

The time bound is set to a value that guarantees all runs to reach a final state.

Analysing the Trajectory of User Journeys. Reaching a final state in a journey with a positive feedback does not ensure a satisfying journey. The user might still visit every pitfall along the way. To provide a pleasant journey, a company is among others interested in minimising the expected number of steps. A strategy minimising the number of steps is refined as follows:

```
strategy goPosFast = minE(steps) [t<=T] :
    <> Journey.finPos under goPos.
```

This strategy can additionally be used to examine the expected lower bound of gas within a journey and the expected maximum value of accumulated gas at the end of a journey (denoted by finalGas):

```
E[t<=T; X] (min: gas) under goPosFast,
E[t<=T; X] (max: finalGas) under goPosFast.
```

These values are computed with a time bound of T and over X runs.

7   Implementing the Pipeline to Analyse User Journeys

This section describes the implementation of the analysis pipeline detailed in Sects. 3–6. We focus on the implementation decisions made along the pipeline to facilitate the analysis. The pipeline is implemented in Python. The input to the pipeline are user logs of a service provided by a company and the output is a UPPAAL model, which can be model checked by either the proposed properties in Sect. 6 or by other custom made properties using UPPAAL STRATEGO. A source repository for our work on user journey games is available online [1].

We first mine the DFG from user logs and then remove transitions that were rarely traversed, to simplify the graph and make it robust. Leemans *et al.* describe two ways to build a robust DFG [26]: One can (1) remove either transitions from the graph or (2) remove journeys from the log and rebuild the graph. We used the first approach with a traversal threshold of three in this paper, since removing journeys requires larger datasets. This modification ensures that the model only contains relevant journeys. We then enrich the graph with knowledge indicating which actions are controllable and uncontrollable. Since companies want to understand why on-boarded users reach their goal or quit in the middle of a journey, we decided to add to the model final states representing a positive endpoint, finPos, and a negative one, finNeg, respectively.

We generate a weighted transition system by computing a weight for each transition, as discussed in Sect. 4. The factor M scales the weights to integer sizes, required by UPPAAL's model checker. However, given that we simplify the DFGs, the log contains journeys that are not re-playable in the graph. Computing the gas of such journeys corresponds to the *alignment* problem [23,26]. The alignment procedure consists of either allowing additional steps in the log without counterparts in the model or allowing steps in the model without steps in the log. Since the simplification of DFGs omits steps in the model, it was here sufficient to use the information given in the trace, without inferring further model steps. Optimal alignments can also be used to compute the gas.

As a final step, we unroll the weighted game with cycles, as described in Sect. 5, to obtain an acyclic weighted game, which is the output of the transformation and the input to UPPAAL for further analysis. Bounded constraints in the properties are introduced to the unrolled model to ensure termination. The analysis described in Sect. 6 is implemented and evaluated.

8   Evaluating the Analysis Pipeline

In this section we evaluate the implemented pipeline described in Sect. 7 in an industrial case study from the company GrepS. The full details of the case study are given in the accompanying artefact.[1]

8.1   Context

GrepS is a company that provides analysis and measurement of programming skills for the Java programming language. The service is research based [6]. Typical customers are organisations hiring or training software developers. The *users* of the service are developers who receive a request from a customer organization to complete a skill analysis within a specific time frame, typically 1–2 weeks.

The service consists of a sign-up phase followed by a phase where the user solves programming tasks in an authentic programming environment, which includes an instructional task and a practice task. Finally, the service analyses the user's skills and requests the user to share the skill report with the customer.

The customer pays GrepS for each skill report it receives. In a *successful* use of the service, a user successfully completes three phases: (1) sign up, (2) solve all programming tasks, and (3) review and share the skill report with the customer. In an *unsuccessful* use of the service, the user permanently stops using the service or does not want to share the skill report with GrepS' customer.

---

[1] An artefact for the implementation and evaluation of the analysis pipeline in this paper is available: https://doi.org/10.5281/zenodo.6962413.

```
strategy goPos = control: A<> Journey.finPos                    TRUE
Journey.finPos --> e > 0 under goPos                            FALSE
control: A[] gas > -41 under goPos                              TRUE
E[t<=100; 500] (max: steps) under goPos                          28.5
E[t<=100; 500] (min: gas) under goPos                           -26.7
E[t<=100; 500] (max: finalGas) under goPos                         60

strategy goPosFast = minE(steps) [t<=100] : <> Journey.finPos under goPos TRUE
E[t<=100; 500] (max: steps) under goPosFast                      20.9
E[t<=100; 500] (min: gas) under goPosFast                       -20.1
E[t<=100; 500] (max: finalGas) under goPosFast                     35
```

Fig. 4. Analysis of the weighed game generated from the user logs of GrepS.

Anonymised user logs were provided by GrepS in the form of tabular data. The logs contain events with various fields; only the fields *Timestamp*, that gives the order of events, and *Metadata*, containing meta-information on the kind of event, were used to generate the weighted game. An extract of the data is shown in Fig. 3.

Timestamp	···	Metadata
5245944	···	Registered
5780525	···	Registered
6104714	···	Activated
6104714	···	Logged in: Web page
⋮	⋮	⋮

Fig. 3. Extract of GrepS' user logs.

For our purposes, only the order of the events was of interest, as given by the *Timestamp*.

The Validation of the Analysis Pipeline. includes observations of the weighted game and the model checking of the properties as outlined in Sect. 6, the results are summarised in Fig. 4. The analysis results were used to provide recommendations for GrepS to improve their service. These recommendations were validated by the third author, a long-term employee of the company who has experience in handling feedback from both users and customers.

8.2   Observations in the Weighted Game

The generated cyclic user journey game, which still contains loops, is shown with events (or touchpoints) T and weighted transitions in Fig. 5. In the figure, the transition thickness indicates how often a transition was traversed and dashed lines represent uncontrollable transitions. Positive (negative) transitions are green (respectively, red). Transitions traversed three times or less were removed from the graph.

The derived weights already allow us to make some interesting observations. The weighted game shows negative weights (about −1 to −2) through Phase 1 (T0–T5), up until the practice task has been completed (T12) in Phase 2 (T6–T20). After that, the weights are positive (about +1 to +5) and increase steadily for each new task. Phase 3 (T21–T26) also has positive weights through the user journey; here, a developer logs back into the web system after having completed all tasks (T19), waits for the report to be ready (T21), and finally approves the sharing of the report with GrepS' customer (T26).

Phase 1 shows two negative weights for some users that involve more touchpoints than what the planned journey entails: (1) T4 captures an error where a virtual computer does not spin up correctly thereby requiring the user to contact support; (2) there are a cyclical negative weights between T6–T8 where a user starts receiving instructions for Phase 2, but stops and then returns to the system again at a later time. Phase 3 also has negative weights due to deviations from the planned journey, for example when the user does not login after the report is available (T24).

The figure also shows a strong negative weight (of −22) when a user does not submit the practice task in T11, resulting in a negative outcome, a transition to finNeg. Seen from a user perspective, Fig. 6 shows the four touchpoints where most users stop using the service: 18% of all users quit after finishing the practice task (T10), which is twice that of users who stop after the first (T12, 9%) and second task (T14, 9%); 12% of the users do not want to share their report (T25). The blue line shows how many users remain using the service in percent after each of the four touchpoints.

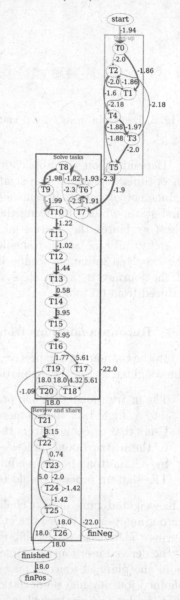

Fig. 5. The weighted game using GrepS' event logs.

8.3 Model Checking the Case Study

The accumulated feedback along the paths of the journey supports the observations on unsuccessful journeys (Sect. 8.2). Figure 7 shows 10 simulations with the goPos and goPosFast strategies; the lines show the amount of gas (accumulated feedback) along the journey. We here used $k = 1$ for the unrolling. For all simulations, the gas has an initial dip with a steep increase afterwards. The results in Fig. 4 support the observations in Sect. 8.2. Observe that the goPos strategy cannot prevent the gas from falling below 0; in fact, it can fall as low as −41 along the journey with an expected minimum of −26.7.

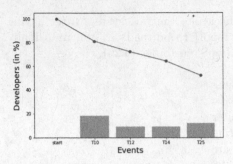
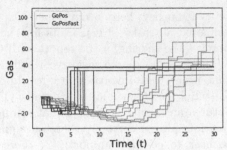

Fig. 6. Events in unsuccessful journeys.   **Fig. 7.** UPPAAL simulations.

Depending on the application context, multiple factors can contribute to an optimised journey. The strategy `goPosFast` was introduced in Sect. 6 as a refinement of `goPos`. It searches for an optimal strategy towards a successful final state, while minimising the expected number of steps. The lower part of Fig. 4 evaluates the queries under `goPosFast`. The simulations of the refined strategy, in Fig. 7, shows a smaller dip than with the `goPos` strategy. It improves the expected minimum feedback by 6.6 units and reduces the expected length of the journey by seven steps. The expected maximum final feedback is also reduced from 60 to 35.

8.4 Recommendations from the Observations and Analysis

From the company's perspective, several key takeaways have been identified from the weighted game, the simulations, and the model checking of properties:

- The instructional task and practice tasks during Phase 2 should be integrated into a single task that is more motivating for the user to complete.
- Users that disconnect from the service for several days after having progressed to the instructional, practice, or first task should be prompted to continue by, e.g., automatically sending a motivational email.
- The sign-up process should be simplified if possible.

The weighted game detects challenges early in Phase 2; in fact this is reassuring for our analysis, as prior work at GrepS has reported that the users struggle more during the first three tasks [6]. However, a question that arises from our analysis of the derived user journey game is whether good user support during deviations from the planned journey may result in better overall satisfaction than if the planned journey had no deviations. It seems plausible that unplanned journeys that involve technical problems result in less motivated users who are less likely to successfully complete the journey. However, interactions with support may also result in additional service to the user that may result in positive weights in the overall game.

In summary, the case study demonstrates that the analysis of games derived from system logs can be used to discover weaknesses in designed user journeys, and to improve and optimise these journeys. For the concrete case study, the company needs to implement additional actions in their service, which will improve user satisfaction and reduce costs in terms of resources.

9   Conclusions and Future Work

This paper proposes a novel analysis pipeline to gain insights into user journeys. We presented a method for the data-driven generation of formal models to analyse user journeys, using weighted games. To the best of our knowledge, this is the first automatic analysis pipeline using formal methods in the context of service science and user journeys. The paper proposes a method to automatically analyse derived models and thereby gain insights into the user journeys in a service, where all decisions and recommendations can be reasoned and explained. The model is not subject to human inference but is generically built from user logs.

The derived model preserves a user-centric point of view. We mine a directly follows graph from user logs, and extend this graph to a game by considering the actions of the user as uncontrollable and those of the service provider as controllable. Weights are introduced to the game by a gas function which maps transitions in the game to numerical values (in the real domain). Cycles in the derived graph are unrolled to generate an acyclic weighted game. The unrolling algorithm preserves weights, actions and final states from the initial graph. The resulting acyclic weighted game can be analysed with respect to properties expressed as UPPAAL STRATEGO queries using the UPPAAL model checker.

The proposed analysis pipeline was evaluated on an industrial case study and revealed challenges to the planned user journey of the service provider. The analysis of the derived game demonstrated that users' experiences fall in their accumulated feedback during the initial phases of the service. Our recommendations were reviewed and approved by an expert on user feedback in the company.

The work presented here opens many interesting possibilities for further work. Our work so far has assumed that users and service providers have perfect knowledge of each other's possible actions, such that the analysis could be done with the STRATEGO extension for UPPAAL [15]. Generally, knowledge about planned user journeys varies between services and between users. We plan to explore imperfect information games, where, e.g., knowledge about user actions is not completely known. In this setting, the analysis could be based on probabilistic priced games, using the model checker PRISM-games [13].

Furthermore, the current analysis is restricted to strategies for unrolled models, which give insights from a k-bounded loop unrolling but does not generalise for unseen values $> k$. We would like to generate strategies for the initial model and not only for the unrolled model. We plan to integrate our work with existing modelling languages for user journeys in the service science domain, such as CJML [18,20], to automate the analysis of user journey models that are manually reviewed today, and to provide feedback from our analysis in the visual language of these models. We are currently investigating the scalability of the proposed method on system logs for user journeys that are significantly larger than the case study considered here.

References

1. User Journey Games Repository. https://github.com/smartjourneymining/User-Journey-Games
2. van der Aalst, W.M.P.: Process Mining - Data Science in Action. Springer, Heidelberg (2016). https://doi.org/10.1007/978-3-662-49851-4
3. Baier, C., Katoen, J.P.: Principles of Model Checking. The MIT Press, Cambridge (2008)
4. Behrmann, G., Cougnard, A., David, A., Fleury, E., Larsen, K.G., Lime, D.: UPPAAL-Tiga: time for playing games! In: Damm, W., Hermanns, H. (eds.) CAV 2007. LNCS, vol. 4590, pp. 121–125. Springer, Heidelberg (2007). https://doi.org/10.1007/978-3-540-73368-3_14
5. Berendes, C.I., Bartelheimer, C., Betzing, J.H., Beverungen, D.: Data-driven customer journey mapping in local high streets: A domain-specific modeling language. In: Proceedings of the International Conference on Information Systems (ICIS 2018). Association for Information Systems (2018)
6. Bergersen, G.R., Sjoberg, D.I., Dyba, T.: Construction and validation of an instrument for measuring programming skill. IEEE Trans. Softw. Eng. **40**(12), 1163–1184 (2014)
7. Bernard, G., Andritsos, P.: CJM-ex: goal-oriented exploration of customer journey maps using event logs and data analytics. In: Proceedings of BPM Demo Track and BPM Dissertation Award co-located with 15th International Conference on Business Process Modeling (BPM 2017). CEUR Workshop Proceedings, vol. 1920. CEUR-WS.org (2017)
8. Bernard, G., Andritsos, P.: A process mining based model for customer journey mapping. In: Proceedings of Forum and Doctoral Consortium Papers at the 29th International Conference on Advanced Information Systems Engineering (CAiSE 2017). CEUR Workshop Proceedings, vol. 1848, pp. 49–56. CEUR-WS.org (2017)
9. Bernard, G., Andritsos, P.: CJM-ab: abstracting customer journey maps using process mining. In: Mendling, J., Mouratidis, H. (eds.) CAiSE 2018. LNBIP, vol. 317, pp. 49–56. Springer, Cham (2018). https://doi.org/10.1007/978-3-319-92901-9_5
10. Bernard, G., Andritsos, P.: Contextual and behavioral customer journey discovery using a genetic approach. In: Welzer, T., Eder, J., Podgorelec, V., Kamišalić Latifić, A. (eds.) ADBIS 2019. LNCS, vol. 11695, pp. 251–266. Springer, Cham (2019). https://doi.org/10.1007/978-3-030-28730-6_16
11. Bitner, M.J., Ostrom, A.L., Morgan, F.N.: Service blueprinting: a practical technique for service innovation. Calif. Manag. Rev. **50**(3), 66–94 (2008)
12. Bouyer, P., Cassez, F., Fleury, E., Larsen, K.G.: Optimal strategies in priced timed game automata. In: Lodaya, K., Mahajan, M. (eds.) FSTTCS 2004. LNCS, vol. 3328, pp. 148–160. Springer, Heidelberg (2004). https://doi.org/10.1007/978-3-540-30538-5_13
13. Chen, T., Forejt, V., Kwiatkowska, M., Parker, D., Simaitis, A.: PRISM-games: a model checker for stochastic multi-player games. In: Piterman, N., Smolka, S.A. (eds.) TACAS 2013. LNCS, vol. 7795, pp. 185–191. Springer, Heidelberg (2013). https://doi.org/10.1007/978-3-642-36742-7_13

14. Crosier, A., Handford, A.: Customer journey mapping as an advocacy tool for disabled people: a case study. Soc. Mark. Q. **18**(1), 67–76 (2012)
15. David, A., Jensen, P.G., Larsen, K.G., Mikučionis, M., Taankvist, J.H.: UPPAAL STRATEGO. In: Baier, C., Tinelli, C. (eds.) TACAS 2015. LNCS, vol. 9035, pp. 206–211. Springer, Heidelberg (2015). https://doi.org/10.1007/978-3-662-46681-0_16
16. Følstad, A., Kvale, K.: Customer journeys: a systematic literature review. J. Serv. Theory Practice **28**(2), 196–227 (2018)
17. Fornell, C., Mithas, S., Morgeson, F.V., Krishnan, M.: Customer satisfaction and stock prices: high returns, low risk. J. Mark. **70**(1), 3–14 (2006)
18. Halvorsrud, R., Boletsis, C., Garcia-Ceja, E.: Designing a modeling language for customer journeys: lessons learned from user involvement. In: Proceedings of 24th International Conference on Model Driven Engineering Languages and Systems (MODELS 2021), pp. 239–249. IEEE (2021)
19. Halvorsrud, R., Haugstveit, I.M., Pultier, A.: Evaluation of a modelling language for customer journeys. In: Proceedings Symposium on Visual Languages and Human-Centric Computing (VL/HCC 2016), pp. 40–48. IEEE Computer Society (2016)
20. Halvorsrud, R., Kvale, K., Følstad, A.: Improving service quality through customer journey analysis. J. Serv. Theory Practice **26**(6), 840–867 (2016)
21. Halvorsrud, R., Mannhardt, F., Johnsen, E.B., Tapia Tarifa, S.L.: Smart journey mining for improved service quality. In: Proceedings of the IEEE International Conference on Services Computing (SCC 2021), pp. 367–369. IEEE (2021)
22. Harbich, M., Bernard, G., Berkes, P., Garbinato, B., Andritsos, P.: Discovering customer journey maps using a mixture of Markov models. In: Proceedings of 7th International Symposium on Data-Driven Process Discovery and Analysis (SIM-PDA 2017). CEUR Workshop Proceedings, vol. 2016, pp. 3–7. CEUR-WS.org (2017)
23. Jagadeesh Chandra Bose, R.P., van der Aalst, W.: Trace alignment in process mining: opportunities for process diagnostics. In: Hull, R., Mendling, J., Tai, S. (eds.) BPM 2010. LNCS, vol. 6336, pp. 227–242. Springer, Heidelberg (2010). https://doi.org/10.1007/978-3-642-15618-2_17
24. Lammel, B., Korkut, S., Hinkelmann, K.: Customer experience modelling and analysis framework a semantic lifting approach for analyzing customer experience. In: Proceedings of 6th International Conference on Innovation and Entrepreneurship (IE 2016). GSTF (2016)
25. Larsen, K.G., Pettersson, P., Yi, W.: UPPAAL in a nutshell. Int. J. Softw. Tools Technol. Transf. **1**(1–2), 134–152 (1997)
26. Leemans, S.J.J., Poppe, E., Wynn, M.T.: Directly follows-based process mining: exploration & a case study. In: International Conference on Process Mining (ICPM 2019), pp. 25–32. IEEE (2019)
27. Legay, A., Delahaye, B., Bensalem, S.: Statistical model checking: an overview. In: Barringer, H., et al. (eds.) RV 2010. LNCS, vol. 6418, pp. 122–135. Springer, Heidelberg (2010). https://doi.org/10.1007/978-3-642-16612-9_11
28. Plotkin, G.D.: A structural approach to operational semantics. J. Log. Algebraic Methods Program. **60–61**, 17–139 (2004)
29. Razo-Zapata, I.S., Chew, E.K., Proper, E.: VIVA: a visual language to design value co-creation. In: 20th Conference on Business Informatics (CBI), pp. 20–29. IEEE (2018)
30. Rosenbaum, M.S., Otalora, M.L., Ramírez, G.C.: How to create a realistic customer journey map. Bus. Horizons **60**(1), 143–150 (2017)

31. Russell, S.J., Norvig, P.: Artificial Intelligence: A Modern Approach. Pearson, Hoboken (2020)

32. Shannon, C.E.: A mathematical theory of communication. Bell Syst. Tech. J. **27**(3), 379–423 (1948)

33. Terragni, A., Hassani, M.: Analyzing customer journey with process mining: from discovery to recommendations. In: Proceedings of 6th International Conference on Future Internet of Things and Cloud (FiCloud 2018), pp. 224–229. IEEE, August 2018

34. Terragni, A., Hassani, M.: Optimizing customer journey using process mining and sequence-aware recommendation. In: Proceedings of 34th Symposium on Applied Computing (SAC 2019), pp. 57–65. ACM Press, April 2019

35. Thrane, C., Fahrenberg, U., Larsen, K.G.: Quantitative analysis of weighted transition systems. J. Logic Algebraic Program. **79**(7), 689–703 (2010)

36. Tueanrat, Y., Papagiannidis, S., Alamanos, E.: Going on a journey: a review of the customer journey literature. J. Bus. Res. **125**, 336–353 (2021)

37. Vandermerwe, S., Rada, J.: Servitization of business: adding value by adding services. Eur. Manag. J. **6**(4), 314–324 (1988)

Safety Controller Synthesis for a Mobile Manufacturing Cobot

Ioannis Stefanakos[1]([✉]) [iD], Radu Calinescu[1] [iD], James Douthwaite[2] [iD],
Jonathan Aitken[2] [iD], and James Law[2] [iD]

[1] University of York, York, UK
{ioannis.stefanakos,radu.calinescu}@york.ac.uk
[2] University of Sheffield, Sheffield, UK
{j.douthwaite,jonathan.aitken,j.law}@sheffield.ac.uk

Abstract. We present a case study in which probabilistic model checking has been used to synthesise the correct-by-construction safety controller for a mobile collaborative robot (*cobot*) deployed in a prototype manufacturing cell alongside a human operator. The case study used an ICONSYS iAM-R mobile cobot responsible for the execution of a complex machining process comprising tasks requiring the use of multiple machines at different locations within the cell. Within this process, the role of the safety controller was to ensure that the cobot carried out its tasks and movements between task locations without harming the human operator responsible for its supervision and for performing additional tasks. The paper describes our generalisable approach to synthesising the mobile cobot safety controller, and its evaluation using a digital twin of our experimental manufacturing cell at the University of Sheffield Advanced Manufacturing Research Centre in the UK.

Keywords: Safety controller · Probabilistic model checking · Collaborative robot · Discrete-event controller synthesis · Markov chain

1 Introduction

Collaborative robotics "have the potential to revolutionise manufacturing" [4,21] and are expected to play a key role in Industry 4.0 [8,23,24]. However, the use of collaborative robots (*cobots*) in industry comes with significant safety concerns. Industrial cobots have been designed to directly operate and share workspaces with human operators, leading to the introduction of additional safety risks and the need to mitigate these [16,20,22].

Ensuring the safety of human operators (e.g., [3,25]) and improving the risk assessment during collaborative tasks with cobots (e.g., [18,19]) has been the primary focus of research in the area of human-robot collaboration in manufacturing environments. However, the effectiveness of this collaboration is still limited, e.g., due to restrictive cobot movement and frequent emergency stops resulting from safety concerns. The rapid technological advancements in robotics introduce increasingly complex robotic systems that confine the ability to assess and mitigate risks. At the same time, to fully benefit from the use of cobots in industry there must be a trade-off between risk and performance. Thus, it is necessary to develop techniques that address these constraints and test their application in case studies with real collaborative robotic processes from the manufacturing domain.

In this paper, we present a case study involving the use of probabilistic modelling and verification for the synthesis of a safety controller for a collaborative robot used in a industrial research lab (Fig. 1). We carried out this case study at the University of Sheffield Advanced Manufacturing Research Centre (AMRC)[1] in the UK.

The main contributions of our case study paper are:

Fig. 1. Collaborative robot in action inside the AMRC gear center

- a new method for augmenting the activity diagram describing the ideal manufacturing process carried out in collaboration by the robot and a human operator with risk mitigation constructs based on the cobot safety operation modes recommended by the international standard ISO/TS 15066 [13];
- a new technique for mapping the mitigation-extended activity diagram of the industrial process to a stochastic model encoded in the high-level probabilistic modelling language of the established model checker PRISM [14];
- the use of probabilistic model checking to synthesise safety controllers that satisfy risk and cost-related constraints for the industrial process;
- the presentation of the end-to-end process we used to synthesise a safety controller for a real mobile cobot (i.e., an ICONSYS iAM-R[2]) deployed in an experimental manufacturing cell.

By considering a mobile cobot with its additional safety concerns due to the cobot moving between task locations, and by providing a detailed description of our safety controller synthesis, these contributions go beyond existing research papers on the safe use of cobots in manufacturing (e.g., [2,10,26]).

The rest of the paper is organised as follows. Section 2 introduces a manufacturing process comprising a number tasks, allocated between a cobot and a

---

[1] https://www.amrc.co.uk/.

[2] The iAM-R is a mobile collaborative robot built on the MiR200 mobile robot base, and carrying a 3 kg, 5 kg, or 10 kg 6-axis Universal Robot collaborative manipulator (the 10 kg version being the focus this case study). The two are combined with an Iconsys modular interface, which provides programmable control over the platform. https://iam-r.iconsys.co.uk/.

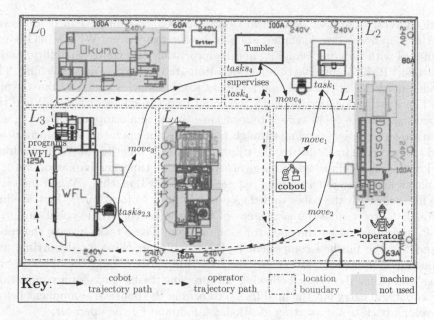

Fig. 2. Floorplan of the AMRC gear center facility (Color figure online)

human operator. Section 3 presents our employed approach for the synthesis of safety controllers, ensuring the safety of the human operator in the introduced manufacturing process. Section 4 describes a two-pronged evaluation methodology for the synthesised safety-controllers, and Sect. 5 compares our solution to existing approaches. Finally, Sect. 6 summarises the benefits and limitations of our approach, and suggests directions for future work.

2   Manufacturing Process

Figure 2 depicts the shop floor for the AMRC manufacturing process used in our case study. As shown in this diagram, the shop floor consists of a main area annotated with information about the location of tasks that need to be carried out both by the cobot and the operator, and their movement between locations.

The boundary of each location is specified by the red dashed lines, and the location identifier is given in the form of L_n where n is the location's number. The trajectory path of the cobot is depicted by the continuous blue line that also captures information about the various movements between locations and tasks that the cobot needs to perform. The movement and task identifiers appear in the form of $move_k$ and $task_l$ where k and l are numbers associated with each of the cobot's planned movements and tasks in an increasing order, respectively. The operator's trajectory path is depicted by the dashed green line, and brief descriptions of the operator's tasks can also be seen on the diagram along this path. Several Computer Numerical Control (CNC) machines[3] can be observed on the shop floor. Two machines are used by the process: an WFL M30G 5-axis turn-mill with hobbing, shaping, and reciprocating broaching capability; and a Sharmic VRM225 abrasive tumbler for automated deburring and polishing. The shaded machines are unused, and represent fixed obstacles the cobot must avoid.

The starting location for both the cobot and the operator is L_2. When the process starts, the cobot travels to location L_1 to pick a component ($task_1$), and then moves to L_3 by traveling through L_4, as does the operator, to perform $task_2$ and $task_3$. These tasks involve the cobot in loading a billet to the WFL machine, and retrieving the finished component. At the same time, the human operator is responsible for any programming required at the WFL machine. When the tasks are finished, both the cobot and the operator move to location L_1 by travelling through L_0 to resume the next steps of the process. At L_1 the cobot performs $task_4$ and $task_5$ under the operator's supervision. These tasks involve the cobot depositing the finished component to the tumbler machine for deburring, and collecting it upon completion. In case something goes wrong, the operator will intervene to fix the issue. Following the previous tasks' successful completion, the cobot will carry out the final $task_6$, returning the polished component before travelling back to the starting location L_0, followed by the operator.

The process carried out by the cobot and a human operator is summarised by the "ideal" activity diagram from Fig. 3[4]. The diagram is consisted of two main branches associated with the cobot's and operator's movements and tasks on the left and right side, respectively. The fork notations lead to synchronisation points ($sync$) where the cobot and the operator need to confirm the completion of the previous tasks before they proceed to the next. Some tasks are performed independently by the cobot and some by the operator. These are standardised tasks that are always eventually performed even if there is a delay in place. On the contrary, there is another group of cobot's tasks that necessitates the operator's supervision as failure in such a task requires the operator's intervention to fix the issue, allowing the cobot to resume carrying out or re-initiating the task ($task_l\_retry$). The probabilities of success ($p_{t_l success}$) and failure ($p_{t_l failure}$) of these tasks and the resulting paths are denoted by decision nodes in the diagram. Finally, after the successful completion of all tasks (i.e., the cobot and the operator travel to their starting locations) the process can either be repeated or terminated.

Synthesising the safety controller as described in the remainder of the paper requires knowledge about the levels of risk and probabilities of hazards occurring during cobot movement and task execution in the proximity of the human operator. These quantities can be obtained experimentally by using sensors (i.e. cameras, or wearables) combined with software tools that track human movements. This ensures the capability of the work cell to recognise situations that

---

[3] CNC machining: computerized manufacturing process in which pre-programmed software and code controls the movement of production equipment.

[4] This is an "ideal" activity diagram (and the starting point for our work) because it does not consider the hazards/risks associated with the process.

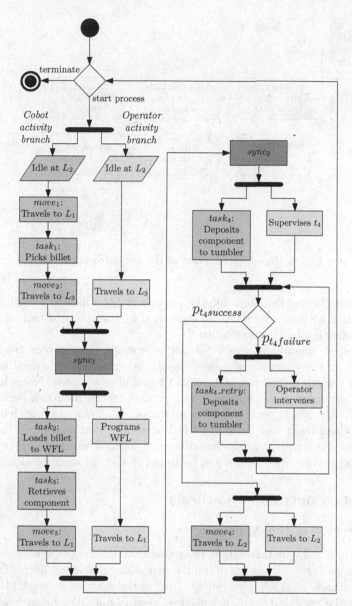

Fig. 3. Activity diagram of the collaborative process

can lead to undesired risks. The Assuring Autonomy International Programme (AAIP) project RECOLL[5] is an example of recent work that collected a considerable amount of data related to a group of operators. The analysis of the

---

[5] https://www.york.ac.uk/assuring-autonomy/demonstrators/flexible-manufacturing/.

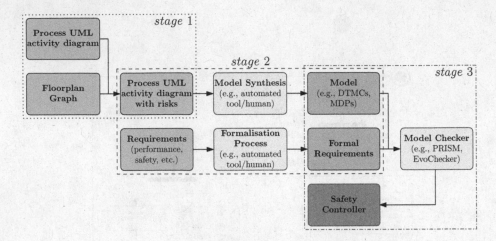

Fig. 4. High-level diagram of the employed approach.

obtained data helped to determine the probability of a hazard's occurrence and its correlation with an incorrect task execution by the operator and/or an incorrect task planning by the system itself.

Given these quantities, which for our case study their values are assumed, we focused on the synthesis of a safety controller considering several mitigation actions for hazards associated with cobot tasks and movements. Note that not all tasks and movements that appear in the process have a high-risk factor. In our case study, only $move_2$, $move_3$, $move_4$ and $task_4$ in combination with operator's movements and tasks have been identified as actions that could lead to hazards.

A detailed description of the hazards, mitigation strategies and their associated risk and probability values can be found in the following section.

3   Safety Controller Synthesis

3.1   Overview of the Approach

As shown in Fig. 4, our three-staged approach carries out the synthesis of safety controllers, and comprises a set of inputs, processing activities, and outputs used for the synthesis of safety controllers. During the first stage, an UML activity diagram and a floorplan graph are used to identify potential hazards in the process. This leads to the annotation of the UML diagram with mitigation strategies for the identified hazards (e.g., slowing down the cobot's speed to avoid collision with the human operator). Stage two of the approach synthesises a discrete-time Markov chain (DTMC) model based on the annotated UML diagram of the previous step, and formalises the requirements of the process. Finally, stage three employs probabilistic model checking and applies an exhaustive search over the discretised parameter space of the model to synthesise combinations of values for the DTMC parameters that correspond to requirements-compliant safety controllers for the industrial process.

3.2 Stage 1: Hazard Identification

In this first stage of the approach, the UML activity diagram from Fig. 3 and the floorplan from Fig. 2 are combined in order to identify hazards in the process. This is currently a manual activity in which the user needs to assess where hazards may appear. The output of this combined analysis is an UML activity diagram annotated with probabilities of hazards occurring when the cobot is performing a high-risk movement or task (i.e., an action that may affect the human operator who is or will be in close proximity to the cobot), and mitigation actions which are also selected based on probabilities. An example of such diagram can be seen in Fig. 5, depicting the last part of our case study's process, where $task_4 retry$ and $move_4$ are replaced by the dashed rectangles that contain the hazard mitigation actions.

These actions are defined following the specifications of the standard ISO/TS 15066 [13] which describes four main techniques for collaborative operation: a) safety-rated monitored stop, b) hand-guiding, c) speed and separation monitoring, and d) power and force limiting. All these apply in our collaborative process, except the hand-guiding.

In case of cobot's failure to complete $task_4$ (Fig. 5), the operator must intervene to correct the issue, so that the cobot can resume performing the task. This introduces a high-risk situation as the operator will be in close proximity to the cobot, and

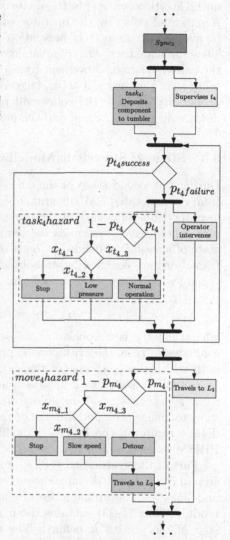

Fig. 5. Activity diagram of the collaborative process with risks

any unpredicted movement could potentially result in injury. To prevent this from happening, a series of hazard identification and mitigation steps are introduced under $task_4 hazard$. Specifically, there is a p_{t_4} probability that a hazard will not occur, leading to the cobot's normal operation and a $1 - p_{t_4}$ probability that a hazard will occur, leading to the following mitigation actions. With probability of $x_{t_{4\_1}}$ the cobot will pause its operation, with $x_{t_{4\_2}}$ will decrease the applied pressure, and with $x_{t_{4\_3}}$ will resume its normal operation as the risk has not exceeded the given threshold.

Following the successful completion of $task_4$, the cobot will try to move to its initial location ($move_4$) to terminate or repeat the process, as does the operator. A potential delay by the operator could cause a collision accident, which can be avoided by the correct prevention mechanisms defined under $move_4 hazard$. These indicate that with a probability of p_{m_4} a hazard will not occur, leading to the cobot's planned movement towards location L_2, and with a $1 - p_{m_4}$ probability that a hazard will occur, triggering the following mitigation actions. With probability of $x_{m_{4\_1}}$ the cobot will pause its movement, with $x_{m_{4\_2}}$ will slow down, and with $x_{m_{4\_3}}$ will find the next available route towards L_2.

3.3   Stage 2: Stochastic Modelling

During the second stage of the employed approach, we built a DTMC derived from the annotated UML diagram of Fig. 5. We specified this DTMC in the high-level modelling language of the probabilistic model checker PRISM [14], which represents a given system as the parallel composition of a set of *modules*. The state of a *module* is defined by a set of finite-range local variables, and its state transitions are encoded by probabilistic guarded commands that modify these variables, and have the general form:

$$[] \, g \; \to \; \lambda_1 : u_1 \, + \, \lambda_2 : u_2 \, + \, \dots \, + \, \lambda_n : u_n; \tag{1}$$

where *guard g* is a boolean expression over all model variables. If the guard evaluates to true, the arithmetic expression λ_i, $1 \le i \le n$ gives the probability with which the u_i change of the module variables occurs. Commands can be (optionally) labelled with *actions* that are placed between the square brackets, e.g., [*sync*], causing all modules comprising commands with the same action to synchronise (i.e., perform one of these commands simultaneously). For more details regarding the PRISM modelling language, we refer the reader to the PRISM manual, available at http://www.prismmodelchecker.org/manual.

Part of the synthesised DTMC, modelling the collaborative process, can be seen in Fig. 6. Line 4 declares the probability of a hazard occurring during $move_2$, and lines 5–7 the probabilities of each of the mitigation actions. The process module (lines 11–23) contains the main functionality of the model where each step of the process is defined. The reward structures, capturing information about states in the model (e.g., a risk of 0 is associated with the mitigation action of state c = 4), are located between lines 27–42. The complete model of our case study's process can be found in our GitHub repository[6].

The process requirements are formally expressed in probabilistic computation tree logic (PCTL) [12] extended with rewards [1]. The syntax of PCTL is as follows:

$$\Phi ::= true \mid a \mid \neg \, \Phi \mid \Phi \, \wedge \, \Phi \mid P_{\bowtie p}[\phi]$$
$$\phi ::= X \, \Phi \mid \Phi \, U^{\le k} \, \Phi \tag{2}$$

---

[6] https://github.com/CSI-Cobot/CSI-artefacts.

```
1   dtmc
2
3   const double p_m2 ;   //hazard probability during move_2
4   const double x_m2_1 ;    //probability of stopping
5   const double x_m2_2 ;    //probability of reducing speed
6   const double x_m2_3 ;    //probability of following an alternative route
7   ...
8   module process
9     c : [0..30] init 0;
10
11    [] c=0 -> 1:(c'=1);    //cobot idle at L0
12    [] c=1 -> 1:(c'=2);    //cobot performs task_1 at L1
13    [] c=2 -> p_m2 :(c'=3) + (1-p_m2 ):(c'=7); // hazard prob. for move_2
14    [] c=3 -> x_m2_1 :(c'=4) + x_m2_2 :(c'=5) + x_m2_3 :(c'=6); //mitigation
15    [] c=4 -> 1:(c'=7);   // cobot stops
16    ...
17    [] c=28 -> 1:(c'=30); // cobot slows speed
18    [] c=29 -> 1:(c'=30); // cobot identifies alternative route
19    [] c=30 -> 1:(c'=0);  // cobot travels to L2
20  endmodule
21
22  rewards "delay"
23    c=4  : 20;    // base - stop
24    c=5  : 13;    // base - reduce speed
25    c=6  : 15;    // base - detour
26    ...
27    c=22 : 4; // arm - low pressure
28  endrewards
29
30  rewards "risk"
31    c=4  : 0; // base - stop
32    c=5  : 2; // base - reduce speed
33    c=6  : 1; // base - detour
34    ...
35    c=22 : 1; // arm - low pressure
36  endrewards
```

Fig. 6. DTMC model representation of the process with hazard mitigation actions.

and cost/reward state formulae are defined by the grammar:

$$R_{\bowtie r}[C^{\leq k}] \mid R_{\bowtie r}[I^{=k}] \mid R_{\bowtie r}[F\ \Phi] \tag{3}$$

where $k \in \mathbb{N} \cup \{\infty\}$, $p \in [0,1]$ and $r \in R_{\geq 0}$ are probability/reward bounds (that can be replaced with '=?' if the computation of the actual probability or reward is required), and Φ and ϕ are state and path formulae, respectively. The definition of PCTL semantics is beyond the scope of this paper; details are available from [5,15].

We use the above PCTL syntax to specify the properties of the DTMC model. In particular, we extract information about the delay introduced in the process by the mitigation actions, and the risk of a hazard occurring:

$$R_{=?}^{delay}[\ F\ \text{``done''}\ ]$$
$$R_{=?}^{risk}[\ F\ \text{``done''}\ ] \tag{4}$$

where "*done*" is a label referring to the end of the process.

3.4   Stage 3: Synthesis

In the third and final stage, an exhaustive search is performed over the discretised parameter space of the output DTMC model, combined with the set of formal requirements to obtain the Pareto-optimal controller configurations. The parameters of the DTMC model are consisted by a) the probabilities obtained from the manufacturing process that cannot be modified (e.g., the probability that a hazard will occur during the $move_3$ action of the cobot), and b) the probabilities associated with mitigation actions for which suitable values must be obtained in order to have an optimal trade-off between risk

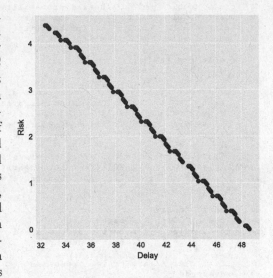

Fig. 7. Pareto-optimal controller configurations

and performance (e.g., the probability $x_{t_{4\_1}}$ that a stop will be triggered to avoid a potential hazard during $task_4$).

Regarding the second group, we go through all the combinations of controller parameters $\{x\_mi\_1, x\_mi\_2, x\_mi\_3\}$, similarly for $\{x\_ti\_1, x\_ti\_2, x\_ti\_3\}$, between $\{0.0, 0.0, 1.0\}$ and $\{1.0, 0.0, 0.0\}$ with step 0.2, where i refers to the number of movement or task associated with the mitigation action. This results to a total of 456,976 combinations of parameter values, i.e. model instantiations, whose analysis using the model checker PRISM required just under one hour on a 2 GHz Quad-Core Intel Core i5 MacBook Pro computer with 32 GB of memory, and which are used in identifying optimal trade-offs between the requirements of the process. Section 4.1 provides an example on how these optimal trade-offs can be obtained.

4   Evaluation

To evaluate the safety-controller synthesis approach used in our case study, we employed a two-pronged evaluation methodology. First, we used our approach to synthesise a set of safety controller instantiations that meet strict safety constraints and achieve optimal trade-offs between the efficiency of the manufacturing process and the level of residual risk. Second, we developed a digital twin of the manufacturing process and used it to trial one of these safety controller instantiations. These results from these stages of our two-pronged evaluation are described in Sects. 4.1 and 4.2.

Fig. 8. The process DT constructed as a test-bed within the DTF. The DT presents a faithful reconstruction of the real-world process used for the evaluation of the proposed safety-controller.

4.1   Generation of Safety Controller Instantiations

Figure 7 depicts the Pareto-front of optimal controller configurations. Using the data collected during stage 3 of the approach (Sect. 3.4) we are able to identify which of these model instantiations provide the most optimal trade-offs between risk and performance. This information is of great use in scenarios where it is necessary to improve the overall performance of the process, while ensuring that risks are below the specified threshold levels. We obtained these results by analysing the output data from PRISM's experiments using python scripts. This process can also be automated by using tools such as EvoChecker [9] that provides more efficient search algorithms.

4.2   Evaluation on a Digital Twin

Digital Twin Description. The digital twin used to evaluate the safety controller was developed within the Digital Twin Framework (DTF), in associated works [6], as part of the Confident Safety Integration for Collaborative Robotics (CSI:Cobot) project. The DTF is versatile sandbox for the development and testing of safety-critical systems[7].

The DTF provides the kinematic, communication and data infrastructure necessary to deploy digital twins on real world systems. Using its integrated APIs for MATLAB ® and the Robotic Operating System (ROS), commands issued inside the DTF may be exchanged with the physical system and demonstrated as a real-time response.

---

[7] For further information on the CSI:project please visit the project's website at: https://www.sheffield.ac.uk/sheffieldrobotics/about/csi-cobots/csi-project, and our associated repository: https://github.com/CSI-Cobot/CSI-artefacts.

Process Twin. In this study, the DTF was used create a faithful recreation of the process as (seen in Fig. 8), from the real-world process description as shown in Fig. 9. In associated works [6,10], we describe the inclusion of entity-modules and behaviour-modules as a system of *actors* and *abstract-actors* respectively. The distinction being those that are *embodied* in the real-world and those that are not. We define A to be this set of actors, but also as the set of communication nodes. Actor $n \in A$ is then able to communicate with other actors through a static interface $I_n = (I_n, O_n)$. Here $I_n = [i_n^1, i_n^2, ..., i_n^k]$ and $O_n = [o_n^1, o_n^2, ..., o_n^h]$ define n's set of input (subscription) and output (publication) channels respectively. Each actor n is modelled a distinct state machine that listens on channels I_n and responds on channels O_n where $I_n, O_n \subseteq X$ where X is the set of all available channels.

The process controller is modelled as *abstract-actor* $n_{pc} \in A$, implementing the interface $I_{n_{pc}} = (I_{n_{pc}}, O_{n_{pc}})$. n_{pc} communicates with the other digital-twin systems via this interface in order to interact with the *iAMR* mobile robot, the human *operator* and other sensors in the environment. The nominal process procedure (seen in Fig. 3) is defined by the state machine of n_{pc} that responds to process updates from process members $n_{i \in 1:k} \subset A$ received on channels $I_{n_{pc}}$ with responses commands $O_{n_{pc}}$.

Safety Controller. Similar to the process controller, the safety controller n_{sc} is introduced as a behaviour module and *abstract-actor*. Here $n_{sc} \in A$, and $I_{sc} = (I_{n_{sc}}, O_{n_{sc}})$ defines its interface. n_{sc} may communicate with both the actor and process controller such that $n_{i \in 1:k} \in A_{sc} \subset A$ and $n_{pc} \in A_{sc}$. To allow n_{sc} to intervene with the nominal process managed by n_{pc}, n_{sc} is introduced as an independent state-machine able to observe channels $I_{n_{sc}}$ and enact changes to the process such that $I_{n_{pc}} \subseteq O_{n_{sc}}$.

For example, upon reception of sensor data received on $I_{n_{sc}}$ indicating that the iAMR and operator are in the same process region. n_{sc} issues a request to n_{pc} to request a change in safety mode for the robot in that region. This command is received on $I_{n_{pc}}$ and issued on $O_{n_{pc}}$, as a request to process member $n_{k=2}$, for a new safety mode-*reduced speed*. $n_{k=2}$ defines the iAMR mobile robot, which in turn enacts a response to this request by changing its active safety mode to *reduced speed*.

Evidencing Safety. Whilst active, the DTF provides connection to the robots via other APIs (such as ROS) and data storage (via SQL) amongst other fundamental DT services necessary for this study. Information broadcast on channels $X = (I_{n=1:k}, O_{n=1:k})$ are timestamped and recorded in a process database. This allows key process and safety signals to be recovered and analysed alongside additional ground-truth data (i.e. absolute positions and decision historicity).

In the following example, the machine-tending DT is used to demonstrate the application of the safety controller to a realistic process interface. The process is implemented as an *abstract-actor* and state-machine whose process is defined by the work-activities (shown in Fig. 3). Work-requests are issued by the process

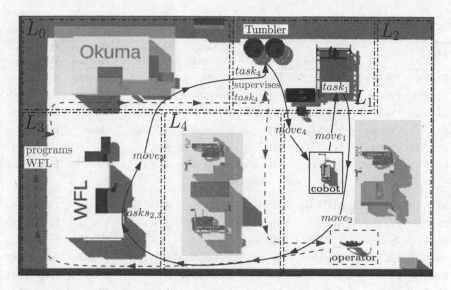

Fig. 9. Transferal of the floor plan from Fig. 2 to the digital environment.

controller, to human and robot *actors* (digital twins) as each step *WState* is completed. The example centers around the collaborative preparation of a component, which must be moved between machines (CNC & WFL) by the robot before being deposited in a tumbler for deburring. An overview of the complete process can be seen in Fig. 9.

The safety controller is implemented similarly, and observes the current process step which is reported as the *Action* of the human and robot by the process controller. The safety controller however, utilises a camera sensor module in order to observe both the *region* (as *L0, l1,.. L4 etc.*) of the robot and human operator and their approximate separation distance in order to evaluate a mitigation action proportional to the hazard (see Sect. 3.2). The state of the process controller, safety controller and all communications are logged upon execution of the example scenario and recovered from the process database post-execution.

Table 1 presents the scenario event-sequence reported by the DTF. The process is shown to begin with both the human operator and robot in their start positions (see Fig. 9). The human operator initially proceeds to work at the WFL before completing a sequence of work actions. At 19.45.41 s the operator's work is completed and proceeds to the collaborative work cell *AtTumbler*. Whilst this occurs, the robot moves from its *AtStart* location to collect a work component from the *AtCnC* location and continues to the *AtWFL* where the component is processed. The component is then collected and taken to the collaborative *AtTumbler* location. The robot arrives first and deposits the component in the tumbler. The human operator later joins at 19.46.00 s, interrupting the cobot by violating the safety controller's *close* condition, which should cause a safety-stop.

At 19.46.14, before the robot begins to work, the safety controller issues a *SafetyReq(Stopped)*. A response from the robot *SafetyRes* is immediately issued

Table 1. The process event time-series during the example case-study.

Time	Type	Robot Location	Robot Action	Robot WState	Human Location	Human Action	Human WState
19:41:51	Process	Start	Idle	Incomplete	Start	Moving	Incomplete
19:42:00	Process	AtCNC	Done	Incomplete	Start	Moving	Incomplete
19:42:08	Process	AtCNC	Done	Incomplete	AtWFL	Done	Incomplete
19:42:15	Process	AtCNC	Idle	Incomplete	AtWFL	Done	Incomplete
19:42:23	Process	AtCNC	Idle	Incomplete	AtWFL	Idle	Incomplete
19:42:23	Process	AtCNC	Idle	Incomplete	AtWFL	Working	Incomplete
⋮	⋮	⋮	⋮	⋮	⋮	⋮	⋮
19:44:46	Process	AtWFL	Moving	Complete	AtWFL	Done	Incomplete
19:45:01	Process	AtWFL	Moving	Complete	AtWFL	Idle	Incomplete
19:45:01	Process	AtWFL	Moving	Complete	AtWFL	Working	Incomplete
19:45:15	Process	AtTumbler	Done	Incomplete	AtWFL	Working	Incomplete
19:45:30	Process	AtTumbler	Idle	Incomplete	AtWFL	Working	Incomplete
19:45:41	Process	AtTumbler	Idle	Incomplete	AtWFL	Done	Incomplete
19:45:41	Process	AtTumbler	Idle	Incomplete	AtWFL	Done	Complete
19:46:00	Process	AtTumbler	Idle	Incomplete	AtTumbler	Done	Incomplete
19:46:14	SafetyReq		Stopped				
19:46:14	SafetyRes		Stopped				
19:46:14	Process	AtTumbler	Idle	Complete	AtTumbler	Done	Incomplete
19:46:15	Process	AtTumbler	Stopped	Complete	AtTumbler	Idle	Incomplete
19:46:15	Process	AtTumbler	Stopped	Complete	AtTumbler	Working	Incomplete
19:46:30	Process	AtTumbler	Stopped	Complete	AtTumbler	Done	Incomplete
19:46:30	Process	AtTumbler	Stopped	Complete	AtTumbler	Done	Complete
19:46:37	SafetyReq		Nominal				
19:46:37	SafetyRes		Nominal				
19:46:47	Process	AtTumbler	Moving	Complete	Start	Done	Incomplete
19:46:56	Process	Start	Done	Incomplete	Start	Done	Incomplete

and at 19.46.15 s the robot enacts *Action(Stopped)*. The human operator continues to inspect the component in *close* proximity of the robot, until at 19.46.30 s, the his work (*WState*) is completed and he moves away from *AtTumbler*. Once the operator complies with the *close* condition again, the safety controller successfully issues a new *SafetyReq(Nominal)* to resume normal operation. The robot and operator then proceed to return to the start locations and the example process is completed. A complete video of the sequence can be found on the CSI:Cobot repository[8].

---

[8] Additional study data and materials can be found on the CSI:Cobot repository: https://github.com/CSI-Cobot/CSI-artefacts.

5   Related Work

Mobile collaborative robots have only emerged as a viable technology in recent years (e.g., [7,17]) and, to the best of our knowledge, no formal approaches have been used so far for the synthesis of their safety controllers.

For static cobots, an approach for safety-controller synthesis has been developed in the earlier stages of our CSI:Cobot project. Like the solution presented in our paper, this approach [10,11] uses stochastic models to capture the interactions between the cobot and the human operator, and probabilistic model checking to analyse these models. However, unlike the approach we employed for the case study presented in this paper, the previous CSI:Cobot solution from [10,11] does not consider the floorplan of the shop floor, nor the risks associated with the cobot travelling between different shop floor locations and the mitigations for these risks. Furthermore, the techniques used to augment the activity diagram of the collaborative manufacturing process risks and mitigations, and to derive the process DTMC from the augmented activity diagram represent new contributions of this paper, as does the ICONSYS iAM-R case study.

These differences also distinguish our work from other approaches to using formal verification for the safety analysis of cobot-human interaction, e.g., [2,25].

6   Conclusion

We presented a case study in which probabilistic model checking was used to synthesise Pareto-optimal safety controller configurations for a mobile cobot from an experimental manufacturing cell. In future work, we intend to deploy the safety controller tested in the digital twin on the actual iAM-R mobile cobot for validation in our experimental manufacturing cell.

We envisage that the multi-stage approach employed for this purpose can be generalised to a broad range of mobile-cobot scenarios, and that many of its activities can be automated. Both of these and assessing the scalability of the approach represent additional directions of future work for our project. Finally, when automating the synthesis of the Pareto-optimal controller configurations, we plan to replace the exhaustive search through the discretised controller configuration space with the much more efficient metaheuristic search provided by the EvoChecker probabilistic model synthesis tool [9].

Acknowledgments. This research has received funding from the Assuring Autonomy International Programme (AAIP grant CSI: Cobot), a partnership between Lloyd's Register Foundation and the University of York, and from the UKRI project EP/V026747/1 "Trustworthy Autonomous Systems Node in Resilience". We are grateful to our industrial collaborator for the gained insights into manufacturing cobots and to the AMRC for allowing us to use the iAM-R mobile collaborative robot, to implement the physical robotic process and evaluate the synthesised safety controller into their facilities.

References

1. Andova, S., Hermanns, H., Katoen, J.-P.: Discrete-time rewards model-checked. In: Larsen, K.G., Niebert, P. (eds.) FORMATS 2003. LNCS, vol. 2791, pp. 88–104. Springer, Heidelberg (2004). https://doi.org/10.1007/978-3-540-40903-8_8
2. Askarpour, M., Mandrioli, D., Rossi, M., Vicentini, F.: SAFER-HRC: safety analysis through formal verification in human-robot collaboration. In: Skavhaug, A., Guiochet, J., Bitsch, F. (eds.) SAFECOMP 2016. LNCS, vol. 9922, pp. 283–295. Springer, Cham (2016). https://doi.org/10.1007/978-3-319-45477-1_22
3. Bi, Z., Luo, C., Miao, Z., Zhang, B., Zhang, W., Wang, L.: Safety assurance mechanisms of collaborative robotic systems in manufacturing. Robot. Comput.-Integr. Manufact. **67**, 102022 (2021). https://doi.org/10.1016/j.rcim.2020.102022
4. Cherubini, A., Passama, R., Crosnier, A., Lasnier, A., Fraisse, P.: Collaborative manufacturing with physical human-robot interaction. Robot. Comput.-Integr. Manufact. **40**, 1–13 (2016). https://doi.org/10.1016/j.rcim.2015.12.007
5. Ciesinski, F., Größer, M.: On Probabilistic Computation Tree Logic, pp. 147–188. Springer, Berlin Heidelberg (2004). https://doi.org/10.1007/978-3-540-24611-4_5
6. Douthwaite, J., et al.: A modular digital twinning framework for safety assurance of collaborative robotics. Front. Robot. AI, **8** (2021). https://doi.org/10.3389/frobt.2021.758099
7. D'Souza, F., Costa, J., Pires, J.N.: Development of a solution for adding a collaborative robot to an industrial AGV. Ind. Robot **47**(5), 723–735 (2020)
8. El Zaatari, S., Marei, M., Li, W., Usman, Z.: Cobot programming for collaborative industrial tasks: an overview. Robot. Auton. Syst. **116**, 162–180 (2019). https://doi.org/10.1016/j.robot.2019.03.003
9. Gerasimou, S., Tamburrelli, G., Calinescu, R.: Search-based synthesis of probabilistic models for quality-of-service software engineering. In: 30th IEEE/ACM International Conference on Automated Software Engineering, pp. 319–330 (2015). https://doi.org/10.1109/ASE.2015.22
10. Gleirscher, M., et al.: Verified synthesis of optimal safety controllers for human-robot collaboration. Sci. Comput. Program. **218**, 102809 (2022). https://doi.org/10.1016/j.scico.2022.102809
11. Gleirscher, M., Calinescu, R.: Safety controller synthesis for collaborative robots. In: 25th International Conference on Engineering of Complex Computer Systems (ICECCS), pp. 83–92 (2020)
12. Hansson, H., Jonsson, B.: A logic for reasoning about time and reliability. Formal Aspects Comput. **6**(5), 512–535 (1994). https://doi.org/10.1007/BF01211866
13. ISO/TS 15066: Robots and robotic devices - Collaborative robots. Standard, Robotic Industries Association (RIA) (2016). www.iso.org/standard/62996.html
14. Kwiatkowska, M., Norman, G., Parker, D.: Prism 4.0: verification of probabilistic real-time systems. In: Computer Aided Verification, pp. 585–591. Springer, Berlin Heidelberg (2011). https://doi.org/10.1007/978-3-642-22110-1_47
15. Kwiatkowska, M.Z., Norman, G., Parker, D.: Stochastic model checking. In: Formal Methods for Performance Evaluation, 7th International School on Formal Methods for the Design of Computer, Communication, and Software Systems. Lecture Notes in Computer Science, vol. 4486, pp. 220–270. Springer (2007). https://doi.org/10.1007/978-3-540-72522-0_6
16. Lee, K., Shin, J., Lim, J.Y.: Critical hazard factors in the risk assessments of industrial robots: causal analysis and case studies. Saf. Health Work **12**(4), 496–504 (2021). https://doi.org/10.1016/j.shaw.2021.07.010

17. Levratti, A., Riggio, G., Fantuzzi, C., De Vuono, A., Secchi, C.: TIREBOT: a collaborative robot for the tire workshop. Robot. Comput.-Integr. Manufact. **57**, 129–137 (2019)
18. Liu, Z., et al.: Dynamic risk assessment and active response strategy for industrial human-robot collaboration. Comput. Ind. Eng. **141**, 106302 (2020). https://doi.org/10.1016/j.cie.2020.106302
19. Marvel, J.A., Falco, J., Marstio, I.: Characterizing task-based human-robot collaboration safety in manufacturing. IEEE Trans. Syst. Man Cybern. Syst. **45**(2), 260–275 (2015). https://doi.org/10.1109/TSMC.2014.2337275
20. Matthias, B., Kock, S., Jerregard, H., Kallman, M., Lundberg, I., Mellander, R.: Safety of collaborative industrial robots: certification possibilities for a collaborative assembly robot concept. In: 2011 IEEE International Symposium on Assembly and Manufacturing (ISAM), pp. 1–6 (2011). https://doi.org/10.1109/ISAM.2011.5942307
21. Maurice, P., Padois, V., Measson, Y., Bidaud, P.: Human-oriented design of collaborative robots. Int. J. Ind. Ergon. **57**, 88–102 (2017). https://doi.org/10.1016/j.ergon.2016.11.011
22. Murashov, V., Hearl, F., Howard, J.: Working safely with robot workers: recommendations for the new workplace. J. Occup. Environ. Hyg. **13**(3), D61–D71 (2016). https://doi.org/10.1080/15459624.2015.1116700
23. Rüßmann, M., et al.: Industry 4.0: the future of productivity and growth in manufacturing industries. Boston Consult. Group, **9**(1), 54–89 (2015)
24. Sherwani, F., Asad, M.M., Ibrahim, B.: Collaborative robots and industrial revolution 4.0 (IR 4.0). In: 2020 International Conference on Emerging Trends in Smart Technologies. pp. 1–5 (2020). https://doi.org/10.1109/ICETST49965.2020.9080724
25. Vicentini, F., Askarpour, M., Rossi, M.G., Mandrioli, D.: Safety assessment of collaborative robotics through automated formal verification. IEEE Trans. Robot. **36**(1), 42–61 (2020). https://doi.org/10.1109/TRO.2019.2937471
26. Zanchettin, A.M., Rocco, P.: Path-consistent safety in mixed human-robot collaborative manufacturing environments. In: IEEE/RSJ International Conference on Intelligent Robots and Systems, pp. 1131–1136 (2013). https://doi.org/10.1109/IROS.2013.6696492

Timely Specification Repair for Alloy 6

Jorge Cerqueira[1,2], Alcino Cunha[1,2], and Nuno Macedo[1,3]($\boxtimes$)

[1] INESC TEC, Porto, Portugal
[2] University of Minho, Braga, Portugal
[3] Faculty of Engineering of the University of Porto, Porto, Portugal
nmacedo@fe.up.pt

Abstract. This paper proposes the first mutation-based technique for the repair of Alloy 6 first-order temporal logic specifications. This technique was developed with the educational context in mind, in particular, to repair submissions for specification challenges, as allowed, for example, in the Alloy4Fun web-platform. Given an oracle and an incorrect submission, the proposed technique searches for syntactic mutations that lead to a correct specification, using previous counterexamples to quickly prune the search space, thus enabling timely feedback to students. Evaluation shows that, not only is the technique feasible for repairing temporal logic specifications, but also outperforms existing techniques for non-temporal Alloy specifications in the context of educational challenges.

Keywords: Specification repair · First-order temporal logic · Formal methods education · Alloy

1 Introduction

Besides their role in traditional formal methods, namely model checking, formal specifications are becoming central in many software engineering techniques, such as property-based testing, automated program synthesis or runtime monitoring. Therefore, software engineers with little expertise on formal methods are increasingly being required to write and validate formal specifications. Unfortunately, students and professionals still struggle with this task, and more advanced tool support is needed if formal specifications are to be embraced by a wider community [10].

Alloy [9] is a formal specification language supported by automated model finding and model checking, being the quintessential example of a lightweight formal method. Its most recent version 6 [11] is based on a first-order relational temporal logic, enabling both structural and behavioural modeling and analysis. For these reasons, Alloy is often used in formal methods introductory courses[1].

---

[1] https://alloytools.org/citations/courses.html

This work is financed by National Funds through the Portuguese funding agency, FCT – Fundação para a Ciência e a Tecnologia within project EXPL/CCI-COM/1637/2021.

B.-H. Schlingloff and M. Chai (Eds.): SEFM 2022, LNCS 13550, pp. 288–303, 2022.
https://doi.org/10.1007/978-3-031-17108-6_18

Alloy4Fun [12][2] is a web-platform for Alloy that supports automated assessment exercises through the creation of specification challenges: instructors write a secret predicate that acts as an oracle, and the students have to write an equivalent predicate given an informal description. If the submitted predicate is incorrect, the student can navigate through counterexamples that witness the inconsistency with the oracle. Unfortunately, in our experience, novice practitioners struggle with interpreting such counterexamples and tracing the problem back to the specification.

The automatic generation of hints to guide students in fixing their code has long been employed in educational coding platforms. One approach to the generation of such hints is to apply automated repair techniques and then derive a hint back from the found sequence of repairs [13]. Although automated repair for specifications is still largely unexplored, recently, a few approaches have been proposed for the previous (non-temporal) version of Alloy, namely ARepair [18] and BeAFix [2]. However, the educational scenario has some characteristics that prevent their adoption for hint generation. The main issue is that their performance (likewise most techniques for code [17]) is still not good enough to support hint generation. Timely feedback is particularly important in this context, to avoid the student hitting bottlenecks and frustration when interacting with the platform. Additionally, ARepair uses test cases as oracles, and it is difficult to manually write a set of test cases that brings its accuracy up to an acceptable level. BeAFix is better suited to repair specification challenges, since it uses the Alloy checks as oracles, but prunes the search space by exploiting multiple suspicious locations and multiple failing oracles, techniques that are useless in this context, where we just want to fix one (usually short) predicate written by the student that failed one specific check against the oracle.

This paper presents a new mutation-based technique for the repair of Alloy 6 specifications that can be used in the educational context for timely hint generation. It is the first repair technique to consider the full logic of Alloy 6, including both its first-order and temporal constructs. Also, it implements a pruning technique based on evaluating previously seen counterexamples, that can be used to optimize repairs in models with a single faulty location, as is the case of specification challenges. Our evaluation shows that the proposed technique considerably outperforms existing automated repair techniques for Alloy (when considering only the first-order subset of the language they support).

The rest of this paper is organized as follows. Section 2 presents existing work on automated specification repair. Section 3 presents the novel specification repair technique and associated pruning strategy, whose performance is evaluated against the existing approaches in Sect. 4. Lastly, Sect. 5 draws conclusions and points directions for future work.

2   Related Work

There is extensive work on automated program repair [6,7], with techniques being broadly classified as search-based (or generate-and-validate) – which search

---

[2] http://alloy4fun.inesctec.pt/.

for possible solutions and test them against the oracle – or semantics-driven (or constraint-based) – where the needed repair is encoded as a constraint from which a correct fix is generated. Most approaches use test cases as oracles, although a few rely on reference implementations (e.g., in the educational context) or program specifications (e.g., in the context of design by contract). In contrast, there is very little work on automated specification repair. In [4] a search-based technique is proposed to fix OCL integrity constraints against existing model instances. SpeciFix [14] is a search-based technique for fixing pre- and post-conditions of Eiffel routines against a set of test cases. Techniques [3,15] for semantics-driven repair in the B-method focus on repairing the state machine rather than the broken specifications. Two techniques – ARepair and BeAFix – have been proposed for automatic repair of Alloy specifications, which we further detail next.

ARepair [18,19] uses test cases as oracle. The downsides of this approach are twofold: it is prone to overfitting, where an accepted fix passes all the tests but not the expected properties; and the user is required write (high quality) unit tests, something that is not common practice for Alloy or specifications in general. ARepair starts by feeding the model and tests into AlloyFL [20], a mutation-based fault localization framework for Alloy, which returns a ranked list of suspicious Abstract Syntax Tree (AST) nodes. Then, it checks if the mutation provided by AlloyFL on the most suspicious node retains currently passing tests and passes some previously failing tests. Otherwise, it creates holes and tries to synthesize code for these holes that make some of the failing tests pass. These tests are performed with Alloy's evaluator, avoiding calls to the solver. This process is repeated until all tests pass. The synthesizer returns complex non-equivalent expressions for a specified type and bounds. Since a huge amount of expressions is synthesized, ARepair presents two search strategies, one which chooses a maximum amount of tries per hole and tries to prioritize certain expressions; and another which iteratively fixes all holes except one for which it it tries all expressions to find the one that makes most tests pass.

In contrast, BeAFix [1,2] uses the check commands of an Alloy specification as oracles, focusing on the repair of the system specification referred to by the check. This is a more natural scenario since defining checks to verify the intended properties of a design are common practice. BeAFix relies on a different fault localization technique for Alloy, FLACK [22], which it only runs once for the initial model, unlike ARepair. To generate the fix candidates, BeAFix defines a set of mutation operators that are then combined up to a certain maximum amount of mutators. Mutated expressions are then tested against the oracles using Alloy's solver. Since the number of candidates grows exponentially with the maximum amount of combined mutations, BeAFix relies on two pruning strategies to discard groups of candidates that are guaranteed to not fix the specification, without calling the solver for a full check. Partial repair checking is used when there is a command $Check_i$ that refers to a suspicious location l_0, but not another suspicious location l_1. If $Check_i$ is still invalid under mutation m_0 for l_0, it is not worth to pair mutations for l_1 with m_0 since they will never render

```
var sig File {
    var link : lone File
}
var sig Trash in File {}
var sig Protected in File {}

//SECRET
pred prop4o {
    eventually some Trash
}
//SECRET
check {
    prop4 <=> prop4o
}
// some file will eventually be sent to the trash
pred prop4 {

}
```

Fig. 1. An example specification challenge in Alloy4Fun

$Check_i$ valid. Variabilization is used when a $Check_i$ fails for a pair of mutations m_0 and m_1 for suspicious locations l_0 and l_1, having yielded a counterexample. To check whether m_0 is a mutation worth exploring, variabilization freezes m_0 and replaces l_1 by an existentially quantified variable and checks whether the counterexample persists for $Check_i$. If so, there is no possible value for l_1 that fixes the specification for m_0 at l_0 and that mutation can be automatically discarded.

3   Alloy Temporal Repair

This sections presents the main contribution of this paper: an automatic repair technique for Alloy 6 temporal specifications, suitable for the educational domain. Required Alloy concepts are introduced as needed, but for a more thorough the reader should consult [8].

3.1   Overview

Our goal is to use automatic specification repair to generate hints to students in autonomous assessment platforms. For Alloy, Alloy4Fun is currently the only framework providing such functionality, by allowing the definition of secret predicates and check commands. A typical usage of this feature is in the creation of specification challenges: the instructor writes a hidden predicate representing a correct answer, and a hidden check command that tests it against an initially empty predicate that the student is expected to fill. As an example, consider the Alloy snippet presented in Fig. 1, modelling a simple file system where a file

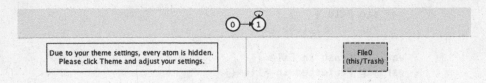

Fig. 2. Counterexample to `prop4`

can link to another file, be put in the trash, or be set in a protected state. This snippet belongs to an exercise given to students in a formal methods course at University of Minho, Portugal [12]. The keyword **sig** declares a new signature in a specification, grouping together a set of atoms of the domain. Signatures can be defined as subsets of other signatures using keyword **in**. Inside signatures, fields can be declared to introduce new relations between atoms, for example the link binary relation. Signatures and fields can have multiplicty constraints, such as the one in link stating that each file links to at most one other file (**lone**). The **var** keyword indicates that the content of a signature or field can change between time instances.

Each exercises has multiple specification challenges. The fourth one of this exercise asks the student to write a formula that evaluates to true iff a file is sent to the trash at any point in time. The student is asked to write such a formula in predicate (**pred**) prop4. Hidden to the student, marked with the special comment *//SECRET*, a check command tests whether the student's predicate is equivalent to the instructor's oracle written in prop4o, written using the temporal operator **eventually** and cardinality test **some**. The most common erroneous solution submitted by the students is the following.

```
pred prop4 {
    some f : File | eventually f in Trash
}
```

Without temporal operators, expressions are evaluated in the initial state, so the outermost existential quantifier is evaluated in the first state. So this predicate is actually stating that a file present in the first state is eventually sent to the trash, disregarding scenarios where a file created after the first state is sent to the trash. Checking against the oracle, Alloy would return a counterexample trace such as the one in Fig. 2, where a file is directly created in the trash in the second state[3]. Students would then interpret the counterexample, trying to find the error in their reasoning.

Search-based automatic repair approaches usually implement a generate-and-validate process: alternative candidate solutions are generated and then tested against the oracle for correctness. Mutation-based approaches generate candidates by mutating nodes of the AST. In this scenario, it is natural to use a repair

---

[3] Note that in this challenge the evolution of the system is not restricted and files are not required to be created before being sent to the trash. The goal of the exercise was precisely to train students to write the weakest specifications of the stated requirement, independent of concrete system implementations.

technique whose oracles are themselves specifications provided in the check commands, rather than test cases, as does BeAFix. For instance, for the incorrect submission above, with search depth 1, mutants like the ones below would be generated and tested against the oracle:

1. **some** f : Trash | **eventually** f **in** Trash
2. **some** f : File | **eventually** f **in** File
3. **some** f : File | **always** f **in** Trash
4. **some** f : File | **after** f **in** Trash
5. **some** f : File | **eventually** f **not in** Trash
6. **all** f : File | **eventually** f **in** Trash
7. **after some** f : File | **eventually** f **in** Trash
8. **eventually some** f : File | **eventually** f **in** Trash

Of these mutants, only the last one is valid and equivalent to `prop4o`. Note that this approach tests the semantic equivalence of the submissions against the oracle, rather than its AST. This also means that validating a mutant amounts to calling the *solver* to run the check command. Calls to the solver are expensive, and since the number of mutants may be overwhelming, this process in general is infeasible without pruning strategies. Unfortunately, BeAFix's pruning strategies are not effective in this scenario: partial repair can optimize the procedure when there are multiple failing checks, but in this scenario each challenge amounts to a single check; variabilization optimizes the procedure when there are multiple suspicions locations, but here we already know that the suspicious location is the single predicate filled by the student.

The idea behind the pruning strategy proposed in this work is that a counterexample for a candidate mutant will likely be a counterexample for similar candidates. For instance, the counterexample returned for the initial student submission in Fig. 2 would actually discard the invalid mutants 1–5 presented above, avoiding 5 additional calls to the solver. Calling the solver for mutant 6 could return a counterexample with some files in the trash in the first state that are then removed in the second, serving also to discard mutant 7. The principal advantage of this reasoning is that testing a mutant specification over a concrete counterexample does not require calling the solver: it can be performed efficiently with Alloy's *evaluator*. Therefore, by storing counterexamples obtained for previously discarded mutants, new candidates can be quickly checked against them before calling the solver to run the check command.

3.2   Mutation-Based Repair with Counterexample-Based Pruning

The technique proposed in this work has in common with BeAFix the fact that it generates fix candidates through a set of mutations. The main differences are twofold: the development of a new pruning technique suitable for specifications with a single check command and suspicious location, and the support for the temporal logic of Alloy 6 that has not been addressed thus far.

In Alloy, a check command with formula ϕ over a specification defined by formula ψ (in Alloy, defined through **fact** constraints) is converted into a model

Table 1. List of mutators for Boolean formulas.

Name	Mutation	Example
REMOVEBINARY	A [bop] $B \leadsto A$ A [bop] $B \leadsto B$	A **and** B $\leadsto$ A
REPLACEBINARY	A [bop] $B \leadsto A$ [bop'] B	A **and** B $\leadsto$ A **or** B
REMOVEUNARY	[uop] $A \leadsto A$	**always no** A $\leadsto$ **no** A
REPLACEUNARY	[uop] $A \leadsto$ [uop'] A	**no** A $\leadsto$ **some** A
INSERTUNARY	$A \leadsto$ [uop] A	**no** A $\leadsto$ **always no** A
BINARYTOUNARY	A [bop] $B \leadsto$ [uop] (A [bop'] B)	A **in** B $\leadsto$ **no** (A + B)
QUANTIFIERTOUNARY	[$qtop$] a:A | $B \leadsto$ [uop] A	**no** a:A | foo[a] $\leadsto$ **no** A
REPLACEQUANTIFIER	[$qtop$] a:A | $B \leadsto$ [$qtop'$] a:A | B	**no** a:A | foo[a] $\leadsto$ **some** a:A | foo[a]

finding problem for a single formula ϕ **and not** ψ. For instance, in the challenge from Fig. 1 ψ is empty, so for the prop4 example shown in Sect. 3.1 the check's formula would simply be converted to

```
not ((some f : File | eventually f in Trash) <=>
    (eventually some Trash))
```

When such a formula is passed to the solver, if the check is invalid it will return a counterexample c (such as the one in Fig. 2 for the example) where the specification facts ψ hold but the check ϕ does not. If there is no such counterexample, the check holds and the solver returns $\bot$. Alloy 6's analyzer checks assertions either with SAT solvers or SMV model checkers, the former only for bounded model checking. Although Alloy's logic is first-order, such analysis is possible because there is a bound imposed on the size of the universe by defining *scopes* for signatures (the default scope is 3). For bounded model checking, the default analysis for temporal properties, it is also possible to define a scope for the temporal horizon (the default being 10 steps). For a concrete counterexample c, Alloy also provides an evaluator that can efficiently calculate the value of any formula ϕ without calling the solver, which simply returns true or false.

A mutation m of a formula ϕ is simply a pair (l, o) of a location l in ϕ (which can be seen as a path through the AST, identifying a concrete node) and an instantiation of a mutator o from Tables 1 or 2 (to be presented shortly). These mutations m are uniquely identified by the location and operation. Each candidate mutant results from the application of a sequence δ of such mutations to the specification that is to be fixed. Order within δ is relevant since a mutation m_1 may refer to a location introduced by a preceding mutation m_0, and a mutation m_1 cannot refer to a location previously removed by a preceding m_0.

A procedure that we abstract as MUTATE takes a specification ϕ and a location l and generates all possible mutations for all AST nodes below l. In our example, l would identify the sub-formula that resulted from the student's submitted predicate (the left-hand side of the equivalence). This procedure is lazy, returning an iterator Δ to generate new mutations on demand. Procedure APPLY represents the actual application of a sequence of mutations δ to a specification, returning a new specification mutant. The skeleton of the available mutation

Table 2. List of mutators for relational expressions.

Name	Mutation	Example
REMOVEBINARY	A [bop] B ⤳ A	A + B ⤳ A
	A [bop] B ⤳ B	
REPLACEBINARY	A [bop] B ⤳ A [bop'] B	A + B ⤳ A - B
REMOVEUNARY	[uop] A ⤳ A	~A ⤳ A
REPLACEUNARY	[uop] A ⤳ [uop'] A	^A ⤳ *A
INSERTPRIME	A ⤳ A'	A ⤳ A'
INSERTBINARY	A ⤳ A [bop] B	A ⤳ A + B
INSERTUNARY	A ⤳ [uop] A	A ⤳ ~A
REPLACERELATION	A ⤳ B	A ⤳ B

operations are presented in Tables 1 and 2 for Boolean formulas – composed of Boolean connectives, first-order quantifications and temporal operators – and relational expressions – composed of relational operations, transitive closure and temporal primes –, respectively. Mutators are guaranteed to not change the type of an expression, so, for instance, REMOVEUNARY for Boolean formulas cannot remove a multiplicity test operator, since its sub-expression is a relational expression, and an operator is always replaced by another of the same type (i.e., Boolean connectives cannot be replaced by relational operators). Operations that require the insertion of relational expressions (namely INSERTBINARY and REPLACERELATION) only introduce a single relation at a time and takes into account type information to avoid creating expressions considered irrelevant according to Alloy's type system [5]. For instance, INSERTBINARY for an expression A only creates intersection expressions A & B for relations B whose type has some elements in common with the type of A. For the particular case of introducing a join operator, INSERTBINARY also only explores mutations that preserve the arity of the original relational expression.

An abstract view of the repair procedure is shown in Algorithm 1. The procedure registers a set *cands* of candidate sequences of mutations δ. At each depth level, the procedure iterates over all *cands* and adds an additional mutation m to a candidate δ. Procedure MUTATE is called over ϕ already mutated with the previous candidate, so that only mutations over valid locations are generated (in case locations from the original ϕ_0 were removed by δ, or new ones introduced). Moreover, to avoid testing redundant mutants, whenever a new candidate is generated it is only analyzed if it has not been previously seen in *cands*. Although abstracted in Algorithm 1, this membership test $\in$ ignores the order of the mutations, meaning that two sequences $[m_0, m_1]$ and $[m_1, m_0]$ are considered the same. This is sound because we assume that a candidate δ cannot contain more than one mutation for the same location l.

Without counterexample-based pruning, for each candidate δ' the procedure would simply calculate a mutant ϕ as APPLY(ϕ_0, δ') and call the solver (here, pro-

Input: A formula ϕ_0 representing an invalid check and a location l in ϕ_0 to fix.
Output: A passing formula or $\bot$

$cands \leftarrow \{[]\};$
$cexs \leftarrow [(\text{SOLVE}(\phi_0), 1)];$
for $d \in 1 \ldots \text{MAXDEPTH}$ **do**
    $cands' \leftarrow \emptyset;$
    while $cands \neq \emptyset$ **do**
        $\delta \leftarrow cands.\text{POP}();$
        $\Delta \leftarrow \text{MUTATE}(\text{APPLY}(\phi_0, \delta), l);$
        while $\Delta.\text{HASNEXT}()$ **do**
            $\delta' \leftarrow \delta \mathbin{+\!\!+} [\Delta.\text{NEXT}()];$
            if $\delta' \notin cands$ **then**
                $\phi \leftarrow \text{APPLY}(\phi_0, \delta');$
                $valid \leftarrow \text{TRUE};$
                $cexs' \leftarrow cexs.\text{CLONE}();$
                while $cexs' \neq \emptyset \wedge valid$ **do**
                    $c \leftarrow cexs'.\text{PULLHIGHEST}();$
                    $valid \leftarrow \text{EVALUATE}(\phi, c);$
                    if $\neg valid$ **then** $cexs.\text{INCPRIORITY}(c);$
                if $valid$ **then**
                    $c \leftarrow \text{SOLVE}(\phi);$
                    if $c = \bot$ **then return** $\phi;$
                    else $cexs.\text{PUSHPRIORITY}(c, 1);$
                $cands'.\text{PUSH}(\delta');$
    $cands \leftarrow cands';$
return $\bot;$

Algorithm 1: Repair procedure with counterexample-based pruning

cedure $\text{SOLVE}(\phi)$). The procedure stops when a specification ϕ is valid according to the SOLVE, or the maximum search depth MAXDEPTH is reached, returning $\bot$. In the example previously presented, the INSERTUNARY mutator can be applied to obtain the expression **eventually some** f : File | **eventually** f **in** Trash. The next most common incorrect submission is

some f : File | **eventually always** f **in** Trash

which, besides the same problem of only quantifying on the files available in the first state, also assumes that a file in the trash must stay there indefinitely (temporal operator **always**). This requires search level 2: one mutation to add an outer-most **eventually**, and another to remove the **always** through REMOVE-UNARY. The third most common is

eventually File **in** Trash

which incorrectly states that at some point in time, all existing files are in the trash. It can be fixed through a single application of BINARYTOUNARY, resulting in **eventually some** File & Trash, which is yet another formula equivalent to prop4o.

To avoid expensive calls to the solver, our technique's pruning strategy first evaluates the candidate formula against previously seen counterexamples. These are kept in a priority queue $cexs$, where the priority of each counterexample c is the amount of candidates they were able to prune. So for each mutant, the evaluator is called (procedure EVALUATE) to test ϕ for every previously found counterexample following the established priority. If ϕ still holds for a counterexample c, then it is still an invalid mutant, so ϕ is discarded and c has its priority increased in $cexs$. Only after passing all previously seen counterexamples is the solver called for ϕ. If the solver returns $\bot$, then ϕ has effectively been fixed. Otherwise, a new counterexample c is found and added to $cexs$ with minimal priority.

3.3 Implementation Details

To improve performance, richer data structures were used in the implementation of Algorithm 1. To avoid repeating the generation of all mutations for all candidate mutants that have ASTs that are still very similar to each other, MUTATE is not freshly called for every candidate. Instead the candidates are stored in a list with a pointer to their predecessor candidate. Thus, to generate all the candidates up to a depth, the index to the candidate being checked is kept, as well as the candidate that generated the latest added candidates. When the end of generated candidates is reached, more are generated from the candidate after the one the latest candidates were generated from. The last counterexample used to prune is also tracked and is tested first, the reasoning being that candidates coming after one another will likely mutate the same locations, and thus, also be more likely to be pruned by the same counterexamples. To prevent combining mutators that would generate incorrect or repeated candidates (for example, when sub-expressions are removed), a mutation also registers blacklisted locations that can no longer be mutated. Lastly, rather than just keep track of mutations δ in $cands$, we also maintain the associated mutant ϕ to avoid re-applying mutations.

The technique was implemented as an extension of Alloy 6. It does not make modifications to original Alloy 6 source code. Instead, it only adds new packages and uses the public methods of the original, hopefully making it easier for anyone to follow the implementation and to update to future Alloy releases. The source code is public and can be found on GitHub[4], as well as a Docker container[5] to allow easier replication of the results. In the implementation, the user has to specify by hand the suspicious predicate that is to be fixed. However, the technique itself has no limitations in terms of compatibility with fault localization techniques, and could have been paired with one of those techniques to automatically identify such predicate.

---

[4] https://github.com/Kaixi26/TAR.
[5] https://hub.docker.com/r/kaixi26/tar.

4   Evaluation

In this section we evaluate the performance of the proposed technique for timely Alloy 6 repair (TAR, in the presented results), with the goal of answering the following research questions:

RQ1 What is the performance of mutation-based repair with counterexample-based pruning for temporal Alloy 6 specifications?

RQ2 How does its performance compare with that of existing automatic repair techniques for static Alloy specifications?

RQ3 What is the actual impact of counterexample-based pruning?

Alloy4Fun stores all submissions made to challenges. These are available to the creators of the challenges for subsequent analysis. Tutors at the Universities of Minho and Porto have been using Alloy4Fun in classes for several years and publicly share the data after anonymization[6]. These challenges follow the shape of the one in presented in Fig. 1, so it is easy to identify the oracle and the student predicate to be repaired in each submission. Thus, for RQ1 we executed TAR for all erroneous submissions to challenges with mutable relations (only allowed in Alloy 6) in the 2021 Alloy4Fun dataset. This amounts to two exercises (`TrashLTL` and `Trains`) composed of 38 challenges, totalling 3671 submissions. These results are summarized in Fig. 3, for different search depth levels, and also in the bottom part of Table 3. BeAFix also used a subset of Alloy4Fun challenges for their evaluation [2] (those compatible with the previous Alloy 5 version). For RQ2, we've also run TAR for submissions to those purely first-order logic challenges. This amounts to 6 exercises (`TrashRL`, `ClassroomRL`, `CV`, `Graphs`, `LTS` and `Production`) composed of 48 challenges with 1935 submissions. ARepair requires the user to specify test cases which are not available for the Alloy4Fun challenges, but writing them ourselves could introduce a bias in the process. Instead, we used counterexamples generated during the counterexample-based pruning process as test cases. For each student submission for a challenge, counterexample-based pruning iterated over a set of counterexamples until a fix was found. Counterexamples more commonly occurring in this process have contributed to fixing the most incorrect submissions, and thus are representative of the challenge. We ran ARepair for the same structural Alloy4Fun challengs as BeAFix using the top 10 and top 25 counterexamples as test cases. For the comparison of BeAFix against ARepair in [2], the authors used AUnit [16] to automatically generate test cases, which resulted in a unusually high rate of incorrect fixes by ARepair. The expectation is that our approach to test case generation is fairer for ARepair. These results are summarized in Fig. 4 for different search depth levels and in the top part of Table 3. ARepair may still report incorrect fixes due to overfitting; the data considers only correct repairs All executions of TAR were also ran with counterexample-based pruning disabled to answer RQ3. Since feedback is expected to be provided quickly, the timeout was set to 1 min for all procedures. All tests were run on a Linux-5.15 machine with docker version 20.10 and an Intel Core i5 4460 processor.

---

[6] https://doi.org/10.5281/zenodo.4676413.

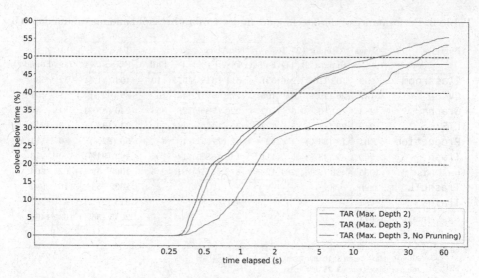

Fig. 3. Percentage of specification challenges repaired by the proposed approach under a certain time threshold, for different search depth levels and with and without pruning

RQ1 The data in Fig. 3 shows that TAR is viable for Alloy 6 repair. It is able to repair about 35% of the specifications by 2 s, and by 1 minute it is able to fix 56%, results that even surpass those for non-temporal Alloy repair, as we will shortly see. Increasing the depth to 3 does not seem to increase significantly the performance of the approach, and with depth 2 the results stagnated at 45% by 10 s. As shown in Table 3, of the 46% challenges that failed to be fixed under 1 minute, 10% were due to time-out while the remainder failed due to an exhausted search space.

RQ2 As can be seen in Fig. 4, TAR consistently outperforms BeAFix, particularly in smaller time thresholds. At 2 s, BeAFix is able to fix 27% of the specifications against the 42% of TAR, a 60% improvement. Although by the 1 minute threshold the difference is reduced to 16%, we consider this to be already too long for a student to wait for automatic feedback. BeAFix was able to successfully fix 47% of the specifications within an 1 h timeout [2], which is still less than the 52% of TAR with a 1 min.

In our evaluation, ARepair was only able to propose a repair that passed the oracle check in less than 5% of the specifications by 2 s, and 22% within 1 minute using the top 25 counterexamples selected using TAR's pruning technique. This strategy for the generation of test cases proved to be fairer than the experiments in [2] where ARepair only proposed fixes that passed the oracle for 9% of specifications for the same dataset within 1 h, but is still well below the performance of TAR and BeAFix. Even disregarding the oracle check, ARepair reported to be able to pass all unit tests in 814 (42%) submissions for the benchmark with 25 unit tests, which is still below TAR and BeAFix.

Table 3. Performance of the 3 techniques under 1 min. threshold and maximum depth 3

Exercise	Cases	ARepair (25 Tests)			BeAFix			TAR		
		Fixed (%)	TO	Failed	Fixed (%)	TO	Failed	Fixed (%)	TO	Failed
Classroom	999	102 (10%)	246	651	311 (31%)	578	110	408 (41%)	52	539
CV	137	26 (19%)	6	105	77 (56%)	44	16	85 (62%)	1	51
Graphs	283	181 (64%)	0	102	220 (78%)	28	35	240 (85%)	4	39
LTS	249	20 (8%)	5	224	35 (14%)	144	70	33 (13%)	5	211
Production	61	18 (30%)	1	42	47 (77%)	10	4	50 (82%)	0	11
Trash	206	89 (43%)	6	111	182 (88%)	14	10	193 (94%)	0	13
total (static)	1935	436 (22%)	264	1235	872 (45%)	818	245	1009 (52%)	62	864
TrashLTL	2890	–	–	–	–	–	–	1832 (63%)	116	942
Trains	781	–	–	–	–	–	–	213 (27%)	47	521
total (temporal)	3671	–	–	–	–	–	–	2045 (56%)	163	1463

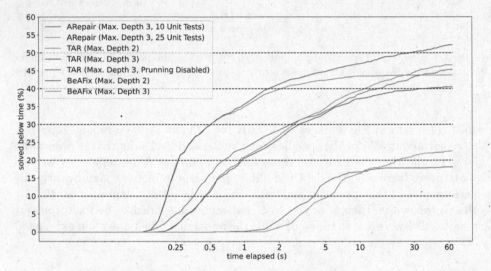

Fig. 4. Percentage of submissions to static challenges correctly repaired by the proposed approach under a certain time threshold, for different search depth levels and with and without pruning

To provide a better understanding of how the specifications fixed by each of the 3 techniques overlap, the Venn diagram in Fig. 5 classifies the specifications according to which tool was able to repair them under a threshold of 1 s. There was no specification that ARepair was able to repair that TAR missed. As for BeAFix, there were 9 specifications that BeAFix repaired and TAR failed within 1 s, against 306 the outer way around. Of those 9 cases, 6 were due to the fact that BeAFix was able to find a repair under 1 s while TAR took longer. The other 3 required the introduction of a join operation that changed the arity of the relational expression, a mutation supported by BeAFix but not by our INSERTBINARY.

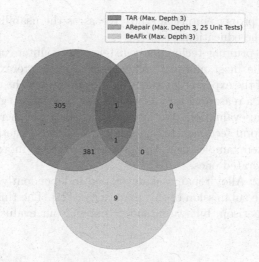

Fig. 5. Classification of submissions to static challenges according to which tool was able to effectively repair them under 1 s

RQ3 Looking at the performance of TAR with pruning disabled shown in Figs. 3 and 4, it is clear that the impact is particularly relevant at lower threshold levels: at 2 s, the technique without pruning is only able to fix about 27% of the specifications, 22% less that the 35% fixed with pruning. As the threshold increases the impact of the pruning technique is reduced. Furthermore, the average amount of generated counterexamples – which amount to calls to the solver – is low, around 5.4 for the static benchmarks; and around 6.4 for the temporal benchmarks. These counterexamples end up being able to prune an impressive amount of candidates, the number being, on average, around 100000 for the static benchmarks, 76% of which are pruned by the same counterexample; and 160000 for the temporal benchmarks, 67% of which are pruned by the same counterexample.

5   Conclusions

This paper presented a mutation-based technique for the automatic repair of Alloy 6 specifications, being the first to consider its full temporal first-order logic. A new pruning technique was proposed that is suitable for target context of the new technique, namely educational scenarios. Evaluation over a dataset of student submissions has shown that, in this scenario, the proposed technique is able to produce timely repairs and that it outperforms existing approaches to Alloy repair (when considering only the non-temporal Alloy subset).

To be effectively used as a hint system in the educational context, the found repairs must be translated back into a hint that can guide the student in the right direction without explicitly providing the correct solution. The technique for the derivation of hints from repairs, and its subsequent implementation in the Alloy4Fun platform, is the next step in our research plan. This is expected to be followed by proper empirical study to assess the usability and efficacy of the technique in the educational context.

The proposed pruning technique registers the counterexamples that were able to discard the most mutants. Arguably, such counterexamples are more "representative" of the expected property as they identified the most semantically different formulas, a reasoning we followed to use this rank to generate test cases for ARepair in the evaluation. We intend to explore whether this information would also be helpful feedback to the students, namely whether returning the top ranking counterexamples from the pruning process is more productive than the randomly generated ones.

A technique for Alloy repair was developed independently of this work and published after the submission of this manuscript [21]. The timing did not allow for a proper comparison, but we intend to expand our evaluation against it in the short term.

References

1. Brida, S.G., et al.: BeAFix: an automated repair tool for faulty alloy models. In: ASE, pp. 1213–1217. IEEE (2021)
2. Brida, S.G., et al.: Bounded exhaustive search of alloy specification repairs. In: ICSE, pp. 1135–1147. IEEE (2021)
3. Cai, C.-H., Sun, J., Dobbie, G.: Automatic B-model repair using model checking and machine learning. Autom. Softw. Eng. **26**(3), 653–704 (2019). https://doi.org/10.1007/s10515-019-00264-4
4. Clarisó, R., Cabot, J.: Fixing defects in integrity constraints via constraint mutation. In: QUATIC, pp. 74–82. IEEE Computer Society (2018)
5. Edwards, J., Jackson, D., Torlak, E.: A type system for object models. ACM SIGSOFT Softw. Eng. Notes **29**(6), 189–199 (2004)
6. Gazzola, L., Micucci, D., Mariani, L.: Automatic software repair: a survey. IEEE Trans. Softw. Eng. **45**(1), 34–67 (2019)
7. Goues, C.L., Pradel, M., Roychoudhury, A.: Automated program repair. Commun. ACM **62**(12), 56–65 (2019)
8. Jackson, D.: Software Abstractions: Logic, Language, and Analysis. MIT Press, revised edn. (2012)
9. Jackson, D.: Alloy: a language and tool for exploring software designs. Commun. ACM **62**(9), 66–76 (2019)
10. Krishnamurthi, S., Nelson, T.: The human in formal methods. In: ter Beek, M.H., McIver, A., Oliveira, J.N. (eds.) FM 2019. LNCS, vol. 11800, pp. 3–10. Springer, Cham (2019). https://doi.org/10.1007/978-3-030-30942-8_1
11. Macedo, N., Brunel, J., Chemouil, D., Cunha, A., Kuperberg, D.: Lightweight specification and analysis of dynamic systems with rich configurations. In: SIGSOFT FSE, pp. 373–383. ACM (2016)
12. Macedo, N., Cunha, A., Pereira, J., Carvalho, R., Silva, R., Paiva, A.C.R., Ramalho, M.S., Silva, D.C.: Experiences on teaching alloy with an automated assessment platform. Sci. Comput. Program. **211**, 102690 (2021)
13. McBroom, J., Koprinska, I., Yacef, K.: A survey of automated programming hint generation: the hints framework. ACM Comput. Surv. **54**(8), 172:1–172:27 (2022)

14. Pei, Yu., Furia, C.A., Nordio, M., Meyer, B.: Automatic program repair by fixing contracts. In: Gnesi, S., Rensink, A. (eds.) FASE 2014. LNCS, vol. 8411, pp. 246–260. Springer, Heidelberg (2014). https://doi.org/10.1007/978-3-642-54804-8_17

15. Schmidt, J., Krings, S., Leuschel, M.: Repair and generation of formal models using synthesis. In: Furia, C.A., Winter, K. (eds.) IFM 2018. LNCS, vol. 11023, pp. 346–366. Springer, Cham (2018). https://doi.org/10.1007/978-3-319-98938-9_20

16. Sullivan, A., Wang, K., Khurshid, S.: Aunit: a test automation tool for alloy. In: ICST, pp. 398–403. IEEE Computer Society (2018)

17. Toll, D., Wingkvist, A., Ericsson, M.: Current state and next steps on automated hints for students learning to code. In: FIE, pp. 1–5. IEEE (2020)

18. Wang, K., Sullivan, A., Khurshid, S.: Automated model repair for alloy. In: ASE, pp. 577–588. ACM (2018)

19. Wang, K., Sullivan, A., Khurshid, S.: Arepair: a repair framework for alloy. In: ICSE (Companion Volume), pp. 103–106. IEEE / ACM (2019)

20. Wang, K., Sullivan, A., Marinov, D., Khurshid, S.: Fault localization for declarative models in alloy. In: ISSRE, pp. 391–402. IEEE (2020)

21. Zheng, G., et al.: ATR: template-based repair for alloy specifications. In: ISSTA, pp. 666–677. ACM (2022)

22. Zheng, G., et al.: FLACK: counterexample-guided fault localization for alloy models. In: ICSE, pp. 637–648. IEEE (2021)

Temporal Logic

BehaVerify: Verifying Temporal Logic Specifications for Behavior Trees

Serena Serafina Serbinowska$^{(\boxtimes)}$ (iD) and Taylor T. Johnson (iD)

Vanderbilt University, Nashville, TN 37235,, USA
{serena.serbinowska,taylor.johnson}@vanderbilt.edu

Abstract. Behavior Trees, which originated in video games as a method for controlling NPCs but have since gained traction within the robotics community, are a framework for describing the execution of a task. BehaVerify is a tool that creates a nuXmv model from a py_tree. For composite nodes, which are standardized, this process is automatic and requires no additional user input. A wide variety of leaf nodes are automatically supported and require no additional user input, but customized leaf nodes will require additional user input to be correctly modeled. BehaVerify can provide a template to make this easier. BehaVerify is able to create a nuXmv model with over 100 nodes and nuXmv was able to verify various non-trivial LTL properties on this model, both directly and via counterexample. The model in question features parallel nodes, selector, and sequence nodes. A comparison with models based on BTCompiler indicates that the models created by BehaVerify perform better.

Keywords: Behavior tree · Model verification

1 Introduction

Behavior Trees are a framework for describing the execution of a task that originated in computer games as a method of controlling Non-Player Characters (NPCs), but have since expanded into the domain of robotics [14,26]. Behavior Trees are split into composite nodes that control the flow through the tree and leaf nodes which execute actions. Behavior Trees have a variety of strengths: they facilitate code re-use (nodes and sub-trees can easily be attached), their modular nature makes reasoning about them easier, and changing one region of a tree doesn't affect how other regions function [1]. However, at present, tools to verify the correctness of a Behavior Tree are scarce. Therefore, we present BehaVerify, a tool for converting a py_tree into a .smv file which can be verified using nuXmv [6].

Contributions. We present BehaVerify, a tool that enables verification with Linear Temporal Logic (LTL) model checking that improves upon BTCompiler, the only previously existing tool for such a task, in terms of run time and in ease of

© The Author(s), under exclusive license to Springer Nature Switzerland AG 2022
B.-H. Schlingloff and M. Chai (Eds.): SEFM 2022, LNCS 13550, pp. 307–323, 2022.
https://doi.org/10.1007/978-3-031-17108-6_19

use with respect to Blackboard variables. Specifically, we present an automatic method to perform the translation and encoding of behavior trees to nuXmv models, a description of this method in a publicly available software tool, a characterization of the verification performance of these different encodings and how they compare to the models created by BTCompiler, and apply the tool to verify key LTL specifications of a challenging robotics case study for an underwater robot used as a controller in an ongoing DARPA project. However, we first define what Behavior Trees are.

1.1 Background

A Behavior Tree (BT) is a rooted tree. Each node has a single parent, save for the root which has no parent. A BT does nothing until it receives a tick event, at which point the tick event propagates throughout the tree. Composite nodes serve to control the flow of execution, determining which children receive tick events. By contrast, Leaf nodes are either actions, such as Accelerate, or guard checks, such as GoingToSlow. Leaf nodes do not have children. Finally, decorator nodes are used to customize the output of their children without actually modifying the children themselves, allowing for greater re-usability. Usually, a Decorator node will have one child.

There are three types of composite nodes: Sequence, Selector, and Parallel. Sequence nodes execute a sequence of children. A Sequence node returns a value if a child returns Failure or Running or there are no more children to run. Sequences return Failure if any child returns Failure, Running if any child returns Running, and Success if every child returned Success. Selector nodes, also known as Fallback nodes [1,24], execute children in order of priority. A Selector node returns a value if a child returns Success or Running or there are no more children to run. Selectors return Success if any child returns Success, Running if any child returns Running, and Failure if every child returned Failure.

Parallel nodes execute all their children regardless of what values are returned. At least three different definitions exist for parallel nodes. The first definition, found in [24], states that parallel nodes return Failure if any child returns Failure, Success if a satisfactory subset of children return Success, and Running otherwise. The second definition, found in [10,11], and [18] is similar, but states that parallel nodes return Success only if all children return Success. The third definition, found in [2,12,14,20,25], and [13], states that parallel nodes return Success if at least m children return Success, Failure if $n - m + 1$ children return Failure, and Running otherwise. Here n is the number of children the parallel node has and m is a node parameter. BehaVerify, the tool created alongside this paper, was designed for py_trees and therefore utilizes the definition presented in [24].

In addition to these differences, Composite nodes can be further characterized into Nodes with Memory and Nodes without Memory. The above definitions describe Nodes without Memory. Nodes with Memory allow the composite nodes to remember what they previously returned and continue accordingly. Thus a Sequence with Memory will not start from its first child if it previously returned

Running and will instead skip over each child that returned Success. Similarly, a Selector with Memory will skip over each child that returned Failure. A Parallel node with Memory will only rerun children that returned Running.

However, memory is also not standardized. In [24], Nodes with Memory 'forget' if one of their ancestors returns Success or Failure. So, for instance, if a Sequence with Memory returns Running, but its Parallel node parent returns Success, the Sequence with Memory will not behave as though it returned Running. However, in Sect. 1.3.2 of [14], the authors state "Control flow nodes with memory always remember whether a child has returned Success or Failure, avoiding the re-execution of the child until the whole Sequence or Fallback finishes in either Success or Failure", and notably makes no mention of Parallel nodes with Memory. Finally, note that py_trees supports Selector with and without Memory, Sequences with and without Memory, and both types of Parallel nodes. However, the Parallel nodes with Memory and without Memory are instead called Synchronized Parallel and Unsynchronized Parallel, respectively.

Decorator nodes are generally used to augment the output of a child. For instance, a RunningIsFailure decorator will cause an output of Running to be interpreted as Failure. As there are many decorators, we omit attempting to fully list or describe them here.

Furthermore, we note that in many of the above works, Selector nodes are represented using ?, Sequence nodes are represented using →, and Parallel nodes are represented using ⇉. However, we will utilize the notation given in py_trees, as seen in Fig. 1.

Fig. 1. Composite Nodes in py_trees.

1.2 The Blackboard

In certain situations, such as when multiple nodes need to use the result of a computation, it can be useful to read and write information in a centralized location. This sort of shared memory is frequently called a Blackboard [5,15, 16,24]. Unfortunately, there are also drawbacks to using Blackboards. As [23] points out, Blackboards can make BTs difficult to understand and reduce subtree reuse. Ultimately, however, the fact remains that in many cases there are substantial benefits to using a Blackboard, and various implementations, such as py_trees seek to alleviate some of the aspects by creating visualization tools for blackboards [24]. Accordingly, BehaVerify supports Blackboard variables.

2   Related Work

First, we clarify that the term "Behavior Tree" sometimes refer to different concepts. Behavior Trees exist as a formal graphical modeling language, as part of

Behavior Engineering and are used for requirement handling [19]. These are not the BTs we are talking about.

2.1   Strengths and Uses of BTs

In [20], the author shows how general Hybrid Dynamical Systems can be written as BTs and how this can be beneficial. Furthermore, the paper provides justifications for why BTs are useful to UAV guidance and control systems. [4] compares BTs to a variety of other Action Selection Mechanisms (ASM) and proves that unrestricted BTs have the same expressive capabilities as unrestricted Finite State Machines. [1] presents a framework for verifying the correctness of BTs without compromising on the main strengths of Behavior Trees, which they identify as modularity, flexibility, and re-usability.

[17] considers the various implementations of BTs, such as BehaviorTree.cpp and py_trees, and examines a variety of repositories that utilize BTs. In [25] the authors propose an algorithm to translate an I/O automaton into a BT that connects high level planning and low level control. The authors of [9] demonstrate how it is possible to synthesize a BT that is guaranteed to be complete a task specified by LTL. This does require restricting LTL to a fragment of LTL, so there are limits to what BTs can be synthesized in this way. [8] describes a tool-chain for designing, executing, and monitoring robots that uses BTs for controlling high level behaviors of the robots while [7] formalizes the context within which BTs are executed.

2.2   Expanded BTs

The capabilities of BTs have been expanded in several papers. In [3], the authors consider how it is possible to expand BTs by introducing K-BTs which replace Success and Failure with K different outputs. [10,11], and [12] introduce Concurrent BTs and expand on them by introducing various nodes designed to better enable synchronization in BTs that deal with concurrency. Meanwhile [18] extends BTs to Conditional BTs, which enforce certain pre and post conditions on various nodes within the tree and introduces a tool which can confirm that the entire tree is capable of being executed based on the pre and post conditions given. [21] extends BTs to Belief BTs which are better suited to dealing with non-deterministic outcomes of actions.

2.3   Verification of BTs

Some of the above works deal with the verification of BTs. [1], for instance, presents an algorithm for the verification of BTs. [9], on the other hand, presents a method by which to synthesize a BT that is guaranteed to be correct, thereby by-passing the need for verification, but the specifications are limited to a fragment of LTL. The only existing tool we were able to find that allows the user to create and verify LTL specifications for BTs is BTCompiler[1]. Unfortunately, we were not able to install the tool, and as such our knowledge of it is somewhat limited. Most of what we understand comes from analyzing the various examples in the smv folder in the github repository.

From what we understand, BTCompiler uses the following assumptions and definitions. All composite nodes are assumed to have exactly 2 children. Parallel nodes do not have memory. Parallel nodes utilize the third definition presented in the background section. Sequence and Selector nodes with and without memory are supported. Unlike the implementation in py_trees, nodes with memory do not 'forget' if an ancestor terminates. Please note that the requirement that composite nodes have only 2 children does not impact expressiveness. By self-composing nodes, it is possible to effectively create a node with any number of children greater than 2. For a proof, see Sect. 5.1 of [14]. Thus the only downside is potential model complexity and readability.

We will compare the models created by BTCompiler and BehaVerify.

3   Overview of Approach

BehaVerify begins by recursively walking a py_tree and recording relevant information. This information includes what the type of each node is, recording any important parameters (like the Success policy for a parallel node), and the structure of the tree. Once this process has finished, BehaVerify begins to create the .smv file. Most of this process is straightforward. For instance, for each node type, BehaVerify creates a module (basically a class) in the .smv file. These modules are static and don't change between runs. For each node, BehaVerify creates an instance of a module with the necessary parameters, like what children the node has.

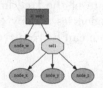

Fig. 2. A simple BT

However, not everything is simple or static. The primary sources of complexity are Nodes with Memory. A lazy approach to implementing Nodes with Memory is to have each node store an integer marking which child returned Running. Such an encoding can greatly increase the number of states in the model. Consider Fig. 2. Seq1 has two children, while sel1 has three. The lazy encoding would therefore produce six states to record which children returned Running.

[1] https://github.com/CARVE-ROBMOSYS/BTCompiler.

However, consider that if we know that node_y returned Running, then sel1 will also return Running. Thus we only need four states.

Next, BehaVerify begins to handle the blackboard. BehaVerify has several ways of doing this. The first method is to have the user provide an input file which is simply included in the .smv file. Assuming no such file is provided, BehaVerify can generate the blackboard. If the user requests, the generated blackboard can be saved. This allows the user to modify the generated blackboard file and use it as an input file on subsequent runs. In addition, BehaVerify also allows the user to specify a file containing LTL specifications which are then included in the .smv file.

At this point, the .smv file is complete, and can be used with nuXmv [6], either for simulation or verification.

4   Encodings

BehaVerify uses two primary encodings: Leaf and Total. The general ideas behind these encodings are presented here. Note that the actual models BehaVerify creates for use with nuXmv differ from what is presented here, but the general motivations are the same. Also note that from this point forward, we write Success as S, Failure as F, Running as R, and Invalid as I. For both encodings, it is useful to consider how a BT operates. A BT remains inactive until it receives a tick. Once a tick is received, it begins to propagate throughout the tree causing various nodes to execute. The path of the tick signal through the Tree is similar to a Depth First Search, though it will sometimes skip over branches of the tree. A basic version of the Leaf encoding explicitly follows the tick signal as it moves throughout the tree, tracing the exact path the tick signal takes through the tree. The Leaf encoding presented here includes some optimizations to improve performance, but the general idea is the same. The Total encoding doesn't follow the path of the signal. The state of the tree in the Total encoding is instead represented by a chain of dependencies and by considering the path of the tick signal through the tree, the chain can be resolved. Additional details follow.

4.1   Leaf

Fig. 3. A selector node with many children.

As was mentioned, an intuitive encoding for BTs follows the path of the tick throughout the tree. At each time step t, one node is the Active Node ($ActNode(t)$), its status is computed, and then another node becomes Active.

Note that in this encoding each time step t does NOT correspond to a tick. A tick instead occurs between any time steps t and $t + 1$ such that $ActNode(t) = -1$. Now consider Fig. 3. In this simple encoding, we would start at wideSel, then move to child1, then back to wideSel, then to child2, back to wideSel, etc., until one of the children returned S or R, or we ran out of children. Thus this encoding spends many steps going through wideSel. The Leaf encoding realizes that the actual points of interest are the leaf nodes themselves. If child1 returns S or R, then the tree returns a status. If child1 returns F, then we need to check child2. Thus we can eliminate many unnecessary steps in the traversal of the tree by jumping from leaf to leaf. Formally, this encoding is as follows:

$$ActNode(t+1) := \begin{cases} \text{if } t + 1 \leq 0, \text{ then } -1 \\ \text{else if } ActNode(t) = -1, \text{ then } NextNode(root, t, -1) \\ \text{else } NextNode(ActNode(t), t, ActNode(t)) \end{cases}$$

So at each time step t, $ActNode(t)$ either indicates a Node that is active or returns -1, which symbolizes the tree returning a value. In $NextNode(n, t, prev)$, n is either -1 or a node, t is an integer indicating the time-step, and $prev$ is either -1 or a node and indicates which node asked for the Next Node. This is used to determine which node should be active next.

$$NextNode(n, t, prev) :=$$

$$\begin{cases} \text{if } n = -1, \text{ then } -1 \\ \text{else if } status(n, t) \neq I, \text{ then } NextNode(parent(n), t, n) \\ \text{else if } IsLeaf(n), \text{ then } n \\ \text{else if } IsSel(n) \wedge prev = parent(n), \\ \quad \text{then } NextNode(Unskipped(FChl(n), t), t, n) \\ \text{else if } IsSel(n), \text{ then } NextNode(rNeigh(prev), t, n) \\ \text{else if } IsSeq(n) \wedge prev = parent(n), \\ \quad \text{then } NextNode(Unskipped(FChl(n), t), t, n) \\ \text{else if } IsSeq(n), \text{ then } NextNode(rNeigh(prev), t, n) \\ \text{else if } IsPar(n) \wedge prev = parent(n), \\ \quad \text{then } NextNode(Unskipped(FChl(n), t), t, n) \\ \text{else if } IsPar(n), \text{ then } NextNode(Unskipped(prev, t), t, n) \\ \text{else if } IsDec(n) \wedge SkipChl(n, t), \text{ then } n \\ \text{else } NextNode(FChl(n), t, n) \end{cases}$$

$parent(Root) = -1$ and otherwise $parent(n)$ returns the parent of n.
$SkipChl(n, t)$ returns True if at time t decorator n does not run it's child.
$IsLeaf(n)$, $IsSel(n)$, $IsSeq(n)$, $IsPar(n)$, and $IsDec(n)$ are all predicates that return True if the node n is of the described type and False otherwise (all return

False if $n = -1$). $FChl(n)$ returns the first child of n, and $rNeigh(n)$ indicates the right neighbor of n.

$$Unskipped(n, t) := \begin{cases} \text{if } Skipped(n, t), \text{ then } Unskipped(rNeigh(n), t) \\ \text{else } n \end{cases}$$

$Unskipped(n, t)$ returns the first right Neighbor of n that is not Skipped (Nodes with Memory can cause their children to be skipped in some cases). If there is no right neighbor, then $rNeigh(n) = -1$.

$$Skipped(n, t) := \begin{cases} \text{if } t \leq 0, \text{ then } \bot \\ \text{else if } \exists a \in Anc(n) \text{ s.t. } status(a, t-1) \in \{S, F\}, \\ \quad \text{then } \bot \\ \text{else if } IsParSynch(parent(n)) \wedge status(n, t-1) = S, \\ \quad \text{then } \top \\ \text{else if } IsSeqWM(parent(n)) \wedge \\ \quad \exists x \geq 1 \text{ s.t. } status(rNeigh(n)^x, t-1) = R, \text{ then } \top \\ \text{else if } IsSelWM(parent(n)) \wedge \\ \quad \exists x \geq 1 \text{ s.t. } status(rNeigh(n)^x, t-1) = R, \text{ then } \top \\ \text{else } Skipped(n, t-1) \end{cases}$$

Here $rNeigh(n)^x := rNeigh(rNeigh(n)^{x-1})$, with $rNeigh(n)^1 := rNeigh(n)$. In other words, $rNeigh(n)^x$ is the xth right neighbor. $Anc(n)$ is the set of nodes that are ancestors to n. This set does not include n or -1. $IsSeqWM(n)$ and $IsSelWM(n)$ check if n is a Sequence/Selector node with memory, respectively.

$$status(n, t) :=$$

$$\begin{cases} \text{if } IsLeaf(n) \wedge ActNode(t) = n, \text{ then } LeafStatus(n, t) \\ \text{else if } IsSel(n) \wedge (\exists c \in Chl(n) \text{ s.t. } status(c, t) \in \{S, R\}), \text{ then } status(c, t) \\ \text{else if } IsSel(n) \wedge status(LChl(n), t) = F, \text{ then } F \\ \text{else if } IsSeq(n) \wedge (\exists c \in Chl(n) \text{ s.t. } status(c, t) \in \{F, R\}), \text{ then } status(c, t) \\ \text{else if } IsSeq(n) \wedge status(LChl(n), t) = S, \text{ then } S \\ \text{else if } IsPar(n) \wedge \\ \quad (\exists c \in Chl(n) \text{ s.t. } (status(c, t) \neq I) \wedge Unskipped(c, t) = -1), \\ \quad \text{then } ParStatus(n, t) \\ \text{else if } IsDec(n) \wedge (ActNode(t) = n \vee status(FChl(n), t) \neq I), \\ \quad \text{then } DecStatus(n, t) \\ \text{else } I \end{cases}$$

$status(n, t)$ describes the status of node n at time step t. $Chl(n)$ is the set of children of n. If both $IsDec(n)$ and $ActNode(t) = n$, then n is a decorator that skipped its child.

$$ParStatus(n,t) := \begin{cases} \text{if } IsFailure(n,t), \text{ then } F \\ \text{else if } NumSucc(n,t) \geq SuccThresh(n), \text{ then } S \\ \text{else } R \end{cases}$$

$$IsFailure(n,t) := \begin{cases} \text{if } \exists a \in Anc(n) \cup \{n\} \text{ s.t. } status(a, t-1) \in \{S, F\}, \\ \quad \text{then } \perp \\ \text{else } IsFailure(n, t-1) \vee \\ \quad \exists c \in Chl(n) \text{ s.t. } status(c, t) = F \end{cases}$$

$$NumSucc(n,t) := \begin{cases} \text{if } \exists a \in Anc(n) \cup \{n\} \text{ s.t. } status(a, t-1) \in \{S, F\}, \\ \quad \text{then } 0 \\ \text{else if } \exists c \in Chl(n) \text{ s.t. } status(n, t) = S, \\ \quad \text{then } NumSucc(n, t-1) + 1 \\ \text{else } NumSucc(n, t) \end{cases}$$

4.2 Total

Unlike the Leaf encoding, in the Total encoding a tick occurs at each time step t and we compute the entire state of the tree in one time step. Consider Fig. 3. By definition, the status of wideSel is S if a child returns S, R if a child returns R, and F if all children return F (a status of I is impossible for the root as the root will always run). The Total encoding uses this sort of definition directly for each node. Thus the status of each child is based on if the child runs and the custom code of the leaf node. As a result, in this case child3 will only run if child2 runs and returns F, and child2 will only run if child1 runs and returns F. This is all directly encoded, though it is done formulaically. The state of the tree is determined by resolving the dependency chain. Formally the encoding is defined as follows:

$$IsActive(n,t) :=$$

$$\begin{cases} \text{if } IsRoot(n), \text{ then } \top \\ \text{else if } \neg IsActive(parent(n), t) \vee Skipped(n, t), \text{ then } \perp \\ \text{else if } n = FChl(parent(n)), \text{ then } \top \\ \text{else if } ResFrom(n, t), \text{ then } \top \\ \text{else if } IsSel(parent(n)), \text{ then } status(lNeigh(n), t) = F \\ \text{else if } IsSeq(parent(n)), \text{ then } status(lNeigh(n), t) = S \\ \text{else if } IsPar(parent(n)), \text{ then } \top \\ \text{else } \perp \end{cases}$$

IsActive(n, t) is True if at time t node n executed. In this encoding multiple nodes can be active at the same time. Notation is reused from the Leaf encoding where applicable. For instance, *IsSel*(n) is defined as before. *lNeigh*(n) functions the same way as *rNeigh*(n), except with the Left Neighbor.

$$Skipped(n, t) := \begin{cases} \text{if } t \leq 0, \text{ then } \perp \\ \text{else if } \exists a \in Anc(n) \text{ s.t. } status(a, t-1) \in \{S, F\}, \\ \quad \text{then } \perp \\ \text{else if } IsParSynch(parent(n)) \wedge status(n, t-1) = S, \\ \quad \text{then } \top \\ \text{else if } IsSeqWM(parent(n)) \wedge \\ \quad \exists x \geq 1 \text{ s.t. } status(rNeigh(n)^x, t-1) = R, \text{ then } \top \\ \text{else if } IsSelWM(parent(n)) \wedge \\ \quad \exists x \geq 1 \text{ s.t. } status(rNeigh(n)^x, t-1) = R, \text{ then } \top \\ \text{else } Skipped(n, t-1) \end{cases}$$

Skipped(n, t) is used to determine if a node with memory caused node n to be skipped at time t.

$$ResFrom(n, t) := IsSeq(parent(n)) \wedge \exists x \geq 1 \text{ s.t. } status(rNeigh(n)^x, t-1) = R$$

Intuitively, *ResFrom*(n, t) tells us if at time t we are supposed to resume from node n or not (only affects certain nodes with memory). As before *status*(n, t) is used to describe the status of a node n at time t.

$$status(n, t) := \begin{cases} \text{if } \neg IsActive(n, t), \text{ then } I \\ \text{else if } IsSel(n), \text{ then } SelStatus(n, t) \\ \text{else if } IsSeq(n), \text{ then } SeqStatus(n, t) \\ \text{else if } IsPar(n), \text{ then } ParStatus(n, t) \\ \text{else if } IsDec(n), \text{ then } DecStatus(n, t) \\ \text{else } LeafStatus(n, t) \end{cases}$$

$$SelStatus(n, t) := \begin{cases} \text{if } \exists c \in Chl(n) \text{ s.t. } status(c, t) \in \{S, R\}, \\ \quad \text{then } status(c, t) \\ \text{else } F \end{cases}$$

$$SeqStatus(n, t) := \begin{cases} \text{if } \exists c \in Chl(n) \text{ s.t. } status(c, t) \in \{F, R\}, \\ \quad \text{then } status(c, t) \\ \text{else } S \end{cases}$$

$$ParStatus(n, t) := \begin{cases} \text{if } \exists c \in Chl(n) \text{ s.t. } status(c, t) = F, \text{ then } F \\ \text{else if } NumSucc(n, t) \geq SuccThresh(n), \text{ then } S \\ \text{else } R \end{cases}$$

$$NumSucc(n, t) := |\{c : c \in Chl(n) \wedge (status(c, t) = S \vee Skipped(c, t))\}|$$

$SuccThresh(n)$ represents the number of nodes that need to return Success for the parallel policy to return S. For the two default policies, Success On One and Success On All, the values would be 1 and $|Chl(n)|$ respectively. Therefore, if a node is a Parallel node and isn't I, then if any of the children returned F the node returns F. Otherwise, it compares against the $SuccThresh(n)$. $NumSucc(n, t)$ is the number of children of n that returned S at time t. Since Leaf Nodes can be customized, it is impossible to fully characterize their behavior, and there are too many Decorator nodes to concisely list here. As such, we have $DecStatus(n, t) \in \{S, F, R\}$ and $LeafStatus(n, t) \in \{S, F, R\}$.

4.3   BTCompiler

The encoding for the BTCompiler, as best we understand it, has been included in [22]. Unfortunately, we were unable to install the tool. However, based on various examples in the BTCompiler repository, we concluded that the file 'bt_classic.smv[2]' contains the relevant encoding. The encoding presented in [22] is meant to approximate this, in the same way that the Leaf and Total encodings approximate the actual encodings used by BehaVerify.

5   Results

We include the results of two main experiments: Checklist and BlueROV. Checklist is a parameterized example that takes as input an integer n and produces a BT that contains n checks which must either succeed or a fallback triggers. For each check we include two LTL specs, one to be proved and one to be disproved. Leaf_v2, Total_v2, Total_v3, and BTC models were used in this experiment, where Leaf_v2 is based on the Leaf encoding, Total_v2 and Total_v3 are based on the Total encoding, and BTC is based on the BTCompiler encoding. The other example is BlueROV, the controller in an ongoing DARPA project. As this example requires blackboard variables which BTCompiler does not support, it is not included, so only the 3 BehaVerify encodings are considered. We include timing results for verifying the LTL spec as well as memory usage. Timing values are based on nuXmv's 'time' command. Maximum Resident Size values are based on nuXmv's usage command, which uses getrusage(2) [6]. Maximum Resident Size is the maximum amount of RAM that is actually used by a process. All tests were run on a computer using Ubuntu 22.04 with 32 gb of ram and an i7-8700K Intel processor. Both the tool and instructions on how to recreate these tests are available[3]. The tests only consider the time to verify LTL specifications in nuXmv. Time spent building the model in nuXmv is not included as it never exceeded .2 s. The time spent converting the BTs to models is not included as it is also fairly negligible, but can be found in [22].

---

[2] https://github.com/CARVE-ROBMOSYS/
BTCompiler/blob/master/smv/bt_classic.smv.

[3] https://github.com/verivital/behaverify.

5.1   Checklist and Parallel-Checklist

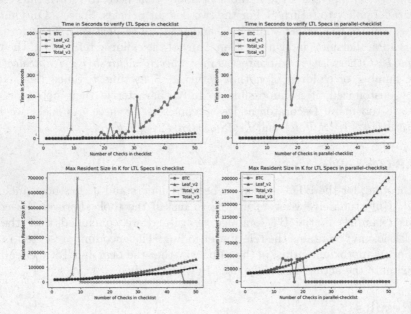

Fig. 4. Timing and memory results for verifying LTL specifications in nuXmv for Checklist and Parallel-Checklist. Timeout is set to 5 min. If a timeout occurred, a value of 350 is used for timing and -1000 for memory. After 3 timeouts, the remaining tests for the version are skipped. BTC is based on BTCompiler, Leaf_v2 is a model based on the Leaf encoding, and Total_v2 and Total_v3 are models based on the Total encoding.

The checklist examples consist of a series of checks that run in order by nested sequence nodes. Each check consists of a selector node, a safety check leaf node that can return S or F, and a backup node that can only return S. Thus if the safety check fails, the selector will run the backup which will return S. This process continues until each check has been run. See [22] for visual examples. Parallel-checklist replaces the sequence nodes with parallel nodes. Each check has two LTL specifications, one True and one False. The True/False specifications require that if a safety check fails, then a backup is triggered/not triggered. Due to differences in encodings, the specifications are slightly different for each version. We include one example here. The remainder can be found in [22].

For Total_v2 and Total_v3:
$$G(safety\_checkX.status = F \implies backupX.status = S);$$
$$G(safety\_checkX.status = F \implies !(backupX.status = S));$$

Checklist Results Discussion. Having re-run the checklist and parallel check-list experiments three times for BTCompiler only, we have found that the spikes are present each time. These results can be found in [22]. The results are extremely similar, so we find it unlikely that this is a fluke. Furthermore, we note that there is a spike at 19 in both the checklist and parallel-checklist experiments. Since nuXmv is using a BDD model to verify the LTL Specifications, we assume that there is some sort of awkward break point with the number of variables that causes the efficiency to greatly suffer at certain points.

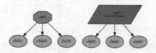

Fig. 5. Two examples with 3 children.

Note that Total_v2 works much better on Parallel-Checklist than on Check-list. This is because of the logic chain created by Selector and Sequence nodes. Consider the Selector Example in Fig. 5. The status of child3 depends on if child3 is active, which depends on the status of child2, which depends on if child2 is active, which depends on the status of child1, which depends on if child1 is active, which depends on if sel0 is active. The chain quickly becomes unmanageable (see [22] for visual examples of the BTs). This is not the case with Parallel-Checklist. Consider the Parallel Example in Fig. 5. The status of child3 depends on if child3 is active, which depends only on par0 and what child3 returned last time. Thus the dependency chain is much shorter and thus Total_v2 performs better on Parallel-Checklist. Total_v3 avoid this by 'guiding' nuXmv through this dependency chain by introducing intermediate variables.

Finally, note that the timing results in Fig. 4 clearly demonstrate that the Total_v3 encoding outperforms the rest.

5.2 BlueROV

We considered three versions of BlueROV: warnings only, small, and full. The differences between these versions is what range of values each blackboard variable is allowed to use. See [22] for an image of the BT. We consider 5 sets of 2 LTL specifications. The timeout for each set of specifications was 10 min. For each warning, the first LTL specification requires that if the warning is set to True, then the appropriate Surface Task is triggered. This specification is False in all cases except battery low warning. The second LTL specification requires that if in a given tick a warning is set, then during that tick a surface task will trigger. This is true for all warnings except the home reached warning.

Table 1. blueROV, time in seconds to compute LTL

Model	LTL Spec	Leaf_v2	Total_v2	Total_v3
Warnings only	Low battery	0.39	4.16	0.12
Warnings only	Emergency stop	0.48	4.21	0.14
Warnings only	Home reached	0.66	–	1.70
Warnings only	Obstacle	0.54	7.79	0.17
Warnings only	Sensor degradation	0.49	4.11	0.13
Small	Low battery	23.43	5.06	0.33
Small	Emergency stop	30.47	6.40	1.02
Small	Home reached	31.48	–	2.58
Small	Obstacle	39.34	9.87	0.39
Small	Sensor degradation	31.73	5.23	0.34
Full	Low battery	79.08	5.54	0.60
Full	Emergency stop	156.20	6.49	1.81
Full	Home reached	107.05	–	3.59
Full	Obstacle	323.00	10.06	1.10
Full	Sensor degradation	106.16	6.57	1.46

For the Leaf_v2 encoding, these look as follows for battery:

$$G(next(battery\_low\_warning) = 1 \wedge active\_node = battery2bb \implies$$
$$(active\_node > -1U(active\_node = surface)));$$
$$G(next(battery\_low\_warning) = 1 \wedge active\_node = battery2bb \implies$$
$$(active\_node > -1U(active\_node \in \{surface, surface1, surface2,$$
$$surface3, surface4\})));$$

For the Total encodings, these look as follows for battery:

$$G(next(battery\_low\_warning) = 1) \wedge battery2bb.active)$$
$$\implies (surface.active));$$
$$G(next(battery\_low\_warning) = 1) \wedge battery2bb.active)$$
$$\implies (surface.active|surface1.active|$$
$$surface2.active|surface3.active|surface4.active));$$

BlueROV Results Discussion. The BlueROV models differ from each other only in the number of values that each blackboard variable can take. Thus based on the results in Table 1, we can see that the Leaf_v2 encoding has the worst scaling of the three with respect to blackboard variable size. Total_v3 improves upon both Total_v2 and Leaf_v2. BTCompiler does not support blackboard variables.

6 Conclusions and Future Work

We introduced BehaVerify, a tool for turning a py_tree into a .smv file for use with nuXmv. We consider several possible encodings for this task and compared them to the encoding that BTCompiler uses. The results indicate that the encoding used by Total_v3 is the best choice.

Future work includes general polish and improvements and expanding support for the various built-in nodes in py_trees. In addition to this, we plan to re-work certain elements of BehaVerify. For instance, currently, in order for BehaVerify to detect blackboard variables in a py_tree using custom leaf nodes, the user must create a field that BehaVerify looks for within the custom node. This could certainly be handled better in the future. In terms of encodings, we plan to focus on Total_v3. An improvement that has been considered, but not yet implemented, would be to restrict the incoming values to the leaf nodes to reduce state space. Specifically, in cases where a leaf node does not run, there is no need to consider the incoming status. Currently, this could be accomplished by tying the incoming value to the active value. However, this would likely cause worse performance for the same reason that Total_v2 performs worse than Total_v3. Therefore, the intended solution would be to, in some sense, enumerate all possible input values, which would hopefully shift some of the burden off of nuXmv and onto BehaVerify.

Acknowledgments. The material presented in this paper is based upon work supported the Defense Advanced Research Projects Agency (DARPA) through contract number FA8750-18-C-0089, the Air Force Office of Scientific Research (AFOSR) award FA9550-22-1-0019, and the National Science Foundation (NSF) through grant number 2028001. Any opinions, findings, and conclusions or recommendations expressed in this publication are those of the authors and do not necessarily reflect the views of DARPA, AFOSR, or NSF.

References

1. Biggar, O., Zamani, M.: A framework for formal verification of behavior trees with linear temporal logic. IEEE Robot. Autom. Lett. **5**(2), 2341–2348 (2020). https://doi.org/10.1109/LRA.2020.2970634
2. Biggar, O., Zamani, M., Shames, I.: On modularity in reactive control architectures, with an application to formal verification (2020). https://doi.org/10.48550/ARXIV.2008.12515, https://arxiv.org/abs/2008.12515
3. Biggar, O., Zamani, M., Shames, I.: A principled analysis of behavior trees and their generalisations (2020). https://doi.org/10.48550/ARXIV.2008.11906, https://arxiv.org/abs/2008.11906
4. Biggar, O., Zamani, M., Shames, I.: An expressiveness hierarchy of behavior trees and related architectures (2021)
5. Broder, D.: Blackboard documentation (2014). https://forums.unrealengine.com/t/blackboard-documentation/1795
6. Cavada, R., et al.: The NUXMV symbolic model checker. In: Biere, A., Bloem, R. (eds.) CAV 2014. LNCS, vol. 8559, pp. 334–342. Springer, Cham (2014). https://doi.org/10.1007/978-3-319-08867-9_22

7. Colledanchise, M., Cicala, G., Domenichelli, D.E., Natale, L., Tacchella, A.: Formalizing the execution context of behavior trees for runtime verification of deliberative policies. In: 2021 IEEE/RSJ International Conference on Intelligent Robots and Systems (IROS). IEEE (2021). https://doi.org/10.1109/iros51168.2021.9636129

8. Colledanchise, M., Cicala, G., Domenichelli, D.E., Natale, L., Tacchella, A.: A toolchain to design, execute, and monitor robots behaviors. CoRR abs/2106.15211 (2021). https://arxiv.org/abs/2106.15211

9. Colledanchise, M., Murray, R.M., Ã-gren, P.: Synthesis of correct-by-construction behavior trees. In: 2017 IEEE/RSJ International Conference on Intelligent Robots and Systems (IROS), pp. 6039–6046 (2017). https://doi.org/10.1109/IROS.2017.8206502

10. Colledanchise, M., Natale, L.: Improving the parallel execution of behavior trees. In: 2018 IEEE/RSJ International Conference on Intelligent Robots and Systems (IROS). IEEE (2018). https://doi.org/10.1109/iros.2018.8593504

11. Colledanchise, M., Natale, L.: Analysis and exploitation of synchronized parallel executions in behavior trees. In: 2019 IEEE/RSJ International Conference on Intelligent Robots and Systems (IROS). IEEE (2019). https://doi.org/10.1109/iros40897.2019.8967812

12. Colledanchise, M., Natale, L.: Handling concurrency in behavior trees. CoRR abs/2110.11813 (2021). https://arxiv.org/abs/2110.11813

13. Colledanchise, M., Natale, L.: On the implementation of behavior trees in robotics. IEEE Robot. Autom. Lett. **6**(3), 5929–5936 (2021). https://doi.org/10.1109/lra.2021.3087442

14. Colledanchise, M., Ã-gren, P.: Behavior Trees in Robotics and AI. CRC Press (2018). https://doi.org/10.1201/9780429489105

15. Crytek: Behavior tree blackboard (2022). https://docs.cryengine.com/display/CEPROG/Behavior+Tree+Blackboard

16. EpicGames: Behavior tree overview (2021). https://docs.unrealengine.com/4.27/en-US/InteractiveExperiences/ArtificialIntelligence/BehaviorTrees/BehaviorTreesOverview/

17. Ghzouli, R., Berger, T., Johnsen, E.B., Dragule, S., Wąsowski, A.: Behavior trees in action: a study of robotics applications. In: Proceedings of the 13th ACM SIGPLAN International Conference on Software Language Engineering. ACM (2020). https://doi.org/10.1145/3426425.3426942

18. Giunchiglia, E., Colledanchise, M., Natale, L., Tacchella, A.: Conditional behavior trees: definition, executability, and applications. In: 2019 IEEE International Conference on Systems, Man and Cybernetics (SMC), pp. 1899–1906 (2019). https://doi.org/10.1109/SMC.2019.8914358

19. Grunske, L., Winter, K., Yatapanage, N.: Defining the abstract syntax of visual languages with advanced graph grammars-a case study based on behavior trees. J. Vis. Lang. Comput. **19**(3), 343–379 (2008). https://doi.org/10.1016/j.jvlc.2007.11.003

20. Ogren, P.: Increasing modularity of UAV control systems using computer game behavior trees (2012). https://doi.org/10.2514/6.2012-4458

21. Safronov, E., Colledanchise, M., Natale, L.: Task planning with belief behavior trees. CoRR abs/2008.09393 (2020). https://arxiv.org/abs/2008.09393

22. Serbinowska, S.S., Johnson, T.: Behaverify: Verifying temporal logic specifications for behavior trees (2022). https://arxiv.org/abs/2208.05360

23. Shoulson, A., Garcia, F.M., Jones, M., Mead, R., Badler, N.I.: Parameterizing behavior trees. In: Allbeck, J.M., Faloutsos, P. (eds.) MIG 2011. LNCS, vol. 7060, pp. 144–155. Springer, Heidelberg (2011). https://doi.org/10.1007/978-3-642-25090-3_13
24. Stonier, D.: PY-trees 2.1.6 module API (2021). https://py-trees.readthedocs.io/en/devel/modules.html
25. Tumova, J., Marzinotto, A., Dimarogonas, D.V., Kragic, D.: Maximally satisfying ltl action planning. In: 2014 IEEE/RSJ International Conference on Intelligent Robots and Systems, pp. 1503–1510 (2014). https://doi.org/10.1109/IROS.2014.6942755
26. Ögren, P.: Convergence analysis of hybrid control systems in the form of backward chained behavior trees. IEEE Robot. Autom. Lett. 5(4), 6073–6080 (2020). https://doi.org/10.1109/LRA.2020.3010747

CHA: Supporting SVA-Like Assertions in Formal Verification of Chisel Programs (Tool Paper)

Shizhen Yu[1,2], Yifan Dong[1,2], Jiuyang Liu[3], Yong Li[1],
Zhilin Wu[1,2(✉)], David N. Jansen[1], and Lijun Zhang[1,2]

[1] State Key Laboratory of Computer Science, Institute of Software, Chinese
Academy of Sciences, Beijing, China
{yusz,liyong,wuzl,dnjansen,zhanglj}@ios.ac.cn, dong-yf18@tsinghua.org.cn
[2] University of Chinese Academy of Sciences, Beijing, China
[3] Huazhong University of Science and Technology, Wuhan, China
jiuyang@hust.edu.cn

Abstract. We present CHA, an assertion language and verification tool
for Chisel programs built on top of ChiselTest, where we extend the Chisel
assertion language with SystemVerilog assertions (SVA)-like temporal
operators. This enables formal verification of Chisel hardware designs
against general temporal properties. The effectiveness of the CHA tool is
validated by two case studies, including an open-source Wishbone protocol adapter design.

Keywords: Chisel · Assertion language · Formal verification

1 Introduction

Working at Register Transfer Level (RTL) is the typical practice in designing
digital systems nowadays. Almost all popular hardware description languages
(HDLs), including Verilog/SystemVerilog [8], create high-level representations of
a digital system at RTL. Recently, Bachrach et al. proposed a new HDL called
Chisel [2], that is embedded in Scala. Chisel features parameterized, modular,
and reusable hardware designs, which greatly enhances the productivity of the
system designers. Since its introduction, Chisel is becoming increasingly popular in RISC-V processor and SoC designs. For instance, the Rocket Chip [1],
BOOM [14], Nutshell [15] and XiangShan [4] are all designed in Chisel.

In contrast to its agility for system designs, the point where Chisel lags
behind other HDLs is its weak support of formal verification, which is vital
to ensure the functional correctness of Chisel designs. Notably, the well-known
SystemVerilog Assertion Language (SVA) provides rich modalities to express and

Supplementary Information The online version contains supplementary material
available at https://doi.org/10.1007/978-3-031-17108-6_20.

to verify general temporal properties, e.g. "Signal p will remain high until signal q becomes low." In contrast, the standard verification tool ChiselTest[1] [10] for Chisel only supports assertions that express simple temporal properties, such as "The value of wire a is equal to the value of wire b in the previous clock cycle".

Contribution. In this work, we fill in this gap and present CHA, a Chisel specification and verification tool, which extends the Chisel assertion language so that SVA-like temporal properties can be specified and verified against Chisel RTL designs. In particular, our tool is easy to use for those who are familiar with SVA, since we follow the constructs of SVA closely to define our specification language.

Related Work. As mentioned above, our work is inspired by SVA; in fact, CHA is built on top of ChiselTest, which only supports simulation and formal verification of Boolean properties and simple temporal properties. Tsai's Master's thesis [13] extends the syntax of the assertion language of ChiselTest and combines it with simulation techniques to verify designs. Nevertheless, CHA is more expressive than the assertions in [13], as we support unbounded sequence repetition; moreover, we target formal verification instead of simulation.

ChiselVerify [5] adapts the Unified Verification Method (UVM) to Chisel, but it focuses on testing, instead of formal verification.

Xiang *et al.* considered also the formal verification of Chisel programs [17]. Nevertheless, CHA uses an approach different from that in [17]: CHA allows us to write the specifications directly in Chisel programs, while Xiang *et al.* first compile Chisel programs down to SystemVerilog programs, then specify the properties in SVA, and finally solve the verification problem by SymbiYosys [16].

The rest of this paper is organized as follows. In Sect. 2, we describe the architecture of CHA. Then in Sect. 3, we describe how CHA can be used to specify and verify hardware RTL designs in Chisel.

2   Tool Data Flow of CHA

In this section, we describe the data flow of CHA (see Fig. 1). The input of CHA consists of a Chisel design and a CHA assertion that states the temporal property the design needs to satisfy.

Our verification procedure works as follows. The Chisel design is first translated to intermediary descriptions in high- and low-level FIRRTL and eventually to a transition system $\mathcal{K}$. Our CHA assertion is wrapped within an **Annotation** metadata container through all levels of FIRRTL descriptions and eventually formalized as a Property Specification Language (PSL) formula φ. We wrap the assertion inside an **Annotation** so that the FIRRTL compiler automatically associates the construct names in FIRRTL intermediates with the original in Chisel, as indicated by the dotted lines between the Annotations and FIRRTL

---

[1] https://github.com/ucb-bar/chiseltest.

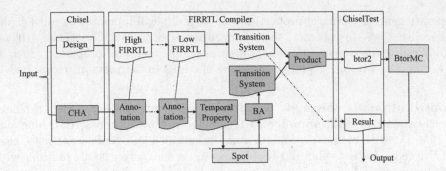

Fig. 1. Detailed data flow of CHA: Upon providing a Design under test and an Assertion, CHA provides the Result ("check passes" or a counterexample trace).—Existing data formats/documents are in white wavy boxes. CHA adds the data in blue wavy boxes and transformations to/from them. Green rectangles show external tools. (Color figure online)

descriptions in Fig. 1. In this way, we can synchronize design and assertion later and easily recover the original Chisel construct names in the witness trace if the assertion is found violated, as indicated by the dotted arrow from the transition system $\mathcal{K}$ to Result in Fig. 1; this helps the designer to locate bugs.

To support the verification of a more powerful assertion language than that of ChiselTest, we adopt automata-theoretic model checking. Once the PSL formula φ of the assertion is ready, the existing tool Spot [6] is used to construct a Büchi automaton (BA) that describes φ being violated at some point. This BA is then translated to a transition system in the same format as the existing translation of the Chisel design under test. The product between the two is stored in btor2 format, which the existing bounded model checker BtorMC [12] uses. If BtorMC finds the product not empty, it stores the trace as a counterexample for easier viewing; an example of such a trace is in Fig. 2.

We now describe the most important steps of this process one by one.

Specifying Properties in CHA. CHA is as expressive as SVA and it supports almost all operators and syntactic sugar in SVA, such as sequence concatenation, sequence repetition, suffix implication and linear temporal logic (LTL) operators. Due to the fact that Chisel and Scala reserve some tokens that are identical to SVA operators, for example "##", we have to use different tokens; the detailed syntax can be downloaded as electronic material from Springer's proceedings webpage or from [18].

Pass Assertion to FIRRTL and Preprocess. FIRRTL is an intermediate representation of Chisel, which is used during compiler optimizations; it can also emit equivalent circuits written in other language (e.g. Verilog).

As described above, we wrap our assertions into Annotation containers of FIRRTL, since the compiler will then maintain the correspondence of the signal and construct names through all transformations.

Generate Transition System from Büchi Automaton. We utilize the external tool Spot [6], which takes as input our given temporal property φ (for example, expressed in PSL syntax) and constructs an ω-automaton that accepts the language of all words that violate φ at some point.

We let Spot output the simplest kind of ω-automaton, namely a Büchi automaton. However, there might be non-deterministic transitions in the automaton (i.e. a state s may have multiple successors upon the same input), while transition systems in FIRRTL need to be deterministic. We make the BA deterministic by using auxiliary input variables to resolve non-deterministic choices. For example, if state s_1 has two successors, say s_2 and s_3, on the same input a, we add a fresh input variable v and let s_1 transition to s_2 on $a \wedge \neg v$ and transition to s_3 on $a \wedge v$. Further, Büchi automata generated by Spot may not be input-enabled, i.e. there may be states that have no successor at all for some inputs. We add a dead state to make the automaton input-enabled.

Transition System Product. At this point, we have obtained two transition systems from design and assertion, and we have to construct the product of the two. Because both transition systems are stored symbolically, we take the design transition system as the backbone and add a state variable *baState*; this variable is initialized and updated according to the transitions of the Büchi automaton.

After constructing the product, we add some auxiliary variables to implement the liveness-to-safety algorithm described in [3].

Model Checking. We reuse the transformation from transition system to the `btor2` file format in ChiselTest. Then, we invoke the hardware model checker BtorMC [12] to verify the property. BtorMC uses bounded model checking (BMC) to verify the property, or to falsify it and find a counterexample. BMC only checks the system up to a given number of steps, and will not find counterexamples that are longer.

ChiselTest computes the trace violating the property based on the witness given by BtorMC and the transition system of design, and we rename the signal names back to their name in Chisel to improve readability. We remark that we can also utilize other model checkers that support `btor2` in this process, such as AVR [7] or Pono [11].

Tool Availability. Our tool CHA is publicly available at https://github.com/iscas-tis/CHA.

3   Case Studies

To demonstrate the effectiveness of CHA, we apply it to two Chisel designs: a simple GCD module and a Wishbone protocol adapter design. The two designs are linked from the above github repository, file `README.md`.

3.1   GCD Module with 4-Bits Inputs

As a proof of concept, we consider a Chisel module that implements the Euclidean algorithm to compute the GCD of two input operands x and y. Besides

Fig. 2. The witness of the property violation (We omit some cycles in the middle.

the result output, we also have an output signal *busy*. When *busy* is low, the module will load the values of the two operands. Then in every cycle, the larger number out of x and y will be reduced by the smaller one until one of them becomes zero. Signal *busy* will stay high during the GCD computation process so to refute possible other input operands, and it will become low one cycle after the computation is completed, as shown in Fig. 2. Thus, we can measure how many cycles the calculation of the GCD takes by counting the number of cycles when *busy* is high. Assume that we want to check whether the program needs at most 15 cycles to compute the GCD. We can formalize this property as:

$$\texttt{ap}(busy) \mathbin{|->} \texttt{\#\#\#}(1,15)\ \texttt{ap}(!busy).$$

Here |-> designates implication: if its left formula ap(*busy*) holds, the right one should hold as well; the operator ### designates a delay of the specified minimum and maximum number of cycles. Therefore, this assertion means that every time the atomic proposition *busy* is high, it must become low again within 1–15 cycles. When we ask CHA to verify this assertion, it concludes that the property can be violated and provides a witness, as shown in Fig. 2.

From this figure, we can see that cycle #0 is an initialization cycle and signal *busy* is initialized to low in cycle #1, indicating the two operands x and y have been successfully loaded. The counterexample operands x and y CHA provides are 1 and 15, respectively, corresponding to the value 1 and F occurring in cycle #2. We can see that in cycle #17, x becomes 0, indicating the termination of the computation. Thus *busy* becomes low in the cycle after that, i.e., cycle #18. It follows that the computation starts in cycle #2 and terminates in cycle #17, yielding in total 16 cycles, so our property is violated.

In fact, we can observe that the GCD module needs at most 16 cycles for operands with 4 bits. If we increase the allowed delay to 1–16 cycles, CHA will not find a counterexample. Since the property is bounded, any counterexample must be of bounded length, and we conclude that the following property holds:

$$\texttt{ap}(busy) \mathbin{|->} \texttt{\#\#\#}(1,16)\ \texttt{ap}(!busy)$$

3.2   Wishbone Interface

The Wishbone protocol provides a standard way of data transfer between different IP cores (predesigned parts of hardware circuits). Basically, in a Wishbone protocol as depicted in Fig. 3, there exists a *host* adapter and a *device* adapter.

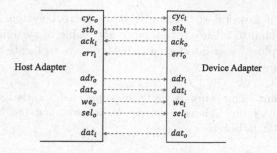

Fig. 3. Interfaces for host adapter and device adapter

The protocol works as follows: the host adapter first sets cyc to announce it wants to use the bus. After that, it sends the address $addr$ and (for writes) the data $data$; we indicates whether it is a write or read operation. Then the host adapter asserts the signal stb. When the device adapter receives the data, it sets ack to high, otherwise it sets err to high. When the host adapter receives this status, the communication is completed and stb will be negated.

We now apply CHA to verify the Chisel implementation of the Wishbone protocol adapter; we modified it based on [9]. We wish to check whether in the program, stb will always stay high before the host adapter receives ack or err from the device adapter, which is formalized as below. (Outputs of the host adapter are annotated with the subscript $_o$ and inputs with $_i$.)

$$\mathrm{ap}(stb_o) \mathrel{|{\rightarrow}} \mathrel{|{-}} \mathrm{ap}(stb_o) \ \mathrm{U} \ \mathrm{ap}(ack_i \| err_i) \mathrel{-|} \ || \ \mathrm{G} \ \mathrm{ap}(stb_o). \tag{1}$$

Since symbols "(" and ")" are reserved in Scala, we use "|–" and "–|" instead here to give priority to the U-operator over |–>. Using CHA to verify the property, we can find it is satisfied within 150 cycles.

ChiselTest has a `past` operator that can also express temporal properties but with an observation range in a fixed number of cycles. For example, if we take three cycles as observation range, the most similar assertion that could be written without CHA would be:

$$(! \, \mathrm{past}\,(stb_o, 2) \ || \ \mathrm{past}(ack_i \ || \ err_i, 2) \ || \ \mathrm{past}(ack_i \ || \ err_i) \ ||$$
$$\mathrm{past}\,(stb_o) \ \&\& \ (ack_i \ || \ err_i) \ || \ \mathrm{past}(stb_o) \ \&\& \ stb_o) \ \&\&$$
$$(! \, \mathrm{past}\,(stb_o) \ || \ \mathrm{past}(ack_i \ || \ err_i) \ || \ (ack_i \ || \ err_i, 2) \ || \ stb_o)$$

This formula cannot catch the full meaning of our formula (1), as Wishbone allows an unspecified number of wait states if one party needs more time to respond. Verification of unbounded behaviors of a Chisel RTL design is needed not only for Wishbone, but in many other instances.

4   Conclusion and Future Work

We have presented CHA, an SVA-like assertion language and a formal verification tool for Chisel. By applying CHA to two Chisel programs, we are convinced that our tool provides a useful step towards more correct system designs. As for future work, we plan to make our tool more accessible to system designers, such as providing graphical user interface and better ways to locate the errors found in the Chisel designs.

Acknowledgement. This work is partially supported by the Strategic Priority Research Program of the Chinese Academy of Sciences and the NSFC grants No. 61872340, 61836005, 62102407.

References

1. Asanović, K., Avizienis, R., Bachrach, J., et al.: The rocket chip generator. Technical report UCB/EECS-2016-17, EECS Department, UC Berkeley (2016). http://www2.eecs.berkeley.edu/Pubs/TechRpts/2016/EECS-2016-17.html
2. Bachrach, J., Vo, H., Richards, B., et al.: Chisel: constructing hardware in a Scala embedded language. In: DAC, pp. 1212–1221. ACM (2012). https://doi.org/10.1145/2228360.2228584
3. Biere, A., Artho, C., Schuppan, V.: Liveness checking as safety checking. Electr. Notes Theor. Comput. Sci. **66**(2), 160–177 (2002). https://doi.org/10.1016/S1571-0661(04)80410-9
4. Chinese Academy of Sciences, Institute of Computing Technology: Xiangshan CPU (2022). https://github.com/OpenXiangShan/XiangShan
5. Dobis, A., et al.: ChiselVerify: an open-source hardware verification library for chisel and scala. In: NorCAS, pp. 1–7. IEEE (2021). https://doi.org/10.1109/NorCAS53631.2021.9599869
6. Duret-Lutz, A., Lewkowicz, A., Fauchille, A., Michaud, T., Renault, É., Xu, L.: Spot 2.0 — a framework for LTL and ω-automata manipulation. In: Artho, C., Legay, A., Peled, D. (eds.) ATVA 2016. LNCS, vol. 9938, pp. 122–129. Springer, Cham (2016). https://doi.org/10.1007/978-3-319-46520-3_8
7. Goel, A., Sakallah, K.: AVR: abstractly verifying reachability. In: TACAS 2020. LNCS, vol. 12078, pp. 413–422. Springer, Cham (2020). https://doi.org/10.1007/978-3-030-45190-5_23
8. IEEE standard for SystemVerilog: unified hardware design, specification, and verification language, pp. 1800–2017. IEEE (2018). https://doi.org/10.1109/IEEESTD.2018.8299595
9. Khan, M.H., Kashif, S.: Caravan (2021). https://github.com/merledu/caravan
10. Laeufer, K., Bachrach, J., Sen, K.: Open-source formal verification for Chisel. In: WOSET (2021). https://woset-workshop.github.io/WOSET2021.html
11. Mann, M., et al.: Pono: a flexible and extensible SMT-based model checker. In: Silva, A., Leino, K.R.M. (eds.) CAV 2021. LNCS, vol. 12760, pp. 461–474. Springer, Cham (2021). https://doi.org/10.1007/978-3-030-81688-9_22
12. Niemetz, A., Preiner, M., Wolf, C., Biere, A.: Btor2, BtorMC and Boolector 3.0. In: Chockler, H., Weissenbacher, G. (eds.) CAV 2018. LNCS, vol. 10981, pp. 587–595. Springer, Cham (2018). https://doi.org/10.1007/978-3-319-96145-3_32
13. Tsai, Y.C.A.: Dynamic verification library for chisel. Master's thesis, University of California, Berkeley (2021). http://www2.eecs.berkeley.edu/Pubs/TechRpts/2021/EECS-2021-132.html, Technical report UCB/EECS-2021-132
14. University of California, Berkeley: BOOM: the Berkeley out-of-order RISC-V processor (2020). https://github.com/riscv-boom

15. University of Chinese Academy of Sciences: NutShell (2021). https://github.com/OSCPU/NutShell
16. Wolf, C., Harder, J., Engelhardt, N., et al.: SymbiYosys: front-end for Yosys-based formal verification flows (2022). https://github.com/YosysHQ/sby
17. Xiang, M., Li, Y., Tan, S., Zhao, Y., Chi, Y.: Parameterized design and formal verification of multi-ported memory. In: ICECCS, pp. 33–41. IEEE (2022). https://doi.org/10.1109/ICECCS54210.2022.00013
18. Yu, S., Dong, Y., et al.: CHA: Supporting SVA-like assertions in formal verification of Chisel programs (2022). https://github.com/iscas-tis/CHA

Runtime Methods

Runtime Verification with Imperfect Information Through Indistinguishability Relations

Angelo Ferrando[1][(✉)] and Vadim Malvone[2]

[1] Department of Informatics, Bioengineering, Robotics and Systems Engineering,
University of Genova, Genova, Italy
`angelo.ferrando@unige.it`
[2] LTCI, Telecom Paris, Institut Polytechnique de Paris, Palaiseau, France
`vadim.malvone@telecom-paris.fr`

Abstract. Software systems are hard to trust, especially when autonomous. To overcome this, formal verification techniques can be deployed to verify such systems behave as expected. Runtime Verification is one of the most prominent and lightweight approaches to verify the system behaviour at execution time. However, standard Runtime Verification is built on the assumption of perfect information over the system, that is, the monitor checking the system can perceive everything. Unfortunately, this is not always the case, especially when the system under analysis contains rational/autonomous components and is deployed in real-world environments with possibly faulty sensors. In this work, we present an extension of the standard Runtime Verification of Linear Temporal Logic properties to consider scenarios with imperfect information. We present the engineering steps necessary to update the verification pipeline, and we report the corresponding implementation when applied to a case study involving robotic systems.

Keywords: Runtime Verification · Autonomous Systems · Imperfect Information

1 Introduction

Developing quality software is a very demanding task [13]. Many are the reasons, but the complexity and presence of autonomous behaviours are definitely amongst them. Techniques that were developed to approach the development of monolithic systems may not work as well for distributed and autonomous ones. This does not only represent a technological issue, but an engineering one as well. In the past decades, we all have been witnesses of technological advances in the software engineering research area, especially when focused on the actual software development. However, the need of re-engineering does not only concern software development, but its verification as well. As software changes, so the ways to verify it need to change. Runtime Verification (RV), as other verification techniques, is not free from such changes.

B.-H. Schlingloff and M. Chai (Eds.): SEFM 2022, LNCS 13550, pp. 335–351, 2022.
https://doi.org/10.1007/978-3-031-17108-6_21

Runtime Verification [1,12] is a formal verification technique that allows the verification of the runtime behaviour of a software/hardware system of interest. Differently from other verification techniques, RV is not exhaustive, since it focuses on the actual system execution. That is, a violation of the expected behaviour is concluded only if such violation is observed in the execution trace. Nevertheless, RV is a lightweight technique, because it does not check all possible system's behaviours, and by doing this, it scales better than its static verification counterparts (which usually suffer from the state space explosion problem).

RV was born after static verification, such as model checking [7], and it inherited much from the latter; especially on how to specify the formal properties to verify. One of the most used formalisms in model checking, and by consequence in RV, is Linear Temporal Logic (LTL) [14]. We will present its syntax and semantics along the paper, but for now, we only focus on the aspect of LTL on which this work is mainly focused on, that is its implicit assumption of perfect information over the system. Indeed, LTL verification is usually performed assuming the system under analysis offers all the information needed for the verification [5]. This is translated at the verification level into the generation of atomic propositions that denote what we know about the system, and are used to verify the properties of interest. However, this is not always the case. Especially when the system to verify contains autonomous, or distributed, or even faulty components (like faulty sensors in real-world environments, e.g. any robotics scenario). In such cases, to assume all the needed information is available is too optimistic. Naturally, as we will better elaborate in related work section, other works on handling LTL RV with imperfect information exist [2,3,10,11,16]. Nevertheless, this is the first work that tackles the problem at its foundations, and without the need of creating a new verification pipeline (which in this case consists on how to synthesise the monitor to verify the LTL property). Specifically, this is the first attempt of extending the standard monitor's synthesis pipeline to explicitly take into consideration imperfect information.

In this paper, we formally define the notion of imperfect information w.r.t. the monitor's visibility over the system, and we then re-engineer the LTL monitor's synthesis pipeline to recognise such visibility information. We also present the details on the prototype that has been implemented to support our claims, and to provide the community an LTL monitoring library that natively supports imperfect information. Moreover, we show some possible uses of such prototype in a realistic case study.

The paper's structure is as follows. Section 2 reports preliminaries notions that are necessary to fully understand the paper contribution. Section 3 formally presents the notion of imperfect information, its implication at the monitoring level and the resulting re-engineering of the standard LTL monitor's synthesis pipeline. Section 4 reports the details on the prototype that has been developed as a result of the re-engineering process, along with some experiments of its use in a realistic case study. Section 5 positions the paper against the state of the art. Section 6 concludes the paper and discusses some possible future directions.

2 Preliminaries

A system S has an *alphabet* Σ with which it is possible to define the set 2^Σ of all its events. Given an alphabet Σ, a *trace* $\sigma = ev_0 ev_1 \ldots$, is a sequence of events in 2^Σ. With $\sigma(i)$ we denote the i-th element of σ (*i.e.*, ev_i), σ^i the suffix of σ starting from i (*i.e.*, $ev_i ev_{i+1} \ldots$), $(2^\Sigma)^*$ the *set of all possible finite traces* over Σ, and $(2^\Sigma)^\omega$ the *set of all possible infinite traces* over Σ.

The standard formalism to specify properties in RV is Linear Temporal Logic (LTL [14]). The relevant parts of the syntax of LTL are the following:

$$\varphi := p \mid \neg\varphi \mid (\varphi \vee \varphi) \mid \bigcirc\varphi \mid (\varphi \ \mathbf{U} \ \varphi)$$

where $p \in \Sigma$ is an atomic proposition, φ is a formula, $\bigcirc$ stands for *next-time*, and $\mathbf{U}$ stands for *until*. In the rest of the paper, we also use the standard derived operators, such as $(\varphi \rightarrow \varphi')$ instead of $(\neg\varphi \vee \varphi')$, $\varphi \ R \ \varphi'$ instead of $\neg(\neg\varphi \ \mathbf{U} \ \neg\varphi')$, $\Box\varphi$ (*always* φ) instead of (*false* $R \ \varphi$), and $\Diamond\varphi$ (*eventually* φ) instead of (*true* $\mathbf{U} \ \varphi$).

Let $\sigma \in (2^\Sigma)^\omega$ be an infinite sequence of events over Σ, the semantics of LTL is as follows:

$$\sigma \models p \text{ if } p \in \sigma(0)$$
$$\sigma \models \neg\varphi \text{ if } \sigma \not\models \varphi$$
$$\sigma \models \varphi \vee \varphi' \text{ if } \sigma \models \varphi \text{ or } \sigma \models \varphi'$$
$$\sigma \models \bigcirc\varphi \text{ if } \sigma^1 \models \varphi$$
$$\sigma \models \varphi \ \mathbf{U} \ \varphi' \text{ if } \exists_{i \geq 0}.\sigma^i \models \varphi' \text{ and } \forall_{0 \leq j < i}.\sigma^j \models \varphi$$

A trace σ satisfies an atomic proposition p, if p belongs to $\sigma(0)$; which means, p holds in the initial event of the trace σ. A trace σ satisfies the negation of the LTL property φ, if σ does not satisfy φ. A trace σ satisfies the disjunction of two LTL properties, if σ satisfies at least one of them. A trace σ satisfies next-time φ, if the suffix of σ starting in the next step (σ^1) satisfies φ. Finally, a trace σ satisfies $\varphi \ \mathbf{U} \ \varphi'$, if there exists a suffix of σ s.t. φ' is satisfied, and for all suffixes before it, φ holds. Thus, given an LTL property φ, we denote $[\![\varphi]\!]$ the language of the property, *i.e.*, the set of traces which satisfy φ; namely $[\![\varphi]\!] = \{\sigma \mid \sigma \models \varphi\}$.

In Definition 1, we present a general and formalism-agnostic definition of a monitor. Informally, a monitor is a function that, given a trace of events in input, returns a verdict which denotes the satisfaction (resp., violation) of a formal property over the trace.

Definition 1 (Monitor). *Let S be a system with alphabet Σ, σ a finite trace, and φ be an LTL property. Then, a monitor for φ is a function $Mon_\varphi : (2^\Sigma)^* \rightarrow \mathbb{B}_3$, where $\mathbb{B}_3 = \{\top, \bot, ?\}$:*

$$Mon_\varphi(\sigma) = \begin{cases} \top & \forall_{u \in (2^\Sigma)^\omega}.\sigma \bullet u \in [\![\varphi]\!] \\ \bot & \forall_{u \in (2^\Sigma)^\omega}.\sigma \bullet u \notin [\![\varphi]\!] \\ ? & otherwise \end{cases}$$

where $\bullet$ is the standard trace concatenation operator.

Intuitively, a monitor returns $\top$ if all continuations (u) of σ satisfy φ; $\bot$ if all possible continuations of σ violate φ; ? otherwise. The first two outcomes are standard representations of satisfaction and violation, while the third is specific to RV. In more detail, it denotes when the monitor cannot conclude any verdict yet. This is closely related to the fact that RV is applied while the system is still running, and future events may still change the verdict. For instance, a property might be currently satisfied (resp., violated) by the system, but violated (resp., satisfied) in the (still unknown) future. The monitor can only safely conclude any of the two final verdicts ($\top$ or $\bot$) if it is sure such verdict will never change. The addition of the third outcome symbol ? helps the monitor to represent its position of uncertainty w.r.t. the current system execution.

A monitor function is usually implemented as a Finite State Machine (FSM), specifically a Moore machine (FSM where the output value of a state is only determined by the state) [4,5]. A Moore machine can be defined as a tuple $\langle Q, q_0, \Sigma, O, \delta, \gamma \rangle$, where Q is a finite set of states, q_0 is the initial state, Σ is the input alphabet, O is the output alphabet, $\delta : Q \times \Sigma \to Q$ is the transition function mapping a state and an event to the next state, and $\gamma : Q \to O$ is the function mapping a state to the output alphabet.

In [5], Bauer *et al.*. present the sequence of steps required to generate from an LTL formula φ the corresponding Moore machine instantiating the Mon_φ function (as summarised in Fig. 1).

Input   (i)Formula   (ii)NBA   (iii)Emptiness per state   (iv)NFA   (v)DFA   (vi)FSM

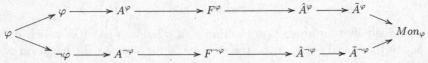

Fig. 1. Steps required to generate an FSM from an LTL formula φ. NBA is Non-deterministic Büchi Automaton, NFA is Non-deterministic Finite Automaton, and DFA is Deterministic Finite Automaton.

Given an LTL property φ, a series of transformations is performed on φ, and its negation $\neg\varphi$. Considering φ in step *(i)*, first, a corresponding NBA A^φ is generated in step *(ii)*. This can be obtained using Gerth *et al.*.'s algorithm [9]. Such automaton recognises the set of infinite traces that satisfy φ (according to LTL semantics). Then, each state of A^φ is evaluated; the states that when selected as initial states in A^φ do not generate the empty language are then added to the F^φ set in step *(iii)*. With such a set, an NFA $\hat{A}^\varphi$ is obtained from A^φ by simply substituting the final states of A^φ with F^φ in step *(iv)*. $\hat{A}^\varphi$ recognises the finite traces (prefixes) that have at least one infinite continuation satisfying φ (since the prefix reaches a state in F^φ). After that, $\hat{A}^\varphi$ is transformed (Rabin-Scott powerset construction [15]) into its equivalent deterministic version $\tilde{A}^\varphi$ in step *(v)*; this is possible since deterministic and non-deterministic finite automata have the same expressive power. The exact same steps are performed on $\neg\varphi$, which bring to the generation of the $\tilde{A}^{\neg\varphi}$ counterpart. The difference between $\tilde{A}^\varphi$ and $\tilde{A}^{\neg\varphi}$ is that the former recognises finite traces which have continuations satisfying φ, while the latter recognises finite traces which have continuations violating φ. Finally, a Moore machine can be generated as a standard automata product between $\tilde{A}^\varphi$ and $\tilde{A}^{\neg\varphi}$ in the final step *(vi)*, where the states are denoted as tuples (q, q'), with q and q' belonging to $\tilde{A}^\varphi$ and $\tilde{A}^{\neg\varphi}$, respectively. The outputs are then determined as: $\top$ if q' does not belong to the final states of $\tilde{A}^{\neg\varphi}$, $\bot$ if q does not belong to the final states of $\tilde{A}^\varphi$, and ? otherwise. This brings us to the revised monitor construction as follows.

Definition 2 (Monitor as FSM). *Given an LTL formula φ and a finite trace σ, the revised monitor is defined as follows:*

$$Mon_\varphi(\sigma) = \begin{cases} \top & \sigma \notin \mathcal{L}(\tilde{A}^{\neg\varphi}) \\ \bot & \sigma \notin \mathcal{L}(\tilde{A}^\varphi) \\ ? & \sigma \in \mathcal{L}(\tilde{A}^\varphi) \wedge \sigma \in \mathcal{L}(\tilde{A}^{\neg\varphi}) \end{cases}$$

where $\mathcal{L}(A)$ denotes the language recognised by automaton A.

3   Runtime Verification with Imperfect Information

Up to now, we have focused on standard RV of LTL properties. However, such standard approach, as presented in Sect. 2, is based upon a strong assumption:

The absence of an atomic proposition is the same as the negation of the latter.

This might be true when we apply formal verification to systems with perfect information (*i.e.*, systems where each involved component has a perfect understanding and vision of the entire system). Unfortunately, even though this may be the case for monolithic and traditional systems, it is not the case for autonomous systems, or in general, systems exploiting artificial intelligence. In such scenarios, it is very common to not have a complete vision over the system. Let us just think about robotics scenarios, where a robot can be deployed in an environment of which it can only access what its sensors provide. Such information can be incomplete. Moreover, since RV is based upon the notion of monitoring the system under analysis; if the verified component has no complete access over the system's information, by consequence, also the monitor does not. Thus, we may find ourselves in scenarios where our runtime monitors observe only partial information of the system. Because of this, the trace of events passed to the monitor to analyse may not contain some of the atomic propositions, and this would be erroneously classified as the negation of such atomic propositions. Instead, we need to give importance to the difference between knowing when something is not true, w.r.t knowing when something is simply not known.

3.1   How Can We Formally Represent the Imperfect Information?

As recognised previously in the paper, the problem of using LTL when the system has imperfect information is in confusing the absence of an atomic proposition, with its negation. Since in case of imperfect information, the trace may not contain atomic propositions which are not known (*i.e.*, cannot be observed), we need a way to characterise such absence of information, explicitly. To do this, we follow an approach similar to [6], where atomic propositions are duplicated.

One possible way to represent imperfect information is by allowing indistinguishability on atomic propositions Σ. To do this we introduce an equivalence relation $\sim$ over Σ. Intuitively, given two atomic propositions $p, q \in \Sigma$, we say that they are indistinguishable if and only if $p \sim q$. The relation $\sim$ gives us the information available to the monitor. Moreover, given an equivalence relation $\sim$ we define a witness for each equivalence class. That is, given an equivalence class γ, we define the witness of γ with the symbol $[\gamma]$.

To handle the verification process in the imperfect information context, we need to do some extensions. First of all, we can not simply use the set of atomic propositions Σ. In particular, we need to replace Σ with a new set $\bar{\Sigma}$ that is defined as follows: for each $p \in \Sigma$ we have $p_\top \in \bar{\Sigma}$ and $p_\bot \in \bar{\Sigma}$. That is, we duplicate the set of atomic proposition to make the truth value explicit.

Without losing generality, we only consider LTL formulas in Negation Normal Form (NNF). An LTL in NNF has only negations at the atom levels (*i.e.*, we only have $\neg p$). Given an LTL formula, its NNF can be easily obtained by propagating all negations to the atoms. For instance, if we had $\neg \bigcirc p$, we would rewrite it as $\bigcirc \neg p$. The same goes for the other operators.

First, we present how to generate the explicit version of an LTL formula.

Definition 3. *Given an LTL formula φ in NNF and the set of equivalence classes Γ, we define the explicit version of φ as follows:*

$$\epsilon(p) = [\gamma]_\top$$
$$\epsilon(\neg p) = [\gamma]_\bot$$
$$\epsilon(\varphi \vee \varphi') = \epsilon(\varphi) \vee \epsilon(\varphi')$$
$$\epsilon(\bigcirc \varphi) = \bigcirc \epsilon(\varphi)$$
$$\epsilon(\varphi \, \mathbf{U} \, \varphi') = \epsilon(\varphi) \, \mathbf{U} \, \epsilon(\varphi')$$

where $\gamma \in \Gamma$ and $p \in \gamma$.

We now present how to construct the explicit and visible versions of a trace.

Definition 4. *Given a trace σ and a set Σ, we define the explicit version of σ as σ_e, for each element $\sigma(i)$ as follows:*

- *for all $p \in \sigma(i)$, $p_\top \in \sigma_e(i)$;*
- *for all $p \in \Sigma \setminus \sigma(i)$, $p_\bot \in \sigma_e(i)$.*

Definition 5. *Given an explicit trace σ_e and the set of equivalence classes Γ, we define the visible version of σ_e as σ_v, for each $\sigma(i)$ and $\gamma \in \Gamma$ as follows:*

- *$[\gamma]_\top \in \sigma_v(i)$ if and only if for all $p \in \gamma$, $p_\top \in \sigma_e(i)$;*
- *$[\gamma]_\bot \in \sigma_v(i)$ if and only if for all $p \in \gamma$, $p_\bot \in \sigma_e(i)$.*

Given the above elements, we define a three-valued semantics for LTL:

$$(\sigma \models p) = \top \text{ if } p_\top \in \sigma(0)$$
$$(\sigma \models p) = \bot \text{ if } p_\bot \in \sigma(0)$$
$$(\sigma \models \neg\varphi) = \top \text{ if } (\sigma \not\models \varphi) = \top$$
$$(\sigma \models \neg\varphi) = \bot \text{ if } (\sigma \not\models \varphi) = \bot$$
$$(\sigma \models \varphi \vee \varphi') = \top \text{ if } (\sigma \models \varphi) = \top \text{ or } (\sigma \models \varphi') = \top$$
$$(\sigma \models \varphi \vee \varphi') = \bot \text{ if } (\sigma \models \varphi) = \bot \text{ and } (\sigma \models \varphi') = \bot$$
$$(\sigma \models \bigcirc\varphi) = \top \text{ if } (\sigma^1 \models \varphi) = \top$$
$$(\sigma \models \bigcirc\varphi) = \bot \text{ if } (\sigma^1 \models \varphi) = \bot$$
$$(\sigma \models \varphi \mathbf{U} \varphi') = \top \text{ if } \exists_{i \geq 0}.(\sigma^i \models \varphi') = \top \text{ and } \forall_{0 \leq j < i}.(\sigma^j \models \varphi) = \top$$
$$(\sigma \models \varphi \mathbf{U} \varphi') = \bot \text{ if } \forall_{i \geq 0}.(\sigma^i \models \varphi') = \bot \text{ or } \exists_{0 \leq j < i}.(\sigma^j \models \varphi) = \bot$$

In all the other cases the truth value is undefined (uu).

To help the reader, we conclude the section with the following example.

Example 1. Consider the set $\Sigma = \{p, q, r\}$, the formula $\phi = \bigcirc r$, and a trace σ where $\sigma(1) = \{p, q\}$. Furthermore, assume $p \sim r$, this means that the monitor cannot distinguish between the atomic propositions p and r. In the context of imperfect information, we have $\tilde{\Sigma} = \{p_\top, q_\top, r_\top, p_\bot, q_\bot, r_\bot\}$. By Definition 3, we have the explicit LTL version $\epsilon(\phi) = \bigcirc[\gamma_\top]$, where $\gamma = \{p, r\}$ is the equivalence class defined over $\sim$. By Definition 4–5, we generate the explicit trace σ_e where $\sigma_e(1) = \{p_\top, q_\top, r_\bot\}$ and visible trace σ_v where $\sigma_v(1) = \{q_\top\}$. Thus, given the three-valued LTL semantics, $\epsilon(\phi)$ is undefined. Indeed, to satisfy (resp., falsify) the original formula φ, the monitor has to check that both $p_\top$ and $r_\top$ (resp., $p_\bot$ and $r_\bot$) are verified since they belong to the same equivalence class γ.

3.2   Re-engineering Monitor with Imperfect Information

Given an LTL formula and a visible trace for the monitor, we need a way to use them to perform RV. This can be obtained by extending the standard pipeline for generating LTL monitors (see Fig. 1). Such extension is based on two specific modifications: (i) we use the explicit version of the LTL formula, following Definition 3; (ii) we modify the product between $\tilde{A}^\varphi$ and $\tilde{A}^{\neg\varphi}$ to generate the Moore machine denoting the monitor. The resulting extension is reported in Fig. 2, where the explicit version of the LTL formula is generated in step (ii). While the updated product between the automata is obtained in step (vii). The rest of the steps are left unchanged w.r.t. Fig. 1.

The pipeline presented in Fig. 2 is identical to the one presented in Fig. 1, but the atomic propositions in the formula are duplicated before using the formula to generate the corresponding NBA, and an additional automaton has been added. The former aspect is important, because by duplicating the atomic propositions, we completely change the semantics of the following steps in the monitor synthesis pipeline. Specifically, it is not true that for any given visible trace σ_v, we have $\sigma_v \notin \mathcal{L}(\hat{A}^{\varphi}) \Rightarrow \sigma_v \in \mathcal{L}(\hat{A}^{\neg\varphi})$, nor $\sigma_v \notin \mathcal{L}(\hat{A}^{\neg\varphi}) \Rightarrow \sigma_v \in \mathcal{L}(\hat{A}^{\varphi})$. Which means, it is not true that when a visible trace of events σ_v is not a good prefix for φ (*i.e.*, a prefix that can be extended to an infinite trace satisfying φ), it has to be then a bad prefix for φ (*i.e.*, a prefix that cannot be extended to an infinite trace satisfying φ). This aspect is closely related to the reason why a third formula (*i.e.*, $\otimes\varphi$) has been introduced in Fig. 2. Since by duplicating the atomic propositions in the formula we break the duality between φ and $\neg\varphi$, we need a third automaton (*i.e.*, $\tilde{A}^{\otimes\varphi}$) to recognise all the traces that do not satisfy, nor violate, φ. For this reason, we extended the pipeline by adding $\otimes\varphi$, which is an abbreviation for $\neg\epsilon(\varphi) \wedge \neg\epsilon(\neg\varphi)$. The automaton $\tilde{A}^{\otimes\varphi}$, obtained following the same steps as for the positive $\hat{A}^{\epsilon(\varphi)}$ and negative $\tilde{A}^{\epsilon(\neg\varphi)}$ automata, recognises all prefixes for which no continuation satisfying or violating φ exist.

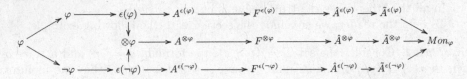

Fig. 2. Extended pipeline to consider imperfect information.

Now, we formalize the above reasoning with the following lemma.

Lemma 1. *Given a visible finite trace σ_v and an LTL formula φ, we have:*

$$\sigma_v \notin \mathcal{L}(\hat{A}^{\epsilon(\varphi)}) \nRightarrow \sigma_v \in \mathcal{L}(\hat{A}^{\epsilon(\neg\varphi)})$$
$$\sigma_v \notin \mathcal{L}(\hat{A}^{\epsilon(\neg\varphi)}) \nRightarrow \sigma_v \in \mathcal{L}(\hat{A}^{\epsilon(\varphi)})$$

Proof. Assume we have a visible trace σ_v and it is not included in the NFA $\hat{A}^{\epsilon(\varphi)}$. To prove our result, we just need to show that σ_v is also not included in $\hat{A}^{\epsilon(\neg\varphi)}$. To do the latter, suppose $\Sigma = \{p, q, r\}$, $\varphi = \bigcirc p$, $p \sim q$, and σ where $\sigma(1) = \{p\}$. Now, given Definition 4–5, we can conclude that $\sigma_v(1) = \{r_\perp\}$. So, σ_v does not satisfy φ and by consequence it is not included in the NFA $\hat{A}^{\epsilon(\varphi)}$. However, it is not included neither in $\hat{A}^{\epsilon(\neg\varphi)}$. This is because $p_\top$ and $p_\perp$ are not included in $\sigma_v(1)$. This concludes the first relation. For the second one, we can use a variant of the above reasoning.

By adding the third automaton, the corresponding FSM synthesis needs also to change. In more detail, the revised version is reported in Definition 6. In such definition, we can see how the addition of a third automaton in the equation allows us to synthesise a finer monitor, in the sense of the number of possible outcomes it returns. Indeed, w.r.t. Definition 2, we have three additional outcomes. Specifically, given a visible trace σ_v, the monitor returns $\top$ if there is no continuation of σ_v which either violates $\epsilon(\varphi)$ or makes it undefined. On the other hand, it returns $\perp$ if there is no continuation which either satisfies $\epsilon(\varphi)$ or makes it undefined. Since now we have three automata, there is an additional final outcome to consider, which is uu. So, the monitor returns uu if there is no continuation which either satisfies or violates $\epsilon(\varphi)$. These first three outcomes are all deriving by the three-values semantics for LTL. Then, we may find $?_{\not\perp}$, which is read "unknown, but it will never be violated from the monitor's point of view". Such outcome is returned by the monitor when the visible trace σ_v does not have any continuation which will eventually violate $\epsilon(\varphi)$, but there are · continuations that satisfy $\epsilon(\varphi)$ and make it undefined. Symmetrically, we may find $?_{\not\top}$, which is read "unknown, but it will never be satisfied from the monitor's point a view". This outcome is the dual of the previous one, where no continuations satisfying $\epsilon(\varphi)$ can be found, but continuations that violate $\epsilon(\varphi)$ and make it undefined exist. Last but not least, we may find $?$ denoting the completely unknown case. As before, this outcome concerns the case where the monitor cannot conclude anything yet, because there exist continuations satisfying $\epsilon(\varphi)$, continuations violating $\epsilon(\varphi)$, and continuations that make it undefined.

Definition 6 (Monitor with imperfect information). *Given an LTL formula φ and a visible trace σ_v, a monitor with imperfect information is so defined:*

$$
Mon_\varphi^v(\sigma_v) = \begin{cases}
\top & \sigma_v \in \mathcal{L}(\tilde{A}^{\epsilon(\varphi)}) \wedge \sigma_v \notin \mathcal{L}(\tilde{A}^{\epsilon(\neg\varphi)}) \wedge \sigma_v \notin \mathcal{L}(\tilde{A}^{\otimes\varphi}) \\
\bot & \sigma_v \notin \mathcal{L}(\tilde{A}^{\epsilon(\varphi)}) \wedge \sigma_v \in \mathcal{L}(\tilde{A}^{\epsilon(\neg\varphi)}) \wedge \sigma_v \notin \mathcal{L}(\tilde{A}^{\otimes\varphi}) \\
uu & \sigma_v \notin \mathcal{L}(\tilde{A}^{\epsilon(\varphi)}) \wedge \sigma_v \notin \mathcal{L}(\tilde{A}^{\epsilon(\neg\varphi)}) \wedge \sigma_v \in \mathcal{L}(\tilde{A}^{\otimes\varphi}) \\
?_{\not\perp} & \sigma_v \in \mathcal{L}(\tilde{A}^{\epsilon(\varphi)}) \wedge \sigma_v \notin \mathcal{L}(\tilde{A}^{\epsilon(\neg\varphi)}) \wedge \sigma_v \in \mathcal{L}(\tilde{A}^{\otimes\varphi}) \\
?_{\not\top} & \sigma_v \notin \mathcal{L}(\tilde{A}^{\epsilon(\varphi)}) \wedge \sigma_v \in \mathcal{L}(\tilde{A}^{\epsilon(\neg\varphi)}) \wedge \sigma_v \in \mathcal{L}(\tilde{A}^{\otimes\varphi}) \\
? & \sigma_v \in \mathcal{L}(\tilde{A}^{\epsilon(\varphi)}) \wedge \sigma_v \in \mathcal{L}(\tilde{A}^{\epsilon(\neg\varphi)}) \wedge \sigma_v \in \mathcal{L}(\tilde{A}^{\otimes\varphi})
\end{cases}
$$

Note that, in the above definition, not all the possible combination are included. In particular, it is not possible to have $\sigma_v \notin \mathcal{L}(\tilde{A}^{\epsilon(\varphi)}) \wedge \sigma_v \notin \mathcal{L}(\tilde{A}^{\epsilon(\neg\varphi)}) \wedge \sigma_v \notin \mathcal{L}(\tilde{A}^{\otimes\varphi})$ and $\sigma_v \in \mathcal{L}(\tilde{A}^{\epsilon(\varphi)}) \wedge \sigma_v \in \mathcal{L}(\tilde{A}^{\epsilon(\neg\varphi)}) \wedge \sigma_v \notin \mathcal{L}(\tilde{A}^{\otimes\varphi})$. In particular, the former is not possible because there exists at least one automaton that includes the trace by following the definition of the three-valued semantics for LTL. The latter follows by the fact that it is unfeasible given the nature of a visible trace that a formula will be true or false but not undefined in the future.

In what follows, we provide two preservation results from the monitor with imperfect information to the one with perfect information.

Lemma 2. *Given a finite trace σ, a monitor with its visibility $Mon_\varphi^v(\sigma)$, and a general monitor $Mon_\varphi(\sigma)$, we have that:*

$$
\text{if } Mon_\varphi^v(\sigma_v) = \top \text{ then } Mon_\varphi(\sigma) = \top
$$
$$
\text{if } Mon_\varphi^v(\sigma_v) = \bot \text{ then } Mon_\varphi(\sigma) = \bot
$$

Proof. Suppose $Mon_\varphi^v(\sigma_v) = \top$. This means that the visible trace σ_v satisfies the formula $\epsilon(\varphi)$. We want to prove that the original trace σ satisfies the formula φ. To do this, given σ_v, by Definition 4–5, we know that for each $\sigma_v(i)$, for all $p_\top \in \sigma_v(i)$, $p \in \sigma(i)$ and for all $p_\bot \in \sigma_v(i)$, $p \notin \sigma(i)$. Given the above reasoning, we need to provide an induction proof over the structure of the formula $\epsilon(\varphi)$. Case: $\epsilon(\varphi) = p_\top$. So, $\varphi = p$. By hypothesis, $Mon_\varphi^v(\sigma_v) = \top$, by the semantics of three-valued LTL this means that $p_\top \in \sigma_v(0)$ and by Definition 4–5, $p \in \sigma(0)$. By the latter, $Mon_\varphi(\sigma) = \top$. Case: $\epsilon(\varphi) = p_\perp$. Thus, $\varphi = \neg p$. By hypothesis, $Mon_\varphi^v(\sigma_v) = \top$, by the semantics of three-valued LTL this means that $p_\perp \in \sigma_v(0)$ and by Definitions 4–5, $p \notin \sigma(0)$. By the latter, $Mon_\varphi(\sigma) = \top$. Since in the inductive cases the transformation of Definition 3 does not change the structure and the elements of the formula, we can conclude the proof.

Suppose $Mon_\varphi^v(\sigma_v) = \perp$. This means that the visible trace σ_v does not satisfy the formula $\epsilon(\varphi)$. We want to prove that the original trace σ does the same for the formula φ. As for the previous case, we need to prove the implication by induction over the structure of the formula $\epsilon(\varphi)$ for the base cases. Case: $\epsilon(\varphi) = p_\top$. So, $\varphi = p$. By hypothesis, $Mon_\varphi^v(\sigma_v) = \perp$, by the semantics of three-valued LTL this means that $p_\perp \in \sigma_v(0)$ and by Definition 4–5, $p \notin \sigma(0)$. By the latter, $Mon_\varphi(\sigma) = \perp$. Case: $\epsilon(\varphi) = p_\perp$. Thus, $\varphi = \neg p$. By hypothesis, $Mon_\varphi^v(\sigma_v) = \perp$, by the semantics of three-valued LTL this means that $p_\top \in \sigma_v(0)$ and by Definition 4–5, $p \in \sigma(0)$. By the latter, $Mon_\varphi(\sigma) = \perp$.

Given the above results, we can deduce the following corollary.

Corollary 1. *Given a visible finite trace σ_v and an LTL formula φ, we have:*

$$\sigma_v \notin \mathcal{L}(\hat{A}^{\epsilon(\varphi)}) \Rightarrow \sigma_v \in \mathcal{L}(\hat{A}^{\epsilon(\neg\varphi)}) \vee \sigma_v \in \mathcal{L}(\tilde{A}^{\otimes\varphi})$$
$$\sigma_v \notin \mathcal{L}(\hat{A}^{\epsilon(\neg\varphi)}) \Rightarrow \sigma_v \in \mathcal{L}(\hat{A}^{\epsilon(\varphi)}) \vee \sigma_v \in \mathcal{L}(\tilde{A}^{\otimes\varphi})$$
$$\sigma_v \notin \mathcal{L}(\tilde{A}^{\otimes\varphi}) \Rightarrow \sigma_v \in \mathcal{L}(\hat{A}^{\epsilon(\neg\varphi)}) \vee \sigma_v \in \mathcal{L}(\hat{A}^{\epsilon(\varphi)})$$

4   Implementation

The prototype implementing the theory presented in this paper is publicly available as a GitHub repository[1]. It consists in a Python script which implements the entire pipeline presented in Fig. 2. The reason for choosing Python lies in the presence of a rich library for automaton manipulation, named Spot[2] [8]. In more detail, we used Spot to automatically generate an NBA, given an LTL formula. This corresponds to step (iii) in Fig. 2, which is the most complicated and computationally expensive step in the pipeline. The rest of the pipeline has been directly implemented in Python.

Going a bit deeper in the implementation, the prototype consists in a Python class, named Monitor. To create a Monitor, its constructor requires: (i) an LTL formula to verify; (ii) a set of atomic propositions; (iii) an equivalence relation on atomic propositions; (iv) a trace of events to analyse.

With the previous information, a FSM representing the monitor as in Definition 6 is constructed. Then, such monitor is used to analyse the input trace, and the corresponding verdict is returned back to the user. The trace is assumed

---

[1] https://github.com/AngeloFerrando/RuntimeVerificationWithImperfectInforma
tion.

[2] https://spot.lrde.epita.fr/.

to be stored inside a file (e.g., a log file). These input parameters can be passed as command line arguments to the tool. However, since the monitor is denoted as a single data structure, it is also possible (and quite natural) to import the script and use the monitor as preferred. This can be useful for instance if the monitor is to be used for online verification, rather than offline verification.

4.1 Remote Inspection Case Study

We talked about the theory behind our approach, and we also briefly introduced the resulting prototype. Let us now focus on the experiments we carried out on a robotic case study, as a proof of concept.

Our case study is based on a 3D simulation of a Jackal[3], a four-wheeled unmanned ground vehicle (referred to as the 'rover' from now on), coupled with a simulated radiation sensor, that the rover uses to take radiation readings of points of interest while patrolling around a nuclear facility, and a camera, that the rover uses to inspect images of the nuclear waste barrels in the area. This simulation is based on the work presented in [20], which explains how the simulated sensor works and how radiation was simulated in the environment. In our version of the simulation the rover is autonomously controlled by a rational/intelligent agent [19]. Figure 3 reports a screenshot of the case study.

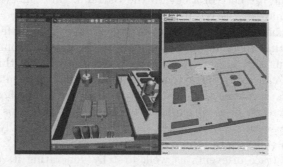

Fig. 3. Simulation in Gazebo of the remote inspection of nuclear plant.

A typical mission in our simulation starts with the rover positioned at the entrance of a nuclear facility. The goal of this mission is to inspect a number of points of interest (*i.e.*, waypoints). Inspecting a waypoint serves two purposes: taking radiation readings to check if the radiation is at an acceptable level, and using a camera to detect abnormalities such as leakage in barrels and pipes. After inspecting all of the waypoints, the rover can either return to the entrance to await for a new mission, or keep patrolling and inspecting the waypoints.

Without losing generality, we assume the image captured by the rover's camera can be represented as a grid. Each cell in such a grid can contain, or not,

---

[3] https://clearpathrobotics.com/jackal-small-unmanned-ground-vehicle.

an abnormality (e.g., a cut in the barrel). This information is translated into propositions, that can be transmitted to the monitor to be analysed at runtime.

Let us assume that, because of the rover's limited resources, the latter is not always capable of sending all the information to the monitor. Because of this, some times the monitor is not able to distinguish a cut from a rust stain. In such cases, from the viewpoint of the monitor analysing the scene, there is imperfect information over the atomic propositions. We assume the presence of a cut on a barrel b with c and the presence of a rust stain with s. So, the set of atomic propositions is $\Sigma = \{b, c, s\}$. Then, we have imperfect information over c and s, which is formalised as $c \sim s$ (i.e., there is an equivalence class γ_{cs} between c and s). Let us now say that the property we want to verify at runtime is whether the rover will not find a cut in the barrel. This information could be used by the software agent controlling the rover to react properly (e.g., by informing a human operator about a possible leakage). Such property can be formulated as the following LTL formula: $\varphi = \Diamond(b \wedge \bigcirc \neg c)$. Nevertheless, this formula would make sense in a case of perfect information over the system, but in this case, where c and s cannot be distinguished (in general), a standard LTL monitor should not be used. To understand this, let us just assume that the trace of events σ observed by the rover is $\sigma(0) = \{\}$, $\sigma(1) = \{b\}$, and $\sigma(2) = \{c\}$. In such trace, the first event means that the rover has not observed anything relevant, the second event means that the rover observed the barrel b, and the third event denotes the presence of a cut on the barrel b. But, since the monitor has imperfect information, the truth value of c cannot be observed. Consequently, if the monitor considered $\neg c$ without caring about the imperfect information, it could report that there are no problems, i.e. the general monitor in this case returns true. But the latter is not correct. Thus, to tackle this aspect in its foundations, we can apply our extended semantics and its resulting monitor.

Since in this scenario we have an equivalence relation between c and s (i.e., $c \sim s$), first we need to explicit the atomic propositions inside the formula, obtaining: $\epsilon(\varphi) = \Diamond(b_\top \wedge \bigcirc [\gamma_{cs}]_\bot)$. By using the newly updated LTL formula, we can generate the three automata as shown in Fig. 2. After that, we can update the trace of events as well, first by generating its explicit version σ_e (see Definition 4), where $\sigma_e(0) = \{b_\bot, c_\bot, s_\bot\}$, $\sigma_e(1) = \{b_\top, c_\bot, s_\bot\}$, and $\sigma_e(2) = \{b_\bot, c_\top, s_\bot\}$. Then by defining its visible version according to the given equivalence class γ_{cs} (see Definition 5), we obtain σ_v, where $\sigma_v(0) = \{b_\bot, [\gamma_{cs}]_\bot\}$, $\sigma_v(1) = \{b_\top, [\gamma_{cs}]_\bot\}$, and $\sigma_v(2) = \{b_\bot\}$. Note that, as expected, the last event in σ_v does not contain information about the atomic proposition c. This is determined by the fact that the atomic propositions $c_\top$ and $s_\bot$ hold in the last event of σ_v, and according to Definition 5, since $c \sim s$, we can have $[\gamma_{cs}]_\top$ (resp., $[\gamma_{cs}]_\bot$) if and only if both $c_\top$ and $s_\top$ hold (resp., $c_\bot$ and $s_\bot$). Thus, having a mismatch between the two atomic propositions (i.e., one is true while the other is false), we cannot safely add any witness for the equivalence class γ_{cs}. Instead, in the first two events of σ_v, since we have both $c_\bot$ and $s_\bot$, we can safely add the witness $[\gamma_{cs}]_\bot$ to the trace. Thanks to our three-value semantics and the presence of explicit atomic propositions, the trace σ which was erroneously classified as satisfying φ from the standard LTL monitor before, now is classified as $?_{\mathcal{Y}}$. The semantics of the two verdicts is fundamentally different, as well as the reaction that the system should have. In the first case, by using a standard LTL monitor, the verdict returned by the monitor was $\top$. Thus, the agent controlling the rover could have used such information to continue the inspection with another barrel and not detecting a danger. In the second case, by using the extended LTL monitor that we presented in this work, the verdict returned by the monitor was $?_{\mathcal{Y}}$. Thus, the agent controlling the rover could use this information to, for instance, ask the rover to check again, maybe taking another picture. Even though this is a simple example, it allows us to show how our extension tackles the foundations of the imperfect information issue.

4.2   Experimental Results

Other than verifying the property previously presented for the remote inspection scenario, we carried out more general experiments to study the execution time of our prototype. In more detail, we focused on two fundamental aspects, the generation and verification time. The former concerns the execution time required to synthesise a monitor given an LTL formula (according to Definition 6). While the latter concerns the execution time required to analyse a given trace of events with the so synthesised monitor. It is important to separate the two experimental evaluations since the monitor's generation is not usually performed online, but ahead of the system execution. Thus, the most critical aspect to consider when evaluating runtime verification techniques is the verification time, since it is the only one which is performed online. Consequently, it is the only part that influences the execution; this is also referred to as the monitor's overhead.

We carried out experiments for both aspects. Specifically, for the monitor's synthesis, we did experiments varying the size of the LTL formula; where the size of the formula consists in the number of operators inside the formula. We picked the size of the formula as target of our experiments because it is the input driving the generation of the monitor[4]. Instead, for the verification part, we carried out experiments varying the length of the trace of events to analyse. Also in this case, we picked the length of the trace because it is the only input which influences the monitor's verification time. This can be easily understood by considering the fact that once the FSM has been generated, it will not change. Thus, its size is fixed and is determined by the size of the formula. So, at runtime, the only aspect that changes is the length of the trace, which is populated by events generated through the system execution.

Figure 4 reports the results obtained with our experiments, where both LTL formulas and traces are randomly generated. Specifically, Fig. 4a reports the execution time to synthesise a monitor given an LTL formula, while Fig. 4b reports the execution time to analyse a given trace of events with the so synthesised monitor. In Fig. 4a, we may find the size of the LTL formula on the x-axis, and

---

[4] Let us remember that steps (iii) and (vi) in Fig. 2 are very expensive and require exponential time w.r.t. the size of the formula.

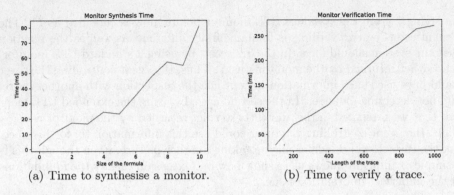

(a) Time to synthesise a monitor.   (b) Time to verify a trace.

Fig. 4. Experimental results.

the execution time on the y-axis (in milliseconds). Note that, as expected, the execution time for the monitor synthesis grows exponentially w.r.t. the size of the formula. In Fig. 4b we may find the length of the trace of the events on the x-axis, and the execution time on the y-axis (in milliseconds). Note that, the execution time is linear w.r.t. the length of the trace; this is crucial for using the monitor at runtime, while the system is running. Since the execution time is linear w.r.t. the length of the trace, the time required for the monitor to analyse a single event in the trace is constant. Thus, the monitor can be used to incrementally analyse events generated at runtime by the system[5].

5   Related Work

The closest work to our contribution is [18], where Past-Time LTL is verified at runtime in case of uncertainty over the observed events. In such work, the verification is carried out on abstract traces of events. An abstract trace corresponds to a trace where not all concrete events are present, but only samples taken with a certain time step. The uncertainty comes from unknown event interleaving, while in our case comes from indistinguishability relations amongst events. Differently from [18], we do not sample the events, and the uncertainty is determined by the monitor's visibility. Thus, the abstraction is not on the order amongst the events in a trace, but on the kind of events the trace contains.

In a completely different line of research, we may find [2,3,10,11,16], where the uncertainty in the verification is caused by the absence of information. In such works, the trace of events may contain gaps, which means at certain point of the system execution, the monitor is not capable of observing the system behaviour. This problem has been tackled in different ways, but in general, the solution consists in filling the gaps with events. Naturally, since there is uncertainty on what was exactly the event in the gap, these approaches depend on probabilities

---

[5] Where with incrementally, we mean the monitor analyses the events one by one (not as in offline RV where the monitor expects the entire trace all at once).

to guess which events to use to fill the gap. These works are different from ours in principle, because we do not assume to miss information, indeed we do not have gaps in our traces. Our uncertainty is not based on the monitor missing events, but on the monitor not being capable of recognising (discerning) some events from other events (according to a indistinguishability relation).

A recent work on RV with uncertainty can be found in [17]. There, the concept of uncertainty is abstracted by considering multi-traces, instead of uni-traces (standard traces). A multi-trace allows multiple evaluations for the same atomic proposition inside the trace. The authors present a monitor to handle such multi-traces and prove its soundness. Like for [2,3,10,11,16], also [17] is focused on missing events, even though partially missing ones are considered too.

Differently from our contribution, all the works previously mentioned explicitly represent the notion of uncertainty (e.g. through a gap). When the trace contains concrete events, the semantics is the standard one. Our approach is less invasive, since it is constructed on top of the standard RV pipeline for the verification of LTL properties. We do not require the addition of gaps. We mainly focus on how to update the standard RV technique for LTL when the monitor can have imperfect information over the system. From an engineering perspective, our approach aims at extending the standard LTL approach to be used in case of imperfect information over the system, while the other works in literature are more focused on proposing completely new techniques to handle the absence of information (usually caused by noise or technical issues).

6 Conclusions and Future Work

In this paper, we presented an extension of the standard LTL runtime verification approach. We introduce the problem of imperfect information at the monitor level, and how such lack of information can bring a standard LTL monitor to conclude a wrong verdict. We present theoretically the notion of imperfect information (through equivalence classes) and how it influences the LTL property verification. In particular, we propose how to extend the standard LTL monitor synthesis [5], we show the resulting Python prototype, and we report its use on a relevant case study along with additional experiments to stress test it.

As future work, we are planning to further extend our approach by considering a post-processing function to add additional information to the monitor's verdict. Such function would depend on the trace of events, the LTL property and the monitor's verdict to establish a level of confidence on the final outcome. Up to now, we mainly focused on how to tackle the problem of imperfect information at the foundations of LTL runtime verification, however, once we obtain the final outcome from the monitor, we can still refine it more. In more detail, when the outcome concluded by the monitor is uu, we could elaborate it further and assign a probability value. For instance, instead of saying uu, we could say that the property is undefined w.r.t. the trace, but according to some probability distribution over the involved equivalence classes, we can claim the property would be satisfied (resp., violated) with a certain probability threshold.

References

1. Bartocci, E., Falcone, Y., Francalanza, A., Reger, G.: Introduction to runtime verification. In: Bartocci, E., Falcone, Y. (eds.) Lectures on Runtime Verification. LNCS, vol. 10457, pp. 1–33. Springer, Cham (2018). https://doi.org/10.1007/978-3-319-75632-5_1
2. Bartocci, E., Grosu, R.: Monitoring with uncertainty. In: Bortolussi, L., Bujorianu, M., Pola, G. (eds.) Proceedings Third International Workshop on Hybrid Autonomous Systems, HAS 2013, Rome, Italy, 17 March 2013. EPTCS, vol. 124, pp. 1–4 (2013). https://doi.org/10.4204/EPTCS.124.1
3. Bartocci, E., Grosu, R., Karmarkar, A., Smolka, S.A., Stoller, S.D., Zadok, E., Seyster, J.: Adaptive runtime verification. In: Qadeer, S., Tasiran, S. (eds.) RV 2012. LNCS, vol. 7687, pp. 168–182. Springer, Heidelberg (2013). https://doi.org/10.1007/978-3-642-35632-2_18
4. Bauer, A., Leucker, M., Schallhart, C.: Monitoring of real-time properties. In: Arun-Kumar, S., Garg, N. (eds.) FSTTCS 2006. LNCS, vol. 4337, pp. 260–272. Springer, Heidelberg (2006). https://doi.org/10.1007/11944836_25
5. Bauer, A., Leucker, M., Schallhart, C.: Runtime verification for LTL and TLTL. ACM Trans. Softw. Eng. Methodol. 20(4), 1–64 (2011). https://doi.org/10.1145/2000799.2000800
6. Belardinelli, F., Lomuscio, A., Malvone, V., Yu, E.: Approximating perfect recall when model checking strategic abilities: theory and applications. J. Artif. Intell. Res. 73, 897–932 (2022). https://doi.org/10.1613/jair.1.12539
7. Clarke, E.M.: Model checking. In: Ramesh, S., Sivakumar, G. (eds.) FSTTCS 1997. LNCS, vol. 1346, pp. 54–56. Springer, Heidelberg (1997). https://doi.org/10.1007/BFb0058022
8. Duret-Lutz, A., Poitrenaud, D.: SPOT: an extensible model checking library using transition-based generalized büchi automata. In: DeGroot, D., Harrison, P.G., Wijshoff, H.A.G., Segall, Z. (eds.) 12th International Workshop on Modeling, Analysis, and Simulation of Computer and Telecommunication Systems (MASCOTS 2004), 4–8 October 2004, Vollendam, The Netherlands, pp. 76–83. IEEE Computer Society (2004). https://doi.org/10.1109/MASCOT.2004.1348184
9. Gerth, R., Peled, D., Vardi, M.Y., Wolper, P.: Simple on-the-fly automatic verification of linear temporal logic. In: PSTV 1995. IAICT, pp. 3–18. Springer, Boston, MA (1996). https://doi.org/10.1007/978-0-387-34892-6_1
10. Kalajdzic, K., Bartocci, E., Smolka, S.A., Stoller, S.D., Grosu, R.: Runtime verification with particle filtering. In: Legay, A., Bensalem, S. (eds.) RV 2013. LNCS, vol. 8174, pp. 149–166. Springer, Heidelberg (2013). https://doi.org/10.1007/978-3-642-40787-1_9
11. Leucker, M., Sánchez, C., Scheffel, T., Schmitz, M., Thoma, D.: Runtime verification for timed event streams with partial information. In: Finkbeiner, B., Mariani, L. (eds.) RV 2019. LNCS, vol. 11757, pp. 273–291. Springer, Cham (2019). https://doi.org/10.1007/978-3-030-32079-9_16
12. Leucker, M., Schallhart, C.: A brief account of runtime verification. J. Log. Algebraic Methods Program. 78(5), 293–303 (2009). https://doi.org/10.1016/j.jlap.2008.08.004
13. Miguel, J.P., Mauricio, D., Rodriguez, G.: A review of software quality models for the evaluation of software products. CoRR abs/1412.2977 (2014). https://arxiv.org/abs/1412.2977

14. Pnueli, A.: The temporal logic of programs. In: 18th Annual Symposium on Foundations of Computer Science, Providence, Rhode Island, USA, 31 October–1 November 1977, pp. 46–57. IEEE Computer Society (1977). https://doi.org/10.1109/SFCS.1977.32

15. Rabin, M.O., Scott, D.S.: Finite automata and their decision problems. IBM J. Res. Dev. **3**(2), 114–125 (1959). https://doi.org/10.1147/rd.32.0114

16. Stoller, S.D., et al.: Runtime verification with state estimation. In: Khurshid, S., Sen, K. (eds.) RV 2011. LNCS, vol. 7186, pp. 193–207. Springer, Heidelberg (2012). https://doi.org/10.1007/978-3-642-29860-8_15

17. Taleb, R., Khoury, R., Hallé, S.: Runtime verification under access restrictions. In: Bliudze, S., Gnesi, S., Plat, N., Semini, L. (eds.) 9th IEEE/ACM International Conference on Formal Methods in Software Engineering, FormaliSE@ICSE 2021, Madrid, Spain, 17–21 May 2021, pp. 31–41. IEEE (2021). https://doi.org/10.1109/FormaliSE52586.2021.00010

18. Wang, S., Ayoub, A., Sokolsky, O., Lee, I.: Runtime verification of traces under recording uncertainty. In: Khurshid, S., Sen, K. (eds.) RV 2011. LNCS, vol. 7186, pp. 442–456. Springer, Heidelberg (2012). https://doi.org/10.1007/978-3-642-29860-8_35

19. Wooldridge, M., Rao, A. (eds.) Foundations of Rational Agency. Kluwer Academic Publishers, Applied Logic Series (1999)

20. Wright, T., West, A., Licata, M., Hawes, N., Lennox, B.: Simulating ionising radiation in gazebo for robotic nuclear inspection challenges. Robotics **10**(3), 86 (2021). https://doi.org/10.3390/robotics10030086

Runtime Enforcement for IEC 61499 Applications

Yliès Falcone, Irman Faqrizal$^{(\boxtimes)}$, and Gwen Salaün

Univ. Grenoble Alpes, CNRS, Grenoble INP, Inria, LIG, 38000 Grenoble, France
irman.faqrizal@inria.fr

Abstract. Industrial automation is a complex process involving various stakeholders. The international standard IEC 61499 helps to specify distributed automation using a generic architectural model, targeting the technical development of the automation. However, analysing the correctness of IEC 61499 models remains a challenge because of their informal semantics and distributed logic. We propose new verification techniques for IEC 61499 applications. These techniques rely on the concept of runtime enforcement, which can be applied to systems for preventing *bad* behaviours from happening. The main idea of our approach is to integrate an enforcer in the application for allowing it to respect specific properties when executing. The techniques begin with the definition of a property. The language of this property supports features such as discarding and replacing events. Next, this property is used to synthesise an enforcer in the form of a function block. Finally, the synthesised enforcer is integrated into the application. Our approach is illustrated on a realistic example and fully automated.

1 Introduction

The emerging industrial revolution, Industry 4.0, affirms that the innovation of technologies has become the main driving force in the advancement of industrial activities [15]. Stakeholders in the industry appeal for new technologies in every aspect of industrial processes. These include the improvements of development tools for industrial automation to increase efficiency and productivity. The International Electrotechnical Commission (IEC) 61499 [1] is a recent standard for developing industrial automation. It conceptualises interconnected function blocks to express an industrial process. Each Function Block (FB) encapsulates some logic describing its behaviour, while the connections with other FBs are defined using input and output interfaces.

The main benefit of IEC 61499 is that it is suitable for developing a fully distributed system [19]. A single application can be distributed among several control devices to optimise efficiency. However, this advantage also raises a challenge because when the system is complex and composed of many control devices and FBs, it becomes error-prone. This a critical issue since IEC 61499 does not define how to handle bugs (e.g., there is no exception handling). Furthermore,

B.-H. Schlingloff and M. Chai (Eds.): SEFM 2022, LNCS 13550, pp. 352–368, 2022.
https://doi.org/10.1007/978-3-031-17108-6_22

the execution of industrial systems is heavily influenced by the environment. In contrast to conventional programs with mostly user interactions, industrial applications also accept inputs from the connected sensors. In complex systems, there can be many sensors, and each of them is associated with the outside world, which has unpredictable behaviour.

IEC 61499 applications can be verified during design time using static verification techniques such as model checking [3,14,20].

Such an approach is useful for finding unexpected behaviour before the application is deployed. However, industrial applications can be huge, and state space explosion may become an issue. On top of that, the debugging process might introduce new bugs since it is done manually by the users. Also, IEC 61499 has loosely defined semantics, which causes the faithfulness of its translation from an application into a model can not be guaranteed (i.e., the model may not really represent the actual behaviour of the application). Furthermore, as previously mentioned, industrial applications often interact with nondeterministic behaviours of the environments, which can not be observed during design time. The work in [5] and [12] propose alternative methods to verify IEC 61499 applications by applying runtime verification techniques [7]. The main idea of both works is to integrate a monitor that can check during runtime whether some properties hold. These techniques can be applied regardless of the application's size, and there is no modelling phase required, which means that it is not necessary to define the application's formal semantics. In addition, the approach involves analyses of execution traces that are obtained directly from executing the application (taking into account the influence of environments). However, the users are still required to manually debug the application when the properties are violated. Moreover, in this case, the properties' violations can be detected only when the application is already running. This is an issue since applications with incorrect behaviours may cause a critical impact on industrial activities.

A practical solution for supporting IEC 61499 applications is to integrate verification techniques that can ensure correctness during runtime. To do so, we propose to rely on runtime enforcement [8] techniques for preventing systems from producing incorrect behaviours. It guarantees correctness by modifying the system execution. There exist multiple enforcement mechanisms such as *input sanitation*, which ensures correctness by altering inputs that enter the system, and *output sanitation*, which modifies outputs such that they follow certain requirements. In our case, we enforce the system's correctness by altering the outputs of existing components (i.e., FBs) in the application.

The main idea of our runtime enforcement techniques is to change the execution of IEC 61499 applications such that they can respect some given properties. For this purpose, the application is modified by integrating a new component called *enforcer* in the form of an FB. This enforcer is synthesised from an input property. Its purpose is to instrument the modification of the application's execution. Therefore, the property does not only specify the correctness of an application but also describes how the enforcement mechanism can react when the property violation happens. To achieve this, we define properties as automata extended with different types of transitions. A transition in the property can either let outputs be forwarded to the next component, discarded, or replaced with modified outputs. Since an enforcer is a type of basic FB, the synthesis process includes the creation of FB interfaces, Execution Control Chart (ECC), and algorithms. Every element in this FB is derived from the input property. After an enforcer is synthesised, then it should be integrated into the application by appropriately connecting the input and output interfaces without changing the initial execution flow.

More precisely, our contributions are as follows: (i) a property language for enforcing IEC 61499 applications, (ii) a technique for synthesising enforcers (in the form of IEC 61499 FBs) from given properties, (iii) a sequence to integrate enforcers into IEC 61499 applications. The approach is illustrated on a realistic example, and tool support was developed to automate the synthesis of enforcers.

The paper is organised as follows. Section 2 introduces background notions. Section 3 describes the runtime enforcement techniques. Section 4 presents the supporting tools. Section 5 surveys related work and Sect. 6 concludes.

2   Background

We first present the necessary concepts from IEC 61499 (Sect. 2.1), followed by a description of the essential idea of runtime enforcement. In the next section, we show a running example to illustrate our approach.

2.1   IEC 61499

IEC 61499 is a standard for designing industrial control systems that consist of interconnected Function Blocks (FBs). A FB is connected to other FBs through its input and output interfaces, where each of them distinguishes between event and data interfaces (see Fig. 1 (a)). The standard adopts an event-driven architecture, meaning that the execution of each component (i.e., FB) is triggered by incoming events. Once the FB is activated by an event, it cannot be re-entered by another event before the previous activation has finished. The *WITH* identifiers associate event and data interfaces. When an event arrives, the values on the associated input data interfaces are refreshed, whereas the emission of an event refreshes the associated values on the output data interfaces.

Figure 1 (b) illustrates IEC 61499. The standard allows the event interfaces to be connected in both fan-in and fan-out configurations (e.g., FB 1 to FB 2 and 3, while FB 2 and 3 to FB 4). However, an input data interface can only receive a connection from a single output data interface (i.e., fan-out only). Moreover, in the same picture, all the FBs (FB 1 to 5) are part of a single application (Application 1). However, as we can see, some of the FBs are mapped into different control devices. This emphasises the fact that IEC 61499 allows for designing distributed applications.

Function Block is the fundamental component of IEC 61499 architecture. There are three types of FBs: basic, composite, and service interfaces. A basic

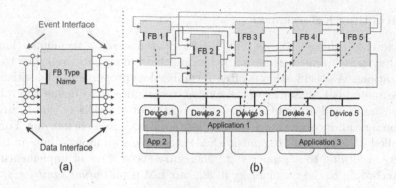

Fig. 1. Example of (a) Function block and (b) IEC 61499 application.

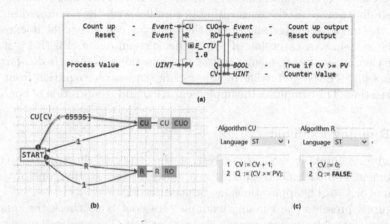

Fig. 2. (a) E_CTU FB, (b) ECC, (c) Algorithms.

FB defines its behaviour using a state machine called Execution Control Chart (ECC). When a state is visited, it may perform two actions: emit an output event and/or execute an algorithm written in structured text. Some conditions on the data interfaces can guard the transitions in an ECC. A composite FB is composed of a network of FBs. A service interface FB concerns FBs that have behaviours specific to their control devices (i.e., vendor dependent).

In our work, we use 4DIAC-IDE [2] as a development environment, an open-source tool to build IEC 61499 applications. Figure 2 (a) shows an example of FB represented with 4DIAC-IDE. This FB is called E_CTU and behaves as a counter. The ECC in Fig. 2 (b) describes the FB behaviour in each activation. Starting from $START$ state, if the FB receives an event CU and the value of CV is below the threshold (65535), then the current state transitions into CU. Such transition with a boolean condition is called guarded transition. Next, in state CU, algorithm CU (Fig. 2 (c)) is executed and output event CUO is fired. The algorithm increments CV and updates the boolean value Q. Finally, it goes back directly to the initial state because the transition going from state CU to $START$ is an empty transition. The same mechanism also applies when the FB receives event R, which resets the counter value CV.

2.2   Runtime Enforcement

Runtime enforcement [17] (see [6,8,10] for overviews) is a technique that can prevent systems from *misbehaving* by forcing them to execute according to their specifications. A specification is often formalised as properties to be satisfied.

The main goal of runtime enforcement techniques is to define the relation between input and output sequences of events. More precisely, the techniques describe how an incorrect sequence can be modified into a correct one. For this, a so-called *Enforcement Mechanism* (EM) transforms an input σ into an output $EM(\sigma)$ according to a property φ. There are three ways of implementing an EM. According to the terminology in [8], our EM is an *output sanitiser* since it prevents a system from generating incorrect traces.

There exist several (mathematical) models of EM. A *Security Automaton* [17] (SA) is a finite-state machine executing in parallel with the monitored program. When the model observes an action, the enforcer can either let it execute or halt the system. An extension of SA is the *edit-automata* [13] (EA), it has a feature that can suppress, memorise and replay actions. *Generalised enforcement monitors* [9] (GEMs) go further by separating sequence recognition from action memorisation. This simplifies the implementation and composition of operations.

2.3   Running Example

A running example is used in the rest of the paper to illustrate the runtime enforcement approach. The example is a conveyor test station, one of the case studies of IEC 61499 applications introduced in [21].

Figure 3 presents the running example. Its goal is to check the quality of industrial materials passing through a conveyor belt. The application consists of four main components. Firstly, a conveyor drive (C1) is connected to a control panel where the user can either start or stop the conveyor. Secondly, the component feeder (C2) is in charge of feeding materials onto the conveyor. Next, a quality acceptance station (C3) evaluates the materials as they pass through. Lastly, depending on the test results, the roll-off mechanism (C4) allows the materials either to be distributed onto the next industrial process or to be dropped into a hopper by opening the reject gate.

The IEC 61499 application of the conveyor test station is presented in Fig. 4. Each of the main components is mapped to a composite FB. *DriveCntl1* corresponds to the conveyor drive (C1), *Feed1* represents the material feeder (C2), *QualStation1* deals with the quality acceptance station (C3), and *RollOff1* takes care of the roll-off mechanism (C4). The two additional FBs, *Exec1* and *Inventory1*, respectively correspond to the initialisation of the application and the database which stores the materials data. In these FBs, there are event and data interfaces that correspond to the application's functionalities. For instance, *Running* data interface in *DriveCntl1* has a boolean value which represents the state of the conveyor belt. When the conveyor is running then *Running* = *true*, otherwise *Running* = *false*. Inside each of these composite FBs, service interface FBs interact with the physical sensors and actuators such as *IO_READER* and

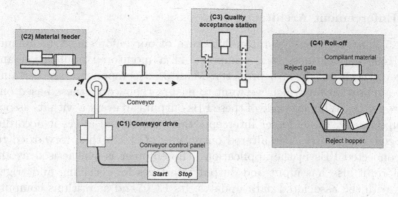

Fig. 3. Conveyor test station

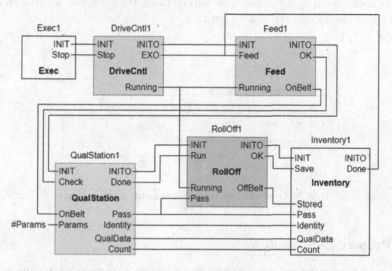

Fig. 4. IEC 61499 application of the conveyor test station

IO_WRITER. For example, an *IO_READER* FB in *Feed1* interacts with the input sensor to detect that a piece of material is successfully fed onto the conveyor. For brevity, we leave out the details of what is internal of every composite FBs; a more comprehensive description can be found in [21].

3   Runtime Enforcement Techniques

This section describes the runtime enforcement techniques for IEC 61499 applications. First, the enforcement architecture is presented, and the property language is explained. We then describe the synthesis of an enforcer and how to integrate it into the application. The section ends with a description of preserved characteristics.

3.1   Enforcement Architecture

Figure 5 illustrates the general architecture of our enforcement techniques for IEC 61499 applications. It is composed of a monitored application and an enforcer synthesised from a property. Monitored components are certain FBs in the application for which we want to ensure their correctness based on specific properties, Whenever one of these FBs outputs an event e with its associated data updates D, the enforcer intercepts this output and alters it according to the specified property. The altered outputs (e', D') are then forwarded to the next connected FBs in the application. The enforcer is synthesised as an FB. Therefore, it also has input and output interfaces for receiving and triggering events with the associated data updates. Its ECC and algorithms compute the output every time an input is received. Lastly, an enforcer has to be integrated into the application by creating new connections between the interfaces of the enforcer and the monitored components.

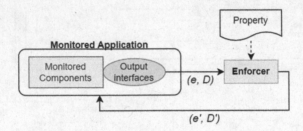

Fig. 5. Overview of the enforcement architecture

3.2   Property Automaton

A property is required as an input of the runtime enforcement techniques. We express properties as automata. This allows enforcing properties in any alternative declarative logical formalisms (e.g., Linear Temporal Logic) that translate to automata. Each automaton consists of states interconnected with transitions. A state can either be a correct state or an incorrect state, which we denote using the colours green and red. A property is satisfied when the current state is green and violated when red. A transition outgoing to a red state corresponds to the property violation itself.

Transitions are extended with types that are used to describe the behaviour of the synthesised enforcer every time it receives an input. There are four types of transitions:

- A *forward* transition indicates that the triggered event and its associated data updates are forwarded (i.e., nothing changed).
- A *discard* transition indicates that the event is discarded and no data is updated.

- A pair of transitions *replace* and *replacement* outgoing from the same state indicates that the triggering of an event and the updating of data interfaces on transition typed as *replace* should be replaced with the triggering of an event and the updating of data interfaces on another transition typed as *replacement*.

A transition typed as *forward* or *replacement* is always outgoing from a green state to another green state. Meanwhile, *discard* and *replace* transitions are outgoing from green states to red states.

Definition 1. *(IEC 61499 property) A property for IEC 61499 enforcement mechanism is an automaton* $P = (S, s^0, E, B, \Gamma, T, va)$, *where*

- S *is a (finite) set of states, and* s^0 *is the initial state,*
- E *is a set of events,*
- B *is a set of boolean expressions,*
- $\Gamma = \{forward, discard, replace, replacement\}$ *is a set of transition types,*
- T *is the set of transitions and each* $t \in T$ *is a transition* $t = (s, e, G, \gamma, s')$, *where* $s, s' \in S$ *are source and target states,* $e \in E$ *is an event,* G *is a boolean guard composed of* $b \in B$ *and generated by the grammar* $G:: = true \mid b \mid \neg b \mid G \wedge G \mid G \vee G$, *and* $\gamma \in \Gamma$ *is the transition's type,*
- $va : S \rightarrow \{green, red\}$ *is the verdict function associating each state to a colour.*

Boolean expressions existing in a transition's guard represent the values of data interfaces when the associated event is triggered. The expression *true* implies that the event on that transition is triggered regardless of the data interfaces' current values. When a transition is typed as *replacement*, the guard must refer to a single possible combination of values, i.e., every boolean expression uses only equality operator (=) and only conjunction (∧) is allowed before or after each expression. The purpose is to ensure a unique replacement when performing data updates on transitions typed as *replace*.

Two examples of properties are shown in Fig. 6. Both of them are specified for IEC 61499 application introduced in Sect. 2.3. We call the first property as Regulate Buttons. It is associated with conveyor drive component (C1) or *DriveCntl1* FB. It specifies that every time event *EXO* is triggered, the value of *Running* can only alternate between *true* and *false*. This is done by discarding event *EXO* guarded with *Running = false* outgoing from state 0 and *EXO* guarded with *Running = true* outgoing from state 1. In practice, this property helps to suppress the impact of users consecutively pressing the same button on the control panel.

The property in Fig. 6 (B) is called Force Accept. It enforces the behaviour of the quality acceptance station component (C3) or *QualStation1* FB. It permits the application to reject industrial materials only twice in a row, and the third rejection is forced to be an acceptance instead. This is done by specifying that the event *Done* guarded by *Pass = false* (i.e., material is rejected) can only be triggered twice in a row (i.e., transitions *Done.{Pass = false}.(forward)* from state 1 to 2 and from state 2 to 3). The third time it is triggered (from state 3 to -1), then it is replaced with the transition *Done.{Pass = true}.(replacement)* from state 3 to 1, where *Pass = true* means that a material is accepted.

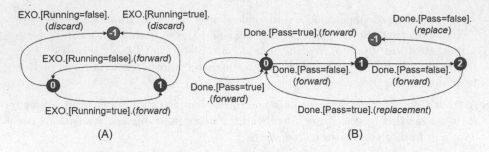

Fig. 6. Examples of properties, (A) Regulate Buttons and (B) Force Accept

3.3 Enforcer Synthesis

An enforcer is an FB synthesised from a given property. It is in the form of a basic FB, and it has interfaces, ECC, and algorithms. The idea is to integrate the enforcer as an additional FB in the IEC 61499 application to enforce its behaviour according to the property. The components of an enforcer are derived from the property.

Definition 2. *(Enforcer) An enforcer is a basic FB $ef = (ei, ecc, A)$, where:*

- *$ei = (E_i, E_o, D_i, D_o, W_i, W_o)$ is an enforcer interface, where E_i, E_o are sets of input and output event interfaces, D_i, D_o are sets of input and output data interfaces, W_i and W_o are WITH input and output identifiers associating events and sets of data interfaces,*
- *$ecc = (S_c, s_c^0, B_c, T_c)$ is an Execution Control Chart (ECC) specifying the enforcer's behaviour, where S_c is a set of states and $s_c^0 \in S_c$ is the initial state and each $s_c \in S_c$ consists of state actions $s_c = q_1, q_2, ..., q_n$, each action is a pair $q = (a, e_o)$, where $a \in A$ is an algorithm and e_o is an output event, B_c is a set of boolean expressions on D_i, T_c is the set of ECC transitions, each $t_c \in T_c$ is a transition $t_c = (s_c, e_i, G_c, s_c')$, where $s_c, s_c' \in S_c$ are source and target states, $e_i \in E_i$ is an input event, G_c is a boolean guard composed of $b_c \in B_c$ and generated by the grammar $G_c ::= true \mid b_c \mid \neg b_c \mid G_c \wedge G_c \mid G_c \vee G_c$,*
- *A is a set of algorithms, where $a \in A$ consists of assignments for variables in D_o.*

The enforcer interface serves as a connection for integrating the enforcer into the application. It is synthesised based on the events and boolean expressions present in the property. For each event or expression variable in the property, a pair of input and output interfaces are created in the enforcer. The *WITH* identifiers are created from the associated events and expressions in guards. ECC is built by traversing the states and transitions in the property. It specifies the behaviour of an enforcer every time it receives an input event from one of the monitored components. Algorithms reside in the ECC's states; they contain value assignments of the data interfaces.

Algorithm 1 describes the synthesis of an enforcer. It takes as input a property P and returns an enforcer ef. Interfaces E_i, E_o, D_i, D_o are created by

---

Algorithm 1: Synthesis of enforcer

    Inputs : $P = (S, s^0, E, B, \Gamma, T)$
    Output: $ef = (ei, ecc, A)$
1 $E_i := \{e_i \mid e \in E\}$
2 $E_o := \{e_o \mid e \in E\}$ /* getVars() returns a set of variable */
3 $D_i := \{d_i \mid d \in getVars(B)\}$ /* names from a set of boolean expression */
4 $D_o := \{d_o \mid d \in getVars(B)\}$ /* or a Guard */
5 **foreach** $(s, e, G, \gamma, s') \in T$ **do**
6     $D_i' := \{d_i' \mid d \in getVars(G)\}$
7     $D_o' := \{d_o' \mid d \in getVars(G)\}$
8     $W_i := W_i \cup \{(e + "\_I", \ D_i')\}$
9     $W_o := W_o \cup \{(e + "\_O", \ D_o')\}$
10 **end**
11 $e_i = (E_i, E_o, D_i, D_o, W_i, W_o)$
12 $Visited := \varnothing, \ s_c^0 := (\varnothing, \varnothing)$
13 **Function** TraverseProperty$(s, s_c, P, ecc, A, Visited)$:
14    $Visited := Visited \cup \{s\}$
15   **let** $T' \subseteq T$ be the set of transitions outgoing from state s **in**
16   **foreach** $(s, e, G, \gamma, s') \in T'$ **do**
17   **foreach** $b \in getExpressions(G)$ **do**
18         $a := a + getVars(b) + "\_O :=" + getVars(b) + "\_I;"$
19         $A := A \cup \{a\}$ /* getExpressions() returns a set of boolean */
20         $e_i := e + "\_I"$ /* expressions from a Guard, whereas, getVal() */
21         $e_o := e + "\_O"$ /* returns a value of data in an expression */
22         $s_c' := (a, e_o)$
23   **if** $\gamma \neq discard \ \& \ \gamma \neq replace$ **then**
24           $T_c := T_c \cup \{(s_c, e_i, G, s_c')\}$
25   **if** $\gamma = replace$ **then**
26           $(s_r, e_r, G_r, \gamma_r, s_r') := t \in T'$ where $\gamma_r = replacement$
27   **foreach** $b_r \in getExpressions(G_r)$ **do**
28             $a_r := a_r + getVars(b_r) + " :=" + getVal(b_r) + ";"$
29             $s_c'' := (a_r, e_r)$
30             $T_c := T_c \cup \{(s_c, e_i, G, s_c'')\}$
31         $S_c := S_c \cup \{s_c, s_c', s_c''\}$
32   **if** $s' \notin Visited$ **then**
33   TraverseProperty $(s', s_c', P, ecc, A, Visited)$
34   **end**
35 **End Function**
36 TraverseProperty $(s^0, s_c^0, P, ecc, A, Visited)$
37 **return** $ef = (ei, ecc, A)$

---

concatenating property's events or variable names with the corresponding suffixes (lines 1 to 4). The suffixes are added since every interface in an FB must have a unique name. The *WITH* identifiers W_i, W_o are obtained by iterating through transitions in the property (lines 5 to 9) and associating each event with the set of data interfaces taken from variable names on the guard.

ECC is built by traversing the property using a recursive function *Traverse-Property* to visit every state. In each recursion:

1. an ECC's algorithm is written by obtaining every variable in the transition's guard and creating an assignment of input data interfaces to output data interfaces,
2. an ECC's transition is created and added into the set only when the type of property's transition is not *discard* (lines 21 and 25),
3. an additional ECC's transition is added when there are a pair of *replace* and *replacement* transitions (lines 26 to 30),
4. the set of ECC's states is updated and proceeds to the next state when it is not yet visited (lines 31 to 33).

Table 1. Synthesised enforcers interfaces

Interface	Regulate buttons	Force accept
Input event	EXO_I	$Done\_I$
Output event	EXO_O	$Done\_O$
Input data	$Running\_I$	$Pass\_I$
Output data	$Running\_O$	$Pass\_O$
WITH input	$(EXO\_I, \{Running\_I\})$	$(Done\_I, \{Pass\_I\})$
WITH output	$(EXO\_O, \{Running\_O\})$	$(Done\_O, \{Pass\_O\})$

As examples of synthesis results, we first present synthesised enforcers interfaces in Table 1. These are enforcer interfaces generated from the properties presented in Fig. 6 (A) and (B). Enforcer interfaces are generated from the property Regulate Buttons in the second column, whereas enforcer interfaces are generated from the property Force Accept in the third column. For each property, there is a pair of event input and output interfaces (e.g., EXO_I and EXO_O) generated from an event. There is also a pair of data input and output (e.g., $Running\_I$ and $Running\_O$) since there exists only one variable in the boolean expression. The *WITH* identifiers associate each event interface with a set of data interfaces according to events and guards in the properties' transitions. For instance, in Regulate Buttons EXO_I is associated with $Running\_I$ because, in property, there is a transition with event EXO associated with a guard that contains data variable *Running*.

Figure 7 depicts the synthesised ECCs of enforcers from both properties, and Table 2 shows the algorithms. The Regulate Buttons property contains *discard* transitions. It translates into an ECC where the corresponding transitions are removed. For instance, in state 1 when the enforcer has just triggered EXO and set *Running* to *true*, there is only a single transition where it can receive EXO with *Running* set to *false*. When the enforcer receives an event EXO with $Running = true$, then that event is discarded, and the current state stays at state

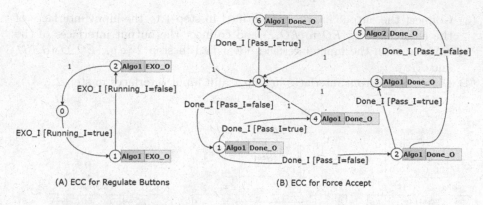

(A) ECC for Regulate Buttons   (B) ECC for Force Accept

Fig. 7. Synthesised execution control charts

1. Hence, the value of *Running* always alternates between *true* and *false* every time *EXO* is triggered. Meanwhile, in the enforcer ECC for the Force Accept property, state 2 corresponds to state 3 of property. In this state, the enforcer has received *Done* with *Pass* set to *false* (i.e., material rejection) twice in a row. Notice that from this state when the enforcer receives event *Done* with *Pass* set to *false* for the third time, state 5 executes *Algo2* where the value of *Pass* is enforced to be *true*. Furthermore, when the property's transition is typed as *forward*, the generated ECC's target state simply uses an algorithm where we assign the value of the input data interface to the output data interface. As an example for the property Force Accept, *Algo1* which assigns $Pass\_I$ to $Pass\_O$ is used in every state except state 5.

Table 2. Synthesised algorithms

	Regulate buttons	Force accept
Algo1	Running_O := Running_I;	Pass_O := Pass_I;
Algo2		Pass_O := true;

3.4 Enforcer Integration

A synthesised enforcer must be integrated into an IEC 61499 application in order to enforce the property's correctness at runtime. Enforcer integration is illustrated in Fig. 8; below is the description of every step:

(1) Identify the subset of output interfaces in the application by matching their names with enforcer input interfaces (e.g., *EO* and *DO*).
(2) Identify the subsets of input interfaces connected with output interfaces identified in step 1 (e.g., $\{EI1, EI2\}$ and $\{D\}$).

(3) Connect the output interfaces identified in step 1 to the input interfaces of the enforcer (e.g., *EO* to *EO_I*) and connect the output interfaces of the enforcer with the input interfaces identified in step 2 (e.g., *EO_O* to *EI1* and *EI2*).

(4) Disconnect output interfaces in step 1 and input interfaces in step 2.

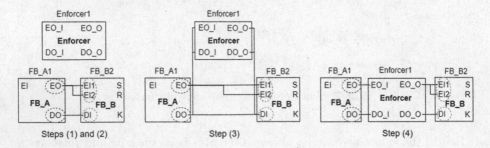

Fig. 8. Four steps of enforcer integration

Figure 9 shows excerpts of enforcers for properties in Fig. 6 that are integrated into the application. Integrating an enforcer essentially places a new FB between sets of connections. For instance, output event interface *EXO* in *DriveCntl1* was initially connected to *Feed* in *Feed1*. After the enforcer is integrated, this connection is replaced with *EXO* to *EXO_I* and *EXO_O* to *Feed*.

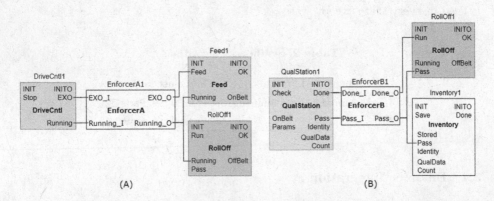

Fig. 9. Integrated enforcers

3.5   Characteristics

Our approach involves the modification of the application. It is essential to make sure that this modification respects some common characteristics. The first characteristic, *soundness* is satisfied if, for any input, it produces the correct output which satisfies the property. This criterion is fulfilled because we synthesise enforcers directly from properties. In a property, transitions outgoing to an incorrect state are either typed as *discard* or *replace*. Hence, any incorrect input is always either discarded or replaced. The second characteristic, *transparency*, is satisfied if the enforcer only intervenes when a property violation happens. This is also true in our approach since the enforcer only replaces events and data when there is a transition typed as *replace* outgoing to an incorrect state (i.e., property's violation). Also, the enforcer only discards an event when there is a transition typed as *discard* outgoing to an incorrect state.

4   Tool Support

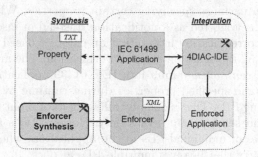

Fig. 10. Implementation overview

We have developed tool support in Java programming language to synthesise enforcers automatically. The tool takes as input a property and outputs an enforcer. The resulting enforcers can be visualised and simulated using Eclipse 4DIAC-IDE [18]. Figure 10 overviews our implementation. A property is written in a text file for a certain IEC 61499 application. The enforcer synthesis takes this property as an input to generate an enforcer in XML format. 4DIAC-IDE is then used to integrate the enforcer into the application. The application with an integrated enforcer is then ready to be simulated. The tool support, along with the running example in Sect. 2.3 integrated with enforcers for properties in Fig. 6 are available online [11]. By taking advantage of this tool support, we have also done several experiments using other examples such as capping station [22] and temperature control [21], both with a variety of properties.

5   Related Work

Several formal verification techniques for IEC 61499 applications have been proposed [4]. The work in [14] introduces a technique based on model checking to visually explain properties' violations. The approach begins with automatic translations of IEC 61499 applications into Symbolic Model Verifier (SMV) specifications. Then, a model checker generates counterexamples from those specifications and some given properties. Finally, the counterexamples are utilized to infer influence paths in a graphical interface. These paths are presented visually to the users to help them debug IEC 61499 applications. Earlier work in [20] uses Esterel for verifying safety properties. These works focus on avoiding properties from being violated by checking them before the application's deployment, whereas our approach ensures those properties are satisfied during runtime by applying modifications. Moreover, in this approach, the state explosion can be a challenge when the application is huge since it has to explore all possible executions. In contrast, our approach is not limited by the application's size.

A runtime verification technique is proposed in [12]. The authors propose a method for monitoring adapter connections in IEC 61499 application. The monitor contains state machines specifying certain properties. When a property is violated, an event is triggered as a notification. Instead of inserting a monitor, our work ensures correctness by integrating an enforcer based on a given property. The work in [5] also relies on runtime verification. The authors propose to integrate so-called *contract monitors* into IEC 61499 applications. These monitors can ensure some specified properties during runtime by constraining the behaviour of existing FBs. This is done by allowing data input and output interfaces to receive and send certain values only. However, this approach ensures only the correctness of individual FBs in the application, whereas our enforcer can ensure a property that involves multiple FBs at once.

The work in [16] introduces a technique to generate sequences of dynamic reconfiguration for IEC 61499 applications. The purpose of a reconfiguration sequence is to guarantee the continuity of a running application when component modifications are being applied. The technique takes as inputs an initial application and a target application. It outputs the sequence of reconfiguration steps to achieve the input target application from the initial input application. The technique starts by using predefined dependency rules on the input application to produce a dependency tree. This tree is then used to generate the sequence of reconfiguration. This approach does not guarantee that the target application is correct since it is an input the users give. In contrast, our approach involves automatically synthesising enforcers that guarantee correct behaviour when integrated into the application.

Compared to the existing models of enforcement monitors (EMs) [8], we consider output sanitisers that alter the outputs of existing components (i.e., FBs) in the application and forward them to the following connected components. Contrarily to the standard runtime enforcement scenario, EMs do not run in parallel with the application but are instead incorporated into the application. The EMs modify the application execution during runtime. Our EMs resemble edit automata [13] and generalised enforcement monitors [9] in that they can suppress and replace actions from the underlying application. However, they are synthesised from richer properties where events are not propositional (as with EAs and GEMs) but carry data values from the application that directly influence the decisions of our EMs.

6   Concluding Remarks

We propose new techniques to support industrial applications developed using the IEC 61499 standard. The novelty of this work is that we apply runtime enforcement to prevent IEC 61499 applications from violating certain properties during runtime. This approach allows the developers to guarantee correctness without manual intervention. Our enforcement techniques involve integrating a new component called an enforcer into the application. This component is in the form of a basic function block which is synthesised from a property. The approach is illustrated on a realistic running example, and tool support was developed to automate the synthesis process.

For future work, the property and the synthesised enforcer can be extended to support buffering. This feature would allow the enforcer to buffer events and trigger them in the future. This could be useful, for instance, when we need to postpone some actions due to a lack of resources in the system. With this feature, we could buffer the events corresponding to those actions and trigger them consecutively when the data corresponding to the resources are available. Another perspective is to construct an enforcer that can interpret properties dynamically. We may achieve this by designing enforcers as service interface FBs. With this type of FB, a program which implements a property interpreter can be written directly into the enforcer. Users could thus dynamically provide properties as inputs to change the enforcer behaviour at runtime. Furthermore, according to our preliminary experiments, the proposed enforcement techniques did not induce noticeable overheads. However, we plan to run more exhaustive analysis to verify that the approach does not significantly impact the application's performance.

Acknowledgements.. This work was supported by the Région Auvergne-Rhône-Alpes within the *"Pack Ambition Recherche"* programme, the French ANR project ANR-20-CE39-0009 (SEVERITAS), and LabEx PERSYVAL-Lab (ANR-11-LABX-0025-01).

References

1. International Electrotechnical Commission, Functional blocks - Part 1: Architecture, 2nd edn. IEC 61499-1. IEC Geneva (2012)
2. 4DIAC-IDE. Framework for Distributed Industrial Automaton (4DIAC) (2010). www.eclipse.org/4diac/
3. Baier, C., Katoen, J.: Principles of Model Checking. MIT Press, Cambridge (2008)
4. Blech, J.O., Lindgren, P., Pereira, D., Vyatkin, V., Zoitl, A.: A comparison of formal verification approaches for IEC 61499. In: 2016 IEEE 21st International Conference on Emerging Technologies and Factory Automation (ETFA), pp. 1–4 (2016)
5. Do Tran, D., Walter, J., Grüttner, K., Oppenheimer, F.: Towards time-sensitive behavioral contract monitors for IEC 61499 function blocks. In: 2020 IEEE Conference on Industrial Cyberphysical Systems (ICPS), vol. 1, pp. 27–34 (2020)

6. Falcone, Y.: You should better enforce than verify. In: Barringer, H., et al. (eds.) RV 2010. LNCS, vol. 6418, pp. 89–105. Springer, Heidelberg (2010). https://doi.org/10.1007/978-3-642-16612-9_9

7. Falcone, Y., Havelund, K., Reger, G.: A tutorial on runtime verification. Eng. Dependable Softw. Syst. **34**, 141–175 (2013)

8. Falcone, Y., Mariani, L., Rollet, A., Saha, S.: Runtime failure prevention and reaction. In: Bartocci, E., Falcone, Y. (eds.) Lectures on Runtime Verification. LNCS, vol. 10457, pp. 103–134. Springer, Cham (2018). https://doi.org/10.1007/978-3-319-75632-5_4

9. Falcone, Y., Mounier, L., Fernandez, J.-C., Richier, J.-L.: Runtime enforcement monitors: composition, synthesis, and enforcement abilities. Formal Methods in System Design **38**, 06 (2011)

10. Falcone, Y., Pinisetty, S.: On the runtime enforcement of timed properties. In: Finkbeiner, B., Mariani, L. (eds.) RV 2019. LNCS, vol. 11757, pp. 48–69. Springer, Cham (2019). https://doi.org/10.1007/978-3-030-32079-9_4

11. Faqrizal, I.: Enforcer synthesis 2022. https://gitlab.inria.fr/ifaqriza/enforcer-synthesis

12. Jhunjhunwala, P., Blech, J.O., Zoitl, A., Atmojo, U.D., Vyatkin, V.: A design pattern for monitoring adapter connections in IEC 61499. In: 22nd IEEE International Conference on Industrial Technology, ICIT 2021, Valencia, Spain, 10–12 March 2021, pp. 967–972. IEEE (2021)

13. Ligatti, J., Bauer, L., Walker, D.: Enforcing non-safety security policies with program monitors. In: di Vimercati, S.C., Syverson, P., Gollmann, D. (eds.) ESORICS 2005. LNCS, vol. 3679, pp. 355–373. Springer, Heidelberg (2005). https://doi.org/10.1007/11555827_21

14. Ovsiannikova, P., Vyatkin, V.: Towards user-friendly model checking of IEC 61499 systems with counterexample explanation. In: 2021 26th IEEE International Conference on Emerging Technologies and Factory Automation (ETFA), pp. 01–04 (2021)

15. Philbeck, T., Davis, N.: The fourth industrial revolution: shaping a new Era. J. Int. Aff. **72**(1), 17–22 (2018)

16. Prenzel, L., Steinhorst, S.: Automated dependency resolution for dynamic reconfiguration of IEC 61499. In: 2021 26th IEEE International Conference on Emerging Technologies and Factory Automation (ETFA), pp. 1–8 (2021)

17. Schneider, F.B.: Enforceable security policies. ACM Trans. Inf. Syst. Secur. **3**(1), 30–50 (2000)

18. Strasser, T.: Framework for distributed industrial automation and control (4DIAC). In: IEEE International Conference on Industrial Informatics (INDIN), pp. 283–288 (2008)

19. Vyatkin, V.: IEC 61499 as enabler of distributed and intelligent automation: state-of-the-art review. Ind. Inf. IEEE Trans. **7**, 768–781 (2011)

20. Yoong, L.H., Roop, P.S.: Verifying IEC 61499 function blocks using Esterel. IEEE Embed. Syst. Lett. **2**(1), 1–4 (2010)

21. Zoitl, A., Lewis, R.: Modelling control systems using IEC 61499, 2nd Edition. Institution of Engineering and Technology (2014)

22. Zoitl, A., Strasser, T.I., Ebenhofer, G.: Developing modular reusable IEC 61499 control applications with 4DIAC. In: IEEE International Conference on Industrial Informatics, INDIN, pp. 358–363. IEEE (2013)

Author Index

Printed in the United States
by Baker & Taylor Publisher Services